THE HANDBOOK FOR THE FUTURE OF WORK

The Handbook for the Future of Work offers a timely and critical analysis of the transformative forces shaping work and employment in the twenty-first century.

Focusing on the past two decades, the handbook explores how technological advancements, automation and a shifting capitalist landscape have fundamentally reshaped work practices and labour relations. Beyond simply outlining the challenges and opportunities of automation, the handbook integrates these emerging realities with established discussions of work. Importantly, it moves beyond dominant technology-centric narratives, probing into broader questions about the nature of capitalism in a time of crisis and the contestation for alternative economic models. With contributions from established and emerging authors, based in institutions around the world, the handbook offers a systematic overview of the developments that have sparked radical shifts in how we live and work, and their multifaceted impacts upon social relations and identities, practices and sectors, politics and environments.

The handbook is unique in its exploration of the potential for economic transformations to reshape the centrality of work in our social and political imaginaries. A useful resource for students and researchers, the handbook serves as an essential guide to this new intellectual landscape.

Julie MacLeavy, School of Geographical Sciences, University of Bristol, UK.

Frederick Harry Pitts, Department of Humanities & Social Sciences, University of Exeter, Cornwall, UK.

ROUTLEDGE INTERNATIONAL HANDBOOKS

ROUTLEDGE INTERNATIONAL HANDBOOK OF COMPLEXITY ECONOMICS
Edited by Ping Chen, Wolfram Elsner and Andreas Pyka

THE ROUTLEDGE INTERNATIONAL HANDBOOK OF PUBLIC ADMINISTRATION AND DIGITAL GOVERNANCE
Edited by Sarah Giest and Ian Roberge

ROUTLEDGE INTERNATIONAL HANDBOOK OF CRITICAL POLICING STUDIES
Edited by Nicole L. Asquith, Jess Rodgers, James Clover, Gary Cordner, Angela Dwyer and Rishweena Ahmed

THE ROUTLEDGE INTERNATIONAL HANDBOOK OF SOCIAL WORK AND DISASTER PRACTICE
Edited by Carole Adamson, Margaret Alston, Bindi Bennett, Jennifer Boddy, Heather Boetto, Louise Harms, and Raewyn Tudor

THE ROUTLEDGE INTERNATIONAL HANDBOOK OF CRIMINAL RESPONSIBILITY
Edited by Thomas Crofts, Louise Kennefick and Arlie Loughnan

THE ROUTLEDGE INTERNATIONAL HANDBOOK OF CRITICAL DISABILITY STUDIES
Edited by Katie Ellis, Mike Kent and Kim Cousins

THE ROUTLEDGE INTERNATIONAL HANDBOOK OF SIGNIFICANCE AND MATTERING
Edited by Arie Kruglanski, Isaac Prilleltensky and Amiram Raviv

THE HANDBOOK FOR THE FUTURE OF WORK
Edited by Julie MacLeavy and Frederick Harry Pitts

THE HANDBOOK FOR THE FUTURE OF WORK

Edited by
Julie MacLeavy and Frederick Harry Pitts

Routledge
Taylor & Francis Group
LONDON AND NEW YORK

Designed cover image: Shutterstock

First published 2025
by Routledge
4 Park Square, Milton Park, Abingdon, Oxon OX14 4RN

and by Routledge
605 Third Avenue, New York, NY 10158

Routledge is an imprint of the Taylor & Francis Group, an informa business

This work was supported by the Engineering and Physical Sciences Research Council [grant ES/S012532/1]

British Library Cataloguing-in-Publication Data
A catalogue record for this book is available from the British Library

ISBN: 9781032355924 (hbk)
ISBN: 9781032355917 (pbk)
ISBN: 9781003327561 (ebk)

DOI: 10.4324/9781003327561

Typeset in Times New Roman
by codeMantra

CONTENTS

List of Figures — *xi*
List of Tables — *xiii*
List of Contributors — *xv*
Acknowledgements — *xxiii*

PART 1
Introduction — **1**

1 An Introduction to *The Handbook for the Future of Work* — 3
Julie MacLeavy and Frederick Harry Pitts

PART 2
Futures of Work in Context — **15**

2 The Future of Work: A History — 17
Tim Strangleman

3 What is the Fourth Industrial Revolution? Towards a Critical Theory of the Future of Work — 29
Greig Charnock

4 Financialisation of Work Futures — 42
Jean Cushen and Paul Thompson

PART 3
Automation, Technology and the Future of Work **55**

5 The Political Economy of Labour and Technological Disruptions in Capitalism 57
Eleni Papagiannaki

6 Automation and the Future of Work 69
James Steinhoff

7 Resisting Determinism(s): Unpacking Cognitive Technology and Automation 79
Abigail Gilbert

PART 4
Platforms, Platform Labour and Gig Work **91**

8 Platform Labour and Gig Work Futures: Uncovering Women's Hidden Digital Labour 93
Al James

9 Non-labour Platforms and Their Effects on Work in Specific Sectors: A Major Gap in Recent Research on Work and Employment 108
David Hesmondhalgh and Charles Umney

10 Fighting the Algorithm: The Rise of Activism in the Face of Platform Inequality 123
Kalie M. Mayberry, Lindsey D. Cameron and Hatim A. Rahman

PART 5
Identity and Difference in the Future of Work **133**

11 A Future of Racial Capitalism: Reproducing Coercion through New Digital Labour in South Africa 135
Bridget Kenny

12 Disability and the Future of Work 145
Melanie Jones, Kim Hoque, Victoria Wass and Nicholas Bacon

13 Work, Wealth and the Future: Evolving Class Structures and Social Mobility in a Changing World of Work 161
Julie MacLeavy

PART 6
Gender, Care and Social Reproduction **173**

14 Gender and the Future of Work in the Affective and Agile Economies 175
M. Winter

15 Queering the Future of Work: Queer and Trans Temporalities for (Re)thinking Work and Social Reproduction 185
Lizzie Richardson and Daniel Cockayne

16 Care and the Future of Work 195
Karin Schwiter

PART 7
Sectoral Case Studies **209**

17 Services Are the Future of Work 211
Matthew Cole

18 Industry 5.0 and the Future of Work in Manufacturing in Australia 225
Darryn Snell, Mark Dean and Al Rainnie

19 A Means to an End? The Role of Technology in Growth and Post-growth Futures of Agrifood Work in a European Context 237
Constantine Manolchev, David Watson, Laura A. Colombo, Patrick Elf and James Scott Vandeventer

PART 8
Labour Market Transitions and Insecurity **251**

20 Young Workers: Understanding Labour Market Transitions and Improving Job Quality 253
Edward Yates

21 Considering the Futures of Unpaid Work 264
Nancy Worth

22 Navigating Self-Employment in the Evolving Landscape of Work: Reflecting on the Past and Anticipating the Future 274
Paolo Borghi

PART 9
Mobilities and Geographies of Work Futures **287**

23 Global Production and the Future of Work: Past, Present, and Futures of Just-in-Time 289
Rutvica Andrijasevic, Julie Yujie Chen and Marc Steinberg

24 Reshaping the Geography of Work: Remote Worker Migration and Regional Dynamics in the Post-Pandemic Era 299
Julie MacLeavy, Suzanne Mills, Katie Mazer and Darja Reuschke

25 Resisting Precarity in City-Regions 314
David Etherington, David Beel and Martin Jones

PART 10
Policy and the Politics of Work Futures **329**

26 Industrial Relations and the Futures of Work: Efficiency, Equity and Voice in the Twenty-first Century 331
Huw Thomas and Peter Turnbull

27 Welfare Policy: The Role of Social Protection and Active Labour Market Programmes in the Future of Work 344
Jo Ingold

28 Politics and the Future of Work: Routine Work, Automation Risk and Redistributive Preferences in the Age of Populism 359
Frederick Harry Pitts and M. Winter

PART 11
Environment and the Future of Work **373**

29 Green Jobs, Just Transition, and the Future of Work 375
Ed Atkins

30 Energy Transitions and the Future of Decent Work in Asian Garment Factories 388
Evie Gilbert

31 Thermal Futures of Work: Intertwined Economic and Environmental Trajectories under Climate Change 400
Laurie Parsons

PART 12
Conclusion **409**

32 Conclusions and Future Challenges: The End of Work and the End of History 411
Frederick Harry Pitts and Julie MacLeavy

Index *419*

FIGURES

4.1	Financialisation of five work domains	43
12.1	The UK disability prevalence rate (%) 2013–2023	146
12.2	The UK disability employment gap (percentage points) 2013–2023	148
12.3	The UK prevalence-adjusted DEG (%) 2013–2023	149
12.4	Disabled employees experience of the great recession in Great Britain	150
13.1	Asset-based class schema	165
19.1	Ivan showing a hand-held scanning device running the 'Crop-picker' software, martenitsa around his wrist	242
19.2	Dana, wearing a blue hoodie under her high-visibility jacket, is processing a tray of daffodils	243
19.3	Members at Tangled Trees making tomato preserves in the coop's production plant	247
22.1	Proportion of independent professionals relative to self-employed workers/self-employed workers without employees, Europe, 2013–2022. Own elaboration on Eurostat data (2023)	276

TABLES

8.1	Women's presence across prominent digital labour platforms	97
8.2	Worker-led data leverage tools for platform worker empowerment – key examples	102
10.1	Understanding algo-activism among workers	125
21.1	Categorizing unpaid work, a beginning	265
27.1	Public policy instruments for individuals and employers	349
27.2	A proposal for a demand-driven activation strategy	352

CONTRIBUTORS

Rutvica Andrijasevic is a Professor of Work and Employment at the University of Bristol Business School, UK. Her most recent work examines the interdependences between software, hardware and labour. Previously, she studied how states' immigration policies foster vulnerability and exploitation of migrant women in human trafficking. She has published on these topics extensively and her writings have been translated into several languages: German, French, Spanish, Italian, Czech, Polish, Greek, Croatian and Mandarin. What drives her research is the desire to improve marginalised groups' access to rights and justice. She serves on the Board of Trustees of Electronics Watch and works towards achieving responsible public procurement and rights of workers in electronics supply chains.

Ed Atkins is a Senior Lecturer working on energy transitions and energy justice at the University of Bristol, UK. His research broadly explores how place-based approaches might allow for more equitable climate action.

Nicholas Bacon is a Professor in Human Resource Management at Bayes Business School and a Founding Member of Disability@Work. His research publications have shaped policies in relation to private equity-owned firms (advising EVCA and the EU's AIFMD), disability and employment (through Disability@Work and the RSA Inclusive Work, Disability and Ageing Network steering group), and industrial relations legislation (amendments to the Trade Union Bill 2016). He has edited the *Industrial Relations Journal,* the *Sage Handbook of Human Resource Management*, and the *Sage Handbook of Industrial Relations.*

David Beel is a Senior Lecturer in Political Economy at Manchester Metropolitan University, based in the Business School and Future Economies team. His research is on the links between economic development and devolution, primarily how city regions frame the interactions between actors, the economy, and the politics of regeneration. David's latest book, *City Regions and Devolution in the UK*, provides a critique of city-region building and considers how governance restructuring shapes the political, economic, social, and cultural geographies of devolution.

Paolo Borghi is currently Senior Assistant Professor at the Department of Political and Social Sciences of Pavia University where he works on different research projects related to digitalisation processes and welfare system, sustainability and data management, platform work, self-employment, collective representation. He employs a mixed-methods approach in his investigations. He worked as a postdoctoral researcher at the Work and Employment Relations Division of the Leeds University Business School and at the Department of Social and Political Sciences of the University of Milan conducting the qualitative fieldwork in Italy and in the UK within the ERC project SHARE – Seizing the Hybrid Areas of work by Representing self-Employment (2018–2023).

Lindsey D. Cameron is an Assistant Professor of management at the Wharton School, University of Pennsylvania and an Assistant Professor of sociology (by courtesy) at the School of Arts and Science, University of Pennsylvania. She is currently a fellow at the Institute for Advanced Studies in Princeton, NJ, and at the Berkman Klein Center for Internet and Society at Harvard University. Previously, she was a fellow at the Data and Society Research Institute. Her research focuses on algorithmic management, the gig economy, and the future of work with an emphasis on how these changes affect work and workers. She earned her PhD in management from the Ross School of Business, University of Michigan.

Greig Charnock teaches global international political economy at The University of Manchester. He is the co-author of *David Harvey: A Critical Introduction to His Thought* (2023) and *The Limits to Capital in Spain* (2014), and he is the co-editor of *The New International Division of Labour* (2016).

Julie Yujie Chen is an Assistant Professor in the Institute of Communication, Culture, Information, and Technology (ICCIT) and Faculty of Information at the University of Toronto, Canada. She is the co-author of *Media and Management* (University of Minnesota Press, 2021) and *Super-Sticky WeChat and Chinese Society* (Emerald, 2018). Her research on digital labor and platform studies has appeared in journals, including *New Media & Society*, *Socio-Economic Review*, *Javnost - The Public*, *Work, Employment and Society, Chinese Journal of Communication, China Perspectives*, and *Triple C* and so on. Her latest publications include a co-edited special section on "worker resistance in digital capitalism" in *International Journal of Communication* and a co-authored paper entitled "A regional and historical approach to platform capitalism: The cases of Alibaba and Tencent" in *Media, Culture & Society.*

Daniel Cockayne is a Feminist Economic Geographer working at the University of Waterloo in Canada. His research explores cultures of work with a focus on employment-based and high-status work through the lenses of feminist, queer, Marxist, and affect theory. His current research explores the transition to working from home for previously office-based workers as a result of the COVID-19 pandemic.

Matthew Cole is a Lecturer in Technology, Work and Employment at the University of Sussex, UK. He is also an Associate Fellow of the DIGIT Centre and the Oxford Internet Institute His research spans the political economy of work and employment, industrial relations, and technological change in the labour process. He has been published in journals such as *Work, Employment and Society*, *Antipode*, *Global Networks*, and the *Socialist Register*. He is also on the Editorial Board of *Work and Employment and Society*.

Laura A. Colombo is a Senior Lecturer in Management Studies, Exeter Business School, UK. Laura's research focuses on issues of scaling in relation to social and co-operative enterprises and alternative food networks. Her academic work further focuses on critical pedagogies, exploring how the business school can be repurposed around civic management education.

Jean Cushen is an Associate Professor of HRM within the School of Business, Maynooth University. Jean is a member of the University 'Political Economy of Work' research cluster and her research explores the contemporary employment experience focusing on financialisation, the labour process and human resource management (HRM).

Mark Dean is a National Research and Planning Officer at the Australian Manufacturing Workers Union and Adjunct Principal Research Fellow of RMIT University's Graduate School of Business and Law. Mark has previously held research roles at the Centre for Future Work at The Australia Institute, The University of Adelaide and Flinders University and has contributed a range of publications on topics, including advanced manufacturing industry policy, the future of work, Australian politics, economic theory, and trade union leadership.

Patrick Elf is a Senior Research Fellow in Sustainable Business, Centre for Enterprise and Economic Development Research (CEEDR), Middlesex University, UK. Patrick's research focuses on investigating avenues for behaviour change approaches towards the adoption of more sustainable lifestyles, and mechanism towards the adaptation of sustainable business models. He has a particular interest in sustainable, inclusive and transformative consumption.

David Etherington is a Professor of local and regional economic development at Staffordshire University. His research focuses on the political economy of welfare reform and employment relations in the UK and Nordic countries. David's latest book, *Austerity, Welfare and Work*, demonstrated the links between welfare policy and employment relations to understand the geographical foundations of social inequalities.

Abigail Gilbert is the Co-Director of the Institute for the Future of Work, and a Policy Advisory Board Member of the University of Manchester Work and Equalities Institute. Her academic background is in institutional and regulation theory, having completed her PhD within a critical geography department at the University of Manchester. In her current role, her focus is on ensuring multi-disciplinary research conducted by IFOW reveals the mechanisms driving new forms of inequality through technological transition, in order that effective interventions can be developed by those with the power to affect change, ranging from workers through to parliamentarians.

Evie Gilbert is a Human Geography PhD student at Royal Holloway University of London. Her research focuses on the imagined futures of work for female garment workers in Cambodia, drawing on technological displacement, resilience-building and non-formal training. This research is positioned at the cross-section between labour and feminist geography with the intention of engaging with speculative and anticipatory knowledge in futures of work studies.

David Hesmondhalgh is a Professor of Media, Music and Culture at the University of Leeds, UK. He is the author or co-author of a number of books, including *The Cultural Industries* (4th edition, 2019), *Why Music Matters* (2013), *Creative Labour* (2010) and a major book-length report for the UK government's Intellectual Property Office on *Music Creators' Earnings in the Digital Era* (2021). He is also the lead author of a literature review of music recommender systems (2023), commissioned by the UK government's Centre for Data Ethics and Innovation. From 2021 to

2026, he is leading a five-year research project, funded by a European Research Council Advanced Research Grant, on *Music Culture in the Age of Streaming*.

Kim Hoque is a Professor of Human Resource Management and Vice Dean (People and Culture) at King's Business School and a founding member of Disability@Work. He has researched and published widely in the HRM and diversity fields. He co-founded the Disability Employment Charter and previously co-provided the secretariat of the All Party Parliamentary Group for Disability. He was a commissioner on the Centre for Social Justice Disability Commission (2022–2021). He serves on the editorial boards of *Human Relations* (of which he was formerly an Associate Editor), *Journal of Management*, and *Industrial Relations Journal*.

Jo Ingold is a Professor in the Peter Faber Business School at the Australian Catholic University. Her research covers employability and skills, employer engagement, recruitment and talent acquisition and workplace inclusion. Jo is the Editor of the academic journal *Work, Employment and Society* and co-edited with Patrick McGurk *Employer Engagement: Making Active Labour Market Policies Work* (Bristol University Press, 2023).

Al James is a Professor of Economic Geography and Head of Geography at Newcastle University with research interests in labour; gendered work-lives; social reproduction; digital work futures; and the platform economy. His first book *Work-Life Advantage* was published in the RGS-IBG book series (2018) and explores the benefits that accrue to employers and workers from family-friendly working provision. He is currently working on a follow-up book that extends these ideas to women's experiences of juggling gig work and family in the platform economy. This research has been funded by the UK's Economic and Social Research Council, Nuffield Foundation, British Academy and Arts and Humanities Research Council. For more information, go to https://geoworklives.com

Martin Jones is the Vice Chancellor and Chief Executive of Staffordshire University, and also a Professor of Human Geography. His research is on the interfaces between economic and political geographer, exemplified by looking at how the state intervenes in economic development through spatialities of governance. Martin's latest book, *Cities and Regions in Crisis*, examined the governance geography of sub-national economic development in the UK and was awarded the Regional Studies Association Best Book Award 2021.

Melanie Jones is a Professor of Economics at Cardiff University and a founding member of Disability@Work (www.disabilityatwork.co.uk). Her research interest is in applied labour economics and focuses on labour market inequality, including health and disability, and gender. This work has been published in high-quality international journals. She is currently an editor at the *British Journal of Industrial Relations*, Member of the Economic and Social Research Council Grant Assessment Panel C and Royal Economic Society Council, and an IZA and ONS Research Fellow. She has previously advised the Welsh Government on Teachers Pay and is a Member of the Review Body on Doctors' and Dentists' Remuneration.

Bridget Kenny is a Professor of Sociology at the University of the Witwatersrand, Johannesburg. She works on labour, gender, race and consumption with specific focus on service work, precarious employment, and political subjectivity in South Africa and comparatively. Her books include *Retail Worker Politics, Race and Consumption in South Africa: Shelved in the Service Economy*

(Palgrave Macmillan, 2018) and the co-edited *Wal-Mart in the Global South* (University of Texas Press, 2018). She serves on the editorial boards of African Studies, *Work in the Global Economy* and the *Global Labour Journal*. She is the past President and Secretary of Research Committee 44-Labour Movements section of the International Sociological Association.

Julie MacLeavy is a Professor of Economic Geography at the University of Bristol, UK, specialising in feminist political economy, economic transformations and new forms of work. She is the Theme Lead for the 'Innovation, Transition, Change' challenge within the new Academic Research Hub for the Prevention of Gambling Harms at the University of Bristol, co-Editor-in-Chief of *Geoforum* and Treasurer of the Royal Geographical Society (with the Institute of British Geographers) Economic Geography Research Group. Julie is the co-editor of *The Handbook of Neoliberalism* (Routledge) and author of *Enduring Austerity: The Uneven Geographies of the Post-Welfare State* (University of Bristol Press), which examines how austerity policies create an uneven landscape of work and welfare opportunities across different communities.

Constantine Manolchev is a Senior Lecturer in Sustainable Futures, Exeter Business School, UK. Constantine studies organisations as sites of precarity and violence. His academic research further focuses on decent work, community resilience and regional development. In 2022, Constantine led a research project on circular textile practices in Cornwall, commissioned by the Secretary of State for Environment, Food and Rural Affairs.

Kalie M. Mayberry is a Social Impact Researcher and Educator, exploring activism practices and community governance models of organisations, specifically through digital and online communities. She is currently the Senior Research Coordinator for the Berkman Klein Center for Internet and Society at Harvard University, and she has held previous roles as a research fellow at Columbia Business School and Wharton School. She holds a double Bachelor of Arts from the University of California Santa Barbara, and a Master of Public Administration from the University of Pennsylvania.

Katie Mazer is an Assistant Professor of Environmental and Sustainability Studies and Women's and Gender Studies at Acadia University, Canada. Her research focuses on natural resources, work and unemployment, and feminist political economy.

Suzanne Mills is an Associate Professor of Labour Studies at McMaster University, Canada. Her current research concerns labour market restructuring and labour relations in declining and northern regions in Canada.

Eleni Papagiannaki is an Assistant Professor/Lecturer in Economics at Edinburgh Napier University and Research Fellow at the Institute for the Future of Work.

Laurie Parsons is a Senior Lecturer in Human Geography at Royal Holloway, University of London and Principal Investigator of the projects Oppressive Heat, Hot Trends, and Disaster Trade. In these and other projects, he explores the experience of climate change in the global economy, exposing the hidden environmental impacts of global production and unequal landscape of exposure to climate change impacts. His books include *Carbon Colonialism: How Rich Nations Export Climate Breakdown*, *Going Nowhere Fast: Inequality in the Age of Translocality*, and *Climate Change in the Global Workplace: Labour, Adaptation and Resistance*.

Frederick Harry Pitts is a Senior Lecturer in Politics at the University of Exeter's Cornwall Campus in his hometown of Penryn, where he is also the Director of Business Engagement and Innovation for Humanities and Social Sciences. He is a Co-Investigator of the Economic and Social Research Council Centre for Sociodigital Futures, a Fellow of the Institute for the Future of Work, Secretary of the British Universities Industrial Relations Association and an Honorary Senior Research Fellow at the University of Bristol Business School. He is the author or coauthor of five previous books, most recently *Marx in Management and Organisation Studies: Rethinking Value, Labour and Class Struggles* (Routledge).

Hatim A. Rahman is an Assistant Professor of Management and Organizations at Northwestern University's Kellogg School of Management. His research focuses on the intersection of new technology, work, labour markets, platforms, and organisations. He earned his PhD from the Center of Work, Technology, and Organization at Stanford's Department of Management Science and Engineering.

Al Rainnie is a Researcher based in Adelaide, South Australia. He is currently working on regional development, hydrogen, renewable energy and Just Transitions. Al is also a co-coordinator of the SA Modern Slavery Network. He has worked at a number of universities in the UK and Australia.

Darja Reuschke is an Associate Professor at the City-Region Economic Development Institute (City-REDI) in the Birmingham Business School at the University of Birmingham, UK. She is a geographer by background and has researched links between home-based working, migration, housing and employment choices.

Lizzie Richardson is a Human Geographer working at Goethe University in Frankfurt am Main, Germany. Her research focuses on the geographies of work and the workplace in the UK, drawing conceptually on approaches to performance and performativity, together with feminist and queer theories for making sense of and constructing the economic.

Karin Schwiter is an Assistant Professor of Labour Geography at the University of Zurich in Switzerland. She works with feminist and discourse theoretical lenses to explore precarious labour. Her current research focuses on the commodification and platformisation of care work.

Darryn Snell is an Associate Professor in the School of Management and Coordinator of the Work in Transition Research Group at the Business and Human Rights Centre at RMIT University, Melbourne. Darryn has worked extensively on employment and workforce development questions. He has conducted research in a range of industries, including manufacturing, agri-foods, transport and logistics, cleantech and the electricity generation industry. He has completed major research projects for the Australian Research Council, the National Centre for Vocational Education Research, the Department of Regional Australia, Local Government Arts and Sport, the Department of Education, Employment and Workplace Relations and The Gordon Institute.

Marc Steinberg is a Professor of Film Studies at Concordia University, Montreal, and the Director of The Platform Lab. He is the author of *Anime's Media Mix: Franchising Toys and Characters in Japan* (University of Minnesota Press, 2012), *The Platform Economy: How Japan Transformed the Commercial Internet* (University of Minnesota Press, 2019), and *Media and Management* (University of Minnesota Press, 2021) (co-authored). Recent publications include "From

Automobile Capitalism to Platform Capitalism: Toyotism as a Prehistory of the Digital Economy" in *Organization Studies* and a special issue of *Media, Culture & Society* on "Media Power in Digital Asia: Super Apps and Megacorps."

James Steinhoff is an Assistant Professor in the School of Information and Communication Studies at University College Dublin. He is the author of *Automation and Autonomy: Labour, Capital and Machines in the Artificial Intelligence Industry* (2021, Palgrave Macmillan) and co-author of *Inhuman Power: Artificial Intelligence and the Future of Capitalism* (2019, Pluto).

Tim Strangleman is an Emeritus Professor of Sociology, SSPSSR, University of Kent, UK. He has written widely on work and deindustrialisation using archives, oral histories and visual methods. He is the author of three books, including *Voices of Guinness* (Oxford, 2019) and the *Routledge International Handbook of Working-Class Studies* (2020). He is currently editing a handbook on deindustrialisation. Throughout his career, he has collaborated with artists, photographers and filmmakers. These creative productions are reflections on work meaning, transition and loss. Tim was a founding member of the Working-Class Studies Association and served as the organisation's president in the past. He regularly blogs for the Working-Class Perspectives blog based in the USA.

Huw Thomas is an Assistant Professor of Employment Relations at the College of Business at University College Dublin.

Paul Thompson is an Emeritus Professor of Employment Studies at the University of Stirling, UK. He is a globally recognised theorist of the labour process with research interests that span diverse issues from financialisation, organisational misbehaviour and social media in the workplace.

Peter Turnbull is a Professor of Management at the University of Bristol Business School.

Charles Umney is a Professor of International Work and Employment at the University of Leeds, UK. He is the co-author of *Marketization* (2022) and author of *Class Matters* (2018). He is currently a Primary Investigator on the *Humans in Digital Logistics* project which examines how digital technologies are transforming work in warehousing workplaces, and also works on the Leeds *Index of Platform Labour Protest*, which documents and analyses global instances of protest on labour platforms. He is a Co-Investigator at the ESRC-funded Digital Futures at Work Research Centre.

James Scott Vandeventer is a Senior Lecturer in Sustainability, Manchester Metropolitan University, UK. James' research interests are situated at the nexus of processual approaches to organising, human geography, and transformative change. These guide his research into diverse economies and alternative organisational practices; housing and urban futures; and the role of organisations in post-growth and degrowth transitions.

Victoria Wass is an Emerita Professor at Cardiff Business School and a founding member of Disability@Work. Her research spans labour economics, sociology of work and HRM, and includes studies of disability at work, formal and informal care and gender pay gaps. She works as an expert witness advising on valuing loss of earnings claims (personal injury, clinical negligence and employment discrimination) which normally have a disability dimension (https://victoriawass.co.uk/).

David Watson is a Senior Lecturer in Organisation Studies and Human Resource Management, University of Essex. An interdisciplinary researcher interested in the concept of well-being and its relationship with work, David has a particular interest in 'alternative' forms of organisation. Other research interests include Marx's concept of alienation, well-being theory – in particular, the capabilities approach and the role of well-being in guiding policy.

M. Winter is a Postdoctoral Researcher at Tallinn University of Technology in Estonia. She is also a Research Fellow at the Institute for the Future of Work in London, UK. Her work is to do with gender, technology, and work.

Nancy Worth is an Associate Professor in the Department of Geography & Environmental Management at the University of Waterloo, Canada. Her research examines the lived experience of the economic; recent projects examine work-from-home freelancing and international student families' housing coping strategies.

Edward Yates is a Lecturer in Employment Relations at The University of Sheffield, UK. His research examines how global processes of political economy shape work and employment conditions and seeks to discover how work and employment can be materially improved in a way that benefits workers and their dependents, employers, and society more generally. His research grounds and operationalises these conceptual ideas through an analytical focus on two interlinked empirical areas of young workers, and local labour markets and local economies.

ACKNOWLEDGEMENTS

The creation of this book would not have been possible without the support of several key individuals and groups. Firstly, we would like to express our gratitude to Andrew Mould at Routledge. His vision for a *Handbook for the Future of Work* and belief in our ability to bring it to life were instrumental in getting this project started. We are also deeply indebted to Claire Maloney and Niamh Hitchmough for their expert editorial assistance throughout the entire process. Their guidance and support have been invaluable. Our heartfelt thanks go out to all the authors who contributed chapters. Your insightful and engaging writing not only inspired us but also made the editing process genuinely enjoyable. We are also grateful to colleagues at (and beyond) our universities for stimulating conversations on the future(s) of work over the years, in particular the Faculty Research Group for Perspectives on Work at the University of Bristol and the *Futures of Work* blog it publishes via Bristol University Press. Additionally, Julie would like to extend a special thanks to the students on her 'State, Economies and Societies' unit, and Harry to students on several modules taught at Bristol and Exeter, for their thought-provoking discussions on this topic, which undoubtedly helped to shape the development of this book. Finally, and most importantly, we owe a debt of gratitude to our families. Julie would like to thank Columba, Cillian, Darragh and Aisling, and Harry would like to thank Laura, Elsie and Nico.

PART 1

Introduction

1

AN INTRODUCTION TO *THE HANDBOOK FOR THE FUTURE OF WORK*

Julie MacLeavy and Frederick Harry Pitts

Introduction

The Handbook for the Future of Work brings together a range of established and emerging scholars to examine the multifaceted consequences of recent developments that are reshaping how we live and work. This encompasses the ongoing debates surrounding the transformation of social relations and identities, work practices and sectors, the evolving political landscape and the environmental pressures arising from these changes. At the outset, we wish to convey to readers that there is no single conception of the future of work, and engagement with technological change, processes of automation and capitalist transformation is common but uneven across (and beyond) academic disciplines. This book is therefore not intended to identify and 'bound' this emerging body of scholarship but rather to provide a series of avenues through which readers might start to comprehend the changing nature of work and employment, and what different conceptions of the future imply for the present, as well as commonly held understandings of the past. *The Handbook for the Future of Work* thus comprises a series of chapters that mobilise a concern for transformations in work and working lives, while reminding readers of the relative openness of the field. It is precisely this openness that has led to the liveliness of debates and the broadening of concerns with automation and technological development to also include matters of unemployment, depreciating wages, job insecurity, precarity and so forth.

The divergent and contested understandings of the future of work are such that there are a range of pathways that readers might take as they move through the Handbook. While we seek to offer a comprehensive overview of our curational and organisational choices within this introductory chapter, readers might choose to focus upon a specific thematic focus (e.g., flexibility and digital infrastructures), certain empirical case studies (e.g., the future of work in deindustrialising economies and urban futures of work) or a particular question or point of debate (e.g., are jobs disappearing? Are the middle classes being 'hollowed out'?). With the use of the Handbook as a guide, we aim for readers to be able to better navigate the emerging body of literature that uses the observed technological, generational and social shifts in how work gets done to call into question the centrality that 'work' occupies in visions of the future (including in contemporary politics), while also opening up other ways of narrating the economy as it exists in the present.

DOI: 10.4324/9781003327561-2

Recognising the inherent complexity and dynamism of the future of work as a subject, we – as editors – have actively sought contributions from a range of geographical and disciplinary perspectives. Accordingly, the Handbook brings together authors working at institutions spanning Europe, North America, South Africa and Australia. Even where authors, as many of them do, work in Anglophone institutions (particularly in the UK or the US), they have often moved from other countries and/or conduct research that brings multiple places and voices to the book's discussion of the future(s) of work. Moreover, many of the scholars who have contributed chapters are junior (if not early career) and therefore part of the generation most affected by the changes in work detailed. Given their range of disciplinary backgrounds and perspectives, we consider that collectively they bring to the Handbook an interdisciplinary perspective on the future of work.

For our part, we are both scholars located in the English-speaking world and the disciplines and communities of practice of which we are part undoubtedly have implications for the knowledge we produce as how and what we write is an artefact of place and (scholarly) culture. The thematic framing and chapter organisation likely reveal our own intellectual, geographical and generational positionalities. In bringing to the fore the challenge inherent in assembling a handbook to present the 'state-of-the-art' within a given field, we wish to make clear that our ambition is to not only consolidate but also progress the state of knowledge on the future of work by casting wide our "drag net of where we look for relevant scholarship" (Müller, 2021: 1459). Given the propensity for handbooks to constitute a scholarly canon (what might be seen as a pre-approved list of authors to read and topics to consider), we have tried hard to mitigate, if not entirely avoid, a gatekeeping role, even though it is impossible to cover adequately the richness and variety of different ways of knowing in relation to feminist, critical race, postcolonial, decolonial, Indigenous, Marxist, anarchist and more-than-human scholarship, for instance. There is always a challenge in composing a selection of work that may be seen to convey what is (and what is not) important within a field of study. But we have worked closely with authors to ensure good geographical coverage of changes in the nature of work and employment, and seek to frame these chapters appropriately through our introduction and conclusion to ensure that knowledge produced from the UK, the US, etc., is not presented as somehow "more universal, and therefore more valuable, than that produced [elsewhere]" (Müller, 2021: 1441). Ultimately, *The Handbook for the Future of Work* is not intended to ringfence a field of study but rather provide a flexible guide to the number of large-scale and rapid changes that are affecting how workers make a living under capitalism, and how these pose challenges and questions for scholars and practitioners.

The Existing Literature

Several books have been written about the future of work, but none of these contributions have attempted to bring the diverse scope and wide-ranging coverage that we incorporate here. Most of the books that have been published to date see a profound alteration in the status of jobs because of processes of digitisation and globalisation, with concerns raised about the demands and uncertainty of the current world of work provoking dystopian visions of what may be to come, as well as utopian calls for a 'post-work world' that would allow people to be productive and creative without being bound to the capitalist employment relation. In contrast, *The Handbook for the Future of Work* charts a new course through these dystopian and utopian visions by historically, empirically and geographically contextualising the ideas and processes driving the changing world of work. In so doing, the Handbook aims to provide the first comprehensive overview of the field, detailing how the future of work has been theorised, promoted and critiqued, as well as how it has been made manifest in a variety of sectors across the globe.

In recent years, there have been several texts that take the future of work as a central focus. Some of the first relatively modern texts orientated towards the contemporary discourse around the 'future of work' (as opposed to earlier iterations such as the 'end of work', etc.) were intended for the managers of firms, promising to help them to identify the skills they will need to guide their business through the anticipated 'workplace revolution' driven by changes in technology (Malone, 2004). Political scientists, meanwhile (West, 2018), have been keen to stress that the future of work is already with us, and so fundamental changes are needed to reform the welfare system as it is no longer tenable to assume that employment is an appropriate means of distributing income. These accounts have provided depth to our understandings of the consequences of work changing by unpacking the political implications of work no longer offering the opportunity for many to fulfil their ambitions and dreams. Along similar lines, the likes of Guy Standing (2011) have offered a class analysis of global economic development and crucially suggested that the evolution of employment has given rise to a new category of workers – the precariat – who do not possess fixed or stable jobs but rather are defined by their unstable labour relations. Found in all sectors of the economy worldwide, the precariat is theorised to have transformative potential, but this has not (yet) been realised because – Standing argues – these workers do not identify as a class and so have not come together to fight for a radically changed income distribution and the reclamation of the commons.

The discussion of these tendencies developed greater political significance as awareness grew through the mid-noughties and in particular from 2010 onwards. From a mainstream perspective, Martin Ford's book *The Rise of the Robots* (2015) focused on the technological advancements made in the last century and pushed for dramatic policy responses to the unemployment that he saw as resulting. Where he differs from other work is in positioning the IT revolution as fundamentally different from previous technological reforms – elsewhere this is seen as part of a longer-term trajectory, as well as fundamentally related to demographic developments, regulatory reform, changing social values and new organisation practices. The radical Left was the location for some of the most provocative and interesting writing, however. Some of this took inspiration from the likes of Kathi Weeks (2011), who, while positing that work in and of itself is not without value, identified the problem to lie with a specific form of work that is bound to the capitalist employment relation. Her book covers some of the most pertinent debates surrounding the conceptualisation of work and importantly addresses critiques that have been made in relation to this literature – specifically, how work can be a source of pleasure and joy for people, a means by which we can realise our creative potential or achieve things we never thought possible.

However, the vast majority of writing that followed took a more 'anti' or 'post' work direction. Srnicek and Williams produced a provocative text based around an argument that the Left as it exists today will not be able to bring about significant economic change (2015). Srnicek and Williams argued that there is a need to think beyond the capitalist imaginary in order to achieve a post-work world. They set out four demands, each of which can be taken as a goal in and of itself, but which may also work together as an integrated programme of reform: a fully automated economy, the reduction of the working week, the provision of a universal basic income and a diminishment of the work ethic. Paul Mason's *PostCapitalism* (2015), meanwhile, explored the potential for the emerging digital age to bring about a socialist revolution which would ultimately bring an end to neoliberal hegemony and the idea of private ownership. Mason argued that the knowledge content of products is becoming more valuable than the physical things that are used to produce them, laying bare the non-capitalist relations on which the economy now depends. Scarcity is no longer a driver of exchange systems or asset values, but rather it is knowledge, which is in abundance, and this is leading to the creation of new norms and institutions. A critical appraisal of the contemporary labour market written by the late anthropologist David Graeber (2018) popularised the argument that, in contrast to historical predictions, technological advancement has led to people spending more, rather than less time at work. Graeber observed the expansion of jobs that exist only to support those in employment, as well as jobs that to his mind are effectively pointless – their main role is to keep people busy, distracted and tired.

The conversation has become progressively more sophisticated as the realities of the unfolding future of work have become more apparent. An impressive recent contribution, Benanav's *Automation and the Future of Work* (2020), brings rigour to some of these debates and discussions by looking at the structural trends driving the crisis of work and as a corollary socio-economic inequality. In doing so, it makes the case for a new mode of social existence, which goes further than public investments such as a jobs' guarantee programme, or the implementation of universal basic income, by also addressing private property, rentiership and relations of debt. Finally, a recent book, from a similarly critical Marxist perspective (Dinerstein and Pitts, 2021), considers how capitalism has been (mis)represented in contemporary analyses of work and suggests that misunderstanding of the core categories of labour, value, money, the state and social reproduction has led to the promotion of political programmes that risk buttressing rather than dismantling the exploitation and subordination at the heart of capitalist labour market.

Each of the aforementioned books does something very different than what we set out to do here. There are recent contributions that attempt something akin in shorter form. Kochan and Dyer's (2001) *Shaping the Future of Work: A Handbook for Action and a New Social Contract* offers a productive resource, considering the roles workers, business leaders and government actors must play in bringing forth a new (and more emancipatory) world of work, as well as the potential offered by new technologies. In particular, Melanie Simms's (2019) *What Do We Know and What Should We Do about the Future of Work?* is attentive to some of the more negative consequences of economic and labour market restructuring (zero-hour contracts, the gig economy) but primarily orientated towards priority areas where the UK should seek to strengthen regulation in order to ensure processes of automation, robotic developments and artificial intelligence benefit workers. However, it reads as a manifesto more than a detailed empirical examination of trends and developments (not least because of its short length), and we are trying to do something bigger and broader with this collection.

Meanwhile, earlier texts of a more academic character, such as Colin Williams's (2007) book, admittedly bear some similarities in structure to this one, insofar as they tend to start with a discussion of dominant perspectives on the direction of work and then considers key drivers of work-related change (the rise of the information/knowledge society, new flexible forms of work organisation, etc.). However, while such texts tend to move on to consider counter-visions (of post-employment, post-capitalist, localist green futures, etc.) that at the time of writing – some 15 years ago – were surprising or experimental, we write from the perspective of a present where such leftfield visions have become much more mainstream. As such, our Handbook charts a different path in that it examines how these are now being lived and practised, as well as the emergent effects of such 'realised' futures.

There are of course many handbooks and other collections similar to our own which touch upon various aspects of work and broader economic futures (e.g., Gibson-Graham and Dombroski, 2020). *The Sage Handbook of the Sociology of Work and Employment*, which is now nearly a decade old, explores how work and employment are lived and experienced on the ground, the changes that are underway and some potential ramifications. However, while the Sage Handbook is orientated towards a specific disciplinary community (sociology), our book is more explicitly and substantively concerned with providing an interdisciplinary assessment and guide to the constitutive processes underlying work and employment transitions, how these are spatially and temporally constituted, including through recent changes; and the politics at play within these processes, as well as the study of them.

Although none of the texts covered above purport to give a comprehensive overview, the respective scopes and missions of existing texts limit their capacity to offer readers a thorough survey of the field, representing instead catalysts for future enquiry. There have also been significant changes in the employment landscape since many of the texts were written, arguably the most important of which is the COVID-19 pandemic that began in 2020, and so is not addressed in detail. In short, we feel that there is a distinct need to take stock of the current state of the field and provide a comprehensive, up to date, and wide-ranging survey of how the future of work is being understood, implemented and resisted which will also include some focused reflections in the wake of a major health and economic crisis, not to mention the other ruptures and upheavals that have occurred since. Our goal is to advance debates within a field that has grown exponentially over the past two decades, coinciding with the rise of digital and artificial intelligence technologies and an emergent sense that a 'crisis of work' is unfolding with many in society who are overworked, and many others who are condemned to intermittent work or unemployment. In short, the Handbook intervenes by outlining how theorisations of the future of work have evolved and by exploring new research agendas that we hope will inform policy making and activism around the concrete ways in which elements of the future of work are already being lived and experienced in the present.

Who This Book Is for and What It Does

By presenting a comprehensive examination of the field, this edited volume will hopefully serve as an invaluable resource for undergraduates, postgraduate students and professional scholars alike. In terms of student readership, the book is suitable for both undergraduate and graduate students, where the book could be used as a resource for those addressing labour geography, economic geography, critical approaches to capitalism, global political economies, among other topics. We envisioned the book as both a teaching guide and a reference for social scientists across the disciplines, whether management scholars, human geographers, anthropologists, psychologists, sociologists, political scientists, economists, media and communications scholars, lawyers or others working on questions of work, employment and economic transformation.

While it is an academic text, those with a more general interest in the changing nature of work and employment, and the position of 'work' in contemporary politics should also find the book particularly useful. As expectations of the future of work feature prominently in media discourse, and in the work of consultancy firms, think tanks, NGOs and political parties, we expect that this book will be of wider interest to those beyond the academy. The book also has international appeal as the subject matter pertains to the global political economy as a whole, and, accordingly, we hope its readership will be similarly wide-ranging in scholarly communities throughout the English-speaking world, including Europe, North America, South Africa and Australia/New Zealand, where there is growing concern for and recognition of how work is changing global and local relations in terms of politics, social processes, environmental concerns and knowledge productions. This importantly includes consideration of discussions around universal basic income, the four-day week, etc., as well as community economies and Indigenous movements that allow us to consider what futures mean in a non-Western sense.

The structure of the Handbook is intended to guide readers through a discussion of some of the main concepts that run through discussions of the future of work, and how these changes have historically cascaded through numerous iterations of the 'future of work' occurring at intervals since the inception of capitalist society. Indeed, the Handbook charts changing conceptions of what the 'future of work' is, with chapters detailing the early voices seeking to represent, evoke and bring forth a 'new' world of work, as well as critical interrogations of these interventions. This includes detailed examinations of the nature of change via a series of chapters that consider specific issues at stake, from the impacts of globalisation and financialisation, through the evolving landscape of political economic organisation, to the transformative power of technological development and digitisation.

Much of the literature suggests that today's work-centred world is becoming increasingly hostile to the human need for autonomy, spontaneity and community: work is defined by drudgery, by subordination, by boredom, by exhaustion. Rather than 'more' or 'better' work, some authors – as we have signalled – have radically proposed a 'postwork society' that transcends arguments for fair pay and better working rights, which tacitly accept work as a taken-for-granted feature of contemporary society. The chapters in this book thus move from the emergence of debates about the future of work to consider the different dimensions of work as a naturalised feature of everyday lives, and the material and political factors that underpin its transformation in the past, present and future, over space, and in technological and financial terms. Evidencing this, this book adopts a particular focus on the rise of digital platforms and the proliferation of platform labour and gig work – forms of work that so often blur the lines between traditional employment and self-employment, raising concerns about worker exploitation, lack of job security, limited social protections and the erosion of traditional notions of community within the workplace. Several chapters explore these tensions, examining how platform labour reshapes the landscape of work and the challenges it presents for achieving fair and sustainable work practices.

As the book develops, it draws further attention to the implications of the future of work as an embodied experience for individual workers and society. Race, gender, class, sexuality, age and other categories of difference create structural inequalities that may be reconstituted in and through the future of work. We look to disability studies as a particularly salient way in which labour market transitions can help us to rethink questions of embodiment, positionality and intersectionality. By exploring the particular histories and distinctive geographies that give rise to individual and societal impacts, chapters progressively shed light on the experiences of those that are beginning to live the future of work. As pertinent to this discussion, the book considers the growing importance of asset ownership, particularly housing, in shaping class structures. This trend, alongside the decline of traditional welfare systems, is argued to undermine employment-centred models of class. While this shift presents challenges, such as trapping some in a 'perpetual present', it also creates possibilities for new understandings of social mobility that incorporate asset ownership and its influence on social movement. By considering inequalities in asset ownership and speculative practices, the book aims to decentre the employment relationship by highlighting the extraction of value via other means, as well as how present-day capitalism relies upon "the expansive, future orientated time of speculation" (Adkins et al., 2020: 72).

More embodied understandings of work and working lives are further advanced through the inclusion of case study analyses of contemporary conditions of work. A broad although non-exhaustive range of professions and occupations are incorporated, many if not all characterised by rising unemployment rates, stagnant or declining wages, heightened job insecurity and precarious work arrangements, which combine to make employment and increasingly unreliable source of income and identity. Within this, we turn our attention to critical questions surrounding care and social reproduction. By including a specific examination of care work, both paid and unpaid, the book emphasises the interconnectedness of production and social reproduction in shaping work futures. This broadened lens ought help to ensure that (ongoing) discussions on the future of work consider not just economic output, but also the essential labour that sustains and reproduces society. Within the chapter on care, for instance, we underscore the significance of unpaid socially reproductive labour to the economy, while also allowing for a recap of earlier arguments about the potential for the future of work to modify how gender (and race, class, sexuality, age and citizenship) come to have meaning and are experienced by economic subjects. Several chapters also look to modes of resistance that can make visible the dynamics of labour, care, production and social reproduction within everyday life and how can these engender social transformations at local scales.

In addition to illuminating how the future of work is made manifest through different practices and the difference this makes to the lived experiences of workers across diverse sectors, the book considers the interplay between the future of work, political priorities and environmental concerns. It acknowledges that automation, the gig economy and a globalised workforce will have varying impacts depending on a nation's political stance on issues like retraining, social safety nets and green technology investments. The book explores how these factors influence new industrial relations models and approaches to income distribution outside of the labour market. Shifting electoral and geopolitical realities have been shown to exert a significant influence on both labour market regulations (e.g., job retraining programmes) and the composition of the workforce (e.g., focus on STEM education). The book underscores how these transformations are both a driver and a response to the concrete realities of work futures playing out. For instance, the push for a green economy creates new job opportunities in renewable energy, while also leading to job losses in fossil fuels, and requires political action to manage this transition. Similarly, there are potential environmental benefits (reduced commuting emissions) but also pitfalls (increased data centre energy consumption) of economic transitions based on factors like remote work. In this way, discussions around work futures are shown to be entangled with broader debates about human action, especially the consequences of economic production for the environment.

When discussing mechanisms for (re)shaping the unfolding future of work today, we consider how engaging with metanarratives about the future of work gives them a form of legitimacy and further evaluate the utility of this in the short term against the risk of such engagement bolstering the processes within which work changes emerge and become entrenched. The COVID-19 pandemic has accelerated existing future of work trends, but it is important to remember that the multifarious effects of globalisation, digitalisation, financialisation and innovation on workers and working lives are not new. Moreover, they are not fixed and immutable. Indeed, mirroring the discussion of positionality above, we draw the book to a close by reflecting on ways in which we – as critical scholars, actors and practitioners – can contribute to efforts to chart new pathways by engaging with postgrowth, care work, post-work and diverse economies conceptualisations of work and "embrace the very real possibility of meaningful transformation and lasting change" (Springer et al., 2016: 11).

Summary of the Chapters that Follow

The Handbook comprises ten sections (not including this introduction and the conclusion). This structure is intended to lend itself to use over the course of a semester of study on an undergraduate or postgraduate module. Each section consists of three chapters. Having already given a broad overview, we will use the remainder of this introduction to say a little more about what each section consists of. The first section following this introduction – Part 2: Futures of Work in Context – commences with Tim Strangleman's chapter on the history of the future of work. Strangleman shows how ideas about the future of work imply notions of the past and present too. In Chapter 3, Greig Charnock presents a critical theory of the future of work through an interrogation of the notion of the 'fourth industrial revolution' as an expression of capitalist social relations. In the closing chapter of Part 2, Jean Cushen and Paul Thompson relate the future of work to the financialised character of contemporary capitalism and its impacts on the workplace.

Part 3, Automation, Technology and the Future of Work, confronts the technological dimensions that shape the unfolding futures of work against the backdrop of the dynamics charted in the previous part. In Chapter 5, Eleni Papagiannaki drills down into the sometimes conflicting Marxian theoretical underpinnings of current debates about the future of work and the productive and technological tendencies taken to define contemporary capitalism. In Chapter 6, James Steinhoff considers the specific technological manifestations of automation in action, using the concept of 'synthetic automation' to understand the properties of artificial intelligence and machine learning as themselves products of capitalist social relations. In Chapter 7, Abigail Gilbert develops a sophisticated heuristic approach to the definition of automation and augmentation of work with reference to the different forms of value creation and capture represented in various instantiations of workplace technology.

Part 4, Platforms, Platform Labour and Gig Work, looks at one of the most notable and widely discussed aspects of the unfolding futures of work. In Chapter 8, Al James takes a feminist approach to the proliferation of platform and gig work, contextualising them in wider pasts and presents of working life through the prism of women's experiences of precarious and hidden digital labour. In Chapter 9, David Hesmondhalgh and Charles Umney argue for a reconfiguration of the focus in the existing literature upon platforms for the provision and organisation of gig work towards the role that 'non-labour' platforms play in shaping working life for those employed in fields such as retail, hospitality and the cultural and creative industries. In Chapter 10, Kalie Mayberry, Lindsey Cameron and Hatim Rahman consider how platform and gig workers resist algorithmic management through a case study of the #DeclineNow movement as a form of 'algo-activism' addressed to the on-demand platform DoorDash.

Part 5, Identity and Difference in the Future of Work, considers the intersectional ways in which existing divides and inequalities shape the unfolding futures of work. In Chapter 11, Bridget Kenny considers how the digitalisation of work in South Africa reproduces the dynamics of racial capitalism, not only reinforcing but also exacerbating existing inequalities at the intersection of race, class and gender. In Chapter 12, Melanie Jones, Kim Hoque, Victoria Wass and Nicholas Bacon develop a definition of disability-related disadvantage in the context of periods of economic upheaval, including changes in the character of work and employment. The chapter proposes some policies that could help combat this disadvantage as demographic and technological shifts reshape the labour market. In Chapter 13, Julie MacLeavy critically examines the limitations of conventional employment models in explaining social stratification, as asset ownership takes on increasing importance. She contends that concerns about the future of work may pivot from securing specific jobs towards acquiring the skills and opportunities that empower asset accumulation. Consequently, social class could become less tethered to labour market position, instead reflecting one's ability to use asset holdings to navigate the dynamic economic landscape.

Part 6, Gender, Care and Social Reproduction, engages with gender, sexuality and the related divisions of labour that will shape the future of socially reproductive work in fields like care. In Chapter 14, M. Winter first outlines the history of gender at work in the context of technological shifts, going on to consider the implications for the presents and futures of work in the affective economy of caring labour and the 'agile' economy characterised by new means of quantification and surveillance of an 'ideal worker'. In Chapter 15, Lizzie Richardson and Daniel Cockayne bring feminist, queer and trans theory to bear upon the future of work discourse, providing an alternative understanding of temporality and futurity that challenges the economistic and technocratic visions prevalent in the literature. Their chapter then provides some concrete examples of the futures of work that follow from this new understanding. In Chapter 16, Karin Schwiter considers the shifting burden of care work within and beyond families as a consequence of transformations in wage labour, examining how the commodification and marketisation of care have created a precarious workforce largely comprising women and migrant workers. The chapter examines the possible futures that await between digitalisation and alternative ways of organising social reproduction.

Part 7, Sectoral Case Studies, explores the unfolding futures of work experienced in the specific contexts of three key industrial settings: services, manufacturing and agriculture. In Chapter 17, Matthew Cole argues that the service sector will continue to be central to the future of work as a key engine of economic growth, but that the character of the future of work in this sector will be subject to technological and institutional dynamics ultimately determined by the capital-labour antagonism. In Chapter 18, Darryn Snell, Mark Dean and Al Rainnie consider the false promise of the fourth industrial revolution for manufacturing in Australia, as the country's industrial policy is shaped by the sometimes competing imperatives of free trade, extractivism and militarisation. In Chapter 19, Constantine Manolchev, David Watson, Laura Colombo, Patrick Elf and James Scott Vandeventer (members of the Management Educators Navigating Degrowth [MEND] collective) examine how technology is shaping the relationship between workers and nature in the agrifood sector, which consists of industries like agriculture and horticulture. The chapter uses the case study of a daffodil farm in the South West of the UK to chart the possible futures and alternatives incubated in the work-related use of agrifood technologies.

Part 8, Labour Market Transitions and Insecurity, explores the interlinked experiences in(to) and out of work witnessed among young people, unpaid workers such as carers and volunteers, and the self-employed. In Chapter 20, Edward Yates considers the working conditions faced by young workers entering the labour market, how they are likely to change and how they might be improved through a range of policy and practical measures, including education and economic strategy and the role of trade unions. In Chapter 21, Nancy Worth seeks to address the underrepresentation of unpaid work in accounts of the future of work based on formalised labour markets and wage labour, focusing in particular on a case study of self-employment to illustrate the potential uses of unpaid work for illuminating new aspects of work futures. In Chapter 22, Paolo Borghi puts the present and future of self-employed work in recent historical perspective, charting the emergence of 'independent professions' as a new archetype of the self-employed workforce around which may emerge a new understanding of the rights and freedoms associated with self-employment.

Part 9, Mobilities and Geographies of Work Futures, focuses on the temporal, spatial and place-based dynamics that underpin the changing world of work within and between specific national and international contexts. In Chapter 23, Rutvica Andrijasevic, Julie Yujie Chen and Marc Steinberg put global production in its context of both time and space, exploring how the just-in-time methods associated with Toyota have been adapted in manufacturing in China and Europe, including in the digitalisation and automation of work. In Chapter 24, Julie MacLeavy, Suzanne Mills, Katie Mazer and Darja Reuschke consider the spatial reorganisation of labour through and after the COVID-19 pandemic through the prism of remote workers and their migratory movements within both the UK and Canada. In Chapter 25, David Etherington, David Beel and Martin Jones put work futures in their place by examining city regions as a relevant site for contestation and regulation of the terms and conditions of the changing workplace and employment relationship, with a particular focus on Sheffield in the UK.

Part 10, Policy and the Politics of Work Futures, continues where the previous part left off by considering how work futures are shaped by institutions at the level of industrial relations, welfare policy and party politics. In Chapter 26, Huw Thomas and Peter Turnbull argue for the relevance of industrial relations to the future of work against claims of its redundancy as a focus for resistance and collective action, even though its core notions of efficiency, equity and voice require reframing in the context of the changing employment relationship. In Chapter 27, Jo Ingold stresses the importance of welfare policy to the unfolding future of work, and in particular social protection measures and active labour market policies. These represent core components of the state's toolbox in regulating the sphere of employment, Ingold shows, but seldom have empowering consequences for those who stand to benefit from them. In Chapter 28, Frederick Harry Pitts and M. Winter survey the growing political science literature on the role routine workers have played in the electoral upheavals of recent years, the potential salience of automation risk as a factor driving this dynamic and the questionable capacity of conventional redistributive measures to respond to the sense of anxiety and anticipated hardship associated with the changing position of some voters in the unfolding future of work.

Part 11, Environment and the Future of Work, relates the variously utopian and dystopian futures projected onto the world of work to the equally pressing reality of climate crisis and the very different futures it implies. In Chapter 29, Ed Atkins examines claims about green jobs as the jobs of the future and the contradictions of current attempts to construct a 'just transition', proposing an alternative approach that may go some way towards realising the inclusive potential of green transformation for the world of work. In Chapter 30, Evie Gilbert situates the experience of workers in garment factories in Asia within debates about energy transitions, exploring how supply chains in labour could be reshaped by the development of 'greener' garment manufacturing through the use of renewables and new technology. In Chapter 31, Laurie Parsons stresses the likely future impacts of a heating planet upon work and the workers who will come to labour in extreme temperatures, bringing to attention a new front in the fight for a better world of work.

The book then closes with Chapter 32, a conclusion which recapitulates some of the key points of the book while also proposing future research agendas and theoretical and empirical directions informed by the preceding chapters. Having devoted specific attention to material and ideological shifts through the course of the book, our intention in this final chapter is to remind readers that the trajectory of employment change is not determined or inevitable. Moreover, internalising passive discourses about the future of work risks disempowerment. Work futures remain subject to social, political and economic struggles. By recognising this, we can actively engage in shaping a future that reflects alternative values and aspirations.

References

Adkins, L., Cooper, M. and Konings, M. (2020). *The Asset Economy: Property Ownership and the New Logic of Inequality*. Cambridge: Polity Press.

Benanav, A. (2020). *Automation and the Future of Work*. London: Verso Books.

Dinerstein, A.C. and Pitts, F.H. (2021). *A World beyond Work? Labour, Money and the Capitalist State between Crisis and Utopia*. Bingley: Emerald Publishing.

Edgell, S., Gottfried, H. and Granter, E. (2015). *The SAGE Handbook of the Sociology of Work and Employment*. London: SAGE.

Ford, M. (2015). *The Rise of the Robots: Technology and the Threat of Mass Unemployment*. New York: Basic Books.

Gibson-Graham, J.K. and Dombroski, K. (2020). *The Handbook of Diverse Economies*. Cheltenham: Edward Elgar.

Graeber, D. (2018). *Bullshit Jobs: A Theory*. New York: Simon & Schuster.

Kochan, T. and Dyer, L. (2001). *Shaping the Future of Work: A Handbook for Action and a New Social Contract*. Abingdon: Routledge.

Malone, T.W. (2004). *The Future of Work: How the New Order of Work Will Shape Your Organization, Your Management Style, Your Life.* Cambridge, MA: Harvard Business School Press.
Mason, P. (2015). *PostCapitalism: A Guide to our Future*. London: Allen Lane.
Müller, M. (2021). Worlding geography: From linguistic priviledge to decolonial anywheres, *Progress in Human Geography*, 45(6): 1440–1466. https://doi.org/10.1177/0309132520979356
Simms, M. (2019). *What Do We Know and What Should We Do about the Future of Work?* London: SAGE.
Springer, S., Birch, K. and MacLeavy, J. (2016). *The Handbook of Neoliberalism*. Abingdon: Routledge.
Srnicek, N. and Williams, A. (2015). *Inventing the Future: Postcapitalism and a World without Work.* London: Verso Books.
Standing, G. (2011). *The Precariat.* London: Bloomsbury.
Weeks, K. (2011). *The Problem with Work: Feminism, Marxism and Anti-work Politics*. Durham, London: Duke University Press.
West, D.M. (2018). *The Future of Work: Robots, AI, and Automation*. Washington D.C.: Brookings Institution Press.
Williams, C.C. (2007). *Re-thinking the Future of Work: Directions and Visions*. London: Bloomsbury Publishing.

PART 2

Futures of Work in Context

2

THE FUTURE OF WORK

A History

Tim Strangleman

Introduction

In the late 1970s, Italian automotive giant Fiat made an advert for its new model the Strada. Unlike most car commercials of the time, the Italian car company chose to stress the modernity of its production process, in particular the near-complete absence – from the advert at least – of any form of human labour. The tagline at the end of the commercial was 'The New Fiat Strada – Hand Built By Robots'.[1]

I have shown the advert to my sociology of work students for a number of years now. While the film is a little grainy, the only thing that really dates it are the cars themselves and the transporter lorry they drive onto at the finale. Before this, we see robots constructing frames, moving sub-assemblies on driverless platforms, robotic arms caught in showers of sparks and even choreographed robots spray-painting the near-finished product. 'What', I ask my students, 'has changed?'. If the Strada production line of the late 1970s was the future of work then, how are the various projections of an automated future different now?

I think the 'Hand Built By Robots' commercial can tell us a lot about the futures of work. Fundamentally, it is about technology and its relationship to the labour of human beings. It alerts us to continuities and changes in the way we think about work in the past, present and future. The commercial appears at a pivotal moment in capitalism, at a moment of growing mass unemployment, of huge shakeouts of industrial workforce, the ending of the long postwar boom – *the Glorious Thirty* as the French describe those three decades. This is an era when the crisis in the modern welfare state was matched by a crisis in the Fordism which had underpinned it (Harvey 1989).

Societies have always imagined their futures and an important element of that imagination has been focused on the question of work. The imagining of a future of work almost always tells us more about past and present relationships to labour; it reveals hidden hopes, fears, desires and concerns (see Anthony 1977; Clayre 1974; Hays 1995; Jennings 1985; Thomas 1999). This concern for the future is amplified by modernity itself. Industrialisation created moral, economic, ethical, political and social questions about the relationship of both individuals and society to economic life. Fears about the future often stimulated a backward-looking nostalgia for an idealised labouring past, or at other moments allowed progressives to imagine a more humane and dignified account of what could be to come (Anthony 1983; Stansky 1985). One of the signature themes in

DOI: 10.4324/9781003327561-4

discussions of the relationship between work and the future has been technology. In one register, technology liberates humans from drudge labour, allowing them to fulfil themselves through what they do. In another register, technology is itself oppressive, devaluing the intrinsic rewards of craft and creativity, reducing activity to animalistic repetition owing to its relentless pursuit of efficiency and standardisation (see Jay and Jay 1986; Kropotkin 1974; Meakin 1976). This chapter gives an overview of this rich history of the future, allowing the reader to make links to older ways of understanding work in the context of contemporary debates.

Past Futures

In his famous Preface to *The Making of the English Working Class*, social historian E. P Thompson writes:

> I am seeking to rescue the poor stockinger, the Luddite cropper, the obsolete hand-loom weaver, the 'utopian' artisan, and even the deluded follower of Joanna Southcott, from the enormous condescension of posterity. Their crafts and traditions may have been dying. Their hostility to the new industrialism may have been backward-looking. Their communitarian ideals may have been fantasies. Their insurrectionary conspiracies may have been foolhardy. But they lived through these times of acute social disturbance, and we did not. Their aspirations were valid in terms of their own experience: and, if they were casualties of history, they remain, condemned in their own lives, as casualties.
>
> (Thompson 1963, 12)

Thompson's project was to understand how a working class emerged in a distinctly English way in the late eighteenth and early nineteenth centuries – the classic early period of the industrial revolution. Thompson's argument was that the English people were not blank slates going into or emerging from that process, but rather were fully formed actors with their own autonomous and vibrant cultures, ethics and feelings – what Raymond Williams (1973) described as a structure of feeling. It was this set of values that working people carried with them into the process of change, rooted as it was in the moral economy of preindustrial life. Their experience of change, and by extension their visions of the future of work were embedded in a preindustrial sensibility and value system. Thompson later went on to write an historical biography of William Blake, entitling it *Witness Against the Beast*, reflecting religious ideas about the absence of a moral order in the newly emerging industrial capital (Thompson 1993). The point to note here is how the future of work is critiqued through moral sentiment, something shared in wider public and philosophical discourse in the eighteenth century and evidenced in essayists such as Adam Smith (1999 [1776]) and David Hume (1969 [1739]).

English polymath Humphrey Jennings was engaged in a similar project to E.P. Thompson, albeit slightly earlier, and developed his ideas on a wider historical canvas. Jennings was interested in the experience of industrial culture, and the problem of how to capture responses to the future of work as it unfolded through the long industrial revolution. In his book *Pandaemonium*, Jennings (1985) compiled hundreds of fragments of writing – reportage, diary entry and creative – by people who had lived through and witnessed the industrial revolution in Britain between the seventeenth and nineteenth centuries. Posthumously published 35 years after his death, *Pandaemonium* comprises 372 excerpts, or 'images' to use Jennings own phrase, which reflect the coming of the machine-age over two centuries from 1660 to 1886. The images are arranged chronologically from John Milton's 1660 'The Building of Pandaemonium', through to William Morris' 1886 'The Day of the Earth'.

Pandaemonium is important in both form and content for this current chapter. The collection and structuring of the material is an illustration of Jennings' surrealist sensibility – the juxtaposition of differing images that allow us to look anew upon the process and events of industrialisation. While interested in differing views of industrial transition his collection seeks to capture a poetic sensibility for that change. He described these passages as 'images', and his intention was to create what he called an *imaginative history*.

What Jennings alerts us to is the sublime power of the forces unleased by industrial change, but also how these transitions were rendered into normal life. This is in itself a significant aspect of the processes Thompson was attempting to capture – not simply the shock of the new and the eclipse of the old, but also the process by which the new was rendered intelligible, accepted, normalised and, in turn, acted upon – to forge a future.

Both Thompson and Jennings form part of the English romantic tradition which at its root has a concern with the relationship between culture and labour. This moment was refreshed in industrial Britain by artists and writers such as John Ruskin, William Morris and the Pre-Raphaelite brotherhood (see Anthony 1983; Stansky 1985). The reaction here to the future of work was to seek solace and inspiration in the past, and in particular the act of craft. Here authenticity was sought in the pleasure of labour and a rejection of mass production. Contained within this attitude was a strong moral concern for the collective labourer, an emerging proletariat cut adrift from place, older forms of work and social relationships in which they were embedded. We can also see here elements of Marxian thought about the process of industrialisation and emerging capitalism. In his essay 'A Note on Nostalgia', Bryan Turner highlights the imprint of nostalgia on early sociology, explicitly represented in a concern with loss – skills, tradition, cultures and ways of life. This, he argues, frames, at least in part, how later sociologists have thought about the present and where they have about the future (Turner 1987).

It is worth thinking here about Raymond Williams and his concept of 'structure of feeling'. In *The Country and the City*, Williams (1973) stresses the centuries-old tradition of seeing the past as better than the present, and the future as lacking intelligibility. He likens this to each generation stepping on to an escalator and looking back over their shoulder to see the past as more real, authentic and positive. This speaks to the modern condition of uncertainty both about the present and by extension the future. It is that lack of certainty that is profoundly part of modernity itself, the sense that 'All that is solid melts into air' as Marx and Engels (1986 [1848]) noted in the *Communist* Manifesto (see also Berman 1983). In the literary tradition that Williams was an integral part of, we can see this in David Meakin's (1976) *Man and Work*, especially a chapter entitled 'The nostalgia of permanence at work'. Meakin draws on a range of authors such as George Eliot and Thomas Hardy who evoke settled communities on the cusp of industrialisation, or where rural areas which were threatened by modernity. The nature of work and its vulnerability is central here. While many of these accounts primarily focus on the past, they effectively convey a sense of apprehension regarding the future of work, emphasising concerns about the gradual devaluation and disruption of established value systems and societal order (see Strangleman 2007).

Two slightly later works of fiction that do speak to the future of work, albeit in a dystopian manner, are H.G. Wells' *The Time Machine* of 1895 and Aldous Huxley's *Brave New World* of 1932 (Wells 2012 [1895]; Huxley 1970 [1932]). In *The Time Machine*, Wells projects a future where two distinct species of humans, the Eloi and Morlocks, have evolved. The former are essentially an upper class, untroubled by labour of any kind, living a seemingly utopian, prelapsarian existence – the one fly in the ointment being that they are regularly eaten by the simian-like Morlocks, a kind of future proletariat. The story is highly reflective of contemporary Victorian concerns for the effects of urban industrial labour on the working-class body, and by extension the perils of leisure on that of the upper-class body. Wells, like others who shared his politics, was influenced by eugenicist ideas of breeding and degeneration. *Brave New World* equally projects a division of labour rooted in a caste system ordained at conception. This later interwar vision of the future of work reflects the concern with mature Fordist mass production.

Fears of the future of work in the interwar period are also reflected in influential films of the period. In Fritz Lang's 1927 *Metropolis*, wealthy industrialists preside over a world where subterranean dwellers live to work on vast machines. An altogether more light-hearted version of the present/future of work can be seen in the 1936 Charlie Chaplin movie *Modern Times*. Here Chaplin's famous tramp character is transformed into a Fordist production line worker. He is at one point literally pulled into the production process becoming embedded in the machine. The future of work here is portrayed as unrelentingly monotonous and destructive of humanity.

The interwar period is a fascinating one for debates about the past, present and potential futures of work. Leaving aside the fictional dystopian accounts outlined above, we can see a society coming to terms with a maturing capitalism and with it mass society based on mass consumption and production. Importantly here too we see how modern work is often unfavourably juxtaposed to more heroic labour deemed to have been eclipsed (see Strangleman 2007). This kind of attitude is apparent in various places in the interwar period in the UK. In 1933, for instance, essayist J.B. Priestley set out on what was to become his *English Journey*, a kind of state of the nation of the depression era. Early on in his account he passes through the newly industrialised suburbs of outer London and notes:

> After the familiar muddle of West London, the Great West Road looked very odd. Being new, it did not look English. We might have suddenly rolled into California. Or, for that matter, into one of the main avenues of the old exhibitions, like the Franco-British Exhibition of my boyhood. It was the line of new factories on each side that suggested the exhibition, for years of the West Riding have fixed for ever my idea of what a proper factory looks like; a grim blackened rectangle with a tall chimney at one corner. These decorative little buildings, all glass and concrete and chromium plate, seem to my barbaric mind to be merely playing at being factories.
>
> (Priestley 1984 [1934], 10)

Priestley refused to see these new factories as authentic, as he continued:

> You could go up to any one of these charming little fellows, I feel and safely order an ice-cream or select a few picture postcards. But as for industry, real industry with double entry and bills of landing, I cannot believe them capable of it.

Priestley argued that their cosmetic appeal and prominent positioning on a main arterial road stressed the shift of industry from the 'old' North to the 'new' South. But his concern with authenticity does not end with the new architecture in which they are self-consciously wrapped. For these new places of work produced not tangible heavy industrial products, but rather 'Potato crisps, scents, tooth pastes, bathing costumes, fire extinguishers'. These sites of industry, the work that goes on in them and the products made there, had a certain weightlessness about them; they were somehow trivial, insubstantial and inauthentic.

This lionising of heroic work and workers associated with traditional labour and industry was a common trope in the interwar period and especially the 1930s. The left-leaning Documentary Film Movement (DFM) self-consciously sought out workers in traditional industries as subjects for their films of the period. Influenced by European socialist realism, the group attempted to capture the 'dignified labour' of steel workers, shipbuilders and coal miners. Paul Swann, in his fascinating account of the DFM, quotes Edgar Anstey, an influential member of this group, on his attitude to the representation of manual labour: 'the workingman can only be a heroic figure. If he's not heroic, he can't be a workingman almost' (Swann 1989, 88).

In this register, the future of work is projected as being inauthentic, insubstantial, unheroic less able to furnish (male) workers with real identity. There is a strong link here between the type of work and industry, the commodities being made and sold and the workers and consumers involved in these new processes. Fears of automation in the future are certainly there, especially in fictional portrayals of work futures, but non-fictional commentators on work display a kind of nostalgia for passing heavy industry and what might replace it (see Strangleman 2004, 2007).

The Postwar Futures of Work

The developed economies of Europe, the UK and North America experienced an unprecedented period of growth and affluence in the period after 1945. This was the era of the long boom, the *Glorious Thirty* – a three decades long rise in living standards for working people (Piketty 2014; Rosanvallon 2013). This era of relative growth allowed a variety of ways of thinking about the future to flourish. In many ways, the positive accounts of the future of work were born out of the negativity of the post-WW1 and interwar period – marked by high levels of unemployment and joblessness. During and just after WW2, by contrast, a range of liberal, social democratic and socialist thinking aimed to prioritise full employment coupled to a broader commitment to better work and social conditions. This postwar optimism was rooted in social, economic and industrial planning – illustrated in the 1945 book *There's Work For All,* written by Michael Young and Theodor Prager (1945), one of a number of volumes in *The New Democracy* series. On one level, rising affluence led to greater amounts of holiday and leisure time, meaning that work, if measured in time, was decreasing in importance, albeit modestly. As long ago as 1931, Keynes had predicted that the problem of work in the future would be the question of how to share out what little labour there was to be had. As he noted, within a hundred years would see the dawn of 'the age of abundance' (Keynes quoted by Basso 2003, 27).

In UK terms, possibly the most obvious attempt at futurology by work sociologists are the Affluent Worker studies which had their roots in the 1950s and early 1960s but were published in three volumes in 1968 (Goldthorpe et al. 1968). Their importance for the current chapter is that Goldthorpe and his colleagues were essentially trying to understand future trajectories of work through studying both the past and present. They were attempting to design a research project which would allow them to understand and explain postwar voting patterns of working-class electors. After the success of the postwar Attlee Labour government of 1945, voters subsequently rejected Labour and chose the Conservative Party in the 1951, 1955 and 1959 general elections. In each instance the Conservatives increased their majority. Of the various explanations put forward, the most interesting was that the working-class electorate was becoming bourgeois, the so-called 'embourgeoisement' thesis, as a result of growing postwar affluence. Goldthorpe and Lockwood attempted to test this thesis by researching workers attracted to newer, lighter industries coalescing around the Bedfordshire town of Luton. Through their research they developed a typology of workers – 'Deferential', 'Traditional' and 'Affluent' or 'Instrumental'. It was this last group that were seen as being in the vanguard of a new type of orientation to work – the worker of the future. These 'affluent workers' held an instrumental orientation to work that valued monetary reward over any intrinsic benefits. This was not to say that they were inherently more conservative in their general life or voting intentions. Rather, Goldthorpe and his colleagues argued that these workers could in the future be extremely militant if their wages did not rise in line with expectations. To some extent, these projections were born out as the long boom faltered then ended in the early 1970s and wages became squeezed by inflation and the industrial workforce became increasingly restless.

During the 1970s, there started to develop a trend to think about the by now obvious trends in the economy. Central to this was the shift away from traditional industries to a wide variety of service work (see Chapter 17). One of the earliest thinkers here was the Harvard sociologist Daniel Bell whose 1973 book *The Coming of the Post-Industrial Society* spoke to many of these themes. Interestingly, Bell's book was subtitled '*A Venture in Social Forecasting*', emphasising that this was futurology based on likely trends rather than firm prediction. The essential argument was that society was experiencing a shift away from production to services and that the future jobs were likely to be those requiring higher levels of education and training. Less qualified manual labour was likely to be rapidly reduced or disappear altogether as a result of new technology or job export.

Slightly later in the 1970s, Krishan Kumar wrote his *Prophecy and Progress: The Sociology of the Industrial and Post-Industrial Society*. Kumar noted how accounts of the future of industrial society tended towards the negative, even after WW2 a brief period of optimism was dashed by nascent ecological worries about the pollution caused by modern industrialism. But arguably the most interesting insights in *Prophecy and Progress* centred around computer technology and its role in the future shaping of work. In a fascinating speculative account of work futures, Kumar notes:

> Computers in particular hold out the strongest potential for the de-centralisation and domestication of work, especially white-collar work. In this they are even more promising than the telephone, whose de-centralizing possibilities have still barely been touched. … There is consequently no need for a worker in a computerized office to do anything physically in some central location. … In practice then he can perfectly well work at home for at any rate a great proportion of the time.
>
> (Kumar 1978, 319)

Kumar's vision of the future is strikingly accurate in some aspects – he predicts the power of computer technology to decentre work, while in other senses the positive aspects of this home working have not come to fruition. For example, he thought that home working would increase leisure and family-friendly child raising. Both Bell and Kumar point out that the future of work, and more broadly society, must be allowed to shift beyond the models that emerged in industrial society, echoing older nineteenth-century utopian projections and pre-empting later writings.

Coterminous with Kumar's *Prophecy and Progress* was Jonathan Gershuny's (1978) *After Industrial Society: The Emerging Self-Service Economy*. Gershuny shared some of Kumar's optimism about what *could be*, but thought the shape of post-industrial society would be somewhat different than others predicted. For Gershuny, the service sector was likely to shrink, in part driven by self-provisioning in the household unit. Families were likely to purchase goods that allowed them to do things for themselves rather than buy-in services provided by other paid workers. There would, however, be a growth in technical and managerial occupations.

This interest in self-provisioning strategies was also reflected in Ray Pahl's (1984) *Divisions of Labour*, his long-term study of work and economic life on the Isle of Sheppey on the North Kent Coast. The study examined a number of household strategies for coping with low-wage work or unemployment on the relatively isolated island of Sheppey. Pahl described the Island as his 'post-industrial laboratory' (see Strangleman 2017b, 55). Pahl clearly saw a shift in industrial society occurring in the 1970s and 1980s and that this had a variety of causes and outcomes, impacting different households differently. Pahl was also prescient in the way he identified and discussed the process of deindustrialisation, itself both cause and effect of new ways of working.

Deindustrialisation is itself one work future, a kind of negative absence of work projected forward. This is a huge issue in itself and one that is the subject of a very large body of literature. For the purposes of this piece, deindustrialisation is important for the way it allows the exploration of economic futures, revealing the aspirations and fears of a wide variety of actors; deindustrialisation reveals expectations, norms, values and future orientations. In my research and writing I have often noted the way deindustrialisation acts as a breaching experiment – how loss or change in routine exposes taken for granted norms of behaviours and expectation (see Strangleman 2019). In this sense, the large-scale loss of industrial employment acts as a time for reflection on the past, present and future of work. The taken for granted assumptions about an individual and collective unfolding of working life were profoundly shaken. One aspect of the literature on deindustrialisation is how researchers projected their findings into the future. Pahl himself did this in *Divisions of Labour* but it was also apparent in other studies, especially on coalfield areas (see Strangleman 2022). A good example of this is in Warwick and Littlejohn's (1992) *Coal, Capital and Culture* which studied four former coalfield communities in Yorkshire, UK. As the authors say:

> The mining communities which we have discussed are being restructured by such forces, largely out of the control of the people who live there. The certainty of employment in a local industry, always subject to the constraints of the market for coal, the geological conditions and the organisation of production, has now virtually disappeared. What may have been a dream, or a nightmare, for boys in these localities [coal employment] is now no more than a fading shadow.
>
> (Warwick and Littlejohn 1992, 206)

Coal, Capital and Culture drew out the historical specificity of coalfield areas like West Yorkshire in understanding both the problems being faced concurrently around closure as well as projecting the likely trajectory of the long-term effects of decline. Using Bourdieu's notion of different types of capital, Warwick and Littlejohn struck a depressing note as to the fate of the communities they study:

> The local cultural capital which has been created in the four communities is likely to be eroded within a generation as the reality of coal mining as employment as that basis for social and political organisation disappears. The disadvantage which this will reinforce ought to be the subject of much more scrutiny than it is receiving.
>
> (Warwick and Littlejohn 1992, 206)

The future of work here is bleak. What is projected are communities, particularly the young and immobile being trapped in a cycle of unemployment, underemployment or at best precarious work – pre-empting later discussions on insecure work by two decades.

One way in which deindustrialisation scholars have thought about the future – with or without work – is by developing Sherry Linkon's notion of the 'half-life of deindustrialisation' (Linkon 2018). Using the metaphor of the degrading of radioactivity over an extended period of time, Linkon and others have projected out from the discrete event of plant closure and shutdown to think about the myriad ways in which deindustrialisation unfolds – economically, politically, socially and culturally (see Emery 2018; Fraser and Clark 2021; Strangleman 2017a). Like Warwick and Littlejohn's analysis, the notion of the half-life draws on historical and present conditions to project forward potential trajectories. The concept of half-life is rich as it allows for complexity in terms of variability of geographic location, type and nature of industry, alternative employment opportunities and the intervention strategies of local, regional and national politicians which have the propensity to change envisioned futures.

The 'End of Work' as the Future of Work

A notable feature of debates about work from the 1990s onwards was the tendency to proclaim an end, or rupture in work (see Crow 2005 for a wider account of this trend). This body of literature – one I described elsewhere as the 'end of work' debate – said many interesting things about perceptions of the past, present and by implications the futures of work (Strangleman 2007). The difficulty with this very amorphous literature was that it tended to be quite ahistorical, while often not especially concerned with the empirical reality of the present in which it was situated. Broadly speaking the end of work literature was written by social theorists, rather than sociologists who were specialists in economic life. It was these non-specialists who projected an evolving detraditionalisation and individualising from current patterns. In the process, they created almost ideal typifications of work in the past. Initially it was US journalist Jeremy Rifkin (1995) who wrote his provocatively titled *The End of Work* that led the way. He argued two main points were shaping contemporary work. Firstly, the rapid introduction of new technology was accelerating the process of job loss, without the creation of the volume of new employment to replace them. Second, with the rise of globalisation and non-interventionist neo-liberal policies, there was no longer a political will, nor coordinated policy response, that could react to these shifts.

For more sociologically inclined writers, the 'end' did not imply the absolute destruction of employment but more the individual and collective hollowing out of workplace meaning and identity. Catherine Casey's 1995 *Work, Self and Society after Industrialism* stated that:

> The industrial legacy of the centrality of production and work in social and self formation hovers precipitously with the post-industrial condition in which work is declining in social primacy. *Social meaning and solidarity must, eventually, be found elsewhere.*
>
> (Casey 1995, 2, emphasis added)

Work, it was theorised, no longer offered the chance to build and sustain identity. Zygmunt Bauman argues along these lines in *Work, Consumerism and the New Poor* stating that in the past: '… work was the main orientation point, in reference to which all other life pursuits could be planned and ordered' (1998, 17). He goes on to claim that:

> A steady, durable and continuous, logically coherent and tightly-structured working career is however no longer a widely available option. Only in relatively rare cases can a permanent identity be defined, let alone secured, through the job performed.
>
> (Bauman 1998, 27)

This leads, he posits, to a greater sense of individualisation in terms of an orientation to life in general and work in particular. There are a number of other writers, mostly high-profile social theorists, who discuss work in near-identical ways. Here we could think of the writing of Ulrich Beck (2000), Andre Gorz (1999) and especially Richard Sennett (1998). The thread running through these works is the idea that employment was once collective, solid and stable and that late modernity – however one may characterise it – has in various ways eroded, or in Sennett's phrase 'corroded', the basis of this order. There are a number of 'futures' which emerge from this analysis. On one level, left unchecked work will continue to become increasingly unstable and devoid of meaning. However, some – notably Beck and Gorz – believe that the contemporary nature of work represents an opportunity for radical change, a breaking away of the 'tyranny of work', a kind of neo-Marxist opportunity for reform. The future of work would mean a more equitable sharing of work across society, and possibly a guaranteed income – a proto-Universal Basic Income (see Hasdell 2020).

There was some pushback from more empirically minded academics against the more dire predictions of the 'end of work' tendency; most notably authors like Kevin Doogan (2009) and Ralph Fevre (2007), who argued that such bleak assessments didn't stand up to evidential scrutiny. Nonetheless, there remains an enduring attraction in the idea of work being eroded and devalued. In the second decade of the new century in the wake of the 2008 financial crisis, a new iteration of this discussion emerged with economist Guy Standing's 'precarity' thesis (see Standing 2011, 2014). Essentially, Standing's thesis was that precarious work was becoming normalised across the developed economies of the West. In turn, this was creating an ever-larger body of people he described as the *Precariat*, defined by their shared experience of work – devoid of permanency, prospects, training and good pay. Without greater state regulation – Standing in his 2014 follow-up book suggests dozens of regulatory changes – the future of work would be marked by ever greater insecurity and instability.

In many ways, the literature that has emerged around the gig economy or platform work could be seen as the precariat made flesh (see Chapter 8). Here, the future of work would seem to consist of atomised workers eking out a living through a series of small, short-term parcels of work allocated by an algorithmically driven platform (Srnicek 2017). Workers here seemingly have little or no power, few opportunities for advancements and no collective interest (although see Chapter 10, which points to some emergent developments). Arguably, an even greater existential threat to the future of work comes from a mixture of big data, AI and robotics (Brynjolfsson and McAfee 2014; Ford 2015). Some commentators suggest that the Fourth Industrial Revolution really will abolish many types and forms of work we current witness around the globe.

One way to think about the contemporary attitude to work and its future is to look at the rejection of work in its mainstream contemporary form. One strand of this rejection takes the form of a revival of meaningful work through 'craft', echoing Romantic ideas of the Arts and Crafts Movement. Matt Crawford (2009) makes this case in *Shop Class as Soulcraft* where he argues for a re-evaluation of work away from a privileging of white-collar careers and back towards skilled blue-collar work (see also Korn 2015; Langlands 2017; Ocejo 2017). Another position around the future/contemporary divide is the emergence of a body of literature which questions work and the work ethic completely. Here we could discuss David Graeber (2018) and his *Bullshit Jobs: The Rise of Pointless Work and What We Can Do About It*. From a psychoanalytic position, Josh Cohen (2018) argues for inactivity in *Not Working: Why We Have to Stop*. Finally, journalist Sarah Jaffe (2021), in *Work Won't Love You Back*, seeks to persuade readers against thinking they will be rewarded for corporate loyalty.

Conclusions

What to make of all of these past and present work futures? Do they share any timeless collective insights for us today? There is certainly a sense that technological change continues to offer a threat or opportunity for humanity. Historically, shifts in work create losers as well as new winners. This may continue in the future, but it may not. As we have seen, in the *Communist Manifesto* Marx and Engels characterised the essential condition of capitalism as being inherently unstable – 'All that is solid melts into air'. To be modern, they argued, was to know no certainty or stability, the only surety being that change would, if anything, speed up as this economic system matured. The challenge for our own time is to confront the possibility of smaller amounts of work with the need for a form of income. Additionally, the pressing environmental crisis compels us to make changes to the way we consume, produce and approach work. This challenge presents both threats and genuine opportunities to critically examine the fundamental purpose of work and explore its potential trajectories in the future.

Note

1 Fiat Strada – Hand Built by Robots (1979, UK) – YouTube.

References

Anthony, P. D. (1977) *The Ideology of Work*, London, Tavistock.

Anthony, P. D. (1983) *John Ruskin's Labour: A Study of Ruskin's Social Theory*, Cambridge, Cambridge University Press.

Basso, P. (2003) *Modern Times, Ancient Hours: Working Lives in the Twenty-First Century*, London, Verso.

Bauman, Z. (1998) *Work, Consumerism and the New Poor*, Buckingham, Open University Press.

Beck, U. (2000) *The Brave New World of Work*, Cambridge, Polity.

Bell, D. (1973) *The Coming of the Post-Industrial Society: A Venture in Social Forecasting*, London, Penguin.

Berman, M. (1983) *All That Is Solid Melts into Air: The Experience of Modernity*, London, Verso.

Brynjolfsson, E. & McAfee, A. (2014) *The Second Machine Age: Work, Progress, and Prosperity in a Time of Brilliant Technologies*, New York, Norton.

Casey, C. (1995) *Work, Self and Society after Industrialism*, London, Routledge.

Clayre, A. (1974) *Work and Play: Ideas and Experience of Work and Leisure*, London, Weidenfeld & Nicholson.

Cohen, J. (2018) *Not Working: Why We Have to Stop*, London, Granta.

Crawford, M. (2009) *Shop Class as Soulcraft: An Inquiry into the Value of Work*, New York, Penguin.

Crow, G. (2005) 'Towards a sociology of endings', *Sociological Research Online*, 10, 3, 159–168.

Doogan, K. (2009) *New Capitalism? The Transformation of Work*, Cambridge, Polity.

Emery, J. (2018) 'Geographies of deindustrialization and the working-class: Industrial ruination, legacies, and affect', *Geography Compass*, 13, 2, 1–14.

Fevre, R. (2007) 'Employment insecurity and social theory: The power of nightmares, *Work, Employment and Society*, 21, 3, 517–535.

Ford, M. (2015) *The Rise of the Robots: Technology and the Threat of Mass Unemployment*, London, Oneworld.

Fraser, A. & Clark, A. (2021) 'Damaged hardmen: Organized crime and the half-life of deindustrialization', *British Journal of Sociology*, 72, 4, 1062–1076.

Gershuny, J. (1978) *After Industrial Society: The Emerging Self-Service Economy*, London, MacMillan.

Goldthorpe, J., Lockwood, D., Bechhofer, F. & Platt, J. (1968) *The Affluent Worker: Industrial Attitudes and Behaviour*, Cambridge, Cambridge University Press.

Gorz, A. (1999) *Reclaiming Work: Beyond the Wage-Based Society*, Cambridge, Polity.

Graeber, D. (2018) *Bullshit Jobs: The Rise of Pointless Work and What We Can Do about It*, London, Penguin.

Harvey, D. (1989) *The Condition of Postmodernity: An Enquiry into the Origins of Cultural Change*, Oxford, Blackwell.

Hasdell, R. (2020) *What We Know about Universal Basic Income: A Cross-Synthesis of Reviews*, Stanford, CA, Basic Income Lab.

Hays, S. (1995) *The Response to Industrialism 1885–1914* (2nd ed.), Chicago, IL, University of Chicago Press.

Hume, D. (1969 [1739]) *A Treatise of Human Nature*, London, Penguin.

Huxley, A. (1970 [1932]) *Brave New World*, London, Penguin.
Jaffe, S. (2021) *Work Won't Love You Back: How Devotion to Our Jobs Keeps Us Exploited, Exhausted and Alone*, London, Hurst.
Jay, E. & Jay, R. (eds.) (1986) *Critics of Capitalism: Victorian Reactions to 'Political Economy'*, Cambridge, Cambridge University Press.
Jennings, H. (1985) *Pandaemonium: The Coming of the Machine Age as Seen by Contemporary Observers*, London, Picador.
Korn, P. (2015) *Why We Make Things and Why It Matters: The Education of a Craftsman*, London, Square Peg.
Kropotkin, P. (1974) *Fields, Factories and Workshops Tomorrow*, London, George Allen & Unwin.
Kumar, K. (1978) *Prophecy and Progress: The Sociology of the Industrial and Post-Industrial Society*, London, Penguin.
Langlands, A (2017) *Craft: How Traditional Crafts Are about More Than Just Making Money*, London, Faber.
Linkon, S. (2018) *The Half-Life of Deindustrialization: Working-Class Writing about Economic Restructuring*, Ann Arbor, University of Michigan Press.
Marx, K. & Engels, F. (1986 [1848]) *The Communist Manifesto*, London, Penguin.
Meakin, D. (1976) *Man and Work: Literature and Culture in Industrial Society*, London, Methuen.
Ocejo, R. (2017) *Masters of Craft: Old Jobs in the New Urban Economy*, Princeton, NJ, Princeton University Press.
Pahl, R. (1984) *Divisions of Labour*, Oxford, Blackwell.
Piketty, T. (2014) *Capital in the Twenty-First Century*, Cambridge, Harvard University Press.
Priestley, J. B. (1984 [1934]) *English Journey*, London, Penguin.
Rifkin, J. (1995) *The End of Work: The Decline of the Global Labor Force and the Dawn of the Post-Market Era*, New York, Putnam.
Rosanvallon, P. (2013) *The Society of Equals*, Cambridge, MA, Harvard University Press.
Sennett, R. (1998) *The Corrosion of Character: The Personal Consequences of Work in the New Capitalism*, London, Norton.
Smith, A. (1999 [1776]) *The Wealth of Nations Books I-III*, London, Penguin.
Srnicek, N. (2017) *Platform Capitalism*, London, Polity Press.
Standing, G. (2011) *The Precariat: The New Dangerous Class*, London, Bloomsbury.
Standing, G. (2014) *A Precariat Charter: From Denizens to Citizens*, London, Bloomsbury.
Stansky, P. (1985) *Redesigning the World: William Morris, the 1880s, and the Arts and Crafts*, Princeton, NJ, Princeton University Press.
Strangleman, T. (2004) *Work Identity at the End of the Line: Privatisation and Culture Change in the UK Rail Industry*, Basingstoke, Palgrave.
Strangleman, T. (2007) 'The Nostalgia for permanence at work? The end of work and its commentators', *The Sociological Review*, 55, 1, 81–103.
Strangleman, T. (2017a) 'Deindustrialization and the historical sociological imagination: Making sense of work and industrial change', *Sociology*, 51, 2, 466–482.
Strangleman, T. (2017b) 'Portrait of a deindustrialising island', in Crow, G. & Ellis, J. (eds.) *Revisiting Divisions of Labour: The Impacts and Legacies of a Modern Sociological Classic*, Manchester: Manchester University Press. pp. 25–68.
Strangleman, T. (2019) *Voices of Guinness: An Oral History of the Park Royal Brewery*, New York, Oxford University Press.
Strangleman, T. (2022) 'Contextualising the coalfields: Mapping the socio-economic and cultural loss of the coal industry', in Simmons, R. & Simpson, K. (eds.) *Education, Work and Social Change in Britain's Former Coalfield Communities: The Ghost of Coal*, Basingstoke, Palgrave. pp. 13–36.
Swann, P. (1989) *The British Documentary Film Movement 1926–1946*, Cambridge, Cambridge University Press.
Thomas, K. (ed.) (1999) *The Oxford Book of Work*, Oxford, Oxford University Press.
Thompson, E. P. (1963) *The Making of the English Working Class*, London, Penguin.
Thompson, E. P. (1993) *Witness against the Beast: William Blake and the Moral Law*, Cambridge, Cambridge University Press.
Turner, B. S. (1987) 'A note on Nostalgia', *Theory, Culture & Society*, 4, 147–156.
Warwick, D. & Littlejohn, G. (1992) *Coal, Capital and Culture: A Sociological Analysis of Mining Communities in West Yorkshire*, London, Routledge.

Wells, H. G. (2012 [1895]) *The Time Machine*, London, Penguin.
Williams, R. (1973) *The Country and the City*, Oxford, Oxford University Press.
Young, M. & Prager, T. (1945) *There's Work for All*, London, Nicholson & Watson.

Films

Charlie Chaplin (1936) *Modern Times*.
Fritz Lang (1927) *Metropolis*.

Recommendations for Further Reading

Beer, S. (2018) 'Living the cruel futures of industrial change', *Social & Cultural Geography*, 19, 1, 102–119.
Cowie, J. (1999) *Capital Moves: RCA's 70-Year Quest for Cheap Labor*, Ithaca, NY, Cornell University Press.
Donkin, R. (2010) *The Future of Work*, Basingstoke, Palgrave.
Linkon, S. (2018) *The Half-Life of Deindustrialization: Working-Class Writing about Economic Restructuring*, Ann Arbor, University of Michigan Press.
McIvor, A. (2013) *Working Lives: Work in Britain Since 1945*, Basingstoke, Palgrave.
Potter, J. (2015) *Crisis at Work: Identity and the End of Career*, Basingstoke, Palgrave.
Strangleman, T. (2023) 'Sociological futures and the importance of the past', *Sociology*, 57, 2, 305–314.

3

WHAT IS THE FOURTH INDUSTRIAL REVOLUTION? TOWARDS A CRITICAL THEORY OF THE FUTURE OF WORK

Greig Charnock

Introduction

Humankind stands on the brink of an unprecedented epoch of transformation and progress, or so we are told. Today, technoscientific innovations are driving what one world-renowned economist calls a 'globotics upheaval' that is reshaping the future of work and with it 'our economies, our lives, our communities' (Baldwin, 2019: 83). Innovations in robotics, together with those associated with a so-called Fourth Industrial Revolution based on cyber-physical systems, the Internet of Things, cloud computing, and advanced machine learning, are dramatically reconfiguring how products and services are produced, distributed, and consumed across the world. If Klaus Schwab, the Founder and Executive Chair of the influential World Economic Forum is to be believed, the sheer scale, scope, and complexity of this Fourth Industrial Revolution will reduce the preceding three to mere prologue (Schwab, 2016). Much more so than even the epoch-making advent of large-scale industry and machine-based manufacturing in the nineteenth century, in distinct localities like Manchester in North West England, it will allegedly redefine economic, social, environmental, and political relations simultaneously across the *entire* globe. It will, Schwab (2016: 3) claims, have profound implications for humanity: for 'the way we live, work, and relate to each other' as human beings, and not just for the '"what" and the "how" of doing things but also "*who*" we are'. From this vista, the Fourth Industrial Revolution portends no less than the lifting of humanity 'into a new collective and moral consciousness based on a shared sense of destiny' (2016: 109; see also Marr, 2016).

We are also warned, however, that the 'super-disruptive' potency of such a seismic and exponential revolution in the production, distribution and consumption of goods and services could have deleterious impacts well beyond industry – on social inequality, government, and even human identity and morality (Lee et al., 2018: 6). While some will undoubtedly thrive in this new epoch, swathes of firms will go out of business, wages will diminish, job roles will be automated and disappear, and many middle-income earners will struggle to maintain standards of living (Brynjolfsson and McAfee, 2014). Governments and citizens stand on a knife-edge between 'empowerment' and 'disempowerment' (Schwab, 2016: 95): they must 'adapt' to this new context

DOI: 10.4324/9781003327561-5

or risk being left behind by a fast-moving, intensely competitive race for innovation and prosperity (see Chapter 25) (2016: 69, 97, 106).

Amid recent debates about what opportunities and challenges the Fourth Industrial Revolution brings, there are some who have expressed scepticism about its newness and significance. The very idea of a Fourth Industrial Revolution has been mocked as science fiction and eschatology (Geiger, 2020). It has been dismissed in some quarters as hyperbole or something 'people pretend is original' (Edgerton, 2017). Such scepticism is understandable, to a degree, and this chapter will argue that the essential and underlying *content* of industrial development means that there most certainly are continuities between past and successive industrial revolutions which are just as important to recognise as the more visible innovations and transformations that might be used to distinguish one industrial epoch from the next. But an overly sceptical posture runs the risk of downplaying the seriousness of the kinds of disruption that are associated with the Fourth Industrial Revolution and which are already plain to see in the here and now. These disruptions are indeed cause for immediate concern. The question that animates this chapter, therefore, is not whether the Fourth Industrial Revolution is real, but rather whether the transformations the concept signals (however imperfectly) are inevitable or for the common good. And we must ask whether the kinds of disruption depicted as the unfortunate collateral damage of inexorable, rapid, and wide-reaching technological change can be explained on a different, critical basis that can better inform political debate about our common future in a world that is still largely defined by the social necessity to engage in productive work.

Capital, Labour, and the Impetus for Technological Change

> [T]he development of machinery … occurs only when large industry has already reached higher stage, and all the sciences have been pressed into the service of capital … Invention then becomes a business, and the application of science to direct production itself becomes a prospect which determines it and solicits it.
>
> (Marx, 1973: 704)

Capitalism, or rather the capitalist mode of production, is today the general world-wide form through which we, as human beings, organise the process of metabolism with nature upon which our very survival depends. It has always been a fact of human life that we need to transform the powers inherent in our environment for our own reproduction (Schmidt, 1971; Foster, 2000), though the specific *forms* this metabolic exchange with nature assumes is an historical outcome of centuries of human sociality, ingenuity, conflict, and development. Where capitalism has long been established, it rests upon specific kinds of social relations between classifications of people depending upon their objective relation to the means of production; upon certain political and juridical rules, rights, norms and 'freedoms'; upon negotiated and fragile systems of social provisioning and welfare; and in good part upon large-scale extractive and industrial processes that harness and, in turn, reshape world ecology at a variety of interdependent scales. Of course, the particular way in which these conditions arise and come together over many years varies the world over, meaning that such 'ingredients' can appear to be lacking in some parts of the world; and it is very much the case that the early advancement of industrialisation in particular corners of the world market required as an indispensable precondition of their development that other parts of the world be subjugated to – and held in check by – colonialism, racialisation, and dynamics of oppression and control that have perpetuated their so-called backwardness (see Chapter 13). In general terms, however, we can assert that capitalist industry is a specific form of social-ecological metabolism that is configured around processes of production, market exchange, and profitmaking by private and independent producers of goods and services, and which today spans and subsumes most of the planet (albeit unevenly) within its operational and environmentally transformative dynamics (Moore, 2015).

From its emergence, capitalism has been disruptive to its very core. This can be *explained*, rather than merely narrated, on the basis of capitalism's own immanent, material dependence upon human labour. Within capitalism, human labour is expended under specific general conditions configured around private property. Capitalist society is essentially a *value*-producing society (Pitts, 2021). The daily labouring activities of millions of people around the world are brought into a corresponding social relation, *value*, only by means of the reduction of all that concrete human labour to homogenised and cumulative metrics of abstract labour-time. Under such conditions, the human capacity to labour can be given a price, just as the products of human labour (commodities) bearing differential magnitudes of congealed labour-time (Marx, 1976: 130, 297) can also be priced and consequently bought and sold on markets. The purchase of human labour-power by private and independent producers who then use that capacity to appropriate and transform the powers of nature to make new goods and services, the labour market in which this labour-power is bought and sold, the legal and contractual arrangements in place that regulate the terms and conditions of labouring (or, where they are lacking, the struggles to secure them), and, of course, the wage that is paid to the labourer in remuneration for their working time all signal that there exists an objective *class relation* within this society. On one side of the class divide stands the capitalist. Their immediately conscious goal is to make money out of money; usually, but not always, by investing in, organising and overseeing a process in which labour-power is used to transform other inputs like raw materials and machinery into new goods and services which can then be sold on the market, and under conditions of competition against other producers that compel each of them to organise the labour process under their control as cheaply and efficiently as possible. On the other side of the divide stands the worker: a social subject specific to capitalism insofar as they are, for the most part, bearers of two 'freedoms'. Untethered from any direct access to their means of subsistence and of production, they are at liberty to sell their capacity to work to the capitalist so as to secure their own reproduction (and, it goes without saying, they are therefore free to suffer deprivation should they fail to do so). The differentiation of society into classes based on relations of property, and heavily mediated by ascribed and reproduced social constructions of gender, race, ethnicity, and so forth, signals that the capitalist mode of production is a form of social-ecological metabolism that is inherently antagonistic and divisive. Based on this recognition alone, we can safely assert that disruptiveness is very much coded within capitalism's 'DNA'.

But another genetic source of capitalism's disruptiveness lies within the very business of the production of value. It is a source that is less immediately visible, and which requires the exercise of critical thought and recognition to be seen. To both capitalist and worker, value is immaterial and invisible – though it has very real, material social effects and consequences. This value-objectivity can only be experienced through an encounter with various concrete modes of appearance through which value attains its materiality, most conspicuously through the movement of money (Bonefeld, 2020). Human subjects born into capitalism are therefore raised and become active subjects in a society whose fundamental material premises are hard to make out and decipher. Put simply, we all come to understand (intellectually and, too often, as a harsh fact of life) that most of us need to work for a living, that money does not grow on trees, and that our labour may be priced at a greater or lower rate of pay that the labour of others (so, for example, we feel we must invest in our education and have a good 'work ethic' if we are going to earn a decent living or enjoy a better standard of living than our forebears). But we rarely question why social-ecological metabolism has assumed this specific social form: one in which humans do not relate to each other in a directly social way, but instead establish their social relations indirectly through *things*: the products of their labour, the movement of money. That some-*thing* like money can often govern and indeed imperil our lives objectively, as if according to fate, therefore appears to most of us as an entirely inescapable and natural state of affairs. As such, 'everyday consciousness and political economy remain imprisoned within [a] fetishism' (Heinrich, 2012: 78). The dominant social tendency to view technological artefacts as having both empowering and disempowering effects almost beyond social control only attests to the material and fetishistic sway things hold over humans in capitalism; that is, as objectified forms or modes of appearance of value-in-movement.

All of this speaks to how both capitalist and worker alike contribute to the production and realisation of value but do so in response to the discipline imposed upon them by an alien social power: *capital* (Mau, 2023). The billions of people all over the world who submit to expending their vital energies to produce value do so under the often dull – sometimes acute – compulsion to earn a wage, to put food on the table, to pay their bills, and perhaps with some sense of reassurance that that they might be making some kind of 'contribution to society', for someone, somewhere. Each capitalist enterprise or firm, however, must hope that the general social conditions are in place for profitmaking to be viable – a healthy economy is a stable and growing economy, after all. But they must do all they can to match or better the rate of profit enjoyed by their competitors, their 'hostile brothers' (Marx, 1968: 29), or risk being put out of business. They will often take the path of least resistance, resorting to financial speculation, renting out their property for use by others, even swindling, if a profit can be turned with minimal possible hassle and effort. But, for the capitalist that commits to concentrating themselves on industry – on mustering together the investment, the machinery, the materials and fuels, the licences, the contracts, and, crucially, the human resources required to produce at scale the commodities that satiate the social demand for tangible goods and services (and all in the optimal quantities and ratios, and in the right place and time) – the competitive pressure to do so with the utmost efficiency and speed is relentless and unforgiving.

All of this points to how capital operates as a totalising spectral agent or pseudo-subject in its own right (Postone, 1993); as an alien social power which engenders inter-capitalist competition, which pushes the extension of the organisation of human labour into an industrial form spanning the globe, which entangles 'all peoples in the net of the world-market' (Marx, 1976: 929), and which subsumes most forms of social-ecological metabolism to its rapacious need to valorise – to make *more of itself* through the systemic imperative imposed on all individual capitalists to 'accumulate, accumulate!' (Marx, 1976: 742).

Capital's social power confronts the capitalist class as 'an external and coercive' law of competition (Marx, 1976: 739), one that compels each and every individual capitalist to continuously work to revolutionise the productivity of social labour under their control on an expansive and (as we will see) qualitative basis, and with minimal collective regard for the disruptive toll this exacts upon broader society and the biosphere (such attendant concerns are externalised as a matter of political regulation or governance). Technology is *integral* to how capitalists respond to this 'law'. In his prescient and still relevant exposition of the character and genesis of capitalism as a (then potentially) world-making system, Marx (1976: 493) was keen to argue that the application of science in industry 'discloses' or reveals the essence of how we organise our metabolic exchange with nature, and thereby encouraged us not to see technological change 'as some sort of *deus ex machina*, some sort of exogenous variable outside the system, attributable to the inherent genius of the entrepreneurs or simply to the immanent capacity of human beings for innovation' (Harvey, 2018: 171). Marx's critique reveals how technoscientific innovation has long been a potent lever for profitmaking by raising the productivity of labour employed within a capitalist enterprise, by reducing unit costs, and thereby undercutting competitors using less productive technologies and methods. As one capitalist innovates, that others will follow suit by staying abreast of, or surpassing, the uptake of fresh organisational and labour process innovations reveals the coercive effect of competition and, with it, the incessant technological dynamism and sometimes 'revolutionary' character of industrial development. At its basis is a systemic tendency for new technologies to simultaneously raise the productivity of competitive industries as a whole, while driving down the costs of everyday wage goods; yielding an upward trend in the ratio of surplus labour-time congealed in the form of goods and services produced relative to the necessary labour-time expended by the working classes in return for the going (socially determined) rate of pay upon which they depend. Technological change therefore makes possible the making of profit on a cumulative basis, by continuously enhancing the productivity of labour deployed in the production of goods and services, and by increasing the rate of appropriation of surplus labour-time which accrues back to the competitive capitalist as profit once those goods and services are sold. Technology even serves as a powerful instrument in the decomposition of workers' collective struggles against the imposition of new techniques and rhythms of labour or in defence or advocacy of improvement to wages and conditions of work.

Notwithstanding the remarkable complexity and dynamism exhibited by capitalist development across time and space, its essential 'logics' remain the same. The kinds of productivity-enhancing technological innovations that fuse together the physical, digital and biological 'worlds', that originate in today's industrial laboratories, R&D centres and startup incubators, and which are then applied within world-spanning industrial divisions of labour to transformative effect, must be seen for what they are: '*first and foremost a means to capital's end, valorisation*' (Smith, 2010: 206, italics in original). As such, technological change itself can therefore be understood as a necessarily incessant and disruptive force and as a process whose effects reverberate not only through entire branches of industry but throughout broader societal and environmental infrastructures whose development – and occasional upheaval – is heavily determined by how capitalists respond to competitive pressures by periodically restructuring the technological and organisational forms they adopt.

Capital, Labour, and Technology in the Second and Third Industrial Revolutions

The automobile was for most of the twentieth century arguably '*the* symbol of progress' (Paterson, 2007: 92): synonymous with modernism and Americanism, with mass consumption, suburbanisation, new forms of leisure, and the emergence of pop culture. Its mass production had direct, stimulating effects on national economies the world over, in particular during the booming decades of the 1950s and 1960s in the West, and after the 1970s in East Asia and pockets of the late industrialising world. Car production was undertaken by the most concentrated and advanced industrial firms of their day – firms that organised large-scale assembly line production in such a way as to have profoundly reshaped factory work, but also the conditions of the reproduction of labour-power and of ecological transformation (and indeed degradation) for decades through associated patterns of urbanisation.

In its post-war heyday, the 'Fordist' form of industry that characterised car production in the United States – the largest and most technologically advanced national economy by the mid-twentieth century – relied upon the technical and organisational principles of the vertical integration of production and standardisation of product (which from an early stage would establish limits to the longer-term competitiveness of Fordist industries), but also worked relentlessly to revolutionise the earlier systems of machinery and detail divisions of labour that had emerged with large-scale industry proper and which so fascinated Marx a century earlier. The process of what Marx (1976: 1034–1048) called 'the real subsumption of labour to capital' had marked a turning-point in the early and localised embedding of capitalism as a system with world-making potential. The systems of machinery deployed by large-scale industry in the first industrial cities like Manchester, UK, had, for the first time in history, created 'an entirely objective organisation of production, which confronts the worker as a pre-existing material condition of production' (Marx, 1976: 508). The productive-subjective attributes of an entire class of labourers – and their skills in particular – could thenceforth be transformed and shaped according to the prevailing forms, rhythms and demands of 'machinofacture' (Dunford and Perrons, 1983): industrial production whose orientation was towards world market competitiveness (Starosta, 2016a: Chap. 8). Workers in other words, were already by then subjected to the alien social power Marx identified as capital in profoundly subjective and corporeal ways (Rioux, 2015). The significance of the Second Industrial Revolution of the mid-twentieth century – typified by Fordism in the United States – was really to have engendered a *further* sea change in the process of the real subsumption of labour to capital, and to the qualitative transformation and differentiation of the industrial workforce in these countries. In other words, and as argued above, epoch-making technological advances were rooted in capital's drive to bend the labour processes of large-scale industry – and, outside the factory, society and the environment – to the evolving requirements of its own self-expansion, and through the instrumentalisation of new automation-enabling technologies and organisational forms.

Under various guises of Fordist systems of the scientific management of production across the industrialised world by the mid-twentieth century, the deskilling of large portions of workers who operated the mass production assembly lines went hand in hand with the emergence of a new stratum of 'polyvalent' worker able to work in a variety of functions as required, as well another stratum of highly skilled workers trained to provide forms of intellectual and scientific labour that could produce the innovations required to continuously improve productivity through incremental, discrete technological changes and upgrades to the labour process (Clarke, 1990: 2; Williams, Haslam and Williams, 1992). Outside the factories and in urban contexts, deepening social divisions of labour marked by processes of housewifisation, the racialisation of labour markets, and patterns of residential differentiation (along increasingly ghettoised lines by even the 1960s) served to underpin and buttress this process of the qualitative and fragmented transformation of the working class and the conditions of its reproduction in post-war advanced industrial economies (Fraser, 2016, 2018; Florida and Feldman, 1988). The results of this 'revolution' in industrial and urban socio-environments still largely define how we tend to look back at the Fordist form of society typified by the United States in the post-war era: 'less as a mere system of mass production and more as a total way of life' (Harvey, 1989: 135).

The deep world recession of the early 1970s marked the beginning of a profound transformation of post-war capitalism. Significantly, it expressed the limits to this Second Industrial Revolution just as the technical and organisational components of a Third Industrial Revolution were beginning to emerge and to portend the eclipse of the automobile industry as the driver of industrial change by micro-electronics and digital industries by the close of the century. Developments in telecommunications and international transport and logistics, together with the introduction of early forms of self-calibrating, computerised machine-tools to large-scale industrial processes in the 1950s and 1960s, permitted the reorganisation of the production process on ever 'leaner' grounds – and exponentially so from the 1970s onwards: kick-starting, for instance, the steadily growing divergence in the rates of growth of productivity relative to real wages in the United States that has persisted to this day (Bivens and Mishel, 2015). The imperative to make production ever leaner and more responsive to fluctuations in costs and demand culminated in the ascendancy of new automobile manufacturing competitors like Japan's Toyota, and the subsequent restructuring of this and other sectors on an international scale in the 1980s. But, crucially, successive innovations in semiconducting materials used to enhance the control and calibration of increasingly automated machinofacture also led to the micro-electronics revolution of the early 1970s, and, with it, a further step-change in the automation of industrial production processes (Coriat, 1992). Advanced industrial firms, it transpired, could take advantage of the productivity enhancements afforded by applied innovations in the computerisation and roboticisation of some parts of the labour process while shifting or subcontracting other parts of the process elsewhere and beyond national borders.

The resulting tendency towards a 'new international division of labour' (Fröbel, Heinrichs and Kreye, 1980), comprising world-wide manufacturing and supply chains and interdependent financial systems, expressed yet a *further* development of capital's ongoing transformation of the international working class as an articulated, labouring, surplus value producing organism (Starosta, 2016b). New information and computer technologies (ICTs) were integral to making this global restructuring process possible, their subsequent growth then being driven for much of the late twentieth century by the growth in demand from manufacturing, financial and military sectors for outsourcing-enabling communications and information processing and software, and giving rise, in turn, to a further transformation of the spatial organisation of the production of service sector work that came to prominence in the former industrial heartlands of the Global North (Baldry, 2011).

The preceding account leads to a straightforward enough proposition: from the numerically controlled machine-tools which were in wide use by advanced industries in the 1950s, through to the introduction of microcomputers and industrial robots by the 1980s, and then on to the physical, digital and biological technologies at the fulcrum of the Fourth Industrial Revolution, the primary technologies upon which these successive 'revolutions' were based were originally developed not to benefit humankind in any immediate sense, but rather to bend industrial labour processes – and, with them, the demands of work and the wider conditions of the reproduction of workers – to the practical imperatives of the valorisation of capital.

The Social-Ecological Realities of 'Disruption' in a Fourth Industrial Revolution

Technological innovation continues to be vaunted in some quarters as

> the reason most people live lives of prosperity and wisdom compared with their ancestors, the overwhelming cause of the great enrichment of the past few centuries, [and] the simple explanation of why the incidence of extreme poverty is in freefall for the first time in history.
>
> (Ridley, 2020: 4)

Superficially, this might indeed be the case for *some* among us today. But celebratory discourses surrounding disruptive innovation – its sources and its benefits – can also be said to represent an especially apologetic form of technological determinism that privileges instrumental reasoning about ineluctable 'progress' over fundamentally social and political questions concerning the impetus, control, and effects of the technoscientific innovations driving capitalism on. In reproducing the dualism between technology and society characteristic of the techno-determinism underpinning the commentaries by Schwab and others, too much of the apologia for the Fourth Industrial

Revolution portrays its 'effects' in largely residual terms, disavowing therefore the recognition that social processes of exploitation, appropriation and 'disruption' explain its very genesis and development, and are but the present stage in the development of industrial capitalism. We ought to repudiate the notion that progress comes at the unavoidable cost of residual social-ecological collateral damage, by first returning to 'fundamentals': to ask how *this* current industrial revolution is transforming labour and the socio-ecological conditions of its reproduction *for capital.*

Attending to the fundamentals, we witness the further fragmentation of the international working class as a labouring collective organism, and with this the further stratification of the conditions of the reproduction of different working classes as bearers of differentiated productive subjectivity (Iñigo Carrera, 2013). In broad terms, this process of fragmentation can be identified in the form of four divergent trajectories that have characterised the shift from Second to Third – and now Fourth – Industrial Revolutions; trajectories heavily mediated, of course, by ascriptive and social constructions of gender, race, and ethnicity, and which materialise *across and within* national borders and labour markets (Starosta, 2016b).

First, capital has persisted in demanding that a relatively small fragment of workers, in global terms, be continuously upskilled: placing emphasis upon the advanced education and training of science, technology, engineering and mathematics (STEM) specialists capable of cutting-edge technoscientific research, design and application (see Rothwell, 2013). Of late, these scientific workers have been proactive in areas such as advanced machine learning and cyber-physical systems, and it is fair to surmise that the likes of Schwab are hopeful about the expansion of economic opportunities for this fragment of the working class as the Fourth Industrial Revolution progresses.

In general terms, for a second fragment of the working class, capital has engendered a transformation from the Fordist worker with polyvalent skills learned mainly through on-the-job training, to the generic 'knowledge worker' possessing skills formed mainly through processes of education and socialisation prior to entry into the labour market (and greatly facilitated by the expansion of university education in many countries since the 1990s). This transformation has not entailed a process of deskilling outright, as famously posited by Braverman (1974), but rather one of the degradation of the *particularistic* skills attained on-the-job under Fordism *along with* the development and diffusion of more *generic* 'head based' or 'soft' skills that can be 'transferred' from job to job – 'from familiarity with computers to flexibility or individual initiative in problem-solving or decision-making' (Starosta, 2016b: 87–88). This trend towards the transformation of the productive subjectivity of this fragment of the working class is better described as one of multi-skilling albeit with a general depreciation in wages (Adler, 1990: 791; Vidal, 2022: 75–76), rather than as outright deskilling, and has been made possible by the technical de-complexification of labour processes through automation and codification as well as a greater facilitation of ICT-based skills acquisition by means of an expansion in the broader social consumption of ICTs, the internet, and new social media among populations since the 1990s.

The third trajectory has carried forward the expansion of manual labour – which has never gone away – into every corner of the Global South, before relocating some production back again into the manufacturing units and sweatshops of the North once more. Somebody somewhere must mine the coltan for the cell phones, assemble the iPads, and stitch the Nike Air shoes; do the necessary work that is difficult to automate or more cost effective to have done by manual labourers (Mezzadri, 2017; Sandoval, 2016).

And, finally, capitalist development and globalisation have systematised the reproduction of (predominantly racialised) relative surplus populations acting – in the most sanguine of interpretations – as a substratum of latent industrial workers or 'micro-entrepreneurs'. Defined by Marx (1976: 782) as a 'relatively redundant working population', 'always ready for exploitation' subject to 'capital's own changing valorisation requirements', today these workers 'live lives often characterised by un- or under-employment, hyper-exploitative work, lack of a living wage, and an increasing inability to meet basic subsistence needs' (Bernards and Soederberg, 2021: 412). In 2020, 68% of the world's poor were in some form of work but earned less than a living wage (Balestra, Hirsch and Vaughan-Whitehead, 2023: 8).

The more disconcerting impact of these transformations is most visible in its effects on the latter three fragments of the working class. Take one vivid effect that is manifest across all three of these fragments. The term 'gig economy' has fast become part of our everyday vocabulary, reflecting how new platform technologies have transformed the lives of millions of workers globally in a very short timescale. Many of us, it is safe to assert, have become as rapidly aware of the disquieting connotations of the 'gig' as an especially precarious form of 'cyberwork' (Huws, 2014), where your boss is an absent yet hypervigilant algorithm. The on-demand means of matching workers to the completion of a small task via a digital platform intermediary has been subject to much controversy for its non-compliance with minimum wage laws, social security contributions, anti-discrimination legislation, sick pay, and holidays (Cammack, 2022: Chap. 5; OECD, 2019). Yet, the gig economy continues to grow unabated. One in six adults in the United Kingdom worked a gig job at least once a week by mid-2022 (Fennell, 2022), while 36% of workers in the United States could be classified as engaging in some form of gig work by the same year (McKinsey & Company, 2022). And across the Global South, in countries like India and the Philippines, 'crowdsourced' gig work has become a rapidly growing form of earning a piecemeal wage (Gray and Suri, 2019; Altenried, 2022). This normalisation of gig work – especially among low-income workers, and with conspicuously gendered and racial patterns of inclusion and exclusion (Zanoni and Pitts, 2023) – is only compounding detrimental physical and affective changes in the daily grind of millions across the world as a result of innovations such as the introduction of digital technologies of 'agile management' and surveillance into the workplace (Greenfield, 2018: 195–200); technologies, for instance, that continuously monitor and quantify the productivity and 'well-being' of workers through the use of tracking software and wearables (Moore, 2018). Thanks to the gig economy, and the digital platforms that profit from it, knowledge workers, manual labourers, and the working poor are all experiencing intensified pressures to work longer hours, along with social isolation, and anxiety induced by precariousness, job insecurity and surveillance (Bérastégui, 2021). Gig work outside the relatively more secure ambit of the knowledge economy is especially detrimental for women workers, who are routinely more likely to experience harassment, abuse, and lower pay (Carnegie, 2023), as well as, of course, for the very many racialised, non-white workers who work for quick commerce platforms whose 'last mile' business model depends implicitly upon couriers' acceptance of the risk of real personal injury, neglect, and dispossession as necessary features of their work (Orr et al., 2023).

Conclusion

This chapter has attended to the question of why our metabolic relation with nature assumes a general social form that reduces human beings to a mere means to an end: the quantitative self-expansion of an alien social power, capital. This process depends upon the real subsumption of human subjects as exploitable and disposable appendages to the technoscientific systems and networks integral to contemporary forms of profitmaking under capitalism. The implication is that the technological determinism, complacency, and apologia characteristic of the Fourth Industrial Revolution thesis, which suggests that the degradation of human labour-power and with it the deleterious impact on quality of life is collateral to ongoing processes of industrial transformation, should be resisted. We should question why it is supposedly the individual responsibility of citizens to self-engender their own 'agility' and 'resilience' as 'inoculations' (Kaika, 2017) against the threat of being rendered surplus to (capital's) requirement. We should instead advocate a deceptively simple political idea: that of the exertion of *conscious* and immediately *social* control over the techno-scientifically mediated process of social-ecological metabolism upon which our future will depend.

With this in mind, it is worthwhile taking more seriously recent ideas emanating from the Marxist tradition. For instance, the programmatic demands for an immediate and technologically facilitated transition to a 'post-capitalist' (Mason, 2015) or 'post-scarcity' society (Benavav, 2020). For these critics, capitalism is already as good as finished. Now unable to produce surplus-value through the system of large-scale industry to any meaningful extent, it must instead appropriate value by other means: by imposing scarcity through intellectual and informational property rights, and the continuing imposition of the wage-work nexus. So, they ask, why should we continue to experience free time as under-employed time? Their answer: let us just by-pass capital; let us turn on the (self-learning) machines, accelerate full automation, pay a universal basic income, finish with the very notion of working for a living, share out the necessary reproductive labour, and enjoy the luxury of *really free* time. This approach has the benefit of calling out digital capitalism on an immanently social basis, of offering with it a critique of the fetishised character of work, and of offering an alternative to digital capitalism. But one criticism of it is that it misreads the reality of the situation: it confuses a general crisis of underemployment and of social reproduction with a vista of a world already abundant in free time, a confusion which makes little sense outside of the established knowledge economies of the Global North. Others argue that this opens the door to a naïve politics of leftist-populism (Dinerstein and Pitts, 2021). There is still much to debate, therefore. But at least these socially grounded attempts to rethink the critique of capitalism (beyond Marx) enable a glimpse of what is really at stake in the Fourth Industrial Revolution, and what we might want to do about it.

References

Adler, P. S. (1990) Marx, machines, and skill. *Technology and Culture*, 31(4), 780–812.

Altenried, M. (2022) *The Digital Factory: The Human Labor of Automation*. Chicago, IL: University of Chicago Press.

Baldry, C. (2011) Editorial: chronicling the information revolution. *New Technology, Work and Employment*, 26(3), 175–182.

Baldwin, R. (2019) *The Globotics Upheaval: Globalization, Robotics, and the Future of Work*. New York: Oxford University Press.

Balestra, C. D. Hirsch and D. Vaughan-Whitehead (2023) Living wages in context: A comparative analysis for OECD countries. *OECD Papers on Well-Being and Inequalities*, 13. Paris: OECD Publishing.

Benavav, A. (2020) *Automation and the Future of Work*. London: Verso.

Bérastégui, P. (2021) *Exposure to Psychosocial Risk Factors in the Gig Economy: A Systematic Review*. Report 2021.01. Brussels: European Trade Union Institute.

Bernards, N. and S. Soederberg (2021) Relative surplus populations and the crises of contemporary capitalism: reviving, revisiting, recasting. *Geoforum*, 126, 412–419.

Bivens, J. and L. Mishel (2015) Understanding the historic divergence between productivity and a typical worker's pay: why it matters and why it's real. *Economic Policy Institute Briefing Paper*, 406, Washington DC, September, 2.

Bonefeld, W. (2020) Capital *par excellence*: on money as an obscure thing. *Estudios de Filosfia*, 62. https://revistas.udea.edu.co/index.php/estudios_de_filosofia/article/view/340420.

Braverman, H. (1974) *Labor and Monopoly Capital: The Degradation of Work in the Twentieth Century*. New York: Monthly Review.

Brynjolfsson, E. and A. McAfee (2014) *The Second Machine Age: Work, Progress, and Prosperity in a Time of Brilliant Technologies*. New York: Norton.
Cammack, P. (2022) *The Politics of Global Competitiveness*. Oxford: Oxford University Press.
Carnegie, M. (2023) The gig economy is much worse for women. *Wired*, 8 May. https://www.wired.co.uk/article/the-gig-economy-is-much-worse-for-women.
Clarke, S. (1990) What in the F—'s name is Fordism? *Presentation to the British Sociological Association Conference*, University of Surrey, April, 4. https://homepages.warwick.ac.uk/~syrbe/pubs/Fordism.pdf.
Coriat, B. (1992) *El taller y el robot. Ensayos sobre el fordismo y la producción en masa en la era de la electrónica*. México, DF: siglo veintiuno editores.
Dinerstein, A. C. and F. H. Pitts (2021) *A World Beyond Work? Labour, Money and the Capitalist State between Crisis and Utopia*. Bingley: Emerald.
Dunford, M. and D. Perrons (1983) *The Arena of Capital*. New York: Macmillan Education.
Edgerton, D. (2017) Digital transformation: interview with David Edgerton, King's College London. *YouTube*, 5, 26 mins. https://www.youtube.com/watch?v=bnD3CjrMcm8.
Fennell, A. (2022) Gig economy statistics UK. Standout CV, June. https://standout-cv.com/gig-economy-statistics-uk#:~:text=1%20in%206%20adults%20in,men%20in%20the%20gig%20economy.
Florida, R. L. and M. M. A. Feldman (1988) Housing in US fordism: The class accord and postwar spatial organization. *International Journal of Urban and Regional Research*. 12(2), 187–210.
Foster, J. B. (2000) *Marx's Ecology: Materialism and Nature*. New York: Monthly Review Press.
Fraser, N. (2016) Contradictions of capital and care. *New Left Review*, 100, 99–117.
Fraser, N. (2018) Roepke lecture in economic geography – from exploitation to expropriation: historic geographies of racialized capitalism. *Economic Geography*, 94(1), 1–17.
Fröbel, F., J. Heinrichs and O. Kreye (1980) *The New International Division of Labour: Structural Unemployment in Industrialised Countries and Industrialisation in Developing Countries*. Cambridge: Cambridge University Press.
Geiger, S. (2020) Silicon Valley, disruption, and the end of uncertainty. *Journal of Cultural Economy*, 13(2), 169–184.
Gray, M. L. and S. Suri (2019) *Ghost Work: How to Stop Silicon Valley from Building a New Global Underclass*. Boston, MA: Houghton Mifflin Harcourt.
Greenfield, A. (2018) *Radical Technologies: The Design of Everyday Life*. London: Verso.
Harvey, D. (1989) *The Condition of Postmodernity: An Enquiry into the Origins of Cultural Change*. Oxford: Blackwell.
Harvey. D. (2018) *A Companion to Marx's Capital: The Complete Edition*. London: Verso.
Heinrich, M. (2012) *An Introduction to the Three Volumes of Karl Marx's Capital*. New York: Monthly Review Press.
Huws, U. (2014) *Labor in the Global Digital Economy: The Cybertariat Comes of Age*. New York: Monthly Review Press.
Iñigo Carrera, J. (2013) *El Capital*. Buenos Aires: Imago Mundi
Kaika, M. (2017) "*Don't call me resilient again!*": the New Urban Agenda as immunology … or … what happens when communities refuse to be vaccinated with "smart cities" and indicators. *Environment and Urbanization*, 29(1), 89–102.
Lee, M. et al. (2018) How to respond to the fourth industrial revolution, or the second information technology revolution? Dynamic new combinations between technology, market, and society through open innovation. *Journal of Open Innovation: Technology, Market and Complexity*, 4(21), 1–24.
Marr, B. (2016) Why everyone must get ready for the 4th Industrial Revolution. *Forbes*, April, 5. https://www.forbes.com/sites/bernardmarr/2016/04/05/why-everyone-must-get-ready-for-4th-industrial-revolution/?sh=3a8353483f90.
Marx, K. (1968) *Theories of Surplus Value, Vol. II*. Moscow: Progress Publishers.
Marx, K. (1973) *Grundrisse*. https://www.marxists.org/archive/marx/works/1857/grundrisse/ch14.htm.
Marx, K. (1976) *Capital: Volume I*. Harmondsworth: Penguin.
Mason, P. (2015) *PostCapitalism: A Guide to Our Future*. London: Allen Lane.
Mau, S. (2023) *Mute Compulsion: A Marxist Theory of the Economic Power of Capital*. London: Verso.
McKinsey & Company (2022) Freelance, side hustles, and gigs: many more Americans have become independent workers, August 23. https://www.mckinsey.com/featured-insights/sustainable-inclusive-growth/future-of-america/freelance-side-hustles-and-gigs-many-more-americans-have-become-independent-workers.

Mezzadri, A. (2017) *The Sweatshop Regime: Labouring Bodies, Exploitation and Garments Made in India*. Cambridge: Cambridge University Press.
Moore, J. (2015) *Capitalism in the Web of Life: Ecology and the Accumulation of Capital*. London: Verso.
Moore, P. (2018) *The Quantified Self in Precarity: Work, Technology and What Counts*. London: Routledge.
OECD (2019) *The Future of Work: OECD Employment Outlook*. Paris: OECD Publishing.
Orr, W., K. Henne, A. Lee, J. I. Harb and F. Carneiro Alphonso (2023) Necrocapitalism in the gig economy: the case of platform food couriers in Australia. *Antipode*, 55(1), 200–221.
Paterson, M. (2007) *Automobile Politics: Ecology and Cultural Political Economy*. Cambridge: Cambridge University Press.
Pitts, F. H. (2021) *Value*. Cambridge: Polity.
Postone, M. (1993) *Time, Labor and Social Domination: A Reinterpretation of Marx's Critical Theory*. Cambridge: Cambridge University Press.
Ridley, M. (2020) *How Innovation Works*. London: 4th Estate.
Rioux, S. (2015) Embodied contradictions: capitalism, social reproduction and body formation. *Women's Studies International Forum*, 48, 194–202.
Rothwell, J. (2013) *The Hidden STEM Economy*. Washington, DC: Brookings Metropolitan Policy Program, June.
Sandoval, M. (2016) Foxconned labour as the dark side of the information age: working conditions at apple's contract manufacturers in China. In C. Fuchs and V. Mosco (Eds.), *Marx in the Age of Digital Capitalism* (pp. 350–395). Leiden: Brill.
Schmidt, A. (1971) *The Concept of Nature in Marx*. London: NLB.
Schwab, K. (2016) *The Fourth Industrial Revolution*. Geneva: World Economic Forum.
Smith, T. (2010) Technological change in Capitalism: some Marxian themes. *Cambridge Journal of Economics*, 34, 203–212.
Starosta, G. (2016a) *Marx's Capital, Method and Revolutionary Subjectivity*. Leiden: Brill.
Starosta, G. (2016b) Revisiting the new international division of labour thesis. In G. Charnock and G. Starosta (Eds.), *The New International Division of Labour: Global Transformations and Uneven Development* (pp. 79–103). London: Palgrave Macmillan.
Vidal, M. (2022) *Management Divided: Contradictions of Labor Management*. Oxford: Oxford University Press.
Williams, K., C. Haslam and J. Williams (1992) Ford versus 'Fordism': the beginning of mass production. *Work, Employment and Society*, 6(4), 517–555.
Zanoni, P. and F. H. Pitts (2023) Inclusion through the platform economy? The 'diverse' crowd as relative surplus populations and the pauperisation of labour. In I. Ness (Ed.), *The Routledge Handbook of the Gig Economy* (pp. 33–45). London: Routledge.

Recommendations for Further Reading

Benavav, A. (2020) *Automation and the Future of Work*. London: Verso. (Cuts through much of the popular ideology surrounding automation and its impact on labour and provides both a critical explanation of the structural causes of economic stagnation and underemployment as well as prescriptions for a post-scarcity society.)

Harvey, D. (2014) Technology, work and human disposability. In D. Harvey (Ed.), *Seventeen Contradictions and the End of Capitalism* (pp. 91–111). London: Profile Books. (A classical Marxist treatment of the contradictions attendant to technological change within capitalism.)

Hughes, C. and A. Southern (2019) The world of work and the crisis of capitalism: Marx and the fourth industrial revolution. *Journal of Classical Sociology*, 19(1), 59–71. (A discussion of the utility of Marx when thinking critically about the efficiencies and politics of the Fourth Industrial Revolution and technological change more broadly.)

Huws, U. (2019) *Labour in Contemporary Capitalism: What Next?* London: Palgrave Macmillan. (An introduction to the development of capitalism and its impact on labour over the last 40 years by a leading researcher of work.)

OECD (2019) *The Future of Work: OECD Employment Outlook*. Paris: OECD Publishing. (An empirically rich, candid analysis of the disruptions confronting workers in OECD member countries because of globalisation and technological change, including many workers in 'non-standard' (gig) employment.)

Schwab, K. (2016) *The Fourth Industrial Revolution*. Geneva: World Economic Forum. (The touchstone text for advocates of the Fourth Industrial Revolution, written by the founder of the World Economic Forum.)

Soederberg, S. (2014) *Debtfare States and the Poverty Industry: Money, Discipline and the Surplus Population*. London: Routledge. (An analysis of relative surplus populations in the Global South and North, focusing on how they are forced to subsist on expensive forms of consumer credit.)

Woodcock, J. and M. Graham (2020) *The Gig Economy: A Critical Introduction*. Cambridge: Polity. (A useful introductory text on the gig economy by researchers and advocates of fair work in the digital and platform economies.)

4

FINANCIALISATION OF WORK FUTURES

Jean Cushen and Paul Thompson

Introduction

Discourses and debates around the future of work have been overwhelmingly dominated by notions of technological disruption, with largely negative implications inferred for the quality and quantity of work. Such claims have been critiqued for their frequently deterministic bias and neglect of human agency and other sources of social shaping rooted in capitalist political economy (Thompson, 2019; Warhurst and Hunt, 2019). These contentions are largely beyond the scope of this chapter, which is concerned with the actual and potential impacts of another exogenous force, that of financialisation. This phenomenon is generally taken to refer to the growing influence of financial markets and institutions and their impact on the economy, corporate practices, households and social life more generally.

Connections between work futures and financialisation are, on the surface at least, not as knowable as, for example, employees working with new technologies. The global financial landscape is characterised by immense complexity and systemic fragility (Lagoarde-Segot and Currie, 2018). The ways that localised work is intertwined with these global speculative financialised processes are often not revealed until the systemic volatility prompts a restructuring of work resources, such as in the 2022 near-collapse of British pension funds due to selling pressure in bond markets. As we shall return to later, a wide range of commentators on trends in work and employment have recognised the importance of capital markets and shareholder value regimes, but analysis remains at a fairly general level with financialisation positioned as part of a cluster of contextual influences on workplace and labour market outcomes. However, financialisation literatures themselves are overwhelmingly dominated by macro-level analyses in fields of enquiry such as comparative political economy. While valuable and necessary, such analyses of what regulation theorists would call 'regimes of accumulation' seldom touch directly on work and employment issues and impacts.

In this chapter, we seek to offset these biases by exploring how financialisation shapes the value strategies of non-financial firms, driving future trends for the labour process and worker outcomes and how these arguments have been developed in wider research, including our own (Thompson, 2003, 2013; Cushen and Thompson, 2016; Thompson and Cushen, 2020; Appelbaum et al., 2013; Clark, 2011; Clark and Macey, 2015; Gospel, Pendleton and Vitols, 2014; Gouzoulis, 2023; Gouzoulis et al., 2023). We will set out the core features of financialisation and revisit key arguments on the drivers, mechanisms and impacts of financialised value to offer a more in-depth examination into how financialisation shapes domains of work in key growth sectors, especially

DOI: 10.4324/9781003327561-6

social care and high technology. The latter is emblematic of the ways in which financialised business models challenge emergent notions of essential work, destabilise new forms of work delivery and place constraints and risk on workers. We demonstrate how financialisation results in organisational practices that drive a clash of values playing out in the heart of the labour process, borne by workers in the performance of their work and through precarious redistribution.

Domains of Work and Work Futures

Discussions of changing workplaces take many perspectives and it is not always clear what is covered by the term 'work futures'. For example, are we talking primarily about the quality of work, its availability or other issues? Being clear is important when considering potential impacts of something like financialisation because such pressures do not always operate directly or in a linear manner. The diagram below identifies five work domains that emerge in discussions of work futures and we think it useful to set out briefly the known links to financialised pressures. We identify these domains as work availability, security, rewards, organisation and boundaries (Figure 4.1).

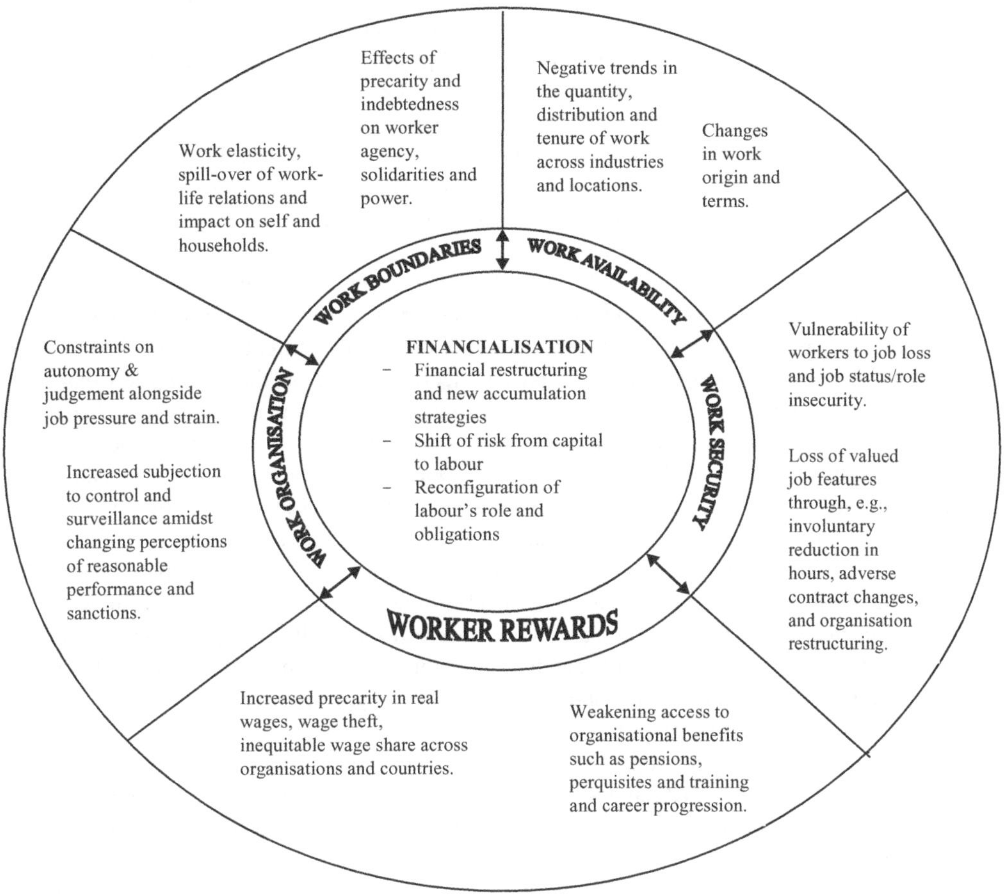

Figure 4.1 Financialisation of five work domains

Source: Created by author.

In this chapter, we do not claim to systematically investigate trends in each domain (see Findlay and Thompson, 2017), but rather we try and tease out some of the connections between financialisation and those trends, where evidence exists to make such inferences.

Financialisation, Firms and Work: General Dynamics

As already indicated, the most prominent contributions to the financialisation literature have primarily focused on macro-level occurrences, with scholars setting out the features of finance-dominated growth or accumulation regimes (Krippner, 2005; Stockhammer, 2008; Lapavitsas, 2011). Capital markets increasingly outweigh the influence of product and labour markets on the economy in general and firm behaviour in particular. Growth models at all levels shift towards the holding and manipulation of financial assets as the primary source of profits. This has become known as the maximising shareholder value (MSV) model in which cash returns, share buybacks and disbursement feature heavily (Findlay et al., 2017).

Such analyses are seldom concerned directly with labour impacts. However, there is a general message that collectively labour is likely to suffer collateral damage from these macro- and meso-level changes (Thompson and Cushen, 2020). Crowding out investment under MSV regimes is a familiar theme, but it is recognised that a key dimension of this process is that there is less room for internal, long-term investment in human and physical capital or research and innovation (Orhangazi, 2008; Lazonick and Mazzucato, 2013; Froud et al., 2014). As a result, there are less opportunities for training and for labour to make claims for wages and other rewards from productivity growth. Workers' assets in pension funds have also proven vulnerable to financial market instability and value transfers within large corporations (Braun, 2022) Across value chains, MSV stimulates incentives for cost-reducing measures that hit job security and quality, notably through offshoring of production (Milberg, 2008).

We are already moving here to the terrain of the micro economy of firm and inter-firm behaviours. Non-financial corporations (NFCs) also become financial actors, often with greater returns from leveraging value from financial assets than operational investment (Milberg, 2008; Müller, 2014). What first became known as financial engineering rested on the assumption that it was advantageous to treat firms as bundles of assets. If those assets are increasingly treated as disposable through disaggregation, delayering and leverage buyouts, then workers were inevitably also potentially disposable and flexible absorbers of risk (Dore, 2008; Lazonick and Mazzucato, 2013). The direct implications for labour and workplace social relations were first set out by Thompson (2003, 2013) in the disconnected capitalism thesis (DCT). Financialisation was increasingly undermining the conditions necessary for mutual gains productivity bargains in NFCs. Workers asked to engage in new participative and partnership practices were increasingly subject to job and role insecurity, work intensification and wage squeeze as a result of the perpetual restructuring associated with corporate management seeking to meet the requirements of capital market targets. The outcome was a fundamental disconnect between employer objectives in the labour process and instability and uncertainty in employment systems.

Though widely influential among work and employment scholars, a challenge for such perspectives was to be clearer about what happened in between the upstream dynamics of corporate strategy and the downstream impacts at workplace level as these links, on the surface at least, looked to be at best indirect (Gospel et al., 2014). While it will always be difficult to demonstrate clear cause and effect between these processes, recent work by Cushen and Thompson (2016) attempts a closer understanding of some of the mechanisms involved. Emphasis is put primarily on financialised targets arising from capital market valuation measures that lead to distinctive accounting metrics and measures that can be operationalised through budgeting processes such as operational expenditure (or OPEX) that drive headcount reduction, work intensification and tightened performance measures.

Firm-Level Mechanisms and Impacts

Taking its cue from this literature and the more general visibility of financialisation in economic life, we can observe a greater recognition of the importance of such processes in contemporary literatures on work and employment trends. Sometimes it is largely an insertion of financialisation as one of the key factors driving a squeeze on labour costs, fragmentation of employment and labour standards, insecurity and precariousness (Dundon and Rafferty, 2018; Doellgast et al., 2021). We can also observe a growing number of case studies of how financialisation shapes large firms such as the Finnish postal service (Vieno, 2023) and France Telecom (Doellgast et al., 2021) in the public and private sectors. Such studies reinforce the point about the financialisation of NFCs, particularly the effects of perpetual restructuring on work intensification, worker health and well-being. The preference for short-term rent-seeking activities that promise immediate returns through reorganisation or work intensification alongside the availability of relatively cheap labour also helps to explain the limited progress towards automation (Howcroft and Taylor, 2023). In other instances, case studies focus on the finance-driven environments that lead firms operating global value chains to drive deteriorating working conditions or 'social downgrading' (Jenkins and Blyton, 2017). Another stream of research focuses more on the reward domain particularly the squeeze and stagnation in real wages, especially in the US and the UK (Palladino, 2021). Aggregate-level studies do not only focus on these countries. A study of 121 countries indicates that financial development and liberalisation increases income inequality (De Hann and Sturm, 2017). Negative impacts for labour are not confined to the workplace, given that financialisation of national economies is often linked to rising household indebtedness. In related work, Gouzoulis (2023) seeks to make innovative connections between the two spheres, arguing that there is an association between such indebtedness and the insecurity and decline of strike activity in many leading industrial countries in recent decades. The inferred factor is heightened fear of job loss due to precarity of living conditions. Though located within comparative case studies of the labour process and organising, Legault and Weststar (2021) also draw pessimistic inferences concerning the impact on collective representation and action. In sectors such as videogames that are characterised by complex logistic structures and modes of organising work, financial players increasingly shape that environment, but are not visible as formal actors or bargaining agents in the employment relations system. The workers in this sector and others such as IT specialists have aspirations for greater collective voice, but this opacity impacts negatively on the propensity to unionise and organise (see Chapter 25).

Gig and platform work have been the focus of much contemporary research. Much of this has highlighted the innovative nature of algorithmic management. Drawing on findings from comparative studies of Chinese and American food delivery platforms, van Doorn and Chen (2021) argue that a specific control mechanism – gamification – acts as a pivot between the value extracted through datafication in platform business models and the wider shift towards more financialised investor expectations. Captured metrics via the worker interactions with the app enable food delivery platforms to manage labour supply, optimise their services and radically reduce labour costs through intensification (see also Iazzolino and Varesio, 2023).

It is clear that financialisation prompts value extracting activities that undermine labours' access to resources across multiple domains of work futures. We turn now to explore events in the care and technology sector to illustrate the immediacy of worker vulnerability within financialised routes to value.

Who Cares? Private Equity and Its Consequences

The private equity (PE) business model has emerged a prominent vehicle for financialised interests. PE funds offer investment to organisations with the goal of increasing the value of the business to then sell on or take public. PE firms typically take on debt to finance PE acquisitions (Horton, 2022). For organisations under PE ownership, the debt financing approach introduces a sharper focus on cost-cutting due to the acquired company being under new pressure to service the debt. Additionally, the PE firm needs to increase the value of the company. Consequently, cost-cutting emerges as an effective and common route to achieve these new dual short-term financial imperatives that acquired firms become instantly saddled with (Kaplan and Strömberg, 2009). PE firms often sell off non-core assets of the acquired company to raise funds to pay down debt (Gregory, 2013). Operating costs are often targeted for reduction resulting in less funds available to run the day-to-day costs of the business, including staffing and wage costs (Gompers et al., 2016). Restructuring becomes more frequent to cut costs via redundancies and centralising of operations (Jensen, 2009). Overhead costs, such as administrative and utility expenditure are also targeted for reduction (Ljungqvist and Richardson, 2003). All of these cost reduction measures have known negative impacts for the availability, security and quality of employment within acquired organisations. While these impacts may not be uniform across sectors and all organisations, they are sufficiently commonplace to be considered an established route to value within PE.

In work and employment literatures, there have been a few prominent case studies detailing job losses and deterioration of working conditions in companies acquired by PE, such as the Automobile Association in the UK, where 3,400 employees were 'managed out' of the business (Clark, 2011). In this section, we want to focus on the care sector, which until recently was under-researched (see Chapter 16). The penetration of the growing care sector by PE has had a significant impact on care quality, as well as the seeming inability to value essential work and workers highlighted during the COVID-19 pandemic. Within the UK, PE firms have acquired some of the largest care home chains in the UK, including Four Seasons, HC-One and Care UK. PE is also increasingly financing and defining the expanding 'aging in place' sector. In addition to controlling the labour needed for home healthcare, PE is investing in the evolving sectoral infrastructure, including telemedicine, data analytics, clinical decision support, mobile health and remote monitoring (Bangerter, 2023). PE is becoming a dominant player in the market and their financialised interests are defining outcomes for stakeholders. PE firms have been accused of prioritising profits over patient care, asset-stripping and financial engineering across the sector. The devaluing of the work of care has allowed PE funds to redirect resources from labour and those in care to financial actors (Horton, 2022; Burns et al., 2016; Kotecha, 2019). For example, Four Seasons, a large care home chain, was heavily indebted after being acquired by a PE firm. The firm used financial engineering techniques, such as high-yield debt and management fees, to extract profits from the care home chain, leading to concerns about the quality of care and the sustainability of the business. In 2019, the UK Centre for Health and the Public Interest published a forensic financial analysis into the adult care home industry and found that PE providers in some of the largest care homes

> operate in a way which hinders accountability of their true profitability; increases their financial fragility; and crucially locks in high future costs for care home beds' while 'At the same time, many of the smaller for-profit and the largest not-for-profit providers are making low levels of profit, without damaging the public interest.
>
> (Kotecha, 2019)

PE firms spend significant amounts on debt repayment, rental costs, and PE management fees which are considered a hidden profit extraction. These profit extraction, disguised as costs, generally add value to the PE firm, are absorbed by the consumer or workforce and have the effect of diverting resources away from those in care.

The PE focus on value extraction, cutting costs and short-term profit maximisation is associated with a lack of investment in the development of long-term care plans for care centres, inadequate staffing levels, lack of investment in training, lack of specialised staff for complex care, poorer facilities, job loss, lower wages and benefits and increasing job turnover rates (Appelbaum, 2019; Armstrong and Baines, 2020; Bos and Harrington, 2017). However, at some point, some semblance of care must be delivered for the business to be viable meaning the labour process is central to and constitutive of financialisation (Horton, 2022). In this way, PE has a parasitic dynamic whereby it feeds off the host but avoids killing it entirely as they are dependent on the host for survival (Bailey et al., 2023). Studies of workers providing care at home have consistently reported the vocational element of their work that enables a highly personalised service and provision of additional tasks that are identified through caring and crucial interaction with those receiving care (Aronson and Neysmith, 1996). This interactive discretionary effort, framed as 'virtuous waste' by PE financial analyses, has become less feasible amidst the PE financialised performance metrics, emphasis on cost-cutting and introduction of virtual, prescriptive and surveillance technologies which increasingly control and discipline the work of care. There is rising evidence that these metric-driven transformations are making workers' lives unbearable, squeezing out the relational element of care work, or forcing employees to undertake relational care without pay (see Chapter 21) (Schneck and Pons-Vignon, 2023). Referred as a shift from care based on 'touch' to care based on 'tech' it means those with a tradition in care are preserving their social work mentality through engaging in additional unpaid and unvalued in-person caring tasks. All the while, PE firms are pushing for change to cheaper forms of virtual care as quickly as possible with minimal in person visits from qualified care givers and health professionals (Thomas, 2019).

To what extent is the care sector indicative of the PE business model more generally? In terms of sectors, PE traditionally focused on industries such as technology, and financial services. Over the last decade, there has been significant growth in PE investments in sectors such as real estate, energy, and infrastructure. PE firms in Europe are increasingly investing in healthcare companies, driven by demographic trends and the increasing demand for care services. In 2021, healthcare accounted for 16% of all European PE deals (PitchBook, 2022). This expansion warrants attention as the techniques of debt-based financial engineering, developed by PE originally for high risk and high return activities such as tech start-ups, are increasingly being applied in disruptive ways to, what should be, low-risk and low-return sectors (Burns et al., 2016). In some sectors, PE firms do fund investments in research and development leading to new jobs and career opportunities; often alongside cost-cutting and high employee turnover (Antoni et al., 2019). However, as a strategy, this investment is more viable in the organisations and sectors that can achieve new revenue in new markets and significant returns. In other sectors, less amenable to high growth strategies, significant investment is less apparent and PE acquisitions are often followed by rapid cutting of costs, selling of assets and restructuring the companies. For example, in the retail sector, PE firms purchase struggling retail chains, restructure them resulting in job losses, store closures and wage freezes for employees. In the healthcare sector, in the US, PE firms have been known to acquire hospitals and introduce cost-cutting measures that lead to staff reductions and a focus on short-term profitability, causing an alarming diminishment in the quality of medical care (Appelbaum, 2019; Cerullo et al., 2022). Across the manufacturing sector, PE purchase is associated with automation and offshoring particularly of lower-skilled work and also high turnover of experienced workers replaced by less experienced lower paid labour (Antoni et al., 2019; Olsson and Tåg, 2017).

The power and proximity of PE owners to their acquired organisations shape the trajectory of financialised pressures and how value extraction is achieved within investee firms (Jones and Search, 2009). We turn now to look at the trajectory of financialisation within some of the largest, most powerful and wealthiest organisations publicly listed organisations.

Availability and Security of Work: The Technology Sector

Big Tech corporations operate at the 'apex of financialization' (Foroohar, 2021:279). Over the course of the 2010s, common corporate financialisation trends have emerged among 'Big Tech' organisations such as Amazon, Apple, Google, Meta and Microsoft (Klinge et al., 2023). Notably, the financialised model of Big Tech is characterised by a feedback loop between mounting value extraction, profitability and growth (Hendrikse et al. 2022; Klinge et al., 2023:15). In this section, we explore how, over the post-pandemic years, it came to be that some of the most financially successful organisations that have ever existed are undermining the availability and security of work for some of the seemingly most privileged of employees. Concerns about technology organisations arose in 2021 when the central banks of leading economies began to signal the end of the pandemic-era stimulus efforts as well as forthcoming rises in interest rates to combat inflation. Shortly after, financial media began speculating about the damaging impact of rising interest rates on technology stocks and the sector more broadly. Concern did not spread to those interested in employment as traditional drivers of job availability and security were strong. Within the product market, technology users and consumer numbers were steady; profits were in a league of their own. Within the labour market, technology related skills were in high demand and this highly compensated class of workers continued to hold power. However, the financialised modes of wealth accumulation that were propping up the share price of technology organisations were about to unravel. In the pandemic years, as other sectors stagnated, many technology products were in greater demand. So, although many technology stocks were expensive, tech products and services were experiencing consumer growth. Additionally, many of the largest technology companies pushed stock prices higher through forecasting even more significant growth in the future via expansionary new technologies. This 'market storytelling' prompted further increase in stock value for investors, so stocks kept going higher which drew more investors in. Tech leaders drove and corroborated the market sentiment of lasting growth so company value soared, as did the value of stock based executive compensation. In addition, low interest rates meant borrowing was cheaper than ever. Technology organisations could use debt to fund internal investments to protect their cash based financial return metrics; for example, debt drives up equity returns. Total debt for the largest seven technology corporations stood at US$318 billion in 2020, up from a US$21 billion in 2011 (Klinge et al., 2023: 8). For firms, interest payments on debt, which are often tax deductible, are likely still cheaper than taxes on repatriated equity. Also, investors were happy to borrow to take a bet on tech, even the smaller unprofitable tech firms. These factors mean the pandemic surge in the stock and value of technology companies was not shaped solely by the long-term earnings fundamentals within organisations and the product market. Instead, macro-economic conditions facilitated financial investors and corporate leaders' engagement in seemingly opportunistic, lucrative, proclamations of ongoing growth that delivered a short-term accumulation of organisational value and investor wealth.

Fast forward a year and almost all of those financialised calculations have changed, far more dramatically than product market dynamics. When interest rates went higher, future profits appeared less valuable, plus debt repayments more costly. For investors, bonds emerged as essentially a risk-free way to get returns, over and above stocks. Waiting for returns, in an era of high inflation and rising interest rates, involves greater risk as the value of money is declining over time; the short-termism becomes even shorter. The opportunity cost of investing in technology stocks rose as the stocks could not deliver returns as quickly as other investments. So, technology shares were sold and stock prices dropped significantly following the rise in interest rates. In response to falling share prices, technology organisations turned away from financialised routes of value accumulation and pivoted, almost instantly, to financialised routes of value distribution. Central to this has been share buybacks and layoffs. The year 2022 was a record year for buybacks which sustain the growth of earnings per share and senior management remuneration (Lazonick, 2014). Employee downsizing is now institutionalised as a shareholder value strategy in the era of financialisation and is often a knee jerk reaction to missed earnings forecasts (Jung and Lee, 2022). Relatedly, financialisation is associated with a misallocation of human and capital resources and hinders labour productivity (Borio et al., 2016). The organisations making layoffs are some of the wealthiest and most powerful on the planet and remain in a class of their own when it comes to profit (Foroohar, 2021). The financial firepower of Big Tech is derived from large reserves and tech's tangible assets now surpass those of major industrial corporations. There are also arguments that, as data or analytics are absent assets in the accounting sense, Big Tech's known value is likely the tip of the iceberg due to their intangible assets which are not captured under accounting standards (Birch et al., 2021). Despite this wealth, over the last year, corporate leaders increased shareholder returns, not via the significant reserves of capital that these organisations hold, but via share price boosting value extracting initiatives, notably share buybacks and firing employees. Many of the technology companies claimed to be 'bloated' and 'stuffed' with unnecessary employees are also hoarding billions of dollars in reserves. As Christy Hoffman, general secretary of UNI Global Union commented. 'It's astonishing that companies that make as much money do these layoffs... [...]...Alternatives to layoffs weren't even considered. Tech companies are just imitating each other' (Sucher and Westner, 2023). The layoffs have also been accompanied by similar rationales, namely that organisations over-hired to meet pandemic demand and now can no longer these employees in a post-pandemic work. It is a simplistic narrative that does not reflect the profits and wealth of the organisations nor the earlier recruitment patterns within the sector. For example, Meta Platforms, the parent company of Facebook, recorded a $23.1 billion gross profit for the 12 months ending December 31, 2022. However, during the fourth quarter of 2022 they reported a second consecutive quarter of declining revenue and warned about rising costs. The stock dropped 25%. In November 2022, Meta announced they were laying off 11,000 employees, followed by an additional 10,000 layoffs in March 2023. As part of the organisation's 'year of efficiency', within four months, the company committed to firing 24% of its work force. However, Meta's rate of employee growth had actually slowed in relative to earlier hiring, moving from 40% to 50% year on year growth in 2017 and in 2018, to more conservative rate of close to 20% annual growth from 2020 to 2022 (Statista, 2022). Ultimately, big tech does not have a cost problem. Rather, big tech has a timing problem, making share-pumping promises to investors about future revenues that are not materialising as quickly as claimed. Consequently, other share price boosting mechanisms were found. In February 2023, Meta reported that first-quarter sales would be better than expected and announced $40 billion in share buybacks, after already buying $28 billion of its own shares last year. Subsequently Meta stock surged by more than 23%, adding nearly $100 billion in market value in a single day following this combination of share buybacks, employee layoffs and better than expected earnings (Isaac, 2023).

There are also assertions that, in addition to boosting the share price, layoffs are enticing for vested interests as they re-assert managerial power and discipline across a sector which has been synonymous with generous compensation and perquisites. In terms of work availability, roles relating to recruitment and learning and development have been targeted in the layoffs. 'It seems to me that these layoffs are in part trying to hit back at the gains in both wage growth and organising', said Brian Merchant, author of 'Blood in the Machine: The Origins of the Rebellion Against Big Tech'.

> Worker power has made some small but real gains at big tech, which has been hostile to unions. These layoffs have the impact of being disruptive to that organising.' 'This is a way for management to say: "We're in charge".
>
> (Cassauwers, 2023)

Certainly, it seems layoffs offer instantly pleasing short-term financial and control benefits to investors and corporate leaders, all paid for through a weakening the availability and security of employment.

Conclusions

In this chapter, we have argued that the increasing prevalence of financialisation across sectors is a key factor impacting, largely negatively, on work futures. Perpetual restructuring and asset disposability reduces the availability and security of work and work rewards while also impacting on intensity and work conditions. Reinforcing the losses for labour are the associated changing boundaries of work and financial precarity which undermine collective solidarities and pursuit of power resources for labour. Studies of employees working in the investigated sectors highlight recurrent tensions that employees experience as they undertake their work. In particular, the clash between value extraction and value creation at the strategic level of these organisations is being mirrored at the heart of the labour process where employees experience a clash of values in their performance of their work. This clash of values is emerging as a novel feature of the financialised labour process. It occurs as employees, through their labour and discretionary effort, are bearing more responsibility for delivering, and sometimes protecting, the productive capacities of the organisation. In this way, the future of work increasingly involves employees delivering new work with precarious resources.

That is not to say that financialisation is a uniform process, or one in which there are no mediating or countervailing tendencies. Indeed, a number of studies of work trajectories that recognise the enhanced importance of financialisation, emphasise this point strongly. Variations derive from two main sources. First, the varieties of capitalism argument that strong national institutions, especially those governing labour market and industrial relations systems, act as a counterweight to financialisation (Kollmeyer and Peters, 2019; Dobbins and Plows, 2023). Second, sectoral and national differences also reflect types of markets, forms of ownership and the extent of integration into global financial circuits, particularly in emerging economies (Karwowski, 2022). Individual unions can also build successful opposition to the effects of financialisation if they can craft discursive and practical strategies that link to mobilising themes such as worker well-being (Doellgast et al., 2021). However, attempts at mitigating the evolving forces of financialisation are not assured. In this chapter, we argue that viewing work futures through multiple work domains reveals how financialised mechanisms have multi-faceted trajectories and reinforcing feedback loops that permeate and undermine working lives. These financialised pressures are playing out alongside other socio-technical developments, and explorations of work futures will be most meaningful where attention is paid to their combined impact.

References

Antoni, M., Maug, E. and Obernberger, S., 2019. Private equity and human capital risk. *Journal of Financial Economics, 133*(3), pp.634–657.

Appelbaum, E., 2019. How private equity makes you sicker: Investment firms have created consolidated hospital empires across America, leading to closures, higher prices, and suffering. *The American Prospect, 30*(4), pp.62–66.

Appelbaum, E., Batt, R. and Clark, I., 2013. Implications of financial capitalism for employment relations research: Evidence from breach of trust and implicit contracts in private equity buyouts. *British Journal of Industrial Relations, 51*(3), pp.498–518.

Armstrong, P. and Baines, D., 2020. Privatization, hybridization and resistance in contemporary care work. In *Working in the Context of Austerity* (pp. 97–108). Bristol: Bristol University Press.

Aronson, J. and Neysmith, S.M., 1996. "You're not just in there to do the work" depersonalizing policies and the exploitation of home care workers' labor. *Gender & Society, 10*(1), pp.59–77.

Bailey, S., Lenglet, M., Lord, G., Pierides, D. and Tischer, D., 2023. Parasitic universes: Organisational and technological meddling in the social. *New Technology, Work and Employment, 38*(1), pp.41–58.

Bangerter, L.R., 2023. The role of private equity in health care for older adults. *Public Policy & Aging Report*, p.prad002.

Birch, K., Cochrane, D.T. and Ward, C., 2021. Data as asset? The measurement, governance, and valuation of digital personal data by Big Tech. *Big Data & Society, 8*(1), p.20539517211017308.

Borio, C.E., Kharroubi, E., Upper, C. and Zampolli, F., 2016. Labour reallocation and productivity dynamics: Financial causes, real consequences. BIS Working Papers No 534. Available at: https://www.bis.org/publ/work534.pdf (Accessed 10th May 2023).

Bos, A. and Harrington, C., 2017. What happens to a nursing home chain when private equity takes over? A longitudinal case study. *INQUIRY: The Journal of Health Care Organization, Provision, and Financing, 54*, p.0046958017742761.

Braun, B., 2022, January. Fueling financialization: The economic consequences of funded pensions. In *New Labor Forum* (Vol. 31, No. 1, pp.70–79). Los Angeles, CA: SAGE Publications.

Burns, D., Cowie, L., Earle, J., Folkman, P., Froud, J., Hyde, P., Johal, S., Jones, I.R., Killett, A. and Williams, K., 2016. *Where Does the Money Go? Financialised Chains and the Crisis in Residential Care*. CRESC Public Interest Report. Available at: https://wiserd.ac.uk/wp-content/uploads/WDTMG-FINAL-01-3-2016-3.pdf (Accessed: 10th May 2023).

Cassauwers, T., 2023. Will tech layoffs silence or galvanise tech workers? Social Europe, 15th March. Available at: https://www.socialeurope.eu/will-tech-layoffs-silence-or-galvanise-tech-workers (Accessed: 10th May 2023).

Cerullo, M., Lin, Y.L., Rauh-Hain, J.A., Ho, V. and Offodile II, A.C., 2022. Financial impacts and operational implications of private equity acquisition of US hospitals. *Health Affairs, 41*(4), pp.523–530.

Clark, I., 2011. Private equity, 'union recognition' and value extraction at the Automobile Association: The GMB as an emergency service? *Industrial Relations Journal, 42*(1), pp.36–50.

Clark, I. and Macey, R., 2015. How is financialization contagious? How do HR practices help capture workplace outcomes in financialized firms? *Paper to 33rd International Labour Process Conference*. Athens, 13–15 April.

Cushen, J. and Thompson, P., 2016. Financialization and value: Why labour and the labour process still matter. *Work, Employment and Society, 30*(2), pp.352–365.

De Haan, J. and Sturm, J.E., 2017. Finance and income inequality: A review and new evidence. *European Journal of Political Economy, 50*, pp.171–195.

Dobbins, T. and Plows, A., 2023. Contesting the politics of neoliberal resilience: Regional labour market resilience from a workers' perspective. *Regional Studies, 57*(1), pp.26–40.

Doellgast, V., Bellego, M. and Pannini, E., 2021. After the social crisis: The transformation of employment relations at France Télécom. *Socio-Economic Review, 19*(3), pp.1127–1147.

Dore, R., 2008. Financialization of the global economy. *Industrial and Corporate Change, 17*(6), pp.1097–1112.

Dundon, T. and Rafferty, A., 2018. The (potential) demise of HRM? *Human Resource Management Journal, 28*(3), pp.377–391.

Findlay, P. and Thompson, P., 2017. Contemporary work: Its meanings and demands. *Journal of Industrial Relations, 59*(2), pp.122–138.

Findlay, P., Thompson, P., Cooper, C. and Pascoe-Deslauriers, R., 2017. *Creating and capturing value at work: Who benefits? Part 1: Thematic literature review*. London: Chartered Institute of Personnel and Development

Foroohar, R., 2021. *Don't Be Evil: The Case against Big Tech*. New York: Currency.

Froud, J., Johal, S., Leaver, A. and Williams, K., 2014. Financialization across the Pacific: Manufacturing cost ratios, supply chains and power. *Critical Perspectives on Accounting*, *25*(1), pp.46–57.

Gompers, P., Kaplan, S.N. and Mukharlyamov, V., 2016. What do private equity firms say they do? *Journal of Financial Economics*, *121*(3), pp.449–476.

Gospel, H., Pendleton, A. and Vitols, S. eds., 2014. *Financialization, New Investment Funds, and Labour: An International Comparison*. Oxford: Oxford University Press.

Gouzoulis, G., 2023. What do indebted employees do? Financialisation and the decline of industrial action. *Industrial Relations Journal*, *54*(1), pp.71–94.

Gouzoulis, G., Iliopoulos, P. and Galanis, G., 2023. Financialization and the rise of atypical work. *British Journal of Industrial Relations*, *61*(1), pp.24–45.

Gregory, D., 2013. Private equity and financial stability. *Bank of England Quarterly Bulletin*, p.Q1. Available at: https://ssrn.com/abstract=2243571 (Accessed 10th May 2023).

Hendrikse, R., Adriaans, I., Klinge, T.J. and Fernandez, R., 2022. The big techification of everything. *Science as Culture*, *31*(1), pp.59–71.

Horton, A., 2022. Financialization and non-disposable women: Real estate, debt and labour in UK care homes. *Environment and Planning A: Economy and Space*, *54*(1), pp.144–159.

Howcroft, D. and Taylor, P., 2023. Automation and the future of work: A social shaping of technology approach. *New Technology, Work and Employment, 38*(2), pp. 351–370.

Iazzolino, G. and Varesio, A., 2023. Gaming the system: Tactical workarounds and the production of antagonistic subjectivities among migrant platform workers in Italy. *Antipode*, *55*(3), pp.877–896.

Isaac, M., 2023. Meta to lay off another 10,000 workers. *The New York Times*, 14th March. Available at: https://www.nytimes.com/2023/03/14/technology/meta-facebook-layoffs.html (Accessed: 10th May 2023).

Jenkins, J. and Blyton, P., 2017. In debt to the time-bank: The manipulation of working time in Indian garment factories and 'working dead horse'. *Work, Employment and Society*, *31*(1), pp.90–105.

Jensen, M.C., 2009. Corporate control and the politics of finance. In Chew, D.H. and Gillan, S.L. eds., *US Corporate Governance*, 2009. *US Corporate Governance* (pp. 243–279). New York: Columbia University Press.

Jones, A. and Search, P., 2009. Proximity and power within investment relationships: The case of the UK private equity industry. *Geoforum*, *40*(5), pp.809–819.

Jung, J. and Lee, Y., 2022. Financialization and corporate downsizing as a shareholder value strategy. *Socio-Economic Review*, *20*(4), pp.1795–1823.

Kaplan, S.N. and Strömberg, P., 2009. Leveraged buyouts and private equity. *Journal of Economic Perspectives*, *23*(1), pp.121–146.

Karwowski, E., 2022. Commercial finance for development: A back door for financialisation. *Review of African Political Economy*, *49*(171), pp.161–172.

Klinge, T.J., Hendrikse, R., Fernandez, R. and Adriaans, I., 2023. Augmenting digital monopolies: A corporate financialization perspective on the rise of Big Tech. *Competition & Change*, *27*(2), pp.332–353.

Kollmeyer, C. and Peters, J., 2019. Financialization and the decline of organized labor: A study of 18 advanced capitalist countries, 1970–2012. *Social Forces*, *98*(1), pp.1–30.

Kotecha, V., 2019. Plugging the leaks in the UK care home industry: Strategies for resolving the financial crisis in the residential and nursing home sector. *Centre for Health and the Public Interest*. Plugging the leaks in the UK care home industry – Strategies for resolving the financial crisis in the residential and nursing home sector—CHPI (Accessed: 10th May 2023).

Krippner, G.R., 2005. The financialization of the American economy. *Socio-Economic Review*, *3*(2), pp.173–208.

Lagoarde-Segot, T. and Currie, W.L., 2018. Financialization and information technology: A multi-paradigmatic view of IT and finance–Part II. *Journal of Information Technology*, *33*(1), pp.1–8.

Lapavitsas, C., 2011. Theorizing financialization. *Work, Employment and Society*, *25*(4), pp.611–626.

Lazonick, W., 2014. Profits without prosperity: Stock buybacks manipulate the market and leave most Americans worse off. *Harvard Business Review*, *92*(9), pp.46–55.

Lazonick, W. and Mazzucato, M., 2013. The risk-reward nexus in the innovation-inequality relationship: Who takes the risks? Who gets the rewards? *Industrial and Corporate Change*, *22*(4), pp.1093–1128.

Legault, M.J. and Weststar, J., 2021. Organising challenges in the era of financialisation: The case of videogame workers. *Work Organisation, Labour & Globalisation, 15*(2), pp.7–24.

Ljungqvist, A. and Richardson, M., 2003. The cash flow, return and risk characteristics of private equity. *Journal of Business, 76*(4), pp.491–534. doi: 10.1086/375035.

Milberg, W., 2008. Shifting sources and uses of profits: Sustaining US financialization with global value chains. *Economy and Society, 37*(3), pp.420–451.

Müller, J., 2014. An accounting revolution? The financialisation of standard setting. *Critical Perspectives on Accounting, 25*(7), pp.539–557.

Olsson, M. and Tåg, J., 2017. Private equity, layoffs, and job polarization. *Journal of Labor Economics, 35*(3), pp.697–754.

Orhangazi, Ö., 2008. Financialisation and capital accumulation in the non-financial corporate sector: A theoretical and empirical investigation on the US economy: 1973–2003. *Cambridge Journal of Economics, 32*(6), pp.863–886.

Palladino, L., 2021. Financialization at work: Shareholder primacy and stagnant wages in the United States. *Competition & Change, 25*(3–4), pp.382–400.

PitchBook, 2022. European private equity report 2022. Available at: https://pitchbook.com/reports/european-private-equity-report-2022

Schneck, J. and Pons-Vignon N., 2023. Quality care on a conveyor belt? *Paper presented at the 41st International Labour Process Conference*. April, 2023.

Statista, 2022. Number of Facebook employees from 2004 to 2021. Statista. Available at: https://www.statista.com/statistics/273563/number-of-facebook-employees/ (Accessed: 10th May 2023).

Stockhammer, E., 2008. Some stylized facts on the finance-dominated accumulation regime. *Competition & Change, 12*(2), pp.184–202.

Sucher, S.J. and Westner, M.M., 2023. What companies still get wrong about layoffs. Social Europe [online] 15th March. Available at: https://www.socialeurope.eu/will-tech-layoffs-silence-or-galvanise-tech-workers (Accessed: 10th May 2023).

Thomas, K., 2019. Tech meets health care, sometimes Shakily. *The New York Times*, 7th August. Available at: https://www.nytimes.com/2019/08/07/technology/personaltech/tech-meets-health-care-sometimes-shakily.html (Accessed: 10th May 2023).

Thompson, P., 2003. Disconnected capitalism: Or why employers can't keep their side of the bargain. *Work, Employment and Society, 17*(2), pp.359–378.

Thompson, P., 2013. Financialization and the workplace: Extending and applying the disconnected capitalism thesis. *Work, Employment and Society, 27*(3), pp.472–488.

Thompson, P., 2019. The Taylor review: A platform for progress? Good work: The Taylor review of modern working practices', reviewed by Paul Thompson. *New Technology, Work and Employment, 34*(2), pp.106–110.

Thompson, P. and Cushen, J., 2020. Essay forum: Labor in financialization: Value logics and labor: Collateral damage or central focus? In Mader, P., Mertens, D. and Van der Zwan, N. eds., *The Routledge International Handbook of Financialization* (pp.324–329). Abingdon: Routledge.

van Doorn, N. and Chen, J.Y., 2021. Odds stacked against workers: Datafied gamification on Chinese and American food delivery platforms. *Socio-Economic Review, 19*(4), pp.1345–1367.

Vieno, A., 2023. 'It's as if I'm worth nothing'—Cost-driven restructuring and the dignity of long-term workers in Finland's state-owned postal service company. *Journal of Business Ethics, 187*(1), pp.17–31.

Warhurst, C. and Hunt, W., 2019. *The Digitalisation of Future Work and Employment: Possible Impact and Policy Responses* (No. 2019/05). JRC Working Papers Series on Labour, Education and Technology.

Recommendations for Further Reading

Cushen, J., 2013. Financialization in the workplace: Hegemonic narratives, performative interventions and the angry knowledge worker. *Accounting, Organizations and Society, 38*(4), pp.314–331.

Ioannou, S. and Wójcik, D., 2019. On financialization and its future. *Environment and Planning A: Economy and Space, 51*(1), pp.263–271.

Mader, P., Mertens, D. and Van der Zwan, N. eds., 2020. *The Routledge International Handbook of Financialization*. Abingdon: Routledge.

Martin, R., Rafferty, M. and Bryan, D., 2008. Financialization, risk and labour. *Competition & Change, 12*(2), pp.120–132.

PART 3

Automation, Technology and the Future of Work

5

THE POLITICAL ECONOMY OF LABOUR AND TECHNOLOGICAL DISRUPTIONS IN CAPITALISM

Eleni Papagiannaki

Introduction

The recent emergence of digital platforms, platform economies and platformisation, as well as the datafication of labour, are all inextricably linked to the rise of artificial intelligence (AI) and machine learning. While the extent to which financialisation caused economies' platformisation (Varoufakis, 2023) is a matter of debate these technological developments have raised fundamental questions about the future of work and the economy. Computer scientists, such as Daskalakis (2018) have asked whether we are heading towards 'wonderland', a future where AI and machine learning create abundance and prosperity for all; 'pessiland', a future where AI and machine learning lead to mass unemployment and social unrest; or 'stagnatia', a future where AI and machine learning do not lead to significant change and we remain stuck in the same economic and social system. These questions have resonated with social scientists and especially political economists of all schools of thought. From mainstream economists like Nobel laureate Daron Acemoglu to Marxists like Nick Dyer-Witheford to heterodox analysts like Mariana Mazzucato, many scholars have attempted to foresee the future of economy, and to a certain degree, the future of work.

This chapter classifies the literature on the contrasting futures of work into four categories: optimistic, utopian, pessimistic and dismissive (see Chapter 6). Techno-optimistic views assume that capitalism will continue to grow uninterruptedly, leading to positive outcomes for workers. Techno-utopian views assume that capitalist technology will help create a postcapitalist utopia, and that the law of value will automatically collapse under capitalism. Techno-pessimistic views underestimate the power of capital-to-capital competition and assume that capital can infinitely suppress labour. Techno-dismissive views take a variety of different perspectives on the future of work, but they all share a common scepticism about the role of technology in shaping the future. This chapter argues that mainly several of these categories of thought are flawed because they are based on incorrect assumptions about the nature of capitalism and the role of technology.

This chapter aligns with a techno-dismissive view in the sense that it acknowledges the benefits of technological advancements, but does not see full automation as the primary driver of social change. Instead, it argues that the future of work will be shaped by the interplay between technology, capitalism and labour. The chapter also highlights the importance of engaging with Marxist literature in order to accurately foresee the future of work. Marxist theory provides a framework

 DOI: 10.4324/9781003327561-8

for understanding the underlying dynamics of capitalism, including the two antagonisms that are identified in the chapter: *labour-to-capital antagonism* and *capital-to-capital antagonism.*

Labour-to-capital antagonism refers to the conflict between workers and capitalists over the distribution of surplus value. Surplus value is the difference between the value of the goods and services that workers produce and the wages that they are paid. Capitalists seek to maximise surplus value by paying workers as little as possible and selling goods and services for as much as possible, while workers seek to increase their wages and reduce their workload. Capital-to-capital antagonism refers to the competition between capitalists for profits. Capitalists are constantly seeking to reduce costs and increase sales in order to outcompete their rivals. This can lead to technological innovation, mergers and acquisitions, and other forms of restructuring. The chapter argues that these two antagonisms are essential for understanding the complex dynamics of capitalism and the future of work. It concludes by calling for a more nuanced and realistic understanding of the future of work, one that takes into account the complex interplay between technology, capitalism and labour.

Techno-optimism: Growth of Output or Profits?

Mainstream economic thought assumes that capitalism does not recognise the contradiction between the constant growth of output (the production of goods and services), and the growth of profits. Although neoclassical economics acknowledge that the 'profit-maximising quantity' produced is not the maximum that can be achieved, it stills serves the system's growth, where profits accumulated are re-invested in an ever-ending cycle, only to be interrupted by external shocks that cause economic crises. This belief in the necessity of growth feeds through into an optimistic disposition about the transformative potential of technology. However, critics argue that this techno-optimism is misplaced. They point out that capitalism is a system that is inherently exploitative and unsustainable. Businesses are driven to generate profits, not to meet human needs. This means that even if technology leads to increased output and economic growth, the benefits of this growth are not likely to be shared equitably. In fact, there is evidence that technological change is leading to increased inequality and social unrest (see Chapter 28).

Contemporary techno-optimism is well represented by Klaus Schwab (2016), the founder and executive chairman of the World Economic Forum (WEF) who is credited with coining the term 'Fourth Industrial Revolution' (4IR). According to Schwab, 4IR is a new era of technological change characterised by a fusion of technologies that blur the lines between the physical, digital, and biological worlds. This fusion is enabled by a number of emerging technologies, including AI, the Internet of Things (IoT), advanced robotics, 3D printing and biotechnology, which are all creating new possibilities for innovation. The 4IR is differentiated from previous industrial revolutions as it impacts more than one sector: it is theorised to affect all aspects of society and the economy. This includes the way we work, the way we live, and the way we interact with the world around us. For example, AI-powered medical devices are being used to diagnose diseases more accurately and to develop personalised treatments. Robots are being used to perform complex surgeries and to manufacture products. The IoT is connecting billions of devices to the internet, creating new opportunities for data collection and analysis. 3D printing is being used to create everything from custom prosthetics to living tissues, while biotechnology is being used to develop new drugs and therapies, and to create new forms of life. The WEF regards these through a class-collaborative discourse of the *augmented workforce*, which means that these technologies will enhance the capabilities of workers and make them more productive. This, in turn, will benefit both businesses and employees (Moencks et al., 2022).

McKinsey & Company represent another mainstream techno-optimist perspective that is driving the discourse of the 4IR. They emphasise the importance of 'upskilling' and 'reskilling' workers, and they argue the 4IR will be a 'people powered' revolution – as compared to the steam-powered 1IR, the electricity-powered 2IR and the automation-powered 3IR – that will drive productivity and efficiency gains in manufacturing and supply chains. However, there is already empirical evidence to suggest a slowdown in productivity in recent years, which has led some economists to wonder whether Solow's (1987) productivity paradox is back (Mekala et al., 2018). In other words, the drop in labour productivity that was observed when investment in information technology took place in the 1970s raises its head again today, with respect to the 4IR technologies. Neo-Schumpeterian economists, such as Cetrulo and Nuvolari (2019), have also noted that productivity growth has been slower than in previous business cycles. Despite this evidence, techno-optimism continues, with Brynjolfsson et al. (2018) recognising the paradox but arguing that '[i]t isn't until a sufficient stock of the new technology is built' (p. 31) that growth will be detectable by economic data. Other critical voices, such as Cole (2023) (see also in this volume), argue that many firms are currently upgrading; therefore, productivity will be soon evident. However, critics also emphasise the unevenness in technological diffusion that makes productivity data more challenging to capture.

Additionally, it is possible for capitalism to function efficiently even with a steady or declining level of output (Saunders, 2016). While capitalists theoretically may appear as advocates of increased output, their primary goal is always to extract surplus value (profit, rent, interest) and expand their capital. This means that they may be willing to invest in technologies that reduce costs and increase profits, even if it means reduced labour and 'capital' productivity, as we observe in contemporary analyses of capitalist economies (Papagiannaki et al., 2023). It is detected that profits can grow with stagnated labour productivity, as within the years of the economy's digitalisation (especially after 2008). According to neoclassical economics, surplus-driven economic units will generally produce less output than 'cost-revenue break-even' units. This is because surplus-driven units are incentivised to produce less output so as to generate more profit. And this is the importance in analysing the system as it is: a *capitalist commodity production*, not a *simple commodity production*. Indeed, Shaikh (1980) argues that 'mechanisation becomes the dominant form of technical change precisely because it is the production of surplus value, not use-value, which is the dominant aspect of the labour process under capitalism' (p. 75). Thus, the pursuit of profit drives technical change, but it is also because of this pursuit that we do not see rising labour productivity with technological innovation.

While capitalism sees both capital- and labour-saving technologies, it is the latter that attracts more attention in discussions of the apparently 'groundbreaking' changes afoot due to automation and AI. However, capital-saving technologies still persist. For instance, despite the growing popularity in robot vacuum cleaners in households, and efforts to use similar devices in workplaces more generally, the cleaning profession remains alive and well with a continuing dependence on 'traditional' equipment, similar to a lot of 'manual' occupations. The declining cost of technologies might potentially enable the cost of labour becoming less decisive in discouraging investment in new technology. However, the low wages of cleaners and the advantages of the physical flexibility and better vision that humans have currently disincentivise capitalists from substituting cleaners with robots *en masse*. We can, however, observe an opposite trend with the substitution of artistic and intellectual work by new software – one of the reasons being that these professions cost more to employ.

Capital- and labour-saving technologies have co-existed in capitalism throughout history, with labour-saving technologies generally dominating. However, for higher productivity to be observed investment in both is necessary. As Duménil and Lévy (2003) argue, 'it is difficult to find new processes allowing for the growth of labour productivity while not considerably reducing the productivity of capital' under capitalist commodity production. Therefore, to understand the 'people-powered' aspects of the Fourth Industrial Revolution we must consider labour productivities with regard to the dynamics of surplus-value extraction and capital accumulation.

Mainstream techno-optimism, apart from expressing capital's need to invest in new technologies in order to stay competitive, tends to focus on the more technical aspects of technological change rather than the social and economic conditions under which technological advancements take place. As Shaikh (1980, p. 76) highlights, 'technical change is generally reduced to a discussion of *all possible* "technical improvements"'. For Schumpeter (1939), this represents the difference between invention and innovation. He argues that invention is 'without importance to economic analysis' (p. 85) because it is only when an invention is commercialised and becomes a profitable product or process that it has a significant economic impact. Leitner (2017) discusses the concept of 'no' and 'slow' innovation strategies, particularly in European companies, whereby innovation is typically not viewed as an inherent good, but rather as something to be carefully considered in terms of costs and benefits. Walsh (2023) additionally points out that '[f]or capital, the question is never: innovation, yes or no? It is always: when to innovate, how to innovate and what kind of innovation is best' (p. 351). However, several mainstream economists who study the future of work, including the impact of automation, assume that all new technologies will inevitably be implemented and diffused. This approach, which reflects a linear model of innovation (Godin, 2006), is exemplified by Webb's (2020), who utilises a method of mapping technologies to specific job tasks to construct a measure of automation exposure for different occupations. Although this is just one of several economic methods for predicting labour displacement from 4IR-related technologies, it is representative of the above assumptions.

While researchers who adhere to neoclassical economic principles acknowledge that automation exposure does not always lead to technology adoption, they generally persist in viewing production as a technical process, rather than a social relationship between classes. One class extracts surplus value from the other and this dynamic mediates the implementation and impact of the available technologies. In other words, it is the social relationships of production that are the root cause of the inherent tendency to develop technology and labour practices that restrict workers as much as possible in order to extract surplus value. As Ramtin (1991, p. 58) points out, 'it is the very elastic characteristic of human labour-power which is crucial to the complex needs of capital's ceaseless expansionist drive'. Therefore, as long as labour and capital have a conflicting relationship, labour costs will continue to be a decisive factor in discouraging investment.

Techno-Utopianism: 'Immaterial' and Productive Labour

Techno-utopian analyses are best represented by Mason's notion of *postcapitalism* (2015), Williams and Srnicek's *accelerationism* (2015), Bastani's *fully automated luxury communism* (2019), Phillips and Rozworski's (2019) *People's Republic of Walmart* and Muldoon's (2022) *platform socialism*. Explicitly or implicitly, this strand of thought draws inspiration from Marx's *Grundrisse* (1973), especially his 'Fragment on Machines'. The work contained within it either posits that we can repurpose existing technology to create a postcapitalist or socialist 'society of abundance' or lays an emphasis on how the law of value will collapse through automation and the reduction of the labour time that is socially necessary for a commodity to be produced. Both tendencies are seen as leading to the inevitable death of capitalism.

This strand of techno-utopianism tends to overlook that technology is a commodity, which means that it has both exchange-value and use-value. Although most authors in this strand will discuss both of these dimensions, their focus tends to be on the specific use-values of technologies, rather than on the way that technologies are shaped in and through capitalism. For this reason, they see technologies as a way to achieve a postcapitalist future. However, the role of surplus value extraction through labour control and domination inherently shapes technologies to meet the specific needs of capitalist production and this determines precisely which technologies are most developed or advanced. For example, in 2021, $4 billion was invested in research for nuclear fusion (Bloomberg Professional Services, 2021), an environmentally friendly technology which requires a huge fixed initial investment but has the potential to solve humanity's energy needs. This compares to the $600 billion invested in cosmetics research (Petruzzi, 2022) which is less consequential. This demonstrates that capitalist production does not prioritise technologies that benefit humanity if investing in other sorts of technology is deemed more profitable.

Some post-operaist analysts predict a collapse of capitalism due to a crisis in the law of value, which they argue is already underway. This crisis in the law of value – which connects the value of a commodity to the amount of labour required to produce it – is often explained by the increasing importance of 'immaterial' labour (Lazzarato, 1996), generating ideas, information and culture, and the fact that such labour is difficult to quantify and measure. Berardi (2013, p. 75), when discussing measurement issues of immaterial labour, casts doubt on the law of value as he highlights the impossibility of capturing 'how much time it takes to produce an idea'. However, what this chapter argues is that both manual and mental labour are required for value production and both are ultimately material. While humans have evolved and divided labour to the point where manual and mental labour appear separate, for millennia they were fused. For example, the working time of an ancient doctor/priest/wizard curing a patient was the same as the time they would spend performing ritual acts; their ancient 'medicine' was part of the same spiritual/religious activity that they conducted. Similarly, today's knowledge workers perform both manual and mental labour when writing a book or designing a website. And even when there is no physical 'end product' resulting from such labour, the service they produce still requires an expenditure of human energy and the use of instruments and means of labour, which are very material. This means the assumed immateriality of mental labour is a historically bound perspective resultant from a narrow view of labour based on the bodily features of its performance. It is not only impossible to assess workers' manual or mental tasks separately (because these have always been intertwined), but additionally the social division of labour has advanced to a point where the collective worker is more productive than any individual worker. Thus, we are yet to witness the catastrophic results on the law of value ascribed to 'immaterial' labour. As Steinhoff (2021) writes, '[w]hile information technology has yet to catapult the world into communism, post-operaismo continues to advance its immaterial labour theory with little revision' (p. 7).

Although sympathetic to their intentions, post-operaismo, instead of demonstrating the Gramscian balance of 'pessimism of the intellect, and optimism of the will' (Gramsci, 1920), therefore displays an over-optimism of the intellect by selectively focusing on the concept of immaterial labour, while neglecting other important parts of Marx's theory. This over-optimism leads to a pessimism of the will as post-operaists, having become disillusioned with the traditional industrial working class and their ability to overthrow capitalism, place an arbitrary optimism on the agency of a new, expanded proletarian-style subject, such as the social worker (Negri, 1991) or neo-proletarian (as per Gorz, 1982), that despite being detached from the factory, they suggest can bring about societal change.

Techno-Pessimism: Labour-to-Capital vs Capital-to-Capital Antagonism

Techno-pessimism is found in both mainstream analyses and alternative scholarship that emphasises the role of power and class struggle. In terms of mainstream studies, Frey and Osborne (2017) have gained popularity for their forecast that 47% of jobs in the US are at high risk of automation in the next 10–20 years. From a more alternative perspective, Morozov (2013) is one techno-pessimist who argues that technology is not neutral, but rather serves to reinforce existing power structures and inequalities. Although not specifically critiquing the discourse of the Fourth industrial revolution, Morozov argues that the idea of 'internet freedom' is a myth, and that the internet is in fact a highly centralised and controlled space. *Neo-Luddism* is another stream, represented by Sadowski (2020, 2021), Mueller (2021), Merchant (2017) and Marx (2022), which also emphasises the non-neutrality of technology. These writers highlight the politics behind technologies' design arguing that 'each phase of the technical process—from design to use—is loaded with politics' (Sadowski, 2020, p. 4). For Mueller (2021), technology is a field for struggle. He sees Marxism as a theory that 'can suggest a more liberatory politics of work and technology – one that is more easily supported than contemporary post-work utopias (Sadowski, 2020, p. 29). For Mueller, the fact that technology is a struggle means the radical left must promote '*decelerationist* politics, to slow down change, undermine technological progress, and limit capital's rapacity' (pp. 127–128).

Dyer-Witheford, Kjøsen and Steinhoff (2019) use the schema of 'maximalist', 'minimalist' and 'abyss' to describe different visions of the future of automation. By claiming that technological futures are characterised by the 'abyss', they refer to the vast unknowns and uncertainties of the trajectory of AI technologies, while also recognising that automation has an ideological function. Steinhoff, Kjosen, Dyer-Witheford (2024) warn that

> [h]umans may well be upgraded as symbiotic, cyborg partners to AGI [Artificial General Intelligence], but if the AGIs are designed to prioritise the goals of capital, such symbioses will develop in the direction of making more perfect vehicles for commodity production and circulation.
>
> (p. 309)

As meaningful and crucial as it is to analyse the specifics of labour-to-capital antagonism that the above techno-pessimists describe, one must consider the ruthless law of capital-to-capital antagonism too. Regardless of whether workers reactively resist capital that deskills and degrades labour (as Labour Process Theory describes) or whether technology is capital's reaction to the power of industrial mass workers (as in *Operaismo*), capitalists fight workers through technical and technological change. The motivation to supress labour and impose discipline in the 'factory', however, is frequently contradicted by capitalist competition. Shaikh (1980, p. 69) emphasises this contradiction, where

> on one hand, each labour process is privately undertaken as if it is independent of all others, with exchange for profit as the goal. On the other hand, this undertaking assumes in advance that other similar labour processes will also be there at the right time and in the right proportions.

The capital-to-capital antagonism betrays how little control individual capitalists have over the market, and therefore inflates their role in determining macroeconomic patterns beyond their own microeconomic firm-based planning. In the factory, technology and labour are regulated by the capitalist directly, while in society labour and technology are regulated by the market through the exchange of commodities. In the factory, the capitalist can pre-determine the conditions of production, but in the market, even in highly monopolistic (or oligopolistic) markets, the individual capitalist does not have the full control over the pricing and technological diffusion of consumable and capital goods. Vidal (2019) goes further in his analysis by pointing out contradictions within capitalist labour processes themselves which further limit the control that an individual capitalist has: the 'management contradiction' according to Vidal is the conflict managers experience between coordination (with a view to increasing efficiency) and discipline (to ensure valorisation). Despite the increasing use of digital technologies, some of the most automated capitalist economies in the world (IFR, 2021) continue to face labour shortages (e.g., South Korea, see Expat.com, 2023), which highlights the difficulties capitalists often face to fully automate, as they still depend on labour. Capital-to-capital antagonism can be an incentive, but it can also be an impediment to suppressing workers by means of technology. What this implies is that the inherent tendency towards automation springs from the social relations of production and from the labour-to-capital competition in the production process, not primarily from the capital-to-capital antagonism.

However, the capital-to-capital antagonism 'tests these potential weapons in the fire of battle' (Shaikh, 1980, p. 75). A lack of full control over the market dynamics is reflected in capitalists' choice of technique, as 'competition forces capitalists, upon penalty of extinction, to adopt the method of production with the lower cost-price' (Shaikh, 1980, p. 76). This lower cost method is not always the highest profit one, i.e. the one where labour is supressed the most. Only under certain conditions (that is, certain prices) does the low-cost technique coincide with the firm's higher profit margin, leading 'each individual capitalist to adopt methods of production with the higher transitional profit margin, even if it lowers their transitional profit rate' (pp. 76–77). To put it differently, on a microeconomic level, even if capitalists wish to extract maximum surplus value, competition can force them into a non-profit-maximising choice of technique. Uber is such a case of years of non-profitable choices, having only recently made positive profits.

Over the course of capitalist competition, we do observe phenomena that many economists see as anomalous. Individual technologically leading capitalists see their competitors catching up, leading to a fall in the intra-branch rate of profit as the whole sector adopts a given technology. For Ramtin, '[t]he more successful capital is in shaping its technological system to increase surplus labour time, the more the production system itself comes up against the limited foundation of capital' (p. 19). Indeed, the greater the extraction of surplus labour, the more difficult it is for capital to self-expand. That is why we see market structures with close to monopoly status having difficulties in innovating and ending up funding 'start ups' to innovate for them until they buy them off. And it is why we see economists entertaining the idea of *techno-feudalism*, where capitalism is assumed to capitalise in order to appropriate, instead of the reverse, with appropriation (instead of capitalisation) being the ultimate driver of a typical feudalist mode of production.

The concept of *techno-feudalism* presents a narrative whereby big tech controls society and creates digital serfdom. Varoufakis (2023) claims that capital has mutated into what he calls 'cloud capital' and this has demolished capital's two pillars: markets and profits, which 'have been pushed out to its margins and replaced [...] by digital trade platforms which look like, but [...] are not markets'. Capitalists have become the vassals to Big Tech and the rest of us the serfs, providing unpaid labour on top of wage labour. Morozov (2022) in his critique on the narrative of techno-feudalism addresses its differences with capitalism. He emphasises that feudalism is characterised by 'politically enabled expropriation' and capitalism by 'economically enabled exploitation' (p. 94). Here I critique the attempted inversion of the *appropriate-to-capitalise* principle that the techno-feudalism thesis implies, building on Morozov's points. Varoufakis' work similarly launches one of the first analysis of techno-feudalism with politico-economic theoretical foundations, addressing both labour-to-capital and capital-to-capital antagonisms. Nonetheless his assumptions do not reflect a theory of intra- and inter-capitalist competition with regard to rates of profits and their determination, but display an uncritical acceptance that a user's input into a platform counts as labour. It is inter-industrial capitalist competition that leads to a structure where industries with higher composition of capital and lower profit margins are those that become dominant for certain periods in time. What Varoufakis presents as an anomaly that has killed capitalism is then nothing other than predictable outcome of inter-industrial competition. As stated earlier, capital's adoption of methods of production with a higher transitional profit margin, even with lower transitional profit rate, also leads to a new general rate of profit that is lower too. In other words, classical Marxian analysis needs a little if not at all the services of a techno-feudalist analysis to describe the doings of platform economy. And the passage from 'finance capitalism' or 'casino capitalism' that were coined a decade ago to a 'platform capitalism' or 'techno-feudalism' does not necessarily mutate or alter the very nature of the capitalist system, regardless of the dominant form of capital in different periods.

Dismissive and Techno-sceptic Perspectives

The final perspectives we consider here are those which dismiss or express scepticism about some of the visions presented elsewhere in the literature. Mainstream economists challenge Frey and Osborne's grim predictions. Meanwhile, other techno-dismissive scholars attempt to analyse the role of technology from a class struggle perspective, or emphasise the role of institutions as a means to explain the inability of capitalism to reproduce itself. Others aim to critique 'maximalist' approaches by rejecting these analyses for their indebtedness to 'productivism', or 'value substantialism'.

In the first category, we see scholars who have critiqued Frey and Osborne's task-based analysis of labour substitution. Arntz et al. (2016, 2017), for instance, by including additional socioeconomic dimensions in their study ended up predicting a much less grim future of work with only 9% degree of jobs at risk of automation.

The second category includes Spencer (2017, 2018; Spencer and Slater, 2020), Smith (2020) and Benanav (2020). They place analytical stress on economic stagnation, lack of capitalist investment (as withheld capitalist profits are distributed to shareholders), a lack of noticeable productivity improvements and the prevalence of underemployment rather than the mass unemployment many fear. These scholars emphasise the influence of social relations on the trajectory of automation. Benanav (2020) asserts that it is possible to reach a world of abundance through social struggle 'even without the full or nearly full automation of production' (p. 11). Spencer (2020) suggests that arguments for the complete automation of work are deeply flawed because they ignore the capitalistic organisation of labour and instead focus on the belief that work is inherently 'bad', a disutility. Spencer (2018) also suggests that some work may not be suitable for automation. Smith (2020) frames the existing fears and hopes around automation in the context of contemporary conditions of technological stagnation, emphasising the role of productive and unproductive labour and the production of 'toys not tools' (p. 43) that predominates in contemporary capitalist economies.

Other scholars who dismiss both techno-optimist and techno-pessimist narratives locate the discourse of automation and the Fourth Industrial Revolution in capitalist business cycles, Kontratief long waves and the approaches of Regulation School. Fuchs (2018), for instance, identifies Germany's strategic failure to align with other advanced capitalist economies, which led to the 2011 discourse of 'Industrie 4.0', which underpinned a plan to increase the profit rate of the country's manufacturing industry. Moll (2022) meanwhile casts doubt on the existence of the Fourth Industrial Revolution, arguing that there is an absence of the changing labour relations and other phenomena associated with previous periods of transformation. He even suggests that the technologies currently shaping the economic environment are essentially still Third Industrial Revolution technologies. Moll blames Schumpeterian thinking which suggests that long waves come with associated technological disruptions for the prevalence of 4IR claims. Cole (2022), by contrast, attempts to produce a deflationary explanation of the narrative and existence of the Fourth Industrial Revolution using a combination of Schumpeterian and Regulation School insights, claiming that 'platformisation represents an (infra)structural discontinuity from the technological and institutional forms of the information and communication technology (ICT)/post-Fordist era, which were spatially and temporally limited in their capacity to leverage control over workers' (p. 363).

There are also revisionist Marxists that are critical of techno-utopianism. They negate the concept of value as 'substantialist' (Pitts, 2021) or a 'nonempirical reality' (Dinerstein, 2014), reduces it to a 'category of social mediation' (Heinrich, 2007), or even invert the Labour Theory of Value into a 'Value Theory of Labour' (Elson, 2015). Pitts (2017, 2019) notably contributes to the debate by arguing for a greater recognition of the role of class struggle in shaping the future of work. Pitts rejects techno-utopian visions and aligns with Heinrich's (2012) rejection of traditional value theory, which posits a rupture between production and circulation in Marx's work, attempting to bridge it with a monetary theory of value that places great emphasis on circulation as the primary regulator of the socioeconomy. But this has a tendency to simply present an abstract analysis of power relations.

This school of thought, like others, concludes – even as neoclassical economics do – that everything marketable has value. Indeed, by skipping mainstream standard price-taking theories where the higher profit method will be chosen even if it has a higher unit cost, predicting that technical change will always raise the average rate of profit, with given real wages does not recognise a fall in the general rate of profit (similar to standard price-taking theories with an 'excessive' rise in the real wage). Such theories have, in practice, failed to justify why global rates of profit fall (as per Basu et al., 2022), especially since there is no significant increase in employees' incomes globally (UNCTAD, 2020). Indeed, capitalists face real challenges in preventing the falling rate of profit through its countertendencies (e.g., increasing exploitation and saving on constant capital). Yet schools of thought like the New Readings of Marx or Open Marxism tend to be more sober about the discourse of full automation, insufficiently include in their analyses the understanding of surplus value and rate of profit that is needed to fully explain and foresee the future of work.

Conclusion: Materialist Analysis and the Fourth Industrial Revolution

Overall, this chapter highlights the importance of technological advancements in capitalism, but recognises that full automation is not in and of itself the prime mover in social change, as Spencer, Benanav and Smith claim. The chapter also underscores the importance of scholars examining the future of work from a perspective informed by Marxist literature, with a particular focus on utilising the methodological concepts of (i) labour-to-capital relations and (ii) capital-to-capital conflicts as essential tools for predicting the future of work. It posits that is crucial we address the misconceptions that lead to capitalism being framed as a system aimed at achieving the highest economic output rather than the generation of profit, or surplus value. Acknowledging this fallacy can help us to understand why labour productivity is not going up, why investment in high tech technology might not be as fruitful as envisaged, and if and why there is a shift in capitalist decision-making from profits to profit-margins.

From this vantage point it is simply not possible to analyse capitalism's technological dynamics using the insights of neoclassical economics. Moreover, the specific qualitative form assumed by technologies that are envisioned to be used in the future are seen to arise from the specific suppressive social relations of surplus value extraction. This explains why the envisaged automatic collapse of capitalism via the increased presence of 'immaterial' labour is not taking place, and, as importantly, why this should not be an aspiration. What the above approaches miss is that the whole process of automation is intended to increase surplus-value, but capital-to-capital antagonism leads to technical methods that aim to reduce labour time per product. This shrinks the basis from which surplus value is extracted resulting in the recurring falling rates of profit witnessed throughout capitalism's history (Basu et al., 2022).

References

Arntz, M., Gregory, T. and Zierahn, U. (2016). The risk of automation for jobs in OECD countries. *OECD*. Available at: oecd-ilibrary.org

Arntz, M., Gregory, T. and Zierahn, U. (2017). Technology and the future of work aggregate employment effects of digitization. In *Conference Proceeding Paper*, IZA, Institute of Labor Economics. Available at: https://conference.iza.org/conference_files/MacroEcon_2018/zierahn_u25158.pdf

Bastani, A. (2019). *Fully Automated Luxury Communism*. Verso Books.

Basu, D., Huato, J., Jauregui, J. L. and Wasner, E. (2022). World profit rates, 1960–2019. *Review of Political Economy*, 1–16. https://doi.org/10.1080/09538259.2022.2140007

Benanav, A. (2020). *Automation and the Future of Work*. London: Verso Books.

Berardi F (2013). *The Uprising: On Poetry and Finance*. Los Angeles: Semiotext(e).

Bloomberg Professional Services (2021). Nuclear fusion market could achieve a $40 trillion valuation | Insights. (2021) [online] 29 Dec. Available at: https://www.bloomberg.com/professional/blog/nuclear-fusion-market-could-achieve-a-40-trillion-valuation/.

Brynjolfsson, E., Rock, D. and Syverson, C. (2018). Artificial intelligence and the modern productivity paradox: a clash of expectations and statistics. In A. Agrawal, J. Gans, and A. Goldfarb. (Eds.), *The Economics of Artificial Intelligence: An Agenda* (pp. 23–57). Chicago: University of Chicago Press.

Cetrulo, A. and Nuvolari, A. (2019). Industry 4.0: Revolution or hype? Reassessing recent technological trends and their impact on labour. *Journal of Industrial and Business Economics*, *46*(3), 391–402.

Cole, M. (2023), (Infra)structural discontinuity: Capital, labour, and technological change. *Antipode*, *55*(2), 348–372.

Daskalakis, K. (2018). To mellon tora? | Tehniti Noimosini [Online Video]. *Aristotele University of Thessaloniki*: 16 January 2018. Available at: https://www.auth.gr/video/24941 [Accessed: 27 January 2020].

Dinerstein, A. C. (2014). The dream of dignified work: on good and bad utopias. *Development and Change*, *45*(5), 1037–1058.

Duménil, G. and Lévy, D. (2003). Technology and distribution: historical trajectories à la Marx. *Journal of Economic Behavior & Organization*, *52*(2), 201–233.

Dyer-Witheford, N., Kjøsen, A. M. and Steinhoff, J. (2019). *Inhuman Power: Artificial Intelligence and the Future of Capitalism*. London: Pluto Press.

Elson, D. (2015). *Value: The Representation of Labour in Capitalism*. London: Verso Books.

Expat.com. (2023). South Korea: Which sectors are currently facing labor shortages? [online] Available at: https://www.expat.com/en/expat-mag/8052-south-korea-which-sectors-are-currently-facing-labor-shortages.html.

Frey, C. B. and Osborne, M. A. (2017). The future of employment: how susceptible are jobs to computerisation? *Technological Forecasting and Social Change*, *114*, 254–280.
Fuchs, C. (2018). Industry 4.0: the digital German ideology. *Triplec: Communication, Capitalism & Critique*, *16*(1), 280–289.
Godin, B. (2006). The linear model of innovation: the historical construction of an analytical framework. *Science, Technology, & Human Values*, *31*(6), 639–667.
Gorz, A. (1982). *Farewell to the Working Class*. London: Pluto Press.
Gramsci, A. (1920). Discorso agli anarchici. L'Ordine Nuovo. 10 Apr.
Heinrich, M. (2007). Invaders from Marx: on the uses of Marxian theory, & the difficulties of a contemporary reading. *Left Curve*, (31), 83. Available at: http://www.oekonomiekritik.de/205Invaders.htm
Heinrich, M. (2012). *An Introduction to the Three Volumes of Karl Marx's Capital*. New York: NYU Press.
IFR (2021). Robot density nearly doubled globally. [online] IFR International Federation of Robotics. Available at: https://ifr.org/ifr-press-releases/news/robot-density-nearly-doubled-globally.
Lazzarato, M. (1996). Immaterial labor. *Radical Thought in Italy: A Potential Politics, 1996*, 133–147.
Leitner, K. H. (2017). 'No' and 'slow' innovation strategies as response to increased innovation speed. In B. Godin, and D. Vinck (Eds.), *Critical Studies of Innovation: Alternative Approaches on the Proinnovation Bias* (pp. 201–219).
Marx, K. (1973). *Grundrisse: Foundations of the Critique of Political Economy*. London, UK: Penguin.
Marx, P. (2022). *Road to Nowhere: What Silicon Valley Gets Wrong about the Future of Transportation*. London: Verso Books.
Mason, P. (2015) *PostCapitalism: A Guide to Our Future*. London: Penguin.
Mekala, K., Mischke, J. and Remes J. (2018). *Is the Solow Paradox back? | McKinsey*. [online] Available at: https://www.mckinsey.com/capabilities/mckinsey-digital/our-insights/is-the-solow-paradox-back.
Merchant, B. (2017). *The One Device: The Secret History of the iPhone*. New York: Little, Brown.
Moencks, M., Roth, E., Thomas, B., Basso, M. and Betti, F. (2022). Augmented workforce: empowering people transforming manufacturing. *World Economic Forum*, Report, 19 January. Available at: https://www.weforum.org/whitepapers/augmented-workforce-empowering-people-transforming-manufacturing. [Accessed: 19 Jul 2024].
Moll, I. (2022). The Fourth Industrial Revolution: A new ideology. *tripleC: Communication, Capitalism & Critique. Open Access Journal for a Global Sustainable Information Society*, *20*(1), 45–61.
Morozov, E. (2013). *To Save Everything, Click Here: The Folly of Technological Solutionism*. Public Affairs.
Morozov, E. (2022). Critique of techno-feudal reason. *New Left Review*. [online] (133/134), pp. 89–126. Available at: https://newleftreview.org/issues/ii133/articles/evgeny-morozov-critique-of-techno-feudal-reason.
Mueller, G. (2021). *Breaking Things at Work: The Luddites Are Right about Why You Hate Your Job*. London: Verso Books.
Muldoon, J. (2022). *Platform Socialism: How to Reclaim Our Digital Future from Big Tech*. London: Pluto Press.
Negri, A. (1991). *Marx beyond Marx: Lessons on the Grundrisse*. Brooklyn, NY: Autonomedia.
Papagiannaki, E., Philp, B. and Wheatley, D. (2023). Decomposing surplus-value: an analysis of distribution and unproductive labour of the UK economy, 1992–2020. *Centre for Accounting, Finance and Economics:* Working Paper 21.
Petruzzi, D. (2022). Cosmetic market value worldwide, 2018–2025 | Statista. [online] Statista. Available at: https://www.statista.com/statistics/585522/global-value-cosmetics-market/.
Phillips, L. and Rozworski, M. (2019). *The People's Republic of Walmart: How the World's Biggest Corporations Are Laying the Foundation for Socialism*. London: Verso Books.
Pitts, F. H. (2017). Beyond the Fragment: postoperaismo, postcapitalism and Marx's 'Notes on machines', 45 years on. *Economy and Society*, *46*(3–4), 324–345.
Pitts, F. H. (2019). Value form theory, open Marxism & the new reading of Marx. In A. C. Dinerstein, A. G. Vela, E. González, and J. Holloway (Eds.), *Open Marxism IV: Against a Closing World* (pp. 63–75). London: Pluto Press.
Pitts, F. H. (2021). *Value*. Cambridge: Polity Press.
Ramtin, R. (1991). *Capitalism and Automation: Revolution in Technology and Capitalist Breakdown*. Pluto Press (UK).
Sadowski, J. (2020). *Too Smart: How Digital Capitalism Is Extracting Data, Controlling Our Lives, and Taking Over the World*. Cambridge, Massachusetts: MIT Press.

Sadowski, J. (2021). I'm a Luddite. You should be one too. *The Conversation*. Available at: https://theconversation.com/im-a-luddite-you-should-be-one-too-163172.

Saunders, H. (2016). Does capitalism require endless growth? The breakthrough institute. Available at: https://thebreakthrough.org/journal/issue-6/does-capitalism-require-endless-growth.

Schumpeter, J. A. (1939). *Business Cycles* (Vol. 1, pp. 161–174). New York: Mcgraw-Hill.

Schwab, K. (2016). The Fourth Industrial Revolution: what it means, how to respond. *World Economic Forum*. Available at: https://www.weforum.org/agenda/2016/01/the-fourth-industrial-revolution-what-it-means-and-how-to-respond/.

Shaikh, A. (1980). Marxian competition versus perfect competition: further comments on the so-called choice of technique. *Cambridge Journal of Economics*, *4*(1), 75–83.

Smith, J. E. (2020). *Smart Machines and Service Work: Automation in an Age of Stagnation*. London: Reaktion Books.

Solow, R. (1987). We'd better watch out. *New York Times Book Review*, *36*. Available at: http://digamo.free.fr/solow87.pdf

Spencer, D. A. (2017). Work in and beyond the Second Machine Age: the politics of production and digital technologies. *Work, Employment and Society*, *31*(1), 142–152.

Spencer, D. A. (2018). Fear and hope in an age of mass automation: debating the future of work. *New Technology, Work and Employment*, *33*(1), 1–12.

Spencer, D. A. (2020). Attitudes to work and the future of work: the view from economics. In R. Skidelsky, and N. Craig (Eds.), *Work in the Future: The Automation Revolution*, (pp. 53–63). Cham, Switzerland: Springer Nature.

Spencer, D. A. and Slater, G. (2020). No automation please, we're British: technology and the prospects for work. *Cambridge Journal of Regions, Economy and Society*, *13*(1), 117–134.

Steinhoff, J. (2021). *Automation and Autonomy: Labour, Capital and Machines in the Artificial Intelligence Industry*. Cham, Switzerland: Springer Nature.

Steinhoff, J., Kjosen, A. M.,and Dyer-Witheford, N. (2024). Afterword: stagnation, circulation, and the automated abyss. In Fehrle J., Lieber M., and Ramírez J., (Eds.), *(De)Automating the Future: Marxist Perspectives on Capitalism and Technology*, (pp. 288–310). Leiden: Brill.

Varoufakis, Y. (2023). *Technofeudalism: What Killed Capitalism*. London: Penguin.

Vidal, M. (2019). Contradictions of the labour process, worker empowerment and capitalist inefficiency. *Historical Materialism*, *28*(2), 170–204.

Walsh, S. (2023). Marx, subsumption and the critique of innovation. *Organization*, *30*(2), 345–360.

Webb, M. (2019) The impact of artificial intelligence on the labor market. Available at: https://dx.doi.org/10.2139/ssrn.3482150.

Williams, A. and Srnicek, N. (2015). *Inventing the Future: Postcapitalism and a World without Work* (pp. 1–33). Brooklyn, NY: Verso Books.

Recommendations for Further Reading

Benanav, A. (2020). *Automation and the Future of Work*. London: Verso Books.

Morozov, E. (2022). Critique of techno-feudal reason. *New Left Review* [online] (133/134), pp. 89–126. Available at: https://newleftreview.org/issues/ii133/articles/evgeny-morozov-critique-of-techno-feudal-reason

Ramtin, R. (1991). *Capitalism and Automation: Revolution in Technology and Capitalist Breakdown*. London: Pluto Press).

Shaikh, A. (1980). Marxian competition versus perfect competition: further comments on the so-called choice of technique. *Cambridge Journal of Economics*, *4*(1), 75–83.

Smith, J. E. (2020). *Smart Machines and Service Work: Automation in an Age of Stagnation*. London: Reaktion Books.

Spencer, D. and Slater, G. (2020). No automation please, we're British: technology and the prospects for work. *Cambridge Journal of Regions, Economy and Society*, *13*(1), 117–134.

6

AUTOMATION AND THE FUTURE OF WORK

James Steinhoff

Introduction

This chapter argues that to think about automation and the future of work, it is necessary to take account of the particular technologies used to implement automation processes and how they are implicated in the social relations constitutive of the capitalist mode of production. It proposes the concept of synthetic automation as a means for thinking about automation and the future of work. Historically, automation of complex labour processes has required the capture of knowledge from workers and its transfer to capital, after which that knowledge can be reassembled in the form of machines or algorithms. However, synthetic automation utilises the approach to artificial intelligence (AI) known as machine learning to produce algorithms without direct knowledge capture, instead extracting patterns from data. This enables the automation of labour processes about which capital, and even workers, lack knowledge. The concept of synthetic automation thus emphasises the significance of machine learning as a new technological infrastructure for automation. But synthetic automation also implies a theory about how automation develops in the capitalist mode of production. Capitalism, as Karl Marx demonstrated in *Capital* (1990 [1867]), has a fundamental relationship to automation. The very structure of the capitalist system compels individual capitalist firms to automate. To explain how this compulsion occurs, this chapter draws on the work of Alfred Sohn-Rethel (2021 [1978]) who describes automation as a "postulate" of capital. A postulate may not be realised in every possible instance, but it remains a tendency immanent to the capitalist system.

By drawing attention both to the novelty of machine learning and to the historical continuity of the postulate, this chapter demonstrates how and why capital is driven to automate automation itself. Capital is characterised by a dynamism of technological development and this dynamism applies not only to the application of automation technologies but also to their development. This is significant for the future of work, not in terms of pointing to a specific scenario in which particular jobs will be rendered obsolete by a certain year, but rather by demonstrating that when it comes to automation under capitalism, the field of play is continually changing. The central claim made in this chapter is not that there will be more and more automation in the future of work: a quantitative claim. Rather, the central claim is that there will be more advanced technologies

DOI: 10.4324/9781003327561-9

of automation; a qualitative claim. The import of automation for the future of work cannot be discussed productively in abstraction from the development of the particular technologies which implement automation.

Automated Futures

Adjudicating between the diverse positions regarding automation and the future of work is not the point of this chapter. The interested reader may consult Frey (2019), Benanav (2022) and Deranty and Corbin (2022). For the purposes of this chapter, it will suffice to give an extremely brief overview of the major positions. While certainly an oversimplification, we can get a rough idea of the field by dividing existing discourse on automation and the future of work into four non-exclusive categories: (a) Utopian, (b) Optimistic, (c) Pessimistic, (d) Dismissive.

Utopian discourses tend to predict that automation will produce a post-work, post-capitalist society of abundance by freeing humans from wage labour and generating a superabundance of necessary and desirable resources (Mason, 2015; Srnicek and Williams, 2015). Optimistic discourses tend not to imagine the transcendence of capitalism, but hold that automation will, by and large, improve the lot of most people by improving the quality of work, by automating boring and repetitive bits, increasing productivity and raising standards of living. Such predictions tend to be based on the notion that automation ultimately creates more new (and better) jobs than it destroys, or generally improves life in most respects (Drucker, 1957; Kurzweil, 2005). Pessimistic discourses predict massive job losses driven by automation (Frey and Osborne, 2017) and/or worsening conditions in existing jobs (Smith, 2020). They also anticipate the deepening of existing social inequalities as automation decimates middle class jobs, leading to hyper-polarisation between the ultra-rich and ultra-poor (Frey, 2019) and the exacerbation of class antagonism between capital and labour (Dyer-Witheford, Kjøsen and Steinhoff, 2019). Dismissive discourses are distinguished from the other categories in that they argue that automation is not a central concern regarding the future of work. They might hold that automation is a secondary phenomenon to a more fundamental stagnation deriving from overproduction (Benanav, 2019), or they may even argue that automation is primarily a fantasy or a deception, employed mainly to artificially boost the image of a company or to intimidate workers, while requiring hidden human labour to keep supposedly automated systems going (Taylor, 2018; Munn, 2022). These are noted here merely to provide background. While the author holds a decidedly pessimistic view, the conception elaborated in this chapter might usefully be applied by any of the above positions to think about automation and the future of work.

Automation and Capitalism

Concerns about the implications of automatic machines for work go back to antiquity. In the fourth century BCE, the Ancient Greek philosopher Aristotle (1984) reasoned that "if … the shuttle would weave and the plectrum touch the lyre without a hand to guide them, chief workmen would not want servants, nor masters slaves". Millenia later in the 2020s, people are worrying that large language models, such as OpenAI's ChatGPT, which can produce convincing linguistic outputs, including essays and dialogue, will soon "reduce employment for college-educated workers" (Lowrey, 2023). The contemporary moment is, however, distinguished from Aristotle's in many respects beyond technological sophistication. Notably, the technology of today is produced and deployed within a different economic system than the Ancient Greek slave economy: the capitalist mode of production.

Marx observed in the first volume of *Capital* that with the proliferation of large-scale industrial production, tools were being "converted into machines" (1990 [1867], p. 492). According to Marx, once a tool is combined with a "motor mechanism" that provides power and a "transmitting mechanism" which delivers that power to the tool, one has a machine (p. 494). With machines, labour can be augmented: the "organic limitations" of the human body can be overcome (p. 495). This presents the possibility of workers doing different kinds of work than they could without machines, and of doing the same kinds of work with greater strength and speed. Take for instance the steam hammer. First built in 1840, it is a massive machine which harnesses steam pressure to deliver immense kinetic energy and up to 300 blows per minute via a vertical ram weighing up to 22,500 kg (Kaushish, 2010, p. 720). While far exceeding the capacities of an individual worker, the steam hammer is, however, not exactly an automation technology.

For analytic precision, it is useful to follow Ramin Ramtin (1991) and distinguish mechanisation from automation. The steam hammer, and most of the machinery of Marx's time, was predominantly mechanised, rather than automated: specialised machinery animated by a power source that could perform specific movements automatically. The steam hammer did just one thing at a superhuman level: hammering. Mechanisation, in general, entails very narrow functionality, a machine which performs one specific task which is determined by its physical form. Automation, however, occurs only with the development of information machines, or machines which do not have one specific function built-in to their physical form, but "can be programmed to perform an unlimited number of tasks" via the processing of encoded information (Ramtin, 1991, p. 50). In other words, a relatively general-purpose machine. The ability to be guided by information means that a machine may "draw upon information from external sources, or from the progress of its own operation" and thus its "control is no longer dependent upon its specialised internal construction" (Braverman, 1998, pp. 191–192). The essential technology here is the digital computer, which uses a generic hardware architecture (Von Neumann architecture) to store and execute programmes as electric impulses in digital memory. A sort of proto-automation existed in Marx's era in the form of the Jacquard loom, a weaving machine that could execute programmes of a sort stored on hole-punched cards (Essinger, 2004). Similar punch cards would be used in early computers. However, the Jacquard loom, despite its programmability, was far from a general-purpose machine. The automation age would not begin until the first of these – the digital computer – proliferated in the mid-1950s. Automation is thus a qualitative advance over mechanisation. It means, as Ramtin (1991) points out, that cognitive, as well as manual tasks can be performed by machines.

Mechanisation and automation occupy a special place in the capitalist mode of production because they are expressions of an imperative forced upon firms "by the very functioning of the capitalist mode of production" (Ramtin, 1991, p. 101). The type of functioning referred to here is competition, a necessary component of capitalism. Individual firms meet in the market where they compete for consumers and resources. Competition drives firms towards "constantly revolutionising the instruments of production" so as to increase the productivity of their labour force, and thereby capture a larger share of surplus-value (Marx and Engels, 1998 [1848], p. 38). Increased productivity may be obtained by fragmenting complex jobs into tasks performed by specialised workers, and the execution of those tasks can be made more efficient by a variety of incentives and threats from management. However, such means can only go so far since the human body has organic limitations. Mechanisation and then automation are essential to overcoming these corporeal limits. A highly skilled person wielding a hammer can drive a maximum of 42 nails in one minute (according to the Guinness Book of World Records), but an average individual armed with a pneumatic nail gun can easily exceed that with little to no practice. A roofing company driving nails by hand will find it hard to offer competitive timelines compared to a nailgun-using competitor, all other factors being the same.

Increasing the productivity of labour is not the only function of mechanisation and automation under capitalism. Both occur within the labour process, a central site of class struggle between labour and capital, in which the latter seeks to establish greater control over the former (Noble, 1986; Braverman, 1998). Marx even described machinery as capital's "most powerful weapon" in its class struggle against workers (1990 [1867], p. 562). In capitalist production, the capitalist purchases the ability to command the labour-power of the worker and sets the worker to completing the labour process (Marx, 1990 [1867], p. 270). The capitalist is not paid a wage and thus technically should not labour; indeed, the worker is hired precisely to perform this function. As far as the capitalist is concerned, the labour process is something that should be completed "automatically" once the relevant inputs are brought together through capital investment – regardless of whether or not mechanisation or automation technologies are involved. The worker is, for the capitalist, always already a sort of machine or automaton. Thus, there is little reason, from the capitalist perspective, not to replace troublesome workers with machines, if such a replacement is economically and politically feasible.

Sohn-Rethel calls this peculiar capitalist perspective the "postulate of automatism" and he notes that it "does not spring from any source in the technology of production but is inherent in the production relations of capitalism" (2021 [1978], p. 119). Specifically, it inheres in the divide between capital (which owns the means of production) and labour (which owns only its capacity to labour). In capitalist production, automation arrives on the scene to find a place already prepared for it. There is a "formal automaticity" posited by the structure of capitalist production which is rendered into "real automaticity" by the introduction of automation technologies (Steinhoff et al., 2024). The drive to achieve real automaticity plots a trajectory which would seem to culminate in "the total replacement of the subjectivity of a human labour-power" (Sohn-Rethel, 2021 [1976], p. 173). However, a postulate is not a necessity. It may not be realised. In other words, automation is an imperative towards which capitalist production is immanently driven, but its realisation is not a certainty in every particular context nor does it unfold in identical ways across varied contexts. Thus, a critical concept of automation must include recognition of its implications in diverse social and economic relations, the historical divisions of which it tends to follow, and may exacerbate (Munn, 2022).

This is apparent even if we consider the simplest case of automation's implications in social relations via costs and benefits. Automation only becomes an appealing option from a capitalist perspective when it presents an economic benefit. In other words, the costs of implementing a system of automation must be offset by the savings or other benefits it will bring (such as increased control over workers). If a certain job can be performed by very cheap labour due to lack of regulation or low cost of living, there will be little incentive to automate it. For example, rather than automate the mining of coltan, the companies which harvest this essential input to computing technologies rely on economic desperation and lack of regulation in places such as Congo to keep the cost of brutal manual labour at shockingly low levels (Mantz, 2008).

The implication of automation in social relations means it is a more complex phenomenon than a discrete event or linear progression in which jobs are destroyed. Rather, automation is a process which fragments existing labour roles, while introducing new forms of technical mediation and generating needs for new types of labour. Bainbridge (1983) acutely describes automation as characterised by a fundamental "irony" insofar as the more advanced an automation system is, the "more crucial may be the contribution of the human operator" (p. 775). Others argue that automation is not so much about human obsolescence as new forms of human-machine integration; what

Ekbia and Nardi (2017) call "heteromation" and Delfanti and Frey (2021) call "humanly-extended automation". Indeed, a human component remains essential to many contemporary automation applications, especially in the case of machine learning, which requires diverse forms of human input for production, maintenance and fallback in the case of system failure (Tubaro, Casilli and Coville, 2020).

Automation is thus a complex social phenomenon driven by the very structure of the capitalist system, although this does not take the shape of a simplistic determinism. For this reason, the perspective advocated here should not be used to predict a specific future: it does not provide enough information to entail a specific future scenario, nor does it indicate a particular timeline. To make predictive claims, one would need (at minimum) to integrate: broad economic data about the sector(s) of the economy which are of interest, detailed data on the labour processes to be automated and a good understanding of the technical details and capacities of the automation technologies which are to be used. This chapter focuses only on the last of these aspects, and it is to this topic that I turn next.

Automation by Capture

We have seen that the capitalist mode of production exhibits a structural tendency towards automation. But how do individual firms actually achieve the automation of their labour processes? This depends on the particular technologies used to implement automation. Historically, automation has depended on the capture of knowledge from workers. This was formalised with Frederick Taylor's project of "scientific management" (or Taylorism) developed in the late 1800s. Scientific management surveilled workers as they worked, decomposed their labour processes into discrete moments, and optimised them for greater, sometimes brutal, efficiency (Braverman, 1998, p. 55). Taylor was concerned with the discipline and control of labour rather than its automation, but his approach provided a framework for automating complex labour processes. Taylor (1967) called for "Gathering together all of the traditional knowledge which in the past has been possessed by the workmen and then of classifying, tabulating, and reducing this knowledge to rules, laws, and formulae" (p. 111). By dissecting complex labour processes into discrete steps, Taylorism paved the way for building a machine to automate those processes. Indeed, Lillian Gilbreth, who along with her husband Frank Gilbreth were the greatest proponents of scientific management after Taylor, once gave a lecture describing scientific management as the "human side of automation" (Gilbreth, 1957).

In the 1980s and 1990s, Taylorism experienced a kind of revival in the context of AI. The cutting-edge in AI at the time was represented by so-called expert systems which aimed to reproduce expert knowledge in a computer program. Expert systems were produced via a process of "knowledge engineering" in which engineers would interview experts and encode their knowledge into the system as a set of conditional rules (Studer, Benjamins and Fensel, 1998, p. 162). Both Taylorism and knowledge engineering demonstrate how automation depends on the capture of knowledge from labour. However, we have already discussed how capitalist competition compels technical change. Should not technical change also occur in automation technology itself, and could this not disrupt the paradigm of automation by capture?

Synthetic Automation

The outlines of a new paradigm of automation became visible when the technology of machine learning began its rise to prominence in the mid-2010s. Now representing the cutting-edge of automation technology, machine learning both extends the automation by capture paradigm, and indicates how it might be surpassed by something I call synthetic automation.

Machine learning is the generation of algorithms called "models" via the extraction of patterns from large data sets. Models contain statistical representations of the data they were trained on, which can be used to analyse and make predictions on new data. Machine learning is an effective approach to automation when the process required to complete a desired task is unknown. Consider that even though most people can easily identify a cat, writing an algorithm describing precisely how to recognise a cat in a photograph would be a difficult and laborious task since cats come in many shapes, sizes, colours and are photographed from many different angles, with different qualities of image and many other variables. Instead of building a cat-recognising algorithm by hand, one can use machine learning to "extract" or "induce" a model from a large data set of images of cats (Alpaydin, 2014, p. 2; Bommasani et al., 2022, p. 3). By identifying patterns across the data set, the model will be capable of predicting probabilistically whether a given image contains a cat or not, without an engineer ever codifying exactly how to do so. This is the basic process by which machine learning models are trained to recognise faces and other objects (Schroff et al., 2015).

Machine learning is described as exhibiting "emergence" meaning that "the behavior of a system is implicitly induced rather than explicitly constructed" (Bommasani et al., 2022, p. 3). This capacity leads Domingos (2015) to describe machine learning as the "inverse of programming" because with it "computers write their own programs" (pp. 6–7). Such statements should not be taken too literally – intensive human labour is still required to produce machine learning systems. However, the extraction of algorithms from data represents a significant change in the process of automation. Instead of hand-building a system, rule by rule, as with expert systems, an automation system can be synthesised from data. This is synthetic automation, or the automation of automation (Steinhoff, 2021, 195).

Synthetic automation still requires knowledge capture because it relies on data, and data generally comes from surveilling the actions of people (Sadowski, 2019). As Lemov (2016) argues, data "is people". Similarly, Dippel (2021) holds that the machine learning systems developed by Big Tech "should be owned by the people" because they are "fed" a diet of data collected via surveillance (p. 40). That being said, surveillance via data can function in a different way than the traditional knowledge capture from the worker. With machine learning, neither the worker nor management is required to be able to articulate knowledge of the labour process to be automated at all, if relevant data may be obtained. This means that the automation may dispense with both Taylorism and knowledge engineering. In fact, it is possible that even once the process is automated, there is no one that knows how it is done. A machine learning model can function well and remain an inscrutable "black box" in its inner functioning, due to the complexities of the neural network architecture (Pasquale, 2015). Thus, while it offers new synthetic functionalities, machine learning extends the automation by capture paradigm.

One might predict, on the basis of the notion of automation by capture, that the future of work will be characterised by increasingly pervasive surveillance, as capital seeks to capture the requisite knowledge for automating all kinds of labour processes. This is the quite reasonable argument put forth by critics like Zuboff (2019), as well as Andrejevic (2020), who envisions a future of "frameless" surveillance in which nothing is off limits. The development of increasingly invasive surveillance tools, such as eye gaze tracking software for "attentiveness analysis" in remote working employees provides support for such views (Visio.ai, nd). However, plotting a future of intensifying surveillance relies on the assumption that automation technology will not undergo qualitative change such that the automation by capture paradigm could be abandoned. In fact, the seeds of such a qualitative change are visible in recent developments in machine learning which point towards more radical forms of synthetic automation which might reduce or eliminate the need for surveillance.

One such innovation is called synthetic data, or data "that computer simulations or algorithms generate as an alternative to real-world data" (Andrews, 2021). Synthetic data are the output of computational processes and are not collected via surveillance. They can still, however, be used to train machine learning models. For instance, realistic 3D models of synthetic faces may be generated and used to train facial recognition systems (Wood et al., 2021). Data for training computer vision systems for deployment in autonomous vehicles may be synthesised in simulations, rather than on real-world streets. Early experiments showed that this could be done by retrofitting video games like Grand Theft Auto V (Richter et al., 2016) and firms such as graphics card manufacturer NVIDIA are now hawking bespoke simulations for this purpose, such as DRIVE Sim.[1] Because synthetic data presents the possibility of decreasing the dependence of data-intensive capital on human actors as data sources, I have argued that synthetic data is data which has been rendered more "adequate to capital" (Steinhoff, 2022, p. 9).

I contend that synthetic data continues the paradigm shift in automation begun by machine learning. If data can be generated within a simulation, instead of being captured from labour, the extraction of a machine learning algorithm from data can be divorced from the surveillance of labour. This is a different kind of automation and it occurs in a different location in the circuit of capital. Rather than automating production, synthetic data automates "the production of the conditions for production and circulation in data-intensive capitalism" (Steinhoff, 2022, p. 2). In other words, it further automates automation, producing a qualitatively different kind of automation which creates, rather than captures the data which it then uses to train machine learning models.

Yet it must be emphasised that synthetic data is still far from representing full automation. Like previous approaches to automation, synthetic data generates a need for new types of human labour. The synthetic face experiment of Wood et al. (2021) cited above relied on the artistic input of a 3D modeller to create facial components that could then be procedurally combined by an algorithm to generate an array of synthetic faces. The use of Grand Theft Auto V or any other simulation environment for generating synthetic data is only possible because of the labour of the engineers, designers and others who produced that virtual world and its mechanics in the first place. So while synthetic automation stacks automation on automation, it is far from the truth to say that these accruing layers of technical mediation operate without human intervention.

Conclusion: Postulate and Realisation

When talking about automation and the future of work, it is easy to reason by extrapolating from the current state of technology. Yet, as I have argued in this chapter, capitalist economies are compelled to continually pursue the realisation of the postulate of automatism, deploying not only more automation technologies in more sectors, but developing new types of automation technologies. I have introduced the concept of synthetic automation to grasp how automation itself can undergo qualitative change. Speaking about the future of work without recognition of the dynamic nature of automation technology makes for dubious predictions. By way of conclusion, let us consider some examples.

First, take the prediction by business scholars Thomas Davenport and Julia Kirby (2016) that in a future in which AI-powered automation is widespread, the "parts of our jobs we'll keep are just the parts that can't be codified" (p. 14). Davenport and Kirby claim that only tasks which can be explicitly mapped out and turned into algorithms can be automated. They seem to be stuck wholly in the paradigm of automation by capture. As I have shown, machine learning presents the possibility of automating processes which have not been codified by extracting a model from data. Or consider a second example, from the Marxist thinker Paolo Virno (2003), who argues that as capitalism evolves into a post-industrial form, the means of production are no longer "reducible to machines but consist of linguistic-cognitive competencies inseparable from living labor" (p. 61). In other words, in the post-industrial era productive labour is fundamentally social and communicative and beyond the grasp of automation. But here Virno seems not to grasp the essential import of information machines as highlighted by Ramtin – their ability to process all kinds of information. The automation of "linguistic-cognitive competencies" has been achieved with the development of large language models, which now constitute a new category of means of production (Luitse and Denkena, 2021).

Statements like Virno's and Davenport and Kirby's result from holding a static conception of automation rather than conceiving it as a postulate of capital. The postulate of automatism suggests that when speaking about the future of automation and work we should feel justified in making the reasonable assumption that the capitalist mode of production is likely to drive further advances in automation technology. This perspective does not seek to plot the absolute disappearance of jobs, but to track new capacities of machines, the reconfiguration of existing work, and the emergence of needs for new kinds of work; in general, to track a fluctuating and creeping frontier distinguishing what is automatable and what is not in particular places and times. For example, what effects a shift to synthetic data might have on the future of work remains an open question, and a timely direction for research. Instead of making sweeping generalisations about automation and the future of work, I suggest the deployment of the concept of the postulate of automatism alongside a multifaceted study of a wide array of social and economic factors and an attentive eye to the qualitative distinctions of the particular technologies used to implement automation.

Note

1 https://www.youtube.com/watch?v=UoPXzzK_g1Q&t=1s&ab_channel=NVIDIA

References

Alpaydin, E. (2014) *Introduction to Machine Learning*. Cambridge: MIT Press.

Andrejevic, M. (2020) *Automated Media*. New York: Routledge.

Andrews, G. (2021) What is synthetic data? The Official NVIDIA Blog. Available at: https://blogs.nvidia.com/blog/2021/06/08/what-is-synthetic-data/

Aristotle (1984) *Politics*. Princeton, NJ: Princeton University Press.

Benanav, A. (2019) 'Automation and the Future of Work—1', *New Left Review*, 119, pp. 5–38.

Benanav, A. (2022) *Automation and the Future of Work*. New York: Verso.

Bommasani, R. *et al*. (2022) 'On the Opportunities and Risks of Foundation Models', arXiv. Available at: https://arxiv.org/abs/2108.07258 (Accessed: 10 October 2022).

Bainbridge, L. (1983) 'Ironies of automation,' *Automatica*, 19(6), pp. 775–779.

Braverman, H. (1998) *Labor and Monopoly Capital: The Degradation of Work in the Twentieth Century*. New York: NYU Press.

Davenport, T. H. and Kirby, J. (2016) *Only Humans Need Apply: Winners and Losers in the Age of Smart Machines*. New York: Harper Business.

Delfanti, A. and Frey, B. (2021) 'Humanly Extended Automation or the Future of Work Seen through Amazon Patents', *Science, Technology, & Human Values*, 46(3), pp. 655–682. Available at: https://doi.org/10.1177/0162243920943665.

Deranty, J. P. and Corbin, T. (2022) 'Artificial Intelligence and Work: A Critical Review of Recent Research from the Social Sciences', *AI & SOCIETY*. https://doi.org/10.1007/s00146-022-01496-x.

Dippel, A. (2021) 'Metaphors We Live by', in A. Sudmann (ed.) *The Democratization of Artificial Intelligence: Net Politics in the Era of Learning Algorithms*. Bielefeld: transcript. pp. 33-42.

Domingos, P. (2015) *The Master Algorithm: How the Quest for the Ultimate Learning Machine Will Remake Our World*. New York: Basic Books.

Drucker, P. F. (1957) *Landmarks of Tomorrow*. New York: Harper.

Dyer-Witheford, N., Kjøsen, A. M. and Steinhoff, J. (2019) *Inhuman Power: Artificial Intelligence and the Future of Capitalism*. London: Pluto Press.

Ekbia, H. and Nardi, B. (2017) *Heteromation, and Other Stories of Computing and Capitalism*. Cambridge: MIT Press.

Essinger, J. (2004) *Jacquard's Web: How a Hand-Loom Led to the Birth of the Information Age*. Oxford: Oxford University Press.

Frey, C. B. (2019) *The Technology Trap: Capital, Labor, and Power in the Age of Automation*. Princeton: Princeton University Press.

Frey, C. B. and Osborne, M. A. (2017) 'The Future of Employment: How Susceptible Are Jobs to Computerisation?', *Technological Forecasting and Social Change*, 114, pp. 254–280.

Gilbreth, L. (1957) 'The Human Side of Automation, Part 1', in P. Walter (ed.) *Recording from Society of Women Engineers National Convention*. Houston, TX: Reuther Library, Wayne State University. Available at: https://reuther.wayne.edu/node/2135 (Accessed 8 May 2023).

Kaushish, J. P. (2010) *Manufacturing Processes*. New Delhi: PHI Learning.

Kurzweil, R. (2005) *The Singularity Is Near: When Humans Transcend Biology*. New York: Penguin.

Lemov (2016) 'Why Big Data Is Actually Small, Personal and Very Human', *Aeon*. Available at: https://aeon.co/essays/why-big-data-is-actually-small-personal-and-very-human (Accessed: 18 November 2021).

Lowrey, A. (2023) 'How ChatGPT Will Destabilize White-Collar Work', *The Atlantic*. Available at: https://www.theatlantic.com/ideas/archive/2023/01/chatgpt-ai-economy-automation-jobs/672767/ (Accessed: 23 January 2023).

Luitse, D. and Denkena, W. (2021) 'The Great Transformer: Examining the Role of Large Language Models in the Political Economy of AI', *Big Data & Society*, 8(2), pp. 1-14.

Mantz, J. W. (2008) 'Improvisational Economies: Coltan Production in the Eastern Congo', *Social Anthropology*, 16(1), pp. 34–50.

Marx, K. (1990 [1867]) *Capital: Volume I*. London: Penguin.

Marx, K. and Engels, F. (1998 [1848]) *The Communist Manifesto: A Modern Edition*. London/New York: Verso.

Mason, P. (2015) *PostCapitalism: A Guide to Our Future*. London: Penguin UK.

Munn, L. (2022) *Automation Is a Myth*. Stanford, CA: Stanford University Press.

Noble, D. (1986) *Forces of Production: A Social History of Industrial Automation*. Piscataway, NJ: Transaction Publishers.

Pasquale, F. (2015) *The Black Box Society: The Secret Algorithms That Control Money and Information*. Cambridge, Massachusetts: Harvard University Press.

Ramtin, R. (1991) *Capitalism and Automation: Revolution in Technology and Capitalist Breakdown*. London: Pluto Press.

Richter, S. R. *et al.* (2016) 'Playing for Data: Ground Truth from Computer Games', *arXiv*. Available at: https://arxiv.org/abs/1608.02192 (Accessed: 13 February 2023).

Sadowski, J. (2019) 'When Data Is Capital: Datafication, Accumulation, and Extraction', *Big Data & Society*, 6(1), pp. 1–12.

Schroff, F., Kalenichenko, D. and Philbin, J. (2015) 'FaceNet: A Unified Embedding for Face Recognition and Clustering', in *2015 IEEE Conference on Computer Vision and Pattern Recognition (CVPR)*. Boston, MA: IEEE, pp. 815–823. Available at: https://doi.org/10.1109/CVPR.2015.7298682.

Smith, J. E. (2020) *Smart Machines and Service Work: Automation in an Age of Stagnation*. London: Reaktion Books.

Sohn-Rethel, A. (2021 [1978]) *Intellectual and Manual Labour: A Critique of Epistemology*. Chicago: Haymarket Books.

Srnicek, N. and Williams, A. (2015) *Inventing the Future: Postcapitalism and a World without Work*. London: Verso Books.

Steinhoff, J. (2021) *Automation and Autonomy: Labour, Capital and Machines in the Artificial Intelligence Industry*. Cham, Switzerland: Springer Nature.

Steinhoff, J. (2022) 'Toward a Political Economy of Synthetic Data: A Data-Intensive Capitalism That Is Not a Surveillance Capitalism?', *New Media & Society*. Available at: https://doi.org/10.1177/14614448221099217.

Steinhoff, J., Kjøsen, A. M. and Dyer-Witheford, N. (2024) 'Afterword: Circulation, Stagnation and the Automated Abyss', in J. Fehrle, J. Ramirez and M. Lieber (eds.) *De-Automating the Future: Marxist Perspectives on Capitalism and Technology*. (pp. 288–310). Leiden: Brill.

Studer, R., Benjamins, V. R. and Fensel, D. (1998) 'Knowledge Engineering: Principles and Methods', *Data & Knowledge Engineering*, 25(1), pp. 161–197.

Taylor, A. (2018) 'The Automation Charade', *Logic Magazine*. Available at: https://logicmag.io/failure/the-automation-charade/ (Accessed: 9 January 2023).

Taylor, F. W. (1967) *The Principles of Scientific Management*. New York: Norton.

Tubaro, P., Casilli, A. A. and Coville, M. (2020) 'The Trainer, the Verifier, the Imitator: Three Ways in Which Human Platform Workers Support Artificial Intelligence', *Big Data & Society*, 7(1), pp. 1–12.

Virno, P. (2003) *A Grammar of the Multitude*. Los Angeles, CA: Semiotext(e).

Visio.ai. (nd) Eye Gaze Detection. https://viso.ai/application/eye-gaze-detection/.

Wood, E., Baltrušaitis, T., Hewitt, C, et al. (2021) 'Fake It Till You Make It: Face Analysis in the Wild Using Synthetic Data Alone', in *International Conference on Computer Vision 2021*. Available at: https://arxiv.org/abs/2109.15102v2.

Zuboff, S. (2019) *The Age of Surveillance Capitalism: The Fight for a Human Future at the New Frontier of Power*. London: Profile Books.

Recommendations for Further Reading

Broussard, M. (2018) *Artificial Unintelligence: How Computers Misunderstand the World*. Cambridge: MIT Press.

Endnotes (2010) 'Misery and Debt: On the Logic and History of Surplus Populations and Surplus Capital', *Endnotes 2*. https://endnotes.org.uk/articles/misery-and-debt.

Gray, M. L. and Suri, S. (2019) *Ghost Work: How to Stop Silicon Valley from Building a New Global Underclass*. New York: Houghton Mifflin Harcourt.

Joque, J. (2022) *Revolutionary Mathematics: Artificial Intelligence, Statistics and the Logic of Capitalism*. London: Verso.

7
RESISTING DETERMINISM(S)
Unpacking Cognitive Technology and Automation

Abigail Gilbert

Introduction

Ideas – mediated by framing, discourse and narrative – can determine outcomes of employment struggles (Carstensen et al., 2022). Ideas about what automation is, and what it can do, shape how technology is designed (Bailey and Barley, 2020); how workers contest, challenge and negotiate technological disruption to the labour process; how firms adopt and deploy technology (Forsythe, 2001) and how governments anticipate and manage risk in order to develop regulatory responses (Aloisi and De Stefano, 2023).

In turn, ideas about what automaton is have performative effects; they can shape the future. This chapter presents a model for making sense of the different ways cognitive automation plays out in practice, viewed through six archetypes. Each of these six archetypes reflects choices, choices which if identified can be held accountable, about the design, development and deployment of cognitive technologies – as these choices are shaped by material and ideological interest struggles. Unpacking these choices and responses, and the conditions under which they are made, is important when thinking about how to redesign and shape technological trajectories (Gilbert et al., 2023). But rather than focusing on those choices – which is not the focus for this piece – the model presented below is intended as a heuristic to equip those negotiating transition, acting within interest struggles, to better tease out changes to work, and the power and position of labour, through adoption.

This chapter begins with an overview of ideas of automation and routes to analysing automation in practice, highlighting their inadequacies. It goes on to present the automation archetypes, highlighting the distinct approach taken to value capture within each of these approaches. The conclusion reflects on what this means, for worker organisation, policy and analysis.

Ideas of Automation

Ideas about the world, and the methods we use to explore it, co-constitute our understanding of reality. Automation can be understood and examined in different ways, reflecting an interplay of ideology and the limits of any given method and its resources. In neoclassical approaches, typically looking at change at the aggregate scale of labour markets and limited by data granularity,

DOI: 10.4324/9781003327561-10

and availability, value creation associated with automation is seen to be derived from labour displacement. This can be at the level of jobs, using binaries of manual vs mental, routine vs non-routine, high vs low skill, rational vs probabilistic, etc. A leading analysis of job-level displacement by Frey and Osborne (2017) deployed a Delphi method to identify 'engineering bottlenecks' – examining skills or knowledges that technology was deemed less capable of displacing to identify 'safe' jobs.

Now it is more popular and common to understand forecasts of automation risk (displacement) or exposure (risk of displacement and other job changes) at the level of tasks (Acemoglu and Restrepo, 2019). Task-based models of automation match the capabilities of new technologies (e.g. through text-based analysis of patents) with registers of the task-based composition of jobs (often relying on a US classification, ONET) to identify likely exposure risk on the basis of level of task match (Webb, 2020).

Such approaches allow for recognition that job design can change, without the entire displacement of a role – i.e. 'complementarity' is a commonplace outcome of cognitive automation reflecting changes in job design, and business redesign (Brynjolfsson et al., 2018). While this begins to understand process-based, institutional factors – technological capabilities, rather than other (e.g. political) factors, are seen as the drivers of these changes – reflect the tendency within methodological individualism for explanations of 'macro' social phenomena (technological development and labour market change) to be underpinned by 'micro' foundations (task complementarity) as the action-theoretic mechanism (Alexander, 1987).

Applications of these approaches in practice can recognise the limitations of skill and task classification systems, and accuracy of patent data (though this is less common, with such approaches often described as 'objective' where an algorithm has detected the task complementarity of tools via patents). However, longstanding tendencies towards socio-economic reductivism – for instance, seeing labour as having objective and comparable hierarchies of value on the basis of formal education – persist, and can lead to a lack of meaningful interrogation of how new value is created or captured where technology plays a complementary role. This is exemplified by recent work on the use of GPTs (General Purpose Transformers) to create a 'revolution' in productivity among knowledge-based services, where the current approach of focusing on individual factors might not adequately capture how these technologies augment the overall productivity and capabilities of knowledge-based sectors (Brynjolfsson et al., 2023). Together, these forces should be understood to interact with supply and demand (Autor, 2022) in ways which re-structure labour markets through the unfolding of 'inevitable' and 'objective' processes of technological disruption. Technological innovation can also create, rather than substitute demand for new tasks (Autor, 2022) and, potentially, jobs – for instance, prompt engineers, where the advent of GPTs has led to the emergence of new jobs specifically related to these tools.

Leading theorists from neoclassical economics analysing automation have identified their own limited ability to understand what is happening in practice because of poor understanding of "the nature of work, microlevel processes (e.g., skill substitution and human–machine complementarity), and understanding of how cognitive technologies interact with broader economic dynamics and institutional mechanisms" (Frank et al., 2019, 6531). To move from these particulars to the aggregate arguably requires a new approach to automation – which is also attentive to the dynamics of the workplace.

Critical approaches that build from a Marxist critique of political economy take a more power-conscious view of the labour process, recognising material and ideological forces which shape outcomes (see Chapters 3, 5 and 6). These have been classified as falling into either 'major' or 'minor' interpretations (Dyer-Witheford et al., 2019). In the major strand, displacement of labour is seen as an inevitable end goal of capitalism, described as the general tendency for capital to increase its organic composition. In minor readings, the role and position of labour are reviewed in more granular detail. In the 'Fragment on Machines', Marx (and others applying 'fragment thinking', Pitts, 2017) envisaged capital mobilising the 'general productive forces of the social brain' (1973, 694) 'general social knowledge… general-intellect' (Marx, 1973, 706) in ways which would not supplant *all* need for human labour but could relegate labour to a *peripheral position*. In the 'Results of the immediate process of production', two stages of subsumption (roughly translated as domination) are presented. While in 'formal' subsumption labour is brought formally into the circuit of commodity production for exchange value, without changing the labour process as such, in the second 'informal' moment of 'real' subsumption the content of labour is transformed to meet the demands of production, with the worker confronted by 'an alien power' mobilised by technological application of the 'general intellect' – leaving capital endowed with 'colossal independence' (cited in Dyer-Withcford et al., 2019).

These themes are picked up by labour process theory, which invites a methodological focus at the scale, and from the perspective, of the worker. This draws attention – as picked up by Frison (1988) – to the positioning and re-positioning of labour. Braverman's (1998) view – the key theorist of labour process theory – is that while mechanisation and automation can each drive deskilling, it is automation, over and above mechanisation, which holds greater import for questions of control and agency, *in its codification of information and decision making*. How this impacts upon bargaining power, beyond ideas of skill and compensation, therefore merits investigation. Readings that consider the relationship between 'man and machine' through the prism of power become ever more important in an era of rapid rollout of cognitive technologies – technologies which also change the distribution of judgement in the labour process. Technologically mediated 'judgements' could substitute workers' own assessments about how to conduct their work, or managers' decisions about how to organise workers. In this sense, technology crafts and reconfigures non-economic power in new ways, while simultaneously reconfiguring economic power in conventional ways. However, fair criticisms have been levelled at this literature by those within it, for placing too much emphasis on the *personal* pursuit of power, by managers for instance (Vidal, 2022) rather than focusing on the political and structural dynamics of how choices are shaped and dominated, but never fully determined. This is what Mau (2021), channelling Marx, has described as the 'mute compulsion' of the market, referencing the subtle, unspoken pressures or influences exerted by market forces that compel individuals or entities to make certain choices or decisions.

In the model outlined below, novel, objective and evolving capabilities of cognitive technologies – shaped by their design, development and deployment – are shown to have varying consequences for the position of labour, and outcomes for work quality. Each archetype can be associated with a specific approach to value capture, which is argued could provide some coherence in analysing alternative trajectories of automation, which can exist at the same time but with different outcomes for different parts of the workforce.

Displacement

Displacement is the most popularly imagined outcome of automation. In this scenario, technology is designed, developed and deployed in ways which allow a sufficient enough share of tasks within a role to be substituted that a position can be eliminated (elsewhere described as labour 'obsolescence'). This generates value by reducing expenditure on labour. Exploring this impact at the level of labour markets, the theory of 'Routine-Biased Technological Change' (RBTC) (Autor et al., 2003; Goos et al., 2014) ought to explain the polarisation of labour markets through displacement effects of early digitalisation. Computerisation was seen as best suited to conducting routine tasks, and routine tasks most characteristic of work in jobs within the 'middle pay' range of the labour market. This fits the archetype of an accountant or retail manager responsible for shift scheduling.

More recent work exploring the impacts of 'more capable AI' – such as GPTs – have increased sympathy for models anticipating significant impacts on 'professional' work (Susskind and Susskind, 2015). However, as some studies note these workers are frequently more equipped to resist marginalisation and devaluation. This is achieved – if not through formal labour organisation – through 'boundary work', which involves workers clearly defining their responsibilities and asserting their expertise to maintain a strong sense of identity and worth, as well as workplace dynamics which afford them a voice (Faulconbridge et al., 2023).

Where displacement increases supply of labour in specific geographies and sectors this can drive competition for work and exert downward pressure on wages. It may, then contribute to phenomena such as 'underemployment', whereby individuals find themselves overqualified for their roles, and 'malemployment' (Benanav, 2020), a scenario in which under-demand for labour weakens bargaining conditions for workers, reducing the quality of their settlement.

The consequences of displacement should also be viewed beyond the position or role which is – or is presented to have been – displaced. The displacement effects of automation are difficult to forecast and have a political dimension (identifying what the core tasks of work are; identifying what is a fair burden for the leftover work as reallocated if at all consciously). Equally, it has been observed that in an era of AI, work is often allegedly – falsely – displaced, with services advertised as automated when in practice a worker, typically hidden from sight (e.g. in a 'dark kitchen' that has been set up solely for delivery work) or in the global south (e.g. Chat GPT's use of Kenyan labourers to classify and filter harmful text from its training data) may produce 'artificially' intelligent products or services (Gray and Suri, 2019; Perrigo, 2023). This may also work in real time, through telepresence (see below).

High-Discretion Augmentation

Augmentation of work sees labour remain within the labour process, but with altered task profiles (including decisions about when, where and how to do work). The concept of augmentation has recently been broken into 'high' vs 'low' discretion augmentation. Shollo et al. (2022) define high-discretion augmentation as applications of Machine Learning which support decision-making in ways which still leave judgement to the discretion of their user. In contrast, low-discretion augmentation allows users little influence over final decisions made about their work. By focusing on discretion, this conceptualisation offers a more expansive lens than 'up' vs 'de'-skilling.

High-discretion augmentation was assumed to be the predominant outcome of technology adoption in early neoclassical models of the effect of computerisation on the labour market – described as 'skills-biased automation' (Spitz-Oener, 2006). In this process, those with the ability to use technology (using it as their tool) can command higher compensation in wages due to the scarcity of their complementary skillsets within new productive industries. This is encapsulated by the 'Bill Gates effect': with the Microsoft co-founder famed to have taken mathematics and computing at Harvard yet dropped out early to start the business which made him a millionaire in his mid-20s.

Noting Braverman's views above on automation vis-à-vis mechanisation, Vidal (2022) challenges the idea that management are solely seeking to extend control when transforming the labour process through a series of case studies in advanced manufacturing (whereby cognitive technologies are being deployed). He finds discretion was being actively promoted in many cases. Rather than negating a capital-labour antagonism, Vidal's point is that the primary motivation of management is to drive the creation of surplus value. This can include equipping workers with resources – including technologies – that *increase* their autonomy, if this were found to increase surplus value creation.

Recognising that this is a possibility, and where and how to achieve it through the design, development and deployment of technology is an important antidote to pessimistic discourses and could reignite a strong history of participatory design in computer artefacts (Ehn, 2017).

Low-Discretion Augmentation

Where high-discretion augmentation may involve the substitution of 'low value' tasks – seen objectively, or subjectively from the perspective of a worker – cognitive technologies designed, developed and deployed to serve the purpose of low-discretion augmentation seek to reduce the cognitive load of workers by delimiting their choice environment (Shollo et al., 2022). The notion of discretion has been used in quantitative reviews of the consequences of automation on labour markets – examined through the lens of 'effort-biased' automation (Green, 2000, 2001, 2004; Guy and Skott, 2005; Skott and Guy, 2007) which defines work effort as the ability of workers to undertake work that is discretionary, i.e. that which is not directly outlined, coded and specified – that is, controlled – by managers or technology. Managerial approaches (to the design, development and deployment of technology) that reduce discretion reflect 'one best method' styles of management developed during Taylorism (Pruijt, 2003). Workers may need to learn how to use a digital system ('upskilling') while also spending more time on repetitive and standardised tasks. This may contribute to the phenomenon of increased routinisation of work within the economy, despite declining shares of 'routine work' (Bisello et al, 2019; Burgess and Connell, 2020).

Recent advances in AI claim to contribute to low-discretion augmentation via tacit knowledge elicitation. Tacit knowledge elicitation seeks to overcome Polanyi's Paradox – that we know more than we can tell (Autor, 2014) – by progressively tracking work processes, and codifying them through pattern recognition. Engineers are working on routes through to more effective tacit knowledge elicitation (Fenoglio et al., 2022). These impacts are materialising across the economy. A study of connected worker platforms revealed methods to elicit, collect and devise work methods from workers across a range of industries (manufacturing, retail, logistics, food production, telecommunications, utilities) in ways which enable new, less experienced or unskilled workers to conduct tasks supported by real time instructions via 'consumer-app standard' technology (Gilbert and Thomas, 2021).

This is also now popularly recognised in the scriptwriters strike in the US, which centred on how workers are still required to edit AI generated plots (i.e. they are made peripheral and side-lined in production) but not generate them – with less compensation. This typifies the merit of tacit knowledge elicitation for value capture. Role-specific knowledge reduces bargaining power. The capacity for management to substitute one worker for another (to treat them as fungible) could undermine the power of strike action.

Yet another paradox pulls in tension with this. Moravec's Paradox (Moravec, 1988) reflects the fact that "it is comparatively easy to make computers exhibit adult level performance on intelligence tests… and difficult or impossible to give them the skills of a one-year-old when it comes to perception and mobility" (Moravec, 1988, 15). The relationship between these forces may mean that in work which relies on sensory perception – roles also deemed to be 'routine' – workers could become the 'sensing appendage' of machines (Delfanti and Frey, 2021). This was indeed found to be the case in a study of new patent applications by major AI platform leaders (Delfanti and

Frey, 2021) that are arguably pioneering the new model for work and are at the cutting edge of AI capabilities.

This may be 'pre-automation' whereby as much of a role as is possible is automated – often including aspects of judgement and decision-making (cognition) – until such time the role can be fully automated (Vertesi et al., 2020). Ultimately, what determines this progress is the relative affordability of both labour and new technology. These effects would not only be shaped by industry and firm but also the labour market – a spatialised, uneven terrain – with the potential to travel in either direction. For instance, recent work has demonstrated a decline in automated carwashes in areas with high supply of vulnerable persons who fall victim to modern slavery (University of Nottingham Rights Lab, 2018).

Intensification

Intensification can be technologically instigated where cognitive technologies are designed, developed or deployed to support or enforce increased density of task completion. Increasing productivity of labour (neoclassical lens) or surplus value (critical lens) of work is core to automation from all standpoints. Cognitive technologies can enable this as a more or less consciously designed outcome; for instance, having more meetings online each day when travel time is saved (as aligned to telepresence below) or setting an algorithmic management tool to fire those who do not meet a set delivery rate per hour (see Chapters 8 and 10).

However, determining the difference – to be detected at an aggregate level – between intensification and augmentation remains challenging. Such outcomes have been examined through 'effort-biased automation', as outlined above. Intensification has been understood in psychological theory through the demand control framework (Van der Doef et al., 1999). Such models could inform the development of 'thresholds' for work intensification and build on work which considers the link between well-being and intensification (Green, 2004) (see Chapter 21).

Intensification at work has been directly linked to the phenomenon of algorithmic management (Lager et al., 2021). 'Metricisation' – whereby work and performance are measured by quantitative indicators – is enabled by the greater use of algorithmic systems at work (Willis et al., 2018). This comes to change behaviour in practice through 'algorithmic regulation' (Ulbricht and Yeung, 2022; Eyert et al., 2022; Gilbert and Thomas, 2021). Here, what counts as work becomes measured and monitored (metricised); standards are set for delivery (e.g. 95% task delivery rates within a day); then this is enforced through penalties – such as the loss of a contract or reduced access to working hours – or incentives such as pay or status via ranking boards that entrench competition between workers.

Telepresence

Work being performed remotely has rapidly expanded following the COVID-19 pandemic, supported by improved communication technologies and domestic internet access. While 'telework' literature emerged in the 1980s and focused principally on tools supporting the transmission of information – voice via telephone or written information via computer – the concept has been extended recently to 'telepresence' also covering contexts in which broader aspects of a user's perceptual, cognitive of psychomotor capabilities can be projected into a distant environment (Draper et al., 1999).

Telepresence presents new opportunities for the spatial reorganisation of work and labour. This change to the literal positioning of labour can empower or disempower labour, tending to reflect and entrench existing polarisations of power. The opportunity to work remotely is unevenly distributed by gender (McKinsey, 2020) and geography (Mutebi and Hobbs, 2022), but also stratified by class, with managers more likely to work remotely in the pandemic and people with higher qualifications more likely to be trusted to work remotely (Bartik et al., 2020). While 'digital nomads' who occupy jobs characterised by an autonomy premium can be given sometimes international freedom over their location (Nash et al., 2018; Nichols, 2022), early studies of some contexts of 'workstation telepresence' suggest strategies that seek to overcome Moravec's paradox by capitalising on cheaper offshored (global south) labour to guide not-yet fully sensing robots in the US (Delfanti et al., 2022).

Research has revealed that managerial imperatives to standardise processes increased during COVID-19, low trust in remote workers seeing managers codify and proscribe even creative work with high discretion, driving routinisation (Fana et al., 2020). Telepresence can also be applied to recognise the distinct role of cognitive technologies in extending the managerial role of surveillance, with consequences for a range of rights within the workplace (Duggan et al., 2020; Castillo et al, 2022).

In sum telepresence can be used to reorganise labour with various outcomes for power and reflecting different approaches to value capture.

Matching

In matching information processing capabilities of technology are harnessed to reduce costs – typically for the employer in processes which pair workers with jobs. While this can be seen as an extension of 'management', this form of automation increasingly plays an intermediary role in labour markets, making and shaping them.

This function has become publicly understood and recognised in the increasingly common context and use of AI in hiring whereby prospective employees are matched with jobs, with 98% of FTSE 100 firms allegedly now using AI in recruitment. However, this function is also core to contracting in the gig economy, where models of just-in-time production have become extended to just-in-time labour as workers become part of the commodity chain within a digital thread ('humans as a service', Prassl, 2018). This has been used to pioneer, reinvent and reconfigure industries and business models.

Even within the neoclassical tradition, matching-based business models have been linked to 'capital-biased' technological change and a declining labour share (Autor et al., 2020). However, such work does not identify, as others have, the tendency for business to save up to 30% by removing outlay on standardised employment protections (Rolf et al., 2022) and classifying workers as contractors in ways which have been legally contested.

Treating labour as a commodity like any other, matching can also allow wage elasticities to be exploited through dynamic pricing, setting different rates for jobs on the basis of (alleged) supply (Dubal, 2020). Research has also identified that big data can be used to predict propensity to unionise, explicitly excluding those likely to collectively bargain during automated hiring processes (Newman, 2017).

Conclusion: Beyond Determinisms

As set out by Steinhoff in this volume, academic work on the future of automation tends to fall into *optimistic*, *pessimistic* or *dismissive* discourses and analyses. This reflects ideology, method and scale of analysis. In practice, such determinisms overlook the variegated routes to and forms of automation in practice. This delimits the ways in which actors can consciously shape and engage in interest struggles to direct technological development in the interests of labour in real time.

This chapter presents a heuristic of automation which seeks to negate predominant 'determinisms' and consider how different processes – processes that reflect evolving and objective functionality of technology, and the choices that shape its use – potentially inform the labour movement and regulators.

As set out elsewhere (Gilbert, 2023), each of the archetypes presented in this model tends to be associated with impacts on certain demographic groups – with consequences for specific dimensions of job quality. If this framework becomes commonplace among labour unions, human resource management professionals and regulators or policymakers – it could draw greater attention to the varied, alternative routes to value capture and creation when using cognitive technologies with a view to steer outcomes towards better outcomes. Future work should examine the necessary institutions to ensure choices made in the design, deployment and development of automation steer towards outcomes which advance better work.

References

Acemoglu, D. & Restrepo, P. (2019). Automation and new tasks: How technology displaces and reinstates labor. *Journal of Economic Perspectives*, 33(2), 3–30.

Alexander, J. C. (Ed.) (1987). *The Micro-Macro Link*. Oakland: Univ of California Press.

Aloisi, A. & De Stefano, V. (2023). Between risk mitigation and labour rights enforcement: Assessing the transatlantic race to govern AI-driven decision-making through a comparative lens. *European Labour Law Journal*, 14(2), 283–307.

Autor, D. (2014). Polanyi's paradox and the shape of employment growth. National Bureau of Economic Research Working Paper No. w20485.

Autor, D. (2022). The labor market impacts of technological change: From unbridled enthusiasm to qualified optimism to vast uncertainty. National Bureau of Economic Research Working Paper No. w30074.

Autor, D., Dorn, D., Katz, L. F., Patterson, C., & Van Reenen, J. (2020). The fall of the labor share and the rise of superstar firms. *The Quarterly Journal of Economics*, 135(2), 645–709.

Autor, D. H., Levy, F., & Murnane, R. J. (2003). The skill content of recent technological change: An empirical exploration. *The Quarterly Journal of Economics*, 118(4), 1279–1333.

Bailey, D. E. & Barley, S. R. (2020). Beyond design and use: How scholars should study intelligent technologies. *Information and Organization*, 30(2), 100286.

Bartik, A. W., Cullen, Z. B., Glaeser, E. L., Luca, M., & Stanton, C. T. (2020). *What jobs are being done at home during the COVID-19 crisis? Evidence from firm-level surveys*. No. w27422. National Bureau of Economic Research. Available at: https://www.nber.org/system/files/working_papers/w27422/w27422.pdf

Benanav, A. (2020). *Automation and the Future of Work*. London: Verso Books.

Bisello, M., et al. (2019). *How Computerisation Is Transforming Jobs: Evidence from Eurofound's European Working Conditions Survey*. Seville: European Commission, JRC117167.

Braverman, H. (1998). *Labor and Monopoly Capital: The Degradation of Work in the Twentieth Century*. New York: NYU Press.

Brynjolfsson, E., Li, D., & Raymond, L. R. (2023). Generative AI at work. National Bureau of Economic Research Working Paper No. w31161.

Brynjolfsson, E., Mitchell, T., & Rock, D. (2018). What can machines learn and what does it mean for occupations and the economy? In AEA Papers and Proceedings, vol. 108, pp. 43–47. 2014 Broadway, Suite 305, Nashville, TN 37203: American Economic Association, 2018.

Burgess, J. & Connell, J. (2020). New technology and work: Exploring the challenges. *The Economic and Labour Relations Review*, 31(3), 310–323.

Carstensen, M. B., Ibsen, C. L., & Schmidt, V. A. (2022). Ideas and power in employment relations studies. *Industrial Relations: A Journal of Economy and Society*, 61(1), 3–21.

Castillo, D., Ponce, A., & Naranjo, D. (2022). Regulating algorithmic management. *ETUI Policy Brief*. Available at: https://www.etui.org/sites/default/files/2022-08/Regulating%20algorithmic%20management-

An%20assessment%20of%20the%20ECs%20draft%20Directive%20on%20improving%20working %20conditions%20in%20platform%20work-2022.pdf

Delfanti, A., & Frey, B. (2021). Humanly extended automation or the future of work seen through Amazon patents. *Science, Technology, & Human*, 46(3), 655–682.

Delfanti, A., Posada, J., & Steinhoff, J. (2022). *Robotic Displacement: Automation, Labour and Digital Migration.* Paper presented at International Labour Process Conference 2022, Padua.

Draper, J. V., Kaber, D. B., & Usher, J. M. (1999). Speculations on the value of telepresence. *Cyberpsychology & Behavior*, 2(4), 349–362.

Dubal, V. (2020). The new racial wage code. *Harvard Law & Policy Review*, 15, 511–550.

Duggan, J., Sherman, U., Carbery, R., & McDonnell, A. (2020). Algorithmic management and app-work in the gig economy: A research agenda for employment relations and HRM. *Human Resource Management Journal*, 30(1), 114–132.

Dyer-Witheford, N., Kjosen, A. M., & Steinhoff, J. (2019). *Inhuman Power: Artificial Intelligence and the Future of Capitalism.* London: Pluto Press.

Ehn, P. (2017). Scandinavian design: On participation and skill. In D. Schuler, & A. Namioka, (Eds.). *Participatory Design* (pp. 41–77). Boca Raton: CRC Press.

Eyert, F., Irgmaier, F., & Ulbricht, L. (2022). Extending the framework of algorithmic regulation. The Uber case. *Regulation & Governance*, 16(1), 23–44.

Fana, M., Milasi, S., Napierala, J., Fernández-Macías, E., & González Vázquez, I. (2020). *Telework, work organisation and job quality during the COVID-19 crisis: A qualitative study*. No. 2020/11. JRC Working Papers Series on Labour, Education and Technology.

Faulconbridge, J., Sarwar, A., & Spring, M. (2023). How professionals adapt to artificial intelligence: The role of intertwined boundary work. *Journal of Management Studies*. https://doi.org/10.1111/joms.12936

Fenoglio, E., Kazim, E., Latapie, H., & Koshiyama, A. (2022). Tacit knowledge elicitation process for industry 4.0. *Discover Artificial Intelligence*, 2(6), 1–15.

Forsythe, D. E. (2001). *Studying Those Who Study Us: An Anthropologist in the World of Artificial Intelligence*. Redwood City: Stanford University Press.

Frank, M. R., Autor, D., Bessen, J. E., Brynjolfsson, E., Cebrian, M., Deming, D. J., … & Yang, H. (2019). Toward understanding the impact of artificial intelligence on labor. *Proceedings of the National Academy of Sciences*, 116(14), 6531–6539.

Frey, C. B. & Osborne, M. A. (2017). The future of employment: How susceptible are jobs to computerisation? *Technological Forecasting and Social Change*, 114, 254–280.

Frison, G. (1988). Technical and technological innovation in Marx. *History and Technology*, 6(4), 299–324.

Gilbert, A. (2023). *Reframing Automation: A Model for Predicting Risks and Impacts*. Institute for the Future of Work.

Gilbert, A. & Thomas, A. (2021). The Amazonian Era, Institute for the Future of Work. Institute for the Future of Work Report 13 May. Available at: https://www.ifow.org/publications/the-amazonian-era-the-gigification-of-work

Gilbert, A., Thomas, A., Barnard, G., & Sheir, S. (2023). *Good Work Algorithmic Impact Assessment: A Methodology for Worker Involvement*. Institute for the Future of Work.

Goos, M., Manning, A., & Salomons, A. (2014). Explaining job polarization: Routine-biased technological change and offshoring. *American Economic Review*, 104(8), 2509–2526.

Gray, M. L. & Suri, S. (2019). *Ghost Work: How to Stop Silicon Valley from Building a New Global Underclass*. New York: Eamon Dolan Books.

Green, F. (2000). Why has work effort become more intense? Conjectures and evidence about effort-biased technical change and other stories, Discussion Paper 00/03. Department of Economics, University of Kent. Available at: https://www.kent.ac.uk/economics/repec/0003.pdf

Green, F. (2001). It's been a hard day's night: The concentration and intensification of work in late 20th century Britain. *British Journal of Industrial Relations*, 39(1), 53–80.

Green, F. (2004). Why has work effort become more intense? *Industrial Relations*, 43(4), 709–741.

Guy, F., & Skott, P. (2005). Power-biased technological change and the rise in earnings inequality. Working Paper vol 2005–17, Department of Economics. University of Massachusetts. Available at: https://www.econstor.eu/handle/10419/105759

Lager, H., Virgillito, A., & Buchberger, T.P. (2021). Digitalization of logistics work: Ergonomic improvements versus work intensification. In M. Klumpp, C. Ruiner, (Eds.), *Digital Supply Chains and the Human Factor. Lecture Notes in Logistics*. Cham: Springer. pp. 33–53.

Marx, K. (1973). *Grundrisse*. Harmondsworth: Penguin.
Mau, S. (2021). 'The mute compulsion of economic relations': Towards a Marxist theory of the abstract and impersonal power of capital. *Historical Materialism*, 29(3), 3–32.
McKinsey Global Institute (2020). *What's next for remote work: An analysis of 2,000 tasks, 800 jobs, and nine countries*. 23 November. Available at: https://www.mckinsey.com/featured-insights/future-of-work/whats-next-for-remote-work-an- analysis-of-2000-tasks-800-jobs-and-nine-countries.
Moravec, H. (1988). *Mind children: The future of robot and human intelligence*. Cambridge: Harvard University Press.
Mutebi, N., & Hobbs, A. (2022). *The impact of remote and hybrid working on workers and organisations' UK Parliament POSTbrief 49*. 17th October 2022. Available at: https://post.parliament.uk/research-briefings/post-pb-0049/
Newman, N. (2017). Reengineering workplace bargaining: how big data drives lower wages and how reframing labor law can restore information equality in the workplace. *University of Cincinnati Law Review*, 85, 693–760.
Nichols, A. (2022). Digital nomads: A savvy enterprise's newest HR frontier. *Strategic HR Review*, 21(6), 185–190.
Perrigo, B. (2023). Exclusive: OpenAI used Kenyan workers on less than $2 per hour to make ChatGPT less toxic. *Time Magazine*, January 18. Available at: https://time.com/6247678/openai-chatgpt-kenya-workers/
Pitts, F. H. (2017). Beyond the fragment: Postoperaismo, postcapitalism and Marx's 'notes on machines', 45 years on. *Economy and Society*, 46(3–4), 324–345.
Prassl, J. (2018). *Humans as a Service: The Promise and Perils of Work in the Gig Economy*. Oxford: Oxford University Press.
Pruijt, H. (2003). Teams between neo-Taylorism and anti-Taylorism. *Economic and Industrial Democracy*, 24(1), 77–101.
Rolf, S., O'Reilly, J., & Meryon, M. (2022). Towards privatized social and employment protections in the platform economy? Evidence from the UK courier sector. *Research Policy* 51(5), 104492.
Shollo, A., Hopf, K., Thiess, T., & Müller, O. (2022). Shifting ML value creation mechanisms: A process model of ML value creation. *The Journal of Strategic Information Systems*, 31(3), 101734.
Skott, P., & Guy, F. (2007). A model of power-biased technological change. *Economics Letters*, 95(1), 124–131.
Spitz-Oener, A. (2006). Technical change, job tasks, and rising educational demands: Looking outside the wage structure. *Journal of Labor Economics*, 24(2), 235–270.
Susskind, D. & Susskind, R. (2018). The future of the professions. *Proceedings of the American Philosophical Society*, 162(2), 125–138.
Susskind, R. E. & Susskind, D. (2015). *The Future of the Professions: How Technology Will Transform the Work of Human Experts*. Oxford: Oxford University Press.
Ulbricht, L., & Yeung, K. (2022). Algorithmic regulation: A maturing concept for investigating regulation of and through algorithms. *Regulation & Governance*, 16(1), 3–22.
University of Nottingham Rights Lab (2018). Labour exploitation in hand car washes. [Online]. Available at: 10.13140/RG.2.2.35903.25766
van der Doef, M., & Maes, S. (1999). The job demand-control (-Support) model and psychological well-being: A review of 20 years of empirical research. *Work & Stress*, 13(2), 87–114.
Vertesi, J.A., Goldstein, A, Enriquez, D, Liu, L., & Miller, K.T. (2020). Pre-automation: Insourcing and automating the gig economy. *Sociologica*, 14(3), 167–193.
Vidal, M. (2022). *Management Divided: Contradictions of Labor Management*. Oxford: Oxford University Press.
Webb, M. (2020). The impact of artificial intelligence on the labor market. Available at SSRN 3482150.
Willis, E., Harvey, C., Thompson, S., Pearson, M., & Meyer, A. (2018). Work intensification and quality assurance. *Journal of Nursing Care Quality*, 33(2), E10–E16.

Recommendations for Further Reading

Benanav, A. (2020). *Automation and the Future of Work*. London: Verso Books.
Dyer-Witheford, N., Kjøsen, A. M., & Steinhoff, J. (2019). *Inhuman Power: Artificial Intelligence and the Future of Capitalism*. London: Pluto Press.

Gilbert, A. (2023). Reframing automation: A new model for anticipating risks and impacts. Working Paper for the Pissarides Review into the Future of Work and Wellbeing, Institute for the Future of Work. https://www.ifow.org/publications/reframing-automation-a-new-model-for-anticipating-risks-and-impacts

Pitts, F. H. (2020). *Value*. Cambridge: John Wiley & Sons.

Rahman, K. S. & Thelen, K. (2019). The rise of the platform business model and the transformation of twenty-first-century capitalism. *Politics & Society*, 47(2), 177–204.

Shollo, A., Hopf, K., Thiess, T., & Müller, O. (2022). Shifting ML value creation mechanisms: A process model of ML value creation. *The Journal of Strategic Information Systems*, 31(3), 101734.

PART 4

Platforms, Platform Labour and Gig Work

8

PLATFORM LABOUR AND GIG WORK FUTURES

Uncovering Women's Hidden Digital Labour

Al James

Introduction

This chapter explores the series of dramatic, digital transformations of work and labour relations that have accompanied the exponential growth of the 'platform economy' over the last two decades. Also known as 'crowdsourcing', 'online freelancing', 'on-demand economy', or 'gig economy', the platform economy offers major research opportunities for studying digitally mediated futures of work, algorithmic management, and shifting patterns of self-employment in the wake of austerity and cost of living crisis. Recent International Labour Organization/ Oxford Internet Institute estimates suggest that over 163 million people worldwide now secure income from paid work through digital labour platforms (Kässi et al. 2021), representing a five-fold increase over the last decade (ILO 2021). Underpinning this impressive growth, internet technologies are used to decouple production from formal employment. Platform workers are paid on a project, piece rate, or hourly basis and must supply and maintain their own capital equipment (Stanford 2017). Divergent from standard employment relationships, their labour is instead sold on a one-off, as-needed basis, with platforms eschewing any legal responsibility as 'employer'. And rather than answer to managers in the flesh, workers are managed remotely by online algorithms through apps on their smartphones, tablets, and personal computers. Consequently, workers are recast as 'independent', 'self-employed', 'freelance contractors', and work executed through platforms is relabelled as 'tasks', 'gigs', or 'HITs' (Human Intelligence Tasks) (De Stefano 2016).

Platforms use complex digital architectures to match clients ('requesters') and workers ('suppliers'), allocate gigs, set minimum terms of service, mediate invoicing and payment, and rank worker performance through multiple metrics based on client feedback (and upon which workflows are predicated in a circular loop). Alongside the much-studied and highly visible 'on-demand' gig workers in cities, engaged in *geographically tethered* tasks such as food delivery, couriering, and personal transportation (Moore and Newsome 2018), platform work also includes *remote crowdsourcing* of desk-based tasks. These range from pay-per-click 'microtasks' (parcelled activities, often menial and monotonous, which still require some sort of judgement beyond the capability of AI, such as image categorisation, tagging, content moderation, and information finding), to more

 DOI: 10.4324/9781003327561-12

complex white-collar 'cloudwork' which emerges from the virtual crowdsourcing of higher skills tasks remotely (e.g. web mobile and software development, sales and marketing, HR, legal, social media management, graphic design, writing and translation, data entry, and accounting).

A globally distributed workforce of on-demand 'platform labour' is marketed as instantly available to customers 24/7 and offering major cost savings relative to traditional 'analogue' service providers. In so doing, the human qualities of 'digital labour' become identified as an 'infinitely available commodity for on-demand purchase' (Cockayne 2016: 75), with consumers often forgetting that there is a real living breathing human on the other end of the app (Scholz 2017). *This chapter explores online gig workers' everyday lived experiences of being used as commodified, on-demand 'platform labour' in this way.* In seeking to enrol the next generation of students, scholars, and researchers, the discussion presents a series of go-to references, accessible works, and draws on novel and provocative empirical engagements with platform workers who remain strangely marginalised in debates around platform work futures. Against a stubbornly male-centred digital labour research literature (Barzilay and Ben-David 2016, Churchill and Craig 2019, Howcroft and Rubery 2018, Gregg and Andrijasevic 2019, James 2022), the chapter introduces a growing feminist body of work that engages with 'hidden' women platform workers – including women platform workers in the global South who are 'doubly excluded' by Western-facing studies of platform 'norms'. This important body of feminist labour research explores gendered precarity through women's everyday struggles to make a living using digital labour platforms. It highlights the role of unequal gender divisions of household reproductive labour in simultaneously motivating workers' turn to platforms, and also constraining workers' abilities to compete online for gigs, secure paid work, and to advance in the platform economy.

The chapter is structured around three cuts. The first cut explores the growth of digital labour platforms in relation to earlier employment practices (outsourcing, flexibilisation, intermediation) and a neoliberal crisis of care, and the growing presence of women as 'hidden platform labour'. The second cut juxtaposes widespread celebratory claims around female 'inclusive' and 'emancipatory' work futures with multiple precarities, hardships, and exclusions experienced by women platform workers – and which expose a series of gender pay gaps in the platform economy, and their rootedness in gendered algorithmic bias and discriminatory client feedback. These constraints were brought into even greater relief during the COVID-19 pandemic and consequent lockdowns, and are further reinforced by problems of female health and safety identified across multiple on-demand delivery, ride hailing, and crowdwork platforms. The third cut identifies some innovative coping tactics and resistance strategies that platform workers have developed individually and collectively to reduce their vulnerabilities and to better navigate platform user agreements, algorithmic systems of control, and client feedback in ways which begin to make their everyday work-lives easier. These include worker-led data justice strategies to recapture and operationalise some of the myriad data that platform workers themselves create through their everyday work practices; alongside platform ranking initiatives designed to name and shame platforms with poor worker support and to encourage progressive change through showcasing best practice.

This is an exciting research agenda, with multiple possibilities for engaging with women as hidden platform workers and for feminising platforms in progressive ways. To this end, the chapter closes with some important research questions that might usefully motivate undergraduate and postgraduate independent research projects to get involved and contribute to the advancement of understanding and knowledge in this field, through much-needed engagements with women platform workers.

Explaining the Rise of the Platform Economy and Its Hidden Female Workforce

The *institutional origins of platform work* are found in earlier forms of nonstandard employment practices around temporary staffing and the restless pursuit of worker 'flexibility' underway for four decades (Van Doorn 2017). These include outsourcing, labour 'flexibilisation', individualisation of labour, labour market intermediation, and the neoliberal erosion of worker rights (see e.g. Stanford 2017, Hunt and Samman 2019, Woodcock and Graham 2019). Other scholars draw earlier historical associations, and suggest that platform work resembles preindustrial home-based piece work (Berg et al. 2018). In the wake of the Great Recession (2008–2010), platforms took root in a climate of profound economic uncertainty (Rosenblat 2018), with growth further enhanced through austerity cuts in welfare state provision and a crisis of public care (Huws 2019), which has pushed care down to the 'natural' level of the home. Workers are turning to platforms as a means of generating much-needed income in the context of income uncertainty and tight labour markets (Altenried 2022).

Against a backdrop of economic precarity and jobless growth, platforms are heralded as offering new forms of accessible paid work, with low barriers to entry, and microentrepreneurship. Celebratory claims herald the power of digital labour platforms as an accessible source of microentrepreneurship that disrupts long-standing labour market inequalities and usurps the tyranny of the 9-5 office job. Multiple commentators have celebrated digital labour platforms for giving workers access to an international client base with minimal barriers to entry, to generate income quickly, and to set their own work schedules. Platforms have been lauded as offering new forms of 'flexible ad hoc work' (Slaughter 2016, Hunt 2017) which 'enable workers to benefit from job opportunities that they might not otherwise be able to access otherwise and on a flexible-schedule basis' (De Stefano 2016: 5).

As part of these celebratory claims, commentators glorify *new platform possibilities for female labour market inclusion and advancement* through improved reconciliation of paid work with the demands of motherhood, avoidance of misogynistic bosses through management by 'neutral' algorithms, and the capacity to sidestep discriminatory hiring practices rooted in conscious and unconscious biases by competing anonymously for online work (Milkman et al. 2021, Micha et al. 2022). Exemplifying such claims is the suggestion that: 'For professional women, the on-demand economy is already a godsend... women can continue to advance in their careers or at least stay in the game while being the kind of parents they want to be' (Slaughter 2015: 2). Accordingly, digital labour platforms are argued to represent a fundamental challenge to stubborn gendered labour market inequalities (Schoenbaum 2016, Krieger-Boden and Sorgner 2018). Such enthusiasm is echoed by platforms themselves, through advertising slogans, imagery, and worker testimonies that target women, and celebrate female emancipatory work opportunities. These *claims take on additional significance in the global South*, where digital labour platforms are framed as a panacea to poverty and informality, to eliminate labour market constraints faced by women, and provide them with new streams of income and good-quality jobs, through new opportunities for 'self-empowerment', and flexibility of paid work around domestic responsibilities (Anwar 2022, World Bank 2016, Varanasi et al. 2022).

It is particularly ironic then, given the pervasiveness of these claims, that *within platform labour research women gig workers remain strangely invisible*, and the gendered dimensions of gig work heavily under-researched (Barzilay and Ben-David 2016, Churchill and Craig 2019, Kasliwal 2020, Milkman et al. 2021). Instead, the majority of our understanding of platform work-lives and digital precarity has come from analyses of men doing gig work, or else studies that lump workers into one apparently genderless mass of 'digital labour'. This lack of knowledge perpetuates hardships for millions of platform workers and their families on several levels. It also limits the ability of policy-makers to hold platforms to account (Hunt and Samman 2019), of feminist activists to target resource in pursuit of progressive digital work futures, and of platform workers to identify more (and less) progressive platforms (and vote with their feet).

The *origins of these male-centred approaches* might sympathetically be understood as a function of a strong empirical research focus on geographically tethered (or 'placed-based') labour platforms, whose highly visible, urban public-facing workforces are male-dominated. These include platform workers in food delivery, parcel delivery, ride hailing, and home maintenance segments. At the forefront of these associations, one of the largest and most studied platforms, Uber's US driver workforce is 84% male. Indeed, Uber has moved from a label attached to one transport platform, towards a generic descriptor of platform models across multiple service functions: 'Uber for food, Uber for cleaning, Uber for courier services, Uber for grocery shopping… Uber for everything' (Kessler 2018: 10). These descriptors reinforce common conceptions of Uber as the gig economy masculinist norm. In contrast, women crowdworkers engaged in remote gig work from behind closed doors in the private spaces of the home remain largely invisible to clients, and more difficult to access. This invisibility is reinforced by crowdwork platform financial marketing strategies that deliberately emphasise the technology bases of their company value (rather than embodied labour) as a means of impressing investors. At a deeper level, these female exclusions can also be understood as part of long-standing ontological constructions of the economic subject as 'male' (Nelson 1992, Ferber and Nelson 2003), in which women's economic activities continue to be devalued and excluded from what is necessary or essential (McDowell 2000, see James 2022).

In combination, the consequent 'virtual absence of women' (Gregg and Andrijasevic 2019: 1) is especially problematic, given the celebration of digital labour platforms as disrupting stubborn gendered labour market inequalities and work-family conflict (Slaughter 2015, Manyika et al. 2016, Hyperwallet 2017, Krieger-Boden and Sorgner 2018). It is also problematic given the increasing significance of women within the global platform workforce. Multiple surveys have revealed women's significant presence across multiple digital labour platforms and service segments, representing between 52% (Berg 2016, Huws et al. 2016), and 40% (ILO 2021) of crowdworkers in the EU, the UK, and the US. Applying these various figures to the total 163 million platform workers worldwide, suggests that there are *more than 64 million women platform workers worldwide* – including millions of women platform workers in the global South – labouring to create value on behalf of platforms, clients and shareholders, yet whose lives remain heavily under-researched. Survey data also point to the extensive childcare responsibilities of women platform workers, and their greater incidence compared with male platform workers (Berg 2016, Churchill and Craig 2019). Likewise, studies identify the crucial role of motherhood, female majority responsibilities for childcare, and gendered penalties within previous employment that have collectively prompted their turn to online gig work. These variously include bad bosses, inappropriate questions at job interviews, lack of maternity provision by previous employers, redundancy during pregnancy, non-provision of family-friendly working, demotion after maternity leave, and /or company cultures of long hours working and misogyny (Graham et al. 2017, Berg et al. 2018, James 2022).

Beyond engagement with 'female-appropriate' carework platforms which provide feminised reproductive tasks through online labour markets, women are identified across an impressively diverse range of platforms, segments, and task offerings (see Table 8.1) ranging from Web

Table 8.1 Women's presence across prominent digital labour platforms

Platform segment	*Example platforms*	*Service description*
Online remote		
'Cloudwork' Approx. even gender workforce split	Amazon M-Turk Clickworker Microworkers Appen PeoplePerHour UpWork Fiverr Copify TranscribeMe Workana Prolific Freelancer	Includes desk-based microtask clickwork, in support of AI: e.g. image tagging, transcription of speech, survey participation, digitalisation, data categorisation. More complex white-collar professional work tasks completed remotely by home-based gig workers (e.g. communications, marketing, business development, HR, office support, web, design, and graphics).
Place-tethered on-demand		
Delivery (food, courier) **Ride hailing** Male-dominated workforce	Deliveroo Doordash GrubHub UberEats JustEat Swiggy Pedal Me Stuart Amazon Flex Peyk Uber Ola Cabs Didi Chuxing	Online platforms making delivery more efficient through comprehensive and verified listings, updated information and analytics. Platforms that connect private-hire vehicle drivers with riders who need to travel, typically lower prices than traditional taxis.
Domestic services Female-dominated workforce	Taskrabbit Helpling eMop Assist Handy BookMyBai Didi.com Maidsapp Batmaid Homeservices24 Serado	Online platforms match freelance labour with local demand, allowing consumers to find immediate help with everyday tasks: e.g. home cleaning, domestic services, household maintenance, pet walking, furniture assembly, and errands.
Carework Female-dominated workforce	Care.com Caresourcer KidSitter Bubble Childcare Careship	Online platform to match care workers with clients with family care needs: child care, elderly care, special needs care.

Source: Table by author.

Development, Design, Video Photo & Audio Writing, Admin, Marketing & PR, Business Support, Social Media, Creative Arts, Mobile, Translation, Search Marketing, Extraordinary, Software Development, to ride hailing. Yet their work-lives remain largely 'hidden in the cloud' (Gregory 2018). Strikingly, women account for less than 1% of articles to date published on platform labour and the gig economy – against an expansive platform labour research literature that boasts over 9.7 million articles and counting (James 2022). In short, 'research on gender and the gig economy is particularly sparse' (Milkman et al. 2021: 360). Encouragingly however, a rapidly growing body of feminist digital labour studies research is challenging this lacuna.

Gendering the Platform Economy: Precarity, Algorithmic Visibility, and Cyberviolence

Experiences of platform worker precarity, hardship, and struggle are now widely documented. In contrast to celebratory claims around the opportunities for microentrepreneurship and economic advancement vis-à-vis traditional 'analogue' employers, critical digital labour studies have exposed multiple precarities. Underpinning these hardships, studies point to the ways in which platforms eschew any legal responsibility as 'employers' – this despite workers' terms and conditions of work being defined by extensive platform user agreements. Studies also point to widespread instances of wage theft for completed tasks deemed 'unsatisfactory' by clients, in whose favour extensive platform user agreements are stacked relative to workers; as well as a constant threat of deactivation for workers whose livelihoods ultimately depend on favourable client reviews to stay visible within the platform algorithms that allocate work (Rosenblat 2018, Van Doorn 2022). Despite hefty platform fees (typically 15%–30% of workers' wages), a lack of employee legal status means a lack of social protection, as platforms bypass legal provisions in employment law that would otherwise afford minimum wage protections, unemployment benefits, paid holiday leave, sick pay, parental leave and pensions (Scholz 2017; Graham and Shaw 2017). These problems are reinforced by intense competition between workers, with platforms deliberately recruiting an oversupply of labour to reduce gig worker bargaining power (Cockayne 2016). Alongside pervasive instances of overwork, this also pushes down compensation for work that is often intermittent with frequent periods of unpaid job search (De Stefano 2016). Constrained 'flexibility' also results from algorithmic 'behavioural nudges' encouraging workers to maintain a high acceptance rating of gigs offered, and thereby avoid their platform profiles suddenly being deactivated (Churchill and Craig 2019). Practices of evening, night-time and weekend working are common, as workers chase lucrative gigs – and which fly in the face of platform claims around improved work-life balance and digitally enabled 'flexible' working (Wood et al. 2018, Tubaro et al. 2022).

Extending these insights, a rapidly growing feminist platform labour studies agenda has identified the ways in which platform precarities, vulnerabilities and hardships are exacerbated for women platform workers. This work is based on an impressive variety of methodological strategies that are also feasible for student researchers on a budget. These include signing up to platforms as both requester and worker, in-depth interviews posted to crowdwork platforms as a paid task in which research participants engage, autobiographical image generation by women platform workers, data scraping of platform profiles, and shadowing platform workers at work (see e.g. Hannák et al. 2017, Cant 2019, Rosenblat 2018, James 2022). This work has revealed how the operation of the platform economy is gendered along multiple dimensions.

On one level, studies offer some support to platform claims around *female online labour market advantage.* Through engagement with women crowdworkers in the UK accessing paid work through 28 different crowdwork platforms (including PeoplePerHour, Upwork, Freelancer, Copify,

Appen) James (2022) acknowledges how these platforms allow women returners to engage in paid work tasks that are relevant to their prior experience, training, and core skill sets after significant periods of maternity leave. This is in contrast to other 'flexible' working options, identified by UK women crowdworkers as commonly available to them locally (including working as dinner ladies, at supermarket checkouts, and cleaning) which are typically oversubscribed and low paid. In contrast, crowdwork platforms give access to a global client base beyond the immediate local area, including clients overseas whose real time demands for evening working fit better with some women's time schedules around childcare and home schooling. Likewise, the role of platform work in giving back a sense of self-esteem, especially in the face of previous failed job applications subsequent to having children. Other studies also point to preferences of some clients for female platform workers, underpinning female preferential hiring (Chan and Wang 2018). Studies also report significantly improved crowdworker abilities to reconcile irregular 'pockets' of paid work time around the unpredictable rhythms of family, in contrast with the fixed rigidity of 9-5 'core' office hours (James 2022, Wallis 2021). Platforms are also recognised as reducing the catch-22 needs of some workers to pay expensive childcare fees to enable labour market engagement, this by providing enhanced access to family-friendly working compared with previous employers – these include spatial flexibility of work though homeworking, temporal flexibility of work, annualised platform work hours, term-time only working to make space for childcare during school holidays, all without the need for line-manager sign-off.

However, the everyday reality for female returners using platforms is also contradictory, and evidences *new forms of online labour market disadvantage*, identified in diverse studies of women platform workers in multiple countries, including the US, Europe, Africa, China, Vietnam, Indonesia, Argentina, and Mexico. At the broadest level, these inequalities are evidenced through *platform gender pay gaps* across multiple task segments. This includes on-demand ride hailing platforms, where studies have shown how women Uber drivers receive fewer rides through algorithmic allocation (Cook et al. 2018), based on less favourable reviews from riders. Similarly on remote crowdwork platforms, the ILO has identified a gender pay gap amongst Amazon M-Turk home-based crowdworkers in the US (N = 564, 48% female): women earn on average 82% of male Turkers' average hourly earnings despite similar levels of educational qualification and weekly working hours (Adams-Prassl and Berg 2017). Similarly, Dubey et al.'s (2017) analysis of 37,599 crowdworkers (19% female) on 'a popular freelancing platform', showed that women earn 62–89 cents for every $1 male workers earned, a pattern evident across multiple job categories (administrative, design, business services, networking management, sales and marketing, writing and translation, software development). Similar patterns are found in other large surveys, including Barzilay and Ben-David's (2016) analysis of 4,600 online taskers' requested rates and work hours on 'a global online work platform', which showed that women's average hourly requested rates are 37% lower than men's, after controlling for feedback score, experience, hours of work and educational attainment. Women are also more likely to quit platforms within 12 months of signup (JPM 2016). Intersectional studies also demonstrate how these injustices are amplified for women from ethnic minority backgrounds, and suggest that platforms further entrench gendered and racialised discriminations and neo-colonial insecurities (Kampouri 2022, Rani et al. 2022).

Underpinning these gender inequalities in patterns of platform remuneration and advancement, studies have identified a range of mechanisms. One source of identified constraint emerges from *gender bias in worker evaluations*. These include reduced overall levels of client feedback for women taskers: based on an analysis of 3,707 worker profiles (42% female), Hannák et al. (2017) find women across 30 US cities consistently receiving 10% fewer reviews than men with equivalent platform work experience (and black women receiving reviews with the least positive adjectives). Negative client feedback that invokes gender stereotypes of worker skills is also identified on ride hailing and delivery apps in multiple countries, including common perceptions of women drivers as slower and less safe in China (Kwan 2022) and Mexico (Hiramatsu 2022). Feedback matters because it sustains *gendered constraints on women's abilities to remain visible within the algorithms* that platforms use to allocate work tasks, make taskers visible to requesters, and hence provide opportunities for paid gig work – this based on worker reputational data combining feedback from previous tasks, frequency of gigs completed, responsiveness to clients, and other performance metrics (Wood et al. 2018).

Women also express common anxieties about 'dropping out of the algorithm' and ranking lower in requester search listings as a result of childcare for which they commonly assume majority responsibility. Studies point to gendered reductions in platform income based on three dimensions of reproductive constraint. First, on the *types of gig that women taskers with young children can engage in*, with a common inability to commit to higher paying gigs that require quick turnaround and/or sustained periods of uninterrupted working. Second, constraints on *when women are able to search for lucrative gigs*, based on times of the day when they are simply unavailable due to the school run, meal times, or bedtime. Third, platform expectation of *instant response to existing clients* with potential for negative client feedback in the case of any delay. As such, studies point to multiple 'motherhood penalties' on the pay levels that women are able to achieve through online platforms. Some women crowdworkers choose to increase their hourly fee to include the costs of childcare needed in order to 'make gig work pay'. But this means that their hourly rate is seen by many clients as less competitive. For other women, platform income just breaks even with the costs of childcare in a zero-sum game.

These challenges are reinforced by *violations of female health and safety* experienced by women platform workers. Evidence from Uber in multiple US cities points to acts of violence against women drivers, sexual harassment by intoxicated male riders, being propositioned for sex, other unwanted come-ons, and physical fondling (Schoenbaum 2016). Similar experiences of sexual harassment by male passengers, violence, and exploitation have also been documented amongst women drivers in Indonesia (Zulfiyan 2020), Mexico (Hiramatsu 2022), Argentina (Micha et al. 2022), and China (Kwan 2022) – experiences which differ from those of male ride hailing drivers (Dinh and Tienari 2022). Likewise, powerful research by Badger (2022) identifies sexual harassment of women food delivery riders in form-fitting cyclewear at food pick-up points from kitchen and restaurant workers; as well as the indignities faced by women riders having to change sanitary products behind the bins of pick-up restaurants, urinating in drinks bottles, and being unable to wash their hands due to the lack of employer-provided, safe toilet facilities (Badger 2022). Sexual harassment and gendered cyberviolence is also evident amongst women remote crowdworkers working from home (see James 2022, Stringhi 2022).

In response, growing numbers of women platform workers are sceptical of celebratory claims around platforms as a challenge to stubborn patterns of gendered labour market inequality (Krieger-Boden and Sorgner 2018). Similarly, the contributions of platforms towards workers' long-term livelihoods and employment-led development are also questioned. In contrast to widespread development discourses which position platform work as offering women new opportunities for advancement through microentrepreneurship, studies instead point to reproduction of informality and precarity, low and insecure incomes on platforms, further entrenchment of unequal power relations and discrimination by clients, and erosion of established labour protections for marginalised women platform workers. These problems are documented amongst women crowdworkers using Upwork and Uber in Africa (Ghana, Nigeria, Kenya, and South Africa) (Anwar 2022). They are also evident amongst women using on-demand domestic work platforms in

South Africa and Kenya to provide domestic work tasks in the private homes of an increasingly tech-savvy and affluent middle-class (Hunt and Machingura 2016, Hunt et al. 2019).

These multiple gendered structures of constraint, and consequent patterns of gendered platform precarity, matter because they reinforce a general lack of social protection for 'independent' platform workers, due to their lack of legal employee status, as platforms seek to bypass legal regulations that would otherwise afford minimum wage protections, unemployment benefits, paid holiday leave, sick pay, parental leave, and pensions. They are also significant because they are evident across multiple platforms, task segments, and in multiple cities and countries. In combination, a clear consensus is emerging that in 'the 'gig' economy… we are witnessing what may be a third generation of sex inequality – Discrimination 3.0' (Barzilay and Ben-David 2017: 427).

Platform Worker Agency and Organising for Change

In the absence of widespread trade unionisation of platform workers, recent high-profile platform labour interventions have sought to legally reclassify 'self-employed' gig workers and thereby bring them under existing employment law. However, multiple platform workers resist legal reclassification on the basis of its increased employer demands and expectations of them as formal employees. Instead, many just want better protection as independent platform workers. In the meantime, studies have identified a range of individual and collective strategies and tactics that women have developed to reduce precarity on gig work platforms, to resist and challenge structures of algorithmic constraint, improve platform incomes, and determine better conditions of work in ways which make their everyday work-lives easier.

Amongst remote crowdworkers, a common tactic amongst new entrants is to take on a quick succession of short turnaround low-paying gigs to secure client feedback, and thereby establish a credible tasker profile and build algorithmic visibility. Here, workers accept a short-term pay hit in lieu of a longer-term gain through reputational capital (but also note that tasker work histories and accumulated feedback are not transferrable between platforms). In response to motherhood penalties, other tactics are evident around *targeted selection of clients*, who recognise and accept workers' childcare commitments and hence are unlikely to penalise them in feedback scores for family constraints on availability. To this end, some women include public statements of their childcare responsibilities on their platform profile pages. Where clients raise issues about the quality of gigs completed (e.g. in terms of workers' lesser availability and responsiveness around childcare commitments), studies identify some women deliberately *failing to submit a pay claim* (James 2022): the dashboard option for clients to leave negative feedback only becomes available once a gig is listed as completed and the tasker submits final claim for payment. The loss of income from one gig is identified as a price worth paying in order to maintain a high feedback score for algorithmic visibility, and thereby to secure future workflow.

Crowdworker tactics also extend to *platform selection* based on geographies of requesters and time zone, to offer better fit of client demands around childcare commitments (e.g. overseas clients enabling night working in UK real time). In terms of maximising income, *taking work offline* is identified as a double-edged sword: on the one hand reducing the hefty fees that platforms take for each gig completed, but on the other hand, undermining the threshold regular flow of gigs through the platform needed to retain algorithmic visibility. Registering across multiple platforms or '*multi-apping*' (to counter limited and/or uneven workflow opportunities on a single platform) is similarly problematic for the same reason. Other tactics involve some women accepting gigs and then '*subbing out some work*' (reintermediation) to other crowdworkers during unforeseen childcare demands and during school holidays. And to avoid gender discriminatory client feedback, studies show that one third of women crowdworkers have done work under a username that kept their female identity hidden (Hyperwallet 2017). But while such tactics help individual women to maintain algorithmic visibility, gig workflows, and income streams at the individual worker level, they *do not challenge larger structures of constraint*, including platform design, algorithmic architectures, and uneven gender divisions of unpaid labour in the home which perpetuate an assumed female majority burden of childcare.

Other organising initiatives build on workers' individual tactics of resistance, to develop collective modes of organising. *Worker-led data organising strategies* aim to recapture and operationalise some of the myriad data that platform workers themselves create through their everyday work practices. Platform workers are coming together to conduct their own digital worker inquiries, to compare gig working conditions and opportunities across platforms, and investigate the potential to access their own worker-generated 'data assets' (Van Doorn and Badger 2020, UNI 2019). Workers argue that access to such data can help them make better and informed choices about when and how to work, when to accept jobs, how to track their wages over time, how to port data or work histories across platforms, and how to make better choices about working safely (see Gallagher et al. 2023). Examples are showcased in Table 8.2 and include Turkopticon which allows remote microworkers to rank and rate job sellers and to share information about which sellers to avoid. Worker-built self-track apps such as WeClock equip workers to track and

Table 8.2 Worker-led data leverage tools for platform worker empowerment – key examples

Worker-led tool	*Description/goal*
WeClock	Gig worker-built, open-source self-tracking app to reduce gig work data asymmetries: equips platform workers to quantify their daily labour and productivity, and pool data with other gig workers to fight wage theft and improve worker well-being while preserving workers' privacy. Developed by UNI Global Union's Young Workers' Lab.
Spotlight	'Race against the algorithm' beta tool to give gig workers increased access and control over their platform work data (track working time, total movement, platform app usage, distance travelled). Developed by Andrew Pakes at Prospect Union.
Workerbird	Worker-centred tracking app, to enable platform workers to calculate real hourly rate, enable fair payment and support job transition. Developed by a mixed gender team of Javascript based coders, London Future of Work hackathon.
Turkopticon	Gig worker-run userscript for microtask clickworkers: 'helps people in the 'crowd' of crowdsourcing to watch out for each other', by ranking and rating job sellers and to share information about bad sellers to avoid. Developed by Lilly Irani and Michael 'Six' Silberman, maintained by Tech Workers Coalition.
Alia	Portable benefits app for domestic gig workers, mediates prorated client payments to mimic paid time off and insurance benefits for employees. Developed in the US by National Domestic Workers Alliance.
My Digital Backpack/Deemly	Enables gig workers to create a single online profile with all client reviews from different platforms combined. Workers' combined reputation data profiles become shareable by digital links (widgets and APIs) to third parties. Developed in the Netherlands.

Source: Author analysis.

quantify their workday to fight wage theft and improve mental health while preserving workers' privacy. And Deliveroo riders have recently created an online receipt reader that allows riders to better determine their wages over time. However, there also remains considerable scope to include women's voices and gendered gig work experiences in the design, development, and coding of worker-led platform apps.

Other platform labour activists identify the potential for improving the lives of platform workers through the development of worker-owned cooperative platforms that challenge the expropriation of platform profits by a select group of platform shareholders and venture capitalist backers (Scholz 2016). Other initiatives are concerned to rank platforms against five key principles (fair pay, fair conditions, fair contracts, fair management, fair representation), to name and shame digital labour platforms with poor worker support, and to encourage progressive change through showcasing best practice (see Chapter 10). At the forefront of this agenda, the Fairwork project is led by Mark Graham at Oxford University (Graham et al. 2020) through partnerships with academics, platform activists, and workers in multiple countries worldwide, to encourage platforms to improve their treatment of workers to improve their rankings, and to encourage workers to vote with the feet and move to higher scoring platforms for a better deal.

Concluding Discussion

The dramatic growth of digitally mediated gig work in the platform economy offers major potential for advancing a feminist labour studies research agenda on work futures. This chapter has explored women's platform work-lives – in ways that are both new and depressingly familiar. In sum, while smartphone apps tout instant access to a 'global digital workforce' available 24/7, the gendered reality is one of multiple constraints of motherhood and care on women's geographies of gig search, working hours, algorithmic visibility, and progression. Thus while platform developers continue to tout their digital infrastructures as offering 'female inclusion', this says nothing about *the terms* of that online labour market inclusion.

The studies presented in this chapter point to a potential digital re-inscription of stubborn 'analogue' gendered labour market inequalities, and force us to question the extent to which digital labour platforms genuinely challenge long-standing gendered labour market inequalities and exclusions. Once the novelty of the sophisticated artificial intelligence, platform architectures, and digital algorithms used to govern these women's work-lives is acknowledged, the constraints of motherhood and care on women's patterns of job search, working hours, pay, and labour market advancement are far from novel – at least to feminist scholars. Indeed, these constraints were brought into greater relief during the COVID-19 lockdowns, with homeworking women more likely to be interrupted by childcare than men in dual-earner households, and increased gender inequalities in paid work hours (Andrew et al. 2020, ILO 2020).

The growing research agenda around feminising platforms offers fertile ground for student researchers and established scholars alike. Urgent research questions that might usefully motivate undergraduate and postgraduate independent research projects are concerned with the material circumstances and everyday realities of digitally mediated work, and economic injustices for women crowdworkers in the platform economy: How do the everyday lived experiences of women with young families using online work platforms vary as a function of intersectional identities (class, race, ethnicity, religion, sexuality), household situation, and platform income dependency? What advantages do digital labour platforms offer women over formal employment in different local labour markets? How do women's experiences of being managed by an algorithm vary between platforms? How do the challenges that women experience on digital labour platforms vary between different nation states and gendered welfare regime? And hence, what does an engagement with women, and gender relations of social reproduction and care, tell us about the opportunities and challenges of digital labour platforms that previous work rooted in a masculinist lens of analysis has not? Students at Newcastle have begun to engage with these questions through a series of innovative dissertations, with some also onboarding as platform workers and writing themselves into the analysis.

Much then remains to be done to understand the role of workers' gender identities and uneven household gender divisions of care in shaping the operation and outcomes of digital labour platforms, and to identify alternative platform models that offer a more progressive set of work-life outcomes for women gig workers.

References

Adams-Prassl A. and Berg J. 2017. *When Home Affects Pay: An Analysis of the Gender Pay Gap among Crowdworkers*. ILO. https://dx. doi.org/10.2139/ssrn.3048711

Altenried M. 2022. *The Digital Factory: The Human Labor of Automation*. Chicago, IL: University of Chicago Press.

Andrew A., Cattan S., Costa Dias M., Farquharson C., Kraftman L., Krutikova S., Phimister A. and Sevilla A. 2020. *How Are Mothers and Fathers Balancing Work and Family under Lockdown?* IFS Briefing Note. 27 May 2020. https://www.ifs.org.uk/publications/14860

Anwar M.A. 2022. Platforms of inequality: gender dynamics of digital labour in Africa. *Gender & Development* 30(3): 747–764.

Badger, A. 2022. Labouring at the interface: exploring the rhythms and resistances of working in London's food delivery gig economy, Doctoral dissertation, Royal Holloway, University of London.

Barzilay A.R. and Ben-David A. 2016. Platform inequality: gender in the gig-economy. *Seton Hall Law Review* 47: 393–431.

Berg J. 2016. *Income Security in the On-Demand Economy: Findings and Policy Lessons from a Survey of Crowdworkers*. Geneva: ILO.

Berg J., Furrer M., Harmon E., Rani U. and Silberman M.S. 2018. *Digital Labour Platforms and the Future of Work*. Geneva: ILO.

Cant C. 2019. *Riding for Deliveroo: Resistance in the New Economy*. Oxford: John Wiley & Sons.

Chan J. and Wang J. 2018. Hiring preferences in online labor markets: evidence of a female hiring bias. *Management Science* 64(7): 2973–2994.

Churchill B. and Craig L. 2019. Gender in the gig economy: men and women using digital platforms to secure work in Australia. *Journal of Sociology* 55(4): 741–761.

Cockayne D.G. 2016. Sharing and neoliberal discourse: the economic function of sharing in the digital on-demand economy. *Geoforum* 77: 73–82.

Cook C., Diamond R., Hall J., List J.A. and Oyer P. 2018. *The Gender Earnings Gap in the Gig Economy: Evidence from Over a Million Rideshare Drivers*. Cambridge, Massachusetts: National Bureau of Economic Research.

De Stefano V. 2016. *The Rise of the 'Just-in Time Workforce': On Demand Work, Crowdwork, and Labor Protection in the 'Gig Economy'*. Geneva: ILO.

Dinh T.T.Q. and Tienari J. 2022. Brothers and broken dreams: men, masculinity, and emotions in platform capitalism. *Gender, Work & Organization* 29(2): 609–625.

Dubey A., Abhinav K., Hamilton M. and Kass A. 2017, June. Analyzing gender pay gap in freelancing marketplace. *Proceedings of the 2017 ACM SIGMIS Conference on Computers and People Research*, pp. 13–19. Available at: https://doi.org/10.1145/3084381.3084402

Ferber M.A. and Nelson J.A. (eds.) 2003. *Feminist Economics Today: Beyond Economic Man*. London: University of Chicago Press.

Graham M., Hjorth I. and Lehdonvirta V. 2017. Digital labour and development: impacts of global digital labour platforms and the gig economy on worker livelihoods. *Transfer: European Review of Labour and Research* 23(2): 135–162.

Graham M. and Shaw J. (eds.) 2017. *Towards a Fairer Gig Economy*. Manchester: Meatspace Press.

Graham M., Woodcock J., Heeks R., Mungai P., Van Belle J.P., du Toit D., Fredman S., Osiki A., van der Spuy A. and Silberman S.M. 2020. The Fairwork Foundation: strategies for improving platform work in a global context. *Geoforum* 112: 100–113.

Gregg M. and Andrijasevic R. 2019. Virtually absent: the gendered histories and economies of digital labour. *Feminist Review* 123(1): 1–7.

Gregory K. 2018. *Introducing Gigs, Economies, and Social Reproduction. Artists in the Gig Economy* Research Workshop, University of Edinburgh 24 August 2018.

Gallagher, C., Gregory, K. and Karabaliev, B. 2023. Digital worker inquiry and the critical potential of participatory worker data science for on-demand platform workers. New Technology, Work and Employment. Available at: https://doi.org/10.1111/ntwe.12286

Hannák A., Wagner C., Garcia D., Mislove A., Strohmaier M. and Wilson C. 2017. Bias in online freelance marketplaces: evidence from Taskrabbit and Fiverr. *Proceedings of the 2017 ACM conference on computer supported cooperative work and social computing* (pp. 1914–1933). Available at: https://doi.org/10.1145/2998181.2998327

Hiramatsu A. 2022. Female taxi drivers in Mexico City: facing patriarchal structures as a force of oppression. *Gender, Work & Organization* 29(5): 1638–1657.

Howcroft D. and Rubery J. 2018. Gender equality prospects and the fourth industrial revolution. In Neufiend M., O'Reilly J. and Ranft F. (eds.), *Praise for Work in the Digital Age*. London: Rowman and Littlefield, pp. 63–74.

Hunt A. 2017. *What Policymakers Need to Know about Women and the Gig Economy*. London: ODI Blog, 26 January 2017.

Hunt A. and Machingura F. 2016. *A Good Gig? The Rise of On-Demand Domestic Work*. ODI Development Progress Working Paper 7. https://cdn.odi.org/media/documents/11155.pdf

Hunt A. and Samman E. 2019. *Gender and the Gig Economy: Critical Steps for Evidence-Based Policy*. London: Overseas Development Institute, Working Paper 2019.

Hunt A., Samman E., Tapfuma S., Mwaura G., Omenya R., Kim K., Stevano S. and Roumer A., 2019. *Women in the Gig Economy: Paid Work, Care and Flexibility in Kenya and South Africa.* London: Overseas Development Institute

Huws U. 2019. The hassle of housework: digitalisation and the commodification of domestic labour. *Feminist Review* 123(1): 8–23.

Huws U., Spencer N. and Joyce S., 2016. *Crowd Work in Europe: Preliminary Results from a Survey in the UK, Sweden, Germany, Austria and the Netherlands*. Brussels: Foundation for European Progressive Studies/UNI Europa.

Hyperwallet 2017. *The Future of Gig Work Is Female.* https://www.hyperwallet.com/app/uploads/HW_The_Future_of_Gig_Work_is_Female.pdf

ILO 2020. *Research Brief: Peak-Level Social Dialogue as a Governance Tool during the COVID-19 Pandemic*. Geneva: ILO.

ILO 2021. *World Employment and Social Outlook 2021: The Role of Digital Labour Platforms in Transforming the World of Work.* Geneva: International Labour Organisation.

James A. 2022. Women in the gig economy: feminising 'digital labour'. *Work in the Global Economy* 2(1): 2–26.

JPM 2016. *The Online Platform Economy: Has Growth Peaked?* New York: JP Morgan Chase and Co. Institute.

Kampouri, E. 2022. Gendering platform research: Theoretical and methodological considerations. *Work Organisation, Labour & Globalisation* 16(1): 14–33.

Kasliwal R. 2020. *Gender and the Gig Economy: A Qualitative Study of Gig Platforms for Women Workers*. New Delhi: Observer Research Foundation. ORF Issue Brief May 2020, Issue #359.

Kässi O., Lehdonvirta V. and Stephany F. 2021. How many online workers are there in the world? A data-driven assessment. *Open Research Europe* 1: 53 (May 19, 2021).

Kessler S. 2018. *Gigged: The Gig Economy, the End of the Job and the Future of Work*. London: Penguine Random House.

Krieger-Boden C. and Sorgner A. 2018. Labor market opportunities for women in the digital age. *Economics* 12(28): 1–8.

Kwan H. 2022. Gendered precarious employment in China's gig economy: exploring women gig drivers' intersectional vulnerabilities and resistances. *Gender & Development* 30(3): 551–573.

Manyika J., Lund S., Bughin J., Robinson K., Mischke J. and Mahajan D. 2016. *Independent Work: Choice, Necessity and the Gig Economy*. San Francisco, CA: McKinsey Global Institute.

McDowell L.M. 2000. Economy, culture, difference and justice. In Cook I., Crouch D., Naylor S. and. Ryan J. (eds.), *Cultural Turns/Geographical Turns: Perspectives on Cultural Geography*. London: Prentice Hall, pp. 182–195.

Micha A., Poggi C. and Pereyra F. 2022. When women enter male-dominated territories in the platform economy: gender inequalities among drivers and riders in Argentina. *Gender & Development* 30(3): 575–600.

Milkman R., Elliott-Negri L., Griesbach, K. and Reich, A., 2021. Gender, class, and the gig economy: the case of platform-based food delivery. *Critical Sociology* 47(3): 357–372.

Nelson J.A. 1992. Gender, metaphor, and the definition of economics. *Economics and Philosophy* 8(1): 103–125.

Rani, U., Gobel, N. and Dhir, R.K. 2022. Experiences of women on online labour platforms: insights from global surveys. In Digital Future Society (ed.), *Global Perspectives on Women, Work, and Digital Labour Platforms*, pp. 13–23. Available at: https://digitalfuturesociety.com/app/uploads/2022/11/Global_Perspectives_on_Women_Work_and_Digital_Labour_Platforms.pdf

Rosenblat A. 2018. *Uberland: How Algorithms Are Rewriting the Rules of Work*. Oakland: University of California Press.

Schoenbaum N. 2016. Gender and the sharing economy. *Fordham Urban Law Journal* 43: 1023–1070.

Scholz T. 2016. *Platform Cooperativism. Challenging the Corporate Sharing Economy*. New York: Rosa Luxemburg Foundation.

Scholz T. 2017. *Uberworked and Underpaid: How Workers Are Disrupting the Digital Economy*. Cambridge: Polity Press.

Slaughter A.M. 2015. The gig economy can actually be great for women. *WIRED*. 23 October 2015.

Slaughter A.M. 2016. *Unfinished Business: Women, Men, Work, Family*. London: Oneworld Publications.

Stanford J. 2017. The resurgence of gig work: historical and theoretical perspectives. *The Economic and Labour Relations Review* 28(3): 382–401.

Stringhi E. 2022. Addressing gendered affordances of the platform economy: the case of UpWork. *Internet Policy Review* 11(1): 1–28.

Tubaro P., Coville M., Le Ludec C. and Casilli A.A. 2022. Hidden inequalities: the gendered labour of women on micro-tasking platforms. *Internet Policy Review* 11(1): 1–26.

UNI 2019. *Connective Action: Digital Tools for Trade Unions*. Geneva: Union Network International.

van Doorn N. 2017. Platform labor: on the gendered and racialized exploitation of low-income service work in the 'on-demand' economy. *Information, Communication and Society* 20(6): 898–914.

van Doorn N. 2022. Platform capitalism's social contract. *Internet Policy Review* 11(1): 1–18.

van Doorn N. and Badger A. 2020. Platform capitalism's hidden abode: producing data assets in the gig economy. *Antipode* 52(5): 1475–1495.

Varanasi R.A., Siddarth D., Seshadri V., Bali K. and Vashistha A. 2022, April. Feeling proud, feeling embarrassed: experiences of low-income women with crowd work. *Proceedings of the 2022 CHI Conference on Human Factors in Computing Systems*, New Orleans. pp. 1–18. Available at: https://doi.org/10.1145/3491102.3501834

Wallis M. 2021. Digital labour and social reproduction–crowdwork in Germany and Romania. *Spheres: Journal for Digital Cultures* 6: 1–14.

Wood A.J., Lehdonvirta V. and Graham M. 2018. Workers of the Internet unite? Online freelancer organisation among remote gig economy workers in six Asian and African countries. *New Technology, Work and Employment* 33(2): 95–112.

Woodcock J. and Graham M. 2019. *The Gig Economy: A Critical Introduction*. Cambridge: Polity.

World Bank Group, 2016. *World Development Report 2016: Digital Dividends*. Chicago: World Bank Publications.

Zulfiyan A. 2020. Legal protection for women drivers in the gig economy: evidence from Tulungagung, East Java. *Brawijaya Law Journal* 7(2): 213–224.

Recommendations for Further Reading

Altenried M. 2022. *The Digital Factory: The Human Labor of Automation*. Chicago, IL: University of Chicago Press.

James A. 2022. Women in the gig economy: feminising 'digital labour'. *Work in the Global Economy* 2(1): 2–26.

Kwan H. 2022. Gendered precarious employment in China's gig economy: exploring women gig drivers' intersectional vulnerabilities and resistances. *Gender & Development* 30(3): 551–573.
Rosenblat A. 2018. *Uberland: How Algorithms Are Rewriting the Rules of Work.* Oakland: University of California Press.
van Doorn N. 2017. Platform labor: on the gendered and racialized exploitation of low-income service work in the 'on-demand' economy. *Information, Communication and Society* 20(6): 898–914.

9

NON-LABOUR PLATFORMS AND THEIR EFFECTS ON WORK IN SPECIFIC SECTORS

A Major Gap in Recent Research on Work and Employment[1]

David Hesmondhalgh and Charles Umney

Introduction

Digital platforms have become pervasive across many areas of society, including work and employment. Researchers on work and labour have responded by devoting much attention specifically to "labour platforms"; be these remote ones organising clickwork, that is relatively small jobs carried out at-a-distance on a freelance basis (such as Amazon Mechanical Turk) or geographically tethered ones providing in-person services (such as Uber or Deliveroo). However, the term "platform" covers a vast array of phenomena, including the following:

- Operating system platforms for smartphones and other connected devices, like Android and iOS
- Payment platforms like PayPal
- Crowdfunding platforms like Kickstarter
- Accommodation platforms like Airbnb
- Consumer rating platforms like TripAdvisor and Yelp
- Social media platforms like Facebook, Twitter or Weibo
- Games hardware platforms like PlayStation
- Video, audio and games streaming platforms like Netflix or Spotify

While it is understandable that scholars of work prioritise study of labour platforms specifically, other platforms also have important implications for working lives. Here, we challenge researchers on work to reflect more expansively on the range of interlinked phenomena that are often (simplistically) described as the "platform economy". We prioritise looking beyond "labour platforms"; here denoting any platform which permits "individuals, families or companies in need of a service to hire a worker who is willing to offer the relevant activity" (Aloisi and De Stefano, 2018: 10). Non-labour platforms (i.e. any digital platform not meeting this definition) often have profound implications for labour, which have not attracted sufficient attention in research on work. Such research, while it has extensively investigated the conditions facing platform workers on labour

DOI: 10.4324/9781003327561-13

platforms, may also need to focus more on how *non-platform work* is being impacted by, and interacts with, *non-labour platforms*. We seek to catalyse this discussion.

We argue, against the monolithic idea of the "platform economy", that the impacts of platforms are pluralistic and variegated. We are sceptical of supposed macro-level shifts towards "platformisation" or "platform capitalism", and advocate a sharper focus on the logic of specific industrial contexts. Digital platforms have particular applications in particular sectors, with different consequences. This variation is obscured partly by platform economy narratives, but also the narrow interest in labour platforms among researchers of work. Hence we observe a gap between two literatures: the literature on digital platforms documents the broad range of platforms but has little to say about work; research on work and employment (one would hope) has much to say about work, but only engages with a small slice of the platform world.

By addressing these gaps, we add our voices to emerging scholarship which has cast a critical eye over current research on labour platforms. Recent interventions have argued that labour platforms have been over-studied by scholars of work (Azzellini et al., 2022b); and also that this over-focus has gone hand-in-hand with a narrow conceptual repertoire concentrated overwhelmingly on the limiting theme of "algorithmic control" (Joyce et al., 2023). Our argument, that the empirical focus of studies of platforms and work has been too limited and requires expansion, builds further on these interventions.

Our chapter proceeds as follows. First, we examine critically the concept of platforms and underline its heterogeneity, arguing research on work should examine a wider range of the phenomena than currently included in the platform concept. We propose that the application of platforms should be understood through a closer focus on sectoral context, questioning the narrative of a monolithic shift. Next, we support this claim by reviewing literature on two industries: retail and hospitality work and the cultural and creative industries (CCIs). In both cases, non-labour platforms have a significant impact, but in sector-specific ways; though particular platform mechanisms may indeed permeate across sectors. Thus, we contribute to understanding the implications of digital platforms as a whole for people's ability to live flourishing lives in and through their work. How are digital platforms tied to old and new forms of exploitation, alienation, and control in work, and how might they enable old and new forms of autonomy, independence and resistance? These questions will often be most effectively addressed by engaging with the digital platforms most apparent in to particular sectors, rather than (overly broad) analyses of "platform capitalism", or an (overly narrow) focus specifically on labour platforms.

Neglect of Work in Platform Research

Partly, this chapter is motivated by some reflections based on our own experiences in Higher Education. Particularly as educators, we have observed quite concretely the role of platforms in our industry. However, it is notable that the most impactful platforms, which have had substantial implications for Higher Education workers, are not "labour platforms".

IT corporations have been heavily involved in education for many years, and various digital technologies and software systems have long been present in schools. But as van Dijck et al. (2018) point out, their presence has now gone far beyond the sale of hardware and software to a "next generation of data-driven, platform-based tool sets", covering "content production and distribution, student performance tracking, class communication, and administrative organization" (119). van Dijck et al. recognise the potential for these technologies to make education "more efficient, accessible, and affordable" (122) but highlight an intensification of managerialism and teacher surveillance, and an erosion of fundamental principles of academic autonomy and independence.

The implications of new educational platforms for teachers as workers are explored by Selwyn (2019) in a study of two Australian high schools. Selwyn shows how the extensive use of a school management system, Compass, brought various advantages, in terms of consistency, error reduction and communication between staff. But it also brought significant standardisation, including widespread use of cut-and-paste in assessment of students and their work. The availability of standardised lesson plans made preparation less intense, but diminished teacher creativity (with Compass, "there's no creativity whatsoever", one teacher observed). The platform also intensified monitoring or surveillance of teacher performance and, as is familiar from various other studies of the spread of digital technologies via the smartphone and laptops, to an intensification of student work and "presence bleed" (Gregg, 2014) beyond established working hours, and a severe difficulty in disengaging from work. Above and beyond teacher experience, van Dijck et al. argue that platformisation of education has catalysed a commodification of education, on the basis of "the processing of learning data by large data hubs that render big data streams monetizable and potentially profitable" (121). Detailed data about the learning habits of young people is potentially gold for advertisers. We observe that the debate on platforms in the sociology of work, given its focus on a relatively narrow set of labour platforms, is unable to tell us a great deal about these developments. Arguably, these developments are closely embedded in sectoral context, meaning the wider "platform economy" narrative is also of limited utility.

These limitations alerted us to the need for a wider view on the relationship between platforms and work, including a reflection on the historical evolution of "platform" terminology. From around the 1980s, the term platform, based on its original meaning of a raised surface on which people or things are placed, began to be used in computing, referring to "an infrastructure that supports the design and use of particular computing applications", e.g. "computer hardware, operating systems, gaming devices, mobile devices or digital disc formats" (Gillespie, 2010: 349). So the 1980s saw "platform wars" between IBM's personal computer (PC) and Apple's Macintosh (Gillespie, 2010: 349). Gradually, the term also began to refer more specifically to "online environments that allow users to design and deploy applications they design or that are offered by third parties" (Gillespie, 2010: 349), like eBay, which from 2000, made public its API (Application Programming Interface), allowing other businesses to gain detailed insights about eBay's users. The idea of "open APIs" spread, and Facebook made its API open in 2009, spreading the term further, so that "platform" is now often used to mean something as general as "a service made available via computers". While the term is unlikely to disappear any time soon, the diversity of phenomena described as platforms raises concerns over the term's validity and coherence.

Nevertheless, a meaningful core remains, and some analysts have sought to go beyond casual and clumsy uses. "At the most general level", Srnicek writes, platforms are "digital infrastructures that enable two or more groups to interact", positioning themselves as intermediaries, and providing tools enabling users to build their own products, services and marketplaces (Srnicek, 2017: 43). van Dijck et al. (2018: 4) provide a fuller delineation: a platform is "a programmable digital architecture … designed to organize interactions between users… geared toward the systematic collection, algorithmic processing, circulation, and monetization of user data". They identify key elements constituting any platform's anatomy, arguing platforms are fuelled by *data*; are automated and organised through *algorithms, interfaces* and *protocols* which shape *usage* in particular ways; are characterised by certain *ownership* relations; adopt certain *business models* and govern usage through *user agreements*.

Platforms have sometimes been welcomed as ways of achieving greater business efficiency (McAfee and Brynjolfsson, 2017). Other writers hail the datafication that is crucial to their operations as having enormous potential for business, science and culture (Mayer-Schönberger and Cukier, 2013). However, research also identifies various dangers of digital platforms, and of associated processes such as datafication and the extensive use of recommendation algorithms.

Some of these critical writers have contextualised these developments within a wider narrative of capitalist transformation. The catchy title of Srnicek's (2017) *Platform Capitalism* has been widely cited. However, its suggestive analysis has rarely been scrutinised, although some recent contributions in studies of work and employment have sought to more explicitly critique the platform capitalism narrative (Azzellini et al., 2022b; Joyce et al., 2023). Srnicek saw the rise of platform companies as a response by capitalists to the economic crises afflicting rich countries from the 1970s onwards. For Srnicek, platforms developed as ways for capitalist firms to take advantage of new opportunities for profit afforded by data, and thereby to become the means by which other businesses sought to gain competitive advantage. Similarly, though in more detail, Zuboff (2018) argued that Google played a crucial role in bringing together various technologies to use data to develop personalised advertising, thus generating "click throughs" whereby viewers of an advertisement (or other online content) opt by clicking to purchase a product or service or to learn more about it, or undertake some other interaction, thereby providing data that the company might, in turn, use for future product development. For Zuboff, this enabled a new type of capitalism (with Google playing an equivalent role to Ford's transformation of manufacturing systems in the twentieth century) based on the collection and analysis of massive amounts of user data, with significant implications for surveillance by corporations and states.

Such research makes only passing reference to implications for workers. Equally importantly, the admirable macro-historical scope of these sources leaves little room for analysing how platforms are embedded and used in particular sectors. Research undertaking this humbler sociological strategy has mainly developed within media, communication and information studies, where analyses of social media platforms like Facebook and Twitter have explored "the construction of these digital spaces, user activities on them, and the political economy of data within them" (Ajunwa and Greene, 2019: 63). van Dijck et al. (2018: 101), for example, see mechanisms of datafication, commodification and selection as essential to how platforms translate information into value, and show these mechanisms at work across many sectors, including news, urban transport, healthcare and health research, and education. In health, for example, they highlight the multiplication of platforms, from personal fitness apps to medical apps for self-diagnosis, symptom monitoring and illness management. These platforms collect abundant data given freely by users and purport to offer public health benefits by doing so (see also Chamakiotis et al., 2021). van Dijck et al. also stress the importance of understanding any one platform as part of an ecosystem of related platforms rather than seeing platforms as operating autonomously from each other.

van Dijck et al.'s normative focus is on how digital platforms favour private convenience and corporate power over the common good – focusing not only on privacy, safety and consumer protection concerns (values that do receive abundant if inconsistent attention from within the tech world behind platforms), but also "fairness, equality, solidarity, accountability, transparency and democratic control" (van Dijck et al., 2018: 3). They and other critical analysts of digital platforms have little to say about platforms' implications for workers. Some media, communication and information research *has* paid attention to implications of digital platforms for workers, but mainly in terms of one important but particular group of platforms, social media, which we discuss further below. Next, however, we discuss scholarship specifically focused on work and employment, considering how platforms figure in this literature.

Neglect of Platforms in Research on Work

It may seem counterintuitive to suggest that scholars focused on work have neglected platforms, since there has been huge growth in studies of labour platforms and platform work. At sociology of work conferences, personal experience suggests that sessions on platform work are often among the most well-attended. However, there is growing recognition that this scholarship is often rather narrow, being strongly concentrated on a rather specific set of labour platforms (what might be termed the Uber or Deliveroo models of platform-mediated in-person service work) (Azzellini et al., 2022b; Joyce et al., 2023).

To this emerging critique of scholarship on platform work, we add another line of argument: platforms are neglected insofar as this narrow focus on labour platforms overshadows study of non-labour platforms. To study *platform workers*, we need to focus on labour platforms. However, to study the wider category of *non-platform workers whose jobs are affected by platforms*, a focus on labour platforms is inadequate.

We should clarify that our discussion is distinct from the issue of how digitalisation more broadly is transforming work and employment (Neufeind et al., 2018; Howcroft and Taylor, 2014), since platforms represent a particular (though currently crucial) manifestation of digitalisation. We are also less concerned with the labour undertaken behind certain prominent platforms (Gray and Suri, 2019), though this is clearly important too.

Research on work and labour has extensively typologised platforms and forms of platform work. Typically, however, these typologies are divisions *within* an implicit or explicit broader category of the "labour platform". In many cases, the starting point is distinguishing between platforms enabling people to buy and sell labour, and other kinds of platform, where it is then assumed that the former is primarily or even exclusively relevant (Aloisi and De Stefano, 2018; Ilsøe and Larsen, 2020; Vallas and Schor, 2020).

Once the labour platform is singled out and other platforms sidelined, the next step for researchers on work and labour is often to distinguish where platforms involve work done online, from cases where platforms involve arranging offline services. Aloisi and De Stefano (2018), for example, distinguish between online "crowdsourcing" platforms and, platforms enabling on-demand in-person services. Wood and Lehdonvirta (2019) similarly distinguish between the "offline service gig economy" (mainly food delivery ride-sharing) and the "remote gig economy" (e.g. clickwork). Schmidt (2017) differentiates between "cloud work" and "gig work": the former corresponding to Wood and Lehdonvirta's "offline service economy" and the latter to their "remote gig economy". Hence a conventional analytical starting point appears to be distinguishing between online and offline types of labour platform.

Further distinctions can be drawn within these types. Schmidt (2017) divides each type into three sub-types. "Cloud work" includes freelancer markets; microtasking crowdwork; and competition based creative crowdwork. "Gig work" includes transport and delivery; household and personal services; and counterintuitively, accommodation (e.g. Airbnb). Howcroft and Bergvall-Kareborn (2020) have a different approach, identifying four sub-types of "crowdwork". These are situated on a 2 × 2 matrix where the axes are worker-initiated versus requester-initiated; and paid work versus "non-paid or speculative work". This method cuts across the remote-online/offline services distinction. Requester-initiated paid work is "online task crowdwork"; requester-initiated non-paid/speculative work is "playbour", where requesters post jobs which people do out of passion (e.g. creating modifications for games), or as part of a competition; worker-initiated paid work involves "asset based services" like Uber, TaskRabbit or Airbnb; worker-initiated speculative work is professional freelancer crowdwork (such as the development of mobile apps or providing photos for iStockphoto). Notably, their third category (worker-initiated paid work) brings together services other authors would tend to separate.

As noted, all these typologies introduce further classificatory divisions into the category of the "labour platform". The latter is the starting point, designating non-labour platforms as of less interest. There are partial exceptions to this. Maffie (2020) encourages scholars of work to distinguish between the "gig" and "sharing" economy. The gig economy largely corresponds with the labour platform, while the sharing economy (e.g. Etsy, where individuals can sell their own craft products) denotes situations where platforms' centralisation of information is less problematic for users, facilitating wider exchange of assets rather than a subordinate labour relationship. Both centralise and organise digital markets, but the latter expands, rather than constrains, user choices. Maffie's work is important in addressing the industrial relations implications of certain types of non-labour platform. However, his contribution remains unusual in this respect. Moreover, we will later highlight less benign characteristics of non-labour platforms. Another case where scholarship on work engages with non-labour platforms is debates about social media usage. These discussions interrogate whether individuals' social media activity can be considered a form of labour from which value is extracted (Hesmondhalgh, 2016; Fumigallie et al., 2018). Nonetheless, such debate remains relatively confined to Marxist debates on value and has not made wider inroads into research on work and labour.

Vallas and Schor (2020) take a slightly different approach, categorising five types of *platform work*, rather than platform model, which includes phenomena outside strictly defined labour platforms:

- technologists and instigators of platforms
- professionals and freelancers who do professional work over platforms such as UpWork and Freelance
- gig workers who provide offline services arranged through a platform
- clickworkers
- those who carry out often-unpaid "aspirational labour", like social media influencers.

Schor and Vallas arrange these types of work into a 2 × 2 matrix, along axes of spatial dispersion and task complexity. The distinctive feature of their account is that rather than examining types of platform, they are identifying types of platform work. This enables them to acknowledge other platforms beyond the labour platform – such as content producers seeking to monetise output over sites like YouTube. However, despite this exception, the focus overall remains on labour platforms and those who work for them.

What points should be taken from this discussion of platform (and platform worker) typologies in research on work, labour and employment? A first comment is that it reveals a strong focus on labour platforms, which is a relatively narrowly defined segment of platforms. From the perspective of researching work, this is a limitation, because studying work on labour platforms is a much narrower research agenda than the effects of platforms on work. Hence, a second comment is that while research on work and platforms tells us much about *different types of platform* and *different types of platform work*, it is unable to provide a more complex picture of the multifaceted role of platforms, particularly how their role is variably embedded in different sectoral contexts. The focus on the labour platform risks overlooking other types of platforms which are reshaping work, and the way their effects vary depending on context.

To reiterate, the deficiencies of the wider platform literature include not only its neglect of work, but its need for a more sociological focus on sectoral context, in contrast to broader platform economy narratives. Next, we will look at two sectors (retail/hospitality and CCIs), examining their specificities, to show the importance of non-labour platforms among working populations way beyond platform workers themselves.

Platform Effects in Different Sectors

In this section, we develop our earlier claim that other kinds of platforms often have as much relevance for work and employment as labour platforms, having major implications for working conditions in some sectors. To properly address implications of non-labour platforms for work, a detailed sectoral focus is required, since platforms reshape sectors in specific ways that cannot be grasped with a wider focus on the platform economy (Azzellini et al., 2022a). We examine two sectors to make this point: frontline service work in retail and hospitality; and the cultural and creative industries.

Frontline Service Work in Retail and Hospitality

At the broadest level, the transition from bricks-and-mortar retail to online retailers, most notably Amazon, is well-documented. Moreover, the seismic implications of the Amazon model for industrial relations are attracting a much wider literature, particularly concerned with authoritarian forms of work organisation in the warehousing sector (Delfanti, 2021), and with casualisation and work intensification in distribution and delivery work (Moore and Newsome, 2018).

However, other forms of retail and customer service work are also being reshaped by platforms, including by non-labour platforms which are less well-documented in research on work and labour. An important example is the implications of customer review platforms such as TripAdvisor and Yelp. While customer-driven ratings systems have received much attention from scholars of work and labour, the focus has been on labour platforms that have their own in-house customer ratings systems, such as Uber's star ratings and similar (Rosenblat et al., 2017; Prassl and Risak, 2015). It has also been examined among "Uberised" legal professionals who offer services over platforms (Yao, 2020) and in relation to online crowdwork platforms (Schörpf et al., 2017). However, these are all cases of platform enterprises using their own rating systems to discipline platform workers. TripAdvisor and Yelp differ, because they are not integrated into labour platforms. They are separate platforms where users can submit reviews of third party businesses. In many cases, these are bricks-and-mortar businesses, meaning that platformisation here has implications for management and workers who, ostensibly, are completely separate from "the platform economy" (Paul, 2018; Sperber, 2014). So the issue here is not platform labour firms disciplining platform workers, but non-labour platforms disciplining non-platform workers. Intriguingly, much of the literature examining these implications emanates from other fields dealing only tangentially with work and labour issues (Bradley et al., 2015; Jeacle and Carter, 2011; Sahin et al., 2017; Prayag et al., 2018; Ranard et al., 2016).

These types of platform are increasingly relevant for working conditions and the employment relationship in retail and hospitality work. Local retailers and small-scale hospitality businesses are increasingly dependent on sites like Yelp. Evidence from the US restaurant sector shows that their profitability appears connected to reviews on platforms, with favourable Yelp reviews enabling independent restaurants to develop a profile, even re-gaining market share against chains (Luca, 2016).

Moreover, evidence also reveals that one of the most important influences on the feedback provided on consumer review platforms is customer perceptions of staff performance. Perceived deficiencies in staff performance are one of the most frequent causes of negative TripAdvisor feedback, and managers have increasingly implemented "recovery plans" (such as training or performance management and warnings) in response (Sahin et al., 2017). Importantly, while consumer review platforms are most obviously and immediately applicable to retail and hospitality work, consumer ratings platforms have sought to extend their influence. For instance, Ranard et al. (2016) study Yelp's influence on frontline healthcare work.

Hence, there are numerous implications of consumer ratings platforms of relevance to scholarship on work and labour. First, they may cause work intensification and increased emotional strain. Negative ratings may have a deep affective impact both on small business owners and on staff within them (Bradley et al., 2015; Prayag et al., 2018). Bradley et al. describe this as a particularly insidious threat to well-being which evades containment within designated working hours. While, of course, retail workers have long had to deal with complaints, the difference is that review-based platforms facilitate and publicise grievances and criticisms. Responding to such criticism is not only labour-intensive, it may also, as Bradley et al. (2015) point out, involve the kind of "emotional dissonance" discussed by Hochschild (1983) in her famous study of the emotional labour of (mainly female) flight attendants. Notably, these studies of the affective and well-being-related consequences of consumer review platforms for workers stem from hospitality and tourism management, rather than critical scholarship on work and labour.

Second, consumer review platforms constitute an additional third party "stick" with which workers can be threatened. Sperber (2014: 69), one of the few critical scholars of labour to study consumer review platforms, writes:

> Yelp reviews are frequently read by restaurant owners and have been invoked to discipline, and even fire, restaurant employees who have been criticized on the site. In this way, Yelp contributors not only enrich Yelp but function as unpaid managers, or "secret shoppers," for the restaurant industry.

Thus they might act as a kind of free, outsourced provider of labour discipline. Sperber argues that these sites are inherently dangerous for workers since criticism voiced on them tends to focus on what is immediately visible, and ignores less obvious power structures and imbalances:

> For instance, a long wait for one's lunch is more easily blamed on the server, not on ownership's decision to reduce the afternoon staff, and thus lower costs by giving servers more work than they can handle… Similarly, it is easier to blame a disappointing meal on the cook, not the cook's accelerating workload that produces burnt omelets or the dubious ingredients purchased by a parsimonious owner. In short, online consumer criticism encourages people to critique merely what is apparent, obfuscating the less visible societal and historic relations undergirding society's effects.
>
> (Sperber, 2014: 70–71)

Sperber also notes that workers have little recourse against criticisms voiced over consumer review platforms. They are also vulnerable to customer biases which are less constrained by institutional and legal protections (Paul, 2018). Hence, while the danger of customer bias is well-documented in relation to labour platforms themselves (Rosenblat et al., 2017), the threat of the same problem affecting non-platform work is potentially more diffuse and extensive, but less well-understood.

Finally, it is possible that consumer review platforms may qualitatively alter important aspects of the labour process itself. This is potentially a profound process requiring detailed investigation, which is so far lacking among scholars of work and labour. While this effect may be pronounced in retail and frontline service sector work, the most detailed treatments of it emerge once again from other fields. For instance, Chen (2018), a health economist, investigates the consequences of Yelp reviews on doctors' performance. Chen asks whether the need for favourable reviews leads to perverse incentives and short-termism; for instance, accelerating treatment to impress patients, to the detriment of clinical quality. Although Chen's study of US clinicians rejects this hypothesis, suggesting a positive correlation between clinical quality, measured by other indicators, and Yelp reviews, we cannot exclude that these dynamics may have traction in other circumstances. However, at this stage scholars of work and labour can only speculate on this question. A broader theoretical consideration here relates to the assessment of value and expertise. Jeacle and Carter (2011), in an accounting journal, reflect on the question of how trust is created in industries, arguing that it has "come increasingly to be placed in lay opinion over expert knowledge" (307). This issue is potentially of deep and multifaceted interest for scholars of work and labour, particularly as consumer ratings platforms are extending their influence. What does it mean when the "quality" of work is assessed by laypeople whose understanding of a job stems from their role as customers? Does this undermine workers' ability to do their work as they see fit, or in line with their professional and ethical frameworks, or is this threat overstated? We currently have little systematic answer.

We can therefore see how platforms which have thrived in specific industries (in this case retail and service/hospitality work) have wider implications, including for theory, and that these implications remain poorly understood in the absence of closer scrutiny of the sectoral contexts in which specific platform technologies may become embedded. Concepts such as platformisation and the platform economy are too broad to capture these dynamics, and the focus on labour platforms is too narrow.

Cultural and Creative Industries

Another sector where non-labour platforms are affecting working conditions is the CCIs.[2] When studying work in the CCIs, the need for an approach rooted in a sociological understanding of sectoral context is underlined, because in doing so we quickly see the dangers of over-focusing on labour platforms, and that non-labour platforms often have a bigger impact on the nature of work. Indeed, in some parts of the CCIs, such as live music, evidence suggests that more authentic "labour platforms" that organise offline service provision remain stunted and ineffectual (Azzellini et al., 2022a; Greer and Umney, 2022).

CCI labour markets are notoriously precarious, and it is notable that the very term "gig economy" derives from a major CCI, the live music industry. Numerous studies confirm that work is often carried out on a project basis, with high levels of freelance work, with many workers compelled to hold multiple jobs (Towse, 1992). Where more secure work is available, it is often in less prestigious and creative sectors (e.g. public relations rather than journalism). Yet despite the exploitative conditions they potentially face, there has long been an over-supply of willing workers (Miege, 1989), and analysts have sought to explain this, often via young workers' (often unrealistic) hopes that they will be able to achieve high levels of autonomy and self-realisation through creative labour (Menger, 1999). Competition for salaried, secure and unionised positions is ferociously intense, often favouring those with high levels of economic and cultural capital (O'Brien and Oakley, 2015). This contributes to elevated class, gender and racial inequality and to occupational segregation, with less powerful groups taking less prestigious roles (Hesmondhalgh and Baker, 2015; Hesmondhalgh, 2019).

The project-based, insecure nature of many cultural jobs has encouraged the growth of sector-specific cultural labour platforms. However, in some cases, sociological and organisational aspects of sectors have stunted the growth of labour platforms, keeping them a relatively marginal presence. In live music, for example, developers of platforms that seek to co-ordinate bookings have not been able to displace the mix of offline and online arrangements that currently organise the higher value market segments of the live music economy (Azzellini et al., 2022a).

Although many cultural workers make use of general labour and work-related platforms (such as LinkedIn), the more significant developments for them have been new digital platforms that have changed how distribution operates, with huge implications for labour markets and potentially for working conditions. By distribution, we mean the way in which cultural products are matched with audiences: often acknowledged as the locus of power and profit in the CCIs (Garnham, 1990: 161). The best-known examples of digital cultural platforms exercising such forces of change are famous names. In the realm of video, including the vast industries of television and film, YouTube, Netflix, Amazon Prime Video, Apple TV+ and other platforms have transformed the way in which many people consume culture – but they are also shifting labour markets and labour conditions. YouTube is perhaps the most striking example, as it has given rise to entire new sub-sectors of production, and generates payments for vast numbers of creators. While it established itself as a site for amateurs, and it is still used to upload amateur content, it also hosts vast amounts of older and more recent content produced by media companies, as professional content produced by small groups of content makers (occasionally lone producers), usually known within the industry as "creators". An important way in which content is presented is via "channels". These are not akin to traditional broadcast channels, which presented television live in a linear flow, and were run by powerful commercial or public service networks. Instead, they are entities to which users subscribe by simply clicking on a button, so that they will receive updates, notifications and recommendations associated with that channel. Many creators work directly with YouTube via its "partner programme", which offers a cut of the revenues generated by YouTube's advertising. A new set of intermediaries has arisen around these channels, called "multi-channel networks", which offer services to creators in return for a cut of income (Lobato, 2016; Vonderau 2016).

The number of creators making a living from these sources is unclear. There are currently around two million creators in YouTube's partner programme, which is accessible only to creators (which includes companies as well as individuals) who achieve more than a thousand subscribers and 4,000 watch-hours. Income is concentrated among the biggest stars, as with previous cultural labour markets, and few creators are likely to earn a sustainable living from YouTube, or even from YouTube plus other activities such as merchandise sales. Nevertheless, YouTube represents a remarkable expansion of the ability of cultural workers to find audiences and income for their cultural productions. This is nothing like the kind of democratising participation hailed by early commentators on "user-generated content". Instead a new industry has arisen not only of creators but also of intermediaries servicing them via marketing and publicity deals and know-how. Cunningham and Craig (2019: 5) make the following claim:

> It would be little overstatement to claim that these dynamics are a huge experiment in seeking to convert vernacular or informal creativity into talent and content increasingly attractive to advertisers, brands, talent agencies, studios and venture-capital (VC) investors on a near global scale.

Yet this is also likely to increase dynamics of "reluctant entrepreneurship" (Haynes and Marshall, 2018), whereby creators who are committed to notions of cultural autonomy are compelled to undertake self-promotional activities, downplaying the cultural aspects of their work at the expense of the economic. It is these cultural aspects that tend to offer CCI workers opportunities for the self-expression and self-realisation that many such workers value highly.

Another example of how non-labour platforms are transforming work in the CCIs is provided by music streaming platforms (Lal et al., 2023). Spotify and Apple are (outside China) the major players in terms of revenues, because of their substantial subscription revenues. Along with YouTube (which has an increasingly popular subscription version), Amazon and others, they have brought about a partial recovery of the recording industry, devastated by the collapse of CD sales in the face of easy, "free" downloading from the early 2000s onwards (Sun, 2018). It is easy and cheap for musicians and intermediaries to upload content to music streaming platforms. However, it is very difficult to make a sustainable living from music, leading to considerable protest from musicians, fans and media commentators, many of whom blame the music streaming platforms for musicians' plight (Marshall, 2015; Hesmondhalgh et al., 2021). Much content on these platforms gets zero plays, and the vast majority get very few. Much of it is old. More successful recordings tend to be owned by the three large corporations or sizeable independents, who pay musicians a percentage based on contracts, meaning that these rights-owners are arguably as much to blame as the platforms if musicians are not paid sufficiently. Yet it is undoubtedly true that more musicians are earning money from music than ever before, even if only a tiny proportion make a sustainable living from recorded music alone (Hesmondhalgh, 2021). Moreover, it seems unlikely that significant numbers of musicians were able to make sustainable incomes from recorded music, even when CDs were generating high levels of income in the 1980s and 1990s. A vast amount of that money went to the rights-owners, and royalty rates were (even) lower back then.

What both YouTube and the music streaming platforms have done is to bring the vast sector of willing, aspiring and informal workers, who used to exist "outside" the formal industry where revenues were generated by copyright, *inside* that system, where their products become part of vast datafied systems. This is an unprecedented capture of the "reservoirs" (Miege, 1989) of creative labour that have long characterised CCIs. Moreover, the tech corporations that run the platforms have no responsibility for the welfare of workers. To be sure, the rights-holders who contract musicians for recording and songwriting have outsize power over most musicians, and there is a long history of dubious relations, often exploitative in nature (Stahl, 2012). However, the music streaming platforms produce no music of their own. Unlike video streaming platforms, they do not even commission content from production companies; they merely licence content from record companies.

Platforms such as YouTube and Spotify, then, are considerably more important than labour allocation platforms in the CCIs for understanding the conditions facing cultural workers. In some senses, they might even be thought of as the real labour platforms for the CCI sector. They are therefore indicative of what is missed in terms of the reconfiguration of working life when sector-specific platforms, seemingly unrelated to labour, are not considered as a central part of labour conditions in the platform era.

Conclusions and Implications for Future Research

This chapter began by identifying shortcomings in our understanding of the effects of platforms on work. While scholarship on platforms neglects questions of work (van Dijck et al., 2018; Srnicek, 2017), scholarship on work tends to focus on a relatively narrow range of platforms: specifically labour platforms, and their workers (the latter being what is normally meant by "platform workers"). Indeed, while there is much attention given to typologising platforms, these attempts often take the labour platform as the starting point (Aloisi and De Stefano, 2018; Wood and Lehdonvirta, 2019; Schmidt, 2017). We have, by contrast, shifted focus to the relationship between non-labour platforms and non-platform labour. While scholars of work and employment have tentatively started to engage with non-labour platforms, as in Maffie's (2020) application of industrial relations frames to the "sharing economy", there have been relatively few systematic engagements with this issue.

The wider question of the effects of platforms on work has received less interest than the more specific issue of labour platforms and platform workers. We also argued that to properly investigate this question, a focus on individual sectors is required. *Contra* notions of "platformisation" and "platform capitalism", we suggest that specific contexts give rise to specific dynamics with regard to the implications of platform technologies within them. These dynamics mean that non-labour platforms play a vital role in reshaping questions of work and employment. They do so in ways which are not easy to generalise beyond specific industrial contexts. The development of independent consumer review platforms is a case in point. While the issue of customer-driven ratings systems is well established in research on work (Yao, 2020; Rosenblat et al., 2017; Schörpf et al., 2017), this emphasises the use of platforms' own systems applied to workers on that platform. In other words, they have been addressed as examples of labour platforms disciplining platform workers. Consumer review platforms like Yelp and Trip Advisor are cases of non-labour platforms disciplining non-platform workers, including in small-scale service and hospitality work, and potentially in professional domains like medicine and accounting. Yet the scholars investigating these potentially more widespread and insidious phenomena are largely from other fields (in this case, such as tourism and hospitality management studies) where questions of work quality and power relations in workplaces are a tangential concern, if of interest at all (Chen, 2018; Jeacle and Carter, 2011; Bradley et al., 2015). Likewise, in the CCIs, the platforms with the biggest implications for questions of work and labour *are not labour platforms*. They are platforms which define and re-engineer the way CCI outputs are circulated and in so doing alter the relationships between the "reservoir" of potential cultural workers, and their audiences or users (some of them subscribers, some of them purchasers, some of them "paying" for their consumption by being exposed to platform advertising). More creators can share their work, but their activities and relationships become prone to datafied surveillance, and the general precariousness and insecurity of cultural work are further entrenched.

Hence in each of these cases, we argued that, to understand changes in the nature of working life, non-labour platforms were more important than labour platforms. However, the kinds of non-labour platforms that mattered were radically different and could not be fit into a wider narrative of the platform economy, or "platform capitalism". This suggests the need for scholars of work and labour to be more sceptical of narrative-building about the transitions of the platform economy. To some degree, this chimes with recent contributions underlining the limits to platformisation and expressing scepticism over the prevalence of labour platforms and platform work (Azzellini et al., 2022b; Greer and Umney, 2022; Fleming et al., 2019). However, while we share these contributions' scepticism about the labour platform as a pre-eminent focus on scholarship on work and employment, we differ insofar as we want to draw attention to the importance of non-labour platforms. These comments expand Azzellini et al.'s (2022a) argument, which stresses the organisational and sociological characteristics of individual sectors in shaping platform trajectories.

Ultimately, then, our chapter is a two-pronged call, on the one hand for a wider focus on the full spectrum of phenomena grouped under the "platform" concept, and on the other, for a more defined focus on the way different aspects of these phenomena play out within specific sectors.

It will still of course be necessary for critical analysis to investigate general processes of digitalisation and platformisation. But only by undertaking this more specific work will such analysis be able to form a comprehensive picture of the effects of those processes on a wide range of workers in a way that would enrich understanding of the future of work.

Notes

1 Our work on this chapter was made possible by The UK Economic and Social Research Council's Digital Futures at Work Research Centre, grant number ES/S012532/1.

2 The CCI terminology is contested, partly because of the very extensive definition adopted by the UK government in its "mapping documents" of the turn of the century, which sought to provide a way of measuring the size of the sector, its contribution to GVA and other measures, and its rapid growth (O'Connor, 2010). We focus here on music, film and television as examples, and follow the increasingly common practice of avoiding naming controversies by referring to cultural and creative industries (CCI), rather than either cultural industries or creative industries.

References

Ajunwa I, Greene D (2019) Platforms at work: Automated hiring platforms and other new intermediaries in the organization of work. In SP Vallas, and A Kovalainen, (eds). *Work and Labor in the Digital Age*. Bingley: Emerald, pp. 61–91.

Aloisi V, De Stefano A (2018) *European Legal Framework for 'Digital Labour Platforms'*. Luxembourg: European Commission. https://publications.jrc.ec.europa.eu/repository/handle/JRC112243

Azzellini D, Greer I, Umney C (2022a) Why isn't there an Uber for live music? The digitalisation of intermediaries and the limits of the platform economy. *New Technology, Work and Employment*, 37(1), 1–23.

Azzellini D, Greer I, Umney C (2022b) Why platform capitalism is not the future of work. *Work in the Global Economy*, 2(2), 272–289.

Bradley GL, Sparks BA, Weber K (2015) The stress of anonymous online reviews: A conceptual model and research agenda. *International Journal of Contemporary Hospitality Management*, 27(5), 739–755.

Chamakiotis P, Petrakaki D, Panteli N (2021) Social value creation through digital activism in an online health community. *Information Systems Journal*, 31(1), 94–119.

Chen Y (2018). User-generated physician ratings—evidence from Yelp. https://www. Softwareadvice.Com/resources/how-patients-use.

Cunningham S, Craig D (2019) *Social Media Entertainment*. New York: NYU Press.

Delfanti A (2021) Machinic dispossession and augmented despotism: Digital work in an Amazon warehouse. *New Media & Society*, 23(1), 39–55.

Fleming P, Rhodes C, Yu KH (2019) On why Uber has not taken over the world. *Economy and Society*, 48(4), 488–509.

Fumigalli L, Lucarelli S, Musolino E, Rocchi G (2018) Digital labour in the platform economy: The case of Facebook. *Sustainability*, 10(6), 1757–1772.

Garnham N (1990) *Capitalism and Communication*. London: Sage.

Gillespie T (2010) The politics of 'platforms'. *New Media & Society*, 12(3), 347–364.

Gray ML, Suri S (2019) *Ghost Work: How to Stop Silicon Valley from Building a New Global Underclass*. London: HMH.

Greer I, Umney C (2022) *Marketization: How Capitalist Exchange Disciplines Workers and Subverts Democracy*. London: Bloomsbury.

Gregg M (2014) Presence bleed: Performing professionalism online. In Banks M, Gill R, Taylor S (eds) *Theorizing Cultural Work*. Abingdon: Routledge, pp. 136–148.

Haynes J, Marshall L (2018) Reluctant entrepreneurs: Musicians and entrepreneurship in the 'new' music industry. *British Journal of Sociology*, 69(2), 459–482.

Hesmondhalgh D (2016) Exploitation and media labor. In Maxwell R (ed) *The Routledge Companion to Labor and Media*. Abingdon: Routledge, pp. 30–39.

Hesmondhalgh D (2019) *The Cultural Industries*, 4th Ed., London: Sage.

Hesmondhalgh D (2021) Is music streaming bad for musicians? Problems of argument and evidence. *New Media and Society*, 23(12), 3593–3615.

Hesmondhalgh D, Baker S (2015) Sex, gender, and work segregation in the cultural industries. *Sociological Review*, 63(S1), 23–36.
Hesmondhalgh D, Osborne R, Sun H, Barr K (2021) *Music Creators' Earnings in the Digital Era*. London: Intellectual Property Office.
Hochschild A (1983) *The Managed Heart.* Berkeley: University of California Press.
Howcroft D, Taylor P (2014) 'Plus ca change, plus la meme chose': Researching and theorising the new, new technologies. *New Technology, Work and Employment*, 29(1), 1–8.
Ilsøe A, Larsen TP (2020) Digital platforms at work – champagne or cocktail of risks. *The Impact of the Sharing Economy on Businesses and Society: Digital Transformation and the Rise of Platform Businesses.* pp. 1–20. Abingdon: Routledge.
Jeacle I, Carter C (2011) In TripAdvisor we trust: Rankings, calculative regimes and abstract systems. *Accounting, Organizations and Society*, 36(4–5), 293–309.
Joyce S, Umney C, Whittaker X, Stuart M (2023) New social relations of digital technology and the future of work: Beyond technological determinism. *New Technology, Work and Employment*, 38(2), 145–161.
Lal A, Hesmondhalgh D, Umney C (2023) The changing shape of the Indian recorded music industry in the age of platformisation. *Contemporary South Asia*, 31(2), 291–310.
Lobato R (2016) The cultural logic of digital intermediaries: YouTube multichannel networks. *Convergence*, 22(4), 348–360.
Luca M (2016) Reviews, reputation, and revenue: The case of Yelp.com (March 15). *Harvard Business School NOM Unit Working Paper* (12–016).
Maffie MD (2020) Are we 'sharing' or 'gig-ing'? A classification system for online platforms. *Industrial Relations Journal*, 51(6), 536–555.
Marshall L (2015) 'Let's keep music special. F—Spotify': On-demand streaming and the controversy over artist royalties. *Creative Industries Journal*, 8(2), 177–189.
Mayer-Schönberger V, Cukier K (2013) *Big Data.* New York: Houghton Mifflin Harcourt.
McAfee A, Brynjolfsson E (2017) *Machine, Platform, Crowd: Harnessing our Digital Future*. New York: WW Norton & Company.
Menger PM (1999) Artistic labor markets and careers. *Annual Review of Sociology*, 25(1), 541–574.
Moore S, Newsome K (2018) Paying for free delivery: Dependent self-employment as a measure of precarity in parcel delivery. *Work, Employment and Society*, 32(3), 475–492.
Neufeind M, O'Reilly J, Ranft F (eds) (2018) *Work in the Digital Age: Challenges of the Fourth Industrial Revolution*. Lanham, MD: Rowman & Littlefield.
O'Brien D, Oakley K (2015) *Cultural Value and Inequality: A Critical Literature Review*. Swindon: Arts and Humanities Research Council.
O'Connor J (2010) *The Cultural and Creative Industries*, 2nd Ed., Newcastle upon Tyne: Creativity, Culture and Education.
Paul CS (2018) The architecture of digital labour platforms: Policy recommendations on platform design for worker well-being. *ILO Future of Work Research Paper Series,* 3. Available at: https://www.ilo.org/publications/architecture-digital-labour-platforms-policy-recommendations-platform
Prassl J, Risak M (2015) Uber, taskrabbit, and co.: Platforms as employers – rethinking the legal analysis of crowdwork. *Comparative Labor Law & Policy Journal*, 37, 619.
Prayag G, Hall CM, Wood H (2018) I feel good! Perceptions and emotional responses of Bed & Breakfast providers in New Zealand toward Trip Advisor. *Journal of Hospitality Marketing & Management*, 27(1), 1–20.
Ranard BL, Werner RM, Antanavicius T, Schwartz HA, Smith RJ, Meisel ZF, Asch DA, Ungar LH, Merchant RM (2016) What can Yelp teach us about measuring hospital quality? *Health Affairs (Project Hope)*, 35(4), 697.
Rosenblat A, Levy KE, Barocas S, Hwang T (2017) Discriminating tastes: Uber's customer ratings as vehicles for workplace discrimination. *Policy & Internet*, 9(3), 256–279.
Sahin I, Gulmez M, Kitapci O (2017) E-complaint tracking and online problem-solving strategies in hospitality management: Plumbing the depths of reviews and responses on TripAdvisor. *Journal of Hospitality and Tourism Technology*, 8(3), 372–394.
Schmidt F (2017) *Digital Labour Markets in the Platform Economy* (FES report). https://library.fes.de/pdf-files/wiso/13164.pdf
Schörpf P, Flecker J, Schönauer A, Eichmann H (2017) Triangular love-hate: Management and control in creative crowdworking. *New Technology, Work and Employment*, 32(1), 43–58.
Selwyn N (2019) What's the problem with learning analytics? *Journal of Learning Analytics*, 6(3), 11–19.

Sperber J (2014) Yelp and labor discipline: How the internet works for capitalism. *New Labor Forum*, 23(2), 68–74.
Srnicek N (2017) *Platform Capitalism*. Cambridge: Polity.
Stahl M (2012) *Unfree Masters*. Durham, NC: Duke UP.
Sun H (2018) *Digital Revolution Tamed*. London: Palgrave.
Towse R (1992) The labour markets for artists. *Ricerche economiche*, 1–2, 55–74.
Vallas S, Schor J (2020) What do platforms do? Understanding the gig economy. *Annual Review of Sociology*, 46, 277–294.
van Dijck J, Poell T, De Waal M (2018) *The Platform Society: Public Values in a Connective World*. Oxford: OUP.
Vonderau P (2016) The video bubble: Multichannel networks and the transformation of YouTube. *Convergence*, 22(4), 361–375.
Wood A, Lehdonvirta V (2019) Platform labour and structured antagonism: Understanding the origins of protest in the gig economy (March 5, 2019). Available at SSRN: https://ssrn.com/abstract=3357804 or http://dx.doi.org/10.2139/ssrn.3357804.
Yao Y (2020) Uberizing the legal profession? Lawyer autonomy and status in the digital legal market. *British Journal of Industrial Relations*, 58(3), 483–506.
Zuboff S (2018) *The Age of Surveillance Capitalism*. London: Profile.

Recommendations for Further Reading

Cohen J (2019) *Between Truth and Power: The Legal Constructions of Informational Capitalism*. Oxford: OUP.
Couldry N, Mesias U (2024) *Data Grab: The New Colonialism of Big Tech and How to Fight Back*. London: Penguin.
Gillespie T (2018) *Custodians of the Internet: Platforms, Content Moderation and the Hidden Decisions That Shape Social Media*. New Haven, CT: Yale UP.
van Dijck J, Poell T, de Waal, M (2018) *Thomas Poell and Martijn de Waal, The Platform Society: Public Values in a Connective World*. Oxford: OUP.

10

FIGHTING THE ALGORITHM

The Rise of Activism in the Face of Platform Inequality

Kalie M. Mayberry, Lindsey D. Cameron and Hatim A. Rahman

Introduction

A long history of labour geography, industrial relations, sociology, and organisational research has examined worker-led activism, defined as how individuals "engage in coordinated action to address a societal problem connected to the company they work for" (Briscoe & Gupta 2021: np), in response to shared grievances or systematic inequalities. Unlike individual resistance efforts (Cardinal et al. 2017; Sutton & Rafaeli 1988; Van Maanen & Kunda 1989), activism is collective in nature, building on shared experiences and group solidarity to coordinate actions for a shared impact, and elicit others to join the shared cause. Work in the on-demand economy challenges traditional pathways to activism. To start, on-demand workers are physically distributed, leading to a lack of relationships with co-workers that are typically at the core of coordinating work-based actions (Cameron 2022; Möhlmann & Henfridsson 2019; Tassinari & Maccarrone 2020; Wood et al. 2019). Moreover, much research has documented the power asymmetries and systemic inequalities embedded within the on-demand workplace (Cameron & Rahman 2022; Rosenblat & Stark 2016; Shapiro 2018; Lee et al. 2015). On-demand platforms depend on opaque algorithm "managers" to hire, evaluate, and discipline workers, leaving individuals with little understanding about how decisions are being made and without a clear pathway to address workplace grievances (see Chapter 8).

To date, existing literature on activism by on-demand workers has focused on two extremes: how workers independently try to resist the algorithm, e.g., declining less favourable rides (see Chapter 21) (Jhaver et al. 2018; Cameron & Rahman 2022), or how workers collectively mobilise offline, e.g., coordinated strikes against platform owners, such as the 2016 strike by Foodora cycle couriers in Italy and the 2022 strike by the Independent Workers' Union of Great Britain (Tassinari & Maccarrone 2017; Wood et al. 2019; Smoke 2022). What remains unclear is the relationship between individual attempts to resist and offline collective action towards platform algorithms. Workers' understanding is largely speculative, based on lay understandings and folk tales (DeVito et al. 2018; Christin 2020; Hancock et al. 2017), often leading them to independently form mental models or "algorithmic imaginaries" (Bucher 2017) of how the technology works. This, in turn, raises the question of how shared understanding and collective action in relation to a platform's algorithm can even occur among dispersed workers each with their own unique understandings.

 DOI: 10.4324/9781003327561-14

In some cases, these shared understandings are created through the online networks found on social media, such as Facebook and Reddit, where workers gather around the proverbial "water-cooler" to exchange questions, raise grievances, and solicit council (Rosenblat & Stark 2016; Maffie 2020; Margetts et al. 2015; Tassinari & Maccarrone 2020; Wood, Lehdonvirta, & Graham 2018; Kochan et al. 2022). Filling in the gap left from the lack of co-located meeting spaces, these online communities allow workers to share information, build connections, and assist in forming solidarity practices (Hedstrom 1994; Fiorito et al. 2006; Kerr & Siegel 1954; Miller & Bernstein 2017; Rosenblat 2018; Qadri 2021).

To shed light on how workers mobilise in a distributed, algorithmically managed environment, we draw on a qualitative case study of workers' involvement in the #DeclineNow movement on DoorDash. Building upon Kellogg et al. (2020), we define algo-activism as a distinct form of dispersed action in which workers use experiences with an algorithmic manager to determine specific actions to redress their grievances. Through our case study, we document three algo-activism practices. As these workers imagine their social existence in relation to the algorithm, they create social solidarity with respect to the shared target of the algorithmic manager: a type of solidarity that is felt by the algorithmic management system, but not necessarily felt by the workers in a dispersed environment. We conclude with implications about how algo-activism will affect the future of activism and the implications of algo-activism for inequality in platform settings.

Research Setting

DoorDash, founded in 2013, is an online food ordering and delivery platform headquartered in San Francisco. As of 2021, the company overtook Uber Eats and GrubHub to become the largest food delivery platform in the United States based on customer spending, with over 65% of the market share (Edison Trends 2021). By late 2022, DoorDash had served 450,000 merchants, and it had 34 million active customers, 6.8 million workers, and had facilitated over a million deliveries worldwide (Philbrook 2023). In 2020, the company went public at a $71.3 billion valuation (Zainab, Hussain & Franklin 2020). During this time, DoorDash has consistently advertised that their drivers can make up to $25 per hour nationally, and can keep 100% of their tips (DoorDash 2021). Despite their financial success, DoorDash has faced scrutiny from the media and its users regarding the company's misleading tipping policy, in which customers' tips were not given directly to drivers and instead were included in their base pay (Newman 2019). Facing rising public pressure and two lawsuits, the company changed its tipping policy in 2019 and issued an apology for its misleading practices (Abril 2019; Lampen 2019; OAGDC 2020).

Around the same time, in late 2019, two DoorDash couriers ("Dashers") living in the Lehigh Valley of Pennsylvania founded the #DeclineNow movement. Initially focused on workers sharing their ideas about how DoorDash's algorithm makes decisions regarding order assignment, payment, and deactivation, the movement quickly grew to include nearly 40,000 Facebook community members and, by early 2022, had developed a set of principles for how Dashers should interact with the DoorDash algorithm. The group receives an average of 19 posts per day, with a majority of posts receiving upwards of 60+ comments and likes from members of the community. The #DeclineNow movement targets DoorDash's algorithmic management system by encouraging drivers to exercise their "right to reject" (Shapiro 2018) orders that pay less than $7 (the base pay for a single order begins at $2.50). In doing so, drivers believe that these actions manipulate the algorithm by decreasing supply of workers. The decrease in supply creates pent-up demand through unfulfilled food delivery orders and creates a logistics "chokehold." Workers reported that these actions led the algorithmic management system to increase the base pay to fulfil an order in hopes of attracting more drivers to work on the DoorDash platform.

Data Collection and Analysis

To capture the perspectives of all actors in the triad, our dataset includes worker interviews and worker web forum data. As of March 2023, we have completed sixty-three (63) semi-structured interviews with drivers across the United States. The average age of participants was 35 (range between 18 and 70), with the majority (52%) identifying as female. Nearly a third of drivers (37%) relied on DoorDash as their main source of income. Then, we collected data from two nationally known web forums (n = 1,634 posts) sampling on any posts that included the words "accept," "decline," and "declinenow." We analysed the data in accordance with best practices of grounded theory (Charmaz 2006).

Findings

In the following sections, we describe how workers engage in algo-activism by placing pressure on the algorithmic management system. Table 10.1 provides an overview of what we derived inductively from our findings. This table provides an overview of how workers use various tactics to place pressure before and during the service encounter, and then turn to online forums to share grievances and form alliances after the service encounter. As algorithmic imaginaries become realised in these shared spaces, workers feel a psychological connection to one another, and they describe feeling like they can influence or pressure the algorithmic management system. We describe three distinct practices of worker algo-activism.

Uninvolved Practices

In *uninvolved practices,* workers express frustration with the algorithm and DoorDash more broadly, but do not apply any pressure on the algorithmic management system, in part because they are concerned about being penalised by the system. Uninvolved worker practices do not actively push back on the algorithm's work assignments, with drivers accepting almost all assignments that come their way and remaining uninvolved with the #DeclineNow movement. By lacking engagement

Table 10.1 Understanding algo-activism among workers

Practice outcome	*Feeling against algorithm*	*Engagement on forums*	*Realisation of algorithmic imaginary*	*Pressure on algorithm*
Uninvolved Practices	Frustrated	Only to share grievances but do not engage	Lacking Understanding	Relies on work as normal and remains uninvolved
Aligned Practices	Motivated	Share information	Partial Construction	Utilises shared tactics but aiming for individual benefit
Coordinated Practices	Empowered	Actively building together	Full Realisation	Strategically build activism together

Source: Table by authors.

and alliance-building within online forums, workers are unable to build mental models of how the algorithm is working, and, in turn, lack a conceptualisation of an algorithmic imaginary.

Workers use the app and the algorithmic manager to obtain a sense of their performance, taking the ratings as "truth" without knowing anything about how they are constructed. Striving to provide good customer service and achieve a high customer rating, uninvolved drivers take pleasure in "accommodating the customer and making sure the order's fulfilled" in order to "never [have] a one-star rating" (Brett). This constant internalised pressure provides insight into the precarity of their economic situation as independent contractors. Other drivers reported feeling pressured to accept all orders because they thought they would be penalised if they did not. Keith explained, "I try to keep my acceptance rate pretty up there – just because I feel like it impacts the type of orders that you get."

But while these workers acknowledge there are issues with the algorithm, and turn to a type of online forum to commiserate about their frustration and mistrust in the algorithm's opaque decision making, they ultimately are not actively searching for relationships with other workers to learn more about the algorithm and coordinate shared actions. Instead, these web forums simply served as spaces for drivers to air their grievances and to share a general awareness of the #DeclineNow movement, while offering some "suspicions," or worrying it might be "a bit small" (Kyle) and not worthwhile to get involved in after the strikes in July 2021 didn't work.

Most workers with uninvolved practices are worried about how the algorithm specifically affects them because they don't fully understand it. Drivers mainly engage with the web forums for "curious reading" before "going on [with the] day" (Brett).

Aligned Practices

In *aligned practices*, workers demonstrate their mental models for how the algorithm works and begin to experiment with applying pressure on the algorithmic management system, largely due to their budding alliances with each other within online forums. Aligned worker practices showcase tactical actions that push back on the algorithm's work assignments through algo-activism, with drivers turning to the forums to engage in dialogues about how to receive higher wages on the platform after a bad experience. Through engagement and alliance-building within online forums, workers begin to build mental models of how the algorithm works and what their relationship is with the algorithm that manages their experience, establishing a partial conceptualisation of the algorithmic imaginary.

In contrast to the uninvolved practices, in which workers are fearful of sanctions from the algorithmic management systems and therefore do not engage fully in solidarity practices, workers engaged in aligned practices seek to understand and take advantage of the gaps in the algorithmic management system, relying on information gleaned in online communities. Workers feel more comfortable experimenting with actions on the platform to increase their earnings, such as avoiding accepting orders from restaurants that are slower:

> if three times, three unique days I go to this restaurant and I'm waiting 20 minutes for this order, what am I doing? It's not worth my time. It's nothing personal, but I can't be a charity. I have to make money.
>
> (Paul)

At the same time, drivers were deeply aware of the risks of trying to thwart the algorithmic management system. Noting how she paid attention to how many orders she declined, Aubrey said,

"It's a super perverse system, if you're not super careful about what you're doing, you're going to lose money. You're not going to make money."

Many drivers describe having a revelation after experiencing an injustice, such as being stilted on a tip, a long delivery route, or having their pay cut because a customer lied about their food not being delivered. For Harold, his moment came when he received a large catering order with a base pay of $3 and no tip: "That was a huge learning experience for me…DoorDash is happy you're taking the low offers because they make more money and you don't get a tip." Rather than quitting, Harold turned to Reddit to hear how others were faring on the platform, noting that there is a "whole bunch of stuff that I think would be beneficial [for new Dashers]…but most people don't even know where to look for it."

Therefore, workers begin to build aligned practices with others on their respective forums by acknowledging others who have faced similar issues, and actively crowdsourcing information from each other about how they can resolve their problems and generate higher earnings. One worker stated:

> My acceptance rate is now at 8%! Gee. What happens at 0? It currently does not affect anything. I fully expect [DoorDash] to put on some minimum acceptance rate to stay active. Otherwise these low ball orders are never gonna get completed.

These shared issues demonstrate another layer of the algorithmic imaginary, where workers realise how the algorithm is working against them, and how they can build active solutions that are then tried and repeated by hundreds of others. However, while workers build aligned algo-activism practices together, the aligned practices are still ultimately completed by each individual, and their individual autonomy keeps them at arm's length from the algorithm.

Coordinated Practices

In *coordinated practices*, workers are actively pushing against the algorithmic manager through parallel algo-activism tactics, and they feel a deeper psychological sense of solidarity and awareness of the larger movement. Coordinated worker practices demonstrate the evolution of workers becoming evangelistic resistors with a dedication to orient new drivers to the tenets of the movement. Therefore, coordinated practices are enacted through the realised collective built around an algorithmic imaginary, in which workers form a shared evidence-based mental model to push back against the algorithm. This algorithmic imaginary allows workers to take back more control over how they interact with the platform's algorithm management system.

In stark contrast to uninvolved practices, individuals deploying coordinated practices are actively building their own targeted solutions to their issues with the algorithm due to their better understanding of how the algorithm works. Similar to workers using aligned practices, coordinated drivers had an experience that led them to turn to forums to learn more about the algorithm, with a particular focus on how to manipulate it to work for them. Within these discussion forums, workers demystify how the algorithm works and share with others. One of the leaders of the #DeclineNow movement shared information about how when drivers declined a low-paying, untipped order DoorDash would add to the base fare until a driver accepted. By sharing how the algorithm works with other drivers, #DeclineNow movement leaders shape practices with the larger community, developing a consensus regarding how to maximise profit. Drivers even show up on customer review sites with the hopes of encouraging customers to join the #DeclineNow movement. One driver said:

> Many of us are going on strike and [are participating in] the DeclineNow movement in order to pressure DD to stop this practice. If you are a Dasher, please stop taking low-ball orders and DD will stop paying us garbage rates. They also manipulate our tips after the order is completed, sometimes saying we earned more. If they can change the payout for the contract, what makes you think they aren't stealing tips in other circumstances?

Importantly, these interactions, albeit limited, continue to highlight how the forums are aiding in the complete realisation of an algorithmic imaginary, where through knowledge about how the algorithm works, its power is well-understood and actions are specifically designed to manipulate it to help others. Many are interested in working together to organise an offline collective action almost mirroring a wildcat strike, asking, "What if a large group of dashers all gathered in one area and all declined orders to jack base pay way up?"

Overall, coordinated practices bring workers closer within the service triangle towards something resembling a more traditional form of activism. However, the ultimate goal of their algo-activism is to solve a specific issue – such as to get a higher-paying order – and is not actually a movement to change the organisation in any significant way. A leader of #DeclineNow succinctly states that the purpose of the movement is to "Simply to help drivers make the most profit. We tell them, 'We don't hate the platform, we love the platform.'"

Implications and Future Directions

The algo-activism practices we uncovered expose the inequality inherent in the gig economy and in the broader institutional work environment. Significantly, our interviews with workers and the examination of web forums revealed a notable absence of encouragement for utilising institutional or legal avenues to tackle the information and power imbalance inherent in platforms. Several scholars highlight how platform companies exploit existing institutional and legal policies in ways that make it difficult for workers to organise effectively (Dubal 2020; Ravenelle 2019). Because gig economy workers, in the U.S. at least, are currently categorised as independent contractors, they do not have the same protections in place that full-time workers have earned through decades of reform. Further, platform companies claim their algorithms are proprietary secrets, making it difficult for workers to gain insight into how they operate. The absence of such protections and recourse options creates the need for algo-activism. Given the relatively slow progress in holding platform companies accountable (Rahman, Karunakaran & Cameron 2024), workers saw algo-activism as one of the few mechanisms to address the inequalities they encountered. Our findings, however, found that not all workers felt comfortable participating in coordinating practices.

Our case study on #DeclineNow on DoorDash found many workers not engaging with algo-activism practices, despite these tactics being understood as largely beneficial to both parties. In part, this may be because workers face pressures on their time, cognitive attention, and resources, limiting their capacity to understand the value of collective action and participate in it. Workers are constantly pressured by both the platform company and by themselves to maximise their time to make as much money as possible. These pressures can frustrate and anger workers so they disengage from the platform instead of taking part in coordinated activism.

Future research should aim to further examine the development of algo-activism in different types of platform work and customers' role in this activism. Workers on other platform companies (e.g., cleaning work and care work) often maintain robust social networks in digital (e.g., WhatsApp groups) and public spaces (e.g., parks) that allow for shared practices to develop. Moreover, these workers often have repeated interactions with customers, which, in turn, allow for more substantial relationships and shared interests that could lead to coordinated action. Algo-activism in these spaces would potentially take a different form than in the food delivery case study we examined, as algo-activism would be based on co-created ideas and could more actively involve the customers. Care workers, for example could include specific keywords in customer reviews and ratings that serve as signal to other care givers (Ticona & Mateescu 2018).

Researchers should continue to investigate ways algo-activism fosters inclusivity and can address the inequalities workers and customers encounter when they are subject to a platform's algorithmic management system. When do algo-activism practices begin to "scale up" and create institutional change, such as by lawmakers proposing new legislation to increase worker insight into platforms' algorithmic management systems? Put another way, at what point do they lead to sustainable changes improving worker conditions? Alternatively, under what conditions do algo-activism practices exacerbate workers' precarious positions within the algorithmic management system? Building upon this case study will offer potential for a broader scholarship on how workers and customers handle interacting with algorithmic management systems.

References

Abril, D. (2019). "DoorDash's New Tipping Policy Has Increased Driver Pay," *Fortune*. https://fortune.com/2019/11/12/doordash-new-tipping-policy-worker-pay/

Briscoe, F., & Gupta, A. (2021). "Business Disruption from the Inside Out," *SSIR*. https://ssir.org/articles/entry/business_disruption_from_the_inside_out

Bucher, T. (2017). "The Algorithmic Imaginary: Exploring the Ordinary Affects of Facebook Algorithms," *Information, Communication & Society* 20(1), 30–44. https://doi.org/10.1080/1369118X.2016.1154086

Cameron, L. (2022). "Making out While Driving: The Relational and Efficiency Game in the Gig Economy," *Organization Science* 33(1), 231–252.

Cameron, L., & Rahman, H. A. (2022). "Expanding the Locus of Resistance: Understanding the Co-constitution of Control and Resistance in the Gig Economy," *Organization Science*. https://doi.org/10.1287/orsc.2021.1557

Cardinal, L. B., Kreutzer, M., & Miller, C. C. (2017). "An Aspirational View of Organizational Control Research: Re-Invigorating Empirical Work to Better Meet the Challenges of 21st Century Organizations," *Academy of Management Annals* 11, 559–592.

Charmaz, K. (2006). *Constructing Grounded Theory: A Practical Guide through Qualitative Analysis*. London: Sage.

Christin, A. (2020). "The Ethnographer and the Algorithm: Beyond the Black Box," *Theory and Society* 49(5), 897–918.

DeVito, M. A., Hancock, J. T., French, M., Birnholtz, J., Antin, J., Karahalios, K., … & Shklovski, I. (2018). The algorithm and the user: How can hci use lay understandings of algorithmic systems? in CHI 2018 - Extended Abstracts of the 2018 CHI Conference on Human Factors in Computing Systems: Engage with CHI., panel04, Association for Computing Machinery, Conference on Human Factors in Computing Systems - Proceedings, vol. 2018-April, 2018 CHI Conference on Human Factors in Computing Systems, CHI EA 2018, Montreal, Canada, 21/04/2018. Available at: https://doi.org/10.1145/3170427.3186320.

DoorDash (2021). *Dasher Pay*. https://dasher.doordash.com/en-us/pay#:~:text=How%20much%20do%20drivers%20make,%2C%20including%20100%25%20of%20tips

Dubal, V. (2020). "A Brief History of the Gig," *Logic Magazine* (10). Available at: https://logicmag.io/security/a-brief-history-of-the-gig/

Edison Trends (2021). *2021 Edison Trends U.S. Convenience Store Delivery Sales Report*. https://trends.edison.tech/research/convenience-store-delivery-sales.html

Fiorito, J., Jarley, P., & Delaney, J. T. (2006). "Change to Win: Can Structural Reform Revitalize the American Labor Movement?" in D. Lewin, and B.E. Kaufman (Eds). *Advances in Industrial & Labor Relations*. Taipei: Emerald Group Publishing Limited. vol. 15, pp. 359–391.

Hancock, J. I., Allen, D. G., & Soelberg, C. (2017). "Collective Turnover: An Expanded Meta-Analytic Exploration and Comparison," *Human Resource Management Review* 27, 61–86.
Hedstrom, P. (1994). "Contagious Collectivities: On the Spatial Diffusion of Swedish Trade Unions, 1890–1940," *American Journal of Sociology* 99, 1157–1179.
Jhaver, S., Karpfen, Y., & Antin, J. (2018). "Algorithmic Anxiety and Coping Strategies of Airbnb Hosts," *Proceedings of the 2018 CHI Conference on Human Factors in Computing Systems* (pp. 1–12). https://doi.org/10.1145/3173574.3173995
Kellogg, K. C., Valentine, M. A., & Christin, A. (2020). "Algorithms at Work: The New Contested Terrain of Control," *Academy of Management Annals* 14(1), 366–410. https://doi.org/10.5465/annals.2018.0174
Kerr, C., & Siegel, A. J. (1954). *The Interindustry Propensity to Strike: An International Comparison.* Bobbs-Merrill Company Incorporated.
Kochan, T., Fine, J., Bronfenbrenner, K., Naidu, S., Barnes, J., Diaz-Linhart, Y., Kallas, J., Kim, J., Minster, A., Tong, D., Townsend, P., & Twiss, D. (2022). "U.S. Workers' Organizing Efforts & Collective Actions: A Review of the Current Landscape. Worker Empowerment Research Network," *MIT Sloan.* https://mitsloan.mit.edu/sites/default/files/2022-06/Report%20on%20Worker%20Organizing%20Landscape%20in%20US%20by%20Kochan%20Fine%20Bronfenbrenner%20Naidu%20et%20al%20June%202022.pdf
Lampen, C. (2019). "Brooklyn Man Sues DoorDash over Grifty, Misleading Tip Policy," *Gothamist.* https://gothamist.com/food/brooklyn-man-sues-doordash-over-grifty-misleading-tip-policy
Lee, M. K., Kusbit, D., Metsky, E., Dabbish, L. (2015). Working with machines: The impact of algorithmic and data-driven management on human workers. Proceedings of 33rd Annual ACM Conference Human Factors Computing Systems. Seoul, Republic of Korea: ACM Press, pp. 1603–1612.
Maffie, M. D. (2020). "The Role of Digital Communities in Organizing Gig Workers," *Industrial Relations: A Journal of Economy and Society* 59(1), 123–149. https://doi.org/10.1111/irel.12251
Margetts, H., John, P., Hale, S., & Yasseri, T. (2015). *Political Turbulence: How Social Media Shape Collective Action.* https://doi.org/10.2307/j.ctvc773c7
Miller, M., & Bernstein, E. H. (2017). "New Frontiers of Worker Power," New York: Roosevelt Institute, Report published 15 February. Available at: https://rooseveltinstitute.org/wp-content/uploads/2020/07/RI-New-Frontiers-Worker-Power-201702.pdf
Möhlmann, M., & Henfridsson, O. (2019). "What People Hate about Being Managed by Algorithms, According to a Study of Uber Drivers," *Harvard Business Review.* https://hbr.org/2019/08/what-people-hate-about-being-managed-by-algorithms-according-to-a-study-of-uber-drivers
Newman, A. (2019). "My Frantic Life as a Cab-Dodging, Tip-Chasing Food App Deliveryman," *The New York Times.* https://www.nytimes.com/2019/07/21/nyregion/doordash-ubereats-food-app-delivery-bike.html
OAGDC (2020). "AG Racine Reaches $2.5 Million Agreement with DoorDash for Misrepresenting That Customer Tips Would Go to Food Delivery Drivers," *Office of the Attorney General for the District of Columbia (OAGDC).* https://oag.dc.gov/release/ag-racine-reaches-25-million-agreement-doordash
Philbrook, T. (2023). "DoorDash Statistics: Revenue, Usage Statistics, & More," *The Rideshare Guy.* https://therideshareguy.com/doordash-statistics/
Qadri, R. (2021). "What's in a Network? Infrastructures of Mutual Aid for Digital Platform Workers during COVID-19," *Proceedings of the ACM on Human-Computer Interaction* 5(CSCW2), 1–20. https://doi.org/10.1145/3479563
Rahman, H., Karunakaran, A., & Cameron, L. (2024). "Taming Platform Power: Taking Accountability into Account, An Integrative Review on Digital Platforms," *Academy of Management Annals* 18(1), 251–294.
Ravenelle, A. J. (2019). *Hustle and Gig: Struggling and Surviving in the Gig Economy.* University of California Press.
Rosenblat, A., & Stark, L. (2016). "Algorithmic Labor and Information Asymmetries: A Case Study of Uber's Drivers," *International Journal of Communication* 10, 27.
Rosenblat, A. (2018). *Uberland: How Algorithms Are Rewriting the Rules of Work.* Oakland, CA: University of California Press.
Shapiro, A. (2018). "Between Autonomy and Control: Strategies of Arbitrage in the "On-Demand" Economy," *New Media & Society* 20(8), 2954–2971. https://doi.org/10.1177/1461444817738236
Smoke, B. (2022). "The UK's Longest Gig Economy Strike Isn't Letting Up," *Huck Magazine.* https://www.huckmag.com/article/the-uks-longest-gig-economy-strike-isnt-letting-up

Sutton, R. I., & Rafaeli, A. (1988). "Untangling the Relationship between Displayed Emotions and Organizational Sales: The Case of Convenience Stores," *Academy of Management Journal* 31(3), 461–487. https://doi.org/10.2307/256456

Tassinari, A., & Maccarrone, V. (2017). "The Mobilisation of Gig Economy Couriers in Italy: Some Lessons for the Trade Union Movement," *Transfer: European Review of Labour and Research* 23(3), 353–357.

Tassinari, A., & Maccarrone, V. (2020). "Riders on the Storm: Workplace Solidarity among Gig Economy Couriers in Italy and the UK," *Work, Employment and Society* 34(1), 35–54. https://doi.org/10.1177/0950017019862954

Ticona, J., & Mateescu, A. (2018). "Trusted Strangers: Carework Platforms' Cultural Entrepreneurship in the On-Demand Economy," *New Media & Society* 20(11), 4384–4404.

Van Maanen, J., & Kunda, G. (1989). ""Real Feelings": Emotional Expression and Organizational Culture," *Research in Organizational Behavior* 11, 43–103.

Wood, A., Lehdonvirta, V., & Graham, M. (2018). "Workers of the Internet Unite? Online Freelancer Organisation among Remote Gig Economy Workers in Six Asian and African Countries," *Social Science Research Network* (SSRN Scholarly Paper ID 3211803). https://papers.ssrn.com/abstract=3211803

Wood, A. J., Graham, M., Lehdonvirta, V., & Hjorth, I. (2019). "Good Gig, Bad Gig: Autonomy and Algorithmic Control in the Global Gig Economy," *Work, Employment and Society* 33(1), 56–75. https://doi.org/10.1177/0950017018785616

Zainab Hussain, N., & Franklin, J. (2020) "DoorDash Valued at $71 Billion in Blockbuster Market Debut," *Yahoo News*. https://www.yahoo.com/now/doordash-shares-set-jump-blockbuster-152812509.html

Recommendations for Further Reading

Cameron, L., & Rahman, H. A. (2022). "Expanding the Locus of Resistance: Understanding the Co-constitution of Control and Resistance in the Gig Economy," *Organization Science*. https://doi.org/10.1287/orsc.2021.1557

Gray, M. L, & Suri, S. (2019). *Ghost Work: How to Stop Silicon Valley from Building a New Global Underclass*. London: HMH.

Pasquale, F. (2016). *The Black Box Society: The Secret Algorithms that Control Money and Information.* Cambridge, Massachusetts: Harvard University Press.

Ravenelle, A. J. (2019). *Hustle and Gig: Struggling and Surviving in the Sharing Economy*. Oakland: University of California Press.

Rosenblat, A. (2019). *Uberland: How Algorithms Are Rewriting the Rules of Work*. University of California Press.

Schor, J. B. (2021). *After the Gig: How the Sharing Economy Got Hijacked*. Oakland: University of California Press.

Shestakofsky, B. (2024). *Behind the Startup: How Venture Capital Shapes Work, Innovation, and Inequality*. University of California Press.

Wells, K., Attoh, K. & Cullen, D. (2023). *Disrupting D.C.: The Rise of Uber and the Fall of the City*. Princeton: Princeton University Press.

Wood, A. J., Graham, M., Lehdonvirta, V., & Hjorth, I. (2019). "Good Gig, Bad Gig: Autonomy and Algorithmic Control in the Global Gig Economy," *Work, Employment and Society* 33(1), 56–75. https://doi.org/10.1177/0950017018785616

Woodcock, J. (2021). *The Fight against Platform Capitalism*. London: University of Westminster Press.

Woodcock, J., & Graham, M. (2019). *The Gig Economy. A Critical Introduction.* Cambridge: Polity.

PART 5

Identity and Difference in the Future of Work

11

A FUTURE OF RACIAL CAPITALISM

Reproducing Coercion through New Digital Labour in South Africa

Bridget Kenny

Introduction

The study of the future of work in South Africa focuses on questions of the labour market, labour process and worker struggles. It builds from a long tradition of labour process studies in the country (see Kenny and Webster 2021). A key intervention of this work is to emphasize the continuities of racialized and gendered segregated labour markets and coercive control reproduced through the introduction of new forms of work. Despite optimistic interest in the possibilities of the Fourth Industrial Revolution ('4IR') for development, the future of work, from the perspective of South Africa, looks much like its divided past and present.

Howcroft and Rubery (2021: 2), in their review of articles on technology and work in the *International Labour Review* for the centenary of the ILO, find a fair amount of "projective speculation that, with hindsight, can be seen to have been off beam". Debates on technology "almost always engage in futurology", they caution (Howcroft and Rubery 2021: 2). Still, they show continuities in attention over the decades to the effects of new technologies on workplace change and their implications for the number and quality of jobs. The overwhelming focus of debate from the global North, then, as they argue, is around job replacement, labour market access and policy frameworks to ameliorate ill-effects and/or to encourage the redistribution of benefits of new technology across stakeholders. For developing countries, Rani and Furrer (2021) highlight how new digital platforms capture a global Southern labour supply where high unemployment means available and relatively highly educated workers, but ultimately offer precarious forms of work, with low autonomy, repetitive tasks, irregular and often long hours of work, and unstable and low income, including non-payment of wages to workers. In some ways, the tension of such realities within debates about 'decent work' pose deeper questions about the possibilities of their attendant futures that move beyond the projective 'futurology' of which Howcroft and Rubery warn.

This chapter argues for expanding detailed labour process analyses and concerns around employment to focus on theorizing about the social reproduction of capitalist relations through enduring and, indeed, deepening divisions of race, class and gender. It does this through a review of South African 'future of work' studies. Indeed, scholars working on South Africa acknowledge the potential of gig economy work to offer income in a context of high unemployment (Anwar and Graham 2022: xxiii), but they also show how existing inequalities are reinforced and exacerbated.

 DOI: 10.4324/9781003327561-16

This chapter presents some key studies to show precisely how changes have affected work and workers. It then interrogates the central theoretical framings of this work to argue for connecting these insights into a wider view of changes to capitalism constituted out of social relations in space/place (Massey 1994). Ultimately, it argues that much of the research on and from South Africa suggests that new forms of work reproduce dynamics of racial capitalism structuring this postcolonial political economy. Even as South African policy debate worries about missing the 'train' of new technology development (our metaphors remain quaintly anachronistic), it simultaneously predicts the devastating effects of these new technologies on already high unemployment and inequality (see Kenny 2021: 134–136); the digitalization of work seems to be taking rather more familiar turns. Our futurologists need only to be reminded of our sobering present.

Studies of the Future of Work in South Africa

Labour studies in South Africa were reinvigorated in the 1970s in response to a militant independent black trade union movement and at a time when Marxist labour process theory was brought into the academy. Eddie Webster (1985) examined changes to engineering labour processes with mechanization, deskilling of work, the incorporation of a new black workforce into semi-skilled manufacturing jobs and the emergence of new worker mobilization and trade union militancy. This tradition combined attention to technology change, work organization and skill redefinition with labour market shifts to explain worker politics. In the 1990s, workplace restructuring and labour market changes posed questions anew about shifts in the standard employment relation precisely when most workers became full citizens and labour law reform extended employment rights broadly, thereby including the majority black workforce. Researchers showed how these processes undercut the labour movement precisely when it gained national political power, and unions when they had secured labour rights. In the twenty-first century, scholars examined the configurations of precarious and informalized labour that reshaped the economy. In each of these moments, researchers paid particular attention to forms of worker and movement organizing (Kenny and Webster 2021). In many ways, then, the 'future of work' literature in South Africa follows this tradition of mapping detailed labour process and labour market analyses with attentiveness to workers' organizing potential.

Sociological studies on the future of work draw out similarities in reorganization of forms of work around such new technologies with a focus on how algorithmic logic shapes labour processes and mediates work, exacerbates conditions of precariousness for workers, but also leads to new worker mobilizations, often, indeed, using new technologies to organize. As outlined below, South African studies attend to the effects of new technology and changes to work through examining automation and its impact on manufacturing workers, the ways that the gig economy, digital platforms, and algorithmic management introduce new forms of control, and how workers and trade unions have been able to respond and organize or resist.

Automation

Studies of automation have focused on manufacturing labour processes and trade union engagement. Hlatshwayo (2015) examines the ability of trade unions to bargain around new technology introduced when ArcelorMittal bought out a South Africa steel plant. He reported little consultation with workers around technology, and unions still focused primarily on wage bargaining (and see also Hlatshwayo and Buhlungu 2017). Mashilo shows how the National Union of Metal and Allied Workers of South Africa (NUMSA) with strong shopfloor organizing traditions, successfully bargained for skills upgrading for multi-skilled operations in auto assembly, but was less successful in components manufacturing (Mashilo 2022). Like Hlatshwayo (2015), ultimately he found trade union bargaining around the introduction of new technology in auto limited to negotiations around retrenchments, partly by how technology was understood as an issue of company competitiveness and not a sectoral matter for the bargaining council (Mashilo 2022: 254). Using the power resources approach, Mashilo and Webster (2021) argue that where any social upgrading was won within their cases of auto components manufacturing, it was when the union strategically used various forms of power to institute gains. Worker agency had to be explained, in short, within layered institutional arrangements, including the state. By contrast, Dor (2023) suggests that because of how trade union bargaining has been institutionalized within a framework of standard employment relationship, when restructuring in manufacturing outsourced units and workforces, trade unions hit the limits of their capacities to organize. Instead manufacturing workers found new forms of organizing outside of trade union structures.

Other research on automation in manufacturing shows the replacement of workers and jobs in capital intensive sectors like automobile manufacturing (Chigbu and Nekhwevha 2022). Despite the increasing role of the auto industry in the GDP in South Africa, employment has overall fallen. Most of these job losses were a result of automation in the sector. Globally integrated car makers use 'robots' on assembly lines. These 'new robotic assembly lines' fragment tasks (Chigbu and Nekhwevha 2022: 727–729). Based on qualitative interviews with managers, workers and unions, Chigbu and Nekhwevha (2022: 733) found that managers felt pressured to increase productivity and thus to support automation. Workers interviewed argued that technology was used to address problems of human control:

> They think technology is more productive, more efficient, there is less absenteeism, no sick leave, no complaints, the payslip is always the same but people get tired, but with robot and technology, it moves fast. Also, technology cut[s] cost and avoids the labour issue of the workers and their unions. Hence, they are more reliable, so I get why they prefer technology.
> (quoted in Chigbu and Nekhwevha 2022: 734)

Yet workers also commented on the time lost when the technology broke down, and the machines had to be tended by workers: "There is no machine that is not being operated or supervised by a human being" (quoted in Chigbu and Nekhwevha 2022: 739). Furthermore, while they found clear evidence of job replacement, managers also argued that new jobs came with the introduction of robotics, requiring higher skills, particularly "the things that are seen by human eyes" and not able to be done by the robots (Chigbu and Nekhwevha 2022: 736). Another study focused on possibilities for retraining of autoworkers in the context of increased automation. It indicated little concrete evidence of programmes to ameliorate workers' anxieties of replacement, and instead found workers were relying on their own plans to retool themselves, including through Bitcoin and FOREX trading (Chigbu and Nekhwevha 2021: 6).

These studies of the introduction and expansion of automation in manufacturing suggest how embedded relations of trade union bargaining and workplace dynamics explained the ways in which technology, skilling and worker agency played out. They further demonstrate how black workers themselves attended to the reproduction of labour as lack of trust became evident in these processes to define any avenue for future inclusion. Such analyses of automation focus on the constituted relations at workplaces and within sectors where unions have been strong and in relation to political processes (and previously contested through labour movement struggles). These studies of automation do not approach the introduction of technology as a 'new' phenomenon, but rather a conjunctural feature of changes within global supply chains and within longer histories of union and worker politics and viz. state building in a post-apartheid context. As such, in these analyses, these processes are clearly contested and changes implemented by capital must be explained through such imbricated relations.

Platform Work

Many 'future of work' studies examine new forms of digitized platform work. Anwar and Graham's research on digital labour in Africa shows how workers across five African countries, including South Africa, conduct the human labour required to train AI programmes, such as tagging images for computer learning, offering their labour power for low wages to support US companies in business process outsourcing, and supplying remote gig labour to a range of platforms (Anwar and Graham 2019, 2021, 2022). They show "the ways in which Africa is embedded into contemporary digital economy activities" thereby highlighting the involvement of African workers in these processes (see Chapter 7) (Anwar and Graham 2022: xviii). Much of the business services performed by African workers is in administrative support, sales and marketing but also includes writing and IT support (Anwar and Graham 2022: 73. Fig. 3.7). Anwar (2022) notes that the optimistic view that digital technologies can assist Africa's development woes is overstated (see also Anwar and Graham 2022: 40–44). As they write, "The gig economy is largely made possible due to the commodification of work into bite-sized small tasks performed by an atomized workforce" (Anwar and Graham 2019: 2). Instead focusing on effects on African workers, this work reveals the hidden forms of exploitation and alienation intensified through remote digital work reliant on African labour, even as workers also find means of resisting some forms of control (Anwar and Graham 2019, 2022).

In the introduction to a special issue of *Gender & Development*, digital work is examined for how it increases inequalities of race, gender, national and sexual difference (Rani et al. 2022). Here, access to technology and access to jobs are assessed along with how the technology also reproduces and re-entrenches race and gender divisions of labour, including issues around the boundaries between paid and unpaid labour. Such analysis focuses on the central themes of precariousness, inequality and policy intervention (Rani et al. 2022).

A major emphasis of studies of the gig economy in South Africa has been focused on on-demand delivery drivers and transport services. Chinguno (2019) analyses new ride services such as Uber and Bolt for how they contribute to forms of labour control. He positions the new platforms within the existing forms of (private) 'public' transport, especially minibus taxis and metred taxis, which expanded as public services declined in late apartheid and transported commuters from segregated residential areas across divided cities. Minibus taxis tend to be poorly serviced and maintained and charge higher fees than state-subsidized transport. He explains that limits to a proper transportation system within the context of dire need because of enduring apartheid spatial geographies opened up a market for Uber and the other apps, which started in 2013 in Johannesburg (Chinguno 2019: 37–39). As in other contexts, drivers are considered 'independent contractors' not employees of Uber or Bolt (see Chapters 8 and 10). In South Africa this was maintained by the Labour Court after a challenge by drivers who were 'deactivated' from the platform without warning. The app works to surveil the workers, and the rating system serves to control the drivers (Chinguno 2019: 49). Nevertheless drivers attempted to organize and collectively bargain with Uber, but this effort went punished, with drivers involved being removed from the platform (Chinguno 2019: 54). The drivers also used WhatsApp groups for sharing information. And, in 2018 when a petrol price increase made conditions difficult for them, they used the WhatsApp groups to discuss their grievances and organize a collective action with demands sent to the company. They embarked on a go-slow, a march and a strike across both companies (Chinguno 2019: 56).

Similarly, Webster and Masikane (2021) studied ride share workers in South Africa, Ghana and Kenya. They found multiple forms of labour control operating through the apps. In addition, urban riders, who are black and often migrant workers in Johannesburg, experienced a range of vulnerabilities, including accidents, xenophobia and gender-based violence for the few women riders. A key finding of their research was how riders in different places organized collectively. Some used trade union or quasi-trade union structures, but in South Africa, new organizations formed through WhatsApp and by meeting in place, where drivers congregated to wait for orders. Through these new forms, riders organized a strike to demand better conditions from the platforms and better regulation from the state (see Chapter 10) (see also Webster et al. 2021).

Studies of platform domestic labour in South Africa make the point that the digitalized conduit only exacerbates racially divided labour markets. Paid domestic work is overwhelmingly conducted by black, working-class women in South Africa. It is a historically definitive employment relation in South Africa's structure of racial capitalism, where under apartheid African women without rights to live in white residential areas served white families, raised their children and lived in small one-room accommodation attached to their employers as a means of accessing urban labour markets (see Cock 1980; Ally 2010). While in a post-apartheid context, domestic workers have gained employment rights as employees, many remain de facto precariously employed, assumed to be low skilled, in reality paid less than minimum wage, and exploited through working time and individualized relationships. Digital platforms slotted into this already existing regime of racialized and gendered precarious labour (Hunt and Samman 2020; Kalla 2022; Sibiya and du Toit 2022).

Kalla researched SweepSouth, a South African start-up backed by Silicon Valley capital. It boasted prioritizing job creation even as it identified as a technology company only and not an employer. The conditions faced by workers interviewed included low wages, particularly as working hours were erratic with uneven bookings, platform surveillance of workers' time, rating systems which served to punitively discipline workers, lack of recourse to abuse or mistreatment by clients, and expectations of deference regardless of treatment by clients (Kalla 2022: 657–663; and see Hunt and Samman 2020: 110–113). In their survey of platform domestic workers, Hunt and Samman (2020: 111) found that not only were wages low but the costs of maintaining gig work were high, including cell phone, airtime and transport costs. Many of their interviewees reported working in other forms of informal or precarious work, including regular domestic labour, to supplement their gig work (Hunt and Samman 2020: 111–112). Furthermore, many workers were migrant women from Zimbabwe, thereby increasing their vulnerability within contexts of rising xenophobia in South Africa (Kalla 2022: 660; Hunt and Samman 2020: 104). While particularly younger workers in studies reported preferring platform domestic work to direct employment with its associated colonial relations, the benefits of platforms did not quite deliver, such as being able to control one's hours of work (Hunt and Samman 2020: 112; Kalla 2022).

In the context of structural unemployment, researchers argue that platforms profit from the low waged reproductive labour of black women in ways that continue unequal racist and sexist relations of apartheid. It could be that platforms assist to mitigate against the fraught intimacies of these relationships, but instead, these studies show how they regenerated through unaccountable digital intermediaries. Indeed, Hunt and Samman (2020) argue that gains won by the labour movement to incorporate domestic work into the labour relations framework after 1994 are potentially being disrupted by these platform services (and see Sibiya and du Toit 2022).

Recent work on digitalized platform work on South Africa, then, emphasizes how its 'newness' shapes labour relations through control by algorithmic management and the distance of the technology, combined with the legal excision of workers from 'employee' status by platforms across sectors, like research elsewhere. Yet all such studies focus on the intertwined and spatial relations of longer histories of racialized, but also gendered, relations of inequality and coercion that reproduce vulnerabilities for these specific workers today. While some research frames its orientation around the quality of these jobs in the context of South African policy debates and possibilities for regulation (Sibiya and du Toit 2022; Hunt and Samman 2020; Webster and Masikane 2021), all explain the effects on workers and work through how low wage precarious jobs remain the fate of working-class and poor black residents. They also show how workers contend with these conditions by individually or collectively resisting the worst infringements.

Logistics

Finally, some recent work engages with the expansion of logistics and the implications for new technological reorganization of work. The full integration of warehouse and logistics operations through the platform, in such new business models as e-commerce, allows companies and consumers to have efficient, timely and cheap delivery (Atzeni and Kenny 2022). Ongoing and current research on the labour process in logistics warehouses in Gauteng Province in South Africa indicates the punitive and stressful effects on shop floor workers, who are almost all demographically 'black', of algorithmic management through hand-held scanners, extensive use of labour broking for picking and packing jobs, erratic hours of work, with workers sometimes being sent home or not scheduled and sometimes being required to work late without overtime pay, variable wages related to fluctuating working times, little union organization, and low recognition of skills and career paths (Kenny 2023b). Dor (2023) finds that the outsourcing of logistics from manufacturing units in a number of firms in Gauteng, even while the logistics operations were located within the same business premises, served to divide workers and set up conditions for redefining skill around operation and not actual substance of work, thereby deskilling logistics workers as 'auxiliary' and dividing workers in sectors historically organized by militant industrial unions (Dor 2023: 88).

As I have written elsewhere, the growth of logistics in Gauteng Province maps changes to capital accumulation and the social reproduction of capitalist relations in this once industrial heartland. Following authors in critical logistics studies, I link the expansion of warehousing and logistics to new forms of employment, labour control and precariousness and use a framework of the circuit of capital to think through these changes to capital investment and labour within these processes. In South Africa, the use of digitized warehouse management systems is a growing trend. Like in other studies above, workers were keen to take up new job opportunities. These warehouses were located in expanding logistics corridors surrounding the airport on land distant from settlements. The primarily black workforce invested in transport and often in their own education from vocational colleges to upskill in logistics curriculum, which went unrecognized by employers. Hourly productivity rates monitored on individualized scanners meant that stress defined daily routines (see Chapter 19). Furthermore, women reported stress from having to stay late without notice when they were required to fulfil a day's orders. Women packers explained how they were unable to budget for their households and plan for childcare with irregular schedules. Workers felt surveilled by biometric clocking and how scanners recorded their every operation. Yet because of few job opportunities, workers faced these conditions with a sense of little choice (Kenny 2023b).

Workers experienced this new work organization through familiar relations of racially segmented labour markets, punitive labour relations, non-recognition of skill and capacities of black workers, and racialized power on the shop floor, which defined the 'apartheid workplace regime' historically (Von Holdt 2003). As one worker said, "Why do we have to know all these things when we are still called general workers. Why know this technology if I am still regarded as a general worker?" Another worker explained, "it's not a matter of [the HR manager] coming to employees …and say[ing], 'Come here, tell me about your dreams, tell me about your vision in the next five years'" (Kenny 2023b). In other words, workers reinterpreted the machinic despotism through well-known human relations of segmentation and power. Thus, the new technologies and work organization in warehousing were incorporated into already existing relations. Workers responded by organizing around issues with which they had long-time experience, particularly they contested (unsuccessfully) the use of labour broking and tried to obtain agreement around minimum hours and wages. This meant that they did not specifically engage the digitalized Taylorism of the technology (i.e. they did not directly contest the use of digital technology to optimize work processes, streamline workflows, and monitor employee performance) because of how this technology segued into already understood dynamics of externalization and devaluation of their labour power

Logistics thus reproduces past divisions and relations of extraction within South Africa's longer history of racialized capitalism (see Hall 1980; Kenny 2023a: 3521–3524). Hence, these new logistics infrastructures remade physical space across the landscape and within firms. The technology divided workers through individualized monitoring of their work and through outsourcing segments of a previously united workforce. While the new technology may have provided a promise of upskilling through digital interfaces, instead the mostly black, working-class labour force across different companies, appears to have experienced the reproduction of a racialized status of manual labour, with the frustrations of ongoing exclusion from economic stability, let alone mobility, and by implication, a 'future' for their families, despite being 30 years into democracy. New logistics labour processes rely on the infrastructural labour of mostly black workers which is invisibilized (as the labour behind-the-scenes ensuring newly efficient consumer distribution) but reproduces relations of abjection all while creating a new terrain of capital accumulation.

Conclusion: Theorizing Digital Labour through Racial Capitalism

Much of the new research within labour sociology in and on South Africa writing on the effects of new technologies on work and labour, then, emphasizes the punitive effects of digitized labour processes, of increased surveillance and, indeed, Taylorist forms of control over workers within South African and now globally restructured labour processes. This expanding body of work offers rich empirical studies of the actual technologies and material practices being implemented. It argues for how labour continues to be central to new technologies in new and often hidden ways, and it amasses an archive of new energies and efforts at contesting intensified work processes by workers collectively.

A number of studies evaluate digital labour in terms of the ILO's framework of decent work, focusing on documenting the gap between conditions of work created by platforms and policy directives (see Sibiya and du Toit 2022; Rani et al. 2022; Webster and Dor 2023). This orientation aims to influence global policy directives within the context of swiftly changing working conditions, with arguments about the distance of developing economies from any benefits of new technological uptake.

Other work positions these insights more broadly within changes to forms of capital accumulation now. For instance, Huws' (2014) book has had an important impact on studies. She emphasizes the interconnections of digital labour within the larger economy and therefore the relationship it has to changing forms of capital accumulation (see for instance, Anwar and Graham 2022: 4–5; Rani et al. 2022: 421). This chapter argues, however, that taken together the studies of the future of work in South Africa suggest not only how work in this context is globally implicated within these 'planetary' processes (Anwar and Graham 2022), but also how it is conjuncturally constituted through relations in place (Hall 1980) in ways that beg questions about the social reproduction of capital through these interconnected processes.

South African studies have much to offer debates about the 'future of work' through such rich research into labour process and labour market shifts while attending to the always-present co-constitution of worker agency and collective resistance within these processes. But, they also offer, especially if taken together, an urgent call for analysis of how conjunctural relations direct changes to work, labour, value and capitalism from concrete spaces and places. That the future of work in South Africa looks so much like its present requires an understanding not of the 'new' and future as much of its past and enduring forms of division, exploitation and oppression.

References

Ally, Shireen (2010) *From Servants to Workers: South African Domestic Workers and the Democratic State*, New York: Cornell University Press.

Anwar, Mohammad Amir (2022) "Platforms of inequality: Gender dynamics of digital labour in Africa," *Gender & Development* 30:3, 747–764, DOI: 10.1080/13552074.2022.2121059

Anwar, Mohammad Amir and Mark Graham (2019) "Hidden transcripts of the gig economy: Labour agency and the new art of resistance among African gig workers," *Environment and Planning A: Economy and Space* 52:7, 1269–1291.

Anwar, Mohammad Amir and Mark Graham (2021) "Between a rock and a hard place: Freedom, flexibility, precarity and vulnerability in the gig economy in Africa," *Competition & Change* 25:2, 237–258.

Anwar, Mohammad Amir and Mark Graham (2022) *The Digital Continent: Placing Africa in Planetary Networks of Work*, Oxford: Oxford University Press.

Atzeni, Maurizio. and Bridget Kenny (2022) "The labour process and workers' rights at Mercado Libre: Hiding exploitation through regulation in the digital economy," SCIS Working Paper, No. 31. The Future of Work(ers) Research Project. Johannesburg: Southern Centre for Inequality Studies.

Chigbu, B. I. and F. H. Nekhwevha (2021) "The future of work and uncertain labour alternatives as we live through the industrial age of possible singularity: Evidence from South Africa," *Technology in Society* 67 (article #101715), 1–9, DOI: 10.1016/j.techsoc.2021.101715

Chigbu, B. I. and F. H. Nekhwevha (2022) "The extent of job automation in the automobile sector in South Africa," *Economic and Industrial Democracy* 43:2, 726–747, DOI: 10.1177/0143831X20940779

Chinguno, Crispen. (2019) "Power dynamics in the gig/share economy: Uber and Bolt Taxi Platforms in Johannesburg, South Africa," *Labour, Capital and Society* 49:2, 31–65.

Cock, Jacklyn (1980) *Maids and Madams: A Study in the Politics of Exploitation*, Johannesburg: Ravan Press.

Dor, Lynford (2023) "Divided workers, divided struggles: Entrenching dualisation and the struggle for equalisation in South Africa's manufacturing sector," in E. Webster and L. Dor (eds.) *Recasting Workers' Power: Work and Inequality in the Shadow of the Digital Age*. Bristol: Bristol University Press, 72–100.

Hall, Stuart (1980) "Race, articulation and societies structured in dominance," in Mary O' Callaghan (ed.) *Sociological Theories: Race and Colonialism*. Paris: UNESCO, 305–345.

Hlatshwayo, Mondli (2015) "Unpacking NUMSA's responses to technological changes at the Arcelormittal Vanderbijlpark Plant," *South African Review of Sociology* 46:2, 77–96.

Hlatshwayo, Mondli and Sakhela Buhlungu (2017) "Work reorganisation and technological change: Limits of trade union strategy and action at ArcelorMittal, Vanderbijlpark," *African Sociological Review* 21:1, 126–153.

Howcroft, Debra and Jill Rubery (2021) "Introduction: Labour and technology: Reflecting on a century of debate in the *International Labour Review*," *International Labour Review* Centenary Issue No. 2, 1–11.

Hunt, Abigail and Emma Samman (2020) "Domestic work and the gig economy in South Africa: Old wine in new bottles?," *Anti-Trafficking Review* 15, 102–121, DOI: 10.14197/atr.201220156

Huws, Ursula (2014) *Labor in the Global Digital Economy: The Cybertariat Comes of Age*, New York: Monthly Review Press.

Kalla, Shaeera (2022) "Hacking platform capitalism: The case of domestic workers on South Africa's SweepSouth platform," *Gender & Development* 30:3, 655–666, DOI: 10.1080/13552074.2022.2136838

Kenny, Bridget (2021) "The new 'Arcadia'? Racial capitalism, technological histories and the 'utopian' future of labour," in T. Ngwane and M. Tshoaedi (eds.) *The Fourth Industrial Revolution: A Sociological Critique*. Johannesburg: Jacana Media, 133–146.

Kenny, Bridget (2023a) "Reproducing 'racial capitalism' through retailing in South Africa: Gender, labour and consumption 1950s–1970s," *Ethnic and Racial Studies*, 46:16, 3520–3541.

Kenny, Bridget (2023b) "The infrastructural labour of logistics: Reorganising warehouse workers and reconfiguring landscapes in South Africa," *Paper Presented at International Conference of Labour and Social History (ITH)*, Linz, Austria, September 7–9.

Kenny, Bridget and Edward Webster (2021) "The return of the labour process: Race, skill and technology in South African labour studies," *Work in the Global Economy* 1:1–2, 13–32.

Mashilo, Alex (2022) "Collective bargaining during and after apartheid: Economic and social upgrading in the automobile global value chains in South Africa," in C. Teipen, P. Dünhaupt, H. Herr, and F. Mehl (eds.) *Economic and Social Upgrading in Global Value Chains*. Cham: Palgrave Macmillan, 227–257, DOI: 10.1007/978-3-030-87320-2_9

Mashilo, Alex and Edward Webster (2021) "Upgrading in automotive global production: Networks: Workers' power in South Africa," *Journal of Labor and Society* 24, 525–555.

Massey, Doreen (1994) *Space, Place and Gender*, Minneapolis: University of Minnesota Press.

Rani, Uma, Ruth Castel-Branco, Shivani Satija and Mahima Nayar (2022) "Women, work, and the digital economy," *Gender and Development* 30:3, 421–435, DOI: 10.1080/13552074.2022.2151729

Rani, Uma and Marianne Furrer (2021) "Digital labour platforms and new forms of flexible work in developing countries: Algorithmic management of work and workers," *Competition & Change* 25:2, 212–236, DOI: 10.1177/1024529420905187

Sibiya, Wandile and David du Toit (2022) "Sweeping up decent work: Paid domestic work and digital platforms in South Africa," *Gender and Development* 30:3, 637–654, DOI: 10.1080/13552074.2022.2126199

Von Holdt, Karl (2003) *Transition from Below: Forging Trade Unionism and Workplace Change in South Africa*, Pietermaritzburg: University of Natal Press.

Webster, Edward (1985) *Cast in a Racial Mould: Labour Process and Trade Unionism in the Foundries*, Johannesburg: Ravan Press.

Webster, Edward and Lynford Dor (2023) *Recasting Workers' Power: Work and Inequality in the Shadow of the Digital Age*, Bristol: Bristol University Press.

Webster, Edward, Carmen Ludwig, Fikile Masikane and Dave Spooner (2021) "Beyond traditional trade unionism: Innovative worker responses in three African cities," *Globalizations* 18:8, 1363–1376.

Webster, Edward and Fikile Masikane (2021) *'I Just Want to Survive': A Comparative Studies of Food Courier Drivers in Three African Cities*, Johannesburg: FES and SCIS.

Recommendations for Further Reading

Anwar, Mohammad Amir and Mark Graham (2022) *The Digital Continent: Placing Africa in Planetary Networks of Work*, Oxford: Oxford University Press (A five country study of digital labour in Africa with a focus on debates around its developmental potential).

Hall, Stuart (1980) "Race, articulation and societies structured in dominance," in Mary O' Callaghan (ed.) *Sociological Theories: Race and Colonialism*. Paris: UNESCO, 305–345 (Classic piece intervening in the race-class debate on South Africa).

Kalla, Shaeera (2022) "Hacking platform capitalism: The case of domestic workers on South Africa's SweepSouth platform," *Gender & Development* 30:3, 655–666, DOI: 10.1080/13552074.2022.2136838 (Sensitive study positioning the forms of control and effects of platform domestic service work on black women workers within longer history of racial and gender oppression of black women as 'maids' in South Africa).

Ngwane, Trevor and Malehoko Tshoaedi, eds. (2021) *The Fourth Industrial Revolution: A Sociological Critique*, Pretoria: Jacana Press (Edited volume presenting and critiquing the discourses and policy use of 'The Fourth Industrial Revolution' in South Africa).

Rani, Uma, Ruth Castel-Branco, Shivani Satija and Mahima Nayar (2022) "Women, work, and the digital economy," *Gender & Development* 30:3, 421–435, DOI: 10.1080/13552074.2022.2151729 (Introduction to a special issue focusing on gender and women workers in the digital economy and focusing on experiences from the global South).

Webster, Edward and Lynford Dor (2023) *Recasting Workers' Power: Work and Inequality in the Shadow of the Digital Age*, Bristol: Bristol University Press (A collection of essays examining worker and labour power through digital technological workplace change).

Webster, Edward and Fikile Masikane (2021) *'I Just Want to Survive': A Comparative Studies of Food Courier Drivers in Three African Cities*, Johannesburg: FES and SCIS (An extended research report on working conditions, workers' experiences and organising models amongst platform food delivery drivers in Johannesburg, South Africa, Nairobi, Kenya and Accra, Ghana).

12

DISABILITY AND THE FUTURE OF WORK

Melanie Jones, Kim Hoque, Victoria Wass and Nicholas Bacon

Introduction

Across the world, disabled individuals still face substantial labour market disadvantage. This is evident in their lower likelihood of being employed, a pay gap relative to non-disabled employees, and gaps in other work-related outcomes, including job satisfaction, well-being, contentment, and fairness perceptions. At the same time, the number of people who report being disabled is increasing. Hence, securing an inclusive future for disabled individuals has become an urgent concern, affecting an ever-growing number of people, as well as garnering attention from both employers and governments.

This chapter will first explore long-term rising trends in the number of people reporting disability, and the limited progress made in mitigating the disadvantage they often experience within the labour market, including in relation to the exacerbating impact of economic shocks. The UK provides the focus of our analysis as it reflects these trends and provides an ideal setting for studying disability employment dynamics.

The chapter then outlines steps the government might take to address this disadvantage and engender a more inclusive future of work for disabled people, particularly in terms of addressing the barriers disabled people continue to encounter within organisations. The final section briefly speculates on the impact of emergent events (an ageing population, the growth of the gig economy and automation/digitalisation) on disabled people's employment. As other chapters in this handbook describe, the UK and other developed countries have witnessed a significant expansion of the gig economy and automation trends which may affect disabled people's employment prospects.

Defining Disability

In the UK, disability is defined by the Equality Act 2010 as a physical or mental impairment that has a 'substantial' and 'long-term' negative effect on a person's ability to do normal daily activities. Our focus is on disability within the working-age population, specifically individuals aged 16–64, and the resulting employment challenges it presents. A key metric in this context is the disability employment gap (DEG), which measures the percentage point difference in employment rates between individuals without disablities and those with disabilities. The DEG

 DOI: 10.4324/9781003327561-17

serves as an indicator of employment disadvantage and of the wider inequalities faced by disabled individuals. These disparities encompass barriers to independent living, as well as economic and social well-being (Barnes and Mercer, 2005). A reduction in the DEG has been a target of government policy since 2015 in order to help meet international obligations as signatories of the United Nations Convention on the Rights of Persons with Disabilities (UNCRPD).

Disability is a complex and multi-faceted concept with legal, social, cultural, and functional components. It may also vary throughout an individual's life stages and in response to their external environment. As such, whether an individual identifies as disabled depends on the importance they attribute to various aspects of functional impairment, and the extent to which this impairment hinders their activities and participation in society. The reporting of disability is influenced by language and context, and this complicates the comparison and interpretation of disability statistics. The primary gauge of disability concerning employment in the UK, and the one used in this chapter, is gathered through the quarterly Labour Force Survey (LFS), which stands as the most extensive household survey in the UK. Based on the UK's Equality Act definition, an individual is classified as disabled if they state they have a long-term health condition or illness that reduces their ability to carry out day-to-day activities.

Trends in Disability Prevalence

The most striking trend in disability research over the last 25 years is the increase in the disability prevalence rate within the working-age population (the percentage of working-age people who self-report disability). Figure 12.1 shows that the prevalence rate from the second quarter of 2013 increased from 16.5% to 19.8% in the first quarter of 2020, and to 23.2% by the second quarter of 2023. This represents an additional 2.9 million people, an increase of 44% over the period

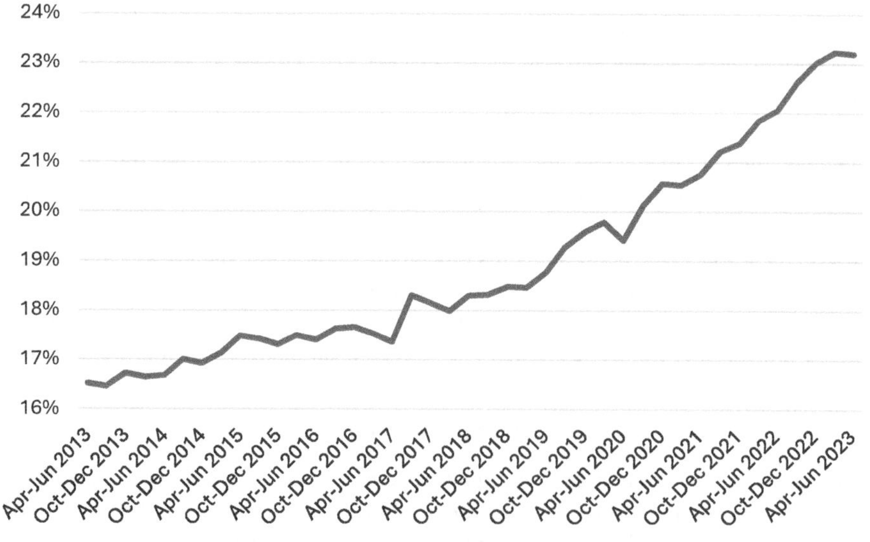

Figure 12.1 The UK disability prevalence rate (%) 2013–2023

Source: UK Office for National Statistics Table A08 Disability and Employment.

Notes: The disability questions in the LFS changed in q2 2013 from which date they have remained the same (see Jones and Wass, 2018).

(or 4% per year), and indicates acceleration in a trend which has been apparent since data collection began in 1998, when the disability prevalence rate was 14.5%.

To comprehend the increasing trend in disability prevalence and its implications for the future of work, we need to understand its drivers. For example, if it is due to socio-legal reasons such as increased awareness, acceptance and confidence in reporting disability, especially in relation to mental ill-health, this might reflect greater inclusion in the workplace. However, if it is due to greater functional impairment and/or activity-limitation, this might indicate that more people are experiencing health issues that make it challenging for them to perform various tasks and activities required in their jobs. It is also possible that job descriptions have evolved to become more complex and demanding, placing requirements on individuals to possess certain skills or abilities that some disabled individuals might find difficult to meet due to impairments or limitations. Understanding these drivers is important given their implications for the interpretation of the underlying dynamics affecting the employment landscape for disabled individuals and in interpreting trends in disability equality indicators (such as the DEG).

Regarding this, in the absence of a war or pandemic, attributing the increase to deteriorating health becomes challenging. The positive influence of medical advances in reducing impairments and their disabling effects appear to outweigh any potential impact on prolonging life in a morbid state, particularly where the working-age population is concerned. The recent COVID-19 pandemic, of course, represented a health shock, and the residual impacts of the disease, lockdowns and the redirection of resources towards COVID-19 care, which resulted in escalating waiting lists for medical treatment, are likely to have increased disability for health reasons from the second quarter of 2020. It is also possible that daily activities (including work) are increasingly designed around non-disabled people (see Foster and Wass, 2013). Nevertheless, this trend towards heightened disability is at least partially counteracted by the enabling impacts from assistive technology in both workplace and home settings, though the impact of the latter may be limited as disabled people are less likely than non-disabled people to be employed in job roles that allow working from home (Hoque and Bacon, 2022).

On balance, it is reasonable to assume that, between 2013 and 2020 before the pandemic, the growing rate of disability in the working-age population was likely not due to an increase in functional impairments, but reflects the influence of socio-legal and cultural factors such as changing societal attitudes, broader definitions of disability, advancements in healthcare, and changing job demands in reshaping the disability landscape (see Wass and Jones, 2020). When more people report disabilities because of socio-legal and cultural factors, it means that statistical indicators will include more people who have fewer limitations in their daily activities and are closer to being able to work, if not in work already. The inclusion of people with less severe limitations makes it tricky to understand trends in how employment opportunities for disabled individuals are changing over time.

Trends in the Disability Employment Gap

Official figures from the Office for National Statistics based on the nationally representative LFS show there has been a decrease in the size of the DEG (see Figure 12.2). Given this is widely viewed as one of the key indicators of work-related disability disadvantage, the government has been quick to claim this as a policy success. The percentage point gap in employment rates fell from 33 percentage points in the second quarter of 2013 to 29 percentage points in the second quarter of 2020 (a 14% fall). It has, however, not fallen since this time.

Despite the government's claim that a falling DEG indicates reduced work-related disability disadvantage, if this arises from an increase in disability prevalence attributed to a cultural expansion

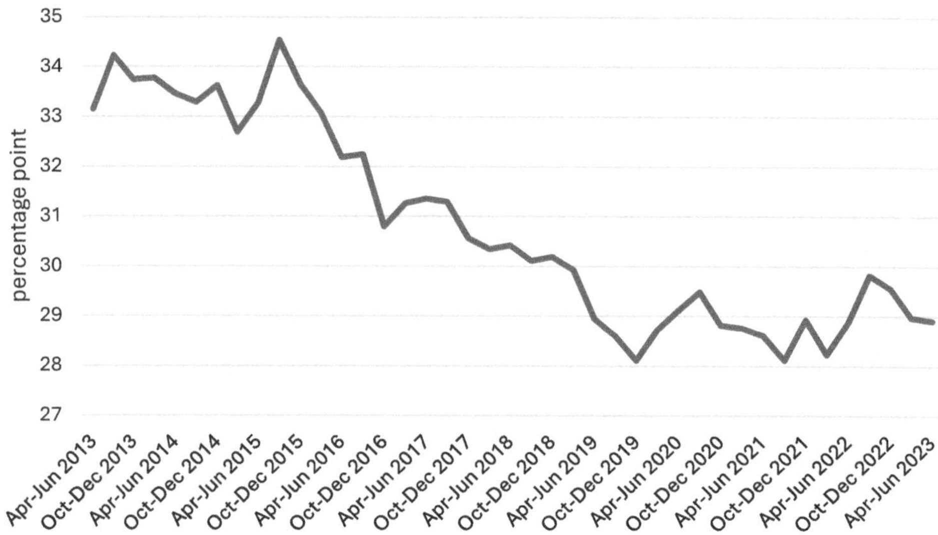

Figure 12.2 The UK disability employment gap (percentage points) 2013–2023
Source: UK Office for National Statistics Table A08 Disability and Employment.

of disability reporting, it does not imply a reduction in disability-related employment disadvantage for any given disabled individual. Without a more functional measure of disability, it is not possible to determine how far the narrowing trend is explained by a reduction in disadvantage, and how far it is explained by the aforementioned change in the composition of disabled people towards those with less severe activity-limitations. Regarding this, three studies (Baumberg et al., 2015; Jones and Wass, 2013; Slade and Edwards, 2015) point to the confounding effects on the DEG of an expanding disability prevalence rate. Jones and Wass's (2013) approach is replicated here in Figure 12.3 for the period 2013–2023. Figure 12.3 tracks a composite measure, in which the DEG is multiplied by the disability prevalence rate, which gives the proportion of the working-age population prevented from working by disability (PWD). We refer to this as a prevalence-adjusted DEG metric. In contrast to the falling DEG 2013 –2020, the prevalence-adjusted DEG fluctuates around 5.6%. There is a sharp increase between 2020 and 2023 suggesting a pandemic-related increase in functional impairment and/or activity-limitation lies behind the stalling in the downward DEG trend in Figure 12.2. This rapidly increasing proportion of the working-age population prevented from working by disability (5.6%–6.7%) includes a COVID effect (e.g., long COVID and increased hospital waiting times) and is part of the observed reduction in labour supply and current labour shortages in the UK following COVID (Haskel and Martin, 2022).

If we accept that the long-term upward trend in disability prevalence in the working-age population from 1998 to 2020 likely reflects a socio-legal broadening in understanding of disability, then the decline in the DEG until 2020 was likely a function of changes in the composition of disabled people rather than a reduction in disability-related employment disadvantage *per se*. This suggests a long-term failure to address disability disadvantage (Wass and Jones, 2020). Given increasing disability prevalance among the working-age population, increased inactivity within the working-age population following COVID, and the effects of an overall relative shrinking working-age population, managing disability inclusion at work is likely to become increasingly important to employers and government policy in the future (Haskel and Martin, 2022).

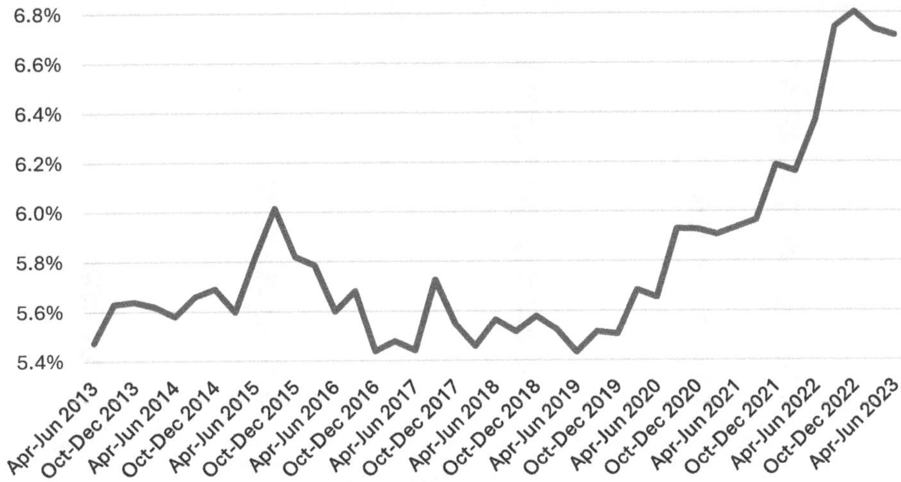

Figure 12.3 The UK prevalence-adjusted DEG (%) 2013–2023

Source: UK Office for National Statistics Table A08 Disability and Employment.

In-Work Disability-Related Disadvantage and Economic Shocks

Having highlighted long-term trends in disability prevalence and the DEG, our analysis now turns to the impact of economic shocks on disabled people's employment outcomes by exploring in greater depth the impact of the Great Recession, and the COVID-19 pandemic. We focus in particular on in-work disability disadvantage, given that disability-related labour market disadvantage does not manifest simply in the DEG, but also exists among workers in the form of disability gaps in experience of work and the quality of employment. While receiving far less policy attention, both are important dimensions of inequality and key drivers of the decision to work.

In addition to the DEG, there is evidence of disability gaps in pay (Jones et al., 2006; Longhi et al., 2012), hours of work (Jones, 2007), skill-mismatch (Jones and Sloane, 2010), self-employment (Jones and Latreille, 2011), and the experience of work (Bacon and Hoque, 2022; Jones, 2016; Hoque et al., 2017), including in relation to well-being at work as measured by anxiety-contentment, job satisfaction, and perceptions of managerial fairness. This disadvantage is not simply a consequence of differences in personal and other job-related characteristics, including average lower levels of education among disabled employees, given that differences remain after controlling for such factors. As such, there is consistent evidence of significant unexplained disability gaps, potentially reflecting unfair treatment (see Jones et al., 2006; Longhi et al., 2012). Consistent with this, in the more limited experimental research on employer discrimination, international studies have found consistent evidence of disability discrimination in hiring across a range of job roles and disabilities (Ameri et al., 2018).

As well as considering long-term trends in labour market disadvantage, it is important to understand fluctuations around the trend, for example, regarding how disabled people fare in recent periods of economic turbulence. Consistent with discrimination theory, US evidence suggests that disabled people are 'last hired, first fired' (Kruse and Schur, 2003: 61), which would imply the DEG widens during a downturn. While the evidence on this is less clear in the UK, recent work using nationally representative data from the 2011 Workplace Employment Relations Study (WERS) shows that disability gaps in in-work indicators widened during the Great Recession

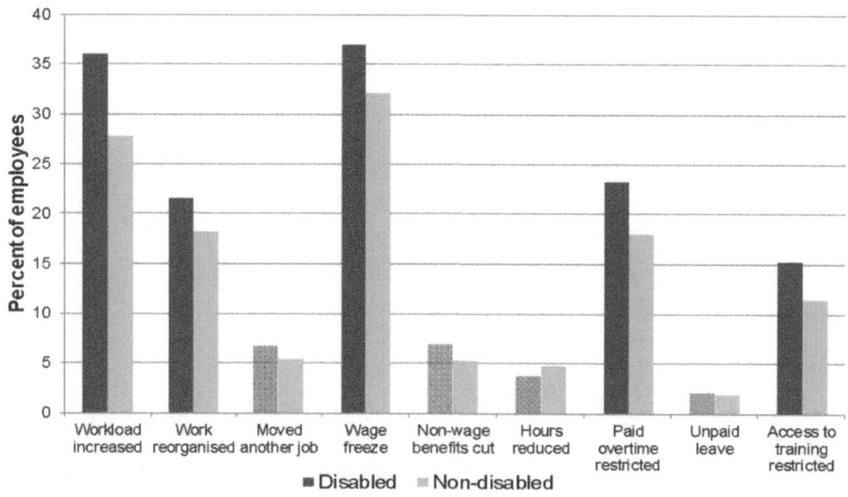

Figure 12.4 Disabled employees experience of the great recession in Great Britain

Notes: Figures are taken from Jones et al. (2021). Data are from the WERS 2011. The darker bars indicate a statistically significant difference between disabled and non-disabled employees.

(Jones et al., 2021). Figure 12.4 reports the percentage of disabled and non-disabled employees reporting being affected by different recession-induced changes to their jobs. Disabled employees were significantly more likely than non-disabled employees to report increased workloads, work reorganisation, a wage freeze or cut, and restricted access to paid overtime and training. Even after controlling for personal, job and workplace characteristics, and thereby capturing pre-existing disadvantage as a source of vulnerability to recessions, unexplained disability gaps in workload, work organisation, wages and access to training remained. Moreover, Jones et al. (2021) find limited evidence that workplace characteristics, including equality practices, working in the public sector and trade union recognition moderate these relationships to protect disabled employees. This could suggest that equality is not a priority for employers during periods of intense financial pressure. Thus, in addition to long-run trends, economic downturns appear to have the potential to change and exacerbate existing disability-related labour market inequality.

A further profound economic and health shock, with implications for disability prevalence and disability inequality in work, was the COVID-19 pandemic. Regarding this, Jones (2022) provides an analysis of labour market outcomes of disabled workers before and during the first year of the pandemic. Pre-pandemic differences in labour market outcomes suggested that disabled workers were more at risk of both adverse economic and health outcomes. For example, disabled employees were over-represented in the hardest hit 'shutdown' sectors, such as retail, accommodation and food, and personal care, and found to have higher occupational COVID-19-related health risks measured by working in proximity to others and exposure to disease. Surprisingly, and in contrast to this, during the first year of the pandemic the DEG and disability pay gaps remained largely unchanged. The explanation appears to lie in the disproportionate increase in being temporarily away from work for disabled people, which is consistent with comparable disabled workers being more reliant on the government job retention 'furlough' scheme. This is true even after accounting for differences in personal and job-related characteristics between disabled and non-disabled people. Bryan et al. (2022) draw similar conclusions with respect to disability arising from mental health problems, which is associated with an increased likelihood of being away from work and working reduced hours during the pandemic relative to non-disabled workers. While it is too early to assess the long-term impact of these trends, the risk is that people who spend time away from the labour market even temporarily will be affected over the longer-term due to human capital depreciation, potentially leading to widening disability-related labour market inequality in the UK.

One feature of the pandemic which is also likely to have long-term implications for the flexibility and location of work is the dramatic increase in working at home. However, when it comes to the relationship between working at home and disability, the existing research offers a mixed picture. While, on average disabled people (when including the self-employed) were more likely to work at home before the pandemic, they are less likely to work in occupations with high potential for homeworking (Jones, 2022; Schur et al., 2020). The latter might explain the absence of a disproportionate increase in homeworking among disabled workers during the pandemic (Jones, 2022), and is likely to restrict disabled workers capitalising on some of the benefits of homeworking in the future. Indeed, while not without potential disadvantages for disabled workers (Hoque and Bacon, 2022) particularly in relation to visibility, the willingness of employers to offer flexible working arrangements in terms of hours, responsibilities and location is likely to be particularly important for the future recruitment and retention of disabled people who might otherwise be unable to work due to their specific needs or circumstances.

An Inclusive Future of Work for Disabled People

There is a central role for government policy in addressing the labour market disadvantage that disabled people encounter, and in ensuring a more inclusive future of work for disabled people. The focus of government policy, both in the UK and internationally, has to date been on supply-side initiatives and labour market activation policies. In the last five years in the UK, this has included the Work and Health Programme, Individual Placement and Support in Primary Care Initiative, Intensive Personalised Employment Support, and the Personal Support Package. These initiatives provide personalised and tailored employment and health support to try and help disabled individuals overcome barriers to work. Although such supply-side initiatives have the potential to improve disabled people's employment outcomes, their potency has been limited by the lack of simultaneous efforts to address the demand-side barriers disabled people encounter in entering and remaining in work, including inflexible jobs, difficulties obtaining reasonable adjustments, and negative employer attitudes. In recognition of this lack of demand-side focus, this chapter will next explore how governments might encourage and support employers to promote greater disability inclusion in the future.

The demand-side workplace barriers disabled people encounter, and hence the challenges governments must help address, are demonstrated by employer responses to the nationally representative 2011 Workplace Employment Relations Study (WERS, 2011). This shows that although most British private sector workplaces with five or more employees have a formal written disability equality policy statement, very few have adopted disability equality practices to underpin this statement. Only approximately 10% monitor or review recruitment and selection by disability; only 5% review promotions by disability; only 2% review pay rates by disability; and only 5% of workplaces have special procedures to attract job applications from disabled people (Bacon and Hoque, 2022). As such, disability equality policy statements in British workplaces are typically little more than 'empty shells' (Hoque and Noon, 2004). Greater employer adoption of such practices is, however, essential for a more inclusive future of work. For example, disability equality practices are especially important to mitigate the potentially disabling effect of modern management practices that assume all employees are polyvalent, with such assumptions being built into competency testing, performance appraisal, individual performance-related pay, teamworking, and functional flexibility (Hoque et al., 2017).

There are several routes by which governments might encourage and/or regulate employers to adopt disability equality practices, and thereby improve disabled people's employment outcomes. These routes include strengthening employer certification and accreditation, introducing mandatory disability employment reporting, leveraging government procurement expenditure for social value, and equality bargaining with trade unions. Below, we address each of these routes, in turn.

Strengthening Certification and Accreditation

Conscious of the need to address the demand-side barriers disabled people encounter, the UK government has created voluntary certifications to which employers can sign up. These certifications aim to encourage employers to improve disability equality practices and outcomes by giving them "the knowledge, skills and confidence they need to attract, recruit, retain and progress disabled people in the workplace" (HM Government, 2021: 54).

The first of these certification schemes was 'Two Ticks', which was introduced in 1990. However, despite the expectations placed on Two Ticks employers to adhere to certain commitments, research indicated that they were no more likely to employ disabled people than non-Two Ticks employers. Also, their adoption of disability equality policies and practices was barely any higher (Bacon and Hoque, 2019; Hoque et al., 2014). In addition, the Two Ticks initiative demonstrated limited effectiveness in enhancing the workplace experiences of disabled employees (regarding well-being, job satisfaction, fair treatment, and contentment) or in closing the disparities in these outcomes between disabled and non-disabled individuals (Bacon and Hoque, 2019; Hoque et al., 2014). These findings reflect the absence of independent inspection to ensure employer adherence to the expected standards; hence, many employers may have sought certification to secure positive reputational effects while not making any improvements to their disability equality practices or outcomes.

Two Ticks was replaced by the Disability Confident scheme in 2016, and over 20,000 employers covering more than 11 million employees have achieved certification (HM Government, 2021: 54). Disability Confident retained many of the same design features as Two Ticks. For example, its certification criteria focus on whether employers have adopted certain processes and practices rather than whether they have achieved certain disability-related outcomes. It also did not introduce independent monitoring to ensure certified employers meet the required standards. There are some differences between the schemes, however, with Disability Confident introducing three levels, the expectation that employers will seek to work their way up to the highest level (Level 3 – leader). However, the first two levels (Level 1 – Committed, and Level 2 – Employer) rely on self-assessment, while the highest level requires peer-assessment of processes and practices by another employer at that level rather than by an independent inspection body. This general lack of assessment suggests Disability Confident is unlikely to have performed any better than Two Ticks in improving disabled people's employment outcomes.

However, to date there have been no systematic assessments of the effectiveness of the revised Disability Confident scheme; hence, further research is needed. Should such research show Disability Confident is indeed no more effective than Two Ticks, this will suggest a need for the assessment criteria to be revised to include rigorous independent monitoring of whether employers have achieved certain disability employment outcomes (e.g., minimum thresholds regarding the number of disabled people they employ as a percentage of their workforce) (Disability@Work, 2022;

Work and Pensions Committee, 2023). This would help ensure that certification sends a stronger signal to disabled job-seekers regarding the employers that are more likely to hire or retain them.

Mandatory Disability Employment Reporting

A further government initiative that might help secure a more inclusive future for disabled people is the introduction of mandatory disability employment reporting (Centre for Social Justice, 2021; Connolly et al., 2016; Institute of Directors, 2022; Work and Pensions Committee, 2021). This would require employers with 250 or more employees to report the number of disabled people they employ as a percentage of their workforce.

Mandatory disability employment reporting would be expected to have several positive effects (Disability@Work, 2022). On the principle of 'what gets measured gets done', it is likely to place the hiring and retention of disability employment firmly on boardroom agendas. It would also provide employers with the necessary data to track the effectiveness of their efforts to improve disabled people's employment outcomes. In addition, if based on a standardised question and data collection process (thus ensuring the data collected are comparable across employers), it would enable employers to benchmark their progress against regional, national and industry averages, and allow government to identify high performers from whom important lessons might be learned. Beyond this, if the Disability Confident certification criteria are revised to focus on disability employment outcomes (as outlined above) the data could be used to assess whether organisations meet these criteria.

However, it is sometimes argued that there are certain practical difficulties in implementing disability employment reporting, including in relation to disabled people's willingness to disclose, for example. Nevertheless, many leading public and private sector employers including EY, Clifford Chance, Capita, and the main television broadcasters already report a range of disability employment metrics (Sayce et al., 2019), thus demonstrating that these practical difficulties are not insurmountable. NHS England's Workforce Disability Equality Standard (WDES) requires NHS employers to report on metrics comparing disabled and non-disabled employees' workplace and career experiences, which are used to develop action plans and measure year-on-year progress (NHS, 2022). Civil service and government department also report workforce disability prevalence by pay and grading levels (Cabinet Office, 2023). In addition, universities are statutorily obliged to report on workforce disability prevalence to the Higher Education Statistics Agency (HESA, 2023). A mandatory approach to disability employment reporting would spread these existing pockets of good practice across the economy more broadly.

Many employers would appear to understand the value of this argument, with only 13% of HR managers reporting that "senior management is not convinced by the business case for disability reporting", and only 25% report their organisation lacks the necessary resources, systems/infrastructure or guidance/support (Chartered Institute of Personnel and Development, 2022: 8). Also demonstrating a mandatory approach can be made to work, in the United States, Section 503 of the Rehabilitation Act 1973 requires employers with federal government contracts to report, using a standard government form that by law cannot be altered, the percentage of disabled workers in their workforce to the Office of Federal Contract Compliance Programs within the Department of Labor (von Schrader and Bruyère, 2018).

Complementing mandatory employment reporting, a further step in ensuring an inclusive future of work for disabled people would be the introduction of mandatory disability pay gap reporting for employers with 250+ employees (mirroring mandatory gender pay gap reporting in the UK) (Centre for Social Justice, 2021; Disability@Work, 2022). This would help demonstrate whether disabled people are equally represented within the organisation's hierarchy, or whether they cluster towards the bottom end. The government argues that gender pay gap reporting "is a key part of building a country that works for everyone", by breaking down barriers to employment and career progression, thus creating 'a more modern workforce' (Government Equalities Office, 2017). These arguments apply equally to disability pay gap reporting.

Leveraging Government Procurement Expenditure for Social Value

A further step that governments might take to engender a more inclusive future of work for disabled people is to leverage government procurement expenditure (Connolly et al., 2016). In the UK, for example, gross spending on public sector procurement was £379 billion in 2021/2022 (House of Commons Library, 2022). This expenditure might be leveraged to increase disability employment in a number of ways. First, contract award decisions for all public sector contracts could take into account the disability employment metrics of tendering employers, thereby requiring them to compete for contracts in part on the basis of their disability employment outcomes. Second, employers that win contracts could be required to uphold certain minimum standards regarding disability employment. Third, failure to work towards these minimum standards could be taken into consideration in future contract award decisions.

Research on the aforementioned federal contractor regulations in the US (Section 503 of the Rehabilitation Act, 1973) highlights the potential for government procurement to be leveraged to improve disability employment outcomes. US regulations since 2014 have required federal contractors to work towards a 7% 'utilisation goal', and report the percentage of their workforce who are disabled using a standard (non-anonymous) self-declaration form. This has led to positive changes to employers' disability policies and practices, with only 15% of employers reporting policies and practices had not changed at all as a result of the regulations, and only 23% disagreeing their firm would employ more disabled people as a result of the regulations (von Schrader and Bruyère, 2018).

The UK government's recent reforms to the *Public Services* (Social Value) Act 2012 might be seen as a step forward in this regard (Cabinet Office, 2020). The new reforms (outlined in PPN 06/20) require government procurement to explicitly evaluate social value in all central government procurement, with a minimum weighting of 10% of the total score for the award of the contract being based on social value. One of the forms of social value that can be used to evaluate tendering firms in contract award decisions is reducing the DEG. This is important in establishing the DEG as an explicit social value outcome against which employer commitments can be evaluated in procurement exercises – indeed, disability is the only protected characteristic that is expressly mentioned within PPN 06/20.

Nevertheless, the recent reforms contain several weaknesses (Centre for Social Justice, 2021; Hoque and Bacon, 2022). For example, contracting bodies are required to select social value contract award criteria that are relevant and proportionate to the contract, hence there is no guarantee that disability will be included as a criterion. Also, where disability is included as a social value objective, the criteria against which employers are judged are arguably weak, as they do not involve evaluation of tendering organisations' disability employment outcomes. In addition, PPN 06/20 specifies KPIs for assessing social value should focus on the 'contract workforce' rather than the 'whole workforce'; only applies to central government procurement, and not to all public sector contracts; and does not outline sanctions for contractors that fail to uphold social value commitments.

However, these weaknesses are not insurmountable. For example, the criteria against which tendering organisations are assessed could be amended to focus on disability employment outcomes, and aspirational targets could be implemented for employers winning contracts, as in the US Federal Contractor Regulations (von Schrader and Bruyère, 2018). PPN 06/20 could also be amended to apply to the employers' whole workforce, and employers found not to have worked towards the achievement of relevant KPIs could be prevented from tendering for future contracts (Centre for Social Justice, 2021; Hoque and Bacon, 2022).

Therefore, notwithstanding the weaknesses of the current regulations, it would appear that there is significant potential for government procurement expenditure to be leveraged to engender a more inclusive future for disabled people.

Equality Bargaining with Trade Unions

There is conflicting evidence regarding the relationship between union membership/recognition *per se* and positive outcomes for disabled employees (Ameri et al., 2019; Jones, 2023). However, this relationship may vary depending on whether employers engage in genuine consultation and negotiation with recognised unions on equality issues. For example, Hoque and Bacon (2014) find that employer adoption of disability equality practices is much greater in union environments where such negotiation and consultation occurs than in union environments where it does not. Governments might therefore further encourage employers to adopt disability equality practices by encouraging (or requiring) them to negotiate or consult with recognised unions on equality issues, via the introduction of a statutory right to equality bargaining.

Trade unions have also promoted disability equality in recent times by recruiting and training Equality Representatives and Disability Champions. Equality Representatives encourage employers to improve equal opportunity practices, offer independent advice and guidance on equality issues and rights to employees, and raise the profile of the equality agenda within their unions. Disability Champions encourage employers to audit and improve disability practices and offer independent advice and guidance on disability issues to employees.

Research highlights the effectiveness of these new forms of union representation. Regarding Equality Representatives, more than three-fifths state they have impacted positively on the employer's disability equality practices (Bacon and Hoque, 2012). This does not vary between the public and private sectors, between SMEs and large organisations, or between industry sectors. Regarding Disability Champions, the majority claim to have impacted positively on employer willingness to conduct disability audits and to amend and improve employer disability equality practices (Bacon and Hoque, 2015).

However, this research also suggests the impact of both Equality Representatives and Disability Champions depends on them having regular contact with management (e.g., via attendance at equality/disability committees), and is also greater where negotiation over equality takes place. The evidence also suggests they have greater impact where they are able to spend least five hours per week on the role. This suggests their future effectiveness is likely to be enhanced by the introduction of statutory rights to time off to perform their role such as those afforded to Union Learning Representatives (ULRs). Such rights may enable them to perform their roles more effectively, thus helping to contribute towards meaningful change in disability-related equality at work (Centre for Social Justice, 2021; Bacon and Hoque, 2012, 2015).

Emerging Trends – Demographic Change, Digitisation, and the Gig Economy

Periods of economic turbulence will be likely to continue to shape the future of work, with potential deleterious labour market consequences for disabled people. Increasing inactivity within the working-age population and an ageing population, which reduces the relative size of the working population, are manifesting in labour shortages. In the UK, the changing composition of the population towards an ageing structure is identified by the Office for Budget Responsibility (OBR) (2022) as one of largest and most certain economic and fiscal risks over the next 50 years, alongside climate change. The proportion of older people dependent on those of working-age is forecast to increase significantly in developed countries (OECD, 2020), driving an ever-increasing shortage of labour. Part of this labour shortage could be met through the greater inclusion of working-age disabled people within organisations.

This suggests the need for the government measures outlined above will become ever more pressing. As argued earlier, responses that rely on supply-side initiatives and labour market activation policies will have limited effectiveness unless more attention is paid to the demand-side barriers disabled people encounter in organisations, including inflexible jobs, difficulties obtaining reasonable adjustments, and negative employer attitudes. UK government assumptions that working from home offers a ready-made solution to demand-side barriers (Department for Work and Pensions, 2023) appear misconceived. Instead, greater focus is needed on demand-side policies including, as outlined above, strengthening employer certification and accreditation schemes, mandatory disability employment reporting, leveraging government procurement expenditure for social value, and greater support for the role of trade unions. Reliance on a voluntary employer-led approach has been insufficient to significantly reduce disability-related disadvantage in the labour market.

However, it is encouraging that support for such measures is increasing across a wide range of stakeholders. This is reflected most clearly by the growing number of signatories to the Disability Employment Charter, which calls for the introduction of the measures outlined here (among others).[1] A more inclusive future for disabled people may be in part dependent on government willingness to introduce these measures, and the growing support for the Charter has increased the likelihood of this happening.

It is possible, though, that the future of work for disabled people will also be impacted significantly by other emergent trends, including the growth in the gig economy, and the possible digitisation and automation of jobs on disabled people. Regarding the gig economy, disabled people in the UK are over-represented in gig economy jobs, and according to the Equality and Human Rights Commission (EHRC, 2023), they are therefore more vulnerable to associated trends in precarious employment and pay inequality. Gig economy work also contains barriers for disabled people. It requires digital skills that disabled people overall are less likely to possess. Gig work relies on automated performance monitoring and job tasks that are likely to pose challenges for any disabled people who require reasonable adjustments. Furthermore, employment and disability benefits are not designed with fluctuating income from gig work in mind (EHRC, 2023). Hence, although gig work offers working time flexibility that might help disabled people enter employment, it also contains inflexibilities that might be to disabled people's detriment.

Turning to the impact of digitisation and automation on disabled people, it is possible that disabled people in jobs undergoing digital transformation might benefit disproportionately if any job tasks affected by their impairments become easier to perform. Hence, an optimistic scenario might emphasise the important role technology can play in helping disabled people overcome physical limitations. A more pessimistic scenario, however, suggests that disadvantage might be exacerbated if digitised platforms and infrastructure are not designed to be fully accessible (OECD, 2023). There is arguably a high risk of this happening, given that most employers have not traditionally taken disabled people's accessibility needs into account when designing jobs and developing related technologies.

However, the impact of digitisation and automation on disabled people will also depend on whether disabled people are more or less likely than non-disabled people to work in affected jobs and industries (OECD, 2023). If digitisation is negatively associated with wages and educational attainment and more likely to affect low-skill jobs (Frey and Osborne, 2017), it will impact more heavily on disabled people who are over-represented in such jobs, and have on average have lower levels of educational attainment. In the UK, it is estimated that disabled workers are slightly more likely than non-disabled workers to be employed in jobs at risk of automation (EHRC, 2023). While the optimistic scenario suggests that this may be to disabled people's benefit, the pessimistic scenario suggests the opposite (especially, of course, if automation means these jobs disappear altogether).

Nevertheless, it is possible that the pressures of demographic change on labour shortages forces employers to take disabled people's accessibility needs into account in the design of digitised and automated systems, suggesting the optimistic scenario will prevail. Government implementation of the proposals outlined above regarding mandatory disability employment reporting, reform of Disability Confident, leveraging of procurement expenditure and support for trade union equality bargaining (as called for within the Disability Employment Charter) may also have a major impact on how far this is likely to happen, and, in turn, on how far the future of work will be more inclusive of disabled people.

Note

1 The Charter (www.disabilityemploymentcharter.org) calls for government to enact a range of proposals to address disability employment disadvantage, including in relation to the areas outlined above (i.e. reform of the government's Disability Confident scheme, disability employment and pay gap reporting, leveraging government procurement, and support for trade union equality representatives and disability champions). Over 150 organisations have signed the Charter, including virtually all of the UK's large disability charities, disabled people's organisations, trade unions (and the Trades Union Congress), and several large employers.

References

Ameri, M., Ali, M., Schur, L. and Kruse, D. L. (2019) *Disability and the Unionized Workplace*. IZA Discussion Papers 12258, Institute of Labor Economics (IZA).

Ameri, M., Schur, L., Adya, M., Bentley, F. S., McKay, P. and Kruse, D. (2018) The disability employment puzzle: A field experiment on employer hiring behavior. *ILR Review*, 71(2): 329–364.

Bacon, N. and Hoque, K. (2012) The role and impact of trade union equality representatives in Britain. *British Journal of Industrial Relations*, 50(2): 239–262.

Bacon, N. and Hoque, K. (2015) The influence of trade union disability champions on employer disability policy and practice. *Human Resource Management Journal*, 25(2): 233–249.

Bacon, N. and Hoque, K. (2019) *Briefing Note: Two Ticks or No Ticks? An Assessment of Two Ticks 'Positive About Disabled People' Certification*. https://www.disabilityatwork.co.uk/wp-content/uploads/2019/02/Disability@Work-Two-Ticks-Briefing-Paper-4.pdf

Bacon, N. and Hoque, K. (2022) The treatment of disabled individuals in small, medium-sized, and large firms. *Human Resource Management*, 61(2): 137–156.

Barnes, C. and Mercer G. (2005) Disability, work, and welfare: Challenging the social exclusion of disabled people. *Work Employment & Society*, 19(3): 527–545.

Baumberg, B., Jones, M. and Wass, V. (2015) Disability prevalence and disability–related employment gaps in the UK 1998–2012: Different trends in different surveys? *Social Science and Medicine*, 141: 72–81.

Bryan, M., Bryce, A., Rice, N., Roberts, J. and Sechel, C. (2022) Exploring mental health disability gaps in the labour market: The UK experience during COVID-19. *Labour Economics*, 78:102253.

Cabinet Office (2020) *Procurement Policy Note – Taking Account of Social Value in the Award of Central Government Contracts. Action Note PPN 06/20.* https://assets.publishing.service.gov.uk/government/uploads/system/uploads/attachment_data/file/921437/PPN-06_20-Taking-Account-of-Social-Value-in-the-Award-of-Central-Government-Contracts.pdf

Cabinet Office (2023) *Statistical Bulletin – Civil Service Statistics: 2022.* https://www.gov.uk/government/statistics/civil-service-statistics-2022/statistical-bulletin-civil-service-statistics-2022#:~:text=Civil%20Service%20Statistics%20shows%20that,of%20the%20Civil%20Service%20workforce

Centre for Social Justice (2021) *Now Is the Time: A Report by the CSJ Disability Commission.* March. https://www.centreforsocialjustice.org.uk/wp-content/uploads/2021/03/CSJJ8819-Disability-Report-190408.pdf

Chartered Institute of Personnel and Development (2022) *Disability Workforce Reporting Submission to the Disability Unit.* https://www.cipd.org/globalassets/media/comms/about-us/influencing-public-policy/misc-policy/cipd-submission-to-disability-workforce-reporting-consultation-final_tcm18-108798.pdf

Connolly, P., Wass, V., Bacon, N., Hoque, K. and Jones, M. (2016) *Ahead of the Arc: A Contribution to Halving the Disability Employment Gap.* All Party Parliamentary Group for Disability. London. https://www.disabilityatwork.co.uk/wp-content/uploads/2016/11/All-Party-Parliamentary-Group-on-Disability-Ahead-of-the-Arc-Report.pdf

Department for Work and Pensions (2023) *Work Capability Assessment: Activities and Descriptors Consultation.* https://assets.publishing.service.gov.uk/government/uploads/system/uploads/attachment_data/file/1182410/work-capability-assessment-activities-and-descriptors-consultation.pdf

Disability@Work (2022) *Submission to the Disability Workforce Reporting Consultation.* March. https://www.disabilityatwork.co.uk/wp-content/uploads/2022/05/Disability@Work-submission-to-the-Disability-Workforce-Reporting-Consultationfinal.pdf

EHRC (2023) *Future of Work Report.* https://www.equalityhumanrights.com/future-work-report Foster, D. and Wass, V. (2013) Disability in the labour market: An exploration of concepts of the 'ideal worker' and organisational 'fit' that disadvantage employees with impairments. *Sociology*, 47(4): 705–721.

Frey, C. B. and Osborne, M. A. (2017) The future of employment: How susceptible are jobs to computerisation? *Technological Forecasting & Social Change*, 114: 254–280.

Government Equalities Office (2017) *Gender Pay Gap: Closing It Together.* https://www.gov.uk/government/news/gender-pay-gap-reporting-goes-live

Haskel, J. and Martin, J. (2022) Economic inactivity and the labour market experience of the long-term sick. Working paper. Available: https://t.co/B06wJvPUJJ

HESA (2023) *Higher Education Staff Statistics: UK 2021/22.* https://www.hesa.ac.uk/news/17-01-2023/higher-education-staff-statistics-uk-202122-released

HM Government (2021) *Welcome to Disability Confident.* https://assets.publishing.service.gov.uk/government/uploads/system/uploads/attachment_data/file/830085/disability-confident-welcome-guide-new-members.pdf

Hoque, K. and Bacon, N. (2014) Unions, joint regulation and workplace equality policy and practice in Britain: Evidence from the 2004 Workplace Employment Relations Survey. *Work, Employment and Society*, 28(2): 265–284.

Hoque, K., Bacon, N., and Parr, D. (2014). Employer disability practice in Britain: Assessing the impact of the Positive About Disabled People 'Two Ticks' symbol. *Work, Employment and Society*, 28(3): 430–451. https://doi.org/10.1177/0950017012472757

Hoque, K. and Bacon, N. (2022) Working from home and disabled people's employment outcomes. *British Journal of Industrial Relations*, 60(1): 32–56.

Hoque, K., Bacon, N., Jones, M. and Wass, V. (2017) Are high performance work practices enabling or disabling? Exploring the relationship between selected HPWPs and work-related disability. *Human Resource Management*, 57(2): 499–513.

Hoque, K., Bacon, N. and Parr, D. (2015) Employer disability practice in Britain: Assessing the impact of the positive about disabled people 'Two Ticks' symbol. *Work, Employment and Society*, 28(3): 430–451.

Hoque, K. and Noon, M. (2004) Equal opportunities policy and practice in Britain: Evaluating the "empty shell" hypothesis. *Work Employment and Society*, 18(3): 481–506.

House of Commons Library (2022) *Procurement Statistics: A Short Guide.* https://commonslibrary.parliament.uk/research-briefings/cbp-9317/

Institute of Directors (2022) *The Future of Business: Harnessing Diverse Talent for Success. Recommendations to Government*. October. London. https://www.iod.com/app/uploads/2022/10/IoD-Future-of-Business-practical-guidance-for-employers-ACCESSIBLE-v11-b0e2942127a9d32722224471624d4f697.pdf

Jones, M. (2007) Does part-time employment provide a way of accommodating a disability? *The Manchester School*, 75(6): 695–716.

Jones, M. (2016) Disability and perceptions of work and management. *British Journal of Industrial Relations*, 54(1): 83–113.

Jones, M. (2022) COVID-19 and the labour market outcomes of disabled people in the UK. *Social Science and Medicine*, 292, article number: 114637. https://doi.org/10.1016/j.socscimed.2021.114637

Jones, M. (2023) Disability and trade union membership in the UK. *British Journal of Industrial Relations*. https://doi.org/10.1111/bjir.12767

Jones, M., Hoque, K., Wass, V. and Bacon, N. (2021) Inequality and the economic cycle: Disabled employees' experience of work during the Great Recession in Britain. *British Journal of Industrial Relations*, 59(3): 788–815.

Jones, M. and Latreille, P. (2011) Disability and self-employment: Evidence from the UK LFS. *Applied Economics*, 43(27): 4161–4178.

Jones, M., Latreille, P. and Sloane, P. (2006) Disability, gender and the British labour market. *Oxford Economic Papers*, 58(3): 407–459.

Jones, M. and Sloane, P. (2010) Disability and skill mismatch. *Economic Record*, 86(s1): 101–114.

Jones, M. and Wass, V. (2013) Understanding changing disability-related employment gaps in Britain 1998–2011. *Work Employment and Society*, 27(6): 982–1003.

Jones, M. and Wass, V. (2018) *Defining Disability in Government Surveys*. Disability@work Briefing Note. https://www.disabilityatwork.co.uk/wp-content/uploads/2018/10/Disability@Work-Defining-disability-in-Government-Surveys-August-2018.pdf

Kruse, D. and Schur, L. (2003) Employment of people with disabilities following the ADA. *Industrial Relations*, 42(1): 31–66.

Longhi, S., Nicoletti, C. and Platt, L. (2012) Interpreting wage gaps of disabled men: The roles of productivity and of discrimination. *Southern Economic Journal*, 78(3): 931–953.

NHS (2022) *Workforce Disability Equality Standard 2022 Data Analysis Report for NHS Trusts and Foundation Trusts*. https://www.england.nhs.uk/wp-content/uploads/2023/09/wdes-summary-report-2022.pdf

OECD (2020) *Promoting an Age-Inclusive Workforce: Living, Learning and Earning Longer*. https://www.oecd.org/employment/promoting-an-age-inclusive-workforce-59752153-en.htm

OECD (2023) *Using AI to Support People with Disability in the Labour Market: Opportunities and Challenges*. OECD Artificial Intelligence Papers, No. 7, OECD Publishing, Paris, https://doi.org/10.1787/008b32b7-en

Office for Budget Responsibility (OBR) (2022) *Fiscal Risks and Sustainability*. OECD Publishing, Paris, https://doi.org/10.1787/59752153-en

Sayce, L., Bacon, N., Hoque, K., Wass, V. and Jones, M. (2019) *Improving Disabled People's Employment and Pay: Proposal for Transparent Reporting by Employers*. London School of Economics/ Disability@Work Briefing Paper. https://www.disabilityatwork.co.uk/wp-content/uploads/2019/12/Proposal-for-transparent-reporting.pdf

Schur, L., Ameri, M. and Kruse, D. (2020) Telework after COVID: A "silver lining" for workers with disabilities? *Journal of Occupational Rehabilitation*, 30(4): 521–536.

Slade, J. and Edwards, R. (2015) *My Voice: The Views and Experiences of Blind and Partially Sighted People in the UK*. London: Royal National Institute for the Blind.

von Schrader, S. and Bruyère, S. (2018) *What Works? How Federal Contractors Are Implementing Section 503*. Cornell University. https://hdl.handle.net/1813/90120

Wass, V. and Jones, M. (2020) *Measuring Disability and Interpreting Trends in Disability-Related Disadvantage*. Briefing Note, Disability at Work. https://www.disabilityatwork.co.uk/wp-content/uploads/2020/08/Briefing-Note-disability-measurement-.pdf

Work and Pensions Committee (2021) *Disability Employment Gap: Second Report of Session 2021–22*. London: HMSO.

Work and Pensions Committee (2023) *Plan for Jobs and Employment Support: Eighth Report of Session 2022–23*. London: HMSO.

Recommendations for Further Reading

Disability@Work (2022) *Written Evidence for the Work and Pensions Committee Plan for Jobs and Employment Support*. https://www.disabilityatwork.co.uk/wp-content/uploads/2023/08/Disability@Work-final-submission-to-Plan-for-Jobs-and-Employment-Support-.pdf

Disability@Work and Disability Rights UK (2018) *Building for Success in Recruiting and Supporting Disabled People in the Workplace*. https://www.disabilityatwork.co.uk/wp-content/uploads/2018/10/DRUK-and-Disability@Work-Disability-Measurement-Advice-for-Employers-Building-for-Success-2018.pdf

OECD (2023) *Using AI to Support People with Disability in the Labour Market: Opportunities and Challenges*. https://www.oecd-ilibrary.org/employment/using-ai-to-support-people-with-disability-in-the-labour-market_008b32b7-en;jsessionid=JO73ZkxzcTKFV2X5tGaCadIHNV4fNKUDxLdd9og-.ip-10-240-5-100

Schur, L., Kruse, D. and Blanck, P. (2013) *People with Disabilities: Sidelined or Mainstreamed?* Cambridge: Cambridge University Press.

13

WORK, WEALTH AND THE FUTURE

Evolving Class Structures and Social Mobility in a Changing World of Work

Julie MacLeavy

Introduction

There is a widespread contention that the global economy is undergoing a significant transformation in which the traditional model of secure, long-term employment is being steadily eroded and replaced by temporary posts in which there is a heightened sense of precarity (Kalleberg, 2018; Standing, 2011). This shift from 'a job for life' to 'a life of jobs' (Gilbert, 1998) is said to be linked to the widespread adoption of neoliberal arguments that increased labour market flexibility is necessary for economic growth and competitiveness in a globalised world (Peck, 2001). Consequently, the anxieties and insecurities present in today's work environment have been framed as the inevitable consequence of prioritising market freedoms. These freedoms include the ability of firms to operate with minimal government regulations – by setting wages without mandated minimums or by hiring and firing at will – engendering a shift in labour market dynamics in which the balance of power tilts away from workers and towards firms. As Herod and Lambert (2016: 2) write, "the changes in labour market practice since the late 1970s have been far reaching and revolutionary and, for many, herald a return to the conditions experienced by workers under nineteenth-century industrial capitalism". Elsewhere, the growing emphasis on labour market flexibility is theorised to have resulted in a breakdown of the post-war class compromise, inducing a "return to the days before the Keynesian euthanasia of the rentier" (Adkins et al., 2020: 5). While the post-war period saw governments, labour unions and firms coexist in a relatively stable economic order, helping to deliver full employment that ensured the availability of stable, long-term jobs and rising wages, the institution of flexible labour markets (underwritten by conditional welfare provisions) is posited as fundamentally restructuring how working lives are organised and experienced. Inequality and economic instability, it is argued, are situating individuals in a space of liminality, where they are vulnerable to the anxieties of precarious work and the frustration of constricted pathways towards social mobility (Garsten, 1999; Purser, 2012; Scott et al., 2022). This liminal space is fostering a pervasive sense of insecurity, fuelled by the constant threat of losing one's wage and the inability to accumulate resources or plan for the future (Standing, 2011).

The widespread narration of the growth of precarious work, encompassing temporary employment agreements (casual work, fixed-term contracts), disguised employment arrangements (where workers are classified as self-employed but lack autonomy) and the burgeoning gig and platform

DOI: 10.4324/9781003327561-18

economy, is not without its detractors. The perceived ubiquity of precarious work arrangements has been challenged and evidence presented to suggest that within advanced capitalist economies, like the UK, temporary jobs are still relatively uncommon and for many job security seems stable (Choonara, 2020). The gig and platform economy, similarly, has been found to primarily supplement existing stable employment, rather than act as a standalone source of income generation (Schor, 2017). Post-pandemic fluctuations notwithstanding, data compiled by the International Labour Organization has even been used to suggest a persistent global decline in the proportion of the workforce employed in the informal sector, which has historically concentrated a high number of precarious workers – although this decline might not necessarily reflect a decrease in the absolute number of workers within this sector, but rather a dilution of the informal sector's relative size due to the demographic expansion of the global workforce (ILO, 2024). Meanwhile, others have challenged the exceptionalism that is currently being ascribed to atypical and non-standard forms employment, contending that the anxieties now associated with forms of precarious work are not solely attributable to contemporary economic shifts but have deeper historical roots embedded within the exploitative and expropriative nature of capitalism itself (Ettlinger, 2007; Waite, 2009).

In this vein, Strauss (2018) outlines how the concept of a standard employment relation, which came to hold dominance, albeit unevenly, within the specific historical context of post-1945 capitalist welfare states, warrants critique for its tendency to obscure the significant influence of factors such as gender, social location, legal status and race/ethnicity on individual employment experiences. By neglecting the way in which the historical organisation of human societies and economies renders some lives inherently more precarious than others, the discourse on precarious work – she contends – fails to acknowledge the 'extra-economic' relations operating both within and alongside the capitalist wage relation to systematically disadvantage certain groups. The consequence of this is that analyses that posit a singular 'precariat class' as the defining feature of the present and future of work fail to convince. This is not to say that there is nothing new about precarious work today, only that to exclude the histories and legacies of global capitalism carries significant risks. These risks include occluding the pervasive role of racism in shaping and developing class structures and embedding a perspective heavily influenced by industrial Europe (Bhambra, 2021; see also MacLeavy, 2023).

Expanding on this critique, I argue here that discussions of the future of work, which often exhibit a narrow understanding of class stemming from an uncritical inheritance of the Keynesian emphasis on traditional employment forms as the paradigm for social mobility, elide both the (longstanding) variety of work forms and how income streams beyond wages can prove crucial for social mobility. As Adkins et al. (2020, 2021) identify, alternative income streams – notably from property and financial assets like stocks, funds and bonds – reduce the importance of (standard and non-standard) employment and are inducing a move away from a labour-based hierarchy towards one that is predicated on asset ownership and capital gains. This observation aligns with arguments suggesting that traditional markers of class, such as occupation and labour-derived income, are specific to a particular historical context and now hold diminishing explanatory power because the detrimental material consequences of asset ownership are becoming increasingly evident (Bhambra, 2021). The nations of Europe and North America, for instance, having arguably escaped the worst aspects of imperialism, while benefitting from it, were for a time places where employment-based understandings of class could flourish, fuelled by a confluence of factors: the rise of industrial jobs and strong labour movements that tied an individual's wealth to their occupation, stable economies that fostered a belief in social mobility through hard work, and the presence of social safety nets that supported this narrative. However, the globalised nature of the contemporary economy, the reach of financial instruments and the erosion of welfare state protections have arguably blurred these historical distinctions, making asset ownership a significant factor in shaping class structures within former colonising countries also.

To further expand these initial outlines, I start with a brief review of the literature on precarious work, which tends to emphasise the centrality of the employment relationship in determining class positions and neglect the importance of other income streams besides wages, before outlining how class is (once again) being shaped by rents derived from the ownership or control of assets and inflating asset prices, particularly in the realm of housing. This, as has already been intimated, undermines employment-centred models of class. But it also creates possibilities for incorporating more nuanced temporalities of social life that may yield new understandings the future (see Chapter 15). As well as disrupting the traditional linear way of thinking about social mobility, whereby the nature of one's job directly determines their class position and trajectory, the dynamics of the (invigorated) asset economy see the emergence of "a new kind of temporal experience, where time doesn't really flow as it used to" (Adkins et al., 2020: 74). This, I go on to outline, may create the documented sense of unease and uncertainty as (some) individuals grapple with stagnant wages despite experience and the ever-evolving skills sets required to stay competitive in the job market (while those who have been able to build asset portfolios can maintain a level of control over their futures by strategically leveraging assets). Considering if and how work translates to social mobility within this new landscape, I review arguments that the dynamics of the asset economy are trapping individuals in a 'perpetual present' with limited economic resources and constantly delayed life goals (Davis and Cartwright, 2019: 96). From this perspective, the future of work – and living – appears less contingent on securing a specific job and more about acquiring the skills and opportunities to accumulate assets, the opportunity for which varies based on factors like education, social background and access to capital. Ultimately, this shift is theorised to usher in a future wherein the notion of class is less tethered to employment and instead becomes a reflection of one's ability use assets to navigate the complexities of a constantly evolving economic landscape.

Work, Class and Asset-Driven Lifetimes

Academic and policy circles have increasingly focused on job insecurity – or 'precarity' – as post-industrial economies have witnessed a decline in workers' bargaining power relative to capital (Alberti et al., 2018; Choonara, 2020). This growing concern for both the redistribution of economic risk through new and revised employment terms, as well as the heightened sense of instability among many workers, has helped frame policy demands for minimum wage increases, portable benefit structures for non-standard work arrangements and stronger legal protections for workers in the digital economy. It has also fuelled the emergence of innovative labour strategies and tactics, such as online organising platforms facilitating cross-sectoral solidarity among gig workers and creative protest actions targeting companies that rely heavily on precarious labour models (see Chapters 8 and 10). But while the anxieties and challenges associated with precarious work have become a potent force for collective action, attempts to define a new social class based solely on this insecurity (Standing, 2011) have been met with significant criticism. Focusing on the contingency of employment relationships in certain sectors of the post-industrial economy, some argue, obscures the fact that similar conditions have existed for a long time and indeed are the norm in many parts of the world. As Munck (2013) writes, the underlying conditions the term 'precarity' describes are not new. In fact, the stable, well-paying jobs associated with Fordism and the welfare state were actually an exception to the historical backdrop against which work has been experienced. The narrative of a bygone era of universally secure employment is problematic insofar as it overlooks the geographically and temporally limited nature of such conditions, systems and standards, even within the most advanced industrialised economies (Breman, 2013; Palmer, 2014). Furthermore, this narrative romanticises the stability of the Fordist era, by failing to acknowledge that the benefits of Fordism, such as long-term contracts and unionisation, were largely confined to a specific segment of the workforce, which was primarily male and concentrated in heavy industries (Hardy, 2017).

Elsewhere, scholars examining the impact of neoliberalism on employment relations in its heartlands (e.g., the UK) have suggested that the relative stability of the majority of the workforce is actually more puzzling than the existence of precarious work (Choonara, 2020). Although they acknowledge the challenge of measuring precarity, they argue that the persistence of stable employment, not the prevalence of precarious work, requires explanation. The stability in employment, which they observe, reminds us that capital does not solely dictate labour's fate through hiring and firing; it is also invested in retaining and reproducing a stable workforce for long-term gain. In other words, the capital-labour relationship exhibits a degree of mutual interdependence, rather than absolute employer dominance, suggesting that "precarization is *more than* the return of insecurity into post-Fordist workers' lives" (Alberti et al., 2018: 449, emphasis added). While data on employment stability offers a valuable metric, Choonara (2020) further cautions that such data can mask stagnation in terms of wages and career progression. Despite questioning the narrated growth of precarity, he proposes that attention be directed towards issues within the world of work such as stagnant pay, long hours, discrimination, decreasing autonomy and rising stress levels, which are not simply problems of precarious workers but of large numbers of non-precarious ones too. It is these elements that, in his view, potentially illuminate the subjective experience of increased worker insecurity, even within the seemingly privileged tiers of the labour market.

From a different vantage, studies investigating the subjective experience of precarity among workers in post-industrial economies have identified the perceived loss of social recognition and a diminished sense of belonging within a group or community as key contributing factors, shaping experiences of security, opportunity and connection to the globalised word (Bromley-Davenport et al., 2019; MacLeod and Jones, 2018). While economic and labour market transformations are seen as drivers, these scholars also conceptualise precarity as the outcome of an (increasingly) uneven distribution of social protections. This broader perspective extends the analysis beyond the labour market, acknowledging the growing influence of the market economy across various life domains, which erodes individuals' sense of agency and control over their own futures. This paves the way for a more comprehensive analysis of class formation by highlighting a potential shift in how class positions are now determined. Occupation may no longer be the sole factor, as the broader distribution of economic capital plays an increasingly significant role (Adkins et al., 2020; Umney, 2018). Hence, an individual might hold a seemingly 'good' or stable job; yet, their overall economic situation, encompassing factors like debt and asset ownership, might leave them feeling vulnerable.

Responding to theorisations of a new precariat class and the reported sense of insecurity despite employment stability, Adkins et al. (2020, 2021) explore how social groups previously thought to be insulated from market forces, such as professionals and managerial staff, are now experiencing a heightened vulnerability. This vulnerability stems, in large part, from the growing importance of asset ownership, which shapes social locations by determining the diversification (or lack thereof) of income sources. Their work argues that traditional class models, given their inherent emphasis on occupations, are unable to fully capture the stratifying effects of asset ownership within contemporary capitalism. Instead, they propose a schema in which people are sorted into categories, with a key dividing line between those who own (housing) assets and those who do not (see Figure 13.1). The upper categories (investors, outright homeowners and homeowners with

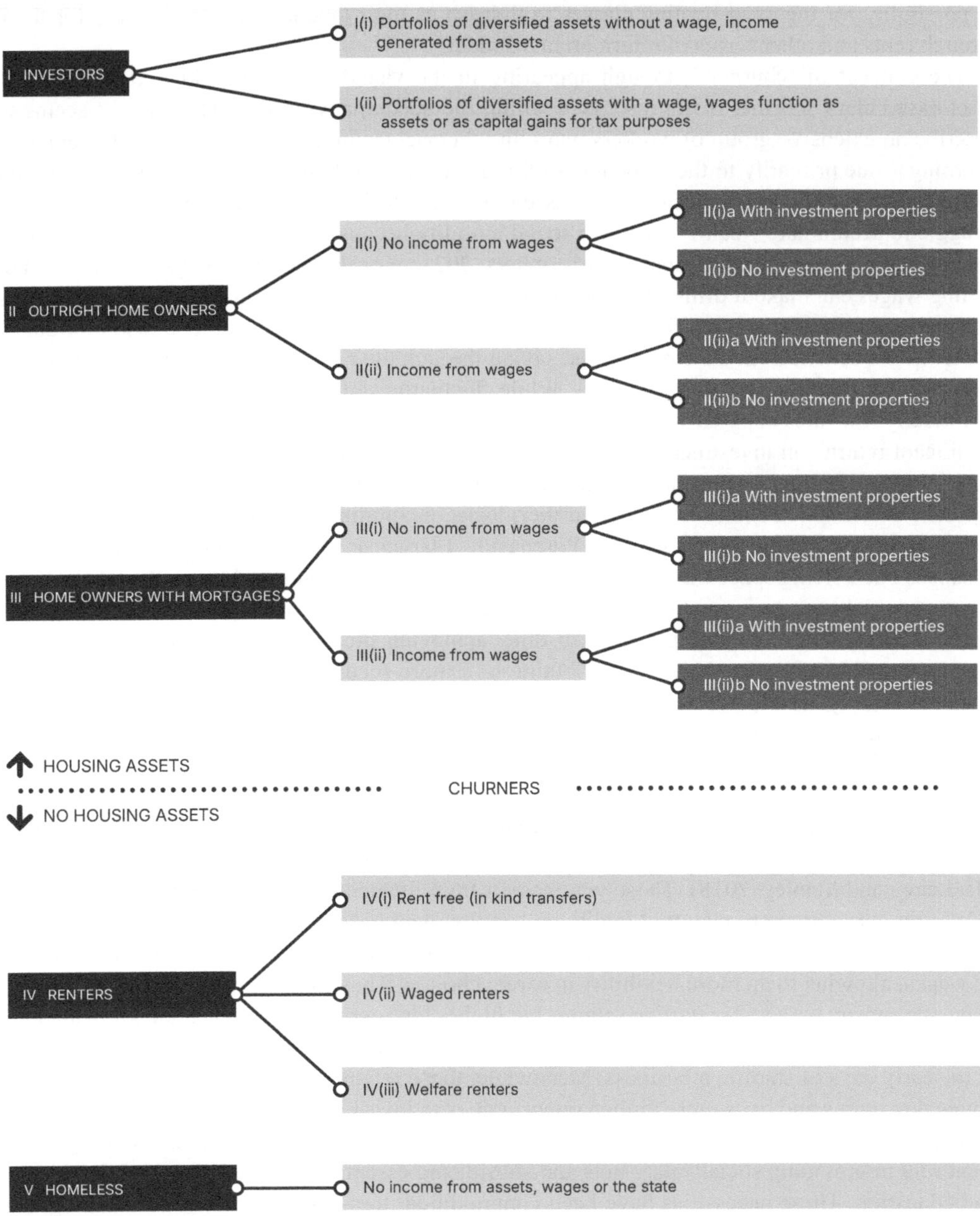

Figure 13.1 Asset-based class schema

Source: Adkins, Cooper and Konings (2021: 565)

mortgages) are seen to have a degree of economic security and the potential for capital appreciation, while the lower categories (who rent or are homeless) have fewer resources and rely primarily on wages, state income streams in the form of welfare benefits or pensions, or charitable support. Moreover, it is the labour of this latter group (primarily the renters) that provides the conditions of possibility for the asset-owning classes to flourish as their labour generates income for them through rents and other forms of return on investment.

The concept of 'churners', though appearing in the visualisation of Adkins et al.'s (2021) asset-based class scheme, is not discussed within the accompanying text. However, it seems to describe an extensive group of workers, who find themselves in a cycle of constant movement – churning – due primarily to the challenge of finding affordable housing. Unstable jobs with fluctuating income may also contribute to this churn. Despite having money coming in, churners struggle to accumulate wealth or achieve social mobility because a significant proportion of their income goes towards housing costs (Christophers, 2021). For this group, the uncertainty of fluctuating wages can make it difficult to secure stable housing, while the limitations of state benefits in covering housing costs may further restrict their options (Taylor, 2024). In contrast, mortgaged homeowners benefit from a form of forced saving through their repayments, which leads to eventual ownership and equity accumulation. While fluctuating interest rates can pose a challenge, historically low rates coupled with rising house prices over the past two decades have resulted in significant returns on investment for many homeowners (Arundel, 2017). Beyond this appreciation, owning a property offers additional avenues for asset appreciation. Homeowners can leverage their accumulated equity to secure (further) loans, facilitating their movement up the housing ladder and corresponding class schema. Purchasing a larger or more desirable property not only enhances one's living space but also has the potential to further wealth. Additionally, some homeowners may choose to invest in rental properties, generating a new stream of income that can further solidify their financial position. In time, achieving mortgage-free ownership eliminates a major monthly expense, thereby contributing to a more secure retirement (Hillig, 2019). This financial security can replace, to some extent, the social safety net benefits that may be lacking in a reduced welfare state, not least because owning a paid-off property later in life provides flexibility for downsizing (Ansell, 2014).

Significantly, homeowners can also release capital that can be gifted or bequeathed to younger generations in a process of intergenerational wealth transfer that potentially solidifies social mobility inheritors, by concentrating wealth within families across generations (Druta and Ronald, 2017; MacLeavy and Manley, 2018). Those who benefit from financial support from parents and/or are able to purchase property may find traditional employment becomes less crucial: owning a property can generate income through appreciation or rental income, which reduces their dependence on wages, allowing them more flexibility in career choices. They may, therefore, be more inclined to pursue careers with lower starting salaries but higher long-term earning potential, knowing they have a financial safety net that can support them through further education, training, internships or the early days of starting a business. Meanwhile, those reliant on wages are vulnerable to economic downturns and have more limited opportunities to invest in themselves, take career risks or access opportunities that might lead to advancement and growth, owing to a diminishing government role in providing social safety nets and subsidising essential needs like housing, healthcare and education. These necessities have been commodified, transforming them from social goods into market-driven commodities with associated costs. For those without asset wealth, therefore, access to these fundamental pillars of human capital development now necessitates significant personal debt (Adkins et al., 2020). While their wealthier counterparts may find income from employment becoming less important, potentially enabling a shift in priorities towards job satisfaction and career fulfilment, those without assets often find the burden of indebtedness creates a cycle of financial constraints and limited resources. Debt acts as a structural restraint, limiting social mobility and career options. In this way, intergenerational wealth transfer through homeownership exacerbates inequalities within the labour market potentially creating a two-tiered system – earners and churners – where those with inherited assets enjoy greater flexibility and potentially less reliance on wages, while those without this advantage remain heavily reliant on a potentially precarious job market, their career options increasingly dictated by the need to service debt and afford ever-increasing rents.

What this indicates is that the Western model of achieving a 'middle class life' through steady employment is becoming increasingly obsolete (Adkins et al., 2020; Christophers, 2021). Soaring housing costs, outpacing wage growth, have eroded the purchasing power of incomes once deemed sufficient for homeownership making it exceedingly difficult for people, particularly those lacking substantial parental support, to acquire the necessary capital for mortgage loans and entry into the housing market. Furthermore, the rental market offers little solace, as rising costs often force young adults to remain living with their parents for longer, hindering their ability to establish independent lives. The growing importance of intergenerational transfers of wealth, which "shape the logic of class in new ways" (Adkins et al, 2021: 551), underlines the historical and geographical contingent nature of understandings of class based solely on employment. While such frameworks have never been universally applicable, this phenomenon further suggests a potential shift in our temporal experience under the asset economy: the traditional employment-centred model offered a more linear and work-orientated conception of time, with well-defined expectations of advancement and social mobility. In contrast, the asset economy introduces a greater degree of uncertainty into how the future unfolds, potentially creating a bifurcated temporality. Those subsisting on a labour-to-wage exchange become constrained by a presentist temporality, their futures inextricably linked to their immediate exertions within the labour market, which offer limited scope for long-term planning. Conversely, those possessing the capital to leverage assets are able to maintain a future-orientated temporality, as they remain able to focus on long-term strategies and potential future gains.

A Divided Landscape of Time and Opportunity

The shift from employment-based to asset-based class structures thus reshapes our experience of time within capitalism, which scholars argue necessitates a broader examination of wealth inequality, access to capital and the very purpose of work in the twenty-first century. As Adkins et al., citing Tadiar (2012, 2013), explain, those whose lives can be capitalised, their assets appreciating in value over time, hold a distinct advantage. Their wealth grows passively, offering long-term security. Conversely, for those whose lives are merely commodified, their labour readily replaceable and offering no long-term value storage, the future becomes increasingly precarious. Arguably, the decline of welfare state provisions in recent years has contributed to this. Previously, robust safety nets enabled (some) workers to consider a longer-term perspective. However, with the rollback of state supports, the pressure to focus on immediate needs has intensified. Latimer (2013: 22) describes how welfare programmes, which once enabled workers to "hold on to a fantasy of the good life, or the life of upward mobility, job security, and political and social equality" have suffered retrenchment and reform such that it is increasingly difficult to inhabit a kind of 'straight time', by "imagining one's futurity in terms of reaching certain points along a life course" (Ahmed, 2006: 554). Similarly, Sharma (2022) posits a link between the kind of work arrangements individuals hold and their temporal experience. Time, she suggests, permeates society in different ways depending on the specific employment structures that people find themselves in.

Unless one has the means to engage in speculative ventures, accumulating assets that have the potential to appreciate in value, this (re)new(ed) sense of the present can give rise to a feeling of stagnation, rather than progress: "of 'going backwards' rather than forwards, and of acting in a sphere of the present, without a clear sense of the future" (Jupp, 2022: 52). This presentist mode of belonging is demonstrative, Latimer (2013) claims, of the cruel optimism that Lauren Berlant (2011: 1) suggests exists when "something you desire is an obstacle to your flourishing". In this case, the desired future – a prosperous life for oneself and future generations – is said to be increasingly out of reach for those without asset wealth: cuts to social safety nets and public services, often presented as necessary for long-term fiscal responsibility and supposedly for the benefit of workers' futures, actually create a more precarious present. This disconnection between the promise of future security and the reality of a precarious present raises important questions for workers considering how to prepare for a future that seems both uncertain and challenging. As traditional pathways to economic mobility like education and training are increasingly inaccessible due to government cutbacks, the images of futurity present undermine the prevailing notion of time, changing what it means to look forward.

The suggestion is that while narratives of precarity have become ubiquitous, their focus on work-related anxieties may overlook a broader and more fundamental sense of insecurity. This insecurity originates from factors external to the workplace and is demonstrably linked to the increasing importance of homeownership, investment properties and stock holdings as determinants of socio-economic status. For many, this is an outcome of a strategy of neoliberal reform that encourages citizens to rethink their status as individuals – funnelling them into debt by promoting a society based on the values of personal responsibility and self-reliance (Grover, 2018; Kelly, 2017). Yet, others note the historical foundation of class phenomena through asset ownership, reminding us that European colonialism established a system where a privileged capitalist class accumulated vast amounts, while many oppressed groups were systematically denied the opportunity to build wealth through asset ownership (Bhambra, 2021). From this perspective, neoliberal austerity reinforces the 'exclusionary tendencies' (Saad-Filho, 2021: 133) of the earlier capitalist phase by exacerbating historical and global inequalities in asset ownership. This not only intensifies the anxieties of the present but (re)entrenches a system characterised by limited economic mobility for a substantial segment of the population (Piketty, 2014).

These enduring inequalities contribute to a growing public perception that neoliberal capitalism is failing to deliver on its promises. While imagined futures of work encompass utopian visions where work is unnecessary (Bastani, 2019; Srnicek and Williams, 2015), they also tap into feelings of discontent with the status quo. As Raynor (2017) notes, a (growing) impression that the system is 'out of control' emerges from the failed promises of social equality, limited upward mobility and homeownership delivering security for only a select few. This sense of unfulfilled expectations is particularly acute for those already economically and socially marginalised within formal labour markets (Reid-Musson et al., 2020). Indeed, Gong (2024) notes how China's youth have embraced 'Tangping' – which translates as 'lying flat' – in response to this bleak future outlook, while in Japan the rise of 'hikikomori' – social withdrawal and isolation – stems from a shared sense that the promise of a better life through work is fading. Similarly, narratives of despair and discontent in neglected 'left behind' areas of the UK have become more prominent in recent years (Jones, 2024). But while extensive critical scholarship has shed light on the historical processes that have culminated in this situation and further charted the uneven geographical distribution of 'futurelessness' (Tutton, 2023), its capacity to envision and actively promote genuinely just and sustainable alternatives to dominant practices remains relatively underdeveloped (Braun, 2015). To progress, Gong, among others, posits that we need to move beyond simplistic linear notions of progress or decline. This framing, whether conscious or unconscious, leads to a selective understanding of developments that "determines the creation of certain versions of the future", whereas recognising the future exists as an 'open temporal category' might serve to empower as it dismantles the illusion of a predetermined fate and unlocks the potential for agency (2024: 4).

Operationalising this collective agency necessitates a multi-pronged approach. This could entail advocacy for policies that promote broader asset ownership and the proliferation of worker cooperatives, fostering economic enfranchisement. Additionally, the development of community-based initiatives that empower individuals to navigate the complexities of the evolving asset economy could cultivate both resilience and adaptability. Ultimately, though, a collective commitment to building a more equitable future is key to unlocking the transformative potential of this open-ended 'futurity' (Grosz, 2005). This collaborative effort would translate the vast spectrum of possibilities into a tangible reality where, for example, work strengthens the social fabric and fosters shared prosperity, dismantling – not reinforcing or exacerbating – the existing stratification of social classes. As Ormerod (2023) details, acknowledging the future's connection to the present and past, but not in a predetermined way, allows for 'otherwise possibilities' to emerge, challenging the limitations imposed by past structures.

Conclusion: Capitalising on the Future in This Unequal Landscape

Centring asset ownership as a primary driver of change, as advocated by Adkins et al (2020), is important insofar as it displaces technology from its exclusive or dominant role in shaping the future of work and invites us to consider the future of work through the lens of workers, their diverse circumstances and the potential for political and organisational transformations (Reid-Musson et al., 2020). This reframing (re)introduces class analysis into discussions about the future of work by placing renewed emphasis on the disparities and resources that shape worker experiences. Crucially, this shift in focus necessitates grappling with important questions of scale, namely the interplay between (localised) experiences of work and the broader global dynamics shaped by asset ownership disparities. Mullings (2021), for instance, emphasises the possibilities of scholarly thinking beyond the normative geographical imaginaries that centre changes occurring within the Global North, pushing us to considers how work, technology and subjectivity are shaped by – and, in turn, perpetuate – colonial violences and silences. This aligns with Bhambra's (2021) encouragement to (re)consider narratives of epochal transformation through an approach that emphasises both continuity and change in the global economy as a means of gaining a more nuanced understanding of how these inequalities (continue to) differentiate life chances and life courses. As Reid-Musson et al. (2020) note, analysing the persistence of past inequalities and unevenness across time and space is crucial for understanding the future of work. Focusing solely on novelty and technological change might overlook the potential for a return to pre-welfare state dynamics, albeit with distinct characteristics.

Additionally, by considering relationships to time as reflections of structural differences, scholars can comprehend the ways in which contemporary society confronts and experiences inequality, strengthening the foundation for a radical politics that actively opposes the injustices perpetuated by the temporal dynamics created within regimes that prioritise asset appreciation, individual responsibility and reducing state involvement. These regimes so often confine the working classes to a predetermined future of limited opportunities, reinforcing a sense of powerlessness. However, by embracing futurity – that is, the open-ended nature of the future – a radical political movement may be able to challenge this narrative (Ormerod, 2023; see also MacLeavy et al., 2021). It could empower workers by highlighting the potential for collective action and systemic change. This shift in focus from a preordained future to an open one becomes a crucial tool for dismantling the very structures that perpetuate and legitimate class stratification through asset accumulation, by presenting a challenge to the current system and enabling the creation of alternative economic models that prioritise shared prosperity over individual wealth concentration.

References

Adkins, L., Cooper, M. and Konings, M. (2020) *The Asset Economy: Property Ownership and the New Logic of Inequality*, Cambridge: Polity Press.

Adkins, L., Cooper, M. and Konings, M. (2021) Class in the 21st century: Asset inflation and the new logic of inequality, *Environment and Planning A: Economy and Space*, 53(3): 548–572. https://doi.org/10.1177/0308518X19873673

Ahmed, S. (2006) Orientations: Toward a queer phenomenology, *GLQ: A Journal of Lesbian and Gay Studies*, 12(4): 543–574. https://doi.org/10.1215/10642684-2006-002

Alberti, G., Bessa, I., Hardy, K., Trappmann, V. and Umney, C. (2018) In, against and beyond precarity: Work in insecure times, *Work, Employment and Society*, 32(3): 447–457. https://doi.org/10.1177/0950017018762088

Ansell, B. (2014) The political economy of ownership: Housing markets and the welfare state, *American Political Science Review*, 108(2): 383–402. https://doi.org/10.1017/S0003055414000045

Arundel, R. (2017) Equity inequity: Housing wealth inequality, inter and intra-generational divergences, and the rise of private landlordism, *Housing, Theory and Society*, 34(2): 176–200. https://doi.org/10.1080/14036096.2017.1284154

Bastani, A. (2019) *Fully Automated Luxury Communism*, New York: Verso.

Berlant, L. (2011) *Cruel Optimism*, Durham, NC: Duke University Press.

Bhambra, G. (2021) Colonial global economy: Towards a theoretical reorientation of political economy, *Review of International Political Economy*, 21(2): 307–322. https://doi.org/10.1080/09692290.2020.1830831

Braun, B. (2015) Futures: Imagining socioecological transformation — An introduction, *Annals of the Association of American Geographers*, 105(2): 239–243. https://doi.org/10.1080/00045608.2014.1000893

Breman, J. (2013) A bogus concept? *New Left Review*, 84: 130–138. https://newleftreview.org/issues/ii84/articles/jan-breman-a-bogus-concept.pdf

Bromley-Davenport, H., MacLeavy, J. and Manley, D. (2019) Brexit in Sunderland: The production of difference and division in the UK referendum on European Union membership, *Environment and Planning C: Politics and Space*, 37(5): 795–812. https://doi.org/10.1177/0263774X18804225

Campbell, I. and Price, R. (2016) Precarious work and precarious workers: Towards an improved conceptualisation, *Economic and Labour Relations Review*, 27(3): 314–332. https://doi.org/10.1177/1035304616652074

Choonara, J. (2020) The precarious concept of precarity, *Review of Radical Political Economics*, 52(3): 427–446. https://doi.org/10.1177/0486613420920427

Christophers, B. (2021) A tale of two inequalities: Housing-wealth inequality and tenure inequality, *Environment and Planning A: Economy and Space*, 53(3): 573–594. https://doi.org/10.1177/0308518X19876946

Davis, M. and Cartwright, L. (2019) 'Deferred lives': Money, debt and the financialised futures of young temporary workers, pp. 91–118, in: Featherstone M. (ed.) *The Sociology of Debt*, Bristol: Policy Press.

Druta, O. and Ronald, R. (2017) Young adults' pathways into homeownership and the negotiation of intra-family support: A home, the ideal gift, *Sociology*, 51(4): 783–799. https://doi.org/10.1177/0038038516629900

Ettlinger, N. (2007) Precarity unbound, *Alternatives: Global, Local, Political*, 32(3): 319–340. https://doi.org/10.1177/030437540703200303

Garsten, C. (1999) Betwixt and between: Temporary employees as liminal subjects in flexible organizations, *Organization Studies*, 20(4): 601–617. https://doi.org/10.1177/0170840699204004

Gilbert, J. (1998) "A job for life" into "A life of jobs", *Empowerment in Organizations*, 6(6): 165–174. https://doi.org/10.1108/14634449810238634

Gong, H. (2024) Futures should matter (more): Toward a forward-looking perspective in economic geography, *Progress in Human Geography*. https://doi.org/10.1177/03091325231224434

Grosz, E. (2005) *Time Travels: Feminism, Nature, Power*, Durham, NC: Duke University Press.

Grover, C. (2018) Developments in loaning social assistance: Support for mortgage interest in Britain, *Journal of Poverty and Social Justice*, 26(3): 401–415. https://doi.org/10.1332/175982718X15244988622812

Hardy, J.A. (2017) (Re)conceptualizing precarity: Institutions, structure and agency, *Employee Relations*, 39(3): 263–273. https://doi.org/10.1108/ER-06-2016-0111

Herod, A. and Lambert, R. (2016) Neoliberalism, precarious work and remaking the geography of global capitalism, pp. 1–36, in: Lambert, R. and Herod, A. (eds.) *Neoliberal Capitalism and Precarious Work*, Cheltenham: Edward Elgar.

Hillig, A. (2019) Everyday financialization: The case of UK households, *Environment and Planning A: Economy and Space*, 51(7): 1460–1478. https://doi.org/10.1177/0308518X19843920

ILO (International Labour Organization) (2024) *World Employment and Social Outlook: Trends 2024*, Geneva: ILO. https://www.ilo.org/publications/flagship-reports/world-employment-and-social-outlook-trends-2024

Jones, R.E. (2024) Myths and realities of "left behind" and "levelling up", *Antipode*, 56(1): 5–25. https://doi.org/10.1111/anti.12974

Jupp, E. (2022) *Care, Crisis and Activism: The Politics of Everyday Life*, Bristol: Policy Press.

Kalleberg, A.L. (2018) *Precarious Lives: Job Insecurity and Well-Being in Rich Democracies*, Cambridge: Polity Press.

Kelly, P. (2017) Growing up after the GFC: Responsibilisation and mortgaged futures, *Discourse: Studies in the Cultural Politics of Education*, 38(1): 57–69. https://doi.org/10.1080/01596306.2015.1104852

Latimer, H. (2013) The straight line: Sexuality, futurity and the politics of austerity, *English Studies in Canada*, 39(4): 21–24. https://ojs.lib.uwo.ca/index.php/esc/article/view/9613/7713

MacLeavy, J. (2023) Class, pp. 59–63, in: Lees, L and Demeritt, D (eds.) *Concise Encyclopedia of Human Geography*, Cheltenham: Edward Elgar.

MacLeavy, J., Fannin, M. and Larner, W. (2021) Feminism and futurity: Geographies of resistance, resilience and reworking, *Progress in Human Geography*, 45(6): 1558–1579. https://doi.org/10.1177/03091325211003327

MacLeavy, J. and Manley, D. (2018) (Re)discovering the lost middle: Intergenerational inheritances and economic inequality in urban and regional research, *Regional Studies*, 52(10): 1435–1446. https://doi.org/10.1080/00343404.2018.1462487

MacLeod, G. and Jones, M. (2018) Explaining 'Brexit capital': Uneven development and the austerity state, *Space and Polity*, 22(2): 111–136. https://doi.org/10.1080/13562576.2018.1535272

Munck, R. (2013) The Precariat: A view from the South, *Third World Quarterly*, 34(5): 747–762. https://doi.org/10.1080/01436597.2013.800751

Mullings, B, (2021) Caliban, social reproduction and our future yet to come, *Geoforum*, 118: 150–158. https://doi.org/10.1016/j.geoforum.2020.11.007

Ormerod, E. (2023) Level with us, regional development is still 'man shaped': Feminism, futurity and leadership, *Regional Studies*, 57(9): 1893–1902. https://doi.org/10.1080/00343404.2022.2153114

Palmer, B.D. (2014) Reconsiderations of class: Precariousness as proletarianization, *Socialist Register*, 50: 40–62. https://socialistregister.com/index.php/srv/article/view/20191/16630

Peck, J. (2001) Neoliberalizing states: Thin policies/hard outcomes, *Progress in Human Geography*, 25(3): 445–455. https://dx. doi.org/10.1191/030913201680191772

Piketty, T. (2014) *Capital in the 21st Century*, London: Harvard University Press.

Purser, G. (2012) The labour of liminality, *Labour, Capital and Society/Travail, Capital et Société*, 45(1): 10–35. https://www.jstor.org/stable/43158419

Raynor, R. (2017) Dramatising austerity: Holding a story together (and why it falls apart ...), *Cultural Geographies*, 24(2): 193–212. https://doi.org/10.1177/1474474016675564

Reid-Musson, E., Cockayne, D., Frederiksen, L. and Worth, N. (2020) Feminist economic geography and the future of work, *Environment and Planning A: Economy and Space*, 52(7): 1457–1468. https://doi.org/10.1177/0308518X20947101

Saad-Filho, A. (2021) Endgame: From 'crisis in neoliberalism' to 'crises in neoliberalism', *Human Geography*, 14(1): 133–137. https://doi.org/10.1177/1942778620962026

Schor, J.B. (2017) Does the sharing economy increase inequality within the eighty percent? Findings from a qualitative study of platform providers, *Cambridge Journal of Regions, Economy and Society*, 10(2): 263–279. https://doi.org/10.1093/cjres/rsw047

Scott, S., Jakobsen, T.S., Rye, J.F. and Visser, M.A. (2022) Labour migration, precarious work and liminality, *Work in the Global Economy*, 2(1): 27–45. https://doi.org/10.1332/273241721X16471891313746

Sharma, S. (2022) Undisciplined time studies, *Time and Society*, 3(1): 44–47. https://doi.org/10.1177/0961463X211073551

Srnicek, N. and Williams, A. (2015) *Inventing the Future: Postcapitalism and a World without Work*, London: Verso.

Standing, G. (2011) *The Precariat: The New Dangerous Class*, London: Bloomsbury.

Strauss, K. (2018) Labour geography 1: Towards a geography of precarity? *Progress in Human Geography*, 42(4): 622–630. https://doi.org/10.1177/0309132517717786

Tadiar, N.X.M. (2012) Life-times of fate playing, *South Atlantic Quarterly*, 111(4): 783–802. https://doi.org/10.1215/00382876-1724183

Tadiar, N.X.M. (2013) Life-times of disposability within global neoliberalism, *Social Text*, 35(1): 19–48. https://doi.org/10.1215/01642472-2081112

Taylor, F.M. (2024) *Precarious Intimacies: Generation, Rent and Reproducing Relationships in London*, Bristol: University of Bristol Press.

Tutton, R. (2023) The sociology of futurelessness, *Sociology*, 57(2): 438–453. https://doi.org/10.1177/00380385221122420

Umney, C. (2018) *Class Matters: Inequality and Exploitation in 21st Century Britain*, London: Pluto Press.

Waite, L. (2009) A place and space for a critical geography of precarity? *Geography Compass*, 3(1): 412–433. https://doi.org/10.1111/j.1749-8198.2008.00184.x

Recommendations for Further Reading

Adkins, L., Cooper, M. and Konings, M. (2020) *The Asset Economy: Property Ownership and the New Logic of Inequality*, Cambridge: Polity Press.

Adkins, L., Cooper, M. and Konings, M. (2021) Class in the 21st century: Asset inflation and the new logic of inequality, *Environment and Planning A: Economy and Space*, 53(3): 548–572. https://doi.org/10.1177/0308518X19873673

Berry, C. (2021) The imperial past of today's asset economy, 16 March 2021. Available at: https://autonomy.work/portfolio/berry-imperialism/#1592467993162-2945af24-5883

MacLeavy, J. (2023) Class, pp. 59–63, in: Lees, L and Demeritt, D (eds.) *Concise Encyclopedia of Human Geography*, Cheltenham: Edward Elgar.

Special Issue: In, Against and beyond precarity: The struggles of insecure workers, *Work, Employment and Society*, 32(3).

PART 6

Gender, Care and Social Reproduction

14

GENDER AND THE FUTURE OF WORK IN THE AFFECTIVE AND AGILE ECONOMIES

M. Winter

Introduction: Gender, Work, and Reproductive Labour, Paid and Unpaid

This chapter considers analyses of affective and agile economic phenomena in the context of ongoing debates about the future of work. These discussions are rife with concerns regarding the profound effects of technology on our economic systems and the ways we experience work in our daily lives. Key areas of focus include the consequences of automation, which can lead to significant worker displacement, as well as the implications of remote work productivity and the rise of platform-based employment. This chapter explores the relationship between work and technology through the lens of gender to uncover aspects of these developments that are often obscured within broader debates. A gender-informed perspective reveals how traditional gender roles, biases, and stereotypes continue to shape technological advancements; it brings into focus the perpetuation and transformation of mechanisms of control and domination within economic systems, demonstrating how these mechanisms are often intertwined with gendered expectations, leading to differential access to opportunities, resources, and decision-making power.

"Progress," technological, economic, or otherwise, ought not to be assumed to garner greater gender equality. Considering work and technology with gender suggests the perpetuation of existing, and evolution of new, mechanisms of control and domination necessary for processes of capital accumulation. Silvia Federici argues that serf women were "less subservient to men's needs than 'free' women were to be later in capitalist society" (2004: 25). This characterisation has been hotly debated, but there is no doubt that the deterioration of feudalism along with the accumulation of capital produced and necessitated new social structures and power relations. Feminists interested in this "transition" note the myriad of mechanisms through which women's work became increasing invisible, excluded from capitalist concepts of value, and recast in essentialist terms. This process included the penalisation and violent punishment of sex workers (as well as, in some places, the decriminalisation of raping a sex worker), campaigns to exclude or expel women from paid work environments, like those of the craft workers of the fifteenth century, and, of course, the systematic murder of "witches," women with expertise in medicine and maternal care (ibid). The impossibility for women to manage their own earnings, often due to policies whereby a man was legally entitled to the wages of his wife, "created the material conditions for their subjection to men and the appropriation of their labor by male workers" (2004: 98).

DOI: 10.4324/9781003327561-20

Therefore, work under capitalism has a subjectification function; it "produces not just economic good and services but also social and political subjects" (Weeks 2011: 8). Most obvious are the ways in which work produces classed subjects through wage setting and occupational status (Marx 1976), but work is also instrumental in the making and organisation of gendered subjects. Vital amongst these mechanisms is the distinction between paid and unpaid work, or more specifically between domestic and waged labour, distinctions upon which gendered work is analogously mapped. Unpaid domestic work produces value through goods and services as much as it produces gender (Berk 2012 [1985]). Unpaid reproductive labour, most often performed by women, enables the (physical, intellectual, emotional, etc.) function of workers engaged in paid labour, and produces future (gendered) workers for the continuity of capitalist state economies. Therefore, the relationship between work and gender is not causal nor hierarchical, but rather co-productive. In contemporary practice, this means that, "sometimes doing gender might be treated as part of doing the job; at other times doing the job is part of what it means to do gender" (Weeks 2011: 10) and to conform to gendered divisions of labour is usually rewarded: it can be a comforting and pleasurable affirmation of gendered identities and relations (Freeman 2000; Willis 1977).

This chapter explores some of the ways in which technology, work, and gender are intertwined, providing a lens through which the future of work can be made sense of. As demonstrative of such a lens, two evolving phenomena, the commodification of care in the affective economy and the quantified self in the agile economy, are excavated accordingly.

Gender and Technology – Techno Fantasies and Utopias

In management literature, technology is regularly conceptualised as a sector or tool where the future of work is at stake. This approach is informed by historical accounts of the industrial revolution, which trace the birth of the machine back to the eighteenth century. However, a much richer and more complex relationship between humans and technologies has existed for centuries, recognition of which can broaden the boundaries – temporal, spatial, and otherwise – within which technological development and innovation are understood (Mumford 2010 [1934]). Acknowledgement of this longer lineage of technics requires a reckoning with the implications of such a history for the ontological and epistemological questions we continue to have about the nature of technology and, its role in our (gendered) future; the relationship between humans and our world of technics is rendered dynamic and culturally specific.

For philosopher Herbert Marcuse, technology is many things: a "social process" (2004 [1941]: 138), as well as a "mode of production, as the totality of instruments, devices and contrivances which characterize the machine age" (138), and a "mode of organizing and perpetuating (or changing) social relationships, a manifestation of prevalent thought and behaviour patterns, an instrument for control and domination" (139). The aspect that holds greater relevance in the context of examining the interplay between gender and technology is the latter dimension, encompassing social relationships, control, and domination. Specifically, this dimension becomes prominent considering the statement that "new technologies help maintain two crucial Euro-American myths: (1) the myth of progress and (2) the myth of white, Western superiority" (Dinerstein 2006: 572). Contemporary techno-revolutionary imaginaries emerge from ahistorical concepts of emancipation where dominant tech-utopian ideals are informed by capitalist expansionism enabled by the capture of racialised and gendered labour (Atanasoski & Vora 2019). Therefore, contemporary techno-future fantasies reify imperial, racial, and gender divisions within capitalism. Technology as it is implicitly embedded within visions for the future, a future where robots relieve humans of menial labour, produces beneficiaries, and disciplines or subjugates others. The next sections, concerning affective and agile economies, provide examples of how power works in and through divisions of labour, how subjects come to be designated as worthy of benefitting, or not.

The Affective Economy: The Commodification of Care

Affective labour, which involves human contact and interaction, constitutes a type of labour producing "an immaterial good, such as a service, knowledge or communication" (Hardt 1999: 94). For instance, caring and affective labour are central to health services, and similarly, affects are created and manipulated in various cultural industries, including forms of entertainment, advertising, and marketing, where emotions and feelings are harnessed to influence consumer behaviour and shape public perception. Affective labour can be said to play a role in the moments of human interaction and communication embedded within service industries where waiting staff advise customers on their orders, or flight attendants calm a customer in distress. The products of such labour are "intangible: a feeling of ease, well-being, satisfaction, excitement, passion" (96). Femininity and affective labour have come to be, at least in the public zeitgeist, irrevocably connected. In practice, this means women often perform affective labour, or at the very least are thought to be best, if not naturally, suited for it. It is no surprise then that feminists have paid affective labour considerable attention, characterising it as "labor in the bodily mode," and even "women's work" (Smith 1987). The use of Foucault's biopower has been particularly powerful for feminist scholars to explicate the governmentality surrounding birthing and maternal, parental, and caregiving labour (Ruddick 1989; Weeks 1998).

Understanding the interplay between the dynamics of women's affective labour and the process of commodification is crucial. Commodification refers to the process through which goods are produced for mass consumption. This process, along with other market relations, continues to puncture and permeate through domains of society previously set outside exchange values (Cherrier & Murray 2004). Humans, their interpersonal relationships, and their culture are increasingly understood as "thing-like"; "they are treated as commodities whose fundamental substance is their value on the open market" (519). This portrayal gains particular relevance when considering affective labour and its role in contemporary economies. Historically, feminists engaged with affective labour, referring to it as kin or care work to emphasise its role in producing collective gendered subjectivities. Despite its placement within the category of immaterial labour, affective labour has been regarded as directly productive of capital (Hardt 1999). The commodification of care work then is demonstrative of the persistent challenge, despite its robust treatment by critical feminists, of dislodging the potential of affective labour from patriarchal constructions of reproduction.

The market for waged care work (see Chapter 16) and its emergent technologically enabled practices, like increased surveillance, is illustrative of the commodification process whereby a person, their attributes, and their affective labour are produced *by and for exchange* (Polyani 1944). The commodification of care in many places, but especially in the global North, has been propagated both by ageing populations and by an increase in employment rates amongst women, with no accompanying reduction to men's working hours, resulting in scarce care provision options of the intra-familial or non-waged variety (Gallagher 2018; McDowell 2014). Employer-driven changes to work with increasingly flexible and intensified hours result in a less predictable working life with more individualised and "unsocial" schedules (see Chapter 8) (James 2017). Coupled with the withdrawal of public services within austerity politics in many countries, these conditions make a global care market not only possible but necessary (MacLeavy 2021).

Global recruitment for the provision of care, and affective labour, in individual homes has become progressively privatised and marketised (Ehrenreich & Hochschild 2003;

England & Henry 2013); "A growing number of middle- and upper-class households across the world delegate the provision of care for their children and elderly or sick relatives to migrant workers from countries with lower income levels" (Schwiter & Steiner 2020: 4). The concept of global care chains emphasises dimensions of inequality within the transfer of reproductive labour and workers across the globe (Lutz 2002). The material and emotional consequences of these migratory patterns include a "care drain" in carers' countries of origin (Pratt 2009), while, in contrast, the affluent families of destination countries benefit from an emotional surplus, some refer to this as emotional imperialism (Hochschild 2015).

There are numerous ways in which technologies, especially digital and communication devices have and continue to enable new forms of and conditions for care work (England 2010). The increasing ubiquity of smart-home technologies carries with it a complex web of privacy, autonomy, and work-related ramifications for domestic workers. The surveillance of nannies (nanny cams) on the private premises of their employers denotes a multi-dimensional context where the home is also a workplace. Recent surveys suggest that nannies themselves consider it an ethical imperative to be told about the use of cameras (Bernd, Abu-Salma & Frik 2020). The level of scrutiny enabled by nanny cams would warrant backlash in other employment contexts where it would be considered invasive or even discriminatory, but the norms of domestic work have been set out as different from the start, as a recognition that entrusting someone with one's child is an intimate and anxiety-inducing experience. In this case, the technology multiplies the affective production of ease and calm offered by the initial care work itself. The beneficiaries of the care work are imbued with a heightened sense of control, while the nannies (often marginalised/minority women) experience working conditions otherwise considered unacceptable to/for workers of greater privilege.

Instead of technology replacing the affective and care work nannies do, it has, in this case, served to discipline workers, reifying their position as subject to their own surveillance. Such surveillance of nannies renders them, and their work, more readily legible as a commodity, especially in the hiring process. The traditional network of agencies and referrals is now rivalled by online marketplaces like Care.com. The site's purpose is to help increase access to opportunities, offering workers profiles on which they can share evidence of their affective abilities with greater ease; they are "encouraged to upload videos of themselves to highlight bubbly, warm, or fun personalities; write up biographical narratives; or add links to their social media accounts" (Mateescu 2018). The implementation of rating systems on these recruitment sites, meant to facilitate trust building between employers and care workers, also reinforces the workers affective labour as measurable and marketable (see Brush & Vasupuram, 2006; Henry 2018). It is not hard to imagine the potential for large language model or facial recognition technologies to further intensify this process of commodification, whereby carers' language and interactions with those they care for can be packaged and sold. A carer's profile today might read "bilingual," while with the help of LLM, it may soon read, "ChatGPT assessed for full integrative bilingualism with language switches four times an hour on average," or even, "diapers are changed within thirteen minutes of soil." Here it is clear that "production for use is systemically displaced by production for exchange" (Prudham 2009: 125).

New forms of resistance and organising are also made possible with the help of digital communication tools, where carers who work in the isolation of private homes can connect with others, participate in grassroots movements, and raise public awareness (Fish 2015; Hobden 2015) (see Chapter 22). Social media platforms also make it easier for interested parties, like journalists and academics, to reach these workers to study and share findings about their experiences (Dalgas 2016). On the whole, technology has increased the visibility of care workers, with online recruitment websites creating digital records of their employment and social media profiles giving them an online presence when they may have limited physical mobility.

Traditional notions of union and worker organising which have enabled the balancing of power in employment relationships are effectively impossible in the context of this domestic care work. In fact, in some places care workers are explicitly excluded from provisions for their freedom of association and any collective bargaining rights (Gomes & Banerjee 2017). Moreover, conventional demarcations between compensated working hours and non-working hours are less relevant in the care sector (Baines & Armstrong 2019). Caring roles, as mentioned above, also include the curation of a persona that maintains employer's expectations of responsibility, meaning carers self-regulate their personal lives to match their employer's implicit desires for an unsexed or sexy, partnered or single, mother or childless, ever available worker who is docile and obedient (Cox 2007; Maher & Staab 2005). The temporal and spatial demands of care work hinder further their availability to engage in organising for better conditions. The future of work in the affective economy is still built upon an underpaid, feminised labour force where workers from economically poorer households provide mitigation to some of the care dilemmas of the time-poor in the global North, while their own care predicaments remain ignored.

The Agile Economy: The Quantified Self

In the context of the agile economy, the notion of flexibility incorporates not only the adaptability of labour to market fluctuations and demands, but also the capacity for responsiveness and adaptiveness at the processual and operational level (Moore 2018). These expectations are not waged, nor experienced equally across the gender spectrum – they are not without their own political context and consequence. Toyota's Just-in-time production system developed between 1948 and 1975 (see Chapter 23) is demonstrative of a rejection of rigidity and routine in factory work and a reorientation towards agility. In 2001, 17 software developers released the "Agile Manifesto," a document extolling the virtues of the "individual and interactions over processes and tools," "working software over comprehensive documentation," "customer collaboration over contract negotiation," and "responding to change over following a plan" (Beck et al. 2001). The manifesto became a blueprint for helping teams shift towards a responsive position in the face of growing unpredictability caused by globalisation and late stage capitalism. Of course, it follows that agile teams, workplaces, and organisations require agile workers. The expectation of agility, in turn, serves to produce gendered difference, whereby agility is culturally associated with masculinity, further marginalising women in the workplace.

The agile worker then is efficient and high-performing, self-managing, and subject to technological evaluation (Moore & Robinson 2016). To begin, the agile worker's efficiency is also about the reduction of "waste." Worker "downtime" is seen as an excess to be eliminated, and methods, such as increased surveillance as mentioned previously, are intended to improve efficiency along these lines. Agile management practices emphasise the mitigation or elimination of excess as far as possible. Worker self-management is also vital to the success of agility. Workers are expected to "self-manage the impact of constant change, including through emotional management and affective control," which becomes an "all-of-life responsibility, where well-being is part of the worker's remit" (Moore 2018: 26). Effectively, an agile worker is not just one who gets the job done, but also one who does so without complaint or evidence of strife. The worker ought not externalise the toll their work might take on them, but rather manage it internally and independently. Lastly, technological evaluation, through surveillance and tracking, renders the worker a constant site for improvement. Therefore, quantification, the process through which things (phenomena of any kind) can be translated to numerical value, is central to the agile economy as the common refrain reminds us "unless something can be measured, it cannot be improved" (Kelly, quoted in Takahashi, 2012).

Quantification for the purposes of self-improvement takes on various forms with the aid of technological devices. In 2017 there were over 160,000 mobile applications available for tracking one's daily habits and behaviours (Lupton 2017). This figure has likely risen sharply since then, but precise accounts are difficult to compile as new applications are developed and others become obsolete continuously. In 2007, two writers from Wired Magazine established the Quantified Self, a community, now operating over 200 local groups in more than 100 cities around the world, which promotes "self-knowledge through numbers" (The Economist 2012). Considerable literature celebrates digital self-tracking practices, describing them as emancipatory and empowering at both the individual and institutional levels. However, there are also sceptics raising concerns about privacy, data ownership, and the never-ending pressure to self-improve. Critical scholars have identified quantification as a process whereby "the body is made amenable to management and monitoring techniques that often echo the ethos of neoliberalism" (Ajana 2017: 1).

The ideal worker paradigm helps to make sense of the quantified worker within the agile economy; the ideal worker represents the most desirable worker as committed and always available to work (Acker 1990; Reid 2015). They have a productive body and a rational mind, which can both be made perfect. The ideal worker then naturalises difference, categorising people into either "rational" or "irrational" actors. And those deemed irrational are understood to be incapable of higher orders of activity. Therefore, it is not necessarily about the assigning of specific forms of activity to specific forms of existence, but rather about the rendering of associations as natural, like gender, race, and ability. Such a sentiment is exemplified in comments like those made by Lord Freud in 2014: "You make a really good point about the disabled. There is a group where actually, as you say, they're not worth the full wage…there is something we can do if someone wants to work for £2 an hour" (Watt & Wintour 2014). Those thought to lack corporeal and/or rational capacity are therefore excluded from high value work and could not possibly meet the expectations of the ideal worker.

Sentiments about women's hormones and apparent emotional instability are also a familiar refrain of the same ilk. Such discourses describe women as unwieldy, at the whim of their menstruating or menopausal bodies, behaving in unpredictable ways that would make them unfit for leadership or decision-making positions (Rowson, Jaworska & Gibas 2023). People who menstruate are increasingly encouraged to manage, conceal, and control their bodies' cycles and phases (Koskenniemi 2023; Whiley et al. 2023), especially in settings where the concept of the logical ideal worker looms large (Sang et al. 2021). In this sense, the auspices of the ideal worker simultaneously encourage women to engage in quantification – tracking their period on mobile applications, for instance, while demarcating them as always already less than ideal. Technology enables women to participate in the quantification of their bodies that the agile economy requires, and yet, its use in relation to menstruation and menopause, denotes their difference.

The concept of the ideal worker is gendered. Research focusing on the "ideal worker" and the act of "performing professionalism" speak to a variety of expectations regarding gender-specific conduct across sectors and roles (Brumley 2014; Trotter 2017). By valorising rationality, the archetype of the ideal worker resists certain aspects of the personal sphere, like motherhood (Thébaud & Taylor 2021) and menopause (Atkinson et al. 2021), which are expected to remain separate from the professional domain. This is termed the work primacy imperative of the ideal worker in the literature (Dumas & Sanchez-Burks 2015). Despite the intention to keep these "personal" issues separate from work, there is evidence that they too can be subjected to quantification. Recent articles, for example, encourage women and people who menstruate to use their monthly periods as a "productivity tool" (Mysoor 2018). Additionally, some articles explore the practice of selling data from period tracking apps to third-party companies (Torchinsky 2022), including insurers or employers. These companies may then use the acquired insights about menstrual cycles, pregnancy status or even menopause to adjust their workforce for optimal agility. These developments underscore the intricate ways in which the ideal worker framework can extend beyond work hours, infiltrating personal domains and potentially leading to privacy concerns and unforeseen adjustments in the workplace.

Undoubtedly, men also encounter challenges in attaining and embodying ideal worker status. However, research has shown that men have more flexibility in their conformity to the image of the ideal worker (Reid 2015). More specifically, men who "stray" from the ideal worker paradigm are far less likely to be targeted by management for strategies of alignment or improvement because of this deviance; men can, in other words, "pass" with relative ease. Women, especially those with families or care responsibilities, are given the least leeway in their compliance to expectations of the ideal worker. The balancing of care responsibilities and work are perceived differently depending on gender, in fact men with children are valued above those without in the workplace (Bear & Glick 2017). Organisational tools for employee management operationalise this inequity. Recent research has illustrated the extent to which formal performance reviews are couched in gendered expectations, and that atypical, gendered behaviour, like when women are perceived as too aggressive, is policed by managers (Correll et al. 2020).

Conclusion

The ideal worker entails more than just the ability to perform tasks efficiently. It also encompasses the embodiment of this ability. It is through control and mastery over one's body that a worker communicates their ability, their ideal-ness. Factors such as a worker's gender, race, weight, age, and overall appearance serve as indicators of their value to an employer or organisation, as well as their ability to produce value. These physical manifestations can be quantified and transformed into SMART goals (Specific, Measurable, Achievable, Relevant, and Time-bound) with the help of technology. Advanced smart watches capable of measuring steps, heart rate, rest duration, and quality amplify the precision and intensity associated with the ideal worker. This process transforms the self and its functioning into a site for increasing quantification towards agile ends.

When discussing this process, this chapter has positioned work, technology, and gender as ontologically intertwined within contemporary capitalist conditions. Through the mechanism of work, individuals are rendered legible in a binary gender system where women's domestic and reproductive labour are denigrated and often unpaid. Moreover, tech-utopian fantasies implicate gendered and raced subjects as surrogates for the realisation of progress. Therefore, the future of work is anticipated to simultaneously recast old, and generate new, work formations along gendered lines. Gender difference, as exemplified in the commodification of care work and the pursuit of the quantified ideal worker, serve to legitimise, and amplify existing inequitable systems. In a somewhat paradoxical twist, the remarkable adaptability of gender reinforces rather than undermines its naturalised status (Weeks 2011: 11).

References

Acker, J., 1990. Hierarchies, jobs, bodies: A theory of gendered organizations. *Gender & Society*, *4*(2), pp.139–158.

Ajana, B., 2017. Digital health and the biopolitics of the quantified self. *Digital Health*, *3*, p.2055207616689509.

Atanasoski, N. and Vora, K., 2019. *Surrogate humanity: Race, robots, and the politics of technological futures*. Durham, North Carolina: Duke University Press.

Atkinson, C., Beck, V., Brewis, J., Davies, A. and Duberley, J., 2021. Menopause and the workplace: New directions in HRM research and HR practice. *Human Resource Management Journal*, *31*(1), pp.49–64.

Baines, D. and Armstrong, P., 2019. Non-job work/unpaid caring: Gendered industrial relations in long-term care. *Gender, Work & Organization*, *26*(7), pp.934–947.

Bear, J.B. and Glick, P., 2017. Breadwinner bonus and caregiver penalty in workplace rewards for men and women. *Social Psychological and Personality Science*, *8*(7), pp.780–788.

Beck, K., Beedle, M., Van Bennekum, A., Cockburn, A., Cunningham, W., Fowler, M., Grenning, J., Highsmith, J., Hunt, A., Jeffries, R. and Kern, J., 2001. The agile manifesto. Dallas: Agile Alliance. http://agilemanifesto.org/

Berk, S.F., 2012 [1985]. *The gender factory: The apportionment of work in American households*. Berlin: Springer Science & Business Media.

Bernd, J., Abu-Salma, R. and Frik, A., 2020. {Bystanders'} Privacy: The perspectives of Nannies on smart home surveillance. In *10th USENIX Workshop on Free and Open Communications on the Internet (FOCI 20)*. https://www.usenix.org/conference/foci20/presentation/bernd

Brumley, K.M., 2014. The gendered ideal worker narrative: Professional women's and men's work experiences in the new economy at a Mexican company. *Gender & Society*, *28*(6), pp.799–823.

Brumley, K.M. and George, M.E.S., 2022. Rules of engagement: Flexplace and ideal workers. *Social Currents*, *9*(6), pp.573–591.

Brush, B.L. and Vasupuram, R., 2006. Nurses, nannies and caring work: Importation, visibility and marketability. *Nursing Inquiry*, *13*(3), pp.181–185.

Campbell, F.K., 2015. Ability. In Adams, R, Reiss, B, and Serling, D (Eds.). *Keywords for Disability Studies* (pp.12–14). New York: New York University Press.

Cherrier, H. and Murray, J.B., 2004. The sociology of consumption: The hidden facet of marketing. *Journal of Marketing Management*, *20*(5–6), pp.509–525.

Correll, S.J., Weisshaar, K.R., Wynn, A.T. and Wehner, J.D., 2020. Inside the black box of organizational life: The gendered language of performance assessment. *American Sociological Review*, *85*(6), pp.1022–1050.

Cox, R., 2007. The au pair body: Sex object, sister or student? *European Journal of Women's Studies*, *14*(3), pp.281–296.

Dalgas, K.M., 2016. Au pairs on Facebook. *Nordic Journal of Migration Research*, *6*(3), pp.175–182.

Dinerstein, J., 2006. Technology and its discontents: On the verge of the posthuman. *American Quarterly*, 58(3): pp. 569–595.

Dumas, T.L. and Sanchez-Burks, J., 2015. The professional, the personal, and the ideal worker: Pressures and objectives shaping the boundary between life domains. *The Academy of Management Annals*, *9*(1), pp.803–843.

Ehrenreich, B. and Hochschild, A.R. (Eds.)., 2003. *Global woman: Nannies, maids, and sex workers in the new economy*. London: Macmillan.

England, K., 2010. Home, work and the shifting geographies of care. *Ethics, Place and Environment*, *13*(2), pp.131–150.

England, K. and Henry, C., 2013. Care work, migration and citizenship: International nurses in the UK. *Social & Cultural Geography*, *14*(5), pp.558–574.

Federici, S., 2004. *Caliban and the Witch*. New York: Autonomedia.

Fish, J.N., 2015. Making history through policy: A field report on the international domestic workers movement. *International Labor and Working-Class History*, *88*, pp.156–165.

Foucault, M., 1990. *The history of sexuality: An introduction, volume I*. Translated by Robert Hurley. New York: Vintage, *95*, pp.1–160.

Freeman, C., 2000. *High tech and high heels in the global economy: Women, work, and pink-collar identities in the Caribbean*. Durham, Massachusetts: Duke University Press.

Gallagher, A., 2018. The business of care: Marketization and the new geographies of childcare. *Progress in Human Geography*, 42(5), pp.706–722.

Gomes, A.V.M. and Banerjee, R., 2017. The guarantee of freedom of association and collective bargaining rights to domestic workers: Two opposite models, Brazil and Canada. *Pensar-Revista de Ciências Jurídicas*, *22*(3), pp. 1–15.

Hardt, M., 1999. Affective labor. *Boundary, 2, 26*(2), pp.89–100.

Harvey, D., 2005. *The new imperialism*. Oxford: Oxford University Press.

Henry, C., 2018. The abstraction of care: What work counts? *Antipode*, *50*(2), pp.340–358.

Hobden, C., 2015. *Domestic workers organize–but can they bargain. Mapping collective bargaining and other forms of negotiation in the domestic work sector*. Geneva: International Labour Organization.

https://www.ilo.org/wcmsp5/groups/public/@ed_protect/@protrav/@travail/documents/publication/wcms_345704.pdf

Hochschild, A.R., 2015. Global care chains and emotional surplus value. In Engster, D. and Metz, T. (Eds) *Justice, politics, and the family* (pp.249–261). Abingdon: Routledge.

James, A., 2017. *Work-life advantage: Sustaining regional learning and innovation*. Chichester: John Wiley & Sons.

Kelly, K., In: Takahashi, D. (2012) *Quantifying our lives will be a top trend of 2012*. http://venturebeat.com/2012/01/21/quantifying-our-lives-will-be-a-top-trend-of-2012/.

Kent, R., 2018. Social media and self-tracking: Representing the 'health self'. In Ajana, B. (Ed.). *Self-tracking: Empirical and philosophical investigations* (pp.61–76). London: Palgrave Macmillan

Kent, R., 2020. Self-tracking and digital food cultures: Surveillance and self-representation of the moral 'healthy' body. In Lupton, D, and Feldman, Z (Eds.). *Digital food cultures* (pp.19–34). Abingdon: Routledge.

Koskenniemi, A., 2023. Taking charge of the menstrual cycle: Discourses of menstruation and the menstruating body in self-help literature. *Women's Reproductive Health*, *10*(3), pp.323–340.

Lupton, D., 2017. Self-tracking, health and medicine. *Health Sociology Review*, *26*(1), pp.1–5.

Lutz, H., 2002. At your service madam! The globalization of domestic service. *Feminist Review*, *70*(1), pp.89–104.

MacLeavy, J., 2021. Care-work, gender inequality and technological advancement in the age of Covid-19. *Gender, Work and Organization*, *28*(1), pp.138–154.

Maher, K.H. and Staab, S., 2005. Nanny politics: The dilemmas of working women's empowerment in Santiago, Chile. *International Feminist Journal of Politics*, *7*(1), pp.71–89.

Marcuse, H., 2004 [1941]. Social implications of technology. In Arato Andrew, A (Ed.). *The Essential Frankfurt School Reader* (pp. 138–162). New York: Urizen.

Marx, K. 1976. *Capital: A critique of political economy.* Translated by David Fernbach. London: Penguin.

Mateescu, A., 2018. *Nannies already felt like they were under constant surveillance. The internet has made it even worse*. Slate (13 August). https://slate.com/human-interest/2018/08/nannies-are-under-constant-surveillance-online-care-sites-are-making-it-worse.html

McDowell, L., 2014. Gender, work, employment and society: Feminist reflections on continuity and change. *Work, Employment and Society*, *28*(5), pp.825–837.

Moore, P., 2018. On work and machines: A labour process of agility. *Soundings*, *69*(69), pp.15–31.

Moore, P. and Robinson, A., 2016. The quantified self: What counts in the neoliberal workplace. *New Media & Society*, *18*(11), pp.2774–2792.

Mumford, L., 2010 [1934]. *Technics and civilization*. Chicago: University of Chicago Press.

Mysoor, A., 2018. *How women an use monthly periods as a productivity tool.* Forbes (10 May). https://www.forbes.com/sites/alexandramysoor/2018/05/10/how-women-can-use-monthly-periods-as-a-productivity-tool/

Polyani, K., 1944. *The great transformation.* New York: Rheinhart.

Pratt, G., 2009. Circulating sadness: Witnessing Filipina mothers' stories of family separation. *Gender, Place & Culture*, *16*(1), pp.3–22.

Prudham, 2009. Commodification. In Castree, N, Demeritt, D, Liverman, D, Rhoads, B (Eds.). *A Companion to Environmental Geography*. London: Blackwell.

Reid, E., 2015. Embracing, passing, revealing, and the ideal worker image: How people navigate expected and experienced professional identities. *Organization Science*, *26*(4), pp.997–1017.

Rowson, T.S., Jaworska, S. and Gibas, I., 2023. Hot topic: Examining discursive representations of menopause and work in the British media. *Gender, Work & Organization*. *30*(6), pp. 1903–1921.

Ruddick, S., 1989. *Maternal thinking: Toward a politics of peace*. Boston: Beacon Press.

Sang, K., Remnant, J., Calvard, T. and Myhill, K., 2021. Blood work: Managing menstruation, menopause and gynaecological health conditions in the workplace. *International Journal of Environmental Research and Public Health*, *18*(4), p.1951.

Schwiter, K. and Steiner, J., 2020. Geographies of care work: The commodification of care, digital care futures and alternative caring visions. *Geography Compass*, *14*(12), p.e12546.

Smith, D.E., 1987. *The everyday world as problematic: A feminist sociology*. Toronto: University of Toronto Press.

The Economist. 2012. Counting Every Moment (03 May). Economist.com/node/21548493

Thébaud, S. and Taylor, C.J., 2021. The specter of motherhood: Culture and the production of gendered career aspirations in science and engineering. *Gender & Society*, *35*(3), pp.395–421.

Torchinsky, R. 2022. *How period tracking apps and data privacy fit into post-Roe v Wade climate* (24 June). NPR. https://www.npr.org/2022/05/10/1097482967/roe-v-wade-supreme-court-abortion-period-apps

Trotter, L.J., 2017. Making a career: Reproducing gender within a predominately female profession. *Gender & Society*, *31*(4), pp.503–525.

Watt, N. and Wintour, P. 2014. Welfare reform minister: Some disabled people 'not worth' minimum wage (15 October). *The Guardian*. https://www.theguardian.com/politics/2014/oct/15/welfare-reform-minister-disabled-not-worth-minimum-wage

Weeks, K., 1998. *Constituting feminist subjects*. New York: Cornell University Press.

Weeks, K., 2011. The problem *with work: Feminism. Marxism, antiwork politics, and post work imaginaries.* Durham, Massachusetts: Duke University Press.

Whiley, L.A., Wright, A., Stutterheim, S.E. and Grandy, G., 2023. "A part of being a woman, really": Menopause at work as "dirty" femininity. *Gender, Work & Organization*, *30*(3), pp.897–916.

Willis, P.E., 1977. *Learning to labor: How working class kids get working class jobs*. New York: Columbia University Press.

Recommendations for Further Reading

Allen, R.C., 2017. Lessons from history for the future of work. *Nature*, *550*(7676), pp.321–324. (A brief provocation about the scope and simplicity of future of work discourse.)

Hochschild, A.R., 2005. "Rent a mom" and other services: Markets, meanings and emotions. *International Journal of Work Organisation and Emotion*, *1*(1), pp.74–86. (An exploration of commercialisation on emotional life.)

Kent, R., 2020. Self-tracking health over time: From the use of Instagram to perform optimal health to the protective shield of the digital detox. *Social Media+ Society*, *6*(3), p.2056305120940694. (A close look at Instagram in the context of the quantified self.)

Limki, R., 2018. On the coloniality of work: Commercial surrogacy in India. *Gender, Work & Organization*, *25*(4), pp.327–342. (A rigorous account of how gender, sexual, and racial difference produce the conditions that make capitalist domination and exploitation possible.)

Moore, P.V., 2017. *The quantified self in precarity: Work, technology and what counts*. Routledge. (A comprehensive investigation into the efficacy of quantification processes in workplaces, where Moore argues that in fact, such measure lead to higher turnover rates, worker stress, etc.)

Pratt, G., 2012. *Families apart: Migrant mothers and the conflicts of labor and love*. Minneapolis: U of Minnesota Press. (A series of stories documenting the experience of migrant workers caught up in the neoliberal policies sending and receiving countries, produced in collaboration with the Philippine Women Centre of British Columbia.)

15

QUEERING THE FUTURE OF WORK

Queer and Trans Temporalities for (Re)thinking Work and Social Reproduction

Lizzie Richardson and Daniel Cockayne

Introduction

The future of work is a contemporary discourse that narrates an economic future modelled on the idea that robotisation, artificial intelligence, and other new technologies put many jobs at risk of being eliminated. Much of today's discourse about the future of work is driven by only a few empirical studies (Spencer 2018, e.g., Frey and Osborne 2017). As Samers (2021) explores in detail, these studies are accompanied by a wide range of "grey literature" about the future of work—too vast a literature to cite here in detail—penned by groups, including think tanks, consultancies, corporations, and the mainstream media. While future of work discourses are perhaps more prevalent on the right of the political spectrum (Ford 2015), they also exist on the left (Bastani 2019): both perspectives present cautionary tales about impending joblessness, though disagree about whether robotisation will also create more and different kinds of work, and if joblessness is read as a problem or a boon. Future of work discourses are persuasive in the sense that they tell a common-sense story about the relationship between technological development and economic transition that has wide affective purchase, and though empirically and conceptually questionable, the link between robotisation and widespread job loss seems intuitive (Samers 2021).

Critiques of the future of work discourse focus on its sensationalist and simplistic explanations of technological development and economic transition. Part of this critique argues that technological change does not have a singular nor deterministic effect on joblessness (or any other economic indicator), that this change is far more complex, and that its effects cannot be easily predicted in advance. Some writers have focussed on a more sober and critical set of reflections concerning what might actually be empirically predictable about a future of work (Benenav 2020). These include the likelihood of increased labour market intermediation, widening inequalities, and specific challenges for young people (Ojanperä et al. 2018) (see Chapter 20). Others have highlighted omissions and exclusions in future of work discourses (Howcroft and Rubery 2019; Reid-Musson et al. 2020), exploring how these discourses are largely focussed on the Global North, typically only centre particular kinds of work, and only focus on particular kinds of workers. Here we build on these critiques to suggest that the future of work discourse presents a narrow understanding of temporality, as well as insufficient emphasis on social difference, including gender and sexuality, and thus excludes queer and trans people in its conceptualisation of the future.

 DOI: 10.4324/9781003327561-21

In this chapter therefore, we "queer" the dominant discussions of the future of work in two ways. First, we outline how queer images of futurity—in particular through the work of Keeling and Muñoz—present a conceptual challenge to the prevailing notion of time in the future of work. Second, we explore several practical ways of understanding the future of work through a queer lens. These are (1) queer and trans experiences of work and modes of labour organising, and (2) queer and trans approaches to social reproduction, including (re)emerging debates around family abolition. These ways of conceptualising the future of work are queer precisely in their centring of mutual aid, collective action, and social reproduction and have a distinctly transfeminist inflection (Gleeson and O'Rourke 2021). While acknowledging that queerness is not always anti-normative by default (see Oswin 2008), we want to hold open, perhaps improperly, provocatively, and inappropriately, the possibility for an anti-normative queerness beyond the mainstream assimilationist and respectability politics of identity-based gay and lesbian movements (Nair 2014) and instead define queer, following Lewis (2022: 9) as "anti-property." An anti-property queerness acknowledges that queer and trans people are disproportionately in positions of economic precarity in contemporary society (Hollibaugh and Weiss 2015). It also points to forms of radical queer and trans resistance to hetero- and cis-normative forms of property status (e.g., parenthood, relationship-status, home ownership, and access to the means of production) that defines the sexual hegemony of our time (Chitty 2020), which are best situated in opposition to property as a violent colonial-capitalist cisheteropatriarchal construct. We argue in this chapter that a substantive theory of the future of work needs to take into account queer and trans subjects and lives, thus recognising the possibility that many people will not or cannot be productive or socially reproductive in the narrow ways prescribed by contemporary neoliberal capitalism and the colonial state.

The Future of Work and Queer Temporalities

Dominant discourses on the future of work centre narrowly on particular kinds of productive subjects and those who have been made unproductive through automation (see Reid-Musson et al. 2020). Frey and Osborne's (2017) report—perhaps the most well-known and oft-cited study (though also widely critiqued, see Benenav 2020)—suggests that the roles most at risk of automation in the near future are workers in manufacturing, transportation, and logistics, together with office and administrative support workers. Given current divisions of labour in the countries from where this discourse originates, the future of work is then, at least in part, an anxiety about the future of young white working-class men, feeding into the perceived crisis of masculinity that commonly accompanies this economic transition (Hopkins 2009; McDowell 2002). The risk posed to office and administrative support workers also implicates low status service sector workers, which demographically does disproportionately include women (Howcroft and Rubery 2019). Mostly though, the future of work discourses ignores subjects beyond white and "productive" men, with a focus on working-class men, and ignores socially reproductive work altogether. "Work" in the future of work discourse is implicitly conceptualised as productive, waged or salaried, and formalised through a legal contract, with the social value of work remaining unquestionably positive (Weeks 2011). The future of work thus appears to be the domain of some productive men and (sometimes) women, robots, and the soon-to-be-unproductive jobless masses, while the essential work of social reproduction, informal work, and the work of the state and civil society, remain largely invisible.

In its current manifestation, this future of work discourse provides an image of futurity that bears similarities with what Oswin (2012) calls "straight time." Exploring Singapore's creative city project, Oswin shows how Singapore offers hollow forms of conviviality to queer people while also maintaining discriminatory legislation that excludes gays and lesbians from full citizenship. Straight time functions through teleological narratives of progress and development, valorising only particular productive subjects, while also positing queer people as marginalised and as having "no future" (see Edelman 2004). One difference between the straight time that Oswin describes and the straight time of the future of work is that the former emphasises how city policy making prescribes particular kinds of heteronormative social reproduction. Conversely, Howcroft and Rubery (2019) argue that most future of work discourses ignore conceptualisations of gender entirely, claiming that if not addressed directly, these futures are therefore likely to exacerbate existing forms of gender inequality. Similarly, the absence of queer subjects in the future of work discourse signals the hiddenness of an implicitly straight and cis social reproduction, that, though undiscussed, remains structurally essential in those futures as a substantial subsidy for capital that is still in most geographic contexts disproportionately undertaken by women.

Approaches to time and temporalities in queer theory provide an alternative orientation for the future of work, one that can contribute to addressing the shortcomings of these existing discourses. Queer temporalities offer a means to broaden definitions of work, and to provide more plural and non-linear temporalities of social life that insist on openness and uncertainty. In using the term "queer temporalities," we pull together different concerns with time and temporality that have risen to prominence in the last two decades in anglophone queer theory. Before further explanation of these queer temporalities, two points need clarification. First, these queer approaches do not singularly address or concern LGBTQ people but rather they hold in question, and often seek to imagine otherwise, broader cultural but also social and economic modes of "apprehension and value production" (Keeling 2019: 17), thus challenging prevailing norms organising societies by conceptualising queer as a relation rather than an identity. In doing so, queer theory and associated scholarship draws attention to how sexuality is not "merely cultural" (Butler 1997) but rather, as a mode of social order, is central to economic questions. Second, we see these queer temporalities as aligned with other critical approaches to futurity (e.g., Black, indigenous, and feminist) that are multidimensional and multi-linear, frequently seeking to bring new things and ideas into being (MacLeavy et al. 2021; Bliss 2015).

The different concerns encompassed by theorisations of queer temporalities arose as theorists began to conceptualise time as important for making sense of queer experience. The turn to temporalities in queer theory in the first decade of the twenty-first century (Dinshaw et al. 2007) was situated at a particular juncture in the social and legal recognition of same-gender relationships in the US (from where some key scholars were writing), in which rights were being established to allow civil unions and marriage in certain states. Although purportedly progressive, some critics suggest that rights-based activism stifled conversations that had been opened by earlier LGBTQ movements that had made more radical political claims for lives outside of existing socio-economic institutions delimiting private life, such as marriage and the nuclear family (Cooper 2017; Nair 2014). With the AIDs epidemic in living memory, the issue of how to make sense of the present in relation to traumatic pasts and apparently narrowing futures became crucial. To address this, queer theorists in different ways challenged the linear sense of time defined by the infinite growth logics of capitalism and the "progressive" and reproductive project of democratic liberalism, which situate the straight couple and nuclear family as the indisputable foundation of these twin projects (Latimer 2013). To retain the force of previous political movements and to challenge cyclical, linear, and generational models of time, Freeman (2010) proposed the notion of "temporal drag" as "a way of forcing the present to touch its own disavowed past or seemingly outlandish possible future" (78) through "resuscitating obsolete cultural signs," "embarrassing pre-histories" or "the love of failure" (68). While some advocated for a refusal of the (straight, singular) future promised through reproduction and organised around the image of "the Child" (Edelman 2004), others saw the potentiality of queer futures outside the paradigmatic markers of life experience (Halberstam 2005).

It is this openness to the future that is particularly helpful for challenging prevailing conceptions of the future of work. Perhaps the most influential thinking in this vein is Muñoz's (2009) *Cruising Utopia* in which he emphasises an understanding of queerness as "the rejection of a here and now and an insistence on potentiality or concrete possibility for another world" (10). This is a vision of queer futurity that remains attentive to the past for the purposes of critiquing the present (18), but nonetheless foregrounds the critical practices of imagination that "lets us feel that this world is not enough, that indeed something is missing" (10). For Muñoz, this queerness—that he conceptualises as the promise of a better world for queer people that is a future yet to come—is not singular but rather collective, and so stands in contrast to modes of "ontological certitude" in understandings of a static (gay or straight) identity that seek to fix the future in a deterministic or singular mode, rather than leave it open. The plurality of queer futurity put forward by Muñoz is present in more recent theorising of queer temporality, some of which has foregrounded race in challenging singular approaches to understanding sexuality. For instance, Keeling (2019) emphasises the co-constitution of queer time with what they term "black futures," as that which "remains unaccountable to existing instruments of measurement" (32). Black futures are "an investment in the risk that already inheres in social life," risk produced through queer temporalities that "names that dimension of the unpredictable and the unknowable in time that governs errant, eccentric, promiscuous and unexpected organisations of social life" (19). Even more explicitly than the earlier work above (Freeman 2010), Keeling emphasises the links between the non-linearity of queer times and the unpredictability of the temporal in financial capitalism, only to suggest that in contrast to the latter that tends towards recognition, the former always allows for both the recognisable and imperceptible.

Taken together then, the future orientation in queer theory—and the broader attempt to foreground time and temporality—was and remains intended to retain a radical queer politics by insisting on the possibility for other worlds, and in doing so queer temporalities broaden and diversify what is understood as the political realm. In addressing what will become of work then, queer temporalities hold open the future as a realm of possibility (including the chance of failure [Halberstam 2011]) and imagining otherwise, instead of seeking a singular prognosis or normative (and intended) outcome. Building on the theories of queer temporality outlined in this section, which centre temporalities distinct from the "straight time" of heteronormative reproduction and progressive and linear liberal capitalism, in the rest of this chapter, we reflect on what a queer future of work might look like. To do so, we place an emphasis on sexuality and gender as the lens through which to consider broader questions of what counts as work and what purposes definitions of work should serve, together with issues of how such work is valued and organised. We explore examples in two areas where foregrounding sexuality and gender offers alternative foundations for the future of work, looking firstly at queer and trans work and labour organising, and secondly at queer theories of social reproduction.

Queer and Trans Work and Labour Organising

Despite the absence of queer and trans subjects from the future of work discourses, there exists a substantial body of research that conceptualises queer and trans people in terms of their work and organising. Indeed, queer and trans theory has been (re)turning to Marxism, theories of class and examinations of work in recent years. Much of this research builds on writers like Hennessy (2006), who examines sexual identity in maquiladoras at the US-Mexico border and its role as both a source of exploitation but also in terms of the possibilities it offers in terms of labour organising.

Theories of "queer work" according to writers like Bérublé (2011) name how certain sectors and kinds of work—at specific times and places—come to attract queers more than others. Bérublé, specifically exploring the Marine Cooks and Steward's Union in the United States in the 1930s (see also Chauncey 2009), points to how some professions provide *relative* safety for queers, allowing, albeit perhaps in only limited ways, the expression of queer subjectivity, and means through which queers are able to help one another to find and retain work and organise for better circumstances. Elsewhere, writers like Lewis (2012) explore how labour markets function as a system of governmentality for queer people, that while perhaps offering some freedoms and relative safety, also prescribe a narrow range of only particularly professionalised and appropriate queer subjectivities. Most recently Sharp et al. (2022) discuss how in hospitality work queer subjectivity itself becomes commodifiable and part of a product to be sold, even as queer people try to push back on this commodification. In part, these discussions are centred around where and how queer and trans people can find and maintain work, and the extent to which they can survive and thrive in that work, given the continuing prevalence of homophobia and transphobia in labour markets (Dilmaghani and Robinson 2024), and given the continued dependence on the market for one's social reproduction.

In the background of this research is a connection between queerness and labour markets. Firstly, labour markets have a disciplinary effect on queer communities, even while that discipline is resisted; secondly, within these labour markets, queer people are often restricted to more precarious forms of work. This contrasts with myths of gay and lesbian affluence that posit gays and lesbians as having access to higher disposable incomes. Empirical research confirms that queer and trans people remain disproportionately poor, precarious, and disenfranchised under contemporary capitalism (Hollibaugh and Weiss 2015). These studies confirm a wage gap between straight men and queer people ranging from 10% to 29%, depending on gender identity and sexual orientation, with bisexual women particularly affected by this wage gap (Waite et al. 2020). Queers and trans people continue to face disproportionate discrimination in labour markets (Dilmaghani and Robinson 2024) and are more likely to be unemployed or working less than full-time when they are employed (Statistics Canada 2022; Waite 2021). That interaction between labour markets and queer people—as a discriminatory mechanism and disciplinary force that queer people unevenly resist—is still an under-recognised and under-explored area of research.

In addition to the examination of queer people in labour markets, there is a related body of research that outlines how sexuality operates in labour organising. Writers like Frank (2014) have explored the role of sexual identity in US unions, showing both how many unionisation efforts have been led by queer and trans people, and how some unions have turned towards advocating for issues that pertain in particular to queer and trans people. These issues include anti-discrimination provisions for trans people (long before state protections), equity in shared benefit plans and parental leave for same-gender couples, and access to healthcare that centre queer and trans people, e.g., access to pre-exposure prophylaxis (PrEP) drugs designed to prevent the spread of HIV, gender-affirming hormones and surgeries, and for equal access to IVF and related reproductive health procedures. O'Brien (2021) draws on a recent example of LGBTQ organisers in retail work in New York City to argue that queer and trans workers can be particularly successful labour organisers. This is based on a more general link between marginalised workers—in Brofenbrenner and Warren's (2007) analysis, amongst Black, Hispanic, and women workers—and a willingness to take on leadership roles in labour organising efforts. O'Brien (2021) suggests that this willingness is linked to a number of factors, including disproportionate workplace alienation, a disaggregated social network not tied directly to class interests, and existing skills related to prior experience in social movements and making connections across affinity groups. More broadly, other writers have explored the relationship between queer people and radical and leftist social movements and labour organising, e.g., in generating queer support for the 1984–1985 miners' strikes in the UK (Kelliher 2014; see also Hobson 2016).

Closely related to the discussions of queer social reproduction below, writers like Ward (2010: 237) explore "gender labour," which describes the work of "bolstering someone's gender authenticity [...], co-producing someone's gender irony, transgression, or exceptionality." Gender labour, Ward argues, might be most commonly thought of as the unthinking and passive work that goes into the everyday performances of heterosexual and cisgender normativity (Butler 1990; Federici 2004). Yet, Ward draws attention to the active work required to affirm non-normative sexualities and gender identities that push back against these iterative performances of (cishetero)normativity. Ward focusses specifically on the gender labour of white women in the affirmation of their trans partner's masculinity (see also Frank 2014), though she argues that the implications of these insights go beyond this. The emotional and therapeutic work of affirming someone's gender and sexuality is most often undertaken informally or voluntarily, but it is increasingly becoming recognised, paid, and formalised. Shange (2019) highlights how gender labour is deeply racialised in the sense that Black queer and trans experience is specific and distinct from white queer and trans experience. Shange's discussion of gender labour in a majority Black high school illustrates how gender labour takes place beyond the home in the context of paid and professionalised work too, even while it may not be formally recognised as part of someone's "official" job description. The advantage of analysing gender and sexuality themselves as forms of work lies in the way that they de-naturalise discussions around gender and sexuality as categories. Gender and sexuality are work, in the sense that they are actively produced and maintained, and in their most normative forms, they are a (usually unrecognised) product of colonial and capitalist systems (Nguyen 2021).

Queer(ing) Social Reproduction

As well as sometimes denoting the biological propagation of the species, social reproduction refers to the practices that ensure the ongoing supply of labour involving subsistence, education and training; together with the provisioning (whether privately or publicly) of caring needs (Bakker 2007: 541). By centring on social reproduction as a focus for the future of work debates, our argument is that production cannot be understood separately from that which is essential to sustaining it. This argument is intrinsic to queer theory and studies of sexuality, firstly because of the historical visibility of social reproduction in and for queer communities in different contexts. Out of necessity, queer people engage in forms of sometimes paid, but frequently unpaid work as means of survival, for example, in activism and collective organising that "are not just political tools enabling the advancement of legal equalities of queer people, but also everyday practices that allow queer families, neighbourhoods, and communities to sustain themselves" (Lewis 2017: n.p.). Social reproduction as the work required to create life-worlds for queer people has "for a portion of the population has always been inherently queer" (Lewis 2017: n.p.) and thus exists outside prevailing models such as the nuclear family.

Secondly, social production is indivisible from production because both function as a mechanism of regulation for sexuality (Hennessy 2006), comprising sets of practices and discourses through which power operates, working to "maintain the stability of gender, the heterosexuality of desire, and the naturalisation of the family" (Butler 1997: 273). These two motivations for focussing on social reproduction in queer theory are not necessarily at odds with, but are nonetheless frequently distinct from, certain traditions of feminist enquiry that have uncovered the ways women's unpaid work subsidised the male breadwinners' wages in industrial capitalism (Andrucki 2021). Queer approaches to social reproduction challenge the institutions of reproduction (marriage and the family) together with the stability of dualistic conceptualisations of gender categories, both of which underpin the sexual division of labour. We touch on two areas that indicate what queer approaches to social reproduction might mean for examinations of the future of work. One concerns the practices that sustain collectives and communities of non-normative sexualities—*queer social reproduction*—and the other draws from some of these practices to focus on critiques of and alternative models for the family as a site for organising social provisioning—*queering social reproduction*.

Regarding queer social reproduction, futures of work involve accounting for the myriad of forms of queer labour that constitute the economy. In part this implies giving due attention to the orthodox and unorthodox "pleasures and labours of mundane queer intimate life" (Andrucki 2021: 1365) that may or may not fall into "heteronormative" patterns of social reproduction. Considering the practices through which, for example, same-gender married couples organise their everyday lives, not only broadens what classifies as socially reproductive activities but also demonstrates how sexuality itself organises social reproduction. As Hennessy (2006: 389) argued, "sexuality" is arranged through affective needs and sensate relations that are crucial to the structuring of activities beyond the formal sphere of production, and frequently of course also those within it. Further, there is a whole host of socially reproductive labour that is necessary to sustain the complexity of queer worlds: from the types of labour expected by queer and trans people to get by in everyday social situations (Raha 2021; Savcı 2021) to gay men's "multivalent acts of caretaking" that "mediate boundaries of public and private" (Andrucki 2021: 1375).

Such queer social reproduction follows conflicting patterns of mainstream complicity and queer diversity (Lewis 2017). For example, the AIDS activism of the early 1990s articulated a radical welfare politics that called for an expansion of social insurance in the US that was detached from a reference to the family wage (and sexual normativity), but was by the turn of the millennium largely forgotten in the demands for gay marriage that were a move for inclusion within an already private model of social reproduction (Cooper 2017: 210). In contrast to this narrowing of the political imaginations and motivations of the broader LGBTQ movement, past and contemporary alternatives to existing modes of organising the family provide a more radical vision for futures of work by queering social reproduction. In Europe, North America and beyond, the regulation of sexuality has long been tied to "a legal instrument of wealth appropriation that takes the form of family genealogy" (Cooper 2017: 23). Family abolitionism is one response to this, espousing a politics that aims to address the "structural and material conditions that are more conducive to [the family's] invention" (Weeks 2021: 16; Lewis 2022).

Central to family abolitionism is a critique of a model of the family that institutionalises the privatisation of care and other reproductive labours (Gregson and Lowe 1995). Creating socially reproductive units that are not normalised along lines of kinship, marriage, or private property has been a project of feminist and queer movements in different contexts with varying degrees of success. Alternative domestic arrangements (e.g., co-living and non-monogamous parenting) raise a variety of questions concerning living space, sharing of income or the undertaking of unpaid domestic work, which are not normally asked in more conventional family set ups and involve additional socially reproductive work to ensure their resolution (Cartledge 1980; Barrett and McIntosh 1980; Wauthier 2022). A well-documented recent and successful example is the "Mums 4 Housing" movement in Oakland, California in which five Black mothers occupied a vacant, corporate investor-owned house and created a network of care that allowed for collective motherhood (Ramírez 2020). By thus putting care and motherhood as central to their opposition to regimes of housing speculation and dispossession, the group made the community "a site of production" (Summers and Fields 2024: 833) for social, intimate, and familial relations. By outlining these queer approaches, our aim is not simply to recognise social reproduction but rather to put forward alternative conceptions and practices of socially reproductive labour as central to the future of work.

Conclusion

Queer and trans theory provide a vital means of opening up both the ideas and practices of the future of work. This is important because, as critiques of prevailing future of work discourses on both the right and the left differently suggest, conceptualisations of both work and the future within mainstream future of work discourses are very narrow, and much is left out of these discourses. Yet, the future of work is also a discourse with wide economic and political purchase. Recognising this, we have argued that it is necessary to address the conception of temporality underpinning prevailing future of work discourses in order to foreground alternative queer temporalities that retain a sense of openness, unpredictability, and the unrecognisable. Through an account of queer and trans work, we have shown that such temporalities allow for a focus on different working subjectivities and types of social relations through work that are not solely orientated around the regime of production, whether critically or otherwise. Theorising queer social reproduction similarly extends the realm of the future of work, demonstrating not only the inextricability of production and social reproduction but also the central role of sexuality and gender in their organisation. Thinking the futures of work alongside a conceptualisation of queer temporalities, and with a lens on queer and trans work, organising, and social reproduction allows for a critical recentring of this concept.

References

Andrucki, M. J. (2021). Queering social reproduction: sex, care and activism in San Francisco. *Urban Studies*, 58, 1364–1379.

Bakker, I. (2007). Social reproduction and the constitution of a gendered political economy. *New Political Economy* 12, 541–556.

Barrett, M., & McIntosh, M. (1980). *The Anti-Social Family*. Verso.

Bastani, A. (2019). *Fully Automated Luxury Communism*. Verso.

Benenav, A. (2020). *Automation and the Future of Work*. Verso.

Bérublé, A. (2011). *My Desire for History: Essays in Gay, Community, and Labour History*. University of North Carolina Press.

Bliss, J. (2015). Hope against hope: queer negativity, black feminist theorising, and reproduction without futurity. *Mosaic*, 48, 83–98.

Bronfenbrenner, K., & Warren, D. T. (2007). Race, gender, and the rebirth of trade unionism. *New Labour Forum*, *16*(3/4), 142–148.

Butler, J. (1997). Merely cultural. *Social Text*, 52/53, 265–277.

Butler, J. (1990). *Gender Trouble*. Routledge.

Cartledge, S. (1980). Bringing it all back home: lesbian feminist morality. In (eds.) The Gay Left Collective, *Homosexuality: Power and Politics*, Verso, pp. 93–103.

Chauncey, G. (2009). *Gay New York: Gender, Urban Culture, and the Making of the Gay Male World, 1890–1940*. Basic Books.

Chitty, C. (2020). *Sexual Hegemony: Statecraft, Sodomy, and Capital in the Rise of the World System*. Duke University Press.

Cooper, M. (2017). *Family Values: Between Neoliberalism and the New Social Conservatism*. Zone Books.

Dilmaghani, M., & Robinson, M. (2024). The blue of the rainbow: queerness and hiring discrimination in blue-collar occupations. *Review of Social Economy*, 82, 367–395.

Dinshaw, C., Edelman, L., Ferguson, R., Freccero, C., Freeman, E., Halberstam, J., Jagose, A., Nealon, C., & Nguyen, T. (2007). Theorizing queer temporalities: a roundtable discussion. *GLQ: A Journal of Lesbian and Gay Studies*, 13, 177–195.

Edelman, L. (2004). *No Future: Queer Theory and the Death Drive*. Duke University Press.

Federici, S. (2004). *Caliban and the Witch: Women, the Body, and Primitive Accumulation*. Autonomedia.

Ford, M. (2015). *The Rise of the Robots*. Basic Books.

Frank, M. (2014). *Out in the Union: A Labour History of Queer America*. Temple University Press.

Freeman, E. (2010). *Time Binds: Queer Temporalities, Queer Histories*. Duke University Press.

Frey, C. B., & Osborne, M. A. (2017). The future of employment: how susceptible are jobs to computerisation? *Technological Forecasting and Social Change*, 114, 254–280.

Gleeson, J. J., & O'Rourke, E. (eds) (2021). *Transgender Marxism*. Pluto Press.

Gregson, N., & Lowe, M. (1995). 'Home'-making: on the spatiality of daily social reproduction in contemporary middle-class Britain. *Transactions of the Institute of British Geographers*, 20, 224–235.

Halberstam, J. (2005). *In a Queer Time and Place: Transgender Bodies, Subcultural Lives*. New York University Press.

Halberstam, J. (2011). *The Queer Art of Failure*. Duke University Press.

Hennessy, R. (2006). Returning to reproduction queerly: sex, labour, need. *Rethinking Marxism* 18, 387–395.

Hobson, E. (2016). *Lavender and Red: Liberation and Solidarity in the Gay and Lesbian Left*. University of California Press.

Hollibaugh, A., & Weiss, M. (2015). Queer precarity and the myth of gay affluence. *New Labour Forum*, 24(3), 18–27.

Hopkins, P. E. (2009). Responding to the 'crisis of masculinity': the perspectives of young Muslim men from Glasgow and Edinburgh, Scotland. *Gender, Place & Culture*, 16(3), 299–312.

Howcroft, D., & Rubery, J. (2019). 'Bias in, Bias out': gender equality and the future of work debate. *Labour & Industry*, 29(2), 213–227.

Keeling, K. (2019). *Queer Times, Black Futures, Sexual Cultures*. New York University Press.

Kelliher, D. (2014). Solidarity and sexuality: lesbians and gays support the miners 1984–5. *History Workshop Journal*, 77(1), 240–262.

Latimer, H. (2013). The straight line: sexuality, futurity, and the politics of austerity. *ESC: English Studies in Canada*, 39(4), 21–24.

Lewis, N. (2012). Gay in a 'government town': the settlement and regulation of gay-identified men in Ottawa, Canada. *Gender, Place & Culture*, 19(3), 291–312.

Lewis, N. (2017). Queer social reproduction: co-opted, hollowed out, and resilient. *Society and Space Blog*. Available at: https://www.societyandspace.org/articles/queer-social-reproduction-co-opted-hollowed-out-and-resilient

Lewis, S. (2022). *After the Family: The Case for Abolition*. Verso.

MacLeavy, J., Fannin, M., & Larner, W. (2021). Feminism and futurity: geographies of resistance, resilience and reworking. *Progress in Human Geography*, 45, 1558–1579.

McDowell, L. (2002). Transitions to work: masculine identities, youth inequality and labour market change. *Gender, Place and Culture*, 9(1), 39–59.

Muñoz, J. (2009). *Cruising Utopia: The Then and There of Queer Futurity*. New York University Press.

Nair, Y. (2014). Against equality, against marriage. In (eds.) Conrad, R., Against Equality, *Against Equality: Queer Revolution Not Mere Inclusion*, AK Press, pp. 15–21.

Nguyen, D. H. (2021). The political economy of heteronormativity. *Review of Radical Political Economics*.

O'Brien, M. E. (2021). Why queer workers make good organisers. *Work, Employment and Society*, *35*(5), 819–836.

Ojanperä, S., O'Clery, N., & Graham, M. (2018). *Data Science, Artificial Intelligence and the Futures of Work*. The Alan Turing Institute.

Oswin, N. (2008). Critical geographies and the uses of sexuality: deconstructing queer space. *Progress in Human Geography*, 32(1), 89–103.

Oswin, N. (2012). The queer time of creative urbanism: family, futurity, and global city Singapore. *Environment and Planning A*, 44(7), 1624–1640.

Raha, N. (2021). A queer Marxist transfeminism: queer and trans social reproduction. In (eds.) Gleeson, J., O'Rourke, E., *Transgender Marxism*, Pluto Press, pp. 85–115.

Ramírez, M. M. (2020). Take the houses back/take the land back: Black and Indigenous urban futures in Oakland. *Urban Geography*, 41, 682–693.

Reid-Musson, E., Cockayne, D., Frederiksen, L., & Worth, N. (2020). Feminist economic geography and the future of work. *Environment and Planning A*, 52(7), 1457–1468.
Samers, M. (2021). Futurological fodder: on communicating the relationship between artificial intelligence, robotics, and employment. *Space and Polity*, 25(2), 237–256.
Savcı, E. (2021). *Queer in Translation: Sexual Politics under Neoliberal Islam*. Duke University Press.
Shange, S. (2019). Play aunties and dyke bitches: gender, generation, and the ethics of black queer kinship. *The Black Scholar*, 49(1), 40–54.
Sharp, M., Farrugia, D., Coffey, J., Threadgold, S., Adkins, L., & Gill, R. (2022). Queer subjectivities in hospitality labour. *Gender, Work & Organization*, 29(5), 1511–1525.
Spencer, D. A. (2018). Fear and hope in an age of mass automation: debating the future of work. *New Technology, Work and Employment*, 33(1), 1–12.
Statistics Canada (2022). Labour and economic characteristics of lesbian, gay and bisexual people in Canada. Available at: https://www150.statcan.gc.ca/n1/pub/89-28-0001/2022001/article/00003-eng.htm
Summers, B. T., & Fields, D. (2024). Speculative urban worldmaking: meeting financial violence with a politics of collective care. *Antipode*, 56, 821–840.
Waite, S. (2021). Should I stay or should I go? Employment discrimination and workplace harassment against transgender and other minority employees in Canada's federal public service. *Journal of Homosexuality*, 68(11), 1833–1859.
Waite, S., Pajovic, V., & Denier, N. (2020). Lesbian, gay, and bisexual earnings in the Canadian labour market: new evidence from the Canadian Community Health Survey. *Research in Social Stratification and Mobility*, 67, 1–13.
Ward, J. (2010). Gender labour: trans men, femmes, and collective work of transgression. *Sexualities*, 13(2), 236–254.
Wauthier, P.-Y. (2022). Stepping off the 'relationship escalator': a spatial perspective on residential arrangements of consensually non-monogamous parents. *Sexualities*, 13634607221080515.
Weeks, K. (2011). *The Problem with Work*. Duke University Press.
Weeks, K. (2021). Abolition of the family: the most infamous feminist proposal. *Feminist Theory*, 14647001211015841.

Recommendations for Further Reading

Cooper, M. (2017). *Family Values: Between Neoliberalism and the New Social Conservatism*. Zone Books. (Details the shifting legal, political and cultural construction of the family in neoliberal USA.)
Keeling, K. (2019). *Queer Times, Black Futures, Sexual Cultures*. New York University Press. (Queer futurities through decentring whiteness implicit in some earlier theorisations.)
Muñoz, J. (2009). *Cruising Utopia: The Then and There of Queer Futurity*. New York University Press. (A foundational exploration of queer futurity from the point of view of hope for queer futures.)
O'Brien, M. E. (2021). Why queer workers make good organisers. *Work, Employment and Society*, 35(5), 819–836. (An examination of queer and trans organizing efforts in retail work in New York City.)
Sharp, M., Farrugia, D., Coffey, J., Threadgold, S., Adkins, L., & Gill, R. (2022). Queer subjectivities in hospitality labour. *Gender, Work & Organization*, 29(5), 1511–1525. (An exploration of queer experiences across different hospitality sector jobs.)
Weeks, K. (2021). Abolition of the family: the most infamous feminist proposal. *Feminist Theory*, 14647001211015841. (Overview of contemporary and historical family abolition debates.)

16

CARE AND THE FUTURE OF WORK

Karin Schwiter

Introduction

"Who does the care work for whom and under what conditions?" remains a fundamental question that accompanies us from the cradle to the grave. Infants start crying when feeling left alone. Older adults worry about being unable to care for themselves as they get older. This chapter aims at exploring care work through the lens of the Future of Work debate. It analyses the options digital technologies offer to shape how we organise care work in the future and it explores alternative futures of care work.

There are manifold ways of exploring current transformations of how we work. The term "Future of Work", however, has become synonym with a very specific narrative. The studies on the Future of Work typically analyse how technological advancements impact on labour markets. They are commonly based on the premise that technology will replace much of the human labour force, i.e. machines will be able to take over many tasks currently done by human beings. Based on this, they ask what kind of jobs will still exist in the future? And how do our societies have to adapt? In his often cited book "The end of work", Jeremy Rifkin (1995: xv), for example, argues that "we are entering a new phase in world history – one in which fewer and fewer workers will be needed to produce the goods and services for the global population" and predicts mass unemployment. For many years the debate circled around "automation" and "robotisation" as buzzwords. Most recently, it has been boosted by the new hype about AI, i.e. artificial intelligence (Schlogl et al. 2021). Many such studies are produced by consultancy firms who typically use dramatic language to suggest the necessity for urgent action. The most recent McKinsey report on the Future of Work, for example, emphasises that "100 million workers may need to switch occupations by 2030" (Lund et al. 2021: 1). The consultancies then advise industry leaders and governments on how to adjust their labour policies to stay competitive.

The debate has received substantial criticism for several problematic aspects (for an extensive critique, see Parts 1 and 2 of this book). Most importantly, scholars problematise its technological determinism, i.e. its often unidirectional and deterministic understanding of technology as impacting society (Joyce et al. 2023). This frames technology as the driving force of change and individuals, firms and governments as its passive victims who struggle to adapt. Such narratives are never merely descriptive, but highly political as they affect how we perceive the future. Spreading

DOI: 10.4324/9781003327561-22

anxieties of large-scale job losses reduces individuals' negotiating power over working conditions: "Be glad you still have a job!", their employers might say. The narrative of job loss thus promotes a neoliberal discourse. It suggests that whoever is not willing to outperform their peers and invest more than others in improving their skills will be left behind.

Instead, social scientists emphasise that technological change is not preordained or fixed by nature. On the contrary, it is societies that govern the development and use of technologies (Howcroft and Taylor 2023). This means that we are not dealing with one impending future of work, but multiple possible futures depending on how we shape the development and use of technologies (MacLeavy and Lapworth 2020; Pitts et al. 2018). As Schlogl et al. (2021: 321) point out, much of the Future of Work scholarship thus poses the wrong question. Instead of asking "what will the future look like?" we need to explore "what kinds of future would we like to create?" This chapter aims to do this with a focus on the future of care work.

The term "care" is conceptualised in a variety of ways. In a broad sense, it is defined as "a species activity that includes everything that we do to maintain, continue and repair our 'world' so that we can live in it as well as possible" (Fischer and Tronto 1990: 40). In this vein, it is often used as a synonym for 'social reproduction', a term stemming from feminist Marxist theory that encompasses all activities required to sustain people's labour power over the life-course and intergenerationally (Bhattacharya 2017). (On the distinct histories and emphases of the two terms, see e.g. Aulenbacher [2020], Haubner [2017], Kofman and Raghuram [2015] and Straussand Meehan [2014].) While care usually refers to activities that humans do to sustain themselves, others and the environment, scholars have recently argued for expanding the notion even further to include non-human actors such as soil (Puig de La Bellacasa 2017) or built environments (Power and Williams 2020) as caring. In the sociology of work, however, the term care is typically used in a narrower sense. There, and also in this chapter, it denotes "the provision of practical or emotional support" (Milligan and Wiles 2010: 737) for another person in the form of paid or unpaid labour. This includes child care, senior care and social care for persons with special needs.

Future of Work reports usually limit their scope to paid employment. Care work is then predicted to be one of the employment fields with a steep increase in demand for additional workers (Lund et al. 2021: 14) and a pronounced labour shortage (World Economic Forum 2023: 36). In the social science literature, which includes both paid and unpaid care, this is reflected in the debate on the care crisis (Dowling 2021).

The Care Crisis

In her book "The Care Crisis: What caused it and how can we end it?" Emma Dowling (2021: 19) defines the care crisis as a twofold societal problem: on the one hand, care recipients are increasingly unable to get the care they need. On the other hand, care workers are increasingly unable to do their work under dignified conditions. Both aspects are caused by the current societal organisation of care labour in many countries around the world: political decisions, economic necessities and changing gender relations have reduced the availability of unpaid care labour within families and communities that was previously done predominantly by women. While women have increased their participation in paid work, men have not equivalently reduced their hours to take over unpaid care work (MacLeavy 2020). Furthermore, many employment fields have witnessed an intensification of work and a growing tendency for work to spread beyond stipulated working hours (Richardson 2018). In consequence, many households find themselves in a "time squeeze" (McDowell 2004) and suffer from "time poverty" (Bücker 2022). They struggle to find time for taking care of their children, older or impaired relatives and other loved ones.

At the same time, governments have not increased public spending for care to an extent that would have filled the emerging care gaps. On the contrary, many countries have witnessed neoliberal policy reforms and austerity politics have led to cut backs in public services (England 2010; Hall 2013; Schwiter et al. 2018). This has not only reduced the availability of affordable care services, but also impacted on working conditions. Under the guise of increasing "efficiency" and saving taxpayers' money, public service care workers have been forced to do ever more in ever shorter hours. Even before the outbreak of the COVID-19 pandemic, there were widespread reports of care workers feeling permanently exhausted and overworked, while trying to keep providing decent care under increasingly difficult conditions (Dowling 2021).

In combination, the domestic time squeeze and the insufficient public provision have fostered the commodification of care (Schwiter and Steiner 2020). To fill care gaps, an increasing number of households are opting to purchase home care services. While this alleviates the care deficit for those who can afford it, it leaves the care deficits of all other households unresolved. Fraser (2016: 104) calls this "a dualized organization of social reproduction, commodified for those who can pay for it, privatized for those who cannot". Furthermore, this commodification of care has fostered the spreading of precarious employment and large-scale migration of workers from poorer to richer countries (Horn et al. 2021). The workers – predominantly women – who migrate as part of these "global care chains" (Hochschild 2000; Parreñas 2001) typically work overlong hours for very low wages (Aulenbacher et al. 2024). Many of them live separated from their own loved ones in the households of their employers (Pratt 2012).

In sum, Fraser (2022: 53) argues that the current organisation of our society "systematically cannibalises" care: "the present form of capitalism is doing just that: diverting the emotional and material resources that should be devoted to care work to other, inessential activities, which fatten corporate coffers". While not all scholars share Fraser's fundamental critique of capitalism, there is a broad consensus within academia and beyond that measures are needed to counter existing care deficits and improve working conditions for care workers.

Tackling Care Deficits with Digital Technologies

In discussions about the Future of Work, several digital technologies emerge as potential solutions to address care deficits for both care recipients and care workers. The spectrum of solutions includes tools that enhance remote work capabilities to facilitate private caregiving through to the automation of caregiving tasks.

Providing Care While Home Officing

Firstly, the development of effective tools for digital data transfer and interaction has boosted possibilities for remote work (Stiles and Smart 2021). This trend dramatically accelerated with the COVID-19 pandemic, during which a major share of the labour force worked from home (Hickman and Saad 2020). With regard to care, home officing promises easier alignment of paid work and care responsibilities. It might mitigate care deficits by either allowing workers to care for dependants while they work or arrange their work more flexibly around their care duties. Indeed, a review of existing studies on remote work demonstrates that home officing improves perceived autonomy and reduces work-family conflicts (Gajendran and Harrison 2007). In addition, remote work opens up opportunities for renegotiating gendered divisions of care responsibilities. Being more exposed to the previously "invisible" labour of child care while in home office might lead to more egalitarian attitudes among men (Reichelt et al. 2020). Research on home officing during the pandemic suggests that it has indeed increased fathers' involvement in childcare. This bears the potential to expand men's commitments to participate in unpaid care work in the future (Carli 2020).

However, scholars draw attention to the fact that home officing does not actually reduce the volume of care work that needs to be done, it just allows for rearranging it and doing part of it while undertaking paid work. Especially the advantages of this multitasking are called into question. Based on a time-use survey, Song and Gao (2019), for example, conclude that working from home reduces happiness and increases stress, especially for parents. Furthermore, studies point to the risk of remote workers for being excluded from important networks, which in turn affects professional career perspectives and income opportunities – particularly for women (Güney-Frahm 2022). This needs further attention, as Munsch (2016), for example, shows in a US study that men who requested home officing to care for a child were perceived more favourably compared to women asking for the same. In the case of online gig labour, James (2022) finds evidence that care duties limit female workers' abilities to compete for gigs. Platform algorithms assess numbers of gigs completed, responsiveness and other variables to assess performance. This disadvantages workers who cannot be online for long periods of uninterrupted time due to care demands. He concludes that there is a danger of a "digital reinscription of stubborn "analogue" gendered labour market inequalities".

Providing Care at a Distance

Second, new visual, oral and audio-visual digital communication tools enable novel ways of caring at a distance. Extended and unpredictable working hours and rising commuting distances limit the time household members spend together. In this situation, digital communication tools allow care givers to keep in touch with care recipients. Parents arrange what their children do after school via chat messenger. Daughters and sons briefly skype with their ailing parents during the day to check whether all is well. Digital communication tools have become indispensable tools for maintaining care responsibilities in the everyday lives of families (Valentine 2006).

In addition, they have become key elements of the migration infrastructure (Lindquist et al. 2012) that allows migrants to maintain care relationships across larger distances (Francisco-Menchavez 2018). Asynchronous platforms such as Facebook, Instagram, Snapchat and TikTok are used to share news, send pictures or short videos and thus let loved ones participate in one's experiences abroad. Synchronous platforms such as Facetime, Skype or Zoom are used to spend time "together" across distance and ensure the well-being of loved ones (Chau 2020). In her analysis of mothering via Skype, Longhurst (2013), for example, demonstrates how digital audio-visual communication has further extended the boundaries of maternal care. While such technologies allow for care relationships that transcend previously perceived binaries of absent/present, material/immaterial and real/virtual (Longhurst 2017), they can also be experienced as intrusive if used to track loved ones against their will or without their consent (Longhurst 2013).

Digital Tools to Support Self-Care

The problem of privacy becomes especially salient when digital technologies are used for live remote surveillance. Today, smart watches can measure heart rates and other biometric data and autonomously alert care givers in case of worrying data levels. Sensor mats or video cameras allow for live monitoring what a person does within their home. GPS trackers can follow their movement outside the home and allow for tracking a child or finding a dementia patient who might have lost their way. On the one hand, these and other novel technologies hold the promise to enable care recipients to live more independently while also reducing the amount of care work required to support them. On the other hand, they pose ethical challenges as they infringe on care recipients' privacy and intimacy (Kaspar and Müller 2020; Mortenson et al. 2015). Furthermore, the push towards self-care that reduces interactions with care givers might exacerbate psycho-social problems of loneliness and isolation – particularly in old age (Sixsmith and Sixsmith 2008).

With regard to care workers, studies foreground that the adoption of such digital tools does not necessarily reduce their workload. The tools have to be set up, monitored and require interventions on short notice. Malfunctioning devices, handling errors and other false alarms might require additional attention. Furthermore, users do not necessarily follow the scripts intended by the designers of the devices, but co-create their usage. As Pols (2010) shows based on an analysis of three self-care devices, care recipients did not take care of themselves more on their own, but used the devices to intensify their exchange with care personnel. Winthereik and Langstrup (2010) draw similar conclusions in the case of a digital pregnancy monitoring interface that was intended to reduce health professionals' workload and promote self-care. Their analysis finds that the tool increased the workload as it led the pregnant women to ask health personnel for more detailed assessments. In sum, such devices may increase the quality of care some of its users receive, but they also often imply a greater workload for the carers.

Digital Tools for Managing Care Workers

Apart from devices to promote self-care, there are various ways in which digital technologies are implemented to manage care workers. Hayes and Moore (2017), for example, explore the introduction of a GPS tracking system for the electronic monitoring of home care workers. As the monitoring was set up not to recognise travel time and any other tasks performed outside care recipients' households as work, it resulted in a de facto reduction of paid hours for the workers. Overall, nearly half of the hours workers spent in uniform remained unremunerated. Apart from redefining what is work, Hayes and Moore also observe a problematic shift in the understanding of care: the digital monitoring led care to be understood first and foremost as time consumption. In this neoliberal logic, care recipients were reduced to "needy, greedy time-consumers" and care workers to "resource-wasting time-takers" (Hayes and Moore 2017: 329).

With regard to time, digital platforms such as Care.com that mediate care as short "gigs" have entered the scene with the promise to make care available more flexibly (Ticona and Mateescu 2018). For care recipients and families with sufficient means, they promise to fill care gaps whenever they appear and on short notice. For gig workers, they offer low entry barriers and flexibility to work when it suits them. With this, digital platforms attract people who need to earn some money in between other commitments – such as unpaid care labour (Churchill and Craig 2019). And they serve as stopgap opportunities for people unable to access formal employment – many of them minorities and newly arriving migrants (Van Doorn 2021). As such, care platforms might contribute to alleviate care deficits as they mobilise a workforce that otherwise remains largely excluded from labour markets.

However, platform labour comes without a guarantee of gigs actually being available (Keller 2023) and without the social protection of regular employment (De Stefano et al. 2022). Scholarship thus emphasises the inherent precarity of platform labour due to its unpredictable working hours, fluctuating and generally insufficient income levels, lacking social protection and unequal power relationships between platforms and workers (Berg et al. 2018). Thus, scholars emphasise that platform labour does not fundamentally alter the devaluation and invisibilisation of care workers but creates novel forms of "flexploitation" (Kluzik 2022: 3). While the current care platforms, dominated by profit-oriented multinational corporations, do indeed not seem to alleviate the care crisis in the sense of providing better working conditions for care workers, Huws et al. (2017: 14) emphasise that "there is no reason in principle why the technologies on which platform services are based could not be used in ways that contribute to the improvement of working conditions". For this, Huws et al. suggest using platform technologies in public care provision. Bor (2018) draws attention to successful platform cooperatives that operate locally and Schor (2020) suggests transforming legislation in favour of non-profit platforms as a means to promote equitable and community-driven care services.

Artificial Intelligence Replacing Care Workers

Last but not least, there is the promise that digital technologies based on AI might be able to take over some of the interactive care work still done by humans today. Compared to other technologies, AI-based tools are able "learn" from the interaction with care recipients and adjust their responses to their human counterparts. Some of them take the form of robots – i.e. humanoid or animal-like shapes that simulate interaction with a living being. In dementia care, they are designed to mimic the look and feel of baby seals, cats or rabbits and to sooth patients by imitating movements and noises that invite petting. In the form of companion robots, they serve to entertain children and older adults. Many of them are able to invite conversation, play games and assist with a variety of simple everyday tasks. Since their inception, the use of robots for care has remained contested. Sparrow and Sparrow (2006) raise ethical concerns about the deception inherent in using robot simulacra to imitate social interaction with a human. One of the key critiques is that robots can pretend to care *for* a person, but they do not actually care *about* them. Others have countered this argument by challenging the underlying categorical distinction between human and non-human. Marquardt (2018), for instance, draws on feminist Science and Technology Studies to question the simple opposition between "cold" technology and "warm" human interaction. She foregrounds the manifold affective relations between humans and technologies and their value as training tools to foster interactions with humans. Similarly, Sumartojo and Lugli (2022) argue that it is exactly the "liveliness", i.e. their relational and open-ended entanglements with humans, that allow robots to contribute to care.

How do robots impact the routines of care workers? Based on a study in a Japanese care home, Wright (2019) finds that they did not reduce the care workload as intended, but actually increased it. Care workers were burdened with the additional labour of managing and mending the robots. In addition, they experienced being increasingly perceived as mere assistants of robots as a further devaluation of their roles as carers. In order to prevent this, Walton-Roberts (2018) demands that care workers are involved as key stakeholders already in the development of robots. This would ensure the development of technology that assists care workers rather than vice versa.

With the current rapid development of AI and digital technologies becoming part of "the new normal" (Leonardi 2021) in the future of work, there is an urgent need for more research to explore to what ends technologies are employed and in what (often unintended) ways they alleviate or exacerbate existing inequalities (Del Casino et al. 2020). With regard to care work, the key challenge is to develop them in such a way that they can not only fill care gaps, or raise the quality of care but also improve working conditions for care workers.

Alternative Futures of Care Work

Reviewing the above body of literature, we find that digital technologies have indeed shown the potential to mitigate some aspects of the care crisis. Some facilitate aligning care with other duties or with being geographically distant. Others ease access to care or improve care quality for care recipients. However, existing technologies have not yet led to a marked reduction in the hours it takes to do the care work or in a marked improvement of the working conditions of care workers. On the contrary, there is evidence that they often imply additional work as they need to be set up, operated, monitored and mended. Furthermore, they sometimes make care work even more invisible and leave it unremunerated to an even greater extent. In sum, Huws (2019: 21) concludes that "there is no simple technological fix for the problem of housework" – or care work, in our case.

Strengthening the Public Provision of Care Services

Thus, what are the alternatives to address the care crisis? Many scholars agree that the problem is inherent in the current social order of neoliberal capitalism. Decades of neoliberal governance have cut down on public spending, forced households to raise the number of hours in paid work to make ends meet and thus squeezed the hours available for care (McDowell 2004). Furthermore, they have brought along a widespread outsourcing of care services (Brennan et al. 2012). In consequence, for-profit companies own and control an increasing share of care service provision (Friendly et al. 2021; Gallagher 2020). Above all, they strive for reducing costs to increase profitability (Farris and Marchetti 2017). Through this, an increasing amount of public funds meant for the provision of care are extracted and transformed into private profit (Dowling 2021).

In response, scholars demand reverting to a public provision of basic care services for all. Huws (2019), for instance, suggests socialising care work by creating good jobs in the public sector. Similarly, Dowling (2021) calls for a massive expansion of state organised care services, funded by progressive taxation. This would allow for improving working conditions, salaries, training and available resources for care workers and put a stop to private wealth extraction from care services. As an example for how this local provision could be organised, she refers to the Dutch neighbourhood care (Buurtzorg). This model of publicly funded home care provision is based on local, self-managed teams of nurses. It relies on the expertise of the trained nurses to assess and address care needs in collaboration with the care recipients in their district. The model has received international attention for its bottom-up design that includes care recipients in the decision making on how their care needs are best addressed and for its successful reduction of costly administrative overhead.

Reducing Working Hours

While an expansion of public care provision could substantially mitigate the care crisis, it is neither possible nor desirable to transform all the care that children, seniors and other adults with special needs require into paid work. Thus, there is still the problem of the domestic time squeeze that limits people's ability to provide unpaid care for their own loved ones. In order to address this, scholars question dominant notions of the "universal breadwinner" (Fraser 1994) or the "adult worker model" (Lewis and Giullari 2005). That is, they challenge the neoliberal norm that all adults in working age should be engaged in full-time employment, which underlies much of the current social policy making. The norm is deemed problematic in that it privileges production over social reproduction and denies that all human beings need care at different stages of their lives (Fraser 2022). In response, they develop alternative societal organisations such as the "universal caregiver model" (Claassen 2011), which assumes that all adults are both carers and earners throughout their working lives.

Scholars emphasise that balancing work and care requires a marked reduction of standard working hours for all workers. Since the coronavirus pandemic, the debate on shortening the working week from five to four days has gained considerable traction. In many countries, firms and governments are implementing trials to gain experience (Joly et al. 2023). While the four-day working week promises to facilitate balancing care and work responsibilities, it holds the danger that the same amount of work will have to be crammed into four instead of five days – with negative effects on workers' health. Instead, alternative models of worktime reduction suggest keeping five workdays, but shortening them to five or six hours of work a day. This would allow for balancing work, care and rest on all days of the week (Bücker 2022).

No matter the preferred solution, scholars emphasise that to facilitate sharing care responsibilities more equally between the genders, a reduction of working hours must be universal and mandatory (Himmelweit 2008). The reduction could be funded, for example, by limiting company profits and redirecting money flows from shareholders' coffers to the workforce that actually produces the goods or provides the services (Fraser 2022). Unlike time, money can be redistributed between people, for example via progressive taxation, setting higher minimum income levels or introducing a universal basic income (Bücker 2022).

Alternative Visions of the Future Worker

Both a substantial reduction of working hours as well as markedly improved public care services have been discussed for many years. How can we make such a future of work that values care happen? Scholars argue that the necessary transformation is hindered by our current understanding of the human being as a "homo oeconomicus", an independent, autonomous actor (Green and Lawson 2011). This self-perception positions people in constant competition with their fellow humans and denies that we are all dependent on others.

Instead, Tronto (2017) suggests fostering an alternative subjectivity, which she calls "homo curans" – the caring human. Defining ourselves as "homines curantes" implies an understanding that we are all inherently interdependent and are both care givers and care recipients. Organising the provision of care thus becomes a primary task of every society. In the same vein, Winker (2015) calls for a "care revolution" that transforms the current capitalist order of competing individuals with a society that centres around care for others. The key feature of this society is its solidary aim to foster the well-being of all its members. A large and growing body of literature is engaged in developing these "ethics of care" from different perspectives (Cox 2013; Lawson 2007; McDowell 2004; Milligan and Power 2009). Based on feminist and anti-racist scholarship, they flesh out how we can foreground this interconnectedness of humans (McEwan and Goodman 2010) against the backdrop of a history of racialised and classed exploitation (Raghuram 2019) and work towards "caring democracies" (Tronto 2013), "caring communities" (Kaspar et al. 2021) or "caring economies" (Wichterich 2019). Recently, these attempts at understanding the world through the lens of care have been further extended to include care relations with our non-human environment (Puig de La Bellacasa 2017) and link existing care debates with concerns about environmental degradation. This perspective acknowledges the need to care for and protect nature, wildlife and ecological systems as an integral part of our care ethics.

Environmental disasters, such as wildfires, hurricanes, floods and (other) climate change effects, have underscored the urgency of caring for the planet and promoting sustainable practices. At the same time, the coronavirus pandemic has illuminated the significance of care not only for individual well-being but also for the wider societal fabric. It has placed the care crisis on the political agenda and on the radar of the wider public, generating an unprecedented awareness that care is essential work (MacLeavy 2020). The current moment in history might thus provide a unique opportunity to foster the proliferation of such alternative visions of the future of work and enable us to envision and realise a more caring future. Such a societal transformation can build on many already existing local initiatives based on an ethic of care (Montes and Paris Pombo 2019). It can draw strength from existing social movements and new alliances among workers. Switzerland, my home country of about eight million inhabitants, for example, has recently witnessed the largest feminist strike in its history with roughly half a million people in the streets. This created promising novel alliances between paid care workers striking for better working conditions and unpaid carers who demanded better public care infrastructures (Schilliger 2022). The activists chanted "Pas de retour à la norme mâle" (No return to nor-male-ity). With this slogan, they called to dismantle existing societal norms and structures that devalue care work and pay inadequate attention to essential care needs. They voiced their refusal to go back to a "normal" state that disproportionally burdens women and marginalised groups with care responsibilities. Instead, they demand building a post-COVID world, in which care receives the attention it deserves. Based on this momentum, now might be a unique moment in time to redirect current debates on the future of work from dystopian scenarios of massive job loss or utopian technophilia towards alternative futures of work that value care.

Acknowledgements

First and foremost, I would like to thank the many care workers who shared their time, their experiences and their expert knowledge with me. Furthermore, I am indebted to my colleagues and friends in the care workers' networks "Respect@vpod" and at UNIA, in the think tank "Denknetz.ch", in the research projects "Decent-Care-Work.net" and "Urban Platform Economies (TICS)", and in the geography department at the University of Zurich. Thank you for offering inspiration, constructive criticism and great support at all times. Finally, I would like to thank the editors Julie MacLeavy and Harry Pitts for their valuable feedback and comments on earlier versions of this chapter. All remaining errors are mine.

References

Aulenbacher, B. (2020) Auf Neuer Stufe Vergesellschaftet: Care Und Soziale Reproduktion Im Gegenwartskapitalismus, in: K. Becker, K. Binner and F. Décieux (eds.) *Gespannte Arbeits- Und Geschlechterverhältnisse Im Marktkapitalismus*. Wiesbaden: Springer, 125–147.

Aulenbacher, B., Lutz, H., Palenga-Möllenbeck, E. and Schwiter, K. (eds.) (2024) *Home Care for Sale*. London: Sage.

Berg, J., Furrer, M., Harmon, E., Rani, U. and Silberman, M. S. (2018) *Digital Labour Platforms and the Future of Work. Towards Decent Work in the Online World.* Geneva: ILO International Labour Organization.

Bhattacharya, T. (ed.) (2017) *Social Reproduction Theory: Remapping Class, Recentering Oppression*. London: Pluto Press.

Bor, L. (2018) "Wisch Und Weg? Welche Chancen Bietet Die Online-Plattform Helpling Für Eine Gerechtere Verteilung Von Hausarbeit?", *Zeitschrift LuXemburg*. online issue of November.

Brennan, D., Cass, B., Himmelweit, S. and Szebehely, M. (2012) "The Marketisation of Care: Rationales and Consequences in Nordic and Liberal Care Regimes", *Journal of European Social Policy* 22(4), 377–391. https://doi.org/10.1177/0958928712449772

Bücker, T. (ed.) (2022) *Alle_Zeit: Eine Frage Von Macht Und Freiheit*. Berlin: Ullstein.

Carli, L.L. (2020) Women, gender equality and COVID-19, *Gender in Management*, 35(7/8), 647–655.

Chau, H. S. (2020) *Brokering Circular Labour Migration: A Mobile Ethnography of Migrant Care Workers' Journey to Switzerland*. London: Routledge.

Churchill, B. and Craig, L. (2019) "Gender in the Gig Economy: Men and Women Using Digital Platforms to Secure Work in Australia", *Journal of Sociology* 55(4), 741–761. https://doi.org/10.1177/1440783319894060

Claassen, R. (2011) "The Commodification of Care", *Hypatia* 26(1), 43–64. https://doi.org/10.1111/j.1527-2001.2010.01146.x
Cox, R. (2013) "Gendered Spaces of Commoditised Care", *Social & Cultural Geography* 14(5), 491–499. https://doi.org/10.1080/14649365.2013.813580
De Stefano, V., Durri, I., Stylogiannis, C. and Wouters, M. (2022) "Introduction", in: V. De Stefano, I. Durri, C. Stylogiannis and M. Wouters (eds.) *A Research Agenda for the Gig Economy and Society*. Cheltenham: Edward Elgar, 1–12.
Del Casino, V., House-Peters, L., Crampton, J. and Gerhardt, H. (2020) "The Social Life of Robots: The Politics of Algorithms, Governance, and Sovereignty", *Antipode* 52(3), 605–618. https://doi.org/10.1111/anti.12616
Dowling, E. (2021) *The Care Crisis: What Caused It and How Can We End It?* London: Verso.
England, K. (2010) "Home, Work and the Shifting Geographies of Care", *Ethics, Place & Environment: A Journal of Philosophy & Geography* 13(2), 131–150. https://doi.org/10.1080/13668791003778826
Farris, S. R. and Marchetti, S. (2017) "From the Commodification to the Corporatization of Care: European Perspectives and Debates", *Social Politics: International Studies in Gender, State & Society* 24(2), 109–131. https://doi.org/10.1093/sp/jxx003
Fischer, B. and Tronto, J. (1990) "Toward a Feminist Theory of Caring", in: E. Abel and M. Nelson (eds.) *Circles of Care*. Albany, NY: SUNY Press, 36–54.
Francisco-Menchavez, V. (2018) *The Labor of Care. Filipina Migrants and Transnational Families in the Digital Age*. Urbana: University of Illinois Press.
Fraser, N. (1994) "After the Family Wage: Gender Equity and the Welfare State", *Political Theory* 22(4), 591–618. https://doi.org/10.1177/0090591794022004003
Fraser, N. (2016) "Contradictions of Capital and Care", *New Left Review* 100, 99–117.
Fraser, N. (ed.) (2022) *Cannibal Capitalism: How Our System Is Devouring Democracy, Care, and the Planet – And What We Can Do About It*. London: Verso.
Friendly, M., Vickerson, R., Mohamed, S., Rothman, L. and Nguyen, N. T. (eds.) (2021) *Child Care Ownership in Canada Past, Present and Future*. Toronto: Childcare Resource and Research Unit.
Gajendran, R. and Harrison, D. (2007) "The Good, the Bad, and the Unknown about Telecommuting: Meta-Analysis of Psychological Mediators and Individual Conse-Quences", *Journal of Applied Psychology* 92(6), 1524–1541. https://doi.org/10.1037/0021-9010.92.6.1524
Gallagher, A. (2020) ""A 'Golden Child' for Investors": The Assetization of Urban Childcare Property in Nz", *Urban Geography* 42, 1–19. https://doi.org/10.1080/02723638.2020.1785257
Green, M. and Lawson, V. (2011) "Recentring Care: Interrogating the Commodification of Care", *Social and Cultural Geography* 12(6), 639–654. https://doi.org/10.1080/14649365.2011.601262
Güney-Frahm, I. (2022) "Erwerbsarbeit Im Homeoffice: (K)Eine Chance Für Die Frauen?", in: Caritas (ed.) *Sozialalmanach: Frauenarmut*. Luzern: Caritas, 193–202.
Hall, E. (2013) "Progressive Localism for an Ethics of Care in an Era of Austerity: Local Area Co-Ordination with People with Learning Disabilities", *Social & Cultural Geography* 14(6), 689–709. https://doi.org/10.1080/14649365.2013.803290
Haubner, T. (2017) *Die Ausbeutung der sorgenden Gemeinschaft*. Frankfurt: Campus.
Hayes, L. and Moore, S. (2017) "Care in a Time of Austerity: The Electronic Monitoring of Homecare Workers' Time", *Gender, Work and Organization* 24(4), 329–344. https://doi.org/10.1111/gwao.12164
Hickman, A. and Saad, L. (2020) "Reviewing Remote Work in the Us under Covid-19", *Gallup*, Issue of 22 May. https://news.gallup.com/poll/311375/reviewing-remote-work-covid.aspx
Himmelweit, S. (2008) "Policy on Care: A Help or a Hindrance to Gender Equality?", in: J. Scott, S. Dex and H. Joshi (eds.) *Women and Employment*. pp. 347–368. Cheltenham: Edward Elgar.
Hochschild, A. (2000) "Global Care Chains and Emotional Surplus Value", in: W. Hutton and A. Giddens (eds.) *On the Edge: Living with Global Capitalism*. London: Jonathan Cape, 130–146.
Horn, V., Schweppe, C., Böcker, A. and Bruquetas-Callejo, M. (eds.) (2021) *The Global Old Age Care Industry. Tapping into Migrants for Tackling the Old Age Care Crisis*. Singapore: Palgrave Macmillan.
Howcroft, D. and Taylor, P. (2023) "Automation and the Future of Work: A Social Shaping of Technology Approach", *New Technology, Work and Employment* 38(2), 351–370. https://doi.org/10.1111/ntwe.12240
Huws, U. (2019) "The Hassle of Housework: Digitalisation and the Commodification of Domestic Labour", *Feminist Review* 123(1), 8–23. https://doi.org/10.1177/0141778919879725

Huws, U., Spencer, N. and Coates, M. (2017) *The Platformisation of Work in Europe. Highlights from Research in 13 European Countries*. Brussles: Foundation for European Progressive Studies.
James, A. (2022) "Women in the Gig Economy: Feminising, Digital Labour", *Work in the Global Economy* 2(1), 2–26. https://doi.org/10.1332/273241721X16448410652000
Joly, J., Hurst, L. and Walsh, D. (2023) "Four-Day Week: Which Countries Have Embraced It and How's It Going So Far?", *Euronews.com*, published on 21 June.
Joyce, S., Umney, C., Whittaker, X. and Stuart, M. (2023) "New Social Relations of Digital Technology and the Future of Work: Beyond Technological Determinism", *New Technology, Work and Employment* 38(2), 145–161. https://doi.org/10.1111/ntwe.12276
Kaspar, H. and Müller, C. (2020) "Digitalisierung in Der Pflege Zwischen Technikinnovation Und Beziehungsarbeit", *Frauenfragen* 1/2020, 72–75. https://arbor.bfh.ch/14624/1/Seiten%20aus%20FF_2020_def_nov.pdf
Kaspar, H., Pelzelmayer, K., Schürch, A. and van Holten, K. (2021) "Les Communautés Compatissantes Peuvent-Elles Améliorer L'accompagnement De Longue Durée À Domicile?", *Primary and Hospital Care Médecine* 6(6), 188–190.
Keller, M. (2023) "Getting the First Gig: Exploring the Affective Relations of Accessing Place-Based Platform Labour", *Digital Geography and Society* 5, 100067. https://doi.org/10.1016/j.diggeo.2023.100067
Kluzik, V. (2022) "Governing Invisibility in the Platform Economy: Excavating the Logics of Platform Care", *Internet Policy Review* 11(1), 1–21. https://doi.org/10.14763/2022.1.1636
Kofman, E. and Raghuram, P. (2015) *Gendered Migrations and Global Social Reproduction*. London: Palgrave Macmillan.
Lawson, V. (2007) "Geographies of Care and Responsibility", *Annals of the Association of American Geographers* 97(1), 1–11. https://doi.org/10.1111/j.1467-8306.2007.00520.x
Leonardi, P. (2021) "Covid-19 and the New Technologies of Organizing: Digital Exhaust, Digital Footprints, and Artificial Intelligence in the Wake of Remote Work", *Journal of Management Studies* 58(1), 249–253. https://doi.org/10.1111/joms.12648
Lewis, J. and Giullari, S. (2005) "The Adult Worker Model Family, Gender Equality and Care: The Search for New Policy Principles and the Possibilities and Problems of a Capabilities Approach", *Economy and Society* 34(1), 76–104. https://doi.org/10.1080/0308514042000329342
Lindquist, J., Xiang, B. and Yeoh, B. (2012) "Opening the Black Box of Migration: Brokers, the Organization of Transnational Mobility and the Changing Political Economy in Asia", *Pacific Affairs* 85(1), 7–19. https://doi.org/10.5509/20128517
Longhurst, R. (2013) "Using Skype to Mother: Bodies, Emotions, Visuality, and Screens", *Environment and Planning D: Society and Space* 31(4), 664–679. https://doi.org/10.1068/d20111
Longhurst, R. (2017) *Skype: Bodies, Screens, Space*. London: Routledge.
Lund, S., Madgavkar, A., Manyika, J., Smit, S., Ellingrud, K., Meaney, M. and Robinson, O. (2021) *The Future of Work after the Covid-19*. New York: McKinsey Global Institute.
MacLeavy, J. (2020) "Care Work, Gender Inequality and Technological Advancement in the Age of Covid-19", *Gender, Work & Organization* 28(1), 138–154. https://doi.org/10.1111/gwao.12534
MacLeavy, J. and Lapworth, A. (2020) "A 'Post-Work' World: Geographical Engagements with the Future of Work", *The Political Quarterly* 91(2), 310–316. https://doi.org/10.1111/1467-923X.12785
Marquardt, N. (2018) "Digital Assistierter Wohnalltag Im Smart Home: Zwischen Care, Kontrolle Und Vernetzter Selbstermächtigung", in: S. Bauriedl and A. Strüver (eds.) *Smart City – Kritische Perspektiven Auf Die Digitalisierung in Städten*. Bielefeld: Transcript, 285–297.
McDowell, L. (2004) "Work, Workfare, Work/Life Balance and an Ethic of Care", *Progress in Human Geography* 28(2), 145–163. https://doi.org/10.1191/0309132504ph478oa
McEwan, C. and Goodman, M. K. (2010) "Place Geography and the Ethics of Care: Introductory Remarks on the Geographies of Ethics, Responsibility and Care", *Ethics, Place & Environment* 13(2), 103–112. https://doi.org/10.1080/13668791003778602
Milligan, C. and Power, A. (2009) "The Changing Geography of Care", in: T. Brown, S. McLafferty and G. Moon (eds.) *A Companion to Health and Medical Geography*. Oxford: Wiley-Blackwell, 567–586.
Milligan, C. and Wiles, J. (2010) "Landscapes of Care", *Progress in Human Geography* 34(6), 736–754. https://doi.org/10.1177/0309132510364556
Montes, V. and Paris Pombo, M. D. (2019) "Ethics of Care, Emotional Work, and Collective Action of Solidarity: The Patronas in Mexico", *Gender, Place & Culture* 26(4), 559–580. https://doi.org/10.1080/0966369X.2018.1553854

Mortenson, W. B., Sixsmith, A. and Woolrych, R. (2015) "The Power(s) of Observation: Theoretical Perspectives on Surveillance Technologies and Older People", *Ageing and Society* 35(3), 512–530. https://doi.org/10.1017/S0144686X13000846
Munsch, C. L. (2016) "Flexible Work, Flexible Penalties: The Effect of Gender, Childcare, and Type of Request on the Flexibility Bias", *Social Forces* 94(4), 1567–1591. https://doi.org/10.1093/sf/sov122
Parreñas, R. (ed.) (2001) *Servants of Globalisation: Women, Migration, and Domestic Work*. Stanford, CA: Stanford University Press.
Pitts, F. H., Bales, K. and Huw, T. (2018) "From the Future of Work to Futures of Work", *Futures of Work* 1, n.p. https://futuresofwork.co.uk/2018/09/05/editorial-from-the-future-of-work-to-futures-of-work/
Pols, J. (2010) "Telecare. What Patients Care About", in: A. Mol, I. Moser and J. Pols (eds.) *Care in Practice. On Tinkering in Clinics, Homes and Farms*. Bielefeld: Transcript, 171–193.
Power, E. R. and Williams, M. J. (2020) "Cities of Care: A Platform for Urban Geographical Care Research", *Geography Compass* 14(1), 1–11. https://doi.org/10.1111/gec3.12474
Pratt, G. (2012) *Families Apart. Migrating Mothers and the Conflicts of Labor and Love*. Minneapolis and London: University of Minnesota Press.
Puig de La Bellacasa, M. (2017) *Matters of Care: Speculative Ethics in More Than Human Worlds*. Minneapolis: University of Minnesota Press.
Raghuram, P. (2019) "Race and Feminist Care Ethics: Intersectionality as Method", *Gender, Place & Culture* 26(5), 613–637. https://doi.org/10.1080/0966369X.2019.1567471
Reichelt, M., Makovi, K. and Sargsyan, A. (2020) "The Impact of Covid-19 on Gender Inequality in the Labor Market and Gender-Role Attitudes", *European Societies* 23(1), 228–245. https://doi.org/10.1080/14616696.2020.1823010
Richardson, L. (2018) "Feminist Geographies of Digital Work", *Progress in Human Geography* 42(2), 244–263. https://doi.org/10.1177/0309132516677177
Rifkin, J. (1995) *The End of Work: The Decline of the Global Labour Force and the Dawn of the Post-Market Era*. New York: Putnam.
Schilliger, S. (2022) "Städtische Care-Infrastrukturen Zwischen Küche, Kinderspielplatz Und Kita", *sub\urban. zeitschrift für kritische stadtforschung* 10(2/3), 171–183. https://doi.org/10.36900/suburban.v10i2/3.818
Schlogl, L., Weiss, E. and Prainsack, B. (2021) "Constructing the 'Future of Work': An Analysis of the Policy Discourse", *New Technology, Work and Employment* 36(3), 307–326. https://doi.org/10.1111/ntwe.12202
Schor, J. (ed.) (2020) *After the Gig: How the Sharing Economy Got Hijacked and How to Win It Back*. Oakaland: University of California Press.
Schwiter, K., Berndt, C. and Truong, J. (2018) "Neoliberal Austerity and the Marketization of Elderly Care", *Social & Cultural Geography* 19(3), 379–399. https://doi.org/10.1080/14649365.2015.1059473
Schwiter, K. and Steiner, J. (2020) "Geographies of Care Work: The Commodification of Care, Digital Care Futures and Alternative Caring Visions", *Geography Compass* 14, e12546. https://doi.org/10.1111/gec3.12546
Sixsmith, A. and Sixsmith, J. (2008) "Ageing in Place in the United Kingdom", *Ageing International* 32(3), 219–235. https://doi.org/10.1007/s12126-008-9019-y
Song, Y. and Gao, J. (2019) "Does Telework Stress Employees Out? A Study on Working at Home and Subjective Well-Being for Wage/Salary Workers", *Journal of Happiness Studies* 21(7), 2649–2668. https://doi.org/10.1007/s10902-019-00196-6
Sparrow, R. and Sparrow, L. (2006) "In the Hands of Machines? The Future of Aged Care", *Minds and Machines* 16(2), 141–161. https://doi.org/10.1007/s11023-006-9030-6
Stiles, J. and Smart, M. (2021) "Working at Home and Elsewhere: Daily Work Location, Telework, and Travel among United States Knowledge Workers", *Transportation* 48(5), 2461–2491. https://doi.org/10.1007/s11116-020-10136-6
Strauss, K. and Meehan, K, (2015) Introduction: New Frontier's in Life's Work, in: Meehan, K and Strauss, K (eds.) *Precarious Worlds: Contested Geographies of Social Reproduction*. Athens: University of Georgia Press, 1–22.
Sumartojo, S. and Lugli, D. (2022) "Lively Robots: Robotic Technologies in Covid-19", *Social & Cultural Geography* 23(9), 1220–1237. https://doi.org/10.1080/14649365.2021.1921245
Ticona, J. and Mateescu, A. (2018) "Trusted Strangers: Carework Platforms' Cultural Entrepreneurship in the On-Demand Economy", *New Media & Society* 20(11), 4384–4404. https://doi.org/10.1177/1461444818773727

Tronto, J. (2017) "There Is an Alternative: Homines Curans and the Limits of Neoliberalism", *International Journal of Care and Caring* 1(1), 27–43. https://doi.org/10.1332/239788217X14866281687583

Tronto, J. C. (2013) *Caring Democracy: Markets, Equality, and Justice.* New York: New York University Press.

Valentine, G. (2006) "Globalising Intimacy: The Role of Information and Communication Technologies in Maintaining and Creating Relationships", *Women's Studies Quarterly* 34, 365–393. https://www.jstor.org/stable/40004765

Van Doorn, N. (2021) "Stepping Stone or Dead End? The Ambiguities of Platform- Mediated Domestic Work under Conditions of Austerity. Comparative Landscapes of Austerity and the Gig Economy: New York and Berlin", in: D. Baines and I. Cunningham (eds.) *Working in the Context of Austerity. Challenges and Struggles*. Bristol: Bristol University Press. 49–70.

Walton-Roberts, M. (2018) Care, Migration and Robotics in Japan's Aged Care Sector. *Paper Presented at the Feminist Geographies Conference of 4th–6th August in Montreal.*

Wichterich, C. (2019) *Care Extractivism and the Reconfiguration of Social Reproduction in Post-Fordist Economies*. Kassel: Working Paper No. 25 of the International Center for Development and Decent Work ICDD.

Winker, G. (2015) *Care Revolution. Schritte in Eine Solidarische Gesellschaft*. Bielefeld: Transkript.

Winthereik, B. R. and Langstrup, H. (2010) "When Patients Care (Too Much) for Information", in: A. Mol, I. Moser and J. Pols (eds.) *Care in Practice. On Tinkering in Clinics, Homes and Farms*. Bielefeld: Transcript, 195–213.

World Economic Forum (2023) *Future of Jobs Report*. Geneva: World Economic Forum.

Wright, J. (2019) "Robots Vs Migrants? Reconfiguring the Future of Japanese Institutional Eldercare", *Critical Asian Studies* 51(3), 331–354. https://doi.org/10.1080/14672715.2019.1612765

Recommendations for Further Reading

Dowling, E. (2021) *The Care Crisis: What Caused It and How Can We End It?* London: Verso (an indepth analysis of the crisis of care).

Fraser, N. (ed.) (2022) *Cannibal Capitalism: How our System Is Devouring Democracy, Care, and the Planet – and What We Can Do about It*. London: Verso (a critique of the current capitalist order).

Lawson, V. (2007) "Geographies of Care and Responsibility", *Annals of the Association of American Geographers* 97(1), 1–11 (on developing an ethics of care).

MacLeavy, J. (2020) "Care Work, Gender Inequality and Technological Advancement in the Age of COVID-19", *Gender, Work & Organization* 28(1): 138–154 (on the potential of digital technologies in care).

Richardson, L. (2018) "Feminist Geographies of Digital Work", *Progress in Human Geography* 42(2), 244–263 (a review of feminist perspectives on work in the digital age).

Schwiter, K. and Steiner, J. (2020) "Geographies of Care Work: The Commodification of Care, Digital Care Futures and Alternative Caring Visions", *Geography Compass* 14, e12546 (an overview of current debates on paid care work).

PART 7

Sectoral Case Studies

17

SERVICES ARE THE FUTURE OF WORK

Matthew Cole

Introduction

Services have often been relegated to a secondary status in discussions of economic growth and industrial strategy. Yet, from the latter part of the twentieth century through to the twenty-first, all G7 and most G20 countries have seen a decline in manufacturing and a rise in services as a proportion of GDP (World Bank, 2023b). The story, overall, is clear. Forty-two countries (controlling for population size and per capita GDP) have seen their share of manufacturing employment and value added steadily decline from 1950 to 2012 (Rodrik, 2016). Every advanced capitalist nation in the world today is essentially a service economy and net employment growth has been accounted for largely by service industries (Schettkat and Yocarini, 2006). Globally, the value of services has experienced significant growth, more than tripling, from 19.9 trillion US dollars in 1997 to 62.19 trillion in 2021 (World Bank, 2023d). Concurrently, the contribution of services value added to overall GDP has also risen, with a global increase from 59.18% in 1997 to 64.40% in 2021 (World Bank, 2023b). However, it is essential to note that the world economy has not deindustrialised in absolute terms during this period. Actually, world manufacturing value added has also more than doubled, from 6.129 trillion in 1997 to 16.05 trillion in 2021 (World Bank, 2023c). Global manufacturing value added as a percentage of GDP fell slightly from 19% in 1997 to 17% in 2021 (World Bank, 2023a). What does the relative decline of manufacturing and the rise of services mean for the present and future of work?

There is emerging evidence that, globally, less developed countries are reaching the limits of industrialisation opportunities sooner than countries that industrialised earlier. If industrialisation is defined as an increase in the share of manufacturing in employment and value added, such findings indicate "premature deindustrialization". This term refers to a phenomenon where countries experience a decline in the share of manufacturing value added in their economies at relatively lower levels of per capita income compared to historical patterns observed in more developed countries (Nayyar, Vargas Da Cruz and Zhu, 2018). From a traditional economic standpoint, this decline spells trouble for capitalist growth, since manufacturing has traditionally been regarded as the primary growth engine of any given economy and the condition of possibility of "good jobs". And yet, a closer look reveals that this may no longer be the case. Many countries around the world – particularly India and the UK, but also Rwanda, China and the United

 DOI: 10.4324/9781003327561-24

States – are seeing services contribute an increasing share of growth over time, creating jobs and driving technological progress (Nayyar, Vargas Da Cruz and Zhu, 2018). Many of the distinguishing attributes once deemed exclusive to manufacturing advancement are now shared by service industries across the world. Take, for instance, ICT services, which bear striking similarities to electronics manufacturing in terms of their classification as "high" or "medium" in various aspects such as learning-by-doing, international trade and innovation effects (Nayyar, Vargas Da Cruz and Zhu, 2018). Such classifications indicate that ICT services have much more in common with manufacturing than more historical conceptions of services, which are low-tech.

As the rest of this chapter shows, advancements in ICT infrastructure, datafication and artificial intelligence have allowed for a degree of technological substitution in service work that was previously not possible. In contrast to the automation hysteria that predicts a jobs apocalypse, we argue that the future will likely have plenty of jobs, though they will be in increasingly technologically mediated services subject to algorithmic control and surveillance. The data collected will continue to feed the accumulation of intangible assets such as databases, intellectual property and AI which hold economic significance for organisations. In sum, services are the future of work and the future of growth in our platform and monopoly mediated era of capitalism.

What Are Services Anyway?

In advanced capitalist economies the world over, many products are hybrids of some sort – they are neither pure "goods" nor pure "services" – and so is the work that produces them. These products rely on complex international production networks in which companies often fail to keep track of which contractor produced what part of the product and where those component parts were made or assembled (Hammer et al., 2015). This complexity can be mitigated by being specific about sectors and occupations involved, rather than aggregating a huge range of different labour processes and industries into one homogenous block. Capturing significant heterogeneity is crucial as it provides valuable insights into the evolving nature of services, particularly concerning the technological and institutional changes that will shape the future.

What is a service? The category "services" obscures a divergent range of sectors and outputs in International Standard Industrial Classification (ISIC) divisions 50–99, including wholesale and retail trade, hotels and restaurants, transport, and government, financial, professional and personal services such as education, health care and real estate services, among others (ILO, 2023). Services are generally defined in terms of the "relative simultaneity" of production and consumption (Urry, 1990; Allen and Gay, 1994; Bélanger and Edwards, 2013). Relative simultaneity refers to the temporal proximity of the final link in the production chain to the point of consumption. Empirical studies of service work are vast and ever-growing. Seminal research includes studies of flight attendants (Hochschild, 1983), fast food workers (Leidner, 1993), call centre workers "smiling down the phone" (Taylor and Bain, 1999), care workers (Zimmerman, Litt and Bose, 2006), hospitality work (Cole *et al.*, 2022) and a wide range of other topics (MacDonald and Sirianni, 1996; MacDonald and Korczynski, 2009). Important concepts and findings emerged from this literature, including emotional labour (Hochschild, 1983; Bolton and Boyd, 2003; Bolton, 2010; Brook, Koch and Wittel, 2013), the "service triangle" (Leidner, 1993, 1999) and the customer-oriented bureaucracy (Korczynski *et al.*, 2000; Korczynski, 2009a, 2009b).

These studies offer crucial insights into the concrete dynamics of the labour process; however, some are also limited by their specificity. A more expansive approach drawing on Marxist political economy can offer multi-level and systemic insights into service work and its futures. For Marx, the commodity, as a materialisation of labour in the form of its exchange value, is an imaginary and "purely social mode of existence", which has "nothing to do with its corporeal reality" (Marx, 1969, p. 171). Abstract labour, as the substance of value, means that the specific physical properties of any given commodity are essentially irrelevant in terms of determining its value-status as a commodity:

> the commodity form and the value relation of the products of labour within which it appears, have absolutely no connection with the physical nature of the commodity and the material relations arising out of this.
>
> (Marx, 1969, p. 165)

In service work, since the commodity is primarily the concrete labour performed, abstract labour in the form of time is arguably a more important factor in determining prices of production than in goods manufacturing.

Marx theorises the production of services as commodities, which are subject to the same imperatives of valorisation that are involved in goods manufacturing (that is, the imperative to produce a surplus). Yet, at the same services are mediated by the consumer of the service. Marx understands services as a peculiar from of commodity, since the concrete labour that produces them does not necessarily leave behind an objectified physical commodity. The use-value tends to vanish when workers finish performing their concrete labour. The value of a service-commodity has a distinctly temporal aspect that is not present in physical goods. This dovetails with the notion of "relative simultaneity" described above. It also places certain limits on valorisation as well as technological substitution.

Harry Braverman was one of the few Marxists in the 1970s who recognised the dynamic role that services play in capitalist economies, defining them as the "characteristic form of production of our time, superior to manufacturing and with a greater future" (Braverman, 1974, p. 252). Crucially, Braverman (Braverman, 1974, p. 250) reminds us that capitalists do not necessarily care, in the last instance, whether they employ workers "to produce automobiles, wash them, repair them, repaint them, fill them with gasoline and rent them by the day, drive them for hire, park them, or convert them into scrap metal". What matters to the capitalist is the rate of exploitation, that is, the difference between the prices of the commodities sold (whether goods or services) and the costs of the means of production and labour-power. A service becomes productive of surplus-value when, "the useful effects of labour themselves become the commodity" (Braverman, 1974, p. 248). In other words, when the workers do not offer their labour-power "directly to the user of its effects", but instead sell it to the capitalist, "who re-sells it [their labour-power as a service] on the commodity market", we find the capitalist form of service production (Braverman, 1974). Such service production has now taken over the globe.

Are Services the Future of Work?

The conversation around the future of work was initially dominated by techno-evangelists. Aaron Benanav (2020) refers to it as the "automation discourse". Benanav is rightly sceptical of the techno-evangelist predictions of a jobless future because he thinks capitalism has lost its dynamism. In his book, Benanav draws on Robert Brenner's (2006) "long downturn" thesis, which claims that the world economy has been stuck in a protracted crisis since the end of the post-war boom in the mid-twentieth century due to deindustrialisation, manufacturing overcapacity, decelerating goods output growth and global competition. A sustained, system-wide overproduction of manufactured goods means that labour productivity and GDP growth is in terminal decline.

Brenner (2006, pp. 21–25) is keen to point out that this downturn was not, as others have argued, due to a "profit squeeze" from class conflict or changes in institutional regulation (see Marglin and Schor, 1990), but rather due to the competitive struggle between national capitals at a global scale, leading to a crisis of overproduction, overcapacity and investment overhang. This approach relies almost exclusively on manufacturing data as a proxy for the health of the global economy and as a basis on which to predict the future of work.

Brenner's "long downturn" thesis has been criticised for many reasons by a wide range of scholars (Clarke, 1999; Duménil and Lévy, 1999; Fine, Lapavitsas and Milonakis, 1999; Fine, Petropoulos and Sato, 2005; Aglietta, 2008; Crafts, 2008; Yamamura, 2008). Simon Clarke (1999, p. 58) points out a crucial limitation to Brenner's approach, namely that he focuses on "the development of particular national economies and branches of [manufacturing] production" – not global capital. Brenner essentially extrapolates from three decades of a relative slowdown in manufacturing in a handful of Western countries to claim the world economy is facing terminal crisis. This assumes that manufacturers, who rely on a substantial amount of fixed capital, will not reorganise or invest in new areas of production (such as ICT services) when confronted with competitive pressures. Such path dependency, for Brenner, explains a secular decline in manufacturing productivity growth rates, rate of investment, labour income and demand. By contrast, Clarke (1999, p. 60) points out that capitalists invest with the anticipation that fixed capital will devalue over time (what Marx called "moral depreciation") and in "discounting their future expected flow of profits, they write off their capacity at an appropriate rate of depreciation". They should therefore be able to recover their fixed costs before the pressure of competition bites and restore growth.

Benanav (2020) takes Brenner's thesis and extends it to labour, arguing that overcapacity has led to a global lowering of labour demand manifesting in underemployment (rather than unemployment). Benanav also extrapolates from the relative slowdown to claim that low labour demand persists and the working class is condemned to underemployment due to the rise of service work. This approach essentially forecloses the possibility of digitally automated services (emerging over the past three decades) providing productivity increases that reconfigure growth regimes (Benanav, 2020). For Benanav, secular stagnation and low wages (taken as low labour demand) are caused by deindustrialisation and global competition in manufacturing goods output.

Clarke's intervention highlights a crucial aspect of capitalist competition – that capitalists are guided by the marginal rate of profit anticipated in the future, rather than the averages realised in the past. Problems may arise if there is an unexpected acceleration in technological innovation and diffusion such that prices fall before capitalists have been able to pay off their fixed costs. However, this does not necessarily lead to a terminal decline in the average rate of profit since growth will be faster in more technologically dynamic sectors, which will also attract more investment. One could argue that this is precisely why we have seen huge investments and growth in service sectors associated with ICT and digital automation technologies.

During the post-war period, the global economic order was based around national export economies and capitalism regulated by redistributive politics, social welfare policies, and collective bargaining. Manufacturing output and employment were dominant in this period because technological developments were labour-enabling. The literature on development emphasises that the shift towards neoliberalism in the 1980s, which involved the abandonment of industrial policy, is a significant factor contributing to early deindustrialisation (Hauge and Chang, 2019). UNCTAD (2016) for example, points out that several countries, particularly in Latin America, experienced premature deindustrialisation due to unilateral trade liberalisation, financial deregulation, regressive income redistribution, and the diminished role of the developmental state. The rise of service industries and neoliberal, monetarist policy in the West, marked a distinct shift in the organisation of capitalist accumulation.

ICT services growth has driven or facilitated much of this change. Yet, conventional accounts of services don't seriously consider the dynamism of services technology. They rely on outdated Baumolian (Baumol, 1967) and Kaldorian (Kaldor, 1967) assumptions that characterise services as inherently labour-intensive activities in which a single person performs labour for another (Moraitis, 2022). This ignores the vast automation that took place across clerical work in the 1980s and 1990s because of computerisation and the widespread dissemination of service robots over the past two decades.

Baumol's model analyses unbalanced growth by dividing the economy into two sectors: those that are technologically progressive and those that are stagnant. He assigns manufacturing to the former and services to the latter. Simply put, he argues that the differences in productivity between the two sectors propel a shift of resources from more dynamic to less dynamic sectors as higher productivity activities require less and less labour to meet demand. The stagnant sector absorbs more labour since the barriers to productivity mean more workers are required to meet demand, relative to the falling number of workers in the technologically progressive sectors. Baumol argues that most services (especially care and hospitality) have an inherent barrier to raising productivity due to their interpersonal nature (a claim that is explored further in Chapters 16 and 21).

The implications of Baumol's model are twofold. First, service economies exhibit a "cost disease" whereby prices in stagnant sectors tend to rise relative to sectors that he deems "technologically progressive". This is due to Baumol's observation that labour costs for services increase with output more rapidly than for manufacturing (Moraitis, 2022). The price of services can only be lowered by compressing wages or intensifying work, since it is assumed that technologies cannot achieve economies of scale and scope similar to those in manufacturing (Esping-Andersen, 1999). As manufacturing jobs decline, services expand, and since they tend to be low-waged, this leads to intersectoral inequality (Goos, Manning and Salomons, 2014). Second, according to Baumol, the relative growth of services depresses aggregate labour productivity as a whole and therefore growth, leading to relative stagnation. This seems logical; yet, Baumol was writing during a time when services were a small part of the global economy and technological innovation had barely scratched the surface of what was possible. The argument was based largely on the assumption that personal services (whether, care, barber, education, retail, etc.) would remain essentially unchanged (Nordhaus, 2008).

Contra Baumol, research shows that manufacturing is actually becoming less profitable and services more profitable through technological advancement. For example, Milberg and Winkler (2013) examine the prices of manufactured imports from developing countries into the United States and observe a 40% decline in import prices for clothing, footwear, textiles, furniture, and toys compared to US consumer prices between 1986 and 2006. This indicates the growing importance of research and development (R&D), product design, branding, advertising, and other "intangibles" that are concentrated in the developed/high-income countries. Furthermore, Triplett and Bosworth (2004) found that jobs growth in the United States was driven primarily by market services specifically ICT, logistics and transport, retail trade, insurance, finance and other business services. These jobs accounted for nearly all new employment in the United States, were characterised by the use of productivity-enhancing ICT and represented most aggregate labour productivity growth. Labour productivity in services-producing industries grew at 2.6% a year between 1995 and 2001, exceeding the 2.3% growth in productivity in goods-producing industries (Triplett and Bosworth, 2004). Twenty-four of the 29 services industries in their analysis had positive growth in labour productivity after 1995. Service industries accounted for 73% of post-1995 labour productivity growth in the United States and 76% of aggregate US multifactor productivity growth. Importantly, growth in these industries is technologically driven, with IT in services industries accounting for 80% of the total IT contribution to US labour productivity growth between 1995 and 2001.

The Kaldorian framework is also problematic. Kaldor maintains that manufacturing is unique due to its growth-inducing properties and capacity to scale up (Kaldor, 1967). In this approach, manufacturing generates endogenous technological improvements, while in agriculture and services they are (apparently) exogenous (Hauge and Chang, 2019). This is because manufacturing merely has to increase output to produce more efficiently and this scalability makes it the "fundamental engine of growth" due to networked effects with other sectors (Kaldor, 1996). For Kaldor, manufacturing is free from productivity barriers such as soil fertility or weather in agriculture and limits to human labour time and intensity in services. However, Kaldor fails to consider supply chain issues, sourcing of materials and skills. Before the first industrial revolution, for example, factories were entirely dependent on human labour, animals and other natural energy sources (Deane, 1980). As Moraitis (2022, pp. 20–21) points out, it is only with the transition to steam power that manufacturing transcended such constraints. Later, with fertilisers and automation, industrial farming also transcended many of its historic natural limitations.

Furthermore, recent innovations and infrastructural changes in ICT, AI and platform technologies along with massive increases in the size of firms have enabled economies of scale for services (Hallward-Driemeier and Nayyar, 2018). It is more profitable to procure some services from specialist providers (Nayyar, 2013). Digital platforms are arguably far more scalable than manufacturing; while fixed assets such as data centres with their servers, cooling systems and cyber security are costly, these costs rapidly decrease with scale (UNCTAD, 2019). Furthermore, many services are not internationally tradable, enhancing the capacity of scale, benefits of export and rents from market share (Nayyar, Vargas Da Cruz and Zhu, 2018). The use of services as intermediate inputs has spillover effects, evidenced by their role in boosting manufacturing productivity (Arnold, Javorcik and Mattoo, 2007).

In a reversal of the Solow Paradox, which highlights how the advancement of ICT did not lead to significant productivity improvements (Solow, 1987), the firm-level productivity literature reveals outcomes that deviate from standard growth accounting assumptions (Bloom, Sadun and Reenen, 2012). This is due to complementary investments in "organizational capital" that are reflected in the coefficients on IT capital (Brynjolfsson and Hitt, 2003). Arguing against the notion that manufacturing still holds a privileged place in advanced economies, Berlingieri (2013) shows that the professional and business services industries now have the greatest influence on these economies, accounting for around 40% of total growth in terms of both GDP and employment. When finance and real estate are also factored in, these three industries alone account for 50% of the service sector growth in terms of employment and 94% in terms of GDP (Berlingieri, 2013). This shift performed across any given economy will inevitably reduce the employment in manufacturing firms and increase the employment in service firms.

Looking beyond rich countries, we also see shifts to ICT-intensive services. While Africa has experienced limited industrialisation, the shift from agriculture to services has been more significant (McMillan, Rodrik and Sepulveda, 2017). The services sector in Africa grew by 5.8% annually from 2000 to 2012, surpassing the global average growth rate of services (UNECA, 2015). There is a strong correlation between growth in services – mainly ICT, transportation (primarily airlines) and tourism – and GDP growth on the continent, although caution should be exercised in asserting a causal relationship in any direction. India is another example of service export growth.

As of 2014, it was the largest global exporter of ICT services with a value of $74 billion (Loungani *et al.*, 2017). The rise in service exports is both due to scale and enhanced productivity of India's ICT Sector (Bosworth and Collins, 2008). Total factor productivity in services grew by 2.4% from 1980 and 2006 – twice the rate of industry and agriculture. Between 1998 and 2008, Hyderabad saw a 45-fold increase in services exports (Ghani, 2010).

In sum, service industries have been long-disparaged as "stagnant sectors" of low-skill and low-wage jobs that are a drag on productivity growth and growth generally. Critics claim that "smart machines" have had a "negligible effect" on labour productivity (Smith, 2020, p. 10). The prevalence of cheap labour is the cause of technological stagnation and the lack of wage gains is due to stagnant productivity, a lack of investment and a crisis of profitability. Yet, this outdated perspective eschews empirical evidence of automation-induced productivity gains in services. It also makes little sense in Marxian framework. If agriculture, manufacturing and so forth have been transformed by productivity-enhancing technological progress, then why would services be the exception? As Triplett and Bosworth (2004, p. 2) note, the notion that services are "a drag on aggregate growth is no longer valid". The *profitability* of a given economic activity determines investment and by all metrics, services are very profitable, particularly in ICT-related activities. The growth dynamics summarised above flatly contradict Baumol's paradox and its deployment by Benanav (2020) and others such as Jason Smith (2020). Baumol's cost disease simply does not apply to the parts of the service industry affected by digital automation.

A New Era for Labour?

Recent scholarship has examined the debate around capitalism's evolution in the platform era (circa 2005–present) (Cole, 2023). This period has been variously referred to as the "second machine age" (Brynjolfsson and McAfee, 2014), the "rise of the robots" (Ford, 2015), the "fourth industrial revolution" (Schwab, 2017), "industry 4.0" (Davis, 2015) and "platform capitalism" (Srnicek, 2016), among other terms. At its core are "Cyber-Physical Systems" (CPS) or "engineered systems that are built from, and depend upon, the seamless integration of computation and physical components" (National Science Foundation, 2021). CPS rely on the Internet Protocol Version 6 (IPv6), exponential advances in computer power and artificial intelligence, the Internet of Things and Services [IoTS], big data, cloud computing, etc. The development of advanced telecommunications and logistical infrastructures along with the digitalisation of the global economy has amplified the scale and scope of international finance and productive capital, largely at the expense of labour. The use of modern, algorithmically controlled surveillance technologies across the labour market from warehouses to hospitals and manufacturing is only possible through such CPS (Cole, Radice and Umney, 2021).

Sceptics of "industry 4.0" or the "fourth industrial revolution" point to lower aggregate productivity growth compared to historical business cycles (Perez, 2017; Soete, 2018); yet, aggregate productivity increases depend on both widespread diffusion of new technologies (which can take a long time) and institutional frameworks that redistribute their benefits to labour (which have been greatly undermined over the past several decades). Computers, for example, took nearly 25 years to reach their now long-term plateau of 5% of non-residential equipment capital (Arntz, Gregory, Terry and Zierahn, Ulrich, 2019). A study by Gentili *et al.* (2020) of Denmark, France, Germany, Italy, the UK and the United States found a complex web of causation between productivity, aggregate demand, employment and wages; yet, greater regional and sectoral investment corresponded to more diffusion and impact of AI and robotics technologies. The uneven scale of upgrading means that only leading firms and sectors in high-income high-investment regions typically see

GDP and productivity growth (see UNCTAD, 2019). Differences in the diffusion of technology tend to correspond with a divergence in productivity, as leading firms maintain or increase productivity growth, while laggard firms stagnate or even turn negative (Andrews *et al.*, 2016). The scale of initial investment and early adoption risks are easier for larger, market-leading firms to justify (OECD, 2019b). Laggard firms tend to find it increasingly difficult to attract workers with necessary skills to facilitate transformation, further compounding the divergence (Brynjolfsson, Rock and Syverson, 2019).

A growing literature takes such changes as paradigm-shifting (Montalban, Frigant and Jullien, 2019; Cole, 2023). The diffusion of these technologies from 2006 to 2017 corresponds to a rise in ICT investment from 2005 to 2015 in OECD countries, constituting an "open-ended burst" in technological development, which also correlates with the acceleration of AI-related patent-making since 2005 (OECD, 2019a). This decade also saw the acceleration of cloud connectivity, enabling web domain expansion and mobile datafication – technologies concentrated in services. Globally, R&D expenditure in services increased from an annual average of 6.7% of total business R&D during 1990–1995 to 17% during 2005–2010 (WTO, 2013). ICT service activities in six low- and middle-income countries are as technology-intensive (as measured by a range of learning-by-doing and innovation metrics) as electronic manufacturing (Nayyar, Vargas Da Cruz and Zhu, 2018).

What does this mean for the future of work? Daron Acemoglu and Pascual Restrepo's work is instructive here and has helped reshaped the automation discourse around three factors: the displacement effect, the productivity effect and the reinstatement effect (Acemoglu and Restrepo, 2018, 2019; Autor and Salomons, 2018). The displacement effect describes machine substitution for labour; it is the effect that has provoked the fear of joblessness or the utopian aspiration of a "world without work". The productivity effect reduces the costs of production while increasing output, thus lowering the price of goods for consumers and businesses. It tends to spur both increased demand for products and increased demand for labour to produce them across sectors. The reinstatement effect is a crucial countervailing factor to displacement and productivity effects and refers to the new tasks that are created as a consequence of automation that spurs a demand for complimentary human skills and new tasks as the market expands (Acemoglu and Restrepo, 2019).

How does automation of work actually work? Automation does not just mean replacing tasks previously performed by labour (the extensive margin); it also increases the productivity of machines performing tasks that have already been automated (the intensive margin). This "deepening of automation", tends to create a productivity effect but no labour displacement and can therefore increase labour demand, which can spur wage increases if, crucially, bargaining power is maintained. Weaker productivity effects combined with partial displacement can lead to a net decline in demand for labour; yet, the reinstatement effect can counteract this entirely. The reinstatement effect tends to be neglected in discussion of the future of work, even though the evidence of job growth, a tightening labour market and high productivity in IT-related industries indicates its importance. For example, in Argentina, Chile and Columbia, manufacturing firms that invest in ICT technology have experienced a net increase in employment (Dutz, Almeida and Packard, 2018).

Digital automation and platformisation continue to transform the labour market. In 2018 alone, over 50% of workers in EU countries were reliant on platforms daily and 40% of workers had to learn to use a new digital tool (OECD, 2019a). The imperative to learn and adapt to the digitalisation of work was amplified during the COVID-19 pandemic. From April 28 to May 20, 2020, for example, digital adoption in Europe jumped from 81% to 95%, which would have taken up to three years at pre-pandemic growth rates (Fernandez, Jenkins and Vieira, 2020). AI and big data analytics used in white-collar job tasks have high complementarity with cognitive skills, compared to robots in manufacturing, which tend to displace and deskill work (Morikawa, 2020). Robots are positively correlated to high-skill occupations and negatively correlated to mid-skill and low-skill ones in manufacturing. All of the above points to *services as the future of work.*

Conclusion

Marx makes it clear that "the way surplus is pumped out of the direct producers" is what determines "the entire configuration of the economic community" (Marx, 1981, p. 927). As service sector growth accelerates, it becomes more central to the economy than manufacturing in terms of both GDP and employment. A deregulated global capitalist system has encouraged rent-seeking activities and increasing returns to capital at the expense of labour, stifling aggregate demand at the same time that new technologies are accelerating a skill-biased polarisation of the labour market. Huge multinational corporations originating from Western countries have extended their influence and have particularly profited from the intangible assets that services produce in global production networks. Since the early 2000s onwards, a select few firms have controlled 50% or more of the market share in nearly every global industry (Chang, Hauge and Irfan, 2016). These global monopolist firms are leveraging their technological superiority to extract ever larger profits within an expanding market, often through rentierism (Christophers, 2019; Sadowski, 2020; Rotta, 2022).

The past several decades have seen the increasing dominance of services over manufacturing in terms of both GDP and employment in OECD countries. Yet, the recomposition of capital at both the national and global scales has reorganised production and expanded production networks to place certain services as a crucial engine of growth. Technological change plays a role in these shifts: less than automation messianists propose, yet more than sceptics allow for. We should not take Solow's (1987, p. 36) paradox that "you can see the computer age everywhere but in the productivity statistics" as given simply because aggregate productivity growth in the United States has not matched the post-war boom. Low wages do not indicate "technological stagnation". Such claims obscure the more complicated story about the present and future of work.

To analyse the evolution of work requires an understanding of the institutions (especially labour) that govern capital's laws of motion as much as the laws themselves. We should not conflate the growth of the service sector with the growth of low-waged or non-standard employment, as if it is an inevitable outcome. Nor should we assume that manufacturing employment has represented the primary source of "good jobs". This bears little resemblance to the reality of manufacturing work across the globe, even at the height of post-war settlement. The rise of services is not a terminal drag on development, but rather a transition dogged by the rise of neoliberal policy. National and international institutions have been reengineered to favour capital through reducing worker social protections and the erosion of worker bargaining power. Indeed, the weakening of trades unions – more so than either processes of automation or globalisation – has led to the degradation of work and declining labour share of income (Baccaro and Howell, 2017). New technologies have also enabled capital to overcome spatial and temporal constraints that previously limited their capacity to conduct surveillance and leverage control over workers. Platforms have enabled new norms of control associated with longer working hours, greater time pressure and more irregular hours. What the future of work looks like will ultimately depend more on the balance of power between capital and labour, since this will determine the way that technology and production systems are designed and implemented at work (Moody, 2017).

References

Acemoglu, D. and Restrepo, P. (2018) 'The Race between Man and Machine: Implications of Technology for Growth, Factor Shares, and Employment', *American Economic Review*, 108(6), pp. 1488–1542. Available at: https://doi.org/10.1257/aer.20160696.

Acemoglu, D. and Restrepo, P. (2019) 'Automation and New Tasks: How Technology Displaces and Reinstates Labor', *The Journal of Economic Perspectives*, 33(2), pp. 3–30. Available at: https://doi.org/10.1257/jep.33.2.3.

Aglietta, M. (2008) 'Into a New Growth Regime', *New Left Review*, NLR54 (November–December 2008), pp. 61–74. Available at: https://newleftreview.org/issues/ii54/articles/michel-aglietta-into-a-new-growth-regime.

Allen, J. and Gay, P. du (1994) 'Industry and the Rest: The Economic Identity of Services', *Work, Employment & Society*, 8(2), pp. 255–271. Available at: https://doi.org/10.1177/0950017094008002007.

Andrews, D., Criscuolo, C. and Gal, P.N. (2016) 'The Best versus the Rest: The Global Productivity Slowdown, Divergence across Firms and the Role of Public Policy', *OECD Productivity Working Papers* [Preprint], (5). Available at: https://doi.org/10.1787/63629cc9-en.

Arnold, J.M., Javorcik, B.S. and Mattoo, A. (2007) 'Does Services Liberalization Benefit Manufacturing Firms? Evidence from the Czech Republic', Rochester, NY. Available at: https://papers.ssrn.com/abstract=956489 (Accessed: 20 June 2023).

Arntz, M., Gregory, T. and Zierahn, U. (2019) *Digitalization and the Future of Work: Macroeconomic Consequences*. Discussion Paper 19-024. ZEW. Available at: https://ftp.zew.de/pub/zew-docs/dp/dp19024.pdf.

Autor, D. and Salomons, A. (2018) *Is Automation Labor Share-Displacing? Productivity Growth, Employment, and the Labor Share*. Working Paper 24871. National Bureau of Economic Research, p. 1. Available at: https://www.nber.org/system/files/working_papers/w24871/w24871.pdf.

Baccaro, L. and Howell, C. (2017) *Trajectories of Neoliberal Transformation: European Industrial Relations Since the 1970s*. Cambridge: Cambridge University Press.

Baumol, W.J. (1967) 'Macroeconomics of Unbalanced Growth: The Anatomy of Urban Crisis', *The American Economic Review*, 57(3), pp. 415–426. Available at: https://ezproxy-prd.bodleian.ox.ac.uk:2154/stable/1812111 (Accessed: 1 December 2022).

Bélanger, J. and Edwards, P. (2013) 'The Nature of Front-Line Service Work: Distinctive Features and Continuity in the Employment Relationship', *Work, Employment & Society*, 27(3), pp. 433–450. Available at: https://doi.org/10.1177/0950017013481877.

Benanav, A. (2020) *Automation and the Future of Work*. London: Verso.

Berlingieri, G. (2013) *Outsourcing and the Rise in Services*. 1199. London: Centre for Economic Performance, London School of Economics and Political Science. Available at: https://eprints.lse.ac.uk/51532/1/dp1199.pdf.

Bloom, N., Sadun, R. and Reenen, J.V. (2012) 'Americans Do IT Better: US Multinationals and the Productivity Miracle', *American Economic Review*, 102(1), pp. 167–201. Available at: https://doi.org/10.1257/aer.102.1.167.

Bolton, S.C. (2010) 'Old Ambiguities and New Developments: Exploring the Emotional Labour Process', in P. Thompson and C. Smith (eds.) *Working Life: Renewing Labour Process Analysis*. Basingstoke: Palgrave (Critical Perspectives on Work and Employment). pp.205–222

Bolton, S.C. and Boyd, C. (2003) 'Trolley Dolly or Skilled Emotion Manager? Moving on from Hochschild's Managed Heart', *Work, Employment & Society*, 17(2), pp. 289–308. Available at: https://doi.org/10.1177/0950017003017002004.

Bosworth, B. and Collins, S.M. (2008) 'Accounting for Growth: Comparing China and India', *Journal of Economic Perspectives*, 22(1), pp. 45–66. Available at: https://doi.org/10.1257/jep.22.1.45.

Braverman, H. (1974) *Labor and Monopoly Capital: The Degradation of Work in the Twentieth Century*. New York: Monthly Review Press (Book, Whole).

Brenner, R. (2006) *The Economics of Global Turbulence: The Advanced Capitalist Economies from Long Boom to Long Downturn, 1945–2005*. London; New York: Verso.

Brook, P., Koch, G. and Wittel, A. (2013) 'Thirty Years after Hochschild's "Managed Heart": Exploring the Commodity Frontier', *Culture and Organization*, 19(4), pp. 275–282. Available at: https://doi.org/10.1080/14759551.2013.827419.

Brynjolfsson, E. and Hitt, L. (2003) 'Computing Productivity: Firm-Level Evidence', *The Review of Economics and Statistics*, 85(4), pp. 793–808.

Brynjolfsson, E. and McAfee, A. (2014) *The Second Machine Age: Work, Progress, and Prosperity in a Time of Brilliant Technologies*. Norton Paperback. New York: W. W. Norton & Company (Book, Whole).

Brynjolfsson, E., Rock, D. and Syverson, C. (2019) 'Artificial Intelligence and the Modern Productivity Paradox: A Clash of Expectations and Statistics', in A. Agrawal, J. Gans, and A. Goldfarb (eds.) *The Economics of Artificial Intelligence*. Chicago: University of Chicago Press. pp. 23–60

Chang, H.-J., Hauge, J. and Irfan, M. (2016) *Transformative Industrial Policy for Africa*. Addis Ababa: United Nations Commission for Africa. https://archive.uneca.org/sites/default/files/PublicationFiles/tipa-full_report_en_web.pdf

Christophers, B. (2019) 'The Rentierization of the United Kingdom Economy', *Environment and Planning A: Economy and Space*, 0(0), p. 0308518X19873007. Addis Ababa: United Nations Commission for Africa. Available at: https://doi.org/10.1177/0308518X19873007.

Clarke, S. (1999) 'Capitalist Competition and the Tendency to Overproduction: Comments on Brenner's "Uneven Development and the Long Downturn"', *Historical Materialism*, 4(1), pp. 57–72. Available at: https://doi.org/10.1163/156920699100414409.

Cole, M. (2023) '(Infra)structural Discontinuity: Capital, Labour, and Technological Change', *Antipode*, 55(2), pp. 348–372. Available at: https://doi.org/10.1111/anti.12887.

Cole, M., Radice, H. and Umney, C. (2021) 'The Political Economy of Datafication and Work: A New Digital Taylorism?', in *Socialist Register 2021: Beyond Digital Capitalism: New Ways of Living*. New York: Monthly Review Press. Available at: https://socialistregister.com/index.php/srv/article/view/34948.

Cole, M., Stuart, M., Hardy, K. and Spencer, D. (2022) 'Wage Theft and the Struggle over the Working Day in Hospitality Work: A Typology of Unpaid Labour Time', *Work, Employment and Society*, p. 09500170221111719. Available at: https://doi.org/10.1177/09500170221111719.

Crafts, N. (2008) 'Profits of Doom?', *New Left Review*, (54), pp. 49–60. Available at: https://newleftreview.org/issues/ii54/articles/nicholas-crafts-profits-of-doom.

Davis, R. (2015) *Industry 4.0: Digitalisation for Productivity and Growth. Briefing*. Brussels: European Parliamentary Research Service. Available at: https://www.europarl.europa.eu/RegData/etudes/BRIE/2015/568337/EPRS_BRI(2015)568337_EN.pdf.

Deane, P.M. (1980) *The First Industrial Revolution*. Cambridge: Cambridge University Press. Available at: https://doi.org/10.1017/CBO9780511622090.

Duménil, G. and Lévy, D. (1999) 'Brenner on Distribution', *Historical Materialism*, 4(1), pp. 73–94. Available at: https://doi.org/10.1163/156920699100414418.

Dutz, M.A., Almeida, R.K. and Packard, T.G. (2018) *The Jobs of Tomorrow: Technology, Productivity, and Prosperity in Latin America and the Caribbean*. Washington, DC: World Bank. Available at: https://doi.org/10.1596/978-1-4648-1222-4.

Esping-Andersen, G. (1999) *Social Foundations of Postindustrial Economies*. Oxford: Oxford University Press, Incorporated. Available at: https://ebookcentral.proquest.com/lib/oxford/detail.action?docID=3052767 (Accessed: 1 December 2022).

Fernandez, S., Jenkins, P. and Vieira, B. (2020) *Europe's Digital Migration during COVID-19: Getting Past the Broad Trends and Averages*. Available at: https://www.mckinsey.com/business-functions/mckinsey-digital/our-insights/europes-digital-migration-during-covid-19-getting-past-the-broad-trends-and-averages# (Accessed: 2 June 2021).

Fine, B., Lapavitsas, C. and Milonakis, D. (1999) 'Addressing the World Economy: Two Steps Back', *Capital & Class*, 23(1), pp. 47–90.

Fine, B., Petropoulos, A. and Sato, H. (2005) 'Beyond Brenner's Investment Overhang Hypothesis: The Case of the Steel Industry', *New Political Economy*, 10(1), pp. 43–64. Available at: https://doi.org/10.1080/13563460500031248.

Ford, M. (2015) *The Rise of the Robots: Technology and the Threat of Mass Unemployment*. London: Oneworld (Book, Whole).

Gentili, A., Compagnucci, F., Gallegati, M. and Valentini, E. (2020) 'Are Machines Stealing Our Jobs?', *Cambridge Journal of Regions, Economy and Society*, 13(1), pp. 153–173. Available at: https://doi.org/10.1093/cjres/rsz025.

Ghani, E. (2010) *The service revolution in South Asia*. Oxford: Oxford University Press.

Goos, M., Manning, A. and Salomons, A. (2014) 'Explaining Job Polarization: Routine-Biased Technological Change and Offshoring', *American Economic Review*, 104(8), pp. 2509–2526. Available at: https://doi.org/10.1257/aer.104.8.2509.

Hallward-Driemeier, M. and Nayyar, G. (2018) *Trouble in the Making: The Future of Manufacturing-Led Development*. Washington, DC: World Bank.

Hammer, N., Plugor, R., Nolan, P. and Clark, I. (2015) *New Industry on a Skewed Playing Field: Supply Chain Relations and Working Conditions in UK Garment Manufacturing*. University of Leicester: Centre for Sustainable Work and Employment Futures. Available at: https://www2.le.ac.uk/offices/press/for-journalists/media-resources/Leicester%20Report%20-%20Final%20-to%20publish.pdf/ (Accessed: 28 February 2017).

Hauge, J. and Chang, H.-J. (2019) 'The Role of Manufacturing Versus Services in Economic Development', *Transforming Industrial Policy for the Digital Age*, pp. 12–36. Available at: https://ezproxy-prd.bodleian.ox.ac.uk:3836/view/edcoll/9781788976145/9781788976145.00007.xml (Accessed: 1 December 2022).

Hochschild, A.R. (1983) *The Managed Heart: Commercialization of Human Feeling*. Berkeley; London: University of California Press (Book, Whole).

ILO (2023) *International Standard Industrial Classification of All Economic Activities (ISIC), ILOSTAT*. Available at: https://ilostat.ilo.org/resources/concepts-and-definitions/classification-economic-activities/ (Accessed: 14 June 2023).

Kaldor, N. (1967) *Strategic Factors in Economic Development*. Ithaca: New York State School of Industrial and Labor Relations, Cornell University (The Frank W. Pierce memorial lectures ; October 1966).

Kaldor, N. (1996) *Causes of Growth and Stagnation in the World Economy*. Cambridge: Cambridge University Press. Available at: https://doi.org/10.1017/CBO9780511559709 (Accessed: 2 December 2022).

Korczynski, M. (2009a) 'The Mystery Customer: Continuing Absences in the Sociology of Service Work', *Sociology*, 43(5), pp. 952–967. Available at: https://doi.org/10.1177/0038038509340725.

Korczynski, M. (2009b) 'Understanding the Contradictory Lived Experience of Service Work: The Customer-Oriented Bureaucracy', in M. Korczynski and C. L. Macdonald (eds.) *Service Work: Critical Perspectives*. London: Routledge, pp. 73–90.

Korczynski, M., Shire, K., Frenkel, S. and Tam, M. (2000) 'Service Work in Consumer Capitalism: Customers, Control and Contradictions', *Work, Employment & Society*, 14(4), pp. 669–687. Available at: https://doi.org/10.1177/09500170022118671.

Leidner, R. (1993) *Fast Food, Fast Talk: Service Work and the Routinization of Everyday Life*. Berkeley; London: University of California Press.

Leidner, R. (1999) 'Emotional Labor in Service Work', *Annals of the American Academy of Political and Social Science*, 561(1), pp. 81–95. Available at: https://doi.org/10.1177/000271629956100106.

Loungani, P., Mishra, S., Papageorgiou, C. and Wang, K. (2017) 'World Trade in Services: Evidence from a New Dataset', Rochester, NY. Available at: https://papers.ssrn.com/abstract=2967432 (Accessed: 20 June 2023).

MacDonald, C.L. and Korczynski, M. (eds.) (2009) *Service Work: Critical Perspectives*. New York: Routledge.

MacDonald, C.L. and Sirianni, C. (1996) 'The Service Society and the Changing Nature of Work', in C.L. MacDonald and C. Sirianni (eds.) *Working in the Service Society*. Philadelphia, PA: Temple University Press, pp. 1–26.

Marglin, S.A. and Schor, J. (1990) *The Golden Age of Capitalism: Reinterpreting the Postwar Experience*. Oxford: Clarendon P.

Marx, K. (1969) *Theories of Surplus-Value: Volume 1*. London: Lawrence and Wishart.

Marx, K. (1981) *Capital, Volume III: The Process of Capitalist Production*. Harmondsworth: Penguin in Association with New Left Review.

McMillan, M., Rodrik, D. and Sepulveda, C. (2017) 'Structural Change, Fundamentals and Growth: A Framework and Case Studies', National Bureau of Economic Research (Working Paper Series). Available at: https://doi.org/10.3386/w23378.

Milberg, W. and Winkler, D. (2013) *Outsourcing Economics: Global Value Chains in Capitalist Development*. Cambridge: Cambridge University Press. Available at: https://doi.org/10.1017/CBO9781139208772.

Montalban, M., Frigant, V. and Jullien, B. (2019) 'Platform Economy as a New form of Capitalism: A Régulationist Research Programme', *Cambridge Journal of Economics*, 43(4). Available at: https://doi.org/10.1093/cje/bez017.

Moody, K. (2017) *On New Terrain: How Capital Is Reshaping the Battleground of Class War*. Chicago, IL: Haymarket.

Moraitis, A. (2022) 'From the Post-Industrial Prophecy to the De-Industrial Nightmare: Stagnation, the Manufacturing Fetish and the Limits of Capitalist Wealth', *Competition & Change*, 26(5), pp. 513–532. Available at: https://doi.org/10.1177/10245294211044314.

Morikawa, M. (2020) *Heterogeneous Relationships between Automation Technologies and Skilled Labor: Evidence from a Firm Survey*. RIETI Discussion Paper 20-E-004. Available at: https://www.rieti.go.jp/en/publications/summary/20010006.html.

National Science Foundation (2021) *Cyber-Physical Systems (CPS): nsf21551*. National Science Foundation. Available at: https://www.nsf.gov/pubs/2021/nsf21551/nsf21551.pdf (Accessed: 22 January 2021).

Nayyar, D. (2013) *Catch Up: Developing Countries in the World Economy*. Oxford; New York: Oxford University Press.

Nayyar, G., Vargas Da Cruz, M.J. and Zhu, L. (2018) 'Does Premature Deindustrialization Matter? The Role of Manufacturing Versus Services in Development', Rochester, NY. Available at: https://papers.ssrn.com/abstract=3252828 (Accessed: 20 June 2023).

Nordhaus, W.D. (2008) 'Baumol's Diseases: A Macroeconomic Perspective', *The B.E. Journal of Macroeconomics*, 8(1). Available at: https://doi.org/10.2202/1935-1690.1382.

OECD (2019a) *Measuring the Digital Transformation: A Roadmap for the Future, Measuring the Digital Transformation: A Roadmap for the Future*. Paris: Organisation for Economic Co-operation and Development. Available at: https://ezproxy-prd.bodleian.ox.ac.uk:3355/science-and-technology/measuring-the-digital-transformation_9789264311992-en.

OECD (2019b) *Productivity Growth in the Digital Age*. Organisation for Economic Co-operation and Development. Available at: https://www.oecd.org/sti/ieconomy/productivity-growth-in-the-digital-age.pdf.

Perez, C. (2017) 'Second Machine Age or Fifth Technological Revolution? (Part 3) – Beyond the Technological Revolution'. Available at: https://beyondthetechrevolution.com/blog/second-machine-age-or-fifth-technological-revolution-part-3/ (Accessed: 24 June 2021).

Rodrik, D. (2016) 'Premature Deindustrialization', *Journal of Economic Growth*, 21(1), pp. 1–33. Available at: https://doi.org/10.1007/s10887-015-9122-3.

Rotta, T.N. (2022) 'Information Rents, Economic Growth and Inequality: An Empirical Study of the United States', *Cambridge Journal of Economics*, 46(2), pp. 341–370. Available at: https://doi.org/10.1093/cje/beac004.

Sadowski, J. (2020) 'The Internet of Landlords: Digital Platforms and New Mechanisms of Rentier Capitalism', *Antipode*, 52(2), pp. 562–580. Available at: https://doi.org/10.1111/anti.12595.

Schettkat, R. and Yocarini, L. (2006) 'The Shift to Services Employment: A Review of the Literature', *Structural Change and Economic Dynamics*, 17(2), pp. 127–147.

Schwab, K. (2017) *The Fourth Industrial Revolution*. London: Penguin.

Smith, J.E. (2020) *Smart Machines and Service Work: Automation in an Age of Stagnation*. London: Reaktion Books, Limited. Available at: https://ebookcentral.proquest.com/lib/oxford/detail.action?docID=6376474 (Accessed: 14 October 2022).

Soete, L. (2018) 'Destructive Creation: Explaining the Productivity Paradox in the Digital Age',in M. Neufeind, J. O'Reilly and F. Ranft (eds.) *Work in the Digital Age: Challenges of the Fourth Industrial Revolution*. London: Rowman & Littlefield International Ltd, pp. 29–46.

Solow, R. (1987) 'We'd Better Watch Out', *New York Times Book Review*, 12 July, p. 36. Available at: https://www.standupeconomist.com/pdf/misc/solow-computer-productivity.pdf.

Srnicek, N. (2016) *Platform Capitalism*. Cambridge: Polity Press (Book, Whole).

Taylor, P. and Bain, P. (1999) '"An Assembly Line in the Head": Work and Employee Relations in the Call Centre', *Industrial Relations Journal*, 30(2), pp. 101–117. Available at: https://doi.org/10.1111/1468-2338.00113.

Triplett, J.E. and Bosworth, B.P. (2004) *Productivity in the U.S. Services Sector: New Sources of Economic Growth*. Washington, DC: Brookings Institution Press. Available at: https://ebookcentral.proquest.com/lib/oxford/detail.action?docID=3004441 (Accessed: 30 October 2022).

UNCTAD (2016) *Trade and Development Report: Structural Transformation for Inclusive and Sustained Growth*. Geneva: United Nations Conference on Trade and Development. Available at: https://unctad.org/system/files/official-document/tdr2016_en.pdf.

UNCTAD (2019) *Digital Economy Report: Value Creation and Capture—Implications for Developing Countries*. Geneva: United Nations Conference on Trade and Development. Available at: https://unctad.org/system/files/official-document/der2019_en.pdf.

UNECA (2015) *Economic Report on Africa 2015: Industrializing through Trade*. Addis Ababa: United Nations Economic Commission for Africa. Available at: https://hdl.handle.net/10855/22767.

Urry, J. (1990) *The Tourist Gaze: Leisure and Travel in Contemporary Societies*. London: Sage.

World Bank (2023a) *Manufacturing Value Added (% of GDP)*. World Bank National Accounts Data, and OECD National Accounts Data. Available at: https://data.worldbank.org/indicator/NV.IND.MANF.ZS.

World Bank (2023b) *Services, etc., Value Added (% of GDP)*. World Bank National Accounts Data, and OECD National Accounts Data. Available at: https://data.worldbank.org/indicator/NV.SRV.TETC.ZS.

World Bank (2023c) *World Bank, Manufacturing, Value Added (Current US$)*. World Bank National Accounts Data, and OECD National Accounts Data. Available at: https://data.worldbank.org/indicator/NV.IND.MANF.CD.

World Bank (2023d) *World Bank, Services Value Added (Current US$)*. World Bank National Accounts Data, and OECD National Accounts Data. Available at: https://data.worldbank.org/indicator/NV.SRV.TOTL.CD.

WTO (2013) *World Trade Report 2013: Factors Shaping the Future of World Trade*. Geneva: World Trade Organisation.

Yamamura, K. (2008) 'More System, Please!', *New Left Review*, (54), pp. 75–85. Available at: https://newleftreview.org/issues/ii54/articles/kozo-yamamura-more-system-please.

Zimmerman, M.K., Litt, J.S. and Bose, C.E. (2006) *Global Dimensions of Gender and Carework*. Stanford: Stanford University Press.

Recommendations for Further Reading

Moody, K. (2017) *On New Terrain: How Capital Is Reshaping the Battleground of Class War*. Chicago, IL: Haymarket.

Socialist Register (2021) *Beyond Digital Capitalism: New Ways of Living*. New York: Monthly Review Press. Available at: https://socialistregister.com/index.php/srv/issue/view/2331

Srnicek, N. (2016) *Platform Capitalism*. Cambridge: Polity.

Steinhoff, J. (2021) *Automation and Autonomy: Labour, Capital and Machines in the Artificial Intelligence Industry*. London: Palgrave Macmillan. Available at: https://doi.org/10.1007/978-3-030-71689-9.

Tregenna, F. (2011) 'What Does the "Services Sector" Mean in Marxian Terms?', *Review of Political Economy*, 23(2), pp. 281–298. Available at: https://doi.org/10.1080/09538259.2011.561563.

18

INDUSTRY 5.0 AND THE FUTURE OF WORK IN MANUFACTURING IN AUSTRALIA

Darryn Snell, Mark Dean and Al Rainnie

Introduction

As captured below by the quote from the Australian Industrial Transformation Institute (AITI), concern with the parlous state of manufacturing in Australia is not new:

> Australia has been on the path of deindustrialisation for the past quarter century. This was not inevitable. More than many people think, it was the cumulative result of policy decisions to reject the concept of industrial policy and strategy. Industrial policies of the time were replaced by comparative advantage ideologies that said countries should concentrate on their natural resources and be guided by freer markets and relative price signals. Policies that favoured particular sectors were unwound, and the idea of an industrial strategy was misrepresented as inherently anti-trade and anti-competitive. At most, generic business support policies were acceptable. The only exception to this has been the defence industry which, on national security and sovereignty grounds, has been deemed worthy of a dedicated sectoral plan. Elsewhere, the emphasis has been on 'business support' limited to generic issues across all industries such as addressing market failures (often broadly defined) and easing the cost of doing business.
>
> (AITI 2021)

In a series of book chapters (Rainnie and Dean 2022), journal articles (Rainnie 2021a; Dean and Rainnie 2020; Rainnie and Dean 2020; Dean et al. 2021) and articles in the *Futures of Work* online magazine (Snell, Dean and Rainnie 2022; Rainnie 2021b; Rainnie, Herod and McGrath-Champ 2020; Rainnie and Dean 2019, 2020), we have critically examined 'Industry 4.0' (i4.0), hype around deglobalisation and reshoring, and the impact of COVID-19 on manufacturing and the future of work in Australia. We have also examined how Australian industrial policy has more recently been revitalised through militarisation. In this chapter, we develop this analysis through, initially, a critical examination of the European Union's advanced manufacturing transformation step-change to 'Industry 5.0' (i5.0) and point to a much more complex and problematic picture for the future of manufacturing and manufacturing employment. Although all the authors are based in Australia, we will take a wider perspective, particularly as i5.0 and its predecessor

DOI: 10.4324/9781003327561-25

tended to be Eurocentric. The current context of an emerging new Cold War, and the ongoing 'polycrisis' (Tooze 2022) are critical in driving the pattern of, and policy towards, manufacturing employment. Ongoing crises since 2008 has been evidenced by almost static investment levels in the 'real' economy, whilst investment in robotics has been largely driven by supply chain impacts like COVID-19 and labour shortages in sectors such as warehousing particularly, and logistics generally.

The war in Ukraine has reinforced and accelerated pre-existing tendencies. In the case of Germany, as The Economist (2022) pointed out, a national business model based on cheap energy from Russia and abundant demand from China was being tested severely. Some companies were looking to relocate abroad, placing the *Mittelstand* under pressure. India, however, was looking to develop a domestic semiconductor industry and seek to replace China in the Apple supply chain. Now, increasing environmental pressures that extend the challenge of these pre-existing tendencies are testing the global capitalist growth model and its ecological limitations.

Beyond Industry 4.0

The idea of a Fourth Industrial Revolution (4IR) emerged in Germany around 2008. In the face of a triple crisis – ongoing economic crisis and a new Cold War, climate change and COVID-19 – i4.0 metamorphosed into i5.0. Even the European Commission (Dixson-Declève et al. 2022) had recognised i4.0 as technologically deterministic. It was deemed 'not fit for purpose' in the context of a climate crisis and planetary emergency, and it had the potential to deepen rather than address social tensions and inequalities. In many ways, this echoed the rebadging of the European regional development policy, Smart Specialisation S3, as S4, now incorporating environmental and social concerns. More generally, as we have argued elsewhere, industrial policy dominated by neoliberalism was softened under the threat of the polycrisis, to include ecological and poverty concerns. The promotion of Mazzucato's (2021) concepts – firstly of the entrepreneurial state and subsequently, the environmental state – has provided a theoretical underpinning to policy change along with the notion that companies embracing new 'disruptive' technologies must remain committed to social responsibilities.

In the 4IR's latest incarnation, i5.0, concerns with human-centred production and sustainable development were added. Industrial innovation now was expected to deliver a fundamental redesign, with three dimensions to be included:

- Regenerative features;
- Social dimension demanding attention to the well-being of workers and
- Mandatory environmental dimensions.

The new model was no less demanding than its predecessor. One aim was to reduce Europe's dependence on imports of strategic materials and energy. Industry was told to 'digitalise or die!' Decentralisation and user sovereignty in Web3.0 would allow for the evolution of work and labour shifts. A large proportion of job creation and new skills development would happen through catalysation of a net-zero carbon, circular and regenerative job market. A major pillar would be the formalisation of at least 50% of informal jobs by 2030.

In *Forbes*, Kraaijenbrink (2022) argues that so far i5.0 has not gained much traction; but that given the current major challenges and crises, it is evident that it is a plausible and preferred policy response in the context of real fears of technology-driven unemployment for both unskilled and professional occupations. Strategy will have to become human-centric, resilient and sustainable.

Scholars have argued that despite a lack of consensus around interpretations of sustainability in the context of i4.0, the digital technology focus of that iteration is the key to the step-change offered by its would-be successor, i5.0 (Sartal et al. 2020). The techno-optimistic approach apparent here is echoed by McKinsey (2022). And the proto-optimistic associated future for workers was echoed by Deloitte (2017: 2) with important implications for skills and recruitment:

> Breaking investments in R&D and robotics will likely make manufacturing more attractive, with fewer repetitive tasks. The next generation of employees needs more stimulation and purpose.

Reality may be slightly more nuanced, and unsurprisingly by 2022 The Economist (2022) had retreated from its earlier tentative support for a COVID-19-driven interventionist policy to a more standard ncoliberal critique.

Industrial Policy in Australia

Since the dismantling of tariff protection from the 1970s and subsequent decline in industry assistance, Australia's manufacturing industry has struggled (Weller and O'Neil 2014). The 2017 closure of the Australian automotive industry illustrated for many how precarious the country's manufacturing sector had become under these policies (Clibborn, Lansbury and Wright 2016). By 2021, manufacturing employed around 908,000 people; less than 7% of the total workforce (ABS 2021). This has made Australia the least self-sufficient country in the OECD for manufacturing, producing the lowest proportion of its own domestic requirements for consumption of manufactures of any OECD country (AITI 2021, 6).

Associated with the embrace of neoliberal policy making has been a shift globally towards 'extractive capitalism' whereby Australia is perceived to have a comparative advantage in attracting global investments and export opportunities in resources. We do not see this as a new phase of capitalist development, but rather as a reflection of the limitations of the increasingly dominant neoliberal paradigm (Upchurch 2020). In the Australian context, it is simply the next wave of resource-based development and its geo-political trade relations with an expanding China.

The legacy of a resource-focused colonial-settler regime was broadly, as Fernandes (2021, 2022) points out, a focus on simple economic growth rather than more complex economic development. Economic development involves changes brought about by a country's own initiative; but if an economy is dragged along by the changes in the surrounding world and adapts itself to them, then there is economic growth without economic development. Australia is therefore anomalous in its lack of economic complexity. Low economic complexity reflects dependency leading to industrial monocultures typical of imperial-colonial relationships. Thus, the 'resources curse' might be better described as the impact of extractive capitalism in Australia. In the Australian context, even before the current crisis, it was argued by Goodman and Worth (2007) that the 'resources curse' had involved three elements:

- Deindustrialisation and social division;
- Regulatory capture and energy insecurity; and
- Ecological degradation and exhaustion.

The undermining of First Nations People self-determination and sovereignty over their land must also be acknowledged as an additional (often overlooked) element. Before COVID-19 impacted, the Australian Manufacturing Forum (Roberts 2019) argued that Australia now had the economic diversity and export profile of a typical developing nation:

> Our antipathy to value-adding activities such as manufacturing in favour of industries that require little more than digging it up and shipping it out, has left us dangerously dependent on quarrying.

In 2017, Australia ranked 93rd in Harvard University's economic complexity ranking. In 2019, Australia ranked 14th out of 63 countries in the World Competitiveness Digital Ranking, a situation that had not improved over the previous five years. In the Institute for Management Development's Global Competitiveness Index, Australia was 34th overall for investment and development and 44th for both apprenticeships and employee training (IMD 2021). Australia was reportedly poorly connected into Global Value Chains (GVC) (apart from the resources sector) and even Australian small businesses did not have a great record of innovation (Cunningham et al. 2016).

Breathing Life into Manufacturing

Despite the dominance of 'quarry vision' (Pearse 2009), reliance on resources for economic growth and the overall decline of manufacturing in Australia, political sentiment for maintaining a manufacturing base has remained. Federal and state governments, particularly Victoria and South Australia where manufacturing has been historically important, regularly revise their policy approaches to manufacturing. The Gillard-Labor Government (2010–2013) established a Taskforce on Manufacturing to address the challenges that Australia's manufacturing industry confronted during the mining boom whilst the conservative Abbott-Coalition Government (2013–2015) promised to build a 'five pillar economy' which included manufacturing, agriculture, services, education and mining. The recent Morrison-Coalition Government (2018–2022) also initiated a Modern Manufacturing Initiative (MMI).

The MMI identified the National Manufacturing Priorities as Space; Medical Products; Resources Technology and Critical Minerals Processing; Food and Beverage; Defence and Recycling and Clean Energy. The strategy to revitalise Australian manufacturing was also underpinned by a vision of reshoring manufacturing jobs. The Productivity Commission (2021) investigated Australia's potential vulnerability to global supply chain disruption resulting from COVID-19. Its report quoted *The Economist* (2021: 58) projecting supply chains becoming shorter, less fragmented, and more regional. The *Australian Financial Review* has advocated more resilient supply chains insulated from the prospect of global disruption and a rebuilding of domestic manufacturing capacity for critical goods:

> The health and well being of Australians is a national security-resilience issue and one that has to be assessed for risks and vulnerabilities just like every other aspect of national security from energy to the economy to the environment to the military.
>
> (Coorey 2020)

Andrew Liveris, then the head of the Federal governments manufacturing taskforce, argued that the domestic shortage of all personal protective equipment (PPE) items had brought the lack of Australian manufacturing to national attention (Coorey 2020). Strategies to 'onshore' or 'reshore' could be outweighed by cost issues or could be complicated by continuing reliance on inputs such as crude oil, and Australia may simply lack the expertise to produce locally and competitively.

Even when firms consider onshoring, this is often accompanied by maintenance of several locations globally to diversify risk (Productivity Commission 2021: 5–6). It is worth noting that *The Economist* (2021) suggested that reshoring had not developed to any significant extent. Supply chains were restructuring but mainly around patterns of logistics. Where businesses had moved production out of China, it had mainly gone to countries that now supplied sources of even lower wages like Thailand and Vietnam. The report concluded that capital goods typically form the highest share of vulnerable imports – the main supplier of vulnerable imports being China. The imports that were vulnerable and most likely to be critical were inputs into the goods-producing industries of petrol refining and medicine manufacturing (Productivity Commission 2021: 7–8).

Addressing climate change concerns was one of the major areas where the newly elected Labor-led Albanese Government sought to chart a new policy direction for Australia. As one of the world's most carbon-intensive economies, the Albanese Government committed to reducing the nation's emissions by 43% on 2005 levels by 2030, and increasing the share of renewable energy in the national electricity market to 82% by 2030. There was also a growing (if overblown) belief that Australia could become a renewable energy 'superpower' (Garnaut 2022) in global decarbonisation efforts if it could move beyond extractivism. We now look at the case of lithium and how far the rhetoric of renewable superpower potential will turn into reality.

Lithium and Battery Production

Securing reserves of lithium for battery and component production now dictates the economic strategies of many of the world's nations and most leading global firms. Data reported by the United States Geological Survey (USGS 2020) highlight that Australia is the world's largest producer of lithium by a significant margin – 42,000 tonnes in 2019 compared to the second-placed Chile with 18,000 tonnes. In comparison with other lithium-exporting nations, Australia holds an advantage, in that the mineral-based form of its lithium means it can be supplied as demanded, whereas liquid brine lithium presents additional complications for extraction and refining.

In Australia, attempts to develop a battery industry have been underpinned by a number of government-commissioned reports and targeted funding streams aimed at advancing value-added lithium ore activities. In 2019, the Future Battery Industry Strategy was launched to better facilitate investment, project facilitation, research and development, and the adoption of new battery technologies. Australian battery manufacturing is generally considered years away with the current focus on additional lithium processing to produce lithium hydroxide and undertake anode or cathode production. The interventionist role of government, for example, was acknowledged in the *Road Map for National Manufacturing Priorities* as far as Resources Technology and Critical Minerals Processing was concerned. The strategy would be deemed a success if, by the end of 2030, a range of critical minerals processing projects had successfully gained financing and were operating at scale; and if these activities were driving jobs growth in the sector and delivering economic outcomes for local communities (Commonwealth of Australia 2021: 16). Critical minerals processing covers businesses and enterprises associated with processing critical minerals for use in value-added manufacturing and manufacturing products using those refined materials. Using the battery value chain as an example, this can be from processing lithium ore into lithium hydroxide or metal, through to battery assembly (Commonwealth of Australia 2021: 3). But the *Road Map*'s conclusion about refining and processing critical materials was not overly optimistic:

> The ability to demonstrate a reliable processing capability which meets the specific requirements of different customers is a critical step in on-shoring manufacturing. This

> typically requires pilot scale demonstrations, for example, constructing a pressure acid leach pilot plant that runs from ore beneficiation through to the refining of high purity metal, reconstructing the entire flow sheet at pilot scale. If this final stage demonstration occurs offshore, the chances of securing the scaled-up advanced manufacturing is very low. Companies can often struggle to access funding to enable this step. Many Australian critical minerals processing projects are therefore 'stuck' at this stage of the project development pipeline.
>
> (Commonwealth of Australia 2021: 15)

There was also little indication that these pilot projects or future battery component factories would make use of i4.0 let alone i5.0 strategies. Efforts, however, continue to be made to move beyond these sticking points through government initiatives. The MMI, for example, has provided government support to companies wanting to pursue lithium upgrading and processing. The Future Batteries Industry Cooperative Research Council (FBICRC 2020), for example, highlighted the need for a more coherent approach to battery manufacturing production and concluded that the 'precursor' production capabilities in Australia's supply chain are not present, presenting a challenge to bridging the gap between extraction and value-adding (Accenture 2021).

The new Cold War between the US and China is likely to further complicate Australia's ability to develop a viable battery industry. The US is showing increased interest in Australia's lithium and other critical mineral resources to reduce its reliance on Chinese processed materials. A recent White House report notes that:

> Australia has an abundance of key commodities needed to produce advanced batteries … These commodities require processing, however, before becoming battery materials. Australia currently has no commercial production of Class 1 chemicals or battery precursors. Australia also has no cell manufacturing, but it does have an active battery pack assembly industry. Australia only recycles two percent of its lithium-ion batteries, and its recycling processes typically disassemble and homogenize materials for export to places like Korea, which have developed battery recycling capabilities.
>
> (The White House 2021: 113–114)

The danger of not developing a more coherent strategy for battery development is that Australia will simply become a battery material resource provider for other nations who are desperate to secure supply. The White House report, for example, commented that the US's economic security would require secure and resilient supply chains. It highlighted long-known challenges of domestic industries experiencing harm from disruption of critical materials supply, and that China's global dominance in the production of the world's lithium (60%) and cobalt (80%) – both core inputs to high-capacity batteries – presented a vulnerability issue to the US automotive manufacturing industry (The White House 2021: 7). The outcome would be that the US will look to ally countries like Australia to supply the bulk of the metals, to be processed into battery parts on American shores. In this scenario, advancing i4.0 or i5.0 in this strategic sector seems highly unlikely. This brings us to characterise Australia as a country struggling to reverse deindustrialisation rather than pursuing i4.0 and i5.0 pathways. Where industrial policy appears to being revitalised it has tended to come about as a result of being increasingly militarised and dominated by US military interests with the emergence of a new Cold War. We turn now to how this new Cold War is working to militarise Australian industry policy in the more explicit area of defence hardware.

The Militarisation of Industrial Policy

For countries like Australia, whose economic fortunes are tied to China but whose political, defence and security interests are deeply aligned with US interests, the rise of China and relative decline of the US has resulted in major policy challenges. The 'Chinese Miracle' drove Australia's new Asia-focused economic strategy throughout the late 1990s to 2010 and helped sustain the longest period of uninterrupted economic growth of any developed country. The Obama administration's 'pivot to Asia' strategy which aimed to curtail China's diplomatic and military rise in the region, however, encouraged Australia to tighten its embrace with the US and its renewed military interests in the region.

Kate Louis of the Australian Industry Group commented that the Coalition Government's 2016 defence industry policy statement signalled a shift away from off-the-shelf purchasing to building a local industrial base in defence (AiGroup 2019). A strategic update released in 2020 foreshadowed a large Australian sovereign defence industry, promotion of defence exports, investment in research and increasing Australian industry capability and content (Middleton 2021a, 2021b). As Middleton pointed out, the figures involved are eye-watering, with the government proposing to spend $270 billion over the next ten years boosting Australia's defence capability. This figure does not include the immense difficulties and cost overruns that defence contracts appear to be susceptible to. This picture is further complicated by the fact that the Department of Defence now employs more contractors than soldiers and the Australian Strategic Policy Institute claimed that this could swallow up more than 10% of the military's budget for acquiring new weapons (ASPI 2021: 68–69).

The question of defence capability, broadly defined, became integrated into the MMI. Beyond Defence itself, Space has obvious military implications. The Australian Army Research Centre (AARC 2020) also pointed to the military implications of food production and medical supplies. The strategic importance of resources and critical minerals is obvious. Unsurprisingly, Australian policy echoed that of the US. The Biden administration (The White House 2021: 7), in a report on vulnerable supply chains, commented that experts:

> ...have consistently argued that the nation's underlying commercial industrial foundations are central to our security. Reports ... have raised concerns about the defense industry's reliance on limited domestic suppliers; a global supply chain vulnerable to disruption; and competitor country suppliers. Innovations essential to military preparedness—like highly specialized lithium-ion batteries—require an ecosystem of innovation, skills, and production facilities that the United States currently lacks.

The policy prescription involved attempts to relocalise strategic production and aim for local supplier support initiatives. Silicon chips were a case in point and with its silicon policy, the Australian government hoped to develop a domestic industry in the face of US initiatives.

Chips with Everything?

In 2022, the CSIRO, Australia's national science agency, published the Australian Silicon Action Plan, arguing that the country needed to develop its own fully integrated domestic solar supply chain. This was necessary as a critical step towards energy security and, it was suggested, to support economic growth and jobs across Australia's regions and cities (CSIRO 2022). One of the greatest risks to Australia's solar ambitions and renewable energy future was said to be reliance on overseas supply chains for solar cell technology. Silicon was identified by the Australian government as a critical mineral, given its importance in new economy technologies such as solar cells, semiconductors, optical alloys, energy storage batteries, etc. This is highlighted by the fact that in 2023 although Australia has a high level of solar cell application both domestic and commercial, there is only one Australian owned manufacturer based in the country and that firm assembles units imported from China. This firm operates with high levels of automation consistent with i4.0 technologies but is small in scale. China currently dominates the solar panel supply chain, hosting more than 70% of all downstream activity, and this includes between 85% and 97% of all ingot, wafers and solar cell manufacturing (How 2022a, 2022b). More generally, Miller (2022) notes that East Asia produces 90% of all memory chips, 75% of all processor (logic) chips and 80% of all silicon wafers. Miller (2022: xxv) argues that:

> …both Washington and Beijing are fixated on controlling the future of computing – and, to a frightening degree, that future is dependent on a small island that Beijing considers a renegade province and America has committed to defend in force.

The emerging Cold War between the US and China is scrambling global semiconductor supply chains, with countries racing to secure stable supplies. In light of these rapidly evolving geopolitical developments, South Korea announced it would build the world's largest chip factory with a $230 billion investment from Samsung in an attempt to further challenge Taiwan for the title of largest chip producer in the world (CNN 2023). For the US, however, chip manufacturing in both Taiwan and South Korea is considered 'vulnerable' to disruption from China and North Korean threats. Rebuilding a domestic chip manufacturing industry is becoming a US strategic priority. The US Government's Inflation Reduction Act provides US$280 billion to boost research and manufacturing of semiconductors in the US. Weaver (2022) argues that more than any other decision by Biden, this is intended to tilt the global balance of power in favour of the US. The implications of the US's Inflation Reduction Act for Australia's struggling manufacturing industry and efforts to revive it are significant. The Australian Financial Review's 2022 Energy & Climate Summit was told that the country could lose its advantage in renewable resources unless it matched incentives such as those on offer in the US and Europe (Ker and Wiggins 2022). Furthermore, the Act would provide US subsidies for every step of the hydrogen supply chain from renewable power to manufacture of electrolysers which would make competition from Australian based companies more than difficult (Energy Matters 2022). There is also an incentive for non-US manufacturers to relocate to, or set up manufacturing operations in the US to overcome restrictions. Developing an indigenous 'high tech' manufacturing industry in these circumstances will be more than difficult.

Renewable Energy – Great Expectations?

Beyond strategic concerns, claims regarding jobs and renewable energy are complex. In an earlier work (Rainnie and Dean 2021), commenting on several employment-focused organisations' policy responses to COVID-19, economic crisis and climate change, we argued that all largely reflected an 'ecological modernisation' framing – essentially, government-framed, market-led sustainable growth. Although focused mostly, if not entirely, on sustainability and job creation, all were firmly in the 'jobs-and-growth' camp. Many drew on the various claims for job creation that have been made in the name of sustainable development in general, and renewable energy in particular. Some have made important claims for job creation in regional Australia. These initiatives have had very little to say about i4.0 and complete silence on i5.0.

Echoing an emerging conventional wisdom, Ross Garnaut (2022) argued that new 'superpower industries' would disproportionately be in provincial and rural Australia, providing early growth of new forms of employment on a 'transformative scale'. An Accenture report (2021) prepared for the trade union movement, business peak bodies and ecological foundations in conjunction claimed that six clean export industry opportunities have the potential to generate $AU89 billion of gross value and 395,000 jobs for Australia in 2040. A study by UTS Institute for Sustainable Futures for the Clean Energy Council (2021) produced estimates for the growth of employment in renewable energy between 2020 and 2035 varying from 21,000 to 34,400. More recently, the Institute has calculated that to get Australia's power grid to 82% renewables by 2030 would require, in the first instance, at least 15,000 workers by 2025 amidst a skills shortage, an infrastructure boom and low levels of unemployment (Rutovitz et al. 2022). However, Ford Chief Executive Jim Farley has pointed out that electric vehicles need 40% fewer workers to assemble than cars and trucks powered by petrol, largely because battery vehicles have fewer parts and are easier to assemble.

Against this, our starting point is that, following Pearse and Bryant (2021: 2), the debate to date has tended to be very narrowly focused and with little engagement with i4.0 agendas:

> Too often debates about labour in energy transition focus narrowly on employment estimates for renewable versus fossil fuel industries ... [renewable industry] transitions involve significant reorganisations of labour and nature, and organised labour acts as a political force in shaping how those transitions unfold.

Pearse and Bryant (2021: 8) point to a more nuanced and spatially sensitive approach:

> Current studies of [renewable industries] employment provide evidence of how surplus value extraction strategies shape the quantity and quality of jobs across geographical space. Aggregate claims about job numbers conceal the differentiated and unequal distributions of work in the sector. The employment intensities in the [renewables] value chain are temporally uneven. [Renewable industry] labour is front loaded with the largest numbers in equipment manufacture, project development and construction and installation.

Hines et al. (2022: 27) also took a critical approach to these claims, putting them into a broader framework:

> Multiple crises and disruptions – climate disasters, the pandemic, geopolitical volatility, and supply chain interruptions – have together created the conditions for fresh rounds of state-capitalist development in regions. Viewed from a regional political-economic perspective, this is the latest phase in an extractivist, profit-orientated, and rent seeking mode of capitalism consistent with the settler-colonial experience... Responding to uncertainty and the decarbonisation imperative, governments have recalibrated modes of state-capitalist large-scale transformation in regional Australia. Aiming to secure mobile investment capital and promising jobs bonanzas in regions, governments and private capital are together forging deals and announcing pump-priming projects.

The low labour intensity of ongoing work in wind and solar utility maintenance and operations means that new rural jobs created are mostly in short bursts of temporary labour in project construction that have little to do with i4.0 advancements. There are further concerns about job quality and gender and racial disparities.

Conclusion

Since Federation, Australia has struggled to escape its position in a global extractivist relationship with emerging economies in Asia, particularly China. A commitment to free trade and neoliberal policies has made it difficult to reverse the declining industrial base and ongoing risks associated with extractivism. The militarisation of industry policy has been presented by the Australian government as an important opportunity to revitalise manufacturing industries and regions impacted by industrial decline. Australia's defence policy, however, is increasingly being defined by a slavish following of US foreign policy.

As we have argued in this chapter, this situation acts to foreshorten options open to Australian governments. This is particularly the case firstly, when governments automatically support US policy in Southeast Asia and elsewhere; and secondly, when they continue to support climate-destroying heavy extractive industries (coal, oil and gas, and iron ore) with a very high level of subsidy.

The rhetoric behind initially i4.0 and COVID-19-driven supply chain restructuring, whilst garnering government support in Australia, has done little to alter dominant patterns of organisation globally in manufacturing. The future is unsurprisingly contradictory. Growth in 'new economy' sectors is problematic in the face of global competition, particularly from the US and emerging economies in Southeast Asia. Employment in renewable sectors faces chronic skill and labour shortages in the short term, but massive differences between employment in construction and development phases versus subsequent operation and maintenance. The platforms are currently shedding jobs in historic numbers, and investment in robotics is mostly driven by labour shortages rather than straightforward job replacement or strategic visions driven by an i4.0 or i5.0 economy. Whilst these findings relate to developments in Australia, it is important to note that similar trends are likely to be found in others countries as they pursue their own efforts to rebuild a manufacturing base in a changed geo-political context.

References

AARC (2020). *Exploring Australian Sovereign Capability to Scale Up in Critical Times*. AARC Research Report No. 1. Canberra: Australian Army Research Centre.

ABS (2021). *Labour Force – Manufacturing Industry*. Canberra: Australian Bureau of Statistics.

Accenture (2021). *Future Charge: Building Australia's Battery Industries*. Perth: Future Batteries Industries Cooperative Research Centre.

AiGroup (2019). *Ai Group Head Defence and Industry Policy Kate Louis – Speaking Notes for ASPI International Conference*, Canberra, 14 June. Sydney: Australian Industry Group.

AITI (2021). *Manufacturing Transformation: High Value Manufacturing for the* 21st *Century*. Adelaide: Australian Industrial Transformation Institute, Flinders University of South Australia.

ASPI (2021). *The Cost of Defence 2020–2021 Part 2: ASPI 2020–21 Defence Budget Brief*. Canberra: Australian Strategic Policy Institute.

Clean Energy Council (2022). *Skilling the Energy Transition*. Melbourne: Clean Energy Council.

Clibborn, S., Lansbury, R.D. and Wright, C.F. (2016). 'Who killed the Australian automotive industry: the employers, government or trade unions?', *Economic Papers: A Journal of Applied Economics and Policy* 35(1): 2–15.

CNN (2023). 'South Korea to build 'world's largest' chip center with $230 billion investment from Samsung', *CNN*, 15 March, available online: https://edition.cnn.com/2023/03/15/tech/korea-chips-investment-hnk-intl/index.html

Commonwealth of Australia (2021). *Resources Technology and Critical Minerals Processing – National Manufacturing Priority Road Map*. Canberra: Commonwealth of Australia.

Coorey, P. (2020). 'Australia dangerously dependent on medical imports', *Australian Financial Review*, 18 February: https://www.afr.com/politics/federal/australia-dangerously-dependent-on-medical-imports-20200217-p541ej

CSIRO (2022). *Media Release: 'Australian Silicon Action Plan: A Blueprint for Jobs and Prosperity in Australia's Solar Future'*. Canberra: CSIRO Newsroom, 9 December.

Cunningham, S., Theilacker, M., Gahan, P., Callan, V. and Rainnie, A. (2016). *Skills and Capabilities for Australian Enterprise Innovation*. Melbourne: Report for the Australian Council of Learned Academies.

Dean, M. and Rainnie, A. (2020). 'Post COVID-19 policy responses to climate change: beyond capitalism?', *Labour & Industry* 31(4): 366–386.

Dean, M., Rainnie, A., Stanford, J. and Nahum, D. (2021). 'Industrial policy making after COVID-19: manufacturing innovation and sustainability', *Economic and Labour Relations Review* 32(2): 283–303.

Deloitte (2017). *The Changing Face of Manufacturing*. New York: Deloitte.

Dixson-Declève, S., Balland, P-A., Bria, F., Charveriat, C., Dunlop, K., Giovannini, E., Tataj, D., Hidalgo, C., Huang, A., Isaksson, D., Martins, F., Mir, M., Roca, A., Morlet, A., Renda, S. and Schwaag Serger, S. (2022). *Industry 5.0: A Transformative Vision for Europe*. ESIR Policy Brief No 3. Directorate General for Research and Innovation. Brussels: European Commission.

Energy Matters (2022). 'US law threatens Australia's global hydrogen superpower ambitions', 25 November. https://www.energymatters.com.au/renewable-news/us-law-threatens-australias-global-hydrogen-superpower-ambitions/

FBICRC (2020). *Li-ion Battery Cathode Manufacture in Australia: A Scene Setting Project*. Report, Future Battery Industries Cooperative Research Council. Canberra: Department of Industry, Innovation and Science, Australian Government.

Fernandes, C. (2021). 'The rules-based order', *Arena Quarterly* 7: 12–21.

Fernandes, C. (2022). *Subimperial Power*. Melbourne: Melbourne University Press.

Garnaut, R. (ed) (2022). *The Superpower Transformation*. Melbourne: La Trobe University Press.

Goodman, J. and Worth, D. (2007). 'The minerals boom and Australia's resources curse', *Journal of Australian Political Economy* 61: 201–219.

Hines, A., Gibson, C. and Carr, C. (2022). 'Green hydrogen regions', *Regional Studies* 58, 8 1618–1635

How, B. (2022a). Pilbara lithium pant', *InnovationAus*, 11 November. https://www.innovationaus.com/250m-loan-for-pilbara-lithium-plant/

How, B. (2022b). 'CSIRO calls for domestic silicon, solar cell manufacturing boost', *InnovationAus*, 9 December.

IMD (2021). *World Competitiveness Ranking 2021 – Country Profile: Australia*. Lausanne: Institute for Management Development.

Ker, P. and Wiggins, J. (2022). 'Albanese must match US on clean energy, Debelle warns', *Australian Financial Review*, 10 October.

Kraaijenbrink, J. (2022). 'What is Industry 5.0 and will it radically change your business strategy?', *Forbes,* 24 May.

Mazzucato, M. (2021). *Mission Economy*. London: Allen Lane.

McKinsey & Co (2022). *McKinsey Technology Trends Outlook 2022: Research Overview*. New York: McKinsey & Co.

Middleton, K. (2021a). 'Australia's big spending on war machines', *The Saturday Paper*, 19–25 July: 10.

Middleton, K. (2021b). 'A militarization of the public service', *The Saturday Paper*, 24–30 July: 8.

Miller, C. (2022). *Chip War*. New York: Simon & Schuster.

Pearse, G. (2009). *Quarry Vision: Coal, Climate Change and the End of the Resources Boom*. Melbourne: Quarterly Essay.

Pearse, R. and Bryant, G. (2021). 'Labour in transition: a value-theoretical approach to renewable energy labour', *Environment and Planning E: Nature and Space* 5(4): 1872–1894.

Productivity Commission (2021). *Vulnerable Supply Chains: Interim Report*. Canberra: Australian Government Productivity Commission, Commonwealth of Australia.

Rainnie, A. (2021a). 'i4.0, 3D Printing, deglobalisation and new manufacturing clusters: the view from Australia', *Economic and Labour Relations Review* 32(1): 115–133.

Rainnie, A. (2021b). 'Technology and deglobalisation: a sceptical view', *Futures of Work* 18. https://futuresofwork.co.uk/2021/03/16/industry-4-0-3d-printing-and-deglobalisation-a-sceptical-view/

Rainnie, A. and Dean, M. (2019). 'Against industry 4.0: putting the fourth industrial revolution in its place', *Futures of Work* 7. https://futuresofwork.co.uk/2019/05/24/against-industry-4-0-putting-the-fourth-industrial-revolution-in-its-place/

Rainnie, A. and Dean, M. (2020). 'Industry 4.0 and the future of quality work in the global digital economy', *Labour & Industry* 30(1):1–18.

Rainnie, A. and Dean, M. (2022). 'i4.0 and Australian manufacturing industry', in Montague, A., Connell, J., Nankervis, A., & Burgess, J. (eds), *The Fourth Industrial Revolution. What Does It Mean for Australian Industry*? Singapore: Springer Nature. 39–56.

Rainnie, A. and Dean, M. (2021). Post Covid-19 policy responses to climate change: Beyond capitalism?. Labour & Industry 31(4): 366–386. DOI: 10.1080.

Rainnie, A., Herod, A. and McGrath-Champ, S. (2020). 'Global pandemic networks: COVID-19 and international business', *Futures of Work* 13. https://futuresofwork.co.uk/2020/05/07/global-pandemic-networks-covid-19-and-international-business/

Roberts, P. (2019). 'Manufacturing decline leaves Australia in the third world of exporters', *Australian Manufacturing Forum*, 14 October.

Rutovitz, J., Briggs, C. and Langdon, R. (2022). 'To clean up Australias power grid, were going to need many thousand more skilled workers – and fast', *Conversation*, 14 December, 2022.

Sadiq, S. and Nirmalathas, T. (2021). 'Digital tech is the future, but a new report shows Australia risks being left in the past', *The Conversation*, 21 September.

Sartal, A., Bellas, R., Mejías, A.M. and García-Collado, A. (2020). 'The sustainable manufacturing concept, evolution and opportunities within Industry 4.0: a literature review', *Advances in Mechanical Engineering* 12(5): 1–17.

Snell, D., Dean, M. and Rainnie, A. (2022). 'Militarising Australian industrial policy', *Futures of Work* 21. https://futuresofwork.co.uk/2022/02/10/militarising-australian-industrial-policy-a-dead-end/

The Economist (2022). 'Marginal revolution', 18–24 September: 58–59.

The White House (2021). *Building Resilient Supply Chains, Revitalizing American Manufacturing, and Fostering Based Growth*. Washington, DC: The White House.

Tooze, A. (2022). 'Defining polycrisis – from crisis pictures to the crisis matrix', *Chartbook*, #130, available online: https://adamtooze.substack.com/p/chartbook-130-defining-polycrisis

Upchurch, M. (2020). 'Is there a new extractive capitalism?', *International Socialism* 168: 109–136.

USGS (2020). *Mineral Commodities Summary 2020*. US Geological Survey, Washington, DC: US Department of the Interior.

Weaver, J. (2022). 'Clampdown on chip exports is the most consequential US move against China yet', *The Conversation*, 25 October.

Weller, S. and O'Neill, P. (2014). 'De-industrialisation, financialisation and Australia's macro-economic trap', *Cambridge Journal of Regions, Economy and Society* 7: 509–526.

Recommendations for Further Reading

Dean, M. and Rainnie, A. (2020). 'Post COVID-19 policy responses to climate change: beyond capitalism?', *Labour & Industry 31*(4): 366–386.

Dean, M., Rainnie, A., Stanford, J. and Nahum, D. (2021). 'Industrial policy making after COVID-19: manufacturing innovation and sustainability, *Economic and Labour Relations Review 32*(2): 283–303.

Rainnie, A. (2021). 'Technology and deglobalisation: a sceptical view', *Futures of Work* 18. https://futuresofwork.co.uk/2021/03/16/industry-4-0-3d-printing-and-deglobalisation-a-sceptical-view/

Rainnie, A. and Dean, M. (2019). 'Against industry 4.0: putting the fourth industrial revolution in its place', *Futures of Work 7*. https://futuresofwork.co.uk/2019/05/24/against-industry-4-0-putting-the-fourthindustrial-revolution-in-its-place/

Snell, D., Dean, M. and Rainnie, A. (2022). 'Militarising Australian industrial policy', *Futures of Work* 21. https://futuresofwork.co.uk/2022/02/10/militarising-australian-industrial-policy-a-dead-end/

19

A MEANS TO AN END? THE ROLE OF TECHNOLOGY IN GROWTH AND POST-GROWTH FUTURES OF AGRIFOOD WORK IN A EUROPEAN CONTEXT

Constantine Manolchev, David Watson, Laura A. Colombo, Patrick Elf and James Scott Vandeventer[1]

Introduction: Food Regimes

Food has been a central part of human society since the dawn of time. The need to provide food was a core historical focus of labour, eventually becoming formalised in the many forms of work – from farming and processing to transport and retail – that comprise modern agrifood systems. Food is also political; its production and consumption are debated, contested and determined as part of what can be described as a 'food regime'.

Food Regime Theory (Friedman and McMichael, 1989) recognises the complex processes through which agriculture aids the accumulation of capital across time and space in the production of food and other commodities (McMichael, 2009). This foregrounds how the intensification of agriculture through mechanisation and chemical inputs has hugely increased yields, while seeking to realise greater surplus value through commodity agriculture and the exploitation of a dwindling labour base. For example, Food Regime Theory conceptualises the rapid and problematic development of processed food and expansion in fast food outlets in terms of the opportunities offered by excessive commodity production, notably corn, soy and more latterly palm oil. The development of food regimes therefore broadly reflects different stages of capitalism: from colonial expansion to the post-war acceleration to the dawn of neoliberalism in the 1980s. The food regime lens highlights the ways in which agrifood systems have historically developed according to a wider, capitalist logic of efficient production, and thereby contributed to multiple forms of ecological degradation. Further, agrifood systems are inextricably linked not only to the exploitation of nature, but also to the alienation of human labour. Food production and consumption disconnect people from the environment and one another through production relations and technologies that predominantly concentrate power in the hands of capital and close down opportunities for meaningful labour (Marx, 1959; Watson, 2021). Despite such negative environmental and human impacts, current systems are,

DOI: 10.4324/9781003327561-26

paradoxically, utopian. They are driven by a blind faith in technological advancement as a key measure of progress; a belief that 'untrammelled' technology will eventually solve all our predicaments creating an earthly paradise (Jonas, 1984: 184).

Agrifood today is rooted in past innovations designed to increase efficiency and growth. Prominent examples include the introduction of new crop varieties capable of producing higher yields and increased use of chemical and industrial inputs to supplement human labour (Fuglie, 2007). Yet, such innovations have led to a number of dysfunctional and paradoxical consequences for both human societies and the wider ecosystem. The abuse of fertilisers and pesticides has caused soil degradation, loss of biodiversity and disruption to the nitrogen and phosphorous cycles, which support life on Earth (Rockstrom et al., 2009). Monitoring technologies and robots have improved work efficiency and yields; yet, hunger and undernourishment remain a constant problem as technologies fail to address inequalities of distribution and access (Alexandratos and Bruinsma, 2012: 5–6). There is increased reliance on food banks at the same time as a rising global obesity epidemic, highlighting trends towards increased cost and decreased availability of fresh nutritious food alongside calorie-rich but nutritionally poor (and aggressively marketed) processed food (Caraher and Dowler, 2014). Technology has removed and improved some forms of agrifood work, yet most of those labouring in the agrifood system are migrants and those with little choice or resources, who are poorly paid and exploited (Besky and Brown, 2015).

Although such 'developments' are driven by seemingly dominant growth approaches to food production and consumption, there are also counter-practices. Such instances, which we refer to as 'post-growth', are not only organised differently but also strive for teleologically different outcomes – more just and sustainable futures after (hence post-) growth. These alternative practices are rooted in the failures of the existing food regime (McMichael, 2009). In other words, the current food regime has already sown the seeds of a different future, distinct but currently intertwined with the present one (Watson, 2020). These counter-movements can be discerned in the growth of agroecology as a basis for ultimately transforming the food system to achieve sustainability (Gliessman, 2016); significant interest in localising food systems (Enthoven and Van den Broeck, 2021) and movements around food sovereignty, food democracy and civic food networks that seek to democratise the agrifood system (Renting, 2012).

In the remainder of the chapter, we examine the role of technology in case studies illustrating instances of both growth and post-growth in the UK's agrifood system. We first present the case of Aurelia Acres (all place and personal names in the chapter are pseudonyms), a daffodil farm, to outline the contours of the prevailing agrifood system, where growth and profit remain the central tasks of the sector. Then, we examine the potential to move away from the imperative of growth by drawing on several case studies of alternative food networks, which show how technology used in support of non-exploitative practices and collaborative relationships can foster conviviality, ecological production, and meaningful work. Throughout, we consider the extent to which technologies in agrifood can contribute towards an 'imperative of responsibility' (Jonas, 1984: 191), critiquing the 'immodesty of utopia' and replacing it with a modesty of goals (ibid.). We conclude with a reflection on how different possibilities might (re)shape our imaginings of future agrifood systems.

The Failings of Growth: 'This Work Is Not for Everyone'

> The conditions are hard: manual labour, field-work for approximately seven hours a day, six days a week. It doesn't matter if it's raining or if it's cold. At each induction session for new workers, I make one thing clear: this work is not for everyone. When new workers join us, I

> show them the caravans, the fields, the daffodils and tell them: the choice is yours, are you going to stay, or are you going to go back home?

This is how Ivan, a human resources (HR) manager at Aurelia Acres, a daffodil farm in the South West of England described the field and warehouse work for over 300 migrant workers, farming 4,000 acres of land, work that you must be 'fit' for. Himself a migrant who had a degree in Economics in his native Bulgaria, Ivan rose through the flower-picking ranks to oversee the whole migrant workforce.

This is perhaps not quite what the Government had in mind when they put in place plans for a highly skilled agrifood sector. The sector strategy envisaged using technological innovation to safeguard the sector's competitive advantage and further develop sustainable food systems, promising well-paid jobs for skilled workers (Food Partnership, 2010: 6). In reality, regardless of how qualified the workers are, many agrifood jobs both in the UK and globally continue to offer manual work, and typically require no previous experience or qualifications (Agar and Manolchev, 2020). Globally, the agrifood system employs 70% of all workers in low-income countries, 40% in middle-income countries and as little as 3% in high-income countries (Böhm et al., 2020). Although this offers entry-level, low-skill positions for many, the work carries a series of ethical and welfare risks. For the UK workers, some of these risks – like the drowning of 23 Chinese cockle-pickers in Morecambe Bay, in North West England (GLAA, 2019) – are disastrous. At the same time, everyday work in the agrifood system tends to be both casual and seasonal (Scherrer and Verma, 2018), exhibiting a significant gender gap in pay (ILO, 2016) and the worst health and safety record of all UK sectors in 2021–2022 (HSE, 2023). In addition, global supply chains separate workers (and consumers) from the 'fruits' of their labour, increase the ecological footprint of food production and weaken the stability of the entire food system (Watson, 2017).

At the same time, agrifood is a critical sector for the UK economy, with a total value of £115 billion in 2021 (DEFRA, 2022), in which technology plays an increasingly fundamental role. For instance, robots are increasingly deployed to monitor crops, automate menial physical tasks, spray insecticides, harvest and so on (Lytridis et al., 2021). This use of technology often amounts to the 'quantification' of the working day: movement and productivity-tracking software can 'invisibly manage' workers outputs, ensuring the latter are monitored and under real time surveillance (Moore, 2017: 3). Such developments marginalise the role of the workers in the production process and commodify them. As a result, workers are not only alienated (Marx, 1959) in their work by the use of technology that removes them from the social and natural context (Marx, 1959), but they also become objects of technological manipulation as they are subject to management, monitoring and surveillance by cutting-edge devices (Jonas, 1984).

This may seem disturbing and even dystopian to some observers. Writing in the late twentieth century, German-born philosopher Hans Jonas (1984) understood the implications of such developments, arguing that humans hold a metaphysical responsibility *beyond* self-interest because of their technologies, which extend human power in ways that have significant impact on, and within, the biosphere. As a result, Jonas (1984:8) demanded a rethinking of our very basis for ethics, which needed not only to attend to the good of current generations, but also to account for the time-span between generations, and for current actions' future impact on both humans and non-human species. This led Jonas to issue an ethical call to "[a]ct so that the effects of your action are not destructive of the future possibility of such life" (Jonas, 1984:10).

At present, the prevailing food regime does not align with Jonas' ethical imperative. We observed this at Aurelia Acres, which we visited as part of a research project involving four weeks of participant observation, interviews and archival research. The farm, an independent holding deep in England's countryside, had implemented a system to track the hourly outputs of each migrant worker. Ivan, whom we met earlier, explained the evolution of Aurelia Acres' use of technology:

> In the past, we used to have a pretend currency. Each worker picked flowers and put them in a tray which, when complete, was taken to the team leader who was supervising the field-work. The team leader would then give the worker cardboard money, which was like 'monopoly' money and the worker would stack his or her tray. (…) Now each worker is issued with a roll, where there are bar-code stickers. Each sticker is put on a completed tray and the supervisors scans it with a hand-held device. Each device is connected to our computer database and we can track worker productivity in real time.

Here, technology infiltrates the everyday management of agrifood work. Supervisors also performed spot-checks of worker trays throughout the day. Each supervisor was armed (both in the physical sense of carrying, and as a symbolic indicator of authority and control), with a hand-held device loaded with the Crop-Picker software, through which individual barcodes were scanned. Each label was a representation of the worker's output, and her or his labour power (Marx, 2004). Checking and scanning barcode stickers was a step away from scanning people.

This use of technology to organise and even hardwire the daily rhythms of work (Reid-Musson, 2017) alienated workers in unexpected ways. Rob, a Romanian fieldworker, felt the dehumanising impact of technology and spoke of 'going on auto-pilot':

> During the day you are constantly counting – one, three, five stems. Ten - good, you have a bunch. Start again, one, two, three. Before long you catch yourself counting your steps from the lane [where he is picking daffodils] to the tractor. 10, 15, 30 steps there, then 29 steps on the way back. One day I was in [the supermarket] and I caught myself counting the boxes of cereal on the shelf.

Our conversations with Ivan, the HR manager, offered no insight into his thoughts on the enforced 'rhythmatisation' and alienation Rob and other workers experienced. Rob was acutely aware of the farm's dependence on the daffodil crop, the quality of the soil and the seasons. However, these were described as symbiotic, rather than exploitative, relationships. If workers did not pick the daffodils, the flowers would rot. Ivan saw this outcome as something of a subversion of the workers' duty. In this sense, technology was a force for good: monitoring worker outputs and tracking trends in their daily performance helped with Aurelia Acres' stewardship of the crops. It helped Ivan identify those who were struggling and allowed him to match them up with more experienced picking partners. To the extent that concerns over workers like Rob's well-being are present, they are clearly guided by the aim of improving employees' welfare and their environment to achieve greater productivity and ultimately profit (Watson et al., 2023). Ivan had learned Romanian and Russian, in addition to his fluent English and native Bulgarian, for the sole purpose of improving communication with workers and building trust. Workers could negotiate leave, contract duration and even rate of pay with farm managers, based on their satisfactory performance and good conduct. Ivan had also sought to create a sense of community at the farm, going as far as making ethnic food products available for purchase at the caravan sites where workers live. In Figure 19.1, he wears his traditional, Bulgarian 'martenitsa' bracelet, made up of interwoven white and red wool and symbolising natural fertility. Undoubtedly, this showed a connection to his own roots, but perhaps also to workers: a means of symbolic communication that, despite his authority, he was 'one of them'.

Aurelia Acres' use of technology did not stop with the optimisation of extraction processes, but was visible in other areas, as well. Take flower processing, which followed the rhythmic and barcode tracked flower-picking activity, where daffodils were sorted into bunches with different stem-lengths and different numbers of stems. Two of the workers we shadowed during fieldwork, Dana and Stella, also came from Bulgaria and worked in the warehouse. Although, as far as we could see, gender was not a strong determinant in being a successful flower-picker, they had found the job taxing and difficult. As a result, the farm had agreed to let them work on the flower sorting conveyor belts.

Flower sorting, the main activity in Aurelia Acres' warehouse, bears many similarities to flower picking. In the field, the natural cycles of morning, noon and evening were replaced by the linearity of clock time (Nash, 2018; Edensor, 2010), where worker productivity was monitored in real time by the number of scanned crates. There were no shift patterns – workers picked or packed flowers until the job was done. In the warehouse, where Dana and Stella worked, it was the conveyor belt with its metronome snaps and crackles that measured this productive, clock time. A forklift loaded crates, full of picked flowers, from the tractor trailer and placed them at the end of each conveyor belt. From there, the supervisor would carry a crate to each 'station' (visible through the table at the left-hand edge of Figure 19.2) and the sorting work would commence. Stella viewed this as a collegial process, which was based on collaboration and allowed each table to work as a team, everybody paid at the same rate and working together.

Dana, however, had a different view. We chatted while she was repackaging bunches of five daffodil stems to bunches of seven, after the client supermarket changed their requirements. She pointed to workers having little to no agency over how their day was organised and what they did. Mid-morning and lunch were 'natural' rest periods Dana was accustomed to but unable to take a break:

> I never get a chance to have my break on time and it makes me so mad. It's 2 pm! I need to have my lunch and I need to have a cigarette, but I can't. Nothing is ever certain, and you never know when and at what time you're going to be able to take your break. There is absolutely no point trying to speak to anyone because nobody cares, and nobody pays attention. Nobody listens.

In other words, work in the warehouse followed the capitalist tendency to apply clock time (Kolinjivadi et al., 2020) on natural rhythms, placing workers in subservience to the mechanical pace of the conveyor belt. In turn, work periods were measured by quotas and required level of output, without consideration of workers' needs.

Technology thus made the flower-picking and sorting processes of workers more efficient while exposing workers to the 'invisible eye' of management (Bhave, 2014). It gave muddy, wind-swept daffodil fields a panoptic character (cf. Foucault, 1980), with workers too preoccupied with the tasks at hand to think about their movements being tracked and quantified at all times. The acquired habit of counting, whether stems or crates – or indeed cereal boxes – became an embodied element of workers' lives. As we saw, daily life in the warehouse was no different. Here, it was client quotas and production targets that dominated and overtook physical, bodily needs. But, perhaps the flattening of natural cycles into a linear, clock time, countable in the rhythmic clangs of the conveyor belt, imposed equality on the workers?

We discovered that even the consolation prize of equal pay for equal work was not available. A shorter conveyor belt around one of the corners in the spacious warehouse was reserved for the experienced, high-speed workers, offering an opportunity for accelerated yet harder work in exchange for an improved hourly pay rate. 'People can ask to be put on it but not everyone lasts', Gemma, one of the warehouse supervisors explained. 'People prefer to work at a slower pace and

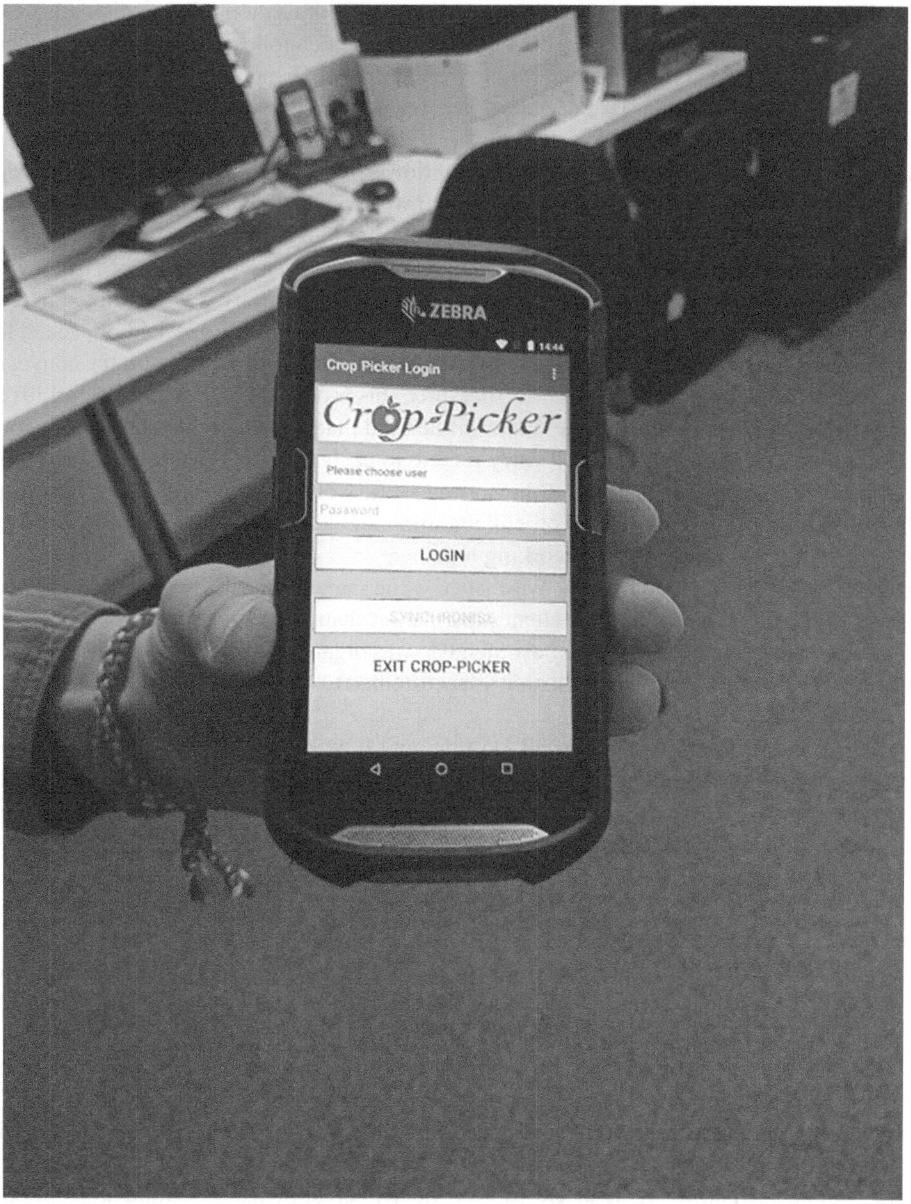

Figure 19.1 Ivan showing a hand-held scanning device running the 'Crop-picker' software, martenitsa around his wrist

Source: Image from author.

Figure 19.2 Dana, wearing a blue hoodie under her high-visibility jacket, is processing a tray of daffodils

Source: Image from author.

talking to those at their station, even occasionally, helps to pass the time'. This explained what felt so intuitively strange and unnatural at the higher-speed belt – all the stations were quiet.

The Responsibility of Post-growth: 'There Is a Different Attitude'

> It's a real sense of achievement, it's different [from getting] some food from the supermarket or something and you just eat (...).If you have an entire plate of food that is all yours and you've put all the work into it (...), there is a different attitude towards the actual meal. And you appreciate it more and everything just tastes nicer, that's probably because also it's fresher (...), it's just a sense of achievement and pride in general that you've put all your work into this.

The previous section revealed technology's use to continually drive productivity forward, at the expense of working conditions and the workers themselves. The above quote from Janet, a participant in a community-supported agriculture (CSA) project in the East of England, provokes an alternative agrifood imaginary. It envisages an agrifood system not driven by the pursuit of growth, where the logic of technology-productivity growth is subverted. As we shall see, technology can instead be an enabler of human purpose, which is inclusive of, rather than in competition with, nature (Jonas, 1984: 32).

In sketching some of the potentialities of a post-growth agrifood system, we draw on data collected from two research projects examining three alternative food networks: Green Gardens, Hazel Haven and Tangled Trees. Green Gardens is a community garden in the East of England, where people work together tending to the garden and producing food. Hazel Haven, also in the East of England, is a CSA scheme bringing together 20 families who exchange money and their labour for a regular share of produce. Tangled Trees is a network of social agricultural cooperatives (SACs) in the South of Italy, combining food production with training and work integration of vulnerable individuals (including those with a disability, mental health conditions and so on).

In all three cases, agrifood practices embraced a radical shift in humanity's approach to economy, society and culture as well as humanity's relationship to nature and the planet. These align with a post-growth vision (Jackson, 2021), where the ultimate purpose of economic activity is not productivity, efficiency or profit, but well-being (Büchs and Koch, 2017). In this approach to (sustainable) well-being, human and environmental needs and priorities are interlinked, and framed in the wider context of environmental limits (Elf et al., 2022). Sustainable well-being moves beyond subjective individuality), and the related notion that well-being is an individual goal achieved through the consumption of products and services. Against this misplaced fulfilment or warped idealisation of consumer culture (Sointu, 2005), sustainable well-being embraces collective and sufficiency-oriented practices of 'being well' in health, work, creativity, fulfilment and more (Jackson, 2021).

The broadness of sustainable well-being as a goal versus the narrowness of growth means that post-growth practices emerge in diverse organisational forms, driven by varied aims. Despite the challenges for small organisations, the numbers of CSAs in the UK continue to increase, as do the amount of community gardens and, in Italy, of SACs (which are specific to the Italian context; Colombo et al., 2023). The COVID-19 pandemic has strengthened this trend though increased appreciation of connection to nature and the need to prioritise well-being and community support. More widely, there has been sustained interest in the possibility of more local place-based, community embedded and ecologically conscious forms of food production and consumption to address problems in the wider food system (Böhm et al., 2022; Watson, 2020).

The experiences of working in these alternative spaces are not governed by profit maximisation and the continual need to conform with demanding production deadlines. As a result, the use of technology is selective and based on its ability to deliver benefits (e.g. enhanced connection to the farm ecosystem, improved relationship with other CSAs and diversification to reach breakeven) in support of more modest goals and purposeful humility (Jonas, 1984; Elf et al., 2022). This fundamentally different role of technology, and its relation to an enhanced connection to the farm ecosystem, is reflected in a field diary entry made during an 18-month ethnographic study at Green Gardens and Hazel Haven:

> The hot weather seemed perfect for scything to me (…). I stopped periodically to sharpen the blade, and when a frog jumped out of a clump of grass I was about to scythe; it narrowly avoided becoming a brasserie dish. As I was relocating the frog it made me wonder how it might have fared had we been attacking the weeds with an industrial mower or herbicide.

Such experiences are at odds with the pressures of productivity observed at the daffodil farm. Here, there was no productivity-tracking software, nor the control operated through the scanning of barcodes. Unlike the quantification of the daffodil workers, who were conditioned to see the world through numbers (in other words, productivity metrics), the Green Gardens member relates to nature through the simple technology of a hand tool; they are not alienated from the context of production and their production practices are conducive to ecological and human well-being. As Jonas would put it, the effects of their actions are compatible with the permanence of ecosystem biodiversity as part of a 'genuine human life' (Jonas, 1984). They are grounded in the reality of production and its consequences, changing their relationship with the food that will eventually be produced. This echoes the earlier quote from Janet, standing in marked contrast to more conventional modes of food provisioning where the consumer is oblivious to the externalised costs of production.

This is not to suggest that a post-growth logic insists on the simplification of technology in the food system. At Tangled Trees in Italy, food processing included multiple activities that are assisted by the use of various machines and technologies. The manner in which this work was undertaken in terms of worker power and control, however, was very different. During the 11 months of fieldwork, including interviews, we observed an attempt to distribute work on a collective basis, in a way that was mutually agreed and accepted by all:

> The day starts with the cooperative gathering in the barn, where Enea has written the jobs for the day on a flipchart. Every task is assigned to a 'champion', who has the responsibility to coordinate work, teach those who are new to the field and make sure that everyone is ok. The champion is often a vulnerable member of the coop. The rest of the team choose a task for the day and sign themselves up (…). Some members return to work in the afternoon, others return to their accommodation (which are managed by the cooperative) or are engaged in lighter tasks.

As a result, the work is not experienced as alienating and dehumanising but rather empowering (Watson, 2020). It pointed to the potentiality inherent to sustainable well-being in practice – a symbiotic and mutually beneficial relationship between people, and people and nature (Elf et al., 2022). Undoubtedly, the experience of greater sustainable well-being was made possible because work was organised around the natural rhythms of a day, rather than sped-up to match the speeds of clock time and mechanised conveyor belts.

Giordano, another 'champion' at Tangled Trees, described how working in an environment focused on sustainable well-being felt:

> Here they make me feel […] that I can manage. How can I tell you? They don't get me to 'command'. […] I feel responsible. I mean, they make me participate. […] I feel at home, I feel important and I feel looked after.

Once again, we observed the stark contrast between work at the daffodil farm and at alternative approaches to agrifood like Tangled Trees. Aurelian Acres enforced a clear hierarchical structure, representative of work organised according to for-profit principles, inadvertently – or inevitably – leading to power inequalities. At the daffodil farm, there was the farm owner, followed by the HR team, of which Ivan was a member. Then, there were the supervisors, and finally, the flower-pickers and sorters. CSAs and SACs asserted an alternative structure, resilient enough to co-exist as a niche with(in) the dominant capitalist-growth paradigm (Vandeventer et al., 2019).

A direct comparison between the opposing approaches to organisational structure was presented by Sarah, a Hazel Haven member, who compared their day-job experience to that of working on the farm.

> I think generally it's, we're more in tune with each other in terms of what needs to be done and stuff like that and so when somebody asks you to do something you think yes that's sensible I'll do it. Whereas at work it's not always the case that somebody they'll ask you to do something out of their own ignorance and they can be a bit uppity if you say, 'I don't think that's the right thing to do' and they just sort of demand that you do it anyway (…).

This internalisation of responsibility provided each CSA participant with agency and choice, which was not imposed on the environment or others but negotiated. Duty was shared and technology used by workers when appropriate. Gone was the prerogative of speed and efficiency, having been replaced with reflection and consideration, driven by felt and enacted responsibility. Shared work in this alternative dimension of post-growth was, however, still hard work. Participants in Green Gardens, Hazel Haven and Tangled Trees tended to their natural environment with the same dedication as flower-pickers in the daffodil farm, yet the alternative food network environment offered conditions circumscribed by empathic and participatory 'managing' (Smith and Reid, 2018). As a result, the availability and use of technology was proportionate and appropriate to the context.

For example, Tangled Trees had access to the same processing plant equipment as conventional agrifood businesses, but this technology was used in line with Jonas' (1984) responsibility imperative. Their processing plant was frequently rented out or simply made available to other organisations in the network. Contrary to a dominant growth paradigm, the plant was not their exclusive technology, a factor of production that increased competitiveness nor a management device, but a means to a different end. It was a tool, which could create community, generate conviviality and strengthen and scale the overall alternative food network (Colombo et al., 2023) (Figure 19.3).

Not externalising responsibility to others meant that challenges had to be faced in the present: pursuing goals other than profit maximisation meant that alternative food network members like Green Gardens, Hazel Haven and Tangled Trees had less investment power than big corporations. Alongside the income they generate to sustain themselves, each relied partly on philanthropy or public grants, which can be difficult to access. Nevertheless, participants were not commodified by technology and always playing catch-up with technologies' demands, like the flow of the conveyor belt. Social relations were woven together through the work rather than work interrupting social relations, as we saw in the case of the daffodil farm. This was a recurring theme throughout our interviews. For example, a Tangled Trees member reflects:

> The best part is that you are not alone. You are always in company – and when there is a problem you can ask.

Figure 19.3 Members at Tangled Trees making tomato preserves in the coop's production plant

Source: Image from author.

And a Green Garden volunteer indicates:

> I get outdoor activity, um fresh air, um meet friends, uh yeah. I live on my own so I've got no, not exactly, no communication, you meet your neighbours, but you just say hello, isn't the weather awful, whatever yeah. Down here, we're in each other's company a lot longer so you can tell people your troubles and they'll listen to you.

The loneliness and isolation of the timed, constantly under surveillance and invisibly managed Aurelia Acres worker were not so palpable in this post-growth potentiality. On a Saturday at Green Gardens you met familiar faces, walked past people ploughing, waved to those fixing their barns or digging. Gone was the constant drone of tractors and processing machinery, unpunctuated by human voices. Instead, our participants were surrounded by the seasonal cacophony of chatters, tree-rustlings, bird-chirps, foot-shuffles, shovel-scrapes and wind-chimes – all the noises produced by humans in their natural habitat.

Conclusion

We have sought to provide a glimpse into possible growth and post-growth futures of the agrifood system. We are unapologetic in our endorsement of a shift towards the latter, which places sustainable well-being, one that is interconnected with nature, at the heart of production and consumption. Such a shift is not without its issues. When employing workers and utilising the same technologies as other enterprises pursuing growth, current post-growth practices need to be viable in order to survive and secure decent work standards. Equally, post-growth organisations must navigate the wider institutional environment which rewards larger scale enterprises geared towards commodity production (as reflected in agricultural subsidies payments, for example).

The difference between growth and post-growth approaches may appear subtle, but is important, nonetheless. Growth offers controlled and restrictive practices through worker commodification and surveillance towards efficiency. Post-growth offers autonomy through the responsible use of technology. It considers the impact on the user, the natural environment, and future generations. Growth offers better earning opportunities for those with access to technology and the skills to use it. Post-growth counters with an opportunity for a more liveable world and a better life.

Crucially, as our case studies show, the current agrifood system contains the conditions for its own transformation. Such a transformation can restore dignity, conviviality and socioecological justice to the future of agrifood work. In this way, work, appropriately aided (rather than organised) by technology, becomes a means to a different end: a way to strengthen social relations, build trust and support both individual and ecological restorative processes.

Note

1 All authors are part of the MEND (Management Educators Navigating Degrowth) collective.

Management Educators Navigating Degrowth (MEND) began as a collective of early career academics exploring ideas and practices of post-growth and degrowth in our pedagogies. We sought to question whether businesses and managers should pursue growth at-all-costs, bringing these debates into management classrooms. We are now bringing others in to form a network of educators interested in what post-growth and degrowth means for management education.

References

Agar, C. C., & Manolchev, C. (2020). "Migrant labour as space: rhythmanalysing the agri-food industry", *Organization*, 27(2), 251–271.

Alexandratos, N., & Bruinsma, J. (2012). "World agriculture towards 2030/2050: the 2012 revision". Available at: https://ageconsearch.umn.edu/record/288998/

Besky, S., & Brown, S. (2015). "Looking for work: placing labor in food studies", *Labor Studies in Working-Class History of the Americas*, 12(1–2), 19–43.

Bhave, D. P. (2014). "The invisible eye? Electronic performance monitoring and employee job performance", *Personnel Psychology*, 67(3), 605–635.

Böhm, S., Spierenburg, M., & Lang, T. (2020). "Fruits of our labour: work and organisation in the global food system", *Organization*, 27(2), 195–212.

Böhm, S., Sandover, R., Pascucci, S., Colombo, L., Jackson, S., & Lobley, M. (2022). "Chapter 10: Circular food systems: a blueprint for regenerative innovations in a regional UK context". In Alexander et al. (2022) (Eds.) *A Handbook of the Circular Economy*. Cheltenham: Edward Elgar Publishing. Available at: https://www.elgaronline.com/view/book/9781800880269/book-part-9781800880269-20.xml (Accessed: 27 February 2023).

Büchs, M., & Koch, M. (2017). *Postgrowth and Wellbeing: Challenges to Sustainable Welfare*. Cham: Springer.

Caraher, M., & Dowler, E. (2014). *Food for Poorer People: Conventional and 'Alternative'* Transgressions? Aldershot: Ashgate.

Colombo, L. A., Bailey, A. R., & Gomes, M. V. (2023). "Scaling in a post-growth era: learning from social agricultural cooperatives", *Organization*, 0(0). Available at: https://doi.org/10.1177/13505084221147480

DEFRA (2022). *Agriculture in the United Kingdom*. Available at: https://www.gov.uk/government/statistics/agriculture-in-the-united-kingdom-2021/chapter-14-the-food-chain#:~:text=In%202020%20the%20agri%2Dfood%20sector%20contributed%20%C2%A3115bn%20to,for%2011%25%20of%20the%20sector

Edensor T. (Ed.) (2010) *Geographies of Rhythm: Nature, Place, Mobilities and Bodies*. Aldershot: Ashgate.

Elf, P., Isham, A., & Jackson, T. (2022). *Self-Transcendent Experiences and Sustainable Prosperity*. CUSP Working Paper No. 31. Guildford: Centre for the Understanding of Sustainable Prosperity. Available at: www.cusp.ac.uk/publications

Enthoven, L., & Van den Broeck, G. (2021). "Local food systems: reviewing two decades of research", *Agricultural Systems*, 193, 103226.

Food Research Partnership (2010). *High-Level Skills for Food*. Available at: https://assets.publishing.service.gov.uk/government/uploads/system/uploads/attachment_data/file/283195/10-929-high-level-skills-for-food.pdf

Foucault, M. (1980). *Power/Knowledge: Selected Interviews and Other Writings, 1972–1977*. New York: Pantheon.

Friedman, H., & McMichael, P. (1989). "The rise and decline of national agricultures, 1870 to the present", *Sociologia Ruralis*, 29(2), 93–117.

Fuglie, K. O. (2007). "Priorities for sweetpotato research in developing countries: results of a survey", *HortScience*, 42(5), 1200–1206.

GLAA (2019). "GLAA remembers Morecambe Bay cockling disaster, 15 years on", Available at: https://www.gla.gov.uk/whats-new/press-release-archive/05022019-glaa-remembers-morecambe-bay-cockling-disaster-15-years-on/#:~:text=Twenty%2Dthree%20Chinese%20cockle%20pickers,with%20a%20further%2015%20surviving.

Gliessman, S. (2016). "Transforming food systems with agroecology", *Agroecology and Sustainable Food Systems*, 40(3), 187–189.

HSE (2023). "Fatal injuries in agriculture, forestry and fishing in Great Britain 2021/22", Available at: https://www.hse.gov.uk/agriculture/resources/fatal.htm

International Labour Organisation (ILO) (2016). *Women at Work: Trends 2016*. Geneva: ILO.

Jackson, T. (2021). *Post Growth: Life after Capitalism*. Cambridge: Polity Press.

Jonas, H. (1984). *The Imperative of Responsibility: In Search of an Ethics for the Technological Age*. Chicago, IL: UCP.

Kolinjivadi, V., Vela Almeida, D., & Martineau, J. (2020). "Can the planet be saved in Time? On the temporalities of socionature, the clock and the limits debate", *Environment and Planning E: Nature and Space*, 3(3), 904–926. https://doi.org/10.1177/2514848619891874

Lytridis, C., Kaburlasos, V. G., Pachidis, T., Manios, M., Vrochidou, E., Kalampokas, T., & Chatzistamatis, S. (2021). "An overview of cooperative robotics in agriculture", *Agronomy*, 11(9), 1818.

Marx, K. (1959) *Economic and Philosophic Manuscripts of 1844. Economica*, vol. 26. Moscow: Progress Publishers.

Marx, K. (2004). *Capital: Volume I* (Vol. 1). London: Penguin UK.

McMichael, P. (2009). "A food regime genealogy", *The Journal of Peasant Studies*, 36(1), 139–169.

Moore, P. V. (2017). *The Quantified Self in Precarity: Work, Technology and What Counts*. Abingdon: Routledge.

Nash, L. (2018). "City rhythms walking and sensing place through rhythm analysis", in Kingma S. F., Dale K., Wasserman V. (Eds.) *Organizational Space and Beyond* (pp. 161–188). London: Routledge.

Reid-Musson, E. (2017). "Grown close to home™: migrant farmworker (Im)mobilities and unfreedom on Canadian family farms", *Annals of the American Association of Geographers*, 107(3), 716–730.

Renting, H. (2012). "Building food democracy : exploring civic food networks and newly emerging forms of food citizenship", *International Journal of Sociology of Agriculture and Food*, 19(3), 289–307.

Rockstrom, J., Steffen, W., Noone, K., Persson, A., Chapin III, F. S., Lambin, E. F., ... & Foley, J. A. (2009) "A safe operating space for humanity: identifying and quantifying planetary boundaries that must not be transgressed could help prevent human activities from causing unacceptable environmental change, argue Johan Rockstrom and colleagues", *Nature*, 461(7263), 472–476.

Scherrer C., & Verma S. (2018). *Decent Work Deficits in Southern Agriculture*. Augsburg; München: Rainer Hampp Verlag.

Smith, T. S. J., & Reid, L. (2018). "Which 'being' in wellbeing? Ontology, wellness and the geographies of happiness", *Progress in Human Geography*, 42(6), 807–829.

Sointu, E. (2005). "The rise of an ideal: tracing changing discourses of wellbeing", *The Sociological Review*, 53(2), 255–274.

Vandeventer, J. S., Cattaneo, C., & Zografos, C. (2019). "A degrowth transition: pathways for the degrowth niche to replace the capitalist-growth regime", *Ecological Economics*, 156, 272–286.

Watson, D. J. (2017). *Well-Being in Community Food Organisations: Responding to Alienation in the Food System* (Doctoral dissertation, University of Essex).

Watson, D. J. (2020). "Working the fields: the organization of labour in community supported agriculture", *Organization*, 27(2), 291–313.

Watson, D. J. (2021). "A Marxian approach to wellbeing: human nature and use value", in Searle B. A., Pykett J.,Alfaro-Simmonds M. J. (Eds.) *A Modern Guide to Wellbeing Research* (pp. 51–67). Cheltenham: Edward Elgar Publishing.

Watson, D. J., Wallace, J., Land, C., & Patey, J. (2023). "Re-organising wellbeing: contexts, critiques and contestations of dominant wellbeing narratives", *Organization* (pp. 51–67). *the 2019 14th ACM/IEE.*

Recommendations for Further Reading

Blanchette, A. (2020). *Porkopolis: American Animality, Standardized Life, and the Factory Farm*. Durham, NC: Duke University Press.

Kirschenmann, F. L. (2010). *Cultivating an Ecological Conscience: Essays from a Farmer Philosopher*. Lexington: University Press of Kentucky.

Lang, T. (2020). *Feeding Britain: Our Food Problems and How to Fix Them*. Penguin UK.

Nelson, A., & Edwards, F. (Eds.) (2020). *Food for Degrowth: Perspectives and Practices*.

Rebanks, J. (2020). *English Pastoral: An Inheritance*. London: Allen Lane.

Simms, A. (2008). *Nine Meals from Anarchy: Oil Dependence, Climate Change and the Transition to Resilience [Schumacher Lecture]*. London: New Economics Foundation.

Smaje, C. (2020). *A Small Farm Future*. Vermont: Chelsea Green.

PART 8

Labour Market Transitions and Insecurity

20
YOUNG WORKERS
Understanding Labour Market Transitions and Improving Job Quality

Edward Yates

Introduction

This chapter considers the future of work for young workers through an examination of their prevailing material conditions in advanced economies, and by exploring how these can be progressively improved. It is important that these changing conditions be explored as understanding young workers and their work futures is critical for the future of society – it is young workers who will become the mainstay of the workforce of the future, and it is young workers' economic contributions which will support both older and younger generations. However, young workers in advanced economies are increasingly likely to find themselves as a marginalised group, one which has experienced progressively worsening material conditions in recent decades, at a time in life and in history when they should be receiving both support and development.

Analysing young workers requires a definition of the unit of analysis. This definitional act is complicated by the tension which exists between the categories of biological age and the socially constructed category of 'youth' (Yates et al., 2021). In the UK, young people are defined as being between the ages of 16 and 24 (ONS, 2022). The age range of 18–24 is also used as 16–18-year-olds cannot enter into and transition through labour markets in the same way as 18 year olds due to the statutory requirement that 16–18-year-olds pursue some form of education or works-based training e.g. an apprenticeship, or volunteering while in education or training.[1] The use of biological age as the category for understanding young workers can be beneficial for statistical analysis, but it can also obfuscate the qualitative dimensions of materiality for young people. A key example of this relates to the notion of 'youth', and how this period of life is extending in advanced capitalist economies as young people take longer to achieve the transitional milestones of adulthood – notably permanent employment, home ownership, living with a partner, and having children (France & Roberts, 2015) (see Chapter 13). When considering the future of work for young people, therefore, the socially constructed notion of youth is more analytically useful than biological age as the extension of youth illustrates a great deal about changing socio-cultural, political, and economic circumstances of young people in advanced economies (Sukarieh & Tannock, 2014).

This chapter presents an overview of young workers, providing historical context and exploring contemporary labour markets, transitions and the labour process for young workers. The chapter also interrogates how the material conditions of young people can be improved, through

DOI: 10.4324/9781003327561-28

consideration of four areas: trade unions, education, industrial policy, and values. The chapter draws on case study evidence from the UK to substantiate its claims.

Contextualising Young Workers

The work and employment conditions of young people have been researched extensively over the last four decades (MacDonald, 2011) and prevailing narrative exists in youth studies research which contrasts two distinct periods. Firstly, a 'golden era' in the post-war period wherein youth transitions (from education-to-employment and inter-employment) were straightforward, and led to the acquisition of good quality jobs with high levels of employment security and regularised real wage increases (Vickerstaff, 2003; Grimshaw & Rubery, 2012). Young workers in this period benefited from sheltered entry points into employment (Ashton et al., 1990), often in form of apprenticeships. These labour market conditions occurred within a framework of embedded liberalism, characterised by buoyant economic conditions, strong trade unions, and a commitment to full-employment (Ruggie, 1982; Helleiner, 2019). The second period begins during the crises of 1970s and stretches to the present day, during which time youth transitions have become increasingly fragmented and extended (MacDonald et al., 2005), and jobs have become less secure and more precarious (Kalleberg, 2011). These changes are part of a generalised trend of worsening work and employment conditions driven by the decline of the post-war institutional order and the intensification of class disciplining in the neoliberal period, whereby capital – often in conjunction with a supportive state apparatus – has empowered itself in relation to labour. This process is complex and multi-faceted, but has entailed increasing the mobility of capital by reducing capital controls and other regulatory restrictions, and expanding the scope from capitalist accumulation through creation of new markets via processes of commodification, privatisation, and financialisation (Greer and Umney, 2022). The ability of labour to respond to these processes has also been reduced by weakening the power of trade unions; limiting labour mobility; and increasing the cost of social reproduction, which increases the compulsion of workers to sell their labour-power (Yates, 2017). The role of the state has been pivotal in these processes, acting as a legislator and as an enforcer of increasingly punitive systems of governance (Jessop, 2019).

Some research has challenged precisely how 'golden' the so-called golden era was, highlighting that job insecurity and poor working conditions for young people were widespread in the post-war period (Goodwin & O'Connor, 2005). Other research has also highlighted how the security and stability of the embedded liberal period era was predicated on a male bread-winner family model, underpinned by systemic chauvinism and racism in labour markets, sometimes enabled by trade unions (Cockburn, 1983). A critical strand in youth studies literature has noted the limitations of youth transitions literature, chiefly its inability to explain *why* large-scale socio-economic changes occurred (Keep, 2012). This has led for calls for the development of a political economy of youth (Cote, 2014; Sukarieh & Tannock, 2016), which has developed more recently into a research agenda which argues that – in order to adequately understand the material conditions of young people – they should by conceptualised as primarily as workers in relation to capitalist accumulation (Yates, 2023b). Doing so allows for a theorisation of how the value of youth labour-power can be decreased as a result of class-based social conflict. Devaluing of youth labour-power on can only be indirectly empirically observed, as the concept of the value of labour-power is an abstract one (Yates, 2023b: 495–500). Youth labour-power could for example decline if wages were to remain stagnant while the price of wage-bundle commodities increased e.g. housing, education, transport, and food. Similarly, decline could be caused by increased work intensification or extensification (Yates, 2023b). The outcome of devaluing youth (or indeed, any age) labour-power is that it increases the potential for increased capitalist accumulation, which can lead to increased profitability for capitalist enterprises at the concrete level.

Conceiving of young people in relation to wage-labour allows for a greater understanding of their historic conditions, contemporary situation, and possible work futures. Young workers have typically occupied a marginalised, peripheral labour market position stemming primarily from lack of employment experience. Younger workers are therefore more likely to be found in occupations characterised by low levels of remuneration e.g. care work, retail, and hospitality. This has meant that, during periods of economic crisis and recession, young workers are most likely to be directly affected by unemployment (youth unemployment was far higher than all-age unemployment following the Great Financial Crisis 2007–2008) (Simms et al., 2011). Young people are also more likely to bear the brunt of state and firm-level budget cuts; graduate schemes and apprenticeships are one of the first areas firms cut during economic downturns, for example. Similarly, state investment in youth focused job policies e.g. training, and broader youth-facing policies were cut heavily in the period of austerity in the UK from 2011 onwards, and have yet to recover (Gray & Barford, 2018); this is due in part to the weakness of young people as a collective, organised, and represented political community.

It is also important when considering the material conditions of young workers in class terms to understand how social categories of race, ethnicity, gender, and (dis)ability overlap and intersect with class-based social relations, often compounding socio-economic disadvantage in various forms. Young people from racial and ethnic minorities often experience multiple forms disadvantage prior to entering labour markets, such as increased likelihood of multiple forms of deprivation which impact health, education, and well-being. Young people from minority backgrounds also have increased likelihood of experiencing discrimination prior to, and once entering, labour markets and the workplace, which can impact their job quality in multiple ways (reduced pay, workplace harassment, reduced opportunities for skills formation and career progression). Similarly, gendered divisions in society can negatively impact on young workers. Historic examples of this included lawful pay discrimination, wherein female workers were paid less than their male counterparts. The Equal Pay Act (1970) and Equality Act (2010) have remedied pay discrimination and act as basis to prevent gender discrimination. However, women are still more likely to be found in lower-paid jobs than men, often caused by imbalances in maternity and paternity allowances, resulting in a 'motherhood pay gap' (Grimshaw & Rubery, 2015)

The conditions of work which young people experience have been shaped by structural processes that have been ongoing for decades. The reassertion of the power of capital following the crises of the 1970s saw the emergence of twin processes of financialisation and globalisation. The former has had major changes on work and employment conditions which impact young workers (and all-age workers), such as the compulsion for firms to become increasingly lean, which can often lead to cuts to workforce size, training budgets, and staff development (Appelbaum, Batt & Clark, 2013). These changes can disproportionately impact young people, who would be most likely to benefit from increased numbers of entry level jobs, workplace training, and staff development.

Processes of globalisation similarly impacted young people in two main ways. Firstly, deindustrialisation removed formerly stable career transitions for young people in many advanced economies, locking-in structural deprivation which remain to this day as communities based around particular industries e.g. shipbuilding in North-East England, or coal mining in Wales, lost their main employer (Telford, 2022). Deindustrialisation also generated follow-on problems of inter-generational unemployment and economic inactivity, and the social ills which follow e.g. poverty, crime, substance misuse, and deaths of despair. Secondly, globalisation compelled advanced economies to pursue strategies which sought to increase competitiveness through expanding higher education in order to compete on the basis of high skill (Nunn, 2008), a policy approach which has had widespread implications for young people.

Initially, the policy of increasing university attendance opened up access to a broader range of students, and could be seen to contribute to social mobility. This supply-side policy was not however matched by demand-side interventions, resulting in a now chronic problem of skills-based underemployment, and the existence of an increasingly marketised, massified higher education system (Tholen, 2022). The costs of higher education the UK for students has been significantly increased following the introduction of tuition fees in 1998[2]; the introduction of fees has resulted in increasing numbers of students working part-time, and in some instances full-time, while undertaking their studies. Fees also potentially deter certain students who may not wish to incur high levels of debt upon graduation, which occurs to those students who must borrow to study. The fees system also increases stratification among students between those who can afford university without taking out loans and those who cannot, and also between home and international students, who pay different levels of fees for the same degree.

Young people born after 2000 have spent their formative years experiencing a severe Global Financial Crisis, a decade of austerity, and then the COVID-19 pandemic, which affected their education, social development, and labour market prospects. This confluence of structural changes in political economy and repeated socio-economic crises underpin the challenging conditions experienced by young people, both in and out of work. Being as they are on the margins of labour markets for the reasons discussed above, young people are more likely to be negatively impacted by these socio-economic processes and events.

Contemporary Labour Markets, Transitions, and the Labour Process for Young Workers

This section examines the future of work for young workers in terms of the quantity and availability of work and employment, the quality of work available, and the regulation of work and employment. It does so by drawing on research exploring labour markets in the post-COVID period, youth transitions, job quality, and the labour process.

Labour Markets for Young Workers in the UK

The historic, structural processes which have shaped contemporary labour markets have resulted in the existence of conditions which are detrimental to young workers. The first area which is of importance is the availability of jobs for young workers. This topic can be conceptualised in multiple ways; one approach is to consider job availability in terms of skill and level of qualification. The notion of skill is contested, and in part socially constructed (Warhurst et al., 2017); however, it is still important when considering availability of jobs, and job security and progression. Labour markets for young people – due to the expansion of higher education in the twenty-first century – can now be conceptualised in terms of a binary between graduate jobs and non-graduate jobs. 'Graduate job' is in some ways a problematic category due to how such jobs are defined. Originally, graduate jobs were those which utilised graduate-level skills; more recently they have become jobs that simply happen to be occupied by graduates (Lloyd & Payne, 2016). Growth in the numbers of graduates has led to three major challenges emerging in graduate labour markets. The first is credentialism, the process whereby employers request applicants have higher levels of qualifications to apply for jobs than was previously required; this is made possible by the increasing number of young people with graduate (and postgraduate) qualifications (UKCES, 2012). One outcome of this is formerly non-graduate jobs becoming graduate jobs, which blocks off access – and limits employment opportunities – for non-graduates. Credentialism is linked to the growing issue of 'entry tournaments' in youth labour markets; which refers to the manner in which applying for and securing employment becomes increasingly challenging and onerous for young people, often involving multi-stage processes with various elements (Marsden, 2011). Again, this places additional challenges on young people, skewing the power dynamic in employment relations further towards employers. Evidence also suggests these entry tournaments have equality, diversity, and inclusion implications as the more complex a recruitment process becomes the more likely there are failings and errors which are detrimental to applicants with protected characteristics (Davies et al., 2023).

Problems of credentialism and entry tournaments relate to the more generalised problem faced by young workers in UK labour markets, namely underemployment (Bell & Blanchflower, 2018), which can be skills-based (when individuals are work in jobs which do not make use of their existing skills, training, and qualifications) or time-based (when individuals do not work as many hours as they would like). The rapid growth of graduates in non-graduate employment is an example the former type of underemployment in the UK (Heyes et al., 2017). Time-based underemployment can impact upon graduates, but it is potentially more likely to impact on those workers – such as non-graduates – with fewer high-level skills and qualifications who occupy lower-occupational jobs. The growth of time-based underemployment leads to the growth of multi-jobbing among these young workers in order to earn sufficient income to survive (Smith & McBride, 2023). One important point to note is there is currently a deficit of research on the 'missing middle' of young people who are neither NEET (not in education, employment, or training) nor in graduate-level employment. The transitional pathways of young people who leave further education at 18 is current being explored (ESRC, 2022).

Job Quality for Young Workers in the UK

Quantity and availability of work are one element of the challenges faced by young workers and their work futures. Another challenge is the issue of in-work job quality. Key challenges for young people in this area are multi-faceted. Firstly, real wage stagnation continues to be a problem for young workers (HoC Library, 2022); wages across many sectors fell following the Great Financial Crisis and remained low due to austerity policies which cut public sector employment, suppressed public sector wages, and inhibited wage growth in the private sector as a result. The sectoral composition of the UK also contributes to these problems, as many sectors are characterised by business models wherein it is profitable to sweat the labour-power of lowly paid workers, rather than investing in productivity enhancing improvements (Yates, 2023a). This problem is compounded by monetary policy which allows businesses to borrow freely, acting as an impediment to productivity enhancement (Evemy et al., 2023).

Related issues of job quality in the UK for young workers also include issues of limited employer-provided skills and training provision, and limited opportunities for career progression in multiple occupations and sectors. Insufficient provision of skills and training has been a long-standing feature of UK labour markets (Simms, 2017), which are characterised by poorly coordinated, market-led systems in which costs of training are individualised, and institutional support for lifelong learning is limited, relative to the rest of Western Europe. Limited career progression opportunities for young workers are driven by multiple factors, including the UK's polarised labour market, and ongoing processes of occupational deprofessionalisation occurring across multiple sectors (Muzio & Kirkpatrick, 2011). The former problem pertains to the decline in mid-level jobs in the UK, limiting opportunities for young people to progress into. Again, the UK suffers from labour market polarisation much more than comparable European countries (Bisello et al., 2020) due to the market-led system of governance which has prevailed in recent decades which has generally shifted power towards capital and away from labour, manifesting through aforementioned processes of financialisation. The impact of this process on the UK is particularly acute due the disproportionate power of the financial sector in the UK, manifest in the form of the City of London, which is a key node in the global financial system.

Labour market polarisation is also related the processes of deprofessionalisation which are evident across multiple occupations in the UK and other advanced economies. Deprofessionalisation is the process whereby well-remunerated, high-status, high-autonomy jobs in professional occupations are degraded across multiple areas. This process has been found to be ongoing in multiple sectors such as medicine (Abbott & Meerabeau, 2020), law (Allan et al., 2019), and higher education in the UK. A driving factor is the introduction of marketised processes, which generally increase workloads, decrease remuneration, increase hierarchical decision making and decrease occupational community cohesion. For young workers the impact is often more challenging entry into the sector, and worse job quality across all areas once employed (Yates, 2023a).

A final, key element shaping job quality (and job availability) for young workers is the role of trade unions. Union membership among young workers – after a period of historic decline – has begun to increase in the last five years. This growth has been driven by improvements in union organising strategies, and also by the increasingly challenging circumstances faced by youth after austerity and COVID-19 (Christie & Swingewood, 2022). The increase in young people joining trade unions is starting to alter their composition, and is leading – in some instances – towards unions adopting more progressive, activist approaches, in a move away from the servicing model which prevailed in the 1990s and 2000s.

Regulation of Local Labour Markets for Young Workers in the UK

A third, key factor shaping job quantity and quality for young workers is the role of the state. Clearly, state regulation of labour markets is a vast topic which cannot adequately be covered in a single chapter. However, one specific aspect of state regulation relevant to young workers is the role played by the local state in seeking to intervene and regulate local labour markets. While the capacity of UK local authorities to substantively shape local economies is limited by the UK's highly centralised system of government, the specific form which local economic governance strategies take can impact young workers in a progressive or regressive manner (Yates & Clark, 2018). Local economic governance can impact young workers directly and indirectly. Direct, progressive impacts can stem from policies aimed specifically at young people e.g. job guarantees or training programmes. However, programmes of this nature are often constrained due to the limited funding available, notably through the severity of cuts to local government budgets over the past decade in the UK. What is often more impactful for young workers, therefore, is the role of indirect policy interventions, including local economic development, infrastructure, and business strategy. There is a degree of flexibility that can be exercised by local authorities over how they intervene to shape the local economy and local labour markets and these powers have been increased by the devolution of certain powers to city-region mayors across England. Various city-regions have illustrated how developmental paths can lead to progressive outcomes for young (and all-age workers) (see Chapter 25). The 'Preston Model' of governance has favoured local procurement and anchor institutions to improve resilience and local employment opportunities (Brown & Jones, 2021), while the 'Manchester Model' adopted business-friendly policies to achieve rapid economic growth in order to generate jobs and create a cycle of investment-led growth (Deas et al., 2021). Both of these strategies are not without limits, but they do highlight how localities can shift away from the conventional model of reliance on limited, often competitive government grants in order to develop localities. For young workers, it is often these somewhat mundane economic governance strategies which can have the most impact on their everyday lives. Recent research has illustrated, for example, how the main factor preventing young people from accessing secure employment in one local authority was the lack of reliable, affordable public transport (Heyes et al., 2022).

What Is the Future for Young Workers?

This final section, rather than making speculative predictions on what the future will look like for young workers, instead focuses on evidence-based suggestions for what can be done to progressively improve the future for young workers. These suggestions are themselves informed by the principle that the best way for individuals and groups to improve their material conditions is through bottom-up processes, which are democratic in nature, rather than relying on elite-led social and policy change from above. It is worth noting that all of the points raised below not entirely new, nor are they overly technical or complex in nature. Indeed, what is necessary to improve the future of work for young people is relatively straightforward. What is far more challenging is overcoming the structural power inequalities which persist in society, and are worsening, and which are they main factor underpinning the conditions faced by young workers. With these ideas considered, four specific areas are of importance.

Firstly, the importance of trade unions for young people remains paramount. The evidence is overwhelming for the positive social role trade unions play in society, both at the level of individual workplaces for improving job quality, and at the level of wider society, where trade union activity has the aggregate effect of reducing socio-economic inequality (Piketty, 2017). That trade unions can have a positive impact is not uncontroversial in employment relations research, it is almost axiomatic. What is however more important – and at times controversial – is *how* trade unions go about their work, and the manner in which they can fall short, particularly with regard to young workers. Again, there is limited scope here to detail the entirety of how unions operate, and how in these actions failures can occur (see Gumbrell-McCormick, & Hyman, 2019 for a review). What is fair to note is that trade unions tend towards particular sectoral focuses which limit more general campaigns for improving young worker right. Trade unions have historically also been large, bureaucratic institutions which can be afflicted by the iron law of bureaucracy, and also by prevailing social prejudices which exist in wider society, including that which views young people as a marginal concern. Rather than focus excessively on negative critique, it is more productive to highlight what can be progressively achieved by young people vis-à-vis unions. The key one is not simply to join unions, but to become an active member. Research has illustrated how active participation in unions is beneficial for remedying democratic deficits, and orienting unions away from servicing models towards activist, campaigning models. The common organising refrain when discussing how to improve work and employment is often '*join a union*', but the modified version for young people should perhaps be '*become active in a union*'.

The second area is the role of education for empowering young workers and facilitating social participation. Education is key for young people, both formalised education provided from 4 to 16, and beyond by colleges and universities, but also a more generalised civic education which empowers young people to become active and engaged members of society. At present, the educational system of many advanced economies – including the UK – are characterised by being driven by metrics and targets, heavily individualised, and increasingly marketised, all with the aim of producing employable young people who will fill labour market gaps and contribute to national competitiveness (Moore, 2010). A thoroughgoing reform of education is needed, one which favours the intrinsic good of learning, and which equips young people with a broad array of critical, analytical tools. However, part of the reason this does not exist is because this is counterproductive to the needs of capitalist society, as much critical pedagogical research has noted (Friere, 1970).

A third key area where change can occur is in the related areas of industrial policy. It is in this area where the UK in particular has an abysmal record, and has failed over recent decades to progressively intervene to develop key industries or to plan to economy, in part because such an approach is seen as ideological anathema to political and state elites (Berry, 2020). The result has been the aforementioned favouring of supply-side interventions, with a failure to develop industries where good jobs for young people could exist. The lack of joined-up policy could be remedied easily, as has occurred in other countries (Chang & Andreoni, 2020). This approach would also facilitate opportunities for development sheltered labour market opportunities for young. A new industrial policy could grow key industries, and in tandem generate job opportunities for young people who leave formal education at 16–18, as well as graduates.

Finally, a broader societal change in values in needed towards young people, one which views youth progressively, as the future of society, rather than the prevailing view which problematises and marginalises youth, leading to ongoing social discrimination (Hart, 2009), as evidenced in workplaces, welfare policy, law, political representation and pay. Older people must become more pro-active in mentoring and engaging with youth, rebuilding the ties of civil society which have been eroded in recent decades (Putnam, 2020). This task is especially urgent for the latest cohort of young people, who are reported as being the most depressed, isolated, and lost generations in the post-war period (Gunnell et al., 2018).

Conclusions

This chapter has explored the material conditions of young workers in advanced economies. It has explored definitional challenges when considering young people, and this has provided a historical contextualisation for the current conditions of young people. The chapter has also examined prevailing material conditions through the presentation of evidence on labour markets, job quality, and state regulation. The chapter then provided four main areas which should be focused on when seeking to improve the future of work for young people. In conclusion, it is important to note that understanding the problems faced by youth people is always less challenging than engaging in the sustained, progressive action necessary to achieve results. It is therefore better to start small and to achieve small wins e.g. increased union participation, policy improvements, and then continue to build from these improvements so as to lock-in progressive change. For this work to be successful, it must necessarily involve people who are not young, due to the transitory nature of youth. While the future for young people is somewhat uncertain, what it is certain is that present is not sustainable for youth, and it must therefore be improved.

Notes

1 The requirement to remain in education or works-based trained until 18 only applies in England. In Scotland, Wales and Northern Ireland young people can enter full-time employment from the age of 16.

2 Students from Scotland – or those who have lived there for five years of more – do not have to pay tuition fees to study in Scotland.

References

Abbott, P., & Meerabeau, L. (2020). Professionals, professionalization and the caring professions. In Abbott, P and Meerabeau, L (Eds.). *The sociology of the caring professions* (pp. 1–19). Abingdon: Routledge.

Allan, S. M., Faulconbridge, J. R., & Thomas, P. (2019). The fearful and anxious professional: partner experiences of working in the financialized professional services firm. *Work, Employment and Society*, *33*(1), 112–130.

Appelbaum, E., Batt, R., & Clark, I. (2013). Implications of financial capitalism for employment relations research: evidence from breach of trust and implicit contracts in private equity buyouts. *British Journal of Industrial Relations*, *51*(3), 498–518.

Ashton, D., Maguire, M., & Spilsbury, M. (1990) *Restructuring the Labour Market: The Implications for Youth.* London: Palgrave Macmillan

Bell, D. N., & Blanchflower, D. G. (2018). Underemployment and the lack of wage pressure in the UK. *National Institute Economic Review*, *243*, R53–R61.

Berry, C. (2020). From receding to reseeding: industrial policy, governance strategies and neoliberal resilience in post-crisis Britain. *New Political Economy*, *25*(4), 607–625.

Bisello, M, Maccarrone, V., & Fernández-Macías, E. (2020). Occupational mobility, employment transitions and job quality in Europe: the impact of the great recession. *Economic and Industrial Democracy*, https://doi.org/10.1177/0143831X20931936.

Brown, M., & Jones, R. (2021). *Paint your town red: how Preston took back control and your town can too.* London: Watkins Media Limited.

Chang, H. J., & Andreoni, A. (2020). Industrial policy in the 21st century. *Development and Change*, *51*(2), 324–351.

Christie, F., & Swingewood, A. (2022). *The impact of Covid-19 on young workers in England: young people navigating insecure work in Greater Manchester during the Covid-19 pandemic.* Manchester: Manchester University Press.

Cockburn, C. (1983). *Brothers.* Boulder, Colorado: Westview Press, Inc.

Côté, J. E. (2014). Towards a new political economy of youth. *Journal of youth studies*, *17*(4), 527–543.

Davies, J., Heasman, B., Livesey, A., Walker, A., Pellicano, E., & Remington, A. (2023). Access to employment: a comparison of autistic, neurodivergent and neurotypical adults'

experiences of hiring processes in the United Kingdom. *Autism*, 13623613221145377.

Deas, I., Haughton, G., & Ward, K. (2021). Scalar postpolitics, inclusive growth and inclusive economies: challenging the Greater Manchester agglomeration model. *Cambridge Journal of Regions, Economy and Society*, *14*(1), 179–195.

ESRC (2022). *Transforming working lives: transitions of young workers in the UK labour market: consequences for careers, earnings, health and wellbeing Research Grant.* University of Sheffield/CIPD.

France, A., & Roberts, S. (2015). The problem of social generations: a critique of the new emerging orthodoxy in youth studies. *Journal of Youth Studies*, *18*(2), 215–230.

Freiri, P. (1970). *Pedagogy of the oppressed.* New York: Continuum,

Goodwin, J., & O'Connor, H. (2005). Exploring complex transitions: looking back at the 'Golden Age' of from school to work. *Sociology*, *39*(2), 201–220.

Gray, M., & Barford, A. (2018). The depths of the cuts: the uneven geography of local government austerity. *Cambridge Journal of Regions, Economy and Society*, *11*(3), 541–563.

Greer, I., & Umney, C. (2022). *Marketization: how capitalist exchange disciplines workers and subverts democracy.* London: Bloomsbury Publishing.

Grimshaw, D., & Rubery, J. (2012). Reinforcing neoliberalism: crisis and austerity in the UK. In *A triumph of failed ideas: European models of capitalism in the crisis*, Steffen Lehndorff (Ed.), Brussels: ETUI. https://www.ilo.org/sites/default/files/wcmsp5/groups/public/@dgreports/@dcomm/@publ/documents/publication/wcms_348041.pdf

Grimshaw, D., & Rubery, J. (2015). The motherhood pay gap: a review of the issues, theory and international evidence. *Conditions of Work and Employment Series,* (p. 57), Geneva: ILO.

Gumbrell-McCormick, R., & Hyman, R. (2019). Democracy in trade unions, democracy through trade unions? *Economic and Industrial Democracy*, *40*(1), 91–110.

Gunnell, D., Kidger, J., & Elvidge, H. (2018). Adolescent mental health in crisis. *BMJ*, *36*, k2608.

Hart, S. (2009). The 'problem' with youth: young people, citizenship and the community. *Citizenship Studies*, *13*(6), 641–657.

Helleiner, E. (2019). The life and times of embedded liberalism: legacies and innovations since Bretton Woods. *Review of International Political Economy*, *26*(6), 1112–1135.

Heyes, J., Tomlinson, M., & Whitworth, A. (2017). Underemployment and well-being in the UK before and after the Great Recession. *Work, Employment and Society*, *31*(1), 71–89.

Heyes, D., Matheson, J., Popli, G., & Yates, E. (2022). *The co-existence of high youth unemployment and high job vacancy rates*. Report for Doncaster Council.

House of Commons Library (2022) Average earnings by age and region. URL: https://commonslibrary.parliament.uk/research-briefings/cbp-8456/ Accessed 3/4/23

Jessop, B. (2019). Authoritarian neoliberalism: periodization and critique. *South Atlantic Quarterly*, *118*(2), 343–361.

Kalleberg, A. L. (2011). *Good jobs, bad jobs: The rise of polarized and precarious employment systems in the United States, 1970s–2000s*. New York: Russell Sage Foundation.

Keep, E. (2012). Where next for vocational education?. *British Journal of Sociology of Education*, *33*(2), 315–322.

Lloyd, C., & Payne, J. (2016). *Skills in the age of over-qualification: comparing service sector work in Europe*. Oxford: Oxford University Press.

MacDonald, R. (2011). Youth transitions, unemployment and underemployment: plus ça change, plus c'est la même chose? *Journal of Sociology*, *47*(4), 427–444.

MacDonald, R., Shildrick, T., Webster, C., & Simpson, D. (2005). Growing up in poor neighbourhoods the significance of class and place in the extended transitions of 'socially excluded' young adults. *Sociology*, *39*(5), 873–891.

Marsden, D. (2011). The growth of extended 'entry tournaments' and the decline of institutionalized occupational labour markets in Britain. In Lee, S and McCann, D (Eds.). *Regulating for decent work: new directions in labour market regulation* (pp. 91–120). London: Palgrave Macmillan UK.

Muzio, D., & Kirkpatrick, I. (2011). Introduction: Professions and organizations-a conceptual framework. *Current sociology*, *59*(4), 389–405.

Moore, P. (2010). *The international political economy of work and employability*. Basingstoke: Palgrave Macmillan.

Nunn, A. (2008). Restructuring the English working class for global competitiveness. *Papers in the politics of global competitiveness, 9.* Policy Research Institute Leeds Metropolitan University, UK. https://www.politicsofglobalcompetitiveness.com/the-politics-of-global-competitiveness.html

ONS (2022) Young people in the labour market by socio-economic background. UK: 2014 to 2021. URL: https://www.ons.gov.uk/employmentandlabourmarket/peopleinwork/empl oymentandemployeetypes/articles/youngpeopleinthelabourmarketbysocioeconomicba ckgrounduk/2014to2021 Accessed 31/3/23.

Piketty, T. (2017). *Capital in the twenty-first century*. Cambridge, Massachusetts: Harvard University Press.

Ruggie, J. G. (1982). International regimes, transactions, and change: embedded liberalism in the postwar economic order. *International Organization*, *36*(2), 379–415.

Simms, M. (2017), Understanding employer engagement in youth labour market policy in the UK. *Human Resource Management Journal*, *27*(4), 548–564.

Simms, M., Elliott, G., & Hudd, D. (2011). Young workers during the Crisis: Hit Hardest and Scarred Longest. London: Unions 21. https://unions21.org/ideas/hit-hardest-scarred-longest-young-workers-during-the-crisis

Smith, A. & McBride, J. (2023). 'It was doing my head in': low-paid multiple employment and zero hours work. *British Journal of Industrial Relations*, *61*(1), 3–23.

Sukarieh, M., & Tannock, S. (2014). *Youth rising?: the politics of youth in the global economy*. Abingdon: Routledge.

Sukarieh, M., & Tannock, S. (2016). On the political economy of youth: a comment. *Journal of Youth Studies*, *19*(9), 1281–1289.

Telford, L. (2022). 'There is nothing there': deindustrialization and loss in a coastal town. *Competition & Change*, *26*(2), 197–214.

UK Commission for Employment and Skills (2012) *The youth employment challenge*. London: UKCES.

Vickerstaff, S. A. (2003). Apprenticeship in the golden age': were youth transitions really smooth and unproblematic back then? *Work, Employment and Society*, *17*(2), 269–287.

Warhurst, C., Tilly, C., & Gatta, M. (2017). *A new social construction of skill* (pp. 72–91). Oxford: Oxford University Press.

Yates, E. (2017). Reproducing low-wage labour: capital accumulation, labour markets and young workers. *Industrial Relations Journal*, *48*(5–6), 463–481.

Yates, E. (2023a). Developing or degrading young workers? How business strategy and the labour process shape job quality across different industrial sectors in England. *Work, Employment and Society*, 37(5): 1186–1205.

Yates, E. (2023b) Work, employment, and the material conditions of young people in developed economies: a Marxist political economy of youth perspective. *Journal of Youth Studies*, *26*(4), 491–506.

Yates, E., & Clark, I. (2021). The strategic economic governance of Greater Manchester's local labour market by the local state: Implications for young workers. *Economic and Industrial Democracy*, *42*(1), 27–49.

Yates, E., Clark, I., & Rossiter, W. (2021). Local economic governance strategies in the UK's post-industrial cities and the challenges of improving local work and employment conditions. *Local Economy*, *36*(2), 115–132.

Recommendations for Further Readings

Fine, B. (2002). *Labour market theory: a constructive reassessment*. Abingdon: Routledge (An excellent account of the operation of labour markets in capitalist societies).

Furlong, A., Goodwin, J., O'Connor, H., Hadfield, S., Hall, S., Lowden, K., & Plugor, R. (2017). *Young people in the labour market: past, present, future*. Abingdon: Routledge (Edited collection of sociological work examining young people prior to COVID19, first authored by the founder of the Journal of Youth Studies).

O'Reilly, J., Leschke, J., Ortlieb, R., Seeleib-Kaiser, M., & Villa, P. (Eds.) (2018). *Youth labor in transition: inequalities, mobility, and policies in Europe*. Oxford: Oxford University Press (Key text on youth labour market transitions, based on findings from a large-scale EU- funded project on Youth Employment in Europe: STYLE).

Simms, M., Holgate, J., & Heery, E. (2013). *Union voices: tactics and tensions in UK organizing*. Ithaca, NY: Cornell University Press (A key text on UK trade union organising, lead authored by a specialist on young workers).

Yates, E. (2023). Developing or degrading young workers? How business strategy and the labour process shape job quality across different industrial sectors in England. *Work, Employment and Society* (online first) (A piece of research linking together ideas discussed in the chapter, including business strategy, the labour process, and job quality for young people).

21

CONSIDERING THE FUTURES OF UNPAID WORK

Nancy Worth

Introduction: What 'Work' is Included in the Future of Work?

My interest in unpaid work began with my research with young people navigating school to work transitions, and further research about millennials' co-residence with parents. In these projects, young people considered interning to bolster their CV, and told me about the work that went into getting by in a precarious labour market (Worth 2016, 2017). These experiences, alongside many others related to care (including care of the self), coping strategies and side hustles, demonstrate the diversity of and broadness of the category 'work' beyond paid work. Yet despite the prevalence and diverse forms of unpaid work encountered throughout participants' narratives about their working lives, this work was at times challenging to conceptualize, especially beyond typical (and problematic) binaries of productive/reproductive work or standard/non-standard work. So, this chapter is an attempt to think through some of the possibilities and potentialities about the future of unpaid work. My approach in this chapter involves a broad scan across disciplines of the literature on unpaid forms of work, emphasizing key debates about the future of these forms of work. This breadth is intentional; most work is unpaid; yet, many academic and popular debates about the future of work centre paid formal employment, while acknowledging its blurry boundaries (Simms 2019) or that paid work often depends on unpaid work (Pettinger 2019). I argue that paid work should be decentred from our thinking about the future of work; instead, a full accounting of work involves reckoning with many different forms of unpaid work, deepening our analysis of what the future of work is and what it means for workers.

This expansive framing of work involves challenging the normative assumption that paid work matters most to the economy, and recognizing that most work that contributes to the economy is unpaid. It's worth reflecting on why paid work remains in a privileged position in future of work debates. This reckoning also involves close attention to who is doing unpaid work—from class (interns with the family wealth to afford to work for free), gender (unfree care labour that is disproportionately borne by women) and race (the emotional labour involved in navigating systemic discrimination), and who is unable to take on unpaid work of volunteering. A spatial attention to where unpaid work happens is also revealing, from the home and the street to countries whose economies are dominated by 'informal' work (Simonet 2022). This matters—in the research highlighted below, what counts in the future of work is already being broadened by a greater attention

DOI: 10.4324/9781003327561-29

to work's breadth. And as the proportion of workers in a standard employment relationship (full time, permanent work for one employer) continues to decline (Stone 2013) (see Chapter 8), there is much to learn about the future of work beyond paid work. In the following sections, I trace the future of unpaid work through self-provisioning, care work, volunteering and the affective labour within paid work. I also feature the unpaid work that happens within self-employment, using a case study from my research with media freelancers. Within each of these sections I highlight a key concept (like *livelihood* or *unfreedom*), considering what we might learn about the future of work by centring unpaid work.

The Future of (Unpaid) Work

Before discussing the diversity of unpaid work, some framing is helpful. The International Labour Organization (ILO) defines work expansively, as "any activity performed by persons of any sex and age to produce goods or to provide services for use by others or for own use" (International Labour Organization [ILO] 2013). This kind of definition is inclusive, but almost too broad to engage with analytically—if everything is work, what then? Some categorizations are useful, although never perfect. Table 21.1 sets out how the ILO's 19th International Conference of Labour Statisticians categorizes work. Of the four forms of work they identify, only one—employment—is paid. It is important to emphasize how much unpaid labour is contributing to the economy. In Miranda's (2011: 4) evaluation of OECD countries, unpaid work accounted for between one-third and half of all valuable economic activity. Where we draw the boundaries around 'work' matter: including unpaid work broadens our conversation about the future of work (Table 21.1).

Self-Provisioning: Learning from *Livelihood*

This section considers own-use 'not-for-market' work, labour that is often excluded from definitions of work, including informal work. Yet, Goldschmidt-Clermont (1990: 279) asks: "When carrying loads of water or firewood on her head, is a woman working? When, returning home at the end of the day, a mason grows vegetables which will be eaten by his family, is he producing economic goods?" For many researchers, the answer is 'yes', but this work is often called something else, including subsistence, household activities and self-provisioning. In development studies, a central concept is '*livelihood*'; it "comprises the capabilities, assets (including both material and social resources) and activities required for a means of living" (Chambers and Conway 1992 in Rakodi 2014: 3). In a livelihoods approach, pay is decentred, and analysis focuses on the variety of activities people engage in—paid and unpaid, for example, farming for one's own

Table 21.1 Categorizing unpaid work, a beginning

	For own final use	*For use by others*			
Forms of work in the 19th ICLS Resolution I	Own-use production work	Employment	Unpaid trainee work	Other work activities	Volunteer work
Type of work	Unpaid work	Work for pay or profit	Unpaid work		

Source: Adapted Table 1.1 from ILO (2018), from Resolution I of the 19th ICLS.

food supply, selling the surplus in a market, and pooling resources with family and community members. Livelihood sits at the blurry boundary between paid and unpaid work, while also capturing the interconnectedness of work. A key strength of the livelihood approach is its attention to workers' basic needs, including food security and well-being rather than simply wages and profit. For example, Dzanku, Tsikata and Ankrah (2021) examine the rise of agricultural commercialization amongst smallholders, finding that commercialization only improves food security up until a threshold point, after which it decreases. In their research, the ideal balance between growing cash crops and food crops was impacted by the location of the farm (north or south Ghana) and gender (where women may seem to be highly involved sellers but are more often driven by survival than profit making). This nuance is only available through a livelihoods approach that takes paid and unpaid work into account.

While discussions on the future of informal labour and self-provisioning have examined formalization (Williams and Round 2007), the focus of research has often focused on defining, measuring and consequently assessing this labour's current economic value. Researchers use time-use surveys and offer calculations about how much it would cost to either replace that labour with paid work (replacement cost), or how much paid work time is lost when a worker does unpaid work instead (opportunity cost) (Antonopoulos and Hirway 2010, Miranda 2011). While an important step towards recognition of the extent and contribution of this work, Langill (2023) offers another productive avenue: her research adds necessary context to livelihoods, as an intersectional and embodied experience; her work with Hmong women in Thailand emphasizes the interconnection of paid and unpaid work, as 'ways of living' rather than only 'making a living'.

Care: Understanding *Unfreedom*

Care labour is at the core of geography's interest in unpaid work, reckoning with the future of socially reproductive labour. As care is the topic of a chapter in this collection (see Chapter 16), this section will specifically examine *unfreedom* within care labour. Unfreedom is a vital concept, where (un)paid work is not freely entered into by the worker (see Strauss 2012 for an excellent discussion of unfreedom). Again, this is a diverse area of labour, including various forms of state-coordinated programmes tied to welfare (the rise of unpaid training and jobs within 'workfare') (Pennisi and Baker Collins 2017) and the carceral system (where prisoners work for nominal or no wages) (Hatton 2020). Strauss and McGrath (2017) call unfreedom a 'continuum of exploitation', from chattel slavery, indentured labour, debt-bondage, as well as the unfreedom of specific migration regimes, where care workers are tied to specific employers. For unfree care labour, unpaid work takes many forms, from withholding promised wages, demands for free overtime or no parameters on the working day, to outright forced or slave labour. The workplace of someone else's home is key to understanding the potential for unfree and unpaid care work. Across national contexts, this work in someone's home is treated differently by regulators—it is often exempted from workplace protections, leaving workers vulnerable. An extreme example is the UAE's kafala system, where workers are under the control of their employer. Parreñas (2021) introduces *Unfree Labour: Migrant Domestic Work in Arab States* with the story of Joy, whose employers witheld her salary under the guise of managing it for her. When Joy discovered this was illegal, she quit but was unable to recoup her wages—instead, she was only able to secure permission to find another job. Yet, being 'released' from a contract was a partial win, as other workers who 'abscond' can be charged with a crime. For children working in Dhaka, the home-as-workspace allowed employers to position work as familial care, where pay might only involve a future dowry for the child worker, rather than full, regular wages (Jensen 2014). Finally, in Waite and Lewis' (2017) examination of transactional labour of irregular migrants (often unpaid care work in exchange for lodging), the moral economy of 'family' blurs boundaries between unpaid work and willingly helping out, in gratitude for a place to stay when paid work is prohibited by migration status.

Some of the future of work discourse about care work, especially outside the family home, examines the role of automation and robotics as a potential solution for the growing labour force need for care workers (Lehdonvirta, Shi et al. 2023; MacLeavy 2021). For unfree care work in particular, replacing labour that is exploitative may be a tempting aim. Yet, Schwiter and Steiner (2020) are ambivalent about the future of potential caring technologies, especially for workers. Instead, the growing role for technology within care work may actually exacerbate precarity for workers, through 'deskilling, distance, and displacement', leading to a 'culturally odorless' care that may increase the demand for precarious migrant care labour (Wright 2019: 347).

Volunteering: Revealing the *Shadow State*

Although volunteering appears in the ILO's framing of work (see Figure 1), it is also conceptualized as non-work leisure time. Within this blurry definitional combination of work/non-work (Overgaard 2019), volunteering can involve mutual aid in support of community, participation in social movements, as well as individual acts of social support for neighbours. Relatedly, interning involves work for an organization, sometimes partially paid by a stipend or rewarded instead with educational credits or the possibility of future paid work (Holdsworth 2017, Allan 2019). Yet if we accept the 'volunteering is work' premise, one (perhaps controversial) way to categorize the diverse labour of volunteering is to ask: who is not paying for this work? This is my approach here, focusing on formal volunteering with organizations supported by or replacing the work of the state. I want to draw attention to the state as a key beneficiary of people's (not just citizens) unpaid labour, using the concept of the *shadow state*. For Trudeau (2012: 442–443), the "shadow state concept refers to the transfer of responsibility for providing integrative functions, such as social welfare services that bring people into specific relations of citizenship, from state institutions to local nonprofits". When work shifts to nonprofits, it is often done by volunteers. Some of these arrangements are longstanding; for example, 80% of French firefighters are volunteers (Pudal 2012). Yet, many others emerge as a response to austerity or crisis, where cuts of public services often involve community volunteering to pick up the slack, from community gardens, food banks, settlement services for newcomers, libraries and more. For Mettenburger and Küpper (2019), replacing basic services with volunteers is a challenge: in their research with young retiree volunteers in rural Germany, motivations to volunteer diminished as expectations and demands mounted; participants wanted their volunteer labour to be an added extra rather than a replacement for missing state services. Being expected to volunteer removed their sense of choice and leisure, decreasing their interest in participating. Volunteering was resisted when it felt exploitative, like unpaid work, rather than a leisure activity.

Given the current trend of decreased state supports and social expenditure, the future of volunteer work may involve a growing demand for volunteers, especially formal volunteering as part of the shadow state. In the height of the COVID-19 pandemic, states mobilized citizens to support fragile health systems and deploy mass vaccination clinics. During this time of 'crisis volunteering', millions of citizens were called upon through discourses of solidarity and civic participation to offer their free labour. Rather than a new phenomenon, the demands of the pandemic made visible a longstanding tradition of volunteering for the civic good, a neoliberal strategy in the wider context of retrenchment (Rosol 2012). This conceptual ambiguity about volunteering as leisure/unpaid work/civic duty helps the shadow state persist, as discourses about the worthiness of the labour complicate calls to value work through pay, or to restore state services.

Unpaid Work within Paid Work: Reckoning with *Invisibility*

This section engages with the concept of *invisibility*, inherent to many forms of unpaid work, but especially unpaid work within paid employment. This section could include analyses of unpaid overtime and other forms of wage theft, the 'gray zone' of unpaid activities related to precarious work (Pulignano and Morgan 2022), or the subtleties of 'family work' where the unpaid work of some family members is hidden by measuring only a larger economic unit (like a family farm, Reid-Musson, MacEachen, et al. 2022). Invisibility helps devalue these forms of work, as the unit of work is structurally uncounted. My focus here centres the lived experience of workers, what Chong (2009: 178) calls: "important unpaid aspects of work that demand identity-based performance that are linked to race, gender and class hierarchies". Building on the germinal work of Hochschild (1983), Chong examines the 'racial silences' of research on emotional labour, calling for an attention not just to the demands on an individual worker, but the wider structural dynamics of emotion work within a global division of labour. A key example is call centre workers in India, who are required to perform 'identity management', changing their name for calls and modifying speech and accent to meet an American ideal, coded as white and middle-class. Here, invisibility operates in two ways—a worker's own identity is hidden beneath strenuous identity work, and the efforts of the identity work itself is also hidden (Hatton 2017) (see Chapter 8). While identity work can lessen a worker's exposure to discriminatory behaviour, it is often mandated by employers mainly to smooth customer service relationships and maximize sales. Andrade-Dixon (2020) explains that identity work also involves managing one's own emotions 'to uphold a palatable image', work that is both self-protective, and again, invisible to others.

Looking to the future, the rapid shift to working from home for many workers and the intensities of the pandemic sparked widespread evaluations about the intensification and extensification of paid work. One outcome was the rise of 'quiet quitting', finding ways to prioritize well-being rather than sacrificing oneself for work (Forrester 2023). Originating from a TikTok, the term 'quiet quitting' involves protecting one's time, avoiding long hours by focusing on work that's valuable (or valued by the employer). Finding ways to minimize the need for identity work can also be part of quiet quitting: situating remote work as an escape from the toxicity of office culture, research on working from home highlights the ability for workers to avoid office microaggressions and the 'minority stress' of the office (Amerikaner, Yan, et al. 2023) (see Chapter 8).

Unpaid Work in Self-Employment: Paying Attention to *Employment Arrangements*

One further aspect of unpaid work that deserves attention involves the unpaid work inherent to non-standard work, including freelance and gig work. While 'extra' tasks of emotional labour fall disproportionally on some workers within salaried employment, within non-standard employment, the *employment arrangement* of this labour can create and perpetuate a wide variety of unpaid work for all, where paid work is centred only on a project, task, or outcome, not a worker's time. This unpaid time is often waiting time, waiting between food deliveries or until a driver picks up their next ride. Franke and colleagues (2023) examine how platform workers actively contest unpaid 'idle time' in delivery work on the Deliveroo app, with strategies, including working between multiple apps, working only in peak hours, stacking orders and refusing orders with remote destinations. This optimization involves careful strategies by workers to minimize their unpaid waiting time. Another form of unpaid time for the self-employed involves looking for work, from managing different apps to find the best gig at a given time, developing an engaging online profile, to pitching editors or bidding for a project. Here, workers often willingly engage in this unpaid labour, as an investment in their future paid work. In both these sources of unpaid work, it is embedded structurally by the *employment arrangement*; this work couldn't be done without the unpaid work that goes alongside it; yet, it's a significant chunk of time that clients are not responsible for.

Examining new varieties of *employment arrangements* within self-employment can help problematize the future of work by destabilizing what counts as work. When having a break is a paid part of your job as a salaried worker and the same kind of break is unpaid 'idle time' as an independent contractor, we can consider how definitions and regulatory choices about work shape the social imaginary about what work could or should be. Moreover, the rise of precarious non-standard work within rich democracies is worthy of our attention because the role this work fulfils in the economy can be quite different (Kalleberg 2018). In some countries, it allows some workers to get experience, to test out fit with both the company and role, and work flexibly before moving into a permanent position. For others, precarious non-standard work can be a dead end, cycling through low-wage, insecure positions with few chances for upwards mobility.

Case Study: Media Freelancing and Unpaid Work

This case study expands on the previous section, examining how the employment arrangement of freelancing creates an expected norm of unpaid productive work. I draw on a wider project, *Home/work*, which examines work-from-home arrangements and job security with media freelancers in Toronto, Canada. Here I focus on one respondent, Yana, an associate producer in broadcast media. The most obvious and perhaps egregious example of unpaid work from her story involves *working for 'exposure'* or working on spec, or speculation, where work is completed with no guarantee of payment. This can be a form of hope labour, what Mackenzie and McKinlay (2021: 1841) define as "unpaid or under-compensated labour undertaken in the present, usually for [...] experience, with the hope that future work may follow". Yana says she worked on a documentary after she graduated from journalism school, with the director promising a payment once the project won a grant—she says:

> I never saw that money, ever, ever. So that was the one and only time that I ever did that, and I told myself I was never ever going to do that again [laughs]. And then what else happened? [...] I would say I was lucky that I found myself in situations where I always got paid.

Feeling lucky to get paid is an unremarkable statement for most freelancers. Yet, Yana immediately caveats her statement by following up with a story about *chasing a late invoice* for five months for some editing work. For the Canadian Freelance Union, this is a key benefit for members: sharing tactics and strategies to get companies to pay you the amount agreed for work already done. Ensuring companies honour contracts is also the centre of advocacy work in the US, with the Freelancing Isn't Free law in New York City requiring timely payment (see also Pitts et al. 2023).

Yana's main experience of unpaid work involves *unpaid overtime* for a powerful employer: "It was unanimous that everyone knew everyone put in at least two or three hours outside of their work hours". She continues,

> I would be told by certain colleagues like, 'Oh be careful about reporting your extra hours because managers don't like that'. [...] So yeah, there was a lot of unpaid work going on there, a lot of too many expectations for the amount of hours that they allocate you in one day.

Even though overtime was technically allowed, freelancers knew it was in their best interests to accept current conditions, to demonstrate 'commitment' in order to have a chance at being hired in the future. The last example of unpaid work from Yana involves *looking for the next project or contract*—for Yana this is emotional labour as well as hours of her time, asking herself what she's going to do next, where the next contract could come from. Another respondent calls the labour of finding new clients her 'Sunday work', beyond the work she explicitly charges for but a necessary part of her job. One more type of unpaid work that wasn't in Yana's narrative, but other freelancers told us about was *bartering*, exchanging goods/services in lieu of cash payment. For some, ad hoc bartering is a way of making a low paying job worthwhile. Overall, this short case reveals how self-employment often limits paid work to the end product, leaving a variety of tasks as necessary but unpaid. These expectations connect to a broader shift in working life, where measuring productivity means measuring the work tasks that 'count', making other work tasks less visible and not worthy of pay. There's a narrowing, towards what can be quantified, but also towards what the employer thinks will maximize their own profit. This begins with hiring freelancers instead of employees. What work we expect to 'count' is a shared construction, yet one that often limits freelance workers' agency and erodes their security.

Conclusion: The Futures of Unpaid Work

This chapter considers the futures of unpaid work in all their diversity. Unpaid work exists alongside paid work, as well as within in, and sometimes instead of it—for Simonet (2022: 167) it is the 'frontier of work'. Importantly, drawing attention to unpaid work is not a call for all work to be paid, but rather that research on work and the economy must be broader (and more integrative) than its current focus on paid labour. Whether measuring unpaid work by time, by its contribution, by its necessity, I echo calls from social reproduction theorists to more fully account for all the work that makes paid work possible (Bhattacharya 2017; Rodríguez-Rocha 2021). Its again worth emphasizing the diversity of this work, and its interdependence with paid work and the formal economy: unpaid care labour supports the domestic lives of workers (and future workers). Volunteering offers a stopgap to reductions in state support, an unpaid workforce often providing critical social services. Unpaid tasks within gig work are an integral part of how this work is organized. Moreover, thinking through how concepts like *livelihood*, *unfreedom*, the *shadow state*, *invisibility* and *employment arrangements* offer contexts to think across the boundary of paid/unpaid work. They contribute to our conceptual language, to question why work exists as it does, where it does and how it endures.

References

Allan, K. (2019). "Volunteering as hope labour: The potential value of unpaid work experience for the un-and under-employed." *Culture, Theory and Critique* 60(1): 66–83.

Amerikaner, L., H. X. Yan, L. C. Sayer, L. Doan, J. N. Fish, K. J. Drotning and R. G. Rinderknecht (2023). "Blurred border or safe harbor? Emotional well-being among sexual and gender minority adults working from home during COVID-19." *Social Science & Medicine* 323: 115850. https://www.sciencedirect.com/science/article/pii/S0277953623002071

Andrade-Dixon, O. (2020). "Racialized emotional labour: The weight of Blackness in White spaces." *Caribbean Quilt* 5: 3–34. https://doi.org/10.33137/caribbeanquilt.v5i0.34373

Antonopoulos, R. and I. Hirway (2010). "Unpaid work and the economy." *Unpaid Work and the Economy: Gender, Time Use and Poverty in Developing Countries*. R. Antonopoulos and I. Hirway (eds.). London, Palgrave Macmillan UK: 1–21.

Bhattacharya, T. (ed.) (2017). *Social Reproduction Theory: Remapping Class, Recentering Oppression*. London, Pluto Press.

Chambers, R. and Conway, G. (1992). "Sustainable Rural Livelihoods: Practical Concepts for the 21st Century, University of Sussex." Institute for Development Studies, DP 296. Brighton.

Chong, P. (2009). "Servitude with a smile: A re-examination of emotional labour." *Just Labour* 14: 177–185. http://www.justlabour.yorku.ca/volume14/pdfs/ss_06_chong_press.pdf

Dzanku, F. M., D. Tsikata and D. A. Ankrah (2021). "The gender and geography of agricultural commercialisation: What implications for the food security of Ghana's smallholder farmers?" *The Journal of Peasant Studies* 48(7): 1507–1536. https://doi.org/10.1080/03066150.2021.1945584

Forrester, N. (2023). "Fed up and burnt out: 'Quiet quitting' hits academia." *Nature* 615: 751–753

Franke, M., V. Pulignano and C. Marà (2023). "Workers' contentions over unpaid labour time in food delivery and domestic work platforms in Belgium." *Work in the Global Economy*: 1–25. https://bristoluniversitypressdigital.com/view/journals/wge/aop/article-10.1332-273241723X16803276410614/article-10.1332-273241723X16803276410614.xml

Goldschmidt-Clermont, L. (1990). "Economic measurement of non-market household activities-is it useful and feasible." *International Labour Review* 129: 279.

Hatton, E. (2017). "Mechanisms of invisibility: Rethinking the concept of invisible work." *Work, Employment and Society* 31(2): 336–351. https://journals.sagepub.com/doi/abs/10.1177/0950017016674894

Hatton, E. (2020). *Coerced: Work Under Threat of Punishment*. Berkeley, University of California Press.

Hochschild, A. R. (1983). *The Managed Heart: Commercialization of Human Feeling*. Berkeley, University of California Press.

Holdsworth, C. (2017). "The cult of experience." *Area* 49: 296–302. https://doi.org/10.1111/area.12201

International Labour Organization (ILO) (2013). "Resolution I Resolution concerning statistics of work, employment and labour underutilization." *19th International Conference of Labour Statisticians (ICLS)*. Retrieved 02-15-2022, from https://www.ilo.org/wcmsp5/groups/public/---dgreports/---stat/documents/normativeinstrument/wcms_230304.pdf

International Labour Organization (ILO) (2018). *Care Work and Care Jobs for the Future of Decent Work*. Geneva, ILO. https://www.ilo.org/wcmsp5/groups/public/---dgreports/---dcomm/---publ/documents/publication/wcms_633135.pdf.

Jensen, K. B. (2014). "Space-time geography of female live-in child domestic workers in Dhaka, Bangladesh." *Children's Geographies* 12(2): 154–169. https://doi.org/10.1080/14733285.2013.783986

Kalleberg, A. L. (2018). *Precarious Lives: Job Insecurity and Well-Being in Rich Democracies*. Cambridge, Polity.

Langill, J. C. (2023). "'I shouldn't have to do this alone': Intersectional livelihoods and single Hmong women in Thailand." *Gender, Place & Culture*: 1–20. https://doi.org/10.1080/0966369X.2023.2171967

Lehdonvirta, V., L. Shi, E. Hertog, N. Nagase and Y. Ohta (2023). "The future(s) of unpaid work: How susceptible do experts from different backgrounds think the domestic sphere is to automation?" *PLoS One* 18(2): e0281282. https://doi.org/10.1371/journal.pone.0281282

Mackenzie, E. and A. McKinlay (2021). "Hope labour and the psychic life of cultural work." *Human Relations* 74(11): 1841–1863. https://journals.sagepub.com/doi/abs/10.1177/0018726720940777

MacLeavy, J. (2021). "Care work, gender inequality and technological advancement in the age of COVID-19." *Gender Work & Organization* 28: 138–154. https://doi.org/10.1111/gwao.12534

Mettenberger, T. and P. Küpper (2019). "Potential and impediments to senior citizens' volunteering to maintain basic services in shrinking regions." *Sociologia Ruralis* 59(4): 739–762. https://onlinelibrary.wiley.com/doi/abs/10.1111/soru.12254

Miranda, V. (2011). "Cooking, caring and volunteering: Unpaid work around the world." *OECD Social, Employment and Migration Working Papers*, No. 116, OECD Publishing. https://doi.org/10.1787/5kghrjm8s142-en

Overgaard, C. (2019). "Rethinking volunteering as a form of unpaid work." *Nonprofit and Voluntary Sector Quarterly* 48(1): 128–145. https://doi.org/10.1177/0899764018809419
Parreñas, R. S. (2021). *Unfree: Migrant Domestic Work in Arab States*. California, Stanford University Press.
Pennisi, S. and S. Baker Collins (2017). "Workfare under Ontario works: Making sense of jobless work." *Social Policy & Administration* 51(7): 1311–1329. https://onlinelibrary.wiley.com/doi/abs/10.1111/spol.12271
Pettinger, L. (2019). *What's Wrong with Work?* Bristol, Policy Press.
Pitts, F., Borghi, P. and Murgia, A. (2023). "Organising the self-employed: Combining community unionism, coworking and cooperativism across contexts." *Open Research Europe* 3(80). https://doi.org/10.12688/openreseurope.15798.1
Pudal, R. (2012). "Travailleurs inachevés et syndicalisation paradoxale: ce que nous apprend le cas des pompiers volontaires." *Sociétés contemporaines* 87(3): 75–97. https://www.cairn.info/revue-societes-contemporaines-2012-3-page-75.htm
Pulignano, V. and G. Morgan (2022). "The social foundations of precarious work: The role of unpaid work in the family." *Faces of Precarity: Critical Perspectives on Work, Subjectivities and Struggles*. J. Choonara, A. Murgia and R. M. Carmo (eds.). Bristol, Bristol University Press: 114–129.
Rakodi, C. (2014). "A livelihoods approach–conceptual issues and definitions." *Urban Livelihoods*. T. Lloyd-Jones, and C. Rakodi (eds.). London, Routledge: 26–45.
Reid-Musson, E., E. MacEachen, M. Beckie and L. Hallström (2022). "Work without workers: Legal geographies of family farm exclusions from labour laws in Alberta, Canada." *Agriculture and Human Values* 39(3): 1027–1038
Rodríguez-Rocha, V. (2021). "Social reproduction theory: State of the field and new directions in geography." *Geography Compass* **15**(8). https://doi.org/10.1111/gec3.12586
Rosol, M. (2012). "Community volunteering as neoliberal strategy? Green space production in Berlin." *Antipode* 44(1): 239–257
Schwiter, K. and J. Steiner (2020). "Geographies of care work: The commodification of care, digital care futures and alternative caring visions." *Geography Compass* 14(12): e12546. https://compass.onlinelibrary.wiley.com/doi/abs/10.1111/gec3.12546
Simms, M. (2019). *What Do We Know and What Should We Do about the Future of Work*. London, Sage.
Unpaid work: Expansion and mobilization of a feminist category, *Shifting Categories of Work: Unsettling the Way We Think About Jobs, Labor and Activities*, L. Herzog and B. Zimmermann (eds.) New York, Routledge: 160–174.
Stone, K. V. W. (2013). "The decline in the standard employment contract: Evidence from ten advanced industrial countries." *After the Standard Contract of Employment: Innovations for Regulatory Design*. K. V. W. S. Stone and H. Arthurs (eds.). UCLA School of Law, Law-Econ Research Paper No. 12–19, Russell Sage Foundation Press. https://ssrn.com/abstract=2181082.
Strauss, K. (2012). "Coerced, forced and unfree labour: Geographies of exploitation in contemporary labour markets." *Geography Compass* 6(3): 137–148. https://onlinelibrary.wiley.com/doi/abs/10.1111/j.1749-8198.2011.00474.x
Strauss, K. and S. McGrath (2017). "Temporary migration, precarious employment and unfree labour relations: Exploring the 'continuum of exploitation' in Canada's Temporary Foreign Worker Program." *Geoforum* 78: 199–208. https://www.sciencedirect.com/science/article/pii/S0016718515301342
Trudeau, D. (2012). "Constructing citizenship in the shadow state." *Geoforum* 43(3): 442–452. https://www.sciencedirect.com/science/article/pii/S0016718511001801
Waite, L. and H. Lewis (2017). "Precarious irregular migrants and their sharing economies: A spectrum of transactional laboring experiences." *Annals of the American Association of Geographers* 107(4): 964–978. https://doi.org/10.1080/24694452.2016.1270188
Williams, C. and J. Round (2007). "Beyond formalization: Rethinking the future of work." *Foresight* 9(3): 30–41. https://doi.org/10.1108/14636680710754156
Worth, N. (2016). "Feeling precarious: Millennial women and work." *Environment and Planning D* 34(4): 601–616.
Worth, N. (2017). "The privilege of a parental safety net: Millennials and the intergenerational transfer of wealth and resources'." *The Millennial City: Trends, Implications, and Prospects for Urban Planning and Policy*. M. Moos, D. Pfeiffer and T. Vinodrai (eds.). London, Routledge: 81–92.
Wright, J. (2019). "Robots vs migrants? Reconfiguring the future of Japanese institutional eldercare." *Critical Asian Studies* 51(3): 331–354. https://doi.org/10.1080/14672715.2019.1612765

Recommendations for Further Reading

Antonopoulos, R. and I. Hirway (eds.) (2010). *Unpaid Work and the Economy. Unpaid Work and the Economy: Gender, Time Use and Poverty in Developing Countries*. London, Palgrave Macmillan UK.

Cohen, N. S. (2016). *Writers' Rights: Freelance Journalism in a Digital Age*. Montreal, McGill-Queen's Press-MQUP.

Gibson-Graham, J. K., J. Cameron and S. Healy (2013). *Take Back the Economy: An Ethical Guide for Transforming Our Communities*. Minneapolis, U of Minnesota Press.

Hatton, E. (2020). *Coerced: Work under Threat of Punishment*. Berkeley, University of California Press.

Hochschild, A. R. (1983). *The Managed Heart: Commercialization of Human Feeling*. Berkeley, University of California Press.

Milligan, C. and D. Conradson (eds.) (2011). *Landscapes of Voluntarism: New Spaces of Health, Welfare and Governance*. Bristol, Policy Press.

Monteith, W. and D.-O. Vicol (2021). *Beyond the Wage: Ordinary Work in Diverse Economies*. Bristol, Policy Press.

22

NAVIGATING SELF-EMPLOYMENT IN THE EVOLVING LANDSCAPE OF WORK

Reflecting on the Past and Anticipating the Future

Paolo Borghi

Introduction

A proper introduction to this chapter requires some necessary groundwork that can also serve as a useful compass for an engaged reflection on self-employment and its possible configuration(s) in the near future. It is worth emphasising that attempting to predict overarching trends in the future of self-employment involves a considerable element of uncertainty. There are indeed several reasons for refraining from using the singular form of the term 'future' when discussing self-employment. The notion of multiple futures should primarily be used due to the multitude of self-employed occupations present not only in the rapidly evolving agricultural and industrial sectors, but also in the expanding tertiary sector. Tertiarisation is a common trend in the Global North, but its significance is also observed in diverse economies, even within sub-Saharan Africa (Kobylatova and Shipulya, 2021). This shift in economic dynamics is highlighted by the fact that tertiary sector activities contribute to over half of the GDP and encompass 45% of employment in economies that are in the process of growth and transformation (Nayyar et al., 2021).

The first section tackles the change in self-employment with a diachronic perspective by looking at the debate that developed at the beginning of the new millennium and the data on the rise of Independent Professionals (I-PROs). We then consider some of the relevant dimensions – flexibility and precarity, online and offline platform work, family and social capital, and individual factors – required to understand self-employment in the present and in the near future(s). Finally, the chapter closes with some brief and tentative conclusions.

Changes in the Landscape of Self-Employment

In 2004, Richard Arum and Walter Müller edited a book that heralded the re-emergence of self-employment. Drawing from cross-national research, it provided an extensive examination of self-employment over the preceding decades in various advanced economies, including countries such as Germany, France, The Netherlands, the United Kingdom, the United States, Australia, Hungary,

DOI: 10.4324/9781003327561-30

Russia, Italy, Japan, and Taiwan. The comparative study was founded on a national perspective, acknowledging that self-employment is intricately woven into specific socio-economic systems with unique historical and legal characteristics. Centring on non-agricultural self-employment, the analysis considered occupational categories and gender, alongside factors such as social class background, educational attainment, and family history as factors influencing labour market outcomes. Amid the diverse forms of self-employment arising from data, the authors identified three significant clusters characterised by distinctive attributes, professional trajectories, and roles in the labour market. These comprised professional and managerial self-employment, skilled nonprofessional self-employment, and unskilled nonprofessional self-employment, signalling the widespread and multifaceted nature of self-employment in contemporary economies. Another pertinent aspect of the comparative analysis, given the ever-changing nature of self-employment, involved a separate examination of both the entry and exit phases. This pointed to cross-national variations in self-employment, owing to the combination of macro factors such as labour market regulation with the impact of family social capital. In certain countries like France, Germany, and the Netherlands (classified as corporatist states) there existed stringent market regulations alongside relatively lower levels of family-based social capital. Conversely, countries such as the United Kingdom, Australia, and the United States (characterised as neoliberal economies) exhibited both low levels of family-based social capital and market regulation. In post-socialist nations, like Russia and Hungary, moderate levels of both dimensions were discernible. The other countries studied – Japan, Italy, and Taiwan – exhibited a contrasting pattern: a strong labour market regulation and simultaneously a family-based social capital. These combinations bore notable repercussions for the transfer of self-employment across generations, particularly during a period when shifts in the labour market were observed to be heightening the instability faced by a fresh cohort of self-employed individuals. In particular, they signalled the crucial role that family social capital could play in alleviating some of the challenges posed by shifts in the labour market through start-up assistance, skill sharing, and access to potential clients and business partners.

Reflecting on this research in light of present circumstances, where self-employment is becoming tougher and less secure due to the rise of the gig economy and, in certain scenarios, limited access to benefits for those who are self-employed, helps in understanding the potential trajectories that may emerge in the times ahead. Subsequent developments over the last two decades have seen increasing heterogeneity in self-employment across both managerial and unskilled occupations. This trend highlights an internal re-composition of self-employment, marked by a gradual decline in traditional self-employed roles occupied by craftspeople, who engage in skilled manual work, and an increase in professional positions aligned with the rapidly expanding tertiary sector. Recent studies confirm the expansion of self-employed workers identified as 'I-PROs' – Independent Professionals – and in parallel with the transformative emergence of digital labour platforms. These platforms have resulted in a rising count of self-employed workers, encompassing both skilled and unskilled individuals, who are seeking access to diverse employment prospects within the service sector. As early as 2012, the first European-wide study of this phenomenon, drawing from an analysis of data from the European Labour Force Survey, highlighted the notable expansion of I-PROs. These professionals were defined as self-employed or independent workers (individuals who work for themselves and operate their own businesses or provide services directly to clients without being employed by a specific employer) engaged in service activities and/or intellectual services, excluding involvement in farming, craft, or retail sectors (Rapelli, 2012). Subsequent updates to this initial study (see, for example, Leighton and Brown, 2014) confirmed these trends, contributing to a robust European public discourse about the emerging necessity for representation of self-employed individuals (Bologna, 2018). Recent Eurozone data has similarly demonstrated consistent growth in the population of I-PROs, both in comparison to overall self-employment and especially among those who are self-employed without employees. While the absolute number of self-employed individuals in Europe decreased slightly over the past ten years from 26,451,000 (2013) to 25,714,400 (2022), there has been a steady increase in the proportion of I-PROs relative to the total number of self-employed workers and in relation to self-employed workers operating without employees over the ten year period (2013–2022) that followed the global economic crisis (Eurostat, 2023), as Figure 22.1 illustrates.

The increasing importance of self-employed professionals within economies that are progressively orientated towards the tertiary sector holds considerable implications for the evolving economic landscape. As economies increasingly pivot towards the tertiary sector, the demand for flexible and specialised skills becomes paramount. The trend underscores the adaptability and agility of self-employed professionals in meeting these demands, driving market development, and contributing to economic growth. This pattern's persistence, even during challenging times like the global economic crisis, further emphasises the resilience and relevance of this type of self-employment in shaping contemporary economies (Rapelli, 2012; Leighton and Brown, 2014; Borghi and Murgia, 2019).

The changes outlined extend beyond a quantitative shift in the internal balance of the contemporary self-employed workforce. They point towards other aspects and policy 'problems' that require appropriate responses in terms of occupational stability, bargaining power, and the inclusion of both traditional and contemporary self-employed professions within national frameworks of welfare support (Semenza and Pichault, 2019). This is especially true for I-PROs and more broadly for solo self-employed individuals, who present a complex profile in contemporary labour dynamics owing to their diverse internal make up and unique attributes (Arum and Müller, 2004; D'Amours and Crespo, 2004; Cieślik, 2015). These attributes transcend the classical dichotomy between employers and employees, resulting in hybrid characteristics that defy straightforward classification (Murgia et al., 2020).

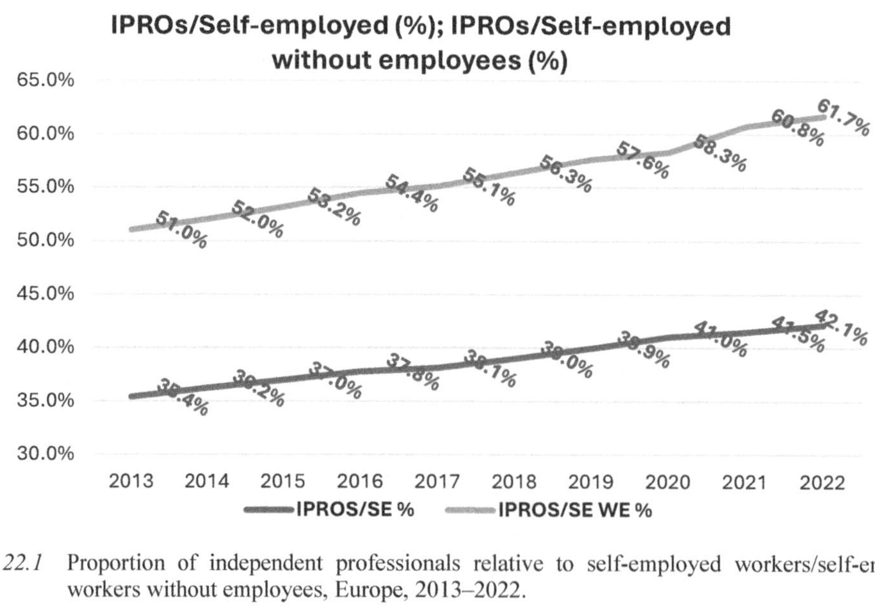

Figure 22.1 Proportion of independent professionals relative to self-employed workers/self-employed workers without employees, Europe, 2013–2022.

Notes: Author's own elaboration of Eurostat data (2023)

Relevant Dimensions for Understanding the Evolution of Self-Employment

As intimated above, self-employment spans a diverse arrange of professional situations and manifests considerable diversity according to the interplay of opportunities and constraints. These disparities are shaped by the distinct employment sectors and geographical settings that are being examined. Nonetheless, within this diversity, the literature identifies specific strategic dimensions, which can act as valuable navigational tools for understanding self-employment in the current landscape of work, while also offering insights into potential trajectories and the spectrum of prospective future scenarios. These are the fragile balance between flexibility and precariousness, the platform work environment and its possible regulation, the role that the family could still play (or not) in supporting self-employed careers, and individual factors interacting with a complex social environment.

Flexibility and Precariousness: Two Sides of the Same Changing Coin

The beginning of the new millennium was characterised by a pervasive and at times mythological rhetoric about the figure of freelancer who, taking full advantage of the rapidly developing connective possibilities, was increasingly becoming a digital nomad. Books such as *We call it work: The digital bohemian or the smart life beyond the fixed job*[1] (Friebe and Lobo, 2006) fuelled imaginaries of freedom that resonated as a promise for entire generations of young people who aspired to reconcile passion, work, freedom of movement, and counterculture. The prevailing narrative at the time depicted a life unburdened by the constraints of wage labour, a theme that dominated numerous popular publications on the emerging realm of self-employment. Words like 'dream', 'independence', 'exploration', and 'fulfilment' guided the discourse that propelled this imaginary.

In a very short time, however, while technological development continued to fuel the growth of new professional profiles and increased the possibilities for remote working, the global economic crisis created turbulence that self-employed workers, the most exposed to market fluctuations, directly and peremptorily experienced. Even the language adapted to the changing times: popular online and traditional publications on freelancing increasingly included tips on how to survive, how to remain attractive to the market and how to improve one's earning possibilities despite the hard times coming. It was implicitly suggested that the golden age of dreams of freedom was gradually turning into an era in which being strategic was necessary in order to avoid turning dreams into a nightmare. This brought about a partial reconfiguration of the imaginary of the autonomous, powerful and exceptional entrepreneurial self (Foucault, 2008 [1979]) capable of capitalising on opportunities in an incessantly expanding market. However, the heterogeneous nature of self-employment also entails – in both favourable and unfavourable market periods – different conditions experienced by self-employed workers operating within the same sector. This diversity encompasses disparities in access to professional and income-generating opportunities, as well as the varying potential of improving one's position in the market.

Furthermore, the first decades of the new millennium were marked by the rise of involuntary self-employed as a result of the economic crisis. The crisis prompted workers who had lost their jobs to turn to self-employment as a temporary alternative to unemployment (Schippers, 2019). This trend, predominantly observed among men, contributed to an uneven increase in the prevalence of male primary caregiving (see Boyer et al., 2017). However, questions remain about the longevity of this trend, especially as gig work continues to be viewed as a means for women to effectively balance work and caregiving responsibilities (see Chapter 8).

An awareness of the increasingly precarious conditions experienced by self-employed workers emerged, raising concerns about the adequacy of existing welfare provisions and safety nets to support individuals navigating self-employment and gig work (Conen and Schippers, 2019; Florin and Pichault, 2019; Pantea, 2022). However, contemporary research indicates that individuals who are self-employed are typically expected to take control and make decisions to address feelings of insecurity or uncertainty that come with their work situation. These individuals are not viewed as passive victims of circumstances; they are expected to proactively employ their own initiative to manage the challenges they face (see Chapter 27). This includes finding ways to deal with conflicting aspects of their home/work life, including striking a balance between contrasting demands or expectations (see Chapter 21). Ultimately, they are compelled to assume responsibility and make informed decisions in navigating the intricacies of their self-employed endeavours, which relates in part to portrayals of the self-employed as entrepreneurial heroes (Murgia and Pulignano, 2021). This nuanced perspective acknowledges the multiplicity and complexity of their working conditions, which are progressively taking on a more hybrid and fluid form, entangled with both risks and opportunities.

Self-Employment, Digital Platforms, and Crowd Work

Linked to the aforementioned developments, platform work has emerged as a relevant economic phenomenon relying mainly on a self-employed workforce. Its impact has been so pervasive that different authors speak of 'platform capitalism', highlighting the profound influence of digital platforms on the economic landscape (Srnicek, 2017; van Doorn, 2018; Vallas, 2019). The core objective of digital labour platforms is attaining market dominance to generate profits for platform companies and maximise returns for shareholders (see Chapter 4). This involves attracting clients by offering self-employed workers at competitive prices and with convenience, which is achieved by exerting pressure on labour rights and minimising costs by fostering intense competition among self-employed workers, whether they are involved in casualised work online or offline (Durri, 2023). Additionally, some platforms are organised to resemble or incorporate elements of games or gaming. In this context, work tasks are structured in a way that resembles a game with features like challenges, rewards, achievements, and competition. The goal of gamified work is to engage workers, motivate them and potentially increase their productivity by incorporating elements of enjoyment and competition to make routine or repetitive tasks more engaging and to encourage workers to achieve specific targets or goals (Caradador et al., 2017; Krzywdzinski and Gerber, 2021).

The organisation of work facilitated by digital labour platforms has effects that go far beyond their immediate operational settings. It has fundamentally altered the nature and practice of self-employment. In placing heavy emphasis on individual autonomy, self-organised work practices, individual bargaining strength, and the freedom to decide when and where one works, digital labour platforms negate the challenges faced by self-employed workers, including job insecurity, inconsistent income, absence of benefits, and constrained labour rights. Of course, digital labour platforms encompass different services and professions, resulting in an inherent diversity that warrants dedicated consideration. When we shift our focus to highly skilled professionals – such as designers, content creators, artists, architects, interpreters, musicians, and music teachers – it becomes evident that many of them merge their conventional undertakings with tasks procured and conducted through these platforms. In these cases, platform work assumes the role of a beneficial earnings supplement, as well as a means to counterbalance periods of reduced client engagement, while also surmounting the constraints posed by conventional social and professional networks. The degree of autonomy held by individual professionals is intricately tied to their economic reliance on platform opportunities (Schor, 2021). Consequently, the liberty to select both the nature and quantity of clients is not uniformly shared among platform-employed workers; instead, it is connected to their bargaining strength. While certain professionals are able to choose when and whether to incorporate platform work into their activities, the converse situation arises within the domain of crowd workers. Crowd workers are a distinct group who engage in tasks, often fragmented and small in scale, through digital platforms. Unlike many highly skilled professionals, crowd workers typically lack the agency to choose the type or timing of tasks they undertake. Instead, they are presented with predefined tasks or projects, leaving them with limited control over the work they perform and the conditions under which they carry it out.

One of the first investigations into crowd workers, specifically those associated with Mechanical Turk and Crowdflower, revealed widespread issues encompassing low and inadequate compensation, unpaid labour, and the absence of social security protections for these workers. Berg's (2016) study revealed instances of mistreatment by clients, including the rejection of completed work and withholding payments. Crowd workers who participated in Berg's investigation denounced the lack of transparency inherent in platforms, revealing that when they raised issues with the responsible corporate entities, their concerns were usually ignored. This illustrated a profound disregard for a work structure in which the advantages are strongly biased towards customers, penalising workers, who often have to navigate unclear instructions.

However, the issues extend further as crowd work platforms have operate on a global scale from the outset, pitting workers from different countries against each other, and consequently fuelling competition for the benefit of customers and triggering 'dumping' dynamics – where tasks and services are offered at extremely low rates – resulting in the erosion of wages and labour standards (Jäger et al., 2019). Crowd work is a global phenomenon that often mirrors the imbalanced dynamics between the Global North and Global South. Operating on a piecework basis for micro-tasks, crowd workers epitomise the most extreme manifestation of self-employment. Although crowd work constitutes a relatively small fraction of overall employment, it raises highly pertinent issues for advanced economies, touching upon issues of tax evasion, workers' rights, and the transparency of algorithms organising work. Similarly, in the developing economies of the Global South, crowd work is seen as a potential employment avenue for the more educated and technologically proficient segments of the population, raising important questions about the potential exploitation of these workers, the effects on local labour markets, and the overall impact on economic inequality and social dynamics.

Wood and colleagues contribute to the emerging analysis of crowd work by analysing data gathered through semi-structured interviews with crowd workers from Southeast Asian and Sub-Saharan African regions (Wood et al., 2019). The outcomes of this research unveil a scenario where, despite the geographical distance that limits direct client oversight of workers (given that most clients are based in high-income countries), the platforms themselves establish the framework for remote monitoring. This includes tracking actions such as keyboard keystrokes, mouse movements and screen captures. This form of invasive control, embedded in the structure of the platforms, poses a significant challenge to the longstanding notion of autonomy that has characterised self-employment for decades. This challenge is so profound that it prompts us to question whether such workers can actually be designated as self-employed. While interviewees indicated that they were able to navigate and sometimes circumvent these control measures, it remains essential to comprehend how work is conceived and organised within this context.

While direct control measures still leave space for workers to exercise self-protection, Wood and colleagues (2019) highlight that the algorithmic control mechanisms governing rating systems on platforms holds significant influence. Such systems intricately shape the reputation of workers, which, in turn, substantially impacts their access to job opportunities. Workers with lower ratings are effectively marginalised, leading to a notable constraint on their earning potential. These situations, which are in some ways unprecedented, disrupt the conventional parameters within which we have been traditionally understood employment and self-employment.

Offline Platform Work: Self-Employed Riders and Drivers

The algorithmic control, reputational pressures, and competition driven by gamification processes emerge as a pervasive concern across various digital labour platforms. The three dimensions combine and take different forms depending on the specific platforms and the underlying business models in place. The first instances of digital labour platforms utilising large numbers of self-employed workers to complete work offline were within the domains of food delivery and ride-hailing platforms. In both cases, notable and early controversies arose in relation to episodes of algorithmic discrimination and the opacity surrounding the algorithms that underpin these platforms' operations (Muller, 2019). Even within these specific cases, the nature of self-employment assumes rather heterodox configurations compared to conventional norms. The theoretical autonomy to establish one's work schedule and locations intersects with algorithmic surveillance that incentivises work at peak times, rewarding those who are willing to work precisely when and where demand is the highest. Moreover, the leverage of ratings and rankings influences and in fact limits the decision-making autonomy of platform workers. These two examples of offline platform work also showed the first signs of collective organisation, no doubt aided by the fact that while such work is mediated by digital platforms, it still requires a physical presence in public spaces.

This dynamic creates the possibility of being visible and recognisable, of gathering in strategic locations in urban spaces while awaiting job assignments from the app, of getting to know fellow workers directly and then exchanging information through social networks and chats. This camaraderie is built upon mutual trust arising from daily interactions within shared spaces and workplaces. These particular characteristics render offline environments of platform work interesting for new and established collective entities eager to experiment with new forms of collective representation (Tassinari and Maccarrone, 2020; Borghi et al., 2021; Woodcock and Cant, 2022). Drawing inspiration from recent developments within the sphere of food delivery and ride-hailing services – which encompass debates over DoorDash's driver deactivation policies, as well as demands from individuals employed by platforms like Uber and Ola for improved compensation, enhanced working conditions, and safeguards against violence – the issue of collective representation in platform work emerges as a forefront concern (see Chapter 10). Indeed, it concentrates in itself the heterogeneity and the contradictions of conventional self-employment alongside new conflicts stemming from the digital organisation of work where its casualisation and fragmentation are merged together with forms of extreme competition and gamification becoming a standard.

Family and Social Capital

Viewing self-employment through a family-orientated lens offers insights into pivotal determinants shaping the choice to pursue self-employment (see Stanworth et al., 1989; Lentz and Laband, 1990; Laband and Lentz, 1992). Different researches have focused on intergenerational entrepreneurship, unveiling how family support can foster entrepreneurial paths (Dunn and Holtz-Eakin, 2000) and career trajectories (Bindah, 2017). The likelihood of opting for self-employment is notably higher if one's father was already engaged in self-employment, compared to those venturing into self-employment without familial precedent (Stanworth et al., 1989). Furthermore, the influence of prior family experiences extends to prospects of success. Lentz and Laband (1990) underscored that second-generation self-employed individuals possess a competitive advantage, entering self-employment at a younger age with more substantial human capital than their first-generation counterparts. Yet it is not only a person's family background (whether family members have been self-employed before), but also their access to social resources like networks, connections, and knowledge (social capital) that shapes their likelihood of entering self-employment and also influences their prospects for success in this endeavour.

The vast literature on social capital has extensively demonstrated its significance in overall economic development, particularly in the context of knowledge-driven economies (see, among others, Dosi, 1988; Maillat and Lecoq, 1992; Storper, 1995; Fountain, 1999). We adopt here Bourdieu and Wacquant's (1992) definition, conceiving social capital as "the sum of the resources, actual or virtual, that accrue to an individual or a group by virtue of possessing a durable network of more or less institutional relationship of mutual acquaintance and recognition". Social capital is therefore the specific surrounding social environment through which social actors can move in developing their strategies. Notably this discussion involves various perspectives concerning 'bridging' and 'bonding' capital, along with a nuanced synthesis acknowledging that both forms of social capital hold value and can complement each other. While 'bridging' capital broadens one's horizons and introduces new resources, 'bonding' capital provides a strong sense of support and unity within a particular group. The interplay between these two facets of social capital shapes various aspects of individual and collective experience, but becomes particularly vital in the context of self-employment, where the relationship between an individual and their social networks can profoundly impact their entrepreneurial journey. The combination of 'bridging' capital's capacity to foster connections that extend beyond immediate social circles and 'bonding' capital's ability to provide nurture and sustain directly influence how self-employed individuals navigate challenges, seize opportunities, and establish a sense of professional identity. In the realm of self-employment, this interplay becomes a critical determinant of not only economic success but also the overall well-being and satisfaction of individuals in their chosen career path.

This perspective on social capital, interwoven with the role trust assumes in professional interactions, provides a lens to navigate the intricate and diverse landscapes that self-employed individuals traverse. Examining social capital within increasingly fluid and mutable professional realms implies a broader shift away from the narrow notion of the solitary entrepreneur as the exclusive architect of their accomplishments or setbacks. Instead, it signifies situating the analysis and comprehension of self-employment dynamics within a collective framework, where the role of not only the individual, but also relationships, interactions, and various other individual and communal actors, comes into play.

Individual Factors

There are several individual characteristics that have traditionally been identified as indicators of a greater propensity to pursue a career in self-employment. In particular, psychological studies show how the propensity to take risks and an individualistic orientation are traits associated with a greater inclination towards entrepreneurial initiatives (Beugelsdijk and Noorderhaven, 2005). Other research underlines how a strong sense of independence influences the likelihood of engaging in independent business ventures (Blanchflower and Oswald, 1998). The combination of individual characteristics, including proactivity, imaginative capacity, adaptability to change, and the ability to navigate through changing and unstable environments, plays a significant role in explaining (often in retrospect) the predisposition for self-employment and the capacity to survive and evolve in this context. However, Fritsch and Rusakova (2010) conducted an empirical study using micro data from the German Socio Economic Panel (SOEP), shedding light on the relative influence of personality traits on becoming self-employed. Their findings suggest that while personality traits do play a role in the decision to become self-employed, the strength of this relationship varies across professions and is generally weak. The authors, through a specific focus on creative professions, show evidence that 'there is, indeed, some positive link between personality structure and self-employment that remains statistically significant after controlling for regional factors, socio-economic indicators, and demographic characteristics. However, according to the estimated marginal effects for the entrepreneurial personality fit, it makes only a minor contribution to the explanation of self-employment' (Fritsch and Rusakova, 2010, p. 25). This implies that while personality attributes contribute to the decision to pursue self-employment, other factors such as contextual conditions and economic forces also play substantial roles in shaping this choice.

Findings indicate the importance of approaching the analysis of individual factors influencing the inclination towards self-employment with caution. It is important to recognise that various professional domains may hold specific values and orientations. Therefore, attempting to generalise specific traits as the sole factors responsible for a heightened or diminished propensity towards self-employment is not only imprecise but also insufficient in capturing the complexity of this phenomenon. It is crucial to acknowledge the multifaceted nature of self-employment and the interplay of various individual, professional, and contextual elements that collectively contribute to shaping one's orientation in this regard.

Conclusions

This chapter has outlined the structural changes in the self-employed workforce (Arum and Müller, 2004). It has pointed out, including through a timely analysis of data for the European area, evidence that affirms the sustained expansion of the skilled component that we have referred to as I-PROs. This trajectory aligns with and reinforces conclusions drawn from earlier studies (Rapelli, 2012; Leighton and Brown, 2014; Borghi and Murgia, 2019). Moreover, the growth of unskilled self-employment, a trend that had already emerged in the 1990s has now been propelled by digital labour platforms. In this context, diverse categories of crowd workers and self-employed individuals have found opportunities for income generation. However, in many cases, the platform environment has entrapped workers in unfavourable circumstances in relation to both their earnings and their working conditions (Berg, 2016; Wood et al., 2019).

Structural changes in self-employment, which appear to be stable at least in the medium term, raise concerns regarding employment security, amid a broader context of cyclical economic crises and international turbulence (Conen and Schippers, 2019; Florin and Pichault, 2019; Pantea, 2022) that make global markets unstable. In addition, structural changes in the production system, driven by the accelerating digitalisation process, reconfigure the roles and centrality of highly skilled self-employed workers on the one hand, and the sustainability of increasingly casualised tasks performed by low-skilled self-employed workers on the other. The opportunities for wielding bargaining power are in many cases shrinking under the weight of increasingly global competition, except in certain market niches where skills are relatively scarce, and bargaining is a real opportunity for self-employed workers.

Questions also remain in terms of the inclusion of new and established self-employed professions into the welfare system (Semenza and Pichault, 2019). This issue takes on different traits and nuances in different countries being bound by welfare systems struggling to maintain the protections guaranteed until a few decades ago, and in need of extending greater protection to those who have hitherto experienced only partial inclusion.

Moreover, I-PROs in particular and solo self-employed in general represent a challenging figure of contemporary work due to their heterogeneity (Arum and Müller, 2004; D'Amours and Crespo, 2004; Cieślik, 2015). Their specific attributes in many cases overcome the classical dichotomy between employers and employees, therefore showing hybrid traits difficult to classify according to standard categories (Murgia et al., 2020).

We have tried to outline here some of the main strategic dimensions to consider to understand the evolution of self-employment and its possible futures. In doing so, we have identified global factors that are partly interlinked. Indeed, digitalisation processes profoundly change the organisation of work, the access to work itself, and the figure of self-employment. The potential they offer goes hand in hand with a growing competition that, on the one hand, is generating opportunities even for low- and middle-income countries, and on the other hand, reproduces, as in the case of crowdwork, power relations that configure digital neo-colonialist approaches. Sub-Saharans and South Asian countries provide labour for customers of the Global North who set fees, delivery times and schedules, effectively defining the obligation to work at night due to the time difference. More generally, the platformisation of work already has a strong impact on work in general and self-employment in particular, fostering flexibility to react to ever faster and more customised demands. Self-employed workers are trapped in this game in the continuous need for new customers and to renew their skills.

We have also identified contingent and place-based factors that contribute to shaping and reshaping the dynamics affecting work in general and self-employed work in particular, especially national and local socio-economic structures more or less favourable for self-employed workers. Indeed, territorial economies, combined with welfare systems, may favour or discourage the concentration of both highly and low-skilled self-employed workers. Moreover, individual and social capital may open up opportunities or, on the contrary, may limit the capacity for taking professional initiative.

Due to all these reasons, thinking about multiple futures for self-employment means recognising a plurality of conditions, experiences, trajectories, expectations and needs, professions and careers that do not fit in a homogeneous and monolithic scenario. Working conditions experienced by the self-employed in the expanding service sector depend on the combination of several variables concerning global competition, national and local markets, regulatory systems and welfare systems, including both individual and collective factors. The main challenge therefore is recognising this irreducible multiplicity and, at the same time, imagining a common framework of rights, and an emancipatory flexibility that is both fair and sustainable.

Note

1 Our translation from the original German title.

References

Arum, R., & Müller, W. (Eds.) (2004). *The reemergence of self-employment: A comparative study of self-employment dynamics and social inequality*. Princeton, NJ: Princeton University Press.

Berg, J. (2016). *Income security in the on-demand economy: Findings and policy lessons from a survey of crowdworkers*. Conditions of Work and Employment Series no.74. Geneva: International Labour Organisation.

Beugelsdijk, S., & Noorderhaven, N. (2005). Personality characteristics of self-employed; an empirical study. *Small business economics*, *24*, 159–167.
Bindah, E. V. (2017). Family dynamics and intergenerational entrepreneurs' leadership style. *Journal of Global Entrepreneurship Research*, *7*(1), 25.
Blanchflower, D. G., & Oswald, A. J. (1998). What makes an entrepreneur?. *Journal of labor Economics*, *16*(1), 26–60.
Bologna, S. (2018). *The rise of the European self-employed workforce*. Milan, IT: Mimesis.
Borghi, P., & Murgia A. (2019). Between precariousness and freedom: The ambivalent condition of independent professionals in Italy. In W. Conen & J. Schippers (Eds.). *Self-employment as precarious work: A European perspective*. Cheltenham: Edward Elgar Publishing, 132–152.
Borghi, P., Murgia, A., Mondon-Navazo, M., & Mezihorak, P. (2021). Mind the gap between discourses and practices: Platform workers' representation in France and Italy. *European Journal of Industrial Relations*, *27*(4), 425–443.
Bourdieu, P., & Wacquant, L. J. D. (1992). *An invitation to reflexive sociology*. Chicago, IL: University of Chicago Press.
Boyer, K., Dermott, E., James, A., & MacLeavy, J. (2017).Regendering care in the aftermath of recession? *Dialogues in Human Geography*, *7*(1), 56–73.
Cardador, M. T., Northcraft, G. B., & Whicker, J. (2017). A theory of work gamification: Something old, something new, something borrowed, something cool? *Human Resource Management Review*, *27*(2), 353–365.
Cieślik, J. (2015). Capturing statistically the intermediate zone. Between the employee and employer firm owner. *International Review of Entrepreneurship*, *13*, 205–214.
Conen, W., & Schippers, J. (Eds.) (2019). *Self-employment as precarious work: A European perspective*. Cheltenham: Edward Elgar Publishing.
D'Amours, M., & Crespo, S. (2004). The dimensions of heterogeneity among own-account self-employed: Elements for a typology. *Industrial Relations*, *59*, (3).
Dosi, G. (1988). Sources, procedures, and microeconomic effects of innovation. *Journal of Economic Literature*, *26*(3), 1120–1171.
Dunn, T., & Holtz-Eakin, D. (2000). Financial capital, human capital, and the transition to self-employment: Evidence from intergenerational links. *Journal of Labor Economics*, *18*(2), 282–305.
Durri, I. (2023). *Casual work arrangements and platform-based work: The casual work agenda as a way to enhance the labour protection of platform workers* (Vol. 115). Alphen aan den Rijn, NL: Kluwer Law International BV.
Eurostat (2023). *Self-employment by sex, age and economic activity (from 2008 onwards, NACE Rev. 2) - 1 000* [Data set]. https://ec.europa.eu/eurostat/databrowser/view/lfsa_esgan2/default/table?lang=en&category=labour.employ.lfsa.lfsa_empself
Florin, L., & Pichault, F. (29 June 2019). *Emerging forms of precariousness related to autonomy at work: Proposals for an Empirical Typology of Self-Employment* [Paper presentation]. 31st Annual meeting of the Society for the Advancement of Socio-Economics, New York, United States.
Foucault, M. (2008[1979]) *The birth of biopolitics: Lectures at the Collège de France 1978–1979*. Basingstoke and New York: Palgrave Macmillan.
Fountain, J. E. (1999). Social capital: A key enabler of innovation. In L. Branscomb & J. Keller (Eds.). *Investing in innovation: Creating a research and innovation policy that works*. Cambridge: The MIT Press, 85–111.
Friebe, H., & Lobo, S. (2006). *Wir nennen es Arbeit: die digitale Bohème oder: Intelligentes Leben jenseits der Festanstellung* (Vol. 60056). Munich, DE: Heyne.
Fritsch, M., & Rusakova, A. (December 10, 2010). *Personality Traits, Self-Employment, and Professions*. Available at SSRN: https://ssrn.com/abstract=1736576 or http://dx.doi.org/10.2139/ssrn.1736576 .
Jäger, G., Zilian, L. S., Hofer, C., & Füllsack, M. (2019). Crowdworking: Working with or against the crowd? *Journal of Economic Interaction and Coordination*, *14*, 761–788.
Kobylatova, M., & Shipulya, M. (2021). *The role of the service sector in the global economy*. Riga: Baltija Publishing.
Krzywdzinski, M., & Gerber, C. (2021). Between automation and gamification: Forms of labour control on crowdwork platforms. *Work in the Global Economy*, *1*(1–2), 161–184.
Laband, D. N., & Lentz, B. F. (1992). Self-recruitment in the legal profession. *Journal of Labor Economics*, *10*, 182–201.

Leighton P., & Brown D. (2014). *Future working: The rise of Europe's independent professionals (iPRos)*. Available online at: chrome-extension://efaidnbmnnnibpcajpcglclefindmkaj/https://iehost.net/pdf/Future_Working_Full_Report.pdf (accessed September 17, 2024).
Lentz, B. F., and Laband, D. N. (1990). Entrepreneurial success and occupational inheritance among proprietors. *Canadian Journal of Economics, 23*, 563–579.
Maillat, D., & Lecoq, B. (1992). New technologies and transformation of regional structures in Europe: The role of the milieu. *Entrepreneurship & Regional Development, 4*(1), 1–20.
Muller, Z. (2019). Algorithmic harms to workers in the platform economy: The case of Uber. *Columbia Journal of Law & Social Problems, 53*, 167.
Murgia, A., Bozzon, R., Digennaro, P., Mezihorak, P., Mondon-Navazo, M., & Borghi, P. (2020). Hybrid areas of work between employment and self-employment: Emerging challenges and future research directions. *Frontiers in Sociology, 4*, 86.
Murgia, A., & Pulignano, V. (2021). Neither precarious nor entrepreneur: The subjective experience of hybrid self-employed workers. *Economic and Industrial Democracy, 42*(4), 1351–1377.
Nayyar, G., Hallward-Driemeier, M., & Davies, E. (2021). *At your service?: The promise of services-led development*. Washington, D.C.: World Bank Publications.
Pantea, S. (2022). Self-employment in the EU: Quality work, precarious work or both? *Small Business Economics, 58*(1), 403–418.
Rapelli, S. (2012). *European I-Pros: A study*. London: PCG Group.
Schippers, J. (2019). Labour market flexibility, self-employment and precariousness. In Conen, W and Schippers, J (Eds.). *Self-employment as precarious work: A European perspective*. Cheltenham: Edward Elgar, 23–39.
Schor, J. (2021). *After the gig: How the sharing economy got hijacked and how to win it back*. Berkley: University of California Press.
Semenza, R., & Pichault, F. (Eds.) (2019). *The challenges of self-employment in Europe*. Cheltenham: Edward Elgar Publishing.
Srnicek, N. (2017) *Platform capitalism*. Hoboken, NJ: John Wiley & Sons.
Stanworth, J., Stanworth, C. B., Granger, B., & Blyth, S. (1989). Who becomes an entrepreneur? *International Small Business Journal, 8*, 11–22.
Storper, M. (1995). The resurgence of regional economies, ten years later: The region as a nexus of untraded interdependencies. *European Urban and Regional Studies, 2*(3), 191–221.
Tassinari, A., & Maccarrone, V. (2020). Riders on the storm: Workplace solidarity among gig economy couriers in Italy and the UK. *Work, Employment and Society, 34*(1), 35–54.
Vallas, S. P. (2019). Platform capitalism: What's at stake for workers? *New Labor Forum, 28*(1), 48–59.
Van Doorn, N. (2018). The parameters of platform capitalism. *Krisis: Journal for Contemporary Philosophy*, 1, 103–107.
Wood, A. J., Graham, M., Lehdonvirta, V., & Hjorth, I. (2019). Networked but commodified: The (dis)embeddedness of digital labour in the gig economy. *Sociology, 53*(5), 931–950.
Woodcock, J., & Cant, C. (2022). Platform worker organising at Deliveroo in the UK: From wildcat strikes to building power. *Journal of Labor and Society, 25*(2), 220–236.

Recommendations for Further Reading

Arum, R., & Müller, W. (Eds.) (2004). *The reemergence of self-employment: A comparative study of self-employment dynamics and social inequality*. Princeton, NJ: Princeton University Press.
Bologna, S. (2018). *The rise of the European self-employed workforce*. Milan: Mimesis.
Bozzon, R., & Murgia, A. (2022). Independent or dependent? European labour statistics and their (In) ability to identify forms of dependency in self-employment. *Social Indicators Research, 160*(1), 199–226.
Cieślik, J., & van Stel, A. (2023). Solo self-employment—Key policy challenges. *Journal of Economic Surveys. 38*(3), 759–792.
Conen, W., & Schippers, J. (Eds.) (2019). *Self-employment as precarious work: A European perspective*. Cheltenham: Edward Elgar Publishing.
Mezihorak, P., Murgia, A., Borghi, P., & Mondon-Navazo, M. (2023). Representing solo self-employed workers: The strengthening of relations between traditional and new collective actors in industrial relations. *Work, Employment and Society, 37*(4), 1013–1031.

PART 9

Mobilities and Geographies of Work Futures

23

GLOBAL PRODUCTION AND THE FUTURE OF WORK

Past, Present, and Futures of Just-in-Time

Rutvica Andrijasevic, Julie Yujie Chen and Marc Steinberg

Introduction

Current global production is driven by an on-demand market imperative. In textiles, automotives, and electronics to mention just several key industries, the general trend is time-based competition propelled by the shortening of product life cycle and price erosion. However, despite this key relevance of time, so far global production has predominantly been investigated from the spatial perspective. This encompasses, just to give a couple of examples, the concept of "spatial fixes" to trace capital's mobility and relocation in search of profitability, control and dispersion of labour struggles (Harvey, 2001; Pun, 2005; Silver, 2003); the debates surrounding the concept of the new international division of labour to understand the geography of global capitalist production (Mezzadra and Neilson, 2013; Starosta, 2016); and that of transnational labour regimes to indicate that the making of labour regimes is as much a local process as its transnational (Baglioni et al., 2022). In addition, feminist scholars showed that the spatial fragmentation of production in the developing economies pivoted on so-called feminisation of manufacturing, given that around 90% of the workforce was female (Bair, 2010). Firms prioritised the recruitment of inexperienced and ununionised women, often internal rural migrants, so as to be able to suppress wages and working conditions to a level, which Wright (2006) has called "disposable labour". As we can see, global production mobilises differences – gender, race, and citizenship status – to expand and to extract value from labour.

Building on these Marxist and feminist analyses of global production, the argument we put forward is that attention to *space* in the analysis of global production needs to be matched by attention to *time*. A temporal approach is pivotal in order to make visible the diverse ways in which capital deploys time to reorganise and expand as well as segment labour along gender and ethnic lines in order to "assemble" workforces best suited for the temporalities of global production. This assembly is aided by electronic forms of communication from the Electronic Data Interchange (EDI) systems adopted in the 1970s onwards in industry to the Internet today, suggesting that the proliferation of networked communication ICTs has engendered a new temporality – instantaneous, simultaneous, and globally networked – that scholars refer to interchangeably as "real-time" and/or "network time" (Adam, 2006; Hope, 2016; Nadeem, 2009). Real time is best understood as a quantitative approach to time, or as Judy Wajcman (2019) put it, an "economic-utilitarian philosophy of

DOI: 10.4324/9781003327561-32

time", that is underpinned by the belief that technology can be successfully employed to achieve time optimisation.

Just-in-time (JIT)'s mobilisation of these technologies *and* of a form of synchronisation needs to be seen as part of a larger shift in the temporalities of production – one that coincides with the rise of networked communication. The managerial consequences for these shifting temporalities of production are significant, and JIT is a crucial, if overlooked, aspect of this. JIT is best summed up as a series of practices associated with the Toyota Production System (TPS), whereby power imbalances are exploited to (1) accelerate production times; (2) reduce inventory space; and (3) extract more profit, efficiency, speed, and space by outsourcing more of the production process. JIT aims at eliminating "unproductive time" and space in the assembly process by synchronising multiple stages of production, so one set of parts is finished as they are needed on the assembly line. The spatial fix is, in other words, directly related in JIT to a temporal fix.

To foreground such a temporal approach, this chapter investigates the notions of JIT and its evolving practices in representative industries to outline past, present and future modalities of global production. Each of these temporalities (past, present, future) will be illustrated through a short case study. This chapter firstly engages Japan in the 1960s and the TPSs typified by JIT and zero-inventory. It shows the extent to which Toyotism and JIT maximise profit by minimising the production time and rapidly identifying mistakes, creating a template for time-based competition, minimum inventory, and labour management organised around an as-needed labour force reliant on underpaid women's labour. Synchronisation between production time and space, we show, is central to this model of control; the as-needed labour force is a template for the on-demand labour forces discussed subsequently. Secondly, the chapter discusses the adaptation of JIT in the electronics manufacturing since early 2000 in China and Central and Eastern Europe (CEE), and shows the way in which the application of JIT model prompted recruitment and labour control practices that attempt to synchronise the supply and assembly of labour to JIT manufacturing. Finally, the chapter discusses how JIT principles informed the transition from analogue to digital capitalism, via a case of data annotation for machine learning (ML)/AI models. It illustrates the new iterations of JIT in data production for AI in which the workforce is designed to be spatially dispersed without formal control boundaries of factories or dormitories.

Synchronisation, we argue throughout, operationalises a very specific idea of time. What we find in all these cases is an exploitation of geographical inequalities through a model of temporal control that operates via an imagined (or in some cases near-real) ideas of instantaneity ("real time") or its closest approximation: JIT. This imagined and constructed real time is materialised through removing socially and culturally lived multiple temporalities and rendering the latter valueless in capitalism. To better historicise this heightened control-and-decentralisation, and doubly spatial-and-temporal nature of this control, it helps to go back to the Toyotist context of development and the way it was described by its analysts.

Past: Toyota Production System

JIT is at the heart of the TPS, which is dedicated – according to its main proponent and innovator Ohno Taiichi – to "the absolute elimination of waste" (Ohno, 1988: 15) via the JIT production method. Waste here is both wasted *time* (an extension here of Taylorist time management practices) and wasted *space* (notably, inventory space). According to Ohno: "Just-in-time means that, in a flow process, the right parts needed in assembly reach the assembly line at the time they are needed and only in the amount needed. A company establishing this flow throughout can approach zero inventory" (Ohno, 1988: 15).

The contrast being made here, albeit implicit, is to the "wasteful" Fordist model of "just-in-case production" (Sayer, 1986). Vertically integrated in its idealised form, Ford and Fordism imagined a "rubber-tree plantation to finished car" model of production that, while being resuscitated now by companies such as Tesla amidst geopolitical struggles over lithium mines and rare earth minerals, fell out of fashion amidst the perceived failures or inefficiencies of vertical integration (Sherman, 2020). Contrary to this, JIT was organised around small inventories, flexible labour forces that had weak union protection, and the ability to quickly ramp up production if demand increased. Producing may be replaced by "procuring" here since it is a system that generally relied on external manufacturers to deliver items on time. The JIT in the name implies the as-needed and *timely* delivery of parts for the assembly line, as parts ran low.

The main tool used in the operationalisation of JIT was the *kanban* system. The kanban was a paper sheet encased in a translucent vinyl plastic cover that allowed workers to order additional parts as they ran low. Kanban informed internal and external suppliers what parts were needed and when, building a real-time dataset about supply levels (Monden, 1994: 9). The elimination of waste meant the elimination of backroom supply; in its ideal form it meant the elimination of storage space in its entirety – a proposition that made sense in a space-constrained nation. Toyotism was hence more than a model for factory work; it was the invention of lean supply chain management.

Contrary to Ford which aimed towards total vertical integration, Toyota disintegrated the factory into different parts of the process, aiming towards zero-inventory, with stock replenished on an as-needed basis. In other words, Toyota aimed "to convert a vast group of suppliers and parts plants into *one large machine*" (Womack et al., 1990: 61). The management of this machine was left to Toyota's assembly line workers, who not only had to build cars but also monitor inventories and fill out kanban cards to indicate when there were too few or too many parts. This required workers to manage stock, frequently change jobs, multitask, and adapt quickly to changes in the assembly line or the assembly process (Dohse et al., 1985: 120). Second- and third-tier suppliers would have to respond by shipping their parts to the main Toyota factory in a timely manner. This often involved multiple deliveries per day. Japan's auto manufacturers may, "in an extreme case, require subcontractors to supply parts eight times a day" – resulting in "increasing distribution costs, traffic jams, and destruction of the environment" (Naruse, 1991: 47). The ethos of "no waste" was simply the externalisation of waste outside of Toyota's factory.

Toyota factories would operate as central hubs around which some ten tiers of subsidiary companies and subcontractors were arrayed. Kenney and Florida (1993: 46) estimate that 70% of production was outsourced (often to suppliers within the country, later to production zones within Southeast Asia), while only 30% was produced in house. The kanban card as managerial technique had quite direct social consequences: the subsidiaries had to take on the risks of production made to order, and both companies and their often-precarious workers bore the consequences in case of any dip in demand for automobiles and their parts. The core companies ensured guaranteed employment to their workers, whereas the further removed subcontractors depend on expendable, precarious, lower-paid labourers who were mobilised contingently to meet the fluctuating demands.

As Taylor (2006) and Andrijasevic (2021) emphasise in their work, JIT was not only about supply of materials or *things*, it was also, from an early moment albeit only later explicitly explained as such, about the supply of labour-power or *people*. The part-time and temporary workers mobilised to meet fluctuating demands were often women and minorities in Japan, and, after the reform of working visitor laws in the 1990s, temporary foreign workers (Allison, 2014; Yamada, 2010), who "make up the periphery of the Japanese economy" (Kenney and Florida, 1988: 129). As Anne

Allison notes, the "family-corporate system" of postwar Japan relied on a system of permanent employment for men, and "low-paid, peripheral jobs" assumed by women (2014: 25) in what has been termed a dual labour market. With Toyotism, women and later migrant workers would be the first to be let go if there was an economic downturn.

Toyota was, then, a kind of sovereign that created a system of vassal companies around it, and contingent workers within these companies who took the brunt of any economic downturn. These companies were sometimes tied to Toyota via relationships of debt which Toyota or Toyota-related banks would lend to allow for subsidiaries' capital expenditures. It also meant that it had inordinate power over its subcontractors. Even apologists for Toyotism like Kenney and Florida acknowledge that "new penetrating forms of corporate control and hegemony appear to be required for the model's success" (1993: 306). Toyota's factories were coercive, gendered, and hierarchical spaces of control – control that radiated from the centre company down throughout its entire supplier chain.

In sum, Toyotism developed a model of time-based competition that sped up the production time by outsourcing production and employment to its parts suppliers, previewing models of the platform economy that would later emerge (Steinberg, 2022). As part of a bid to reduce on-site parts storage – and the space this storage required – Toyota exerted the pressures of time on its own workforce and that of its multiple tiers of suppliers. Put simply, JIT worked by mobilising unequal relations of power to extract more profit, and depended on the synchronous management of time and space in production. What we see from the Toyotist model is that the spatial fix of capital was also, from the start, a temporal fix.

Present: On-Demand Electronics Assembly

Electronics assembly is driven by an on-demand market imperative. The general trend is time-based competition driven by a shortening of product life cycle and price erosion. The dynamics of such time-based competition can be observed in CEE where several Asian electronics manufacturers relocated starting from the early 2000. Being in proximity to customer markets in Western Europe enabled Asian firms to cut lead time required for products to be shipped from China to Europe from 22 to 2 days. Jim Chang, Foxconn's former managing director in Czechia, explained the firm's decision to set up assembly plants in CEE as follows: "Time and distance are crucial for business competitiveness. We need to be close to our major market and deliver products within 48 hours of receipt of a customer's order".[1] In order words, global production pivots on the compression of time and space so as to meet, in the shortest time possible, the production needs of client firms.

Consequently, electronics manufacturers put in place a flexible labour system that enables them to respond quickly and to avail themselves of sufficient workforce when orders are high and to radically decrease the numbers of workers once the orders fall. To this end, assemblers in CEE segment their workforce into core and temporary workers that allows them to expand or contract the workforce, depending on the demands of production. The ratio between core and temporary workers is typically 60:40%, but during periods of high production it gets reversed with temporary migrant workers making up the majority of the workforce. While core workers are employed directly by the manufacturer on full-time contracts, temporary workers are hired by temporary work agencies (TWAs) and originate from across the CEE and beyond: Slovakia, Hungary, Romania, Bulgaria, Croatia, Serbia, Ukraine. Manufacturers use TWAs to manage fluctuations in productive activity, externalise costs and regulatory risks, reduce the contractual responsibilities of direct employment, and weaken workers' protests and demands for higher wages and better working conditions (Andrijasevic et al., 2022).

By positioning themselves between firms and workers, TWAs are in charge of selection, and recruitment of workers in the country of departure; cross-border transportation, direct management of production (including control of workers inside the factory), and management of accommodation in the country of arrival; and finally the return of workers to their country of departure during periods of low production. TWAs also exercise control over workers in the dormitories and on the assembly lines. This is especially because 12-hour night shifts are common. In the dormitories, control is aimed at suppressing behaviours that can decrease productivity, such as excessive drinking, hosting friends and by extension organising. On the assembly line, agency line-leaders implement, on a daily basis and based on manufacturer's requests, decisions regarding worker numbers, placements and working shifts while at the same time monitoring the performance of agency workers.

As we can see, TWAs operate a comprehensive management of migrant labour. Analytically speaking, this is relevant and novel because, in the triangular employment relationship that regulates the interaction between the client firm, TWA, and workers, managerial responsibilities for production commonly lie with the firm and legal responsibilities with the agency. In our case, however, TWAs were directly responsible for organising, controlling and managing agency worker performance on the assembly line.

Within this arrangement, dormitories are key in that they allow TWAs and manufacturers to put in place a model of private and comprehensive management of the workforce, aimed at maximising the short-term utilisation of labour (Andrijasevic et al., 2022). Dormitories not only allow TWAs to recruit and supply labour at short notice, but also they make it possible for TWAs to put workers to work quickly, usually the very next day regardless of the fact that workers may have just travelled some 500–600 km across several international borders (Schling, 2022). Dormitories also function as repositories for migrant labour in that it is quite common for workers to have to wait in the dormitory without work during periods of low production. Dormitories thus enable TWA and manufacturers to avail themselves of a stationary workforce that they can stand down for several days or even weeks without risking a significant shortage of workers.

In light of fluctuating production, TWAs and dormitories facilitate the JIT model for the utilisation of labour. Nowadays short-term labour mobility, involving temporary and repetitive movements between home and a variety of host countries, is on the rise and has already become more widespread than the classic long-term labour migration.

One telling instance is the example of a Croatian female worker residing in Serbia whom we met in Slovakia working for Samsung and staying, once again, in a shared room in a worker dormitory. In the four-year period (October 2015 to June 2019), she was hired eight times by different TWAs for temporary engagements in Slovakia and Czechia. During this period, she worked in electronics, white goods, and logistics for brands ranging from Shin Hueng Precision, to Samsung, and Honeywell, over periods varying from several weeks to several months.

It is urgent, we suggest, to examine how the temporal demands of JIT manufacturing and the prominence of TWAs are obfuscating employment relations, diluting employer's responsibilities, and impeding the effective enforcement of workers' employment and social rights. While it is well established that temporary migrant agency workers do not enjoy sufficient protection in destination states as employment laws and industrial relations are national in scope and character (Berntsen and Lillie, 2016), the real-time model of labour intermediation also gives rise to subcontracting chains that have been referred to as "human supply chains" (Gordon, 2017). In our case this is best illustrated by the case of Serbian workers working for Samsung in Slovakia, they were recruited by a TWA in Serbia, signed the contract with a TWA in Hungary, were paid by a Slovak TWA and then put on a new contract with a Romanian TWA when police shut down the Serbian

TWA subsidiary (Novitz and Andrijasevic, 2020). The notion of chains is also illustrative of the relations of dependency: workers were tied into a contract with a particular employer, live under the menace of penalty and/or non-payment of wages, are subject to illicit deductions from pay, risk homelessness because of tied accommodation, are isolated by geography and language, and lack meaningful legal protection.

To sum up, on-demand electronics assembly makes visible the extent to which JIT manufacturing imposes onto workers the demands and dynamics of JIT organisational temporality. Operationalising this temporality reshapes work and employment relations, in particular via the JIT model aimed at short-term utilisation of labour, and alters transnational labour markets by instantiating novel flows of labour migration. JIT evolves from the management of things to be explicitly about the management of people – migrant workers – on the assembly line, as workforces are themselves organised in a JIT manner.

Future: Data Labour on Demand for Artificial Intelligence (AI)

JIT principle continues to iterate and generate even more sophisticated production networks in the platform economy. How human labour to annotate datasets for AI and ML models – known as data labelling or data annotation – is mobilised and regulated for on-demand data production is emblematic of the new iterations of JIT in the digital era.

The formation of data annotation production networks is inseparable from the preceding spatial-and-temporal orders governing the connected yet geographically dispersed work force in the information economy (Aneesh, 2006) (see Chapter 7). With a deliberate workflow design, data annotation work is divided into very small tasks that can be easily distributed around the world and resembled through ICT networks. These tasks take a few seconds to a couple of days to complete and can be accessed through applications on the mobile phones or digital platforms. Platforms have become critical socio-technical organisations for JIT labour delivery for AI data production and data capital accumulation (Irani, 2015).

In data production, a divergence occurs between control over space and time. Time control is not bound to spatial control (such as in the dormitory regime). Geographical restrictions take new forms other than exclusion. Similar to the call centre sector, JIT data production has been rendered to be scalable in spatial terms (Irani, 2015), requiring no physical migration of workers. The mobility constraints facing data workers are not so much about geographical or locational restrictions imposed by the immigration apparatus and labour intermediary. Instead they are about the persistent trend to distribute the jobs to poor regions, particularly those located within the Global South (Berg et al., 2018; Posada, 2022). AI supply chains also appropriate existing disadvantages facing marginalised populations within labour markets due to social differences, such as women with care responsibilities. Though scheduling flexibility offers job opportunities to these marginalised groups (Berg et al., 2018), it is often mobilised to conceal poor work conditions and a lack of institutional labour protection.

Digital platforms are comparable to conventional TWAs or business process outsourcing (BPO) in allowing clients to access and mobilise a flexible pool of workers to meet fluctuating market demands. But they do not replace or disrupt the existing informal labour systems like BPO or TWAs. Instead BPO and TWAs are grafted onto the platform-mediated labour process, making the labour supply chain ever longer and labour relations more elusive in data production and platform economy in general (Andrijasevic et al., 2021). With the platform's mediatory and institutional roles in governing the labour management and transactions, however, yet another new development from JIT manufacturing is the displacement of any means of employment contractual relation. Data workers are no longer bound to one single employer. Since the annotation jobs are often short-term and extremely unstable, there is no standard production timeline and it is common for the workers on the platforms to work on several projects with different clients simultaneously and to work on multiple platforms (Berg et al., 2018). When BPO is involved in data production networks, workers can also be tasked to work on different projects dealing with different clients (see Chandhiramowuli and Chaudhuri, 2023). They face triple controls from the platforms, managers, and the clients (Miceli et al., 2020).

The divergence between control over space and time in data production also means that time control becomes more prominent, pervading and connecting multi-scalar spaces. The speed and frequency to assemble and disassemble JIT data labour on the basis of projects, the number of workers involved globally, and the degree to which the speed and frequency can be achieved automatically through ICT are unprecedented (Irani, 2015). Indeed, instantaneity and timeliness are the most salient and normative temporal orders of JIT data production. However, speed is articulated and experienced differently by different people – for example, data workers and AI developers – in data production networks. As Sharma reminds us, speed is not a "uniform cultural fact", but "is composed of multiple relational temporalities" (Sharma, 2022: 45). Therefore, a relational lens would shed new light on differentiation of time and immediacy for the clients, developers, and data workers. Specifically, AI developers and clients set respective response times and completion times for each task or project, which vary from project to project. Furthermore, the experimental, and at times speculative, nature of AI development generates uncertainty on the part of developers. This uncertainty sets in motion ripple effects of disruptions in data production and inconsistency in the data annotation rules, making the latter living and constantly updating documents which require adaptable and responsive labour from data workers.

Due to lack of industry-wide standards and information asymmetry preventing the workers from knowing the job complexity and thus anticipating the time commitment needed, the response time and completion time are experienced by the workers as unstable tasks and unpredictable time commitments for each project. To manage the unpredictability and instability of each project, data workers adopt various time strategies such as staying hyper vigilant about new job notifications and staying available (Gray and Suri, 2019), developing atypical work hours such as in the evenings or at night, in the case of workers living in a different time zone from their clients (Berg et al., 2018), and taking on more jobs to buffer the possibility of insufficient pay which may contribute to overwork.

The persistent logic of JIT from lean manufacturing to data production is a redrawing of the temporal boundary for the production process. Capitalism has invented and normalised the distinction between productive and unproductive labour time since its inception; what we see through JIT is this temporal boundary being reset for data workers who get paid by piece rate upon the client's acceptance of their completed job, which generates an ever-growing list of unpaid time. According to a survey-based study conducted by the International Labour Organisation, one third of time spent by the platform-based digital workers is unpaid (Berg et al., 2018) (see Chapter 21). Howson and colleagues argue that unpaid labour time is integral to the platform model of crowdsourcing (Howson et al., 2022). Their conclusion can be extended to the data production process in general with crowdsourcing platforms and outsourcing included. Thus, the critical new development in data labour on-demand is characterised by the dispossession of worker's availability and the trend to dwindle the temporal boundary of paid labour time.

Conclusions

This chapter has treated JIT as it operates a temporal model of coordination and control through Toyotist automobile manufacture, on-demand electronics manufacture, and data annotation for

AI/ML models. The geographical spread and industrial application of JIT points to its pervasiveness in time-based work environments. Indeed, while we have figured these moments as past, present, and future, by placing them together, we see that in truth each moment bleeds into another; they are synchronous in how they operate and how they manage production and labour force.

The synchronisation between production time and space is central to this model of control; and the worker precarisation is both a presupposition and a consequence for the evolving JIT practices that are increasingly dictated by the imperative to maximise the employers' flexibility and minimise their responsibility. Concurrently, synchronicity offers its own benefits for labour activism; better communication among disparate workers, and struggles over work among them. The struggle over working conditions is increasingly a struggle over time. Evidence shows that platform-based drivers organise themselves by simultaneously logging off during peak times (Wells et al., 2021). Knowing the past, present, and futures of JIT management is one step towards enabling temporal pushback of workers against capitalism's continuous tendency to redraw the spatial-and-temporal boundaries of the production process in the interests of the employers.

Note

1 https://taiwantoday.tw/news.php?unit=4&post=4301, consulted on 23 September 2023.

References

Adam, B. (2006). Time. *Theory, Culture & Society*, 23(2–3): 119–126.

Allison, A. (2014). *Precarious Japan*. Durham, NC: Duke University Press.

Andrijasevic, R., Chen, J. Y., Gregg, M., and Steinberg, M. (2021). *Media and Management*. Minneapolis: University of Minnesota Press.

Andrijasevic, R. (2021). "Just-in-Time Labor": Time-based management in the age of on-demand manufacturing. In R. Andrijasevic, J.Y.Chen, M. Gregg, and M. Steinberg (Eds.), *Media and Management*. Minneapolis: University of Minnesota Press, pp. 31–63.

Andrijasevic, R., Sacchetto, D., and Pun, N. (2022). Transnational corporations and the making of global labour markets: The case of Foxconn in China and Europe. In E. Boris, H. Gottfried, J. Greene, & J.-C. Tham (Eds.), *Global Labor Migration: New Directions*. Champaign, IL: University of Illinois Press.

Aneesh, A. (2006). *Virtual Migration: The Programming of Globalization*. Durham, NC: Duke University Press.

Baglioni, E., Campling, L., Coe, M. N., and Smith, A. (Eds.) (2022). *Labour Regimes and Global Production*. Newcastle upon Tyne: Agenda.

Bair, J. (2010). On difference and capital: Gender and the globalization of production. *Signs: Journal of Women in Culture and Society*, 36(1): 203–226.

Berg, J., Furrer, M., Harmon, E., Rani, U., and Silberman, M. S. (2018). *Digital Labour Platforms and the Future of Work: Towards Decent Work in the Online World*. Geneva: International Labour Office.

Berntsen, L., and Lillie, N. (2016). Hyper-mobile migrant workers and Dutch trade union representation strategies at the Eemshaven construction sites. *Economic and Industrial Democracy*, 37(1): 171–187.

Chandhiramowuli, S., and Chaudhuri, B. (2023, January 3). Match made by humans: A critical enquiry into human-machine configurations in data labelling. *Proceedings of the 56th Hawaii International Conference on System Sciences*. Hawaii. https://hdl.handle.net/10125/102882

Dohse, K., Jürgens, U., and Nialsch, T. (1985). From "Fordism" to "Toyotism"? The social organization of the labor process in the Japanese automobile industry. *Politics & Society*, 14(2): 115–146.

Gordon, J. (2017). Regulating the human supply chain. *Iowa Law Review*, 102(445): 445–503.

Gray, M. L., and Suri, S. (2019). *Ghost Work: How to Stop Silicon Valley from Building a New Global Underclass*. Boston, Massachusetts: Houghton Mifflin Harcourt.

Harvey, D. (2001). Globalization and the "spatial fix". *geographische revue: Zeitschrift für Literatur und Diskussion*, 3(2): 23–30.

Hope, W. (2016). *Time, Communication and Global Capitalism*. Basingstoke: Palgrave MacMillan.

Howson, K., Ferrari, F., Ustek-Spilda, F., Salem, N., Johnston, H., Katta, S., Heeks, R., and Graham, M. (2022). Driving the digital value network: Economic geographies of global platform capitalism. *Global Networks*, 22(4): 631–648.

Irani, L. (2015). The cultural work of microwork. *New Media & Society*, 17(5): 720–739.

Kenney, M., and Florida, R. L. (1988). Beyond mass production: Production and the labor process in Japan. *Politics & Society*, 16(1): 121–158.

Kenney, M., and Florida, R. L. (1993). *Beyond Mass Production*. Oxford: Oxford University Press.

Mezzadra, S., and Neilson, B. (2013). *Border as Method, or, the Multiplication of Labor*. Durham, NC: Duke University Press.

Miceli, M., Schuessler, M., and Yang, T. (2020). Between subjectivity and imposition: Power dynamics in data annotation for computer vision. *Proceedings of the ACM on Human-Computer Interaction*, 4(CSCW2): 115:1–115:25. https://doi.org/10.1145/3415186

Monden, Y. (1994). *Toyota Production System: An Integrated Approach to Just-in-Time* (2nd edition). London: Chapman & Hall.Nadeem, S. (2009). The uses and abuses of time: Globalization and time arbitrage in India's outsourcing industries. *Global Networks*, 9(1): 20–40.

Naruse, T. (1991). Taylorism and fordism in Japan. *International Journal of Political Economy*, 21(3): 32–48.

Novitz, T., and Andrijasevic, A. (2020). Reform of the posting of workers regime–An assessment of the practical impact on unfree labour relations. *JCMS: Journal of Common Market Studies*, 58: 1325–1341.

Ohno, T. (1988). *Toyota Production System: Beyond Large-Scale Production*. Portland, OR: Productivity Press.

Posada, J. (2022, March). *The Coloniality of Data Work for Machine Learning (Ethics of AI in Context)*. https://ethics.utoronto.ca/events/julian-posada-the-coloniality-of-data-work-for-machine-learning-ethics-of-ai-in-context/

Pun, N. (2005). *Made in China: Women Factory Workers in a Global Workplace*. Durham, NC: Duke University Press.

Sayer, A. (1986). New developments in manufacturing: The just-in-time system. *Capital & Class*, 10(3): 43–72.

Schling, H. (2022). "Just-in-time" migrant workers in Czechia: Racialisation and dormitory labour regimes. In E. Baglioni, L. Campling, N.M. Coe, and A. Smith (Eds.), *Labour Regimes and Global Production*. Newcastle upon Tyne: Agenda.

Sharma, S. (2022). Undisciplined time studies. *Time & Society*, 31(1): 44–47. https://doi.org/10.1177/0961463X211073551

Sherman, S. (2020). Why Lenin was a fan of Ford. In H. Bratton Benjamin, B. Nicolay, & A. Nick (Eds.), *The New Normal* (pp. 406–410). Moscow: Strelka.

Silver, B. J. (2003). *Forces of Labor: Workers' Movements and Globalization Since 1870*. Cambridge: Cambridge University Press.

Starosta, G. (2016). Revisiting the new international division of labour thesis. In G. Charnock & G. Starosta (Eds.), *The New International Division of Labour* (pp. 79–103). London: Palgrave.

Steinberg, M. (2022). From automobile capitalism to platform capitalism: Toyotism as a prehistory of digital platforms. *Organization Studies*, 43(7): 1069–1090.

Taylor, B. W. K. (2006). A feminist critique of Japanization: Employment and work in consumer electronics. *Gender, Work and Organization*, 13(4): 317–337.

Wajcman, J. (2019). The digital architecture of time management. *Science, Technology, & Human Values*, 44(2): 315–337.

Wells, K. J., Attoh, K., and Cullen, D. (2021). "Just-in-place" labor: Driver organizing in the Uber workplace. *Environment and Planning A: Economy and Space*, 53(2): 315–331. https://doi.org/10.1177/0308518X20949266

Womack, J. P., Womack, J. P., Jones, D. T., et al. (1990). *Machine That Changed the World*. London: Simon and Schuster.

Wright, M. (2006). *Disposable Women and Other Myths of Global Capitalism*. Abingdon: Routledge

Yamada, M. (2010). The current issues on foreign workers in Japan. *Japan Labour Review* 7(3): 5–18.

Recommendations for Further Reading

Andrijasevic, R., Chen, J. Y., Gregg, M., and Steinberg, M. (2021). *Media and management*. Minneapolis: University of Minnesota Press.

Cowen, D. (2014). *The Deadly Life of Logistics: Mapping Violence in Global Trade*. University of Minnesota Press.

Crawford, K. (2021). *Atlas of AI: Power, Politics, and the Planetary Costs of Artificial Intelligence*. New Haven, CT: Yale University Press.

Hope, W. (2006). Global capitalism and the critique of real time. *Time & Society*, 15(2–3): 275–302.

Ohno, T. (1988). *Toyota Production System: Beyond Large-Scale Production*. Portland, OR: Productivity Press.

Tubaro, P., Casilli, A. A., and Coville, M. (2020). The trainer, the verifier, the imitator: Three ways in which human platform workers support artificial intelligence. *Big Data & Society*, 7(1): 2053951720919776. https://doi.org/10.1177/2053951720919776

24

RESHAPING THE GEOGRAPHY OF WORK

Remote Worker Migration and Regional Dynamics in the Post-Pandemic Era

Julie MacLeavy, Suzanne Mills, Katie Mazer and Darja Reuschke

Introduction

The COVID-19 pandemic precipitated a dramatic surge in remote work within most industrialised nations (Özgüzel et al., 2023). Remote working was on the rise before 2020, but the pandemic prompted a fundamental transformation in the *geography* of work. This large-scale shift of employees' jobs from offices to homes has had profound implications for workers, households, communities, regions and nation-states. As the daily commute becomes less essential, traditional patterns of residence have become unmoored, paving the way for new patterns of internal migration. The recent increase in remote working has also led to a surge of new research as geographers and other social scientists seek to understand what the increased prevalence of working remotely means for gender relations, work-life geographies, city structures and broader dimensions of health and well-being (del Boca et al., 2022; Hall et al., 2024; James, 2024; Stevens and Shearmur, 2020). Additionally, researchers have begun to investigate emerging internal migration patterns, often characterised as the 'urban exodus' (Fukuda, 2024; Rowe et al., 2023), to uncover if and how remote work is reshaping not just individual work-life experiences, but also population dynamics across different places (Borsellino et al., 2022; Fielding and Ishikawa, 2021; Nelson and Frost, 2023; Vogiazides and Kawalerowicz, 2023; Wolff and Mykhnenko, 2023). This body of research on the relationship between remote work and migration is, however, still in its infancy.

At the same time, policy interest in attracting remote workers as a means of addressing regional disparities has grown. Governments in declining regions across multiple countries have actively sought to entice remote workers to mitigate population decline and out-migration (see, for example, Chisholm, 2021). At a national scale, there is optimism that remote work might ease population pressure on urban centres while simultaneously fostering economic growth in rural or declining regions (Corbetta, 2022; Davies, 2021). However, concerns have also been raised about the potential for remote worker migration to exacerbate existing inequalities in receiving regions, with identified issues, including rising housing costs, overburdened social services and increased homelessness (Colomb and Gallent, 2022; Gallent et al., 2023; Willet, 2023). Hence, there is a need for a deeper understanding of this phenomenon to inform policy interventions aimed at maximising the potential benefits and mitigating the potential risks associated with this transformative shift in the geography of work.

 DOI: 10.4324/9781003327561-33

In what follows, we review recent literature on internal migration and remote work, defined here as working most of the time at home or outside a central office, mediated by digital technology. By taking stock of the relevant literature at three scales – the national, the regional and the individual – we explore the emergent relationship between internal migration and remote work and highlight relevant questions including the extent to which remote work opportunities are driving internal migration patterns, the potential impacts of remote working on receiving regions in terms of both inequality and prosperity, and the decision-making processes and post-migration experiences of remote workers. We then discuss the relevance of these questions for two countries with high rates of remote work, the United Kingdom and Canada. By placing our discussion within the context of these two policy environments, we aim to contribute to ongoing debates about the future of work, while also charting directions for future research.

Contextualising the Discussion within Economic Geography and Beyond

Our discussion draws on literature from economic geography, urban geography, planning and population geography. This scholarship explores how technological advances are transforming not only the nature of work, but also its geographical distribution. A central focus is on the extent to which digital work reconfigures the spatial organisation of labour markets, labour processes and built environments (Althoff et al., 2022; Knaus et al., 2021; Reuschke and Ekinsmyth, 2021). Economic geographers have brought to light how the rapid expansion of home-based remote working during the pandemic has had wide-ranging implications for work and workers: feminist geographers have explored the gendered impacts of increasingly blurred boundaries between work and life (Cockayne, 2021; del Boca et al., 2022; James, 2024; see also Chapter 8), as well as the effects of remote work on racial and class inequalities (Islam, 2022; Xiang, 2022). Meanwhile scholars specialising in urban and regional development and planning have explored shifts in remote worker mobilities and the use of coworking spaces. Self-employed individuals and employees are noted to have been utilising coworking spaces in addition to their home offices for some time (Akhavan et al., 2021; Mayerhoffer, 2021), underlining that the digital transformation of the economy did not start with COVID-19. But recognising a step-change in the prevalence of home-based remote working alongside other forms of remote working, some scholars have sought to predict the spatial impacts of the increased uptake of remote work on urban structures, transportation systems and residential patterns (see, for example, Stevens and Shearmur, 2020). Our consideration of the relationship between internal migration and remote work builds on this research by highlighting the connections between remote work, population change, regional development and inequality. In essence, we seek to advance three areas of scholarship: population studies exploring the link between the COVID-19 pandemic and internal migration; studies focused on remote work in the context of urban and regional development; and research exploring how remote workers engage with space and place.

How Significant Is Remote Working to Migration-Related Population Dynamics?

Geographers and transport planners have a rich history of studying the spatial effects of remote work, exploring how telecommunication and technological innovations influence urban form and social inequality (Moos and Skaburskis, 2007; Mokhtarian et al., 1998; Shen, 1998). Pre-pandemic research was typically focused on whether remote work leads to longer commutes and urban sprawl, or whether those with longer commutes in suburban or outer urban areas are more likely to adopt remote work (Ory and Mokhtarian, 2006; Mokhtarian et al., 2004). This scholarship was largely disconnected from studies of internal migration in population geography, as well as urban and regional development research. However, the large-scale shift to remote work during the COVID-19 pandemic spurred several new investigations as urban planning scholars started to question whether the growing prevalence of remote work was transforming urban structures by, for instance, diminishing the importance of central business districts (Delventhal et al., 2022; Knaus et al., 2021; Stevens and Shearmur, 2020).

Researchers suggested that the spatial impacts of increasingly blurred labour market boundaries were likely extending well beyond urban areas (Braesemann et al., 2022). Moreover, the pandemic was significantly altering internal migration patterns and demographics (Rowe et al., 2023). International evidence from several industrialised nations showed an initial decline in internal migration during the first lockdown, followed by an increase in the latter half of 2020. This trend occurred in Germany (Dolls and Lay, 2023), Spain (González-Leonardo et al., 2022), Sweden (Vogiazides and Kawalerowicz, 2023) and the United States (Haslag and Weagley, 2023) and sparked research into pandemic-linked population decline in inner-city areas (Sweet and Scott, 2022), along with population growth in rural areas and towns near metropolitan centres (a process of counter-urbanisation) (González-Leonardo et al., 2022). While this identified some important shifts, it also found that internal migration declined in some countries, like Australia (Perales and Bernard, 2022), while in others, such as Great Britain, it fell before rebounding to pre-COVID levels (Rowe et al., 2023). This suggested that projections of a widespread 'urban exodus' (Fukuda, 2024; Rowe et al., 2023) or 'rural revival' (González-Leonardo et al., 2022) linked to remote work were country-specific and that further research was needed to specify and explain country-level differences.

Similarly, claims that remote work migration might reverse decades of exclusionary urban development and so-called 'super-gentrification' warrant further investigation before definitive conclusions can be drawn (MacLeavy and Manley, 2022). While some places experienced clear shifts in population dynamics during the pandemic, many pandemic-era studies have only been able to speculate that remote work was the cause of increased internal migration. Additional research is needed to understand if remote work is an enabler, driver or one of many factors influencing changing migration patterns, and whether these emerging patterns persist. Despite the rise of out-migration, some scholars have speculated that urban centres are likely to remain attractive destinations for the affluent and well-connected (Atkinson, 2020). Moreover, historical precedent suggests that the trend of urban to rural migration may be short-lived, as similar population shifts occurred during the Plague in Tudor London but did not fundamentally alter the long-term trajectory of urbanisation (Roger, 2020).

Can Remote Work Revitalise Regional Development?

From a different vantage, scholarship has considered whether remote work arrangements can address problems of urban and regional development. A key proposition is that remote work-induced migration holds the potential to alleviate problems like urban congestion and pollution (Taneja et al., 2022) while also rejuvenating rural and declining – so-called 'left behind' – regions (Chekmarev et al., 2021). The notion of remote worker in-migration as a development strategy, for rural areas in particular, aligns with the promotion of creative rural spaces (Bosworth et al., 2023; Ceinar and Mariotti, 2021; Krasilnikova and Levin-Keitel, 2022), where regional creative industries' development is framed as a means of achieving economic growth and cultural vitality if potential barriers like limited infrastructure can be overcome (Townsend et al., 2017). As Bell and

Jayne (2010) note, rural areas experiencing economic decline due to the global restructuring of agriculture have been encouraged to embrace the arts and cultural community as a means of fostering new employment and economic opportunities. Yet not only is the creative economy articulated differently in the countryside, there are unique characteristics and employment challenges of rural communities that mean simply replicating the 'creative script' associated with urban centres may not be effective in achieving economic and regional policy aims (Bell and Jayne, 2010).

Similar counterarguments exist to the promoted movement of remote workers to rural towns and villages. Several scholars have noted that there is potential for in-migration to exacerbate pre-existing inequalities. While remote work may offer quality-of-life improvements for some high-skilled, high-income, educated individuals and their households (according to Bonacini et al., 2021), there are clear disparities in who can or cannot move to achieve 'lifestyle goals' (Mancinelli and Germann Molz, 2023). This is particularly evident with regard to the stark divide between digitally enabled remote working that affords location independence and travel opportunities versus low-skilled work that is highly localised, particularly racialised mobile platform work (Braesemann et al., 2022; Islam, 2022; Xiang, 2022). Low earnings and visa restrictions can effectively tether this latter group of workers to specific locations, limiting their residential mobility compared to so-called 'digital nomads' (see Chapter 10). Moreover, remote worker in-migration might shift the class composition of receiving regions, impacting both newcomers and existing residents. Privileged individuals, whose middle-class identities and resources grant them mobility, may thus experience a 'discordant' status (Botterill, 2017). This refers to a mismatch between their socio-economic standing in their origin location and their position within the receiving region's social hierarchy. For instance, a remote worker who works as a middle manager in a large city might find themselves at a higher position in the social hierarchy of a smaller, more rural, receiving region. This newfound social standing could create feelings of alienation or disconnect from their new community. In contrast, for existing residents in low-skilled jobs, the arrival of remote workers with professional and managerial positions and salaries might exacerbate existing social and economic challenges. Certainly, popular media in Canada and the United States have captured local resistance to pandemic-related internal migration and highlighted complex power dynamics at play, both within and between regions (Weeden et al., 2022).

One crucial concern revolves around the risks of gentrification and displacement in receiving regions: an influx of high-income remote workers could lead to rising housing costs and competition for resources, potentially displacing existing residents with lower incomes (Chapple, 2017; Denham, 2021). This aligns with longer-standing concerns about 'amenity migration,' where desirable locations attract wealthier individuals – including second home owners and retirees – exacerbating existing inequalities (Gosnell and Abrams, 2011; Argent and Plummer, 2022). Additionally, a focus on remote work as a *singular* solution to regionally imbalanced economies has been critiqued for diverting attention from deeper structural issues affecting rural or declining regions. These include limited access to essential services, inadequate infrastructure and a lack of diversified economic opportunities beyond resource extraction or low-wage service industries and the recognition that addressing these challenges requires a comprehensive and multifaceted approach that goes beyond simply attracting those able to work remotely (Martin et al., 2021). There is therefore a need to critically evaluate the potential of remote work as a solution for 'levelling up' left-behind regions. This policy discourse, prevalent in many countries, aims to address regional disparities and promote inclusive and sustainable development but the potential for digital divides and social exclusion within receiving regions warrants careful consideration (Martin et al., 2021). Not all residents within rural and declining regions will have the necessary skills, resources or access to technology to capitalise on (expanding) remote work opportunities, and so its continued promotion risks exacerbating existing inequalities and further marginalising economically vulnerable groups because of its potential impact on migration flows (Liddle et al., 2023). Although the effects of remote worker migration on housing, services, class dynamics and the distribution of employment opportunities need a long time span to be investigated, the recent increase in in-migration to specific regions in the early 2020s provides an opportunity for exploratory research. By investigating these areas, we can gain insights how these dynamics have unfolded in the short-term and whether initial policy responses have been effective.

How Does Remote Work Influence Social Embeddedness?

Complementing the body of scholarship investigating the impacts of remote work-induced migration on different places, as well as the factors attracting remote workers to certain locations (Bähr et al., 2021; Krasilnikova and Levin-Keitel, 2022; Zenkteler et al., 2022), researchers have sought to uncover how the shift to remote work impacts workers' relationships with place and space at the community or regional level. This is exemplified by Soroui (2021)'s study of the spatial relationships of those able to escape the daily commute and work from anywhere, which found that some increased their civic engagement after shifting to remote work due to increased non-work time and flexibility. This suggests that the spatial and temporal autonomy offered by increased remote work opportunities not only influences residential choice but also potentially patterns of social interaction and community involvement, with consequences for well-being. Bürgin et al. (2022) similarly discovered that 'multi-local' knowledge workers relocating between rural and urban areas in Switzerland successfully formed social connections and integrated into the social fabric of their new communities. However, their economic integration remained limited as they did not participate significantly in the local job market or contribute meaningfully to the local economy. Such dissonance between social and economic integration highlights the need to consider the specific context of migration, including push and pull factors, individual skills and backgrounds, and pre-existing employment networks. When examining the experiences of remote workers relocating to new communities (moves independent of a specific job change), we must remain cognisant of potential limitations to their economic integration within those communities.

Another emergent concern explored within the literature is the subjective experiences and well-being of remote workers. While some argue that remote working practices can lead to increased stress, longer work hours and blurred work-life boundaries (Ewers and Kangmennaang, 2023), others highlight the potential benefits of flexible spatio-temporal practices, including greater autonomy and job satisfaction (Reuschke, 2019). Additionally, there are some indications that granting workers geographical and temporal autonomy may lead to improved productivity for firms (Choudhury et al., 2021; Felstead and Reuschke, 2023). Much of the debate about individuals' experiences of remote work hinges on how shifting temporal and spatial patterns of work and life alter labour control, worker autonomy and the boundary between work and home (Olson, 1983; Hackney et al., 2022; Felstead, 2022). Although working remotely can increase hours of work and the felt need to be responsive to work-related demands in 'off-work' time, many workers post-pandemic say they prefer working remotely (Richards et al., 2024). Ewers and Kangmennaang's (2023) study of remote work during the pandemic, for instance, found that despite increased technostress (the feeling of anxiety, frustration and overload cause by increased use of technology in a work context) and life disruptions, most workers reported that they had benefited from greater spatial and temporal autonomy. Importantly, they also found that experiences of greater autonomy were contingent on age, race and number of dependents.

Persistent gendered expectations around care and household labour are elsewhere identified as becoming more pronounced with home-based remote work arrangements: the elimination of the physical separation between the workplace and home can lead to women working 'all the shifts' as the traditional expectation of managing household responsibilities extends into the time previously occupied by commuting and office work (Dunne, 2021). This echoes findings that mothers working at home during the pandemic frequently extended their work late into the night (Manzo and Minello, 2020; Parlak et al., 2021). Such studies underscore the need to investigate what types of work and life situations allow workers to harness the greater autonomy and flexibility of remote work to improve their lives (Franken et al., 2021; Chung, 2022). In the case of remote worker migration, gaining a deeper understanding of the subjective experiences and perceptions of relocating remote workers – from their decisions to migrate to their migration journeys to their post-migration lives – requires that explorations into the spatial aspects of remote work be broadened to include the complexities of relocating to and integrating within new communities. This broader analysis could also consider how relocation experiences are shaped by and shape various social factors and life situations. Such a focus on relocation experiences can usefully enable connections to be made between geographical and organisational studies debates around the impacts of remote work on worker well-being.

Considering the 'Remote Revolution' in Canada and the United Kingdom

Approaching the inter-regional migration of remote workers with a feminist political economy lens, we seek here to link population-level questions of counter-urbanisation to questions of regional development and workers' different experiences of autonomy and flexibility. Crucially, this framing posits that economic processes, like regional economic shifts, are fundamentally social in nature, both caused by and often contributing to the production of social inequalities (Massey, 1994; Werner et al., 2017). A key question for scholars, as well as those working within the policy and planning realm, then, is whether and under what circumstances migration triggered by remote work reproduces existing inequalities by further entrenching spatial divisions of labour and regional disparities or whether this migration has the potential to mitigate existing inequalities by contributing to a more balanced distribution of opportunities and resources across regions. Comparison of two divergent policy contexts – in this case, Canada and the United Kingdom – can help to clarify policy factors that shape remote work-induced migration and its impacts on receiving regions, in particular.

What is clear from our review is that the impact of remote work-induced migration on inequalities is not preordained but rather influenced by factors operating at and across different scales. Individual circumstances, such as a worker's socio-economic background, access to technological resources and existing family networks in the relocation destinations under consideration influence their ability to migrate and to capitalise on remote work opportunities. Workers with greater social capital, access to technology and established social networks in potential receiving regions are generally better positioned to benefit from increased work flexibility than those without these assets. These individual factors also help shape the social consequences of migration in receiving regions. Willet (2023), for example, differentiates between return migrants (whose relocation is driven by cultural connections and family ties) and non-return migrants (who typically originate from wealthier regions). Her research in Cornwall, a socio-economically less developed peninsular in South West England, which has long attracted tourists and second home residents, indicates that return migrants can contribute to cultural exchange and population growth, although their skillsets do not often translate to local job opportunities. Conversely, non-return migrants, who tend to possess greater financial resources, can potentially stimulate local economic activity, but their arrival risks exacerbating gentrification and social fragmentation within the receiving community. In this respect, understanding the specific characteristics of who moves (including their socio-economic background and skills but also the location of any work) is crucial. Presently, very little is known about how remote work-induced migration differs from other forms of migration in terms of local impact. This information can not only reveal how technology can entrench pre-existing inequalities between workers, but also how it can potentially be used to mediate these inequalities at the regional or community level.

At the scale of the region, a confluence of diverse factors would seem to influence the appeal of a place for remote worker migration and the impact of this migration on that place. Infrastructure emerges as one crucial factor in determining whether remote worker migration can revitalise struggling economies. Regions boasting robust infrastructure hold a clear advantage in attracting a diverse cohort of workers (Willet, 2023). This is especially true for return migrants seeking to leverage their existing skillsets after relocating. It also holds for remote workers given that reliable, high-speed internet access has transitioned from a luxury to a fundamental prerequisite for this demographic. Furthermore, access to essential services, such as childcare, dependable transportation networks, and quality healthcare, are likely to significantly influence decisions to migrate. Additionally, national and regional policies regarding remote work rights, taxation structures and support for relocation can significantly impact migration patterns. Policies that encourage remote work and facilitate relocation, for example, through financial incentives or streamlined mobility procedures, tend to generate more geographically dispersed migration patterns when compared to historically observed migration patterns, which have been concentrated around major urban centres with high job density (Pagliarin and De Decker, 2021).

Beyond traditional drivers of migration at national and regional scales, relatively little is known about the relative importance of different factors for remote work-induced migration. As noted, Canada and the United Kingdom present contrasting policy environments for relocating workers. These contrasting environments can be harnessed in comparative enquiries to gauge in more detail the relationship between remote work and internal migration and the factors influencing how this migration plays out in receiving regions. Over the course of the pandemic, the share of home-based remote workers increased dramatically in both and remained high such that over 20.1% of all workers in Canada in 2023 worked 'usually from home' (Statistics Canada, 2023) and in the United Kingdom in 2022, 22% of all workers worked in a hybrid way, both at home and in the office, with another 13% working exclusively at home (ONS, 2022). In the United Kingdom, the emerging spatial pattern of remote work suggests intensified suburbanisation rather than migration to rural regions (Gibbs et al., 2023), a trend that is also evident in Germany (Dolls and Lay, 2023). In Canada, meanwhile, the 2021 Census of Population reported a reversal of migration patterns for some peripheral resource regions (Statistics Canada, 2022a), with Newbold et al. (2022) highlighting a net in-migration trend in two of the four Atlantic provinces, Nova Scotia and New Brunswick. These provinces have historically served as net exporters of migrants, particularly to western Canada, but have been experiencing net in-migration since 2015.[1]

While a longstanding gap in rents between regions in Canada likely influenced the recent reversal of migration patterns, particularly in Atlantic Canada, the shift also coincided with government policies designed to promote internal migration. Recognising the potential economic benefits that remote workers can bring to less populated regions, several Canadian provinces and communities have implemented programmes to attract digital nomads and remote workers, including expanding broadband coverage in underserved regions and targeting advertising campaigns aimed at urban professionals seeking a lifestyle change (Chisholm, 2021). Nova Scotia, for example, ran a campaign to attract remote workers, advertising lower housing and land prices, lower population density, and local amenities (Nova Scotia, 2020). These measures connect to an approach to labour market and immigration policy in Canada that emphasises the redistribution of labour between regions, including by incentivising individuals with specific skills to relocate to regions facing labour shortages. For instance, the Canada-wide 'Express Entry' immigration programme for skilled workers prioritises applicants with relevant work experience and qualifications, but also allows individual provinces to nominate candidates, potentially making them more competitive and increasing their chances of receiving an invitation to apply for permanent residency (Government of Canada, 2023). This feature of the Express Entry programme creates an incentive for skilled workers to consider settling outside major urban centres. By contrast, the United Kingdom's Skilled Worker visa system, while seeking to attract skilled workers, does not consider regional distribution as a direct factor in its point-based selection process. The focus remains on national needs for skilled workers. So, while some skilled jobs may exist outside major cities and individual choices might influence location, the visa system itself does not offer incentives to settle in specific regions. Since skilled workers often find remote work opportunities attractive, immigration policies aimed at redistributing skilled labour, like Canada's Express Entry programme, may contribute to the increased in-migration of remote workers in peripheral resource regions.

Despite immigration policies that diverge in their capacity and intent to distribute skilled labour inter-regionally, Canada and the United Kingdom have a similar legislative and policy framework governing remote work arrangements. Crucially, neither country has yet instituted a right to remote work. In Canada, the 1999 Telework Policy established the conditions for employees seeking "to work at alternative locations, thereby achieving a better balance between their work and personal lives" (Government of Canada, 1999 quoted in Champagne et al., 2023). This stipulated that remote work arrangements were subject to managerial approval based on operational feasibility, with participation remaining voluntary for both employees and employers. Importantly, the latter would retain the right to terminate arrangements at their discretion. This was followed in 2019 by the GCcoworking initiative which explored the feasibility and benefits of large-scale telework integration within the public sector and established coworking sites across the National Capital Region and in more remote destinations where public sector employees could access dedicated workspaces to facilitate a hybrid work model (Government of Canada, 2019). Within the next year, the COVID-19 pandemic significantly accelerated the adoption of remote work arrangements, with public and private sector organisations across Canada transitioning to remote models out of necessity. While there is now a growing recognition of the potential benefits of remote working, including hybrid models, some organisations are encouraging a return to the traditional workplace and, in 2022, the Government issued a direction on prescribed presence in the workplace, which encourages a return to in-person work, suggesting two to three days per week, or 40%–60% of regular work schedules in the office for public sector employees (Government of Canada, 2022). At the time of writing, the right to work remotely remains a contested issue. In the spring of 2023, the desire to continue working remotely was one of the motivating factors for 150,000 government workers (members of the Public Service Alliance of Canada) to go on strike. While they did not win the right to work remotely, they did overturn the blanket policy in favour of more individualised decision-making within teams or departments (PSAC, 2023), though some suggest little has changed since this agreement (Morison, 2023).

Like Canada, the United Kingdom is engaged in reconciliation of the potential advantages of remote work practices with the established norms and assumptions of the traditional office model. Debates revolve around employer discretion in approving remote work arrangements, concerns about employee isolation and productivity, and the potential for geographic wage disparities. The COVID-19 pandemic temporarily halted these but, like in Canada, with the return to normalcy, the government preference has been for a return to in-person work (Bowie and Smith, 2023). This stance aligns with a prevailing sentiment amongst some policymakers that telework arrangements can hinder employee focus and collaborative efforts, negatively impact organisational productivity and culture, and even lead to detrimental effects on urban economies due to reduced foot traffic in city centres and a potential decline in local businesses activity (Spicer, 2022). The right to request flexible working, including working at home, was introduced in the United Kingdom in 2003 and expanded in 2023,[2] but still with no right to flexible work, which restricts the bargaining power of employees seeking flexible work options. Proposals have been made to strengthen the right to flexible work, including ensuring the ability of employees to disconnect outside of work hours (Breese and Geraghty, 2023). While these have not been implemented yet, it is important to note that the United Kingdom exhibits regional variation in policy approach. Compared to central government in Westminster, which is primarily focused on fostering a culture of flexibility through employer-employee dialogue, the Welsh Assembly has taken a more proactive stance, having introduced a remote working policy in 2020 with a target of 30% remote work by 2026, demonstrating a willingness to mandate specific remote work goals. The case of the United Kingdom thus allows for comparison across constituent nation-states, as well as cross-country analyses, both of which are useful in evaluating the advantages and disadvantages of expanding remote work practices and informing future policy development.

Concluding Discussion

In closing, we underscore the need for further research on the multifaceted impacts of remote work-induced migration. This research agenda can be productively organised into three key themes, with small-scale projects that could be led by student researchers. The first theme focuses on regional development, examining how remote work migration patterns will (continue to) impact the development of urban and rural areas. Will the increased use of remote work exacerbate existing infrastructure and service disparities or can policies mitigate potential strains on resources in recipient regions? Furthermore, to what extent can remote work create opportunities to attract and retain workers in less populated areas? Ultimately, to what extent and under what conditions can remote work contribute to the revitalisation of declining regional economies? A student project might focus on a specific region and analyse how remote work is impacting a particular industry or demographic group, for example, by conducting surveys of residents to assess changes in service use. Policies encouraging remote workers and their households to spend a greater share of their income in their new communities, along with promoting fair distribution of people and resources across regions, might also be evaluated given their aspiration to distribute the benefits of remote work and prevent the creation of new economic or social disparities.

The second theme concerns the evolving economic/employment landscape of remote work, regionally and nationally. Here, questions arise about how remote work impacts wage compression or inflation across different regions and whether it changes how employers find skilled workers and how/where workers search for jobs. A student project could analyse a specific sector and explore how remote work is impacting pay and pay increases or the spread of talent across locations, perhaps by interviewing employers and remote workers in that industry. Additionally, students might consider, through the use of focus group research, how well existing regulations around labour standards, worker protections and taxation adapt to a more geographically dispersed workforce. Are there potential gaps in regulation that need addressing? Finally, what is the long-term impact of remote work on productivity and innovation? Interviews and surveys with workers, employers and policymakers could shed light on how collaboration and knowledge sharing practices change in a distributed work environment and how policies can foster innovation and knowledge transfer even with geographically dispersed workforces.

The third theme for future research pertains to the individual experiences of remote workers who migrate. The first area of concern is their decision-making processes: How do remote workers make the decision to migrate? What key factors motivate and enable relocation? The second area of concern is workers' post-migration experiences. How do workers and their households adapt to their new work-life circumstances? How do they experience and engage with their new communities? How are these new relationships shaped by the specific experiences of working remotely and by associated social-economic factors, ranging from class to gender to family status? Profiles of key receiving communities and of remote worker migrants versus 'other' migrants, worker focus groups, and interviews with community key informants would begin to address these questions. Across this theme, questions of social power warrant attention. What are the gendered impacts of remote work? How is this altered by migration? How does the digital divide – that is, unequal access to reliable internet connections, affordable devices and digital literacy skills – shape remote work opportunities and dynamics in receiving communities? Finally, what are the long-term implications of remote work on worker well-being? Is it possible for remote work to contribute to a more sustainable lifestyle? What role do class, gender, race, and other factors of social location play in determining lifestyle changes? To answer these questions and fully capture the inequities of remote work opportunities and divergent experiences of migration, research on remote worker experiences must include questions of identity, social power, and work outcomes.

As remote work becomes increasingly commonplace, a comprehensive approach that extends beyond technological advancements is necessary to shape the future of work. While advancements in communication and collaboration tools undoubtedly play a pivotal role, the trajectory of this future hinges not only on the 'what' of technological capabilities but also on the 'how' of policy implementation and establishing fair work practices. Effective policy frameworks will in short be crucial for mitigating potential pitfalls associated with remote work, such as exacerbating regional disparities or hindering social cohesion. Furthermore, fostering fair work practices within the evolving landscape of remote work is essential to ensure equitable access to remote work opportunities, protect worker well-being and minimise the environmental footprint of this new paradigm. By embarking on a comprehensive research agenda that explores the multifaceted impact of remote work across regions, the nature of work itself, and its broader social implications, researchers can equip policymakers and stakeholders with the necessary knowledge to navigate this significant shift and help cultivate a work environment that not only fosters efficiency and innovation but also promotes a sense of connection, shared prosperity and environmental responsibility for generations to come.

Notes

1 Both Nova Scotia and British Columbia, provinces high in natural amenities, saw an increase in the number of people working from home in 2021 who had lived in another province 12 months earlier (Statistics Canada, 2022b). Remote workers, however, represent a fraction (2,100) of the total internal migrants in Nova Scotia in 2020/2021.

2 From 2003, employees were permitted to submit a flexible working request once annually, with no guarantee of employer approval. This right was expanded in 2023 to allow employees to submit requests twice per year.

References

Akhavan, M., Mariotti, I. and Rossi, F. (2021) The rise of coworking spaces in peripheral and rural areas in Italy, *Territorio* 97(2): 35–42. https://doi.org/10.3280/tr2021-097-Supplementooa12925

Althoff, L., Eckert, F., Ganapati, S. and Walsh, C. (2022) The geography of remote work, *Regional Science and Urban Economics*, 93: 103770. https://doi.org/10.1016/j.regsciurbeco.2022.103770

Argent, N. and Plummer, P. (2022) Counter-urbanisation in pre-pandemic times: Disentangling the influences of amenity and disamenity, *Australian Geographer*, 53(4): 379–403, https://doi.org/10.1080/00049182.2022.2043807

Atkinson, R. (2020) *Alpha City: How London Was Captured by the Super-Rich*, London: Verso.

Bähr, U., Biemann, J., Lietzau, J and Hentschel, P. (2021) *Rural Coworking: People, Models, Trends*, Gütersloh: Bertelsmann Stifung. https://www.bertelsmann-stiftung.de/fileadmin/files/user_upload/BS_Coworking_im_laendlichen_Raum_ENG_v04_RZ_Einzelseiten.pdf

Bell, D. and Jayne, M. (2010) The creative countryside: Policy and practice in the UK rural cultural economy, *Journal of Rural Studies*, 26(3): 209–218. https://doi.org/10.1016/j.jrurstud.2010.01.001

Bonacini, L., Gallo, G. and Scicchitano, S. (2021) Working from home and income inequality: Risks of a 'new normal' with COVID-19, *Journal of Population Economics*, 34(1): 303–360. https://doi.org/10.1007/s00148-020-00800-7

Borsellino R., Bernard, A., Charles-Edward, E. and Corcoran, J. (2022) A regional renaissance? The shifting geography of internal migration under COVID-19, *Australian Geographer*, 53(4): 405–423. https://doi.org/10.1080/00049182.2022.2074622

Bosworth, G., Whalley, J., Fuzi, A., Merrell, I., Chapman, P. and Russell, E. (2023) Rural co-working: New network spaces and new opportunities for a smart countryside, *Journal of Rural Studies*, 97: 550–559. https://doi.org/10.1016/j.jrurstud.2023.01.003

Botterill, K. (2017) Discordant lifestyle mobilities in East Asia: Privilege and precarity of British retirement in Thailand, *Population, Space and Place*, 23(5): e2011. https://doi.org/10.1002/psp.2011

Bowie, J. and Smith, B. (2023) Civil servants to be told to spend 60% of time in offices, *Civil Service World*, 15 November 2023. https://www.civilserviceworld.com/professions/article/civil-servants-home-remove-working-60-in-office

Braesemann, F., Stephany, F., Teutloff, O., Kässi, O., Graham, M. and Lehdonvirta, V. (2022) The global polarisation of remote work. *PLoS One*, 17(10): e0274630. https://doi.org/10.1371/journal.pone.0274630

Breese, E. and Geraghty, L. (2023) What is the right to disconnect and does the UK need it to stop people burning out? *Big Issue*, 13 July 2023. https://www.bigissue.com/news/employment/what-is-a-right-to-disconnect-and-does-the-uk-need-one-after-covid/

Bürgin, R., Mayer, H., Kashev, A. and Haug, S. (2022) Far away and yet so close: Urban–rural linkages in the context of multilocal work arrangements, *Regional Studies, Regional Science*, 9(1): 110–131. https://doi.org/10.1080/21681376.2022.2042370

Ceinar, I.M. and Mariotti, I. (2021) The effects of COVID-19 on coworking spaces: Patterns and future trends, pp. 277–297, in: Mariotti, I., di Vita, S. and Akhavan, M. (eds.) *New Workplaces – Location Patterns, Urban Effects and Development Trajectories*, Cham: Springer International Publishing. https://doi.org/10.1007/978-3-030-63443-8

Champagne, E., Choinière, O. and Granja, A.D. (2023) Government of Canada's teleworking and hybrid policies in the aftermath of the COVID-19 pandemic, *Canadian Public Administration*, 66(2): 158–175. https://doi.org/10.1111/capa.12520

Chapple, K. (2017) Income inequality and urban displacement: The new gentrification, *New Labor Forum*, 26(1): 84–93. https://doi.org/10.1177/1095796016682018

Chekmarev, O., Manilov, A., Ulimbashev, A. and Timoshenko, S. (2021) COVID-19 pandemic as a stimulus for sustainable development of rural areas and labour markets, *SHS Web of Conferences*, 129: 1–8. https://doi.org/10.1051/shsconf/202112901007

Chisholm, C. (2021) New work-from-home campaign invites people to move to Nova Scotia, *CBC News*, 3 February 2021. https://www.cbc.ca/news/canada/nova-scotia/work-from-home-campaign-invite-1.5899917

Choudhury, P., Foroughi, C. and Larson, B. (2021) Work-from-anywhere: The productivity effects of geographic flexibility, *Strategic Management Journal*, 42(4): 655–683. https://doi.org/10.1002/smj.3251

Chung, H. (2022) *The Flexibility Paradox: Why Flexible Working Leads to (Self-)Exploitation*, Bristol: Policy Press.

Cockayne, D. (2021) The feminist economic geographies of working from home and "digital by default" in Canada before, during, and after COVID-19, *The Canadian Geographer/Le Géographe Canadien*, 65(4): 499–511. https://doi.org/10.1111/cag.12681

Colomb, C. and Gallent, N. (2022) Post-COVID-19 mobilities and the housing crisis in European urban and rural destinations: Policy challenges and research agenda, *Planning Practice & Research*, 37(5): 624–641. https://doi.org/10.1080/02697459.2022.2119512

Corbetta, M. (2022) Assessing teleworking strategies for local development: A framework proposal, *OECD Report*. https://www.oecd.org/cfe/leed/Assessing-teleworking-strategies-for-local-development-PAT.pdf

Davies, A. (2021) COVID-19 and ICT-supported remote working: Opportunities for rural economies, *World*, 2(1): 139–152. https://doi.org/10.3390/world2010010

del Boca, D., Oggero, N., Profeta, P. and Rossi, M.C. (2022) The impact of COVID-19 on the gender division of housework and childcare: Evidence from two waves of the pandemic in Italy, *IZA Journal of Labor Economics*, 11(1): 27–51. https://doi.org/10.2478/izajole-2022-0003

Delventhal, M.J., Kwon, E. and Parkhomenko, A. (2022) JUE Insight: How do cities change when we work from home? *Journal of Urban Economics*, 127: 103331. https://doi.org/10.1016/j.jue.2021.103331

Denham, T. (2021) The limits of telecommuting: Policy challenges of counterurbanisation as a pandemic response, *Geographical Research*, 59(4): 514–521. https://doi.org/10.1111/1745-5871.12493

Dolls, M. and Lay, M. (2023) Wie wirken sich Homeoffice und steigende Wohnkostenbelastung auf die Wohnortwahl aus? Evidenz aus einergroßangelegten Umfrage in Deutschland, *ifo Schnelldienst*, 76(2): 37–42.

Dunne, K. (2021) All the shifts: Mothering and working in the pandemic era, *Hamilton Digital Commons*. https://digitalcommons.hamilton.edu/student_scholarship/38/

Ewers, M. and Kangmennaang, J. (2023) New spaces of inequality with the rise of remote work: Autonomy, technostress, and life disruption, *Applied Geography*, 152: 102888. https://doi.org/10.1016/j.apgeog.2023.102888

Felstead, A. (2022) *Remote Working: A Research Overview*. London: Routledge.

Felstead, A. and Reuschke, D. (2023) A flash in the pan or a permanent change? The growth of homeworking during the pandemic and its effects on employee productivity in the UK, *Information Technology & People*, 36(5): 1960–1981. https://doi.org/10.1108/ITP-11-2020-0758

Fielding, T. and Ishikawa, Y. (2021) COVID-19 and migration: A research note on the effects of COVID-19 on internal migration rates and patterns in Japan, *Population, Space and Place*, 27(6): e2499. https://doi.org/10.1002/psp.2499

Franken, E., Bentley, T., Shafaei, A., Farr-Wharton, B., Onnis, L. and Omari, M. (2021) Forced flexibility and remote working: Opportunities and challenges in the new normal, *Journal of Management & Organization*, 27(6): 1131–1149. https://doi.org/10.1017/jmo.2021.40

Fukuda, Y. (2024) Urban exodus in Tokyo during the COVID-19 pandemic, *Applied Economics Letters*, 31(3): 202–206. https://doi.org/10.1080/13504851.2022.2130136

Gallent, N., Stirling, P. and Hamiduddin, I. (2023) Pandemic mobility, second homes and housing market change in a rural amenity area during COVID-19 – The Brecon Beacons National Park, Wales, *Progress in Planning*, 172: 100731. https://doi.org/10.1016/j.progress.2022.100731

Gibbs, H., Ballantyne, P., Cheshire, J., Singleton, A. and Green, M.A. (2023) Harnessing mobility data to capture changing work from home behaviours between censuses, *The Geographical Journal*, https://doi.org/10.1111/geoj.12555

González-Leonardo, M., Rowe, F. and Fresolone-Caparrós, A. (2022) Rural revival? The rise in internal migration to rural areas during the COVID-19 pandemic. Who moved and where? *Journal of Rural Studies*, 96: 332–342. https://doi.org/10.1016/j.jrurstud.2022.11.006

Gosnell, H. and Abrams, J. (2011) Amenity migration: Diverse conceptualizations of drivers, socioeconomic dimensions, and emerging challenges, *Geojournal*, 76: 303–322. https://doi.org/10.1007/s10708-009-9295-4

Government of Canada. (1999) Telework Policy. Policies, Directives, Standards, and Guidelines. https://www.tbs-sct.gc.ca/pol/doc-eng.aspx?id=12559

Government of Canada (2019) GCcoworking: New flexible alternative workplaces for government of Canada employees, *Public Services and Procurement Canada*. https://www.canada.ca/en/public-services-procurement/news/2019/06/gccoworking-new-flexible-alternative-workplaces-for-government-of-canada-employees0.html

Government of Canada (2022) Direction on prescribed presence in the workplace, https://www.canada.ca/en/government/publicservice/staffing/direction-prescribed-presence-workplace.html

Government of Canada (2023) Canada launches new process to welcome skilled newcomers with work experience in priority jobs as permanent residents, *News Release*, 31 May 2023. https://www.canada.ca/en/immigration-refugees-citizenship/news/2023/05/canada-launches-new-process-to-welcome-skilled-newcomers-with-work-experience-in-priority-jobs-as-permanent-residents.html
Hackney, A., Yung, M., Somasundram, K.G., Nowrouzi-Kia, B., Oakman, J. and Yazdani, A. (2022) Working in the digital economy: A systematic review of the impact of work from home arrangements on personal and organizational performance and productivity, *PLoS One*, 17(10): e0274728. https://doi.org/10.1371/journal.pone.0274728
Hall, C.E., Brooks, S.K., Mills, F., Greenberg, N. and Weston, D. (2024) Experiences of working from home: Umbrella review, *Journal of Occupational Health*, 66(1): uiad013. https://doi.org/10.1093/joccuh/uiad013
Haslag, P.H. and Weagley, D. (2023) From LA to Boise: How migration has changed during the COVID-19 pandemic, *Journal of Financial and Quantitative Analysis*, 1–31. https://doi.org/10.1017/S002210902300073X
Islam, A. (2022) Work-from/at/for-home: COVID-19 and the future of work: A critical review, *Geoforum*, 128: 33–36. https://doi.org/10.1016/j.geoforum.2021.11.018
James, A. (2024) Platform work-lives in the gig economy: Recentering work-family research, *Gender, Work & Organization*, 31(2): 513–534. https://doi.org/10.1111/gwao.13087
Knaus, K., Margies, N. and Schilling, H. (2021) Thinking the city through work: Blurring boundaries of production and reproduction in the age of digital capitalism, *City*, 25(3–4): 303–314. https://doi.org/10.1080/13604813.2021.1939966
Krasilnikova, N. and Levin-Keitel, M. (2022) Telework as a game-changer for sustainability? Transitions in work, workplace and socio-spatial arrangements, *Sustainability*, 14(11): 6765. https://doi.org/10.3390/su14116765
Liddle, J., Shutt, J. and Forbes, C. (2023) Levelling up or down? Examining the case of North-East England, *Contemporary Social Science*, 18(3–4): 469–484. https://doi.org/10.1080/21582041.2023.2281591
MacLeavy, J. and Manley, D. (2022) Socio-spatial inequalities and intergenerational dependencies, pp.45–61, in: Hujo, K. and Carter, M. (eds.) *Between Fault Lines and Front Lines: Shifting Power in an Unequal World*, London: Bloomsbury
Mancinelli, F. and Germann Molz, J. (2023) Moving with and against the state: Digital nomads and frictional mobility regimes, *Mobilities*. https://doi.org.uk/10.1080/17450101.2023.2209825
Manzo, L.K.C. and Minello, A. (2020) Mothers, childcare duties, and remote working under COVID-19 lockdown in Italy: Cultivating communities of care, *Dialogues in Human Geography*, 10(2): 120–123. https://doi.org/10.1177/2043820620934268
Martin, R., Gardiner, B., Pike, A., Sunley, P. and Tyler, P. (2021) *Levelling Up Left behind Places: The Scale and Nature of the Economic and Policy Challenge*, Abingdon: Taylor and Francis.
Massey, D. (1994) *Space, Place, and Gender*, Minneapolis: University of Minnesota Press.
Mayerhoffer, M. (2021) The impact of Covid-19 on coworking spaces: Evidence from Germany, *Journal of Corporate Real Estate*, 23(3): 170–185. https://doi.org/10.1108/jcre-10-2020-0044
Mokhtarian, P.L., Bagley, N.M. and Salomon, I. (1998) The impact of gender, occupation, and presence of children on telecommuting motivations and constraints, *Journal of the American Society for Information Science*, 49(12): 1115–1134.
Mokhtarian, P.L., Collantes, G.O. and Gertz, C. (2004) Telecommuting, residential location, and commute-distance travelled: Evidence from State of California employees, *Environment and Planning A: Economy and Space*, 36(10): 1877–1897. https://doi.org/10.1068/a36218
Moos, M. and Skaburskis, A. (2007) The characteristics and location of home workers in Montreal, Toronto, and Vancouver, *Urban Studies*, 4(9): 1781–1808. https://doi.org/10.1080/00420980701507639
Morison, C. (2023) PSAC thought it had negotiated a great deal with the government on remote work. But since then, little has changed, *Ottawa Citizen*, *Local News*, 20 October 2023. https://ottawacitizen.com/news/local-news/psac-thought-they-negotiated-a-great-deal-with-the-government-on-remote-work-but-since-then-little-changed
Nelson, P.B. and Frost, W. (2023) Migration responses to the COVID-19 Pandemic: A case study of New England showing movements down the urban hierarchy and ensuing impacts on real estate markets, *The Professional Geographer*, 75(3): 415–429. https://doi.org/10.1080/00330124.2022.2114092
Newbold, K.B., Towle, C. and Vrabic, K. (2022) Exploring human mobilities in the COVID-19 era in urban and rural Canada, pp. 1049–1062, in: Brunn, S. D. and Gilbreath, D. (eds) *COVID-19 and a World of Ad Hoc Geographies*, Cham: Springer. https://doi.org/10.1007/978-3-030-94350-9_58

Nova Scotia (2020) Work from Nova Scotia. https://workfromnovascotia.com/

Olson, M. (1983) Remote office work: Changing work patterns in space and time, *Communications of the ACM*, 26(3): 182–187. https://dl.acm.org/doi/pdf/10.1145/358061.358068

ONS (2022) Public opinions and social trends, Great Britain: 31 August to 11 September 2022, *Office for National Statistics Release*, 16 September 2022. https://www.ons.gov.uk/peoplepopulationandcommunity/wellbeing/bulletins/publicopinionsandsocialtrendsgreatbritain/31augustto11september2022

Ory, D.T. and Mokhtarian, P.L. (2006) Which came first, the telecommuting or the residential relocation? An empirical analysis of causality, *Urban Geography*, 27(7): 590–609. https://doi.org/10.2747/0272-3638.27.7.590

Özgüzel, C., Luca D. and Wei, Z. (2023) The new geography of remote jobs? Evidence from Europe, *OECD Regional Development Papers*, No. 57, Paris: OECD Publishing. https://doi.org/10.1787/29f94cd0-en

Pagliarin, S. and De Decker, P. (2021) Regionalised sprawl: Conceptualising suburbanisation in the European context, *Urban Research & Practice*, 14(2): 138–156. https://doi.org/10.1080/17535069.2018.1539513

Parlak S., Cakiroglu O.C. and Gul F.O. (2021) Gender roles during COVID-19 pandemic: The experiences of Turkish female academics, *Gender, Work & Organization*, https://doi.org/10.1111/gwao.12655

Perales, F. and Bernard, A. (2022) Continuity or change? How the onset of COVID-19 affected internal migration in Australia, *Population Space and Place*, 29(2): 1–20. https://doi.org/10.1002/psp.2626

PSAC Public Service Alliance of Canada (2023) PSAC remote work agreement a 'watershed moment' for workers' rights in Canada. Retrieved April 14, 2024. https://psacunion.ca/psac-remote-work-agreement-watershed-moment

Reuschke, D. (2019) The subjective well-being of homeworkers across life domains. *Environment and Planning A*, 51(6): 1326–1349. https://doi.org/10.1177/0308518X19842583

Reuschke, D. and Ekinsmyth, C. (2021) New spatialities of work in the city, *Urban Studies*, 58(11): 2177–2187. https://doi.org/10.1177/00420980211009174

Richards, A., Convery, S., O'Mahony, M. and Caulfield, B. (2024) Pre and post Covid preferences for working from home, *Travel Behaviour and Society*, 34: 100679. https://doi.org/10.1016/j.tbs.2023.100679

Roger, E.C. (2020) 'To be shut up': New evidence for the development of quarantine regulations in Early-Tudor England, *Social History of Medicine*, 33(4): 1077–1096. https://doi.org/10.1093/shm/hkz031

Rowe, F., Calafiore, A., Arribas-Bel, D., Samardzhiev, K. and Fleischmann, M. (2023) Urban exodus? Understanding human mobility in Britain during the COVID-19 pandemic using Meta-Facebook data, *Population Space and Place*, 29(1): 1–15. https://doi.org/10.1002/psp.2637

Shen, Q. (1998) Spatial technologies, accessibility, and the social construction of urban space, *Computers, Environment and Urban Systems*, 22(5): 447–464. https://doi.org/10.1016/S0198-9715(98)00039-8

Soroui, S. (2021) Understanding the drivers and implications of remote work from the local perspective: An exploratory study into the dis/reembedding dynamics, *Technology in Society*, 64: 101328. https://doi.org/10.1016/j.techsoc.2020.101328

Spicer, A. (2022) What Jacob Rees-Mogg, Alan Sugar and the Daily Mail get wrong about home working, *The Guardian*, 21 December 2022. https://www.theguardian.com/commentisfree/2022/dec/21/jacob-rees-mogg-alan-sugar-daily-mail-home-working-woke

Statistics Canada (2022a) Maritimes population growing at its fastest pace since the mid 1970s, *Statistics Canada Release*, 3 March 2022. https://www.statcan.gc.ca/o1/en/plus/478-maritimes-population-growing-its-fastest-pace-mid-1970s#

Statistics Canada (2022b) Jobs in Canada: Navigating changing local labour markets, *The Daily*, 30 November 2022. https://www150.statcan.gc.ca/n1/daily-quotidien/221130/dq221130b-eng.htm

Statistics Canada (2023) Commuting to work by car and public transit grows in 2023, *The Daily*, 22 August 2022. https://www150.statcan.gc.ca/n1/daily-quotidien/230822/dq230822b-eng.htm#

Stevens, L. and Shearmur, R.G. (2020) The end of location theory? Some implications of micro-work, work trajectories and gig-work for conceptualizing the urban space economy, *Geoforum*, 111: 155–164. https://doi.org/10.1016/j.geoforum.2020.02.010

Sweet, M. and Scott, D. (2022) Insights into the future of telework in Canada: Modeling the trajectory of telework across a pandemic, *Sustainable Cities and Society*, 87: 104175. https://doi.org/10.1016/j.scs.2022.104175

Taneja, S., Rockey, J., Matheson, J., Mizen, P. and de Fraja, G. (2022) Remote working and the new geography of local service spending, *CEPR Discussion Paper DP17431*. https://cepr.org/publications/dp17431

Townsend, L., Wallace, C. and Fairhurst, G. (2017) Broadband and the creative industries in rural Scotland, *Journal of Rural Studies*, 54(8): 451–458. https://doi.org/10.1016/j.jrurstud.2016.09.001

Vogiazides, L. and Kawalerowicz, J. (2023) Internal migration in the time of Covid: Who moves out of the inner city of Stockholm and where do they go? *Population, Space and Place*, 29(4): e41. https://doi.org/10.1002/psp.2641

Weeden, S.A., Hardy, J. and Foster, K. (2022) Urban flight and rural rights in a pandemic: Exploring narratives of place, displacement, and 'the right to be rural' in the context of COVID-19, *Annals of the American Association of Geographers*, 112(3): 732–741. https://doi.org/10.1080/24694452.2021.2003179

Werner, M., Strauss, K., Parker, B., Orzeck, R., Derickson, K. and Bonds, A. (2017) Feminist political economy in geography: Why now, what is different, and what for? *Geoforum*, 79: 1–4. https://doi.org/10.1016/j.geoforum.2016.11.013

Willet, J. (2023) Counter-urbanisation and a politics of place: A coastal community in Cornwall and rural gentrification, *Habitat International*, 141: 102935. https://doi.org/10.1016/j.habitatint.2023.102935

Wolff, M. and Mykhnenko, V. (2023) COVID-19 as a game-changer? The impact of the pandemic on urban trajectories, *Cities*, 134: 104162. https://doi.org/10.1016/j.cities.2022.104162

Xiang, B. (2022) Remote work, social inequality and the redistribution of mobility, *International Migration*, 60(6): 280–282. https://doi.org/10.1111/imig.13085

Zenkteler, M., Foth, M. and Hearn, G. (2022) Lifestyle cities, remote work and implications for urban planning, *Australian Planner*, 58(1–2): 25–35. https://doi.org/10.1080/07293682.2022.2096086

Recommendations for Further Reading

Felstead, A. (2022) *Remote Working: A Research Overview*, London: Routledge.

Hinds, P. J. and Kieslen, S. (eds.) (2002) *Distributed Work*, London: MIT Press.

Wheatley, D., Hardill, I. and Buglass, S. (2021) *Handbook of Research on Remote Work and Worker Well-Being in the Post-Covid-19 Era*, Hershey, PA: IGI Global.

25

RESISTING PRECARITY IN CITY-REGIONS

David Etherington, David Beel and Martin Jones

Introduction

Since the 2008 financial crisis, there has been an increase in labour market inequalities with a rise in low-paid and precarious work. The Trade Union Congress (TUC), the voice of Britain at work, estimate that there are 3.7 million workers who are in work that can be classified as insecure—comprising zero-hour contracts, agency and casualised work with short-term employment contracts, and self-employed paid below the living wage (TUC 2019). The notions of 'precarity' and 'insecurity' have been introduced to shed light on how precarious relationships are actually being produced and reproduced, with Waite calling for a 'critical geography of precarity' (Waite 2009: 412). Following Rubery et al (2018), these terms have been developed further in relation to the concept of 'precarisation', which in the context of work and non-work is a conceptual tool for identifying and analysing processes that undermine social protection and the safety net, linked, in turn, to constant attacks on employment rights and trade union work place organisation (Greer 2016).

Since the 1970s, the imposition of neoliberalism and austerity has involved reducing social protection, wages and labour regulation to make the workforce more 'flexible', which is facilitated by curtailing the bargaining power of labour via industrial relations and deregulation of labour markets. Labour flexibility, capital mobility and global finance are key sources of wage stagnation (Callinicos 2012). Anti-trade union legislation implemented initially by the Thatcher Government in the 1980s and then followed up by the 2016 Trade Union Act has played a key role in reducing employment rights, collective bargaining and the capacity of trade unions to organise and represent workers (Tuckman 2018). Welfare reform by successive governments has been geared towards disciplining labour (as benefit claimants as well as workers) as part of labour market flexibility (see Løedmel and Moreira 2014). As businesses shift the risks of the market on to workers then the 'exit of qualified/skilled benefit claimants into low paying, precarious jobs are uniformly considered a sub-optimal result of activation' (Raffaas 2017: 356).

This is exemplified in the design of Universal Credit (UC) in Britain, which sees tighter controls and requirements placed on claimants for accessing benefit. UC was established to 'simplify' the benefit system, as it merges a number of different benefits into a single payment. UC also involves an in-work benefit (work allowance) to replace working tax credits. Access to both in-work and

DOI: 10.4324/9781003327561-34

out of work elements of UC are subject to demanding work search and progression requirements, and a more punitive sanctions regime, reflecting the way the welfare reform agenda has involved stricter conditionality as a way of moving people into work.

> activation strategies influence the potential pool of labour available for precarious work through combinations of sanctions and financial support. The consequence is a blurring of the unemployed/employed divide and a normalisation of the take up of fragmented, low paid and short-term jobs.
>
> (Rubery et al. 2018: 521)

As Bricken and Taylor (2018: 18) state, it's a matter of 'take the job or get sanctioned, endure workplace tyranny or voluntarily exit and get sanctioned' and, as Greer (2016: 170) notes: 'active labour market discipline translates into workplace discipline through the well-known mechanism of insecurity, which affects both the precariat and workers in stable employment'. We recognise, however, that the influence of welfare conditionality is contingent on negotiation and bargaining within workplaces, which raises the question as to how advocacy organisations for workers/benefit claimants such as trade unions and civil society organisations resist and negotiate around work place practices. We address this through our involvement in the Sheffield Needs A Pay Rise (SNAP) campaign (see Etherington et al 2018; Thomas et al 2020). This was initiated Sheffield Trades Union Council (STUC) responding to a Resolution Foundation report detailing that the South Yorkshire Mayoral Combined Authority (SYMCA) economy—the political designation of the governance space for this 'left behind place' (Rodríguez-Posez 2018)—had an increasingly high proportion of workers paid below the living wage (Clarke 2017). A former old industrial region centred on steel, coal, and manufacturing, Sheffield, along with similar areas, has experienced long-term processes of job destruction and restructuring. The impact of austerity have disproportionally impacted on this region due to the large proportion of people of working age reliant on benefits—including disability and long-term health benefits (Beatty and Fothergill 2017).

The agenda above has been laid onto the SYMCA as part of the broader development of city-regions in the UK (Jonas and Moisio 2016). This means the SYMCA, initially termed the Sheffield City-Region but changing its name in 2016 with the advent of metropolitan mayors to reflect better the political dynamics of South Yorkshire, operates as the research setting in which we consider how work and employment policies operate in a dualistic fashion through city-region building (Beel et al 2017). On the one hand, city-regions are positioned to attract and develop 'better', high-end, GVA uplifiting jobs through processes of agglomeration (see Pike et al 2012); on the other, they are underpinned by an expansion of practices that develop increasingly precious forms of work (see Etherington et al 2023). The chapter details empirically the development of different forms of precarious labour in the SYMCA and more specifically the city of Sheffield.

The research involved an evidence review drawing on a number of mixed-methods sources as well as 42 semi-structured interviews with key actors (trade unions officials, workers, community activists, policymakers, practitioners, and stakeholders in general). Our SNAP research appproach involved targeting workers and claimants who were involved with the campaign and were part of the wider Sheffield TUC network to obtain their experiences of insecure work and welfare.

An important part of the research strategy was to capture the voices in and at the margins of welfare and labour market and this involved contacting relevant voluntary sector stakeholders involved with the Sheffield Equality Hubs, which are coordinated by Sheffield City Council-sponsored advice services such as the Citizens' Advice Bureau. These organisations were important 'gatekeepers' for accessing groups who are more marginalised from the labour market. In addition, a focus group was conducted, comprising eight young people connected to a Big Lottery Group Project on Young People and Employment in the SYMCA. Interviews were carried out with trade union officials and activists to obtain data on experiences of insecure work, trade union strategies and interventions of local policy makers such as those within social and welfare services in Sheffield. Face-to-face interviews were carried out between February and September 2018, were recorded and transcribed and analysed with respect to the key research themes relating to experiences of work and welfare.

Austerity, Insecurity and the South Yorkshire Economy

The South Yorkshire economy displays characteristics of long-term deindustrialisation and employment restructuring based on the creation of low-paid and insecure jobs with significant numbers claiming long-term sickness benefits. It is estimated that the number of those in low-paid and insecure employment in the SYMCA amounts to 185,000. In terms of the 'jobs gap', the number of jobs in the SYMCA that need to be created to bring the employment rate to the national average amounts to around 248,000 (Pike et al 2017).

Many aspects of the welfare system impact on people moving between welfare and work. Earlier research undertaken by Beatty and Fothergill (2014) on the impact of welfare reforms on Sheffield shows the way the reforms are reinforcing labour market and social inequalities. Moreover, between 2010/2011 and 2017/2018, Sheffield City Council experienced a reduction of £430 million in its Government grant (Sheffield City Council 2019). In 2018, the City Council along with the local Department of Work and Pensions (DWP) established a Universal Credit Partnership, with representatives from Sheffield City Council, DWP, Citizens Advice Sheffield and other voluntary, community and faith organisations, to respond to the roll out of UC and deal with the increasing number of claims due the increasingly low-pay nature of local economy. The partnership had been formed in order to mitigate the negative impacts of UC roll out on claimants (Sheffield NHS 2019).

There is an increasing demand for advice services, with knock-on impacts on social and health services. There has also been a reported increase in the demand for food banks, which, in lieu of increased state funding, have formed as another arm of social protection. In this way, we wish to argue that the welfare system perpetuates insecurity and locks people out of employment completely because of the constant struggle to survive (see May et al 2020). According to one account:

> The impact of delays in living costs means nothing to eat and reliance of help from foodbanks. It also impacts on the ability to pay for fuel for cooking and heating with had a particularly detrimental impact on the poorest who use pre-payment meters meaning for some an inability to heat up the tinned food received from the foodbank.
>
> (Sheffield CAB 2018a: 5)

Disability Sheffield, an advocacy organisation promoting independent living for disabled people has highlighted the fact that on many fronts' 'things' are becoming more difficult for disabled people in terms of accessing employment and simply surviving austerity. Approximately 104,000 people in Sheffield said their health condition or disability resulted in them experiencing some degree of difficulties with their day-to-day activities. This represents almost one-fifth (19%) of the population of the City classified as being 'disabled' under the Equality Act (2010) definition (Disability Sheffield 2015), which is higher than the national average. The Sheffield Occupational Health Advisory Service (SOHA) commissioned a survey of their registered carers, with most of the respondents being aged over 40, with 41% reporting that their caring commitments hindered their ability to work (Sheffield Occupational Health Advisory Service [SOHAS] 2019).

The key issue is that incorrect assessments have major implications for benefit entitlement and therefore vulnerability to in and out of work poverty, with knock-on consequences for disabled people's experience of work. According to Disability Sheffield:

> Sheffield Occupational Health Advisory Service (SOHAS) research demonstrates that there is an ambivalent attitude from employers to employing and retaining disabled people. Around 40% of employees employed by organisations who signed up to the Disability Confident scheme have been referred by their GP to SOHAS because their employers have not been helpful in supporting them to manage their long-term health condition and disability.[1]

An additional barrier to work is childcare (see MacLeavy 2011). In Sheffield, a Lone Parent Advocacy Worker highlighted that insufficient and unaffordable nature of this.

> But basically what people are saying is, there's not enough childcare, some women are still having to make up the cost, so they're juggling an additional cost, the provider of childcare sector has been affected because childcare providers cannot, (we're talking about day care here), can't keep going, the lack of flexibility of childcare matters ....

There is evidence that families getting into debt because of having to upfront childcare payments, particularly as most nurseries require advance payments to cover an extended period. Although the 30 hours 'free child care' provision introduced by the Government in 2017 provides some support, the level of funding is insufficient to cover provider costs (see Work and Pensions Committee [WPC] 2018: 20). Lack of affordable childcare has become a key issue in obtaining and retaining employment, which is an additional strand fuelling the geographies of precarity.

Welfare Enforcing Precarious Work and Lives

In this section, we explore two areas. First, experiences of the welfare-to-work system from the perspective of claimants/workers, and second, exploring barriers to representation and organising from the experience of trade union officials. Many aspects of the welfare system impact on people moving between welfare and work. The UC system has inbuilt delays into claimants receiving benefits with foodbanks becoming a safety net for people on benefits and also for those who are in insecure work (Sheffield CAB Worker Interview). What is striking is the way advice services are plugging a gap in the absence of access to trade union representation. Sheffield Citizens Advice Bureaux (CAB) established an Employment Rights project in response to claimants experiencing problems in terms of negotiating their employment rights and wages. An example is the increasing role of agencies in the city-region labour market (with claimants increasingly referred to by the Jobcentre, see Ball and Flynn 2018) and difficulties of obtaining readdress if there has been an issue with employment rights and claiming unpaid wages. As the Sheffield CAB observed:

> Employers (particularly agencies) seem impossible to contact once people start to experience issues with their working arrangements. Often interviewees did not know whom to contact: they had no knowledge of a human resources department and how to approach it, or whether one existed at all. Our findings show that agencies rarely responded to e-mails, phone calls or letters once they learned that a client had a problem. They also appear to be

> largely unresponsive to any interventions made by ACAS [The Advisory, Concilliation and Arbitration Service].
>
> (Sheffield CAB 2018a: 11–12)

Claimants identified the Work Capability Assessment (WCA) as a major source of insecurity. A (former) benefit claimant also experienced problems with the system of assessments:

> I was thrown off DLA (Disability Living Allowance) and during that ATOS [private company undertaking the task] assessment they basically, gave me the impression was that they didn't recognise mental health issues as being, like, a legitimate reason for being unable to participate in wage labour and so, then I was back on to Jobseekers, JSA.
>
> (Interview former Disability Benefit claimant)

The change from Disability Living Allowance (DLA) to Personal Independence Payment (PIP) had created difficulties for disabled people falling through the net, because of the way the WCA is designed to ensure that disability-related benefits are difficult to access. There is evidence that people with health barriers who are in part-time work see their health conditions as a barrier to sustain or improve their position in the labour market (Sheffield CAB 2018b).

This study found strong evidence of work/welfare 'cycling' in particular where claimants were under pressure of accepting jobs in non-union organised workplaces, with the jobs often being 'brokered' through employment agencies.

A case in point is 'Harry', in receipt of UC, who was struggling due to benefit delays—a five-week lead-in time before his first payment, with any hardship loans deducted from his meagre UC allowance, and deductions due to housing overpayments being reclaimed. Unsurprisingly, his view of the system was negative:

> The thing with Universal Credit, they put you under so much pressure. If you are paid and you are on Universal Credit all the money comes off your benefit. It's just the way—I never wanted my life to turn out like this and I am just a pawn of the Universal Credit. That's how I feel, and they are ruthless; the employers are ruthless and Universal Credit is useless as well.
>
> (Interview with Harry)

Such pressures explain what in the summer of 2018 drove Harry to respond to an advert for a courier subcontracted by Amazon (the major distribution company) in Sheffield. The advert promoted the job as 'being your own boss'. He found out that his mandatory two days' training was unpaid, and he had to pay for his own (mandatory) drug and alcohol tests. He was paid £112 a day and calculated that he would need six days' work a week to make the job pay because he had to hire his own van and fuel. He was penalised by £200 if he cancelled a shift at short notice and he claimed that with all these on-costs he was earning around £2 an hour.

Most workers interviewed found that employers were openly hostile to trade unions and could face the sack if they showed an interest in joining a union, as one Unite Organiser noted:

> … this is the thing with zero-hours … it's that you can't join a union. You can't even look like you're going to join a union. That's what I always say to people, that's what it's about. It's about having complete and utter control over everybody.
>
> (Unite Official)

In all cases shifts were changed at very short notice to cover staff shortages and fluctuations in demand. Requirements to 'flex-up' offered challenges for those dependent upon childcare, those with children in general and those on benefits. It could, for instance, minimise rest-breaks between shifts, or require the unscheduled extension of shifts.

People who are outside or at the margins of the labour market (disabled people, lone parents, young people, women) tend to have little contact with the trade unions, whether whilst claiming benefits, or in work. The response of young people for example in the focus group can be seen as typical:

> And the thing is, if you are on a zero hours contract there's just nothing to stop them from just not giving any more hours. I think potentially one of the things that blocks people from joining unions or actively searching them out is that there is so many people who want these jobs and there's not enough jobs for people working, for unskilled or unqualified work. So if there's even something that might risk you losing that job and not having the money to support yourself, is it worth doing?
>
> (Focus Group of young people)

Whilst there are significant numbers of women who are members of trade unions in the city—especially in the public sector, those outside the world of work tend to be detached from their sphere of influence:

> I'm assuming that, you know, most of the people who come to talk to us from the Council are trade unionists, but there's no kind of trade union perspective that I've been aware of on any of this at the Women's Hub, or any of the hubs, as far as I can tell.
>
> (Member of Sheffield Women's Equality Hub)

According to a disability advocacy worker, many disabled people who are in the welfare system or on its margins do not have a great deal of contact with trade unions. There is a view and impression that trade unions will look after their own members and 'their interests' but do not get involved with the 'concerns of disabled people'. Organising efforts for the most vulnerable workers tend to be organised outside of the traditional unions by community activists. MacLeavy (2014) has highlighted that the lack of union response to workfare issues (in the US context) and suggested an opportunity in reclaiming the neoliberal framing of the unemployed as a 'workforce in waiting' to narrow the distance between the concerns of unemployed and non-unionised and low-wage union members.

When trade union branches and officials attempt to reach out to insecure workers and claimants they face a number of challenges. A key contextual factor is the fragmentation of certain sectors particularly with respect to the fast food and retail sectors, which presents difficulties for trade unions and workers' access to representation. According to one dominant trade union view:

> [...] you know that McDonald's is going to be rotten in this country, you know that [restaurants] are going to be stealing tips but yeah, [...] these practices go on right through the whole industry and this is why we're always going to have huge difficulties organising workers when you get down to these three, four, five, six, seven employees level, this is where you need legislation. This is where all these places have got to be legislated for because it's impossible really to have union representation and officers and all these types of things when you've got such a scattered [workforce].
>
> (Unite Official)

This is further compounded by workers having a lack of recognition in terms of Unions. As members in precarious working conditions do not or feel unable to join, they are not then being represented within the unions themselves. According to one source:

> So if you are a regional organiser and you're dealing with half a dozen companies – big companies – and then you might have two or three of these smaller cleaning companies and security companies, who are you going to concentrate on? You know who you're going to concentrate on because you've got fully trained reps there.
>
> (Transport Union Official)

Other difficulties arose due to language barriers. Reinforcing some key contributions in economic geography (see Pratt Wills 2008; Pratt and Migrante 2018), a number of respondents suggested that with some international workers, who would potentially know very little of their employment rights and were hence vulnerable to exploitation, gaining trust alongside raising their awareness of what a trade union is, could be difficult:

> It's left a situation that we've eventually got round to addressing but it's a very, very difficult area because what you have is you have a high turnover, English isn't necessarily the first language, as I said, and there's no trade union culture in a lot of these places.
>
> (Transport Union Official)

Finally, there is the 'low hanging' fruit argument, where trade unions will strategically recruit where it is easier to gain access and organise. According to one account:

> I don't do organising work in unorganised sectors, unorganised workplaces, unless, I'm getting demand for that from those. I would rather recruit more people in the places where we are than use up a lot of energy for no gain because it's really, really difficult.
>
> (Unite Official)

The social care sector serves as a good case study to explore the dynamics of insecurity and challenges for resistance and organising. The care sector is one of the largest employers in Sheffield (over 16,000, 16% of the workforce) characterised by high rates of staff turnover (often linked to cycling between work and welfare), relatively large numbers on zero-hour contracts, and is one of the clearest and direct examples where austerity has impacted on wages and working conditions (Skills for Care 2017). Compulsory competitive tendering adopted during the 1980s forced councils to open up large parts of their service delivery to private sector providers. The major challenge for trade unions is dealing with budget cuts, low pay, zero-hour contracts, shift work and high labour turnover. One Sheffield trade union official stated that the fragmentation of the sector, the high turnover and indeterminate working hours presented challenges to organising and recruiting in the sector.

Local trade union concerns include issues around staffing levels in care homes, with statutory minimum staffing ratios frequently being treated as maximums:

> For instance, at full capacity, say, twenty residents, on a night you would only have two people running the site. That's hourly bed-turns, making sure the residents are able to go to the toilet if they need to go to the toilet and also that they receive water, so especially on warmer nights they have to be watered, with a lot of medication that's then given on

> four-hourly basis, one-hourly basis, depending on the medication, and a lot of paperwork that needs filling in.
>
> (GMB Official)

One aspect of insecurity is the intensification of work often accompanied by oppressive management practices, but a lack of the support necessary to get the job done:

> Yes, it was horrendously stressful, like I went in expecting it would be a lot easier than it actually was. But when you are out there in the community working with a client, you are very aware of the amount of responsibility that you have. And the fact that you have no colleagues around you, there was a bit of mentoring but it was all quite limited. [...] We had this woman we were looking after who had very full-on needs, completely beyond our usual remit as support workers, including a lot of moving and handling using hoists and things like that, which we weren't properly trained on and it was dangerous and people were making mistakes and they were properly equipped with the stuff they needed.
>
> (Sheffield Care Worker 1)

Another perspective is offered from one interviewee:

> [...] there's largely a notion that people who work in care should be expected to be very kind of humble in accepting quite poor conditions, because the reasons that they're doing that care work is because they care about service users, so what happens in reality is you actually get management guilt tripping people, if actually they're bringing up issues and they'll try and pull the focus back to the service user.
>
> (Sheffield Care Worker 2)

Unsurprisingly, trade union officials have described the process of change in the social care sector in Sheffield as a 'race to the bottom' in terms of wages and conditions.

Trade Unions/Communities Building Solidarities with Marginalised Groups

The distinction between workers and claimants is increasingly being blurred and recognised by trade union leaders and officials. As more workers are transferred over to UC which replaces the tax credit system this does raise issues how the trade unions are to address welfare rights needs of workers as UC claimants (Interview with GMB Regional Official). Building solidarities with welfare claimants has been a focus of SNAP and linked campaigns around welfare reform and UC by some trade unions in Sheffield. For example, the closure of the Eastern Avenue Jobcentre in Sheffield serves as a useful case study to demonstrate the role of the Public and Commercial Services union, along with Unite Community trade union and community organisations in terms of taking action to oppose the reduction of employment services to claimants. Union members voted to strike for a total of 26 days until the centre was closed in November 2017. The Union's case against closure focused on the area having already suffered from austerity and the closure of an important social service would exacerbate the problems of deprivation. The alternative locations offered to claimants were deemed inadequate, with overcrowding in one jobcentre located in the centre of Sheffield, which also involves increased travel time and transport costs for claimants (Public and Commercial Services Union [PCS] 2017).

Although the campaign was not successful in preventing the closure of the Jobcentre, it brought together trade unions and community activists around issues relating to welfare reform. Unite Community, along with Sheffield Trade Union Council (and other labour movement organisations) in relation to the campaign to scrap UC, has built on this. The national campaign spear-headed by Disabled People Against the Cuts (DPAC) and Unite Community has raised the profile of trade unions in relation to questions around welfare reform. An important element of the campaign is the work undertaken by Unite Community trade union in Sheffield, which has developed strategies to engage with workers/claimants as a means of promoting unionisation and displaying solidarity with those who feel isolated in the work place. One of the key roles played by the UC campaign is undertaking outreach initiatives in the more deprived parts of Sheffield to connect with claimants and workers by providing support, information and signposting to advice services.

The Sheffield Stop and Scrap Universal Credit campaign follows on from the successes in community organising of the SNAP campaign, introduced above. SNAP was inaugurated in 2016 in response to the Resolution Foundation reports detailing the extent of low pay in the city. Since its inception, it has stimulated efforts to unionise unorganised groups of workers through shaming bad employers and staging solidarity pickets and outreach events. It has distributed thousands of 'Know Your Rights at Work' cards to young people in the city, commissioned research on the extent of low-paid and precarious work in the city and backed the Bakers Food and Allied Workers Union (BFAWU) actions around McDonalds fast food outlets, which seeks to secure a higher minimum wage and the right to union representation (see Etherington et al 2018; Thomas et al 2020). There are also links with other UK campaigns, such as those championing informalised workplaces such as hand car washes, where informalised low-wage, precarious workers are paid less than the minimum wage and experience other forms of labour market exploitation (Clark et al 2020).

A Unite Community Coordinator considered that this activity around welfare reform specifically in terms of embedding unions in the community. He drew a parallel with community organising in other countries, where political parties and trade unions had established themselves in communities through helping individuals with welfare claims, applications to college or university, providing food and clothes banks'.

Whilst in the focus group of young people (see above). we observed that most had little experience and involvement with trade unions, the connection by SNAP with young people is one of the significant features of the campaign. This seems to reflect a trend towards more young people, especially those in insecure employment interested and attracted to trade unions (see Berry and Daniel 2019).

SNAP and Sheffield TUC have been inspired by the successes of innovative new organising strategies being deployed by a range of unions and seeks to share best practice and replicate such work amongst union branches in the city. SNAP/STUC have crowd-funded the hiring of an organiser around the fast food sector as a way of developing the campaign for employment rights and union recognition. This has linked in with the development of more outreach work such as the 'Summer Patrol' organised by the Yorkshire and Humberside TUC. This initiative is developed from a similar one organised by the Norwegian trade unions. The project sent groups of young trade unionists from Yorkshire and Norway into workplaces across Sheffield, Doncaster and Barnsley in order to connect with young workers in a different way, giving them a positive introduction to trade unions. As one regional official commented:

> We need to get back into workplaces and talk to people about their issues (particularly on declining high streets where staff are feeling the squeeze). We also trialled the peer-to-peer

> texting software GetThru to send texts to all the people we met on Patrol to follow up with them on any issues. GetThru allowed us to keep in touch with people who showed an interest and invite them to a follow-up meeting to build a campaign to improve working life in South Yorkshire. But face to face conversations are what makes the difference.

Similar actions have been undertaken by the GMB trade union in relation to drivers delivering for Amazon in Sheffield:

> We've been outside the gates, we've handed them leaflets, we've got Facebook pages set up to say to people, 'You need to get in the union. This is what we can do for you.' And those that are, we're then taking on the challenge for the legal route. How I see it is it works like this: we need to challenge legislation nationally to change law, but we also then need to organise on the ground to hold them employers to account, because even when legislation's change, employers aren't just going to stop doing it.
>
> (GMB Regional Official)

Aiming to draw on the support of the wider community, representative trade unions in the Care Sector (Unison and GMB) have formulated care charters providing a set of demands to campaign around pay and working conditions. Sheffield City Council has signed up to Unison's Care Charter and trade unions are making progress in the city, with membership at one social care provider increasing from 10 to over 50 in the last year and being close to achieving the statutory recognition threshold. In the words of one individual:

> We've got their details, many of them have given us their telephone numbers, you can email them and write to them, but you'll probably never hear back. If you ring them, then they'll speak to you and often they'll speak to you for half an hour, cause they've never had anyone call them before and ask them how it's going.
>
> (Unison Official)

Discussion and Conclusions

The chapter has sought to draw out the complex links between welfare-to-work (workfare) policies and precarious work and secondly, highlight strategies of resistance and negotiation to such insecurity by representative and advocacy organisations such as trade unions and civil society organisations. We highlight here some key salient issues that we consider relevant for our further understanding of theory and practice, which collectively shares our politics of being concerned with futures of work framed about around the dynamics of struggles over the geographies of space and place, as opposed to the positive benefits of technology and the knowledge-based economy.

A key issue is about how trade unions and civil society/social movements relate within the context of increasing insecurity and retrenchment. One of the key research findings is insecure work as a factor in structuring movements in and out of work, where insecure workers tend to be (former or continuing) benefit claimants. The implementation of UC is increasingly blurring the welfare work relationship, intensifying insecurity and posing threats to employment rights. The design of UC guarantees subsidies to low-paid work, including 'mini jobs' and zero-hour work. Work conditionality rules mean that UC claimants will be required to accept zero-hour contract work and then in order to meet the requirements in the claimant commitment of working a set number of hours a week or enhancing take home pay, claimants will be under pressure to look for other mini-jobs. These types of jobs are the main reason for exiting work because of their temporary nature or earnings being unsustainable.

Related to this, the operation of the benefits system locks people out of the immediate labour market—particularly lone parents and people with long-term health conditions. This is not only because work does not pay, but also because employers have little regard for making workplace adjustments to accommodate the employment needs of marginalised groups. So, for a large proportion of the working age population work is not an option. In this way benefit conditionality can reinforce the marginality of disabled people and in particular their families' role as unpaid carers.

Trade unions and their activities can be far removed from the social networks that support disadvantaged groups in the labour market. Also, for most, work is very much of a short-term and unpredictable character and joining a trade union does not appear on people's horizons. Moreover, there is a trend and tendency for the employment rights gap tends to be filled by advice services (see Holgate et al 2012), as these are free to access—exemplified by the increasing role of the Sheffield CAB in this area, but this is highly constrained by the cuts.

This said, in the Sheffield City-Region there has been a distinctive shift of focus by some trade unions towards engaging and joining up with marginalised and disadvantaged groups, as evidenced by the UC and SNAP campaigns (see also Unite Community 2019). There is evidence through the SNAP study (Etherington et al 2018; Thomas et al 2020) of the need for trade unions to reach out to those in insecure work and 'outside' the labour market. This is supported at the national level in relation to work being undertaken between Child Poverty Action Group (CPAG), as part of its Early Warning System, and USDAW (the trade union which represents workers in the retail sector) responding to the impact of UC within workplaces. The Early Warning System, for instance, collates case studies and evidence to demonstrate the impact of changes in the social security system on the wellbeing of children, their families and the communities and services that support them (see Machin et al 2018).

A theoretical contribution of this chapter is the importance of geography vis-à-vis traditions and cultures of mobilising and resistance (see also Etherington et al 2023). The geography of socioeconomic and political processes matters. Gough (2014) argues that both the attacks on the working class and the contradictions of neoliberalism are clearly expressed—and clearly *visible*—on the local scale. Cumbers et al (2010: 68) emphasise that agency and resistance of the more everyday sort continue even in the most coercive and regressive economic environments [and] that past processes of activism and class consciousness remain as latent reserves that can be drawn upon for present and future collective struggles'. This is highly relevant because it informs theoretically the role of localities as sites of (potential) innovation and signposts our focus to understanding the traditions of labour movement and local politics.

Our study of Sheffield TUC demonstrates the need to include Trades Councils as important actors in labour movement and trade union struggles, especially in contexts where the regional economy is in decline. Sheffield TUC SNAP is one of the few initiatives which has focused on the city for mobilising people experiencing insecurity, placing 'grassroots' rank and file organisation at the heart of trade unionism. This has occurred via solidarity actions but also by developing partnerships/ collaboration not only with community organisations but with other trade unions. Perhaps, of more significance, is the national profile of SNAP as illustrated in the 2020 Trades Council Conference in which passed resolutions to adopt the SNAP model under the banner of 'A New Deal for Workers: Precarious Work—a role for Trade Union Councils'. Motions highlight the need for developing across the board initiatives similar to SNAP but to develop the TCs in a way that gears their organisation towards developing "new ways of organizing precarious workers, which some trade unions, both TUC affiliates and others, are already leading in…(and) exploring sources of Trade Union Council support with Peoples Assembly groups and other activists, such as 'Sheffield Needs a Pay Rise' and other similar strategies" (TUC 2020). Other trades councils such as Leeds have embarked on similar initiatives[2] and Leicester TC has played a key role in drawing attention and developing a joint union campaign against exploitative conditions in the garment industry (TUC 2021).

The focus on individual trade unions, whilst essential, provides only a partial analysis of the possibilities and challenges of trade unions addressing the need of precarious workers. It is important to consider the overall role of the TUC in terms of leadership and capacity-building and the way that it can shape individual trade union agendas and policies. This means a more nuanced analysis of the activities and resource Taylor and Mather found, noting there "is also evidence of long-standing enmities between trades union councils and the TUC hierarchy and a feeling that the latter have either no commitment to maintaining trades union councils or would prefer to see their demise". (Taylor and Mathers 2008: 28). In their study of devolution and trade unions in North East England O'Brien et al (2004) (2014) found that regional TUC bodies' role and power to shape policy remains relatively under-developed and circumscribed by national centralism and ambivalent attitudes within affiliated trade unions and the TUC. Trade union officials have commented on the 'remoteness' of the TUC and that more could be done by the major trade unions to support initiatives such as SNAP. The lack of commitment by the TUC to SNAP can be illustrated by the need to crowdfund the campaign rather than providing a long-term sustainable investment.

The structures of traditional unions can be risk-averse, predominantly focused on their membership, and failing to provide an adequate organisational response to precarious workers (see Bertolini and Dykes 2021). Research by Keune (2013) suggests that the resources and efforts of traditional unions have not always been sufficient to implement and sustain organising initiatives for addressing the needs of insecure workers. This situation has been challenged by the STUC who has attempted to bring new resources into the trade union movement through the model of community-based organising, which has allowed a certain freedom from the logics of cost benefit analyses and the focus on 'low hanging fruit'

Although there are some important initiatives by the various individual trade unions concerning engagement beyond the workplace our survey reveals little evidence that the main trade unions have been able to implement a coherent and sustainable strategy for organising unorganised groups or promoting outreach work with communities. This is perhaps in part due to bureaucratic inertia that makes it difficult to reorient their strategies to include workers that lie outside their traditional constituencies (Bertolini and Dykes 2021). The formation of Unite Community has represented a powerful example of the trade union movement responding to the increasing incidence of marginalisation amongst the working class. Nevertheless, Holgate contends that there is an essential tension between the main industrial part of Unite operating along 'traditional lines' whilst Unite Community operates around an orientation towards non-workers and welfare claimants (Gall and Holgate 2018). SNAP and the model of community-funded/supported organising represents a further attempt to bridge such divides and realise the potential of community-based alliances for the trade union movement, but greater support for such experiments, in addition to other kinds of experiments (in different sectors, amongst different categories of workers), will be required to fundamentally reverse the longer term trajectory of the trade union movement.

Notes

1 Information obtained from Disability Sheffield May 2018, http://www:disabilitysheffield.org.uk.
2 https://www.facebook.com/leedsgetorganised/ [accessed November 2023].

References

Ball C and Flynn M (2018) *The UK Labour Market and its Significant Features for Social Dialogue on Active Ageing*. Agediversity.Org. Available: https://www.agediversity.org/wp-content/uploads/2019/04/ASPIRE-UK-National-report.pdf

Beatty C and Fothergill S (2014) *The Uneven Impact of Welfare Reform: The Financial Losses to Places and People*. Sheffield: Sheffield Hallam University.

Beatty C and Fothergill S (2017) The impact on welfare and public finances of job loss in industrial Britain, *Regional Studies, Regional Science*, 4(1), 161–180. DOI:10.1080/21681376.2017.1346481.

Beel D Jones M Jones IR and Escadale W (2017) Connected growth: developing a framework to drive inclusive growth across a city region. *Local Economy*, 32, 565–575.

Berry C and Daniel S (2019) *Young Workers and Trade Unionism in the Hourglass Economy*. Sheffield: Sheffield University Political Economy Research Centre.

BertoliniA and Dykes R (2021) Trade unions and platform workers in the UK: worker representation in the shadow of the law. *Industrial Law Journal*, 50, 662–688.

Bricken K and Taylor P (2018) Fulfilling the 'British Way': beyond constrained choice – Amazon Workers live experience of workfare. *Industrial Relations Journal*, 49, 438–458.

Callinicos A (2012) Contradictions of austerity. *Cambridge Journal of Economics*, 36, 65–77.

Clark I, Hunter J, Pickford R, and Fearnall-Williams H (2020) How do licensing regimes limit worker interests? Evidence from informal employment in Britain. *Economic and Industrial Democracy*, 43, 431–449.

Clarke S (2017) *Forging Ahead or Falling Behind? Devolution and the Future of Living Standards in the Sheffield City Region*. London: Resolution Foundation.

Cumbers A, Helms G and Swanson K (2010) Class agency and resistance in the older industrial city. *Antipode*, 42, 46–73.

Disability Sheffield (2015) *Consultation Response Extra Cost Commission,* Sheffield, Disability Sheffield. Available at: https://disabilitysheffield.org.uk/blog/extra-costs-commission-final-report-recommends-nimbus-access-card-2015-07-20

Equality Act (2010). Available at: https://www.legislation.gov.uk/ukpga/2010/15. (Accessed: 17 May 2022).

Etherington D, Jeffery R, Thomas P, Brooks J, Beel D and Jones M (2018) *Forging an Inclusive Labour Market—Empowering Workers and Communities: An Interim Report on Low Pay and Precarious Work in Sheffield*. Sheffield: Sheffield Hallam University.

Etherington D, Jeffery B, Thomas P, Jones M and Ledger-Jessop B (2023) Trade union strategies to tackle labour market insecurity: geography and the role of Sheffield TUC. *Industrial Relations Journal*, 54, 261–277.

Gall G and Holgate J (2018) Rethinking industrial relations appraisal, application and augmentation. *Economic and Industrial Journal*, 39, 561–576.

Gough J (2014) The difference between local and national capitalisms, and why local capitalisms differ from one another. *Capital and Class*, 38, 197–210.

Greer I (2016) Welfare reform, precarity and the recommodification of labour. *Work Employment and Society*, 30, 162–173.

Holgate J (2018) Trade unions in the community: Building broad spaces of solidarity. *Economic and Industrial Democracy*, 42, 226–247.

Holgate J, Pollert A, Keles J and Kumarappan L (2012) Union decline and voice among minority ethnic workers: do community-based social networks help to fill the gap. *Urban Studies*, 49, 3, 613–630.

Jonas AEG and Moisio S (2016) City regionalism as geopolitical processes: a new framework for analysis. *Progress in Human Geography*, 42, 3, 350–370.

Keune M (2013) Trade union responses to precarious work in seven European countries. *International Journal of Labour Research*, 5, 59–78.

Løedmel I and Moreira A (eds) (2014) *Activation or Workfare? Governance and the Neo-Liberal Convergence*. Oxford: Oxford University Press.

Machin R, Norris D and Jones M (2018) Welfare reform summit. *Poverty*, 161, 10–13.

MacLeavy J (2011) A 'new politics' of austerity, workfare and gender? The UK coalition government's welfare reform proposals. *Cambridge Journal of Regions, Economy and Society*, 4, 355–367.

MacLeavy J (2014) Workfare and resistance in the US: the quietude and ineffectiveness of progressive welfare politics post 1996. *The Geographical Journal*, 181(3), 259–267. Available: https://doi.org/10.1111/geoj.12092

May J, Williams A, Cloke P and Cherry L (2020) Food bank and the production of scarcity. *Transactions of the Institute of British Geographers*, 45, 208–222.

O'Brien P, Pike A, and Tomaney J (2004) Devolution, the governance of regional development and the Trade Union Congress in the North East region of England. *Geoforum*, **35**(1), 59–68.

Pike A, MacKinnon D, Coombes M, Champion T, Bradley D, Cumbers A, Robinson L and Wymer C (2017) *Uneven Growth: Tackling City Decline*. York: Joseph Rowntree Foundation.

Pike A, Rodríguez-Pose A, Tomaney J, Torrisi G and Tselios V (2012) In search of the 'economic dividend' of devolution: spatial disparities, spatial economic policy, and decentralisation in the UK. *Environment and Planning C: Government and Policy*, 30, 1, 10–28.

Pratt G and Migrante BC (2018) Organizing domestic workers in Vancouver Canada: gendered geographies and community mobilization. *Political Power and Social Theory*, 35, 99–119.

Public and Commercial Services Union (PCS) (2017) *PCS DWP Sheffield Branch Response to the Proposed Closure of Eastern Avenue Jobcentre*. Sheffield: PCS.

Raffaass T (2017) Demanding activation. *Journal of Social Policy*, 46, 349–365.

Rodríguez-Posez A (2018) The revenge of the places that don't matter (and what to do about it). *Cambridge Journal of Regions, Economy and Society*, 11, 189–209.

Rubery J, Grimshaw D, Keizer A and Johnson M (2018) Challenges and contradictions in the 'normalising' of precarious work. *Work, Employment and Society*, 32, 509–527.

Sheffield Citizens Advice Bureaux (CAB) (2018a) *Insecure Employment in Sheffield*. Sheffield: Sheffield CAB.

Sheffield Citizens Advice Bureaux (CAB) (2018b) *Just Managing*. Sheffield: Sheffield CAB.

Sheffield City Council (2019) *The End of Austerity? The Impact of Nine Year Austerity Programme on Our City.* Available: https://democracy.sheffield.gov.uk/documents/b21495/Impact%20of%20Austerity%20on%20Sheffield%20Wednesday%2009-Jan-2019%2014.00%20Council.pdf?T=9

Sheffield NHS (2019) *Universal Credit Briefing Note*. Sheffield: Sheffield NHS Clinical Commissioning Group.

Sheffield Occupational Health Advisory Service (SOHAS) (2019) Carers centre survey. *SOHAS Carers Newsletter*. Available: https://sheffieldcarers.org.uk/wp-content/uploads/2019/02/Sheffield-Carers-Centre-Newsletter-024-Winter-2019-3.pdf

Skills for Care (2017) *The State of the Adult Social Care Sector and Workforce in England.* Available at: https://socialserviceworkforce.org/wp-content/uploads/2024/03/State-of-the-adult-social-care-sector-and-workforce-2017.pdf

Taylor G and Mathers A (2008) Organising unions, organising communities? Trades union councils & community union politics in England and Wales. University of West of England Centre for Employment Studies Research. *Working Paper 10.*

Thomas P, Etherington D, Jeffery B, Beresford R, Beel D and Jones M (2020) *Tackling Labour Market Injustice and Organising Workers: The View from a Northern Heartland.* Sheffield: Sheffield Hallam University.

TUC (2019) *Insecure Work Why the New PM Should Put Decent Work at the Top of the to Do List*. London: TUC.

TUC (2020) *TUC Trades Council Programme of Work 2020/21*. London: TUC.

TUC (2021) Fixing Leicester's garment industry one year on: building partnerships ending exploitation. Available: https://www.tuc.org.uk/sites/default/files/2021-10/Fixing_Leicester%27s_Garment_Trade_Report.pdf

Tuckman A (2018) *Kettling the Unions*. Nottingham: Spokesman.

Unite Community (2019) *Universal Credit Not Fit for Purpose: Unite Universal Credit Survey Report.* London: Unite Community.

Waite L (2009) A place and space for a critical geography of precarity. *Geography Compass*, 3, 412–433.

Wills J (2008) Subcontacted employment and its challenge to labor. *Labor Studies Journal*, 34, 441–460.

Work and Pensions Committee (WPC) (2018) *Universal Credit: Childcare*. London: HM Government.

Recommendations for Further Reading

Beel D, Jones M, Jones IR (2021) *City Regions and Devolution in the UK: The Politics of Representation*. Bristol: Policy Press.

Etherington D (2020) *Austerity, Welfare and Work: Exploring Politics, Geographies and Inequalities*. Bristol: Policy Press.

Etherington D and Jones M (2009) City regions: new geographies of uneven development and inequality. *Regional Studies*, 43, 247–265.

Lambert R and Herod A (eds) (2016) *Neoliberal Capitalism and Precarious Work: Ethnographies of Accommodation and Resistance.* Cheltenham: Edward Elgar.

Waite L (2009) A place and space for a critical geography of precarity. *Geography Compass*, 3, 412–433.

PART 10

Policy and the Politics of Work Futures

26

INDUSTRIAL RELATIONS AND THE FUTURES OF WORK

Efficiency, Equity and Voice in the Twenty-first Century

Huw Thomas and Peter Turnbull

Introduction

Concern over the future of work has typically either favoured broad-brushed assumptions of significant paradigm shifts in how, where and what work is conducted or grand narratives between utopia and dystopia (Ainsworth and Knox 2022). Whether assumptions are valid or not, it is clear that work has become worse for many. Jobs have been outsourced or lost through sub-contracting or automation. Contracts have become more precarious. Wages have been squeezed. The right to strike has been progressively constricted. And this is before any discussion is entered into regarding the atrocious human rights violations that continue to be exposed in media headlines (Ilham 2021) or (re)counted by the International Trade Union Confederation (ITUC) (ITUC 2022), but are all too often buried in the depths of global supply chains (ILO 2016). With the decline of trade union power in many advanced economies and its practical insignificance in many other countries (Visser 2019), workers and their representatives are often viewed as passive victims of these trends rather than active constituents of work futures (Cumbers et al. 2008). For some, technology is driving these developments. The future of work has become synonymous with technological change rather than an investigation of the deterioration or, in some rare cases, (re)invigoration of conditions of work. As Peetz (2019: 17) points out, "technology is part of the future, but it is not the whole of the future".

There is certainly no shortage of research on the futures of work. In this chapter, we try to make sense of these developments through an industrial relations lens, which turns our attention to the agentic struggles that are taking place between capital, labour and the state. To this end, we draw on the efficiency, equity and voice (hereafter EEV) framework (Budd 2006). Industrial relations starts with the observation that employment relationships are characterised by a structured antagonism (Edwards and Hodder 2022) between capital and labour and thus any future of work will be one of conflict, the outcome of which is primarily determined by power dynamics in the employment relationship and wider society. The widely recognised objectives of all employment relationships – EEV – may be organisation-centric but are directly impacted and ordered by societal institutions: efficiency rests on the property rights of capital, whereas equity and voice are grounded in employment and human rights. In thinking about the myriad futures of

DOI: 10.4324/9781003327561-36

work, therefore, it is important to look at how disruption globally, nationally, and within different industries will impact the balance of power within, and the ongoing contestation of, the employment relationship.

Overall, we contend that there has been a general trend towards the increasing power of capital (which favours efficiency), growing attacks on labour rights (which undermines equality), and a decline in different forms of industrial democracy (which can silence workers' voice). These underlying trajectories have been overlaid by crises. Indeed, trying to predict the future has proven difficult, especially as disruption to the employment relationship has been the name of the game in recent years. COVID-19 prompted a loss of working hours, unemployment and insecurity, inflation and supply chain disruption, all of which exacerbated poverty and inequality around the world (ILO 2022a). The pandemic not only mainstreamed concerns with vulnerable work(ers), undervalued work(ers), safety and health, etc., but also the importance of collective voice (Doellgast and Wagner 2022). Whilst renewed social pacts that were potentially on the agenda during the pandemic (Dobbins et al. 2023; Meardi and Tassinari 2022) may have not come to fruition in all cases, COVID-19 has stalled various discussions regarding the future of work and has exposed the increasingly fissured employment relationship and its deleterious impact for workers (Weil 2014). We argue that strong(er) mechanisms of voice are the only way to secure the other objectives of efficiency and equity and a future of work fit for all.

The Roots of Industrial Relations and Its Importance to the Futures of Work

Industrial relations take a multidisciplinary approach to studying the employment relationship as one which involves "multiple stakeholders with contrasting and at times conflicting priorities and interests" (Clarke et al. 2011: 243). As a policy-orientated field, it is concerned with not only understanding and analysing the often competing objectives of EEV but finding ways to enhance one or more without detriment to the other(s) (Thomas and Turnbull 2023). Industrial relations has a normative commitment towards more and better jobs rooted in its founding principle that "labour is not a commodity" (ILO 1919; Kaufman 2010).

Whilst industrial relations might have emerged as a study of the 'labour problem' brought about by industrial capitalism (i.e., securing labour peace and labour control), the focus on imperfectly competitive labour markets has remained increasingly relevant. In rejecting the free market, the employment relationship is seen as a plurality of interests underpinned by an asymmetry of power. It is not that the employer wants one thing, and the worker wants something else, but that the employer (which might also be the state) can impose change (e.g. new technology) on the worker. As Kahn-Freund (1972: 19) famously stated, "there can no employment relationship without a power to command and a duty to obey". The focus therefore turns to avenues for 'balancing' a multiplicity of competing yet legitimate employer, employee and state interests in the workplace. However, workers' voice is not merely an end in itself, but also a means to greater efficiency and equality – employees should have a say in the organisation of their work with employers, who can benefit from employees' input in decision-making and most certainly in their commitment to the objectives of the firm, as well as the (ab)use of their labour, including measures to ensure equality in the workplace and beyond (e.g. flexible working time and work-life balance). Put differently, if it comes down to a choice, voice trumps efficiency.

The EEV framework argues that decent jobs are those that deliver on these three objectives (Budd 2006). Budd's argument is that the objective of the employment relationship is to achieve some kind of 'balance' between EEV and that extreme positions are undesirable. Efficiency means economic prosperity, the judicious use of scarce resources and the effective and productive use of labour. Equity refers to fairness in the distribution of rewards, social protection and effective labour laws. Voice means meaningful participation in decision-making. Equity and voice are key objectives rooted in human dignity and citizenship, even when they fail to enhance employee or organisational performance (Budd 2004). The justification for employee voice and equity therefore is not, as advocates of high-performance human resource management (HRM) would have it, as a means to profit-maximisation or higher productivity. Work is as an activity undertaken by human beings who are entitled to certain rights and therefore discrimination or a denial of employee voice is always unacceptable.

The More Things Change, the More They Stay the Same

When industrial relations scholars shine a light on continuity and change in the employment relationship (Blyton and Turnbull 2004), they invariably illuminate the role of labour. Just as past changes have presented challenges, such as outsourcing and the new international division of labour, the same is true of gig work and algorithmic management. Not all is new, but it is different. Changes in the employment relationship have been long on the cards since before the current wave of debate on the future of work (Pitts et al. 2018). Indeed while the technology of algorithmic management is new, the gig economy is "little more than app-based subcontracting", using new technology with forms of risk-shifting lifted from nineteenth-century contractual arrangements (Quinlan and Maxwell-Stewart 2023: 57). The outsourcing of work in the 1990s, facilitated by advances in information communication technology and the new international division of labour, undermined traditional trade union strategies in many industrial sectors (Piven and Cloward 2000). Labour has therefore had to change, adapt and invent new strategies at the scale of international capital. Exemplified by the work of the global union federations, industrial relations plays out on various scales from the local to the global (Donaghey et al. 2014).

In Anglo-American countries, it might seem that the declining power of unions, increasingly fragmented nature of labour relations, decline of the standard employment relationship, and rise in bogus self-employment (where a worker who is acting in the capacity of an employee is classified, often at the request of the employer, as self-employed) has sounded the death knell for the traditional employment relationship and any semblance of 'balance' between efficiency, on the one hand, and equity and voice on the other. However, on the contrary, understanding how workers, both individually and collectively, have responded to these changes is fundamental to understanding the futures of work. As Piven and Cloward (2000: 414) point out: "The worker strategies constructed in the industrial age have been undermined not because globalization has eviscerated labor power but because it weakened old labor strategies and spurred aggressive new elite strategies with which labor has yet to cope".

While much has changed in the world of work, the 'wage-effort bargain' remains at the heart of the employment relationship and therefore the futures of work. Employers and managers always require more than obedience from their workforce: they require effort, and some degree of loyalty or commitment, even if only perfunctory, to the tasks they are required to perform (Behrend 1957). For this reason, control by employers, whether facilitated by technology or not, always invites resistance from workers. Strikes in previously non-unionised companies such as Amazon and Starbucks (Kassem 2023), the successes of movements such as Fight for US$15 (Rolf 2016) and the Fair Food Programme (Mieres and McGrath 2021), and Google employees worldwide walking out to protest its handling of sexual harassment (Weaver et al. 2018) clearly show that collective action to advance workers' rights could divert or even derail attempts by capital and the state to shape a particular future of work(ers) (Vallas and Johnston 2023).

This begs the question: how will the futures of work be 'balanced' through improvements in efficiency, equity and voice? More to the point, can workers promote equality and ensure their voice is heard if employers are determined to drive efficiency at the expense of workers' interests?

Efficiency

Balancing efficiency against equity and voice has proven to be the most difficult to effect under neoliberalism. Neoliberal market ideology emphasises competitiveness and the 'trickle down' benefits of higher profits and economic prosperity. As such, the effective use of scarce resources such as labour and property are an important objective of the employment relationship. However, the employment relationship is far from a purely economic transaction but also one based on social activity in democratic countries; employment should be viewed as having a 'human face' rather than a purely economic one (Budd 2006).

The changing form of the firm, from a managerial hierarchical organisation to a financial hollowed-out enterprise, points to why many employers do not want or need a relationship with employees in order to generate greater efficiency and realise profits (Batt 2018). Instead of a direct employment relationship many organisations now operate through intermediaries creating a triangular contractual relationship that removes a line of responsibility between employer and employee, which helps ensure profitability of capital without protection of workers (Mitlacher 2008). For many activities, companies simply need to contract for services rendered or buy technology, with labour already embedded as an input (Batt 2018). This may be through traditional outsourcing as is common in the footwear and garments sectors or how platforms engage in 'internalised offshoring' (Findlay and Thompson 2017: 132). Many laws that regulate employment assume a direct employer/employee relationship (a contract *of* service as opposed to a contract *for* services) and make presumptions about responsibility and liability. The combination of information communication technology, a reduction in transportation costs and declining trade barriers, has seemingly created a world where "everyone is connected but no one is responsible" (Thomas and Turnbull 2018: 552).

Technology has created opportunities for amplified workplace surveillance and coercion (Colfer et al. 2023) and as a tool to further fragment work thus serving to improve organisational efficiencies. Amazon is a case *par excellence* in how algorithmic management systems have been used to increase labour efficiency. Amazon uses mini hand-held computers to assign tasks to workers and record how quickly those tasks are completed to monitor its warehouse workers, in order to extract valuable information about their workflow that is then used to further exploit, discipline and control (Alimahomed-Wilson and Reese 2021) (see the discussion of similar monitoring in the agricultural sector in Chapter 19). However, whilst technology may bring more control, and thus the more effective use of scarce resources, it is still subject to counter-resistance by workers (Elliott and Long 2016). The drive for efficiency has been met with flash strikes in recent years as workers seek to challenge health and safety, unfair firings (as a result of the monitoring systems) and low pay (Alimahomed-Wilson and Reese 2021).

Technology in particular has been hailed as a way to improve organisational efficiencies by reducing labour inputs and increasing or adapting forms of control. Indeed, the introduction of technology is rooted in the (universal) assumption that technology will be more efficient than that of human labour. However, employers might forgo technical improvements (quantitative efficiency) because labour is still cheaper, easily controlled, or capable of performing tasks that still demand a human touch (qualitative efficiency). For example, human sewer cleaners in India are cheaper than technology-based solutions in the UK (Fleming 2019); garment manufacturing in

Bangladesh is still conducted through a largely gendered workforce with minimal technological advancement (Wickramasingha and Coe 2022) (see Chapter 30); and in Sri Lanka the cultivation of tea is still performed by hand in order to retain the quality of Ceylon tea despite machine picking of tea deployed elsewhere around the world (Thomas 2021). Clearly, the logic for retaining human labour will also reflect market conditions and the wider socio-political and historical nature of work. Plucking tea leaves at the opportune moment is an inherently human skill, but this system of work is also a function of product quality, union organisation and employment laws that give workers significant structural and associational power (Thomas 2021). Irrespective of what technology is available to improve organisational efficiencies, workers will always have, to a greater or less extent, the capacity to contest employers' business and employment practices that threaten equality and quieten voice.

Equity

In the EEV framework, equity refers to how employees are treated in respect to fairness in the distribution of economic rewards, the administration of employment, and the provision of employee security (Budd 2006). Research demonstrates that equity goes hand-in-hand with efficiency when firms invest in more progressive HRM policies (Boxall and Macky 2014), suggesting a potential balance. However, in contrast to proponents of 'high commitment' HRM that emphasises equity as a root to organisational performance, industrial relations has always been concerned with abusive employment practices in and of themselves (Kaufman 2010). Equitable employment outcomes therefore include universal standards – minimum wages, maximum hours, minimum safety standards, protections against discrimination, restrictions on child and forced labour and provision of robust social safety nets as exemplified in the International Labour Organization's (ILO) Decent Work Agenda (ILO 1999). Decent and dignified work is an end in itself rather than the means of organisational performance.

Increasingly, however, the pursuit of productivity to the detriment of decent work is more common. At the global level the power of lead firms, most of which are transnational companies from the global North, have increased in power, in many cases transforming into a monopsonic capitalist market, with a multitude of suppliers captive to one buyer (Kumar 2020). This process has led to what UNCTAD has defined as "a new form of global rentier capitalism to the detriment of balanced and inclusive growth for the many", where living and working conditions deteriorate and "the winner takes most" (UNCTAD 2017) if not 'all'. As UNCTAD (2017) argues, this is not so much a case of a few 'bad apples', allowing policymakers and trade unions to target and regulate the abusive practices of individual firms, but a 'bad barrel' wherein "increasing market concentration in leading sectors of the global economy and the growing market and lobbying powers of dominant corporations" is systematically eroding working conditions and employment standards. The increasing spread of global supply chains has been facilitated by technologies such as advanced robotics and platforms even though the actual production choices are still mainly driven by labour cost (Butollo 2021). In other words, whilst global supply chains can create and bring organisational efficiency (through outsourcing), they systematically fail to guarantee labour rights such as freedom of association and collective bargaining (Thomas 2020a). This was brought to sharp relief when COVID-19 hit and suppliers in developing counties had their contracts cancelled, throwing millions of workers into poverty and destitution (Anner 2022; Thomas 2020b).

COVID-19, initially described as the 'great leveller', exposed increasing inequality for many, particularly for those who still went into a workplace and those who were prohibited from doing so, compounded by the unequal impact of the pandemic according to gender, race, class, age and disability, among others (Bales et al. 2020). One only has to look at the difference between the wages lost (−$3.7tn) (ILO 2021) and the increase in the wealth of billionaires (+$3.6tn) (Chancel et al. 2022) during the pandemic to appreciate the scale of the problem. There was a stark polarisation between those highly protected workers with permanent contracts in secure jobs who were able to work from home and highly precarious workers with unpredictable terms and conditions of employment with limited or no access to social protection should they be unable to continue working. The raft of employment policies that were established in many countries during the pandemic helped provide a buffer against the worst ravages of the pandemic but many of these were rapidly dismantled shortly after. To put it bluntly, it took a global pandemic to make clear that the world's social protection systems were not fit for purpose. However, the outpouring of public support for (frontline) workers did not necessarily translate into meaningful improvements in conditions of work. Following the pandemic, many employers were surprised to discover that they were unable to recruit enough workers under the same conditions as before, largely as a result of workers switching sectors during the pandemic and the reluctance of many to take up jobs in certain sectors because of concerns over wages and working conditions. Recently, with the cost-of-living crisis, focus has shifted more directly to the rewards from work, specifically compensation, and whether it is adequate to sustain a reasonable standard of living.

There is an opportunity to use technology to enhance equity in terms of greater flexibility and autonomy and enabling working from home to improve work-life balance. Greater transparency facilitated by technology apps that enable you to 'know your worth' have helped reduce the gender pay gap (Lobel 2022). There is also the opportunity to reduce the number of dirty, dangerous and difficult jobs by replacing these with robots (Susskind 2020), although in many areas of care there continues to be a preference for the human touch (MacLeavy 2021). However, technology has facilitated a number of new business models such as app-work, crowd-work and platform-work, which have transferred risks and the market pressures of supply and demand directly onto employees (or 'independent contractors' who should in fact be classified as employees) (Wood et al. 2019) (see Chapters 8 and 16). Technology has also created new opportunities and possibilities for control and surveillance (Dörflinger et al. 2021). As always, however, outcomes cannot always be predetermined. To take road haulage as an example, some have argued that the deployment of algorithmic scheduling, automated storage and retrieval systems, advanced robotics, GPS, and digital performance monitoring systems have combined to intensify work (Vallas and Johnston 2023). At the same time, unions such as the European Transport Workers' Federation (ETF) have pushed for digital tachographs (a device fitted to a vehicle that automatically records its speed and distance) as a way to prevent manipulation and ensure that driving and rest times are enforced. The impact of technology therefore depends on a multitude of factors but most importantly the degree to which workers are involved in the decision-making.

Voice

Voice is the ability to have meaningful input into decision-making both individually and collectively. We should be vigilant to avoid letting the definition of voice become so broad that it risks losing meaning. For example, information sharing (tell and sell) is closer to communication than it is to genuine consultation and even further from negotiation. Voice however should not be characterised as just collective voice rooted in trade union organisation but can manifest through individual voice, for example, the ability to speak and be listened to by line managers on a day-to-day basis about workplace concerns as well as more extreme forms such as whistleblowing. At one end of the individual-collective spectrum of voice is employee free speech and at the other end is industrial democracy, namely democratic methods for worker participation in decision-making (Kaufman 2000). Increasing corporate profits, coupled with stagnating or decreasing wage levels and deterioration of labour standards (equity), have sharpened workers' determination to mobilise and exercise their voice.

The collective voice of workers in advanced economies has been under continuous threat for the past 40 years. Although global trade union membership has increased by 3.6% since 2009 (ILO 2022b), collective bargaining coverage (i.e., the proportion of the workforce protected/covered by a union negotiated collective agreement) declined from 46% to 32% in OECD countries between 1985 and 2017 (OECD 2019). Moreover, the ITUC estimates that 77% of countries worldwide deny workers the right to establish and join a trade union and others point to a decline in free speech (ITUC 2022: 20). Increasingly, voice is expressed through voluntarist and private mechanisms, for example, corporate social responsibility along global supply chains or via team-working in firms that purport to practise a form of high-commitment HRM.

The decline of traditional forms of industrial democracy associated with trade unions and collective bargaining is partly as a result of the continued challenges to the right to strike as a foundation of voice at both the national and international levels (Vogt et al. 2020). In many countries, the right to strike has been restricted through limiting secondary action, picketing restrictions, ballot thresholds and advance notice periods. In the UK, for example, the Strikes [Minimum Service Levels] Bill 2022–2023 gives ministers the power to set minimum service levels during industrial action in a number of public sectors, which undermines the effectiveness of strike action and might deter strike action altogether. At the international level the right to strike has been repeatedly challenged at the ILO (Thomas and Turnbull 2021). This is not however to suggest that strikes have been declining in all sectors. In the UK, the cost-of-living crisis sparked strike action by a new generation of mainly public sector workers fighting for their voice to be heard with government.

The fissuring of work occasioned by technology has made it increasingly difficult for workers to organise, voice their grievances and engage in collective action. The OECD (2019) estimates that workers in non-standard jobs are 50% less likely to be unionised than standard workers. There has been an expansion in the number of non-standard jobs, including temporary, fixed-term, casual, part-time, agency and outsourced contracting or seasonal work, but also 'self-employment', such as freelance or gig economy work (Wilkinson et al. 2021). As Rubery (2015: 639) argues, "employers, instead of being held accountable, have become increasingly invisible", hiding behind a web of contractual relationships. These strategies are evident in a range of industries. In aviation, for example, airlines have used (bogus) self-employment (Geary 2022; Harvey and Turnbull 2020) or deliberately fragmented their organisational structures to halt strategies to collective bargaining (Sarina and Wright 2015). This is interlinked with the increasing financialisaton of the firm, mentioned above, which can affect voice by (re)shaping corporate goals, which, in turn, (re)shape strategies towards employee issues generally, and labour unions specifically (Batt 2018) (see Chapter 4).

New technology has the potential to increase rather than curtail worker voice through access to better methods of communication and consultation. Indeed, the availability of social media provides every worker with opportunities to air their discontent and new avenues to engage and communicate with union members and to increase solidarity (Moore and Taylor 2016). Social media also enables employees to circumvent traditional hierarchical voice mechanisms to share or raise grievances (Klaas et al. 2012). What is key with new technology is whether workers and their representatives are involved in the design, development, and deployment of hardware and software. Organisations such as the Institute of Future of Work (IFOW), for example, have been trialling the use of algorithmic assessment tools in order to embed voice in decision-making over the use of technology (IFOW 2023).

That said, new technology can also create barriers to voice. Social media, for example, can help mobilisation but has also been used by employers to monitor and suppress union activities and campaigns (Upchurch and Grassman 2016). To again take the platform economy as an example where the app rather than a direct employer is (supposedly) responsible for terms and conditions of work, there are fewer opportunities for workers (or unions) to resist or be involved in the (algorithmic) decision-making processes (Healy et al. 2017). This is exacerbated by their position as 'independent contractors', which may constrain their ability (or desire) to join and form union organisations (Vandaele 2018). As with all examples in this chapter, this is not to suggest that workers have been powerless in the face of these changes. One such example is the Independent Workers Union of Great Britain (IWGB), which was set up specifically for riders in Deliveroo and to challenge the lack of universal employment rights. Tassinari and Maccarrone (2020) have shown that solidarity among gig workers can create opportunities for voice within non-standard working relationships where the 'disordered nature' of platforms encourages creativity and experimentation (Vandaele 2018).

As with equity, there is a long line of research that links voice to organisational efficiency, whether through communication and consultation with individuals or the collective voice of trade unions (Freeman and Medoff 1984; Turnbull 2003). However, in terms of the balance between EEV, the latter is not simply a means to an end (a mechanism for higher efficiency) but an end in itself – in democratic societies, workers should not surrender their right to a voice when they walk through the factory gate or the office door, step onto the floor of the bourse, or log into an app. Leaving the market or benevolent employers to decide on whether to invest in voice or not is hardly a recipe for increasingly decent work. We need to therefore regulate the future of work by creating institutional safeguards for bolstering voice, creating a buttress against inequity.

Regulating the Future of Work

A policy focus on strengthening or reforming labour laws is essential to achieve the kind of lasting improvement needed to build an economy that provides decent jobs (Wilkinson and Barry 2020). At one level this may manifest as strong employment laws limiting exploitation, for example, the Irish government deciding to ban all zero-hour contracts (O'Sullivan et al. 2020), at another it could be focused on helping workers exercise their voice. For example, the recent developments in Australia to introduce multi-employer bargaining both across sectors and along supply chains suggest alternatives are possible (Wright et al. 2022). Indeed, the OECD has demonstrated that countries with multi-employer bargaining tend to have higher employment, lower wage inequality and more cooperative industrial relations than company- or enterprise-based systems (OECD 2019). Similarly in New Zealand, the Fair Pay Agreements Bill introduces a sectoral bargaining policy again helping to give voice to workers (Pakes and Pitts 2022). Sectoral bargaining is important as a bulwark against resistance by companies to unionisation. For example, as a result of the state's extension of sectoral bargaining in France and the requirement for workplace representation, all of Amazon's fulfilment centres are now formally bound by union agreements (Doellgast 2022). What is important here is a recognition that the future of work is not only shaped by the availability of technology but also employment laws, state policies and workers' organisation, which may have little or nothing to do with the technology itself but instead reflect broader movements to promote better work (Martínez Lucio et al. 2021).

Whilst the national level is most likely to have an impact on firm strategies in technological change (Lloyd and Payne 2021), at the global level soft-law innovations have been proposed to ensure the future of work is beneficial for all. For example, the ILO's human-centred approach to the future of work and promotion of a Universal Labour Guarantee suggested an insurance policy of a base-line of working conditions irrespective of technological change (Thomas and Turnbull 2021).

The OECD has similarly advocated a universal basic income and the inclusion of non-standard workers in collective bargaining, whilst the World Bank recommended a Scandinavian model of labour flexibility and social protection to promote decent work (Silva 2022). More recently, there have been significant developments in regulating platform-work, for example, the EU's Platform Workers Directive as well as a future ILO standard-setting discussion on the platform economy tabled for 2025. In the context of the futures of work the focus of these regulations should be on the degree to which workers are genuinely involved in the process of regulation and, afterwards, how corporate compliance can be ensured.

Concluding Points

In current discussions about the futures of work, there is an overwhelming focus on the quantity of jobs (created or destroyed) and organisational efficiencies rather than the quality of jobs. In other words, efficiency *at the expense of* equity and voice. This is a narrow view that does not consider the wider consequences of labour market and economic transformation for workers, such as employee health and participation in the future of work. In analysing sectors like the gig economy, which account for very few jobs in many countries, it can be difficult to not strike a polemic tone about the state of industrial relations. It should not be forgotten that the standard employment relationship remains the standard in most developed economies (Fudge 2017). However, it is clear that many of the institutions that were once relied upon to protect workers' wages, conditions and job security are being eroded. Trade union membership may be increasing in global terms but joint regulation and collective bargaining are on the decline, despite some positive developments in some countries. While there may be conflicts between equity and voice on the one hand and collective or individual responses on the other, the most significant conflicts arise between efficiency (the property rights of capital) and equity and voice (the human and employment rights of workers). We cannot anticipate that all workers will receive equal material treatment worldwide, but any improvements should aim to give workers a voice in wage setting and the right to negotiate conditions of work. Voice is an end in itself and a means to other ends. It is no surprise that the decline in trade union membership is directly related to an increase in inequality (Montebello et al. 2022).

The future of work(ers) is not predetermined, and it is important therefore to caution against grand assertions (Pitts et al. 2018). While much popular literature sees a context in which universal forces are unleashed upon the world of work there is considerable unevenness in the workplace, not least as institutional arrangements at national level have a major impact on how broad trends play out in the workplace. In other words, automation will be 'bounded', constrained and moulded by a range of organisational and institutional factors (Fleming 2019). What is dangerous about presupposing just one future of work is that it assumes a destination already set, depriving people of the agency to shape and resist that future (single) through organisation and regulation. There is evidently a continuum of futures (plural) from the dystopian and the utopian imaginaries. Whether the future is more dystopian will depend on the power of employers and whether they use technology and other resources to redefine the 'balance' in employment relationships that favours efficiency to the detriment of equity and voice. At the other end, a utopian future for workers will depend in large part on collective organisation and the invention of new repertories of collective action, because if history teaches us anything it is that capital's search for accumulation will often be to the detriment of labour. If we consider multiple futures for workers rather than a single terminus it allows us to imagine a future that is not predetermined and one in which activists, unions, academics, policymakers and others can identify and understand what is needed to support the plight of workers worldwide.

References

Ainsworth, S. and Knox, A. (2022). '"A bridge too far?" Ideas, employment relations and policy-making about the future of work'. *Industrial Relations: A Journal of Economy and Society*. 61 (1): 68–89.

Alimahomed-Wilson, J. and Reese, E. (2021). 'Surveilling Amazon's warehouse workers: Racism, retaliation, and worker resistance amid the pandemic'. *Work in the Global Economy*. 1 (1): 55–73.

Anner, M. (2022). 'Power relations in global supply chains and the unequal distribution of costs during crises: Squeezing suppliers and workers during the Covid-19 pandemic'. *International Labour Review*. 161 (1): 59–82.

Bales, K., Pitts, F. H. and Thomas, H. (2020). 'COVID-19 and the futures of work: Editorial and call for contributions'. *Futures of Work*. (12). https://futuresofwork.co.uk/2020/04/01/covid-19-and-the-futures-of-work-editorial-and-call-for-contributions/

Batt, R. (2018). 'The financial model of the firm, the "future of work", and employment relations'. In: A. Wilkinson, T. Dundon, J. Donaghey, and A. Colvin (eds.). *The Routledge Companion to Employment Relations*. London: Routledge, pp. 465–479.

Behrend, H. (1957). 'The effort bargain'. *Industrial and Labor Relations Review*. 10 (4): 503–515.

Blyton, P. and Turnbull, P. (1994). *The Dynamics of Employee Relations*. Basingstoke: Macmillan.

Boxall, P. and Macky, K. (2014). 'High-involvement work processes, work intensification and employee well-being'. *Work, Employment and Society*. 28 (6): 963–984.

Budd, J. W. (2004). *Achieving Decent Work by Giving Employment a Human Face*. Geneva: International Labour Office.

Budd, J. W. (2006). *Employment with a Human Face: Balancing Efficiency, Equity, and Voice*. Ithaca, NY: Cornell University Press.

Butollo, F. (2021). 'Digitalization and the geographies of production: Towards reshoring or global fragmentation?' *Competition & Change*. 25 (2): 259–78.

Chancel, L., Piketty, T., Saez, E. and Zucman, G. (2022). *World Inequality Report 2022*. Harvard: Harvard University Press.

Clarke, L., Donnelly, E., Hyman, R., Kelly, J., McKay, S. and Moore, S. (2011). 'What's the point of industrial relations?' *The International Journal of Comparative Labour Law and Industrial Relations*. 27 (3): 239–253.

Colfer, B., Harney, B., McLaughlin, C. and Wright, C. F. (2023). 'Introduction: New institutional arrangements for safeguarding labour standards'. In: B. Colfer, B. Harney, C. McLaughlin, and C. F. Wright (eds.). *Protecting the Future of Work: New Institutional Arrangements for Safeguarding Labour Standards*. Leeds: Emerald Publishing Limited, pp. 1–19.

Cumbers, A., Nativel, C. and Routledge, P. (2008). 'Labour agency and union positionalities in global production networks'. *Journal of Economic Geography*. 8 (3): 369–387.

Dobbins, T., Johnstone, S., Kahancová, M., Lamare, J. R. and Wilkinson, A. (2023). 'Comparative impacts of the COVID-19 pandemic on work and employment—Why industrial relations institutions matter'. *Industrial Relations: A Journal of Economy and Society*. 62 (2): 115–125.

Doellgast, V. (2022). *Exit, Voice, and Solidarity: Contesting Precarity in the US and European Telecommunications Industries*. Oxford, New York: Oxford University Press.

Doellgast, V. and Wagner, I. (2022). 'Collective regulation and the future of work in the digital economy: Insights from comparative employment relations'. *Journal of Industrial Relations*. 64 (3): 438–460.

Donaghey, J., Reinecke, J., Niforou, C. and Lawson, B. (2014). 'From employment relations to consumption relations: Balancing labor governance in global supply chains'. *Human Resource Management*. 53 (2): 229–252.

Dörflinger, N., Pulignano, V. and Vallas, S. P. (2021). 'Production regimes and class compromise among European warehouse workers'. *Work and Occupations*. 48 (2): 111–145.

Edwards, P. and Hodder, A. (2022). 'Conflict and control in the contemporary workplace: Structured antagonism revisited'. *Industrial Relations Journal*. 53 (3): 220–240.

Elliott, C. S. and Long, G. (2016). 'Manufacturing rate busters: Computer control and social relations in the labour process'. *Work, Employment and Society*. 30 (1): 135–151.

Findlay, P. and Thompson, P. (2017). 'Contemporary work: Its meanings and demands'. *Journal of Industrial Relations*. 59 (2): 122–138.

Fleming, P. (2019). 'Robots and organization studies: Why robots might not want to steal your job'. *Organization Studies*. 40 (1): 23–38.

Freeman, R. and Medoff, J. (1984). *What Do Unions Do?* New York: Basic Books.

Fudge, J. (2017). 'The future of the standard employment relationship: Labour law, new institutional economics and old power resource theory'. *Journal of Industrial Relations*. 59 (3): 374–392.

Geary, J. F. (2022). 'Securing collective representation in non-union European multinational companies: The case of Ryanair pilots' (partial) success'. *British Journal of Industrial Relations*. 60 (3): 635–661.

Harvey, G. and Turnbull, P. (2020). 'Ricardo flies Ryanair: Strategic human resource management and competitive advantage in a Single European Aviation Market'. *Human Resource Management Journal*. 30 (4): 553–565.

Healy, J., Nicholson, D. and Pekarek, A. (2017). 'Should we take the gig economy seriously?' *Labour and Industry*. 27 (3): 232–248.

IFOW (2023). *Good Work Algorithmic Impact Assessment*. https://www.ifow.org/publications/good-work-algorithmic-impact-assessment-an-approach-for-worker-involvement (accessed 29 March 2023).

Ilham, J. (2021). 'There's a good chance your cotton T-shirt was made with Uyghur slave labor'. *The Guardian*. 9 April. https://www.theguardian.com/commentisfree/2021/apr/09/cotton-slave-labor-uyghur-region-china (accessed 25 April 2023).

ILO (1919). *ILO Constitution*. Geneva: International Labour Organization.

ILO (1999). *Decent Work*. Geneva: International Labour Office.

ILO (2016). *Decent Work in Global Supply Chains*. Geneva: International Labour Organization.

ILO (2021). *ILO Monitor: COVID-19 and the World of Work*. 7th edition. Geneva: International Labour Organization.

ILO (2022a). *ILO Monitor on the World of Work*. 9th edition. Geneva: International Labour Organization.

ILO (2022b). *Social Dialogue Report 2022: Collective Bargaining for an Inclusive, Sustainable and Resilient Recovery*. Geneva: International Labour Organization.

ITUC (2022). *Global Rights Index*. 2022. ITUC Survey of violations of trade union rights. https://survey.ituc-csi.org/?lang=en (accessed 22 March 2016).

Kahn-Freund, O. (1972). *Labour and the Law*. London: Steven & Sons.

Kassem, S. (2023). '(Re)shaping Amazon labour struggles on both sides of the Atlantic: The power dynamics in Germany and the US amidst the pandemic'. *Transfer: European Review of Labour and Research*. 28 (4): 441–456.

Kaufman, B. (2010). 'The theoretical foundation of industrial relations and its implications for labor economics and human resource management'. *ILR Review*. 64 (1): 74–108.

Kaufman, B. E. (2000). 'The early institutionalists on industrial democracy and union democracy'. *Journal of Labor Research*. 21 (2): 189–209.

Klaas, B. S., Olson-Buchanan, J. B. and Ward, A.-K. (2012). 'The determinants of alternative forms of workplace voice: An integrative perspective'. *Journal of Management*. 38 (1): 314–345.

Kumar, A. (2020). *Monopsony Capitalism: Power and Production in the Twilight of the Sweatshop Age*. Cambridge: Cambridge University Press.

Lloyd, C. and Payne, J. (2021). 'Food for thought: Robots, jobs and skills in food and drink processing in Norway and the UK'. *New Technology, Work and Employment*. Early View. 38(2): 272–290.

Lobel, O. (2022). *The Equality Machine: Harnessing Digital Technology for a Brighter, More Inclusive Future*. New York: PublicAffairs.

MacLeavy, J. (2021). 'Care work, gender inequality and technological advancement in the age of COVID-19'. *Gender, Work & Organization*. 28 (1): 138–154.

Martínez Lucio, M., Mustchin, S., Marino, S., Howcroft, D. and Smith, H. (2021). 'New technology, trade unions and the future: Not quite the end of organised labour'. *Revista Española de Sociología*. 30 (3): a68.

Meardi, G. and Tassinari, A. (2022). 'Crisis corporatism 2.0? The role of social dialogue in the pandemic crisis in Europe'. *Transfer: European Review of Labour and Research*. 28 (1): 83–100.

Mieres, F. and McGrath, S. (2021). 'Ripe to be heard: Workers' voice in the fair food programme'. *International Labour Review*. 160 (4): 631–647.

Mitlacher, L. W. (2008). 'Job quality and temporary agency work: Challenges for human resource management in triangular employment relations in Germany'. *The International Journal of Human Resource Management*. 19 (3): 446–460.

Montebello, R., Spiteri, J. and Von Brockdorff, P. (2022). 'Trade unions and income inequality: Evidence from a panel of European countries'. *International Labour Review*. 162(3): 481–503.

Moore, S. and Taylor, P. (2016). '"We planned a dispute by Blackberry": The implications of the trade union bill for union use of social media as suggested by the BA-BASSA dispute of 2009–11'. *Industrial Law Journal*. 45 (2): 251–256.

OECD (2019). *Negotiating Our Way Up: Collective Bargaining in a Changing World of Work | en | OECD*. Washington, DC: OECD. https://www.oecd.org/publications/negotiating-our-way-up-1fd2da34-en.htm (accessed 28 March 2023).

O'Sullivan, M., Turner, T., Lavelle, J., MacMahon, J., Murphy, C., Ryan, L., Gunnigle, P. and O'Brien, M. (2020). 'The role of the state in shaping zero hours work in an atypical liberal market economy'. *Economic and Industrial Democracy*. 41 (3): 652–671.

Pakes, A., and Pitts, F. H. (2022). Fair Pay Agreements: How Labour can help people get on at work—not just get even. *Progressive Britain*. https://www.progressivebritain.org/fair-pay-agreements-how-labour-can-help-people-get-on-at-work-not-just-get-even/

Peetz, D. (2019). *The Realities and Futures of Work*. Acton: ANU Press.

Pitts, F. H., Bales, K. and Thomas, H. (2018). 'From the future of work to futures of work'. *Futures of Work*. (1). https://futuresofwork.co.uk/2018/09/05/editorial-from-the-future-of-work-to-futures-of-work/

Piven, F. and Cloward, R. (2000). 'Power repertoires and globalization'. *Politics & Society*. 28 (3): 413–430.

Quinlan, M. and Maxwell-Stewart, H. (2023). 'Inequality, worker mobilisation and lessons from history: Australia 1788–1900'. *Labour and Industry*. 33 (1): 39–62.

Rolf, D. (2016). *The Fight for Fifteen: The Right Wage for a Working America*. Illustrated edition. New York: The New Press.

Rubery, J. (2015). 'Change at work: Feminisation, flexibilisation, fragmentation and financialisation'. *Employee Relations*. 37 (6): 633–644.

Sarina, T. and Wright, C. F. (2015). 'Mutual gains or mutual losses? Organisational fragmentation and employment relations outcomes at Qantas Group'. *Journal of Industrial Relations*. 57 (5): 686–706.

Silva, V. (2022). 'The Schumpeterian consensus: The new logic of global social policy to face digital transformation'. *Journal of Social Policy*. FirstView. https://doi.org/10.1017/S0047279422000861

Susskind, D. (2020). *A World without Work: Technology, Automation and How We Should Respond*. London: Allen Lane.

Tassinari, A. and Maccarrone, V. (2020). 'Riders on the storm: Workplace solidarity among gig economy couriers in Italy and the UK'. *Work, Employment and Society*. 34 (1): 35–54.

Thomas, H. (2020a). 'Governing global production networks in the new economy'. In: A. Wilkinson and M. Barry (eds.). *The Future of Work and Employment*. Cheltenham: Elgar, pp. 189–203.

Thomas, H. (2020b). 'Pandemic, poverty and power in global exploitation chains'. *Futures of Work*. (14). https://futuresofwork.co.uk/2020/06/05/pandemic-poverty-and-power-in-global-exploitation-chains/

Thomas, H. (2021). 'A "decent cuppa": Worker power and consumer power in the Sri Lankan tea sector'. *British Journal of Industrial Relations*. 59 (1): 114–138.

Thomas, H. and Turnbull, P. (2018). 'From horizontal to vertical labour governance: The International Labour Organization (ILO) and decent work in global supply chains'. *Human Relations*. 71 (4): 536–559.

Thomas, H. and Turnbull, P. (2021). 'From a "moral commentator" to a "determined actor"? How the International Labour Organization (ILO) orchestrates the field of international industrial relations'. *British Journal of Industrial Relations*. 59 (3): 874–898.

Thomas, H. and Turnbull, P. (2023). 'Navigating the perilous waters of partisan scholarship: Participatory Action Research (PAR) with the European Transport Workers' Federation (ETF)'. *Work, Employment & Society*. 37 (3): 703–720.

Turnbull, P. (2003). 'What do unions do now?' *Journal of Labor Research*. 24 (3): 491–527.

UNCTAD (2017). *Trade and Development Report 2017*. https://unctad.org/system/files/official-document/tdr2017_en.pdf (accessed 6 March 2023).

Upchurch, M. and Grassman, R. (2016). 'Striking with social media: The contested (online) terrain of workplace conflict'. *Organization*. 23 (5): 639–656.

Vallas, S. P. and Johnston, H. (2023). 'Labor unbound? Assessing the current surge in labor activism'. *Work and Occupations*. 50 (3): 376–384.

Vandaele, K. (2018). 'Will trade unions survive in the platform economy?' *Emerging Patterns of Platform Workers' Collective Voice and Representation in Europe*. ETUI Research Paper - Working Paper 2018.05, Available at SSRN: https://ssrn.com/abstract=3198546 or http://dx.doi.org/10.2139/ssrn.3198546.

Visser, J. (2019). *Trade Unions in the Balance*. Geneva: ILO ACTRAV Working Paper.

Vogt, J., Bellace, J., Compa, L., Ewing, K. D., QC, J. H., Lörcher, K. and Novitz, T. (2020). *The Right to Strike in International Law*. Chicago, IL: Hart Publishing.

Weaver, M., Hern, A., Bekiempis, V., Hepler, L. and Fermoso, J. (2018). 'Google walkout: Global protests after sexual misconduct allegations'. *The Guardian*. 1 November. https://www.theguardian.com/technology/2018/nov/01/google-walkout-global-protests-employees-sexual-harassment-scandals (accessed 29 March 2023).

Weil, D. (2014). *The Fissured Workplace*. Cambridge, MA: Harvard University Press.

Wickramasingha, S. and Coe, N. M. (2022). 'Conceptualizing labor regimes in global production networks: Uneven outcomes across the Bangladeshi and Sri Lankan apparel industries'. *Economic Geography*. 98 (1): 68–90.

Wilkinson, A. and Barry, M. (2020). 'Understanding the future of work'. In: A. Wilkinson and M. Barry (eds.). *The Future of Work and Employment*. Cheltenham: Elgar, pp. 1–16.

Wilkinson, A., Knoll, M., Mowbray, P. K. and Dundon, T. (2021). 'New trajectories in worker voice: Integrating and applying contemporary challenges in the organization of work'. *British Journal of Management*. 32 (3): 693–707.

Wood, A. J., Graham, M., Lehdonvirta, V. and Hjorth, I. (2019). 'Good gig, bad gig: Autonomy and algorithmic control in the global gig economy'. *Work, Employment and Society*. 33 (1): 56–75.

Wright, C. F., Lansbury, R. and Andersen, S. K. (2022). 'Employers say Labor's new industrial relations bill threatens the economy. Denmark tells a different story'. 31 October 2022. *The Conversation*. https://theconversation.com/employers-say-labors-new-industrial-relations-bill-threatens-the-economy-denmark-tells-a-different-story-193311 (accessed 29 March 2023).

Recommendations for Further Reading

Budd, J. W. (2006). *Employment with a Human Face: Balancing Efficiency, Equity, and Voice*. Ithaca, NY: Cornell University Press.

Doellgast, V. and Wagner, I. (2022). 'Collective regulation and the future of work in the digital economy: Insights from comparative employment relations'. *Journal of Industrial Relations*. 64 (3): 438–460.

Howcroft, D. and Taylor, P. (2023). 'Automation and the future of work: A social shaping of technology approach'. *New Technology, Work and Employment*. 38 (2): 351–370.

Spencer, D. A. (2018). 'Fear and hope in an age of mass automation: Debating the future of work'. *New Technology, Work and Employment*. 33 (1): 1–12.

27

WELFARE POLICY

The Role of Social Protection and Active Labour Market Programmes in the Future of Work

Jo Ingold

Introduction

Historically, social protection and active labour market policies and programmes (ALMP) together have served as carrots, sticks and sermons (Schneider and Ingram, 1990) in respectively incentivising, punishing or persuading individuals to take up employment. These policy drivers have been observed in the organisation of different welfares states (Esping-Andersen, 1990) and political economic approaches (Hall and Soskice, 2001) to protect individuals, families and households against the social risks of unemployment, sickness and infirmity associated with age (Taylor-Gooby, 2004). Such risks are still present but needs have qualitatively changed which require recalibration of social protection to reflect different patterns of participation in employment from female labour market participation to the gig economy and portfolio careers. Debates concerning how welfare states recalibrate their systems to respond to contemporary demographic and labour market changes are not new (Hemerijck, 2013) and full employment is still a policy goal for most governments. However, we now face a crisis regarding what work is in the twenty-first century. This includes dimensions such as the meaning and place of paid work in contemporary and future societies with respect to caring responsibilities and the increasing advances in technology and automation that are shrinking pathways to particular occupations. What should work look like? Should everyone be expected to work? How long should people work? Population ageing, pensions deficits and a lack of health and social care workers speak to a crisis in just one industry. From the climate crisis arises a need for a green jobs agenda and a more even distribution of work across demographic categories and across geopolitical spheres. Crises around work and employment have given rise to calls for radical reforms such as Universal Basic Income paid to all citizens and the need for a restructuring of the standard work week to a Four-Day Week.

ALMP have long been viewed by governments as panaceas for labour market challenges, particularly rising unemployment and more recently the challenge of individuals not in employment for other reasons such as disability or caring ('economic inactivity'). However, surprisingly, in both policymaking and scholarship in this policy domain employers are implicitly considered to be recipients of ALMP rather than key demand-side actors. This 'supply-side fundamentalism' (Peck and Theodore, 2000) has led to a race to the bottom in terms of labour market inequalities, poor workplace practices and low-quality jobs. As such, it could be argued that ALMP have largely

DOI: 10.4324/9781003327561-37

perpetuated the problem they were purported to solve. For too many work is low-paid and insecure and for some degrading and dangerous. Within disability studies there is a lasting debate on disabled people's right not to work (Grover and Piggott, 2015) rather than be subjected to degrading welfare conditionality and sanction regimes designed to coerce individuals into poor-quality work. There is, relatedly, a wider debate about good work (Green and Sissons, 2023) and job quality (Guest et al., 2021). It is at this juncture that this chapter argues that a radical departure is required from predominant ALMP trajectories focused on a supply-sided, work first model underpinned by strict compliance and sanctions.

The chapter begins by outlining the aims and common features of social protection and ALMP, then reflects on extant scholarly critiques. The chapter argues that welfare policy has a key role to play in the future of work but a radical departure is required from current trajectories. Key dimensions that could comprise a future of work welfare policy are outlined: demand-informed policy models; an incentive model for ALMP based on job quality; a focus on rights and choice for individuals utilising ALMP; capacity-building of the employment services sector to better engage employers in delivery; and engaged employers who embrace inclusive Human Resource Management (HRM) in order to leverage overlooked talent.

Welfare Policy

Social Protection

Across welfare states, welfare policies aim to assist individuals outside the labour market into paid employment. This section considers the first pillar of this strategy: social protection. Social protection offers protection against social 'risks', including ill health, unemployment and destitution (Armingeon and Bonoli, 2007). Social protection policies rest on the central concept of whom is primarily responsible for providing protection: the state, the individual or the market. It is worth noting that the father of public administration Richard Titmuss (1974) considered 'welfare' to be a positive commitment by government and the opposite of 'illfare'. However, latterly the term has been appropriated as a deficit model term utilised to problematise recipients of social protection, particularly in liberal welfare states and informed by the US model of residualised and last resort protection.

The principal differentiator between social protection across welfare states is between social insurance and social assistance models, the former being based on entitlement from contributions within employment and the latter being based on means testing of resources such as savings and income. Esping-Andersen's (1990) typology of welfare states, although heavily critiqued particularly for its omission of gender, is nevertheless a useful starting point. The typology provides a way of conceptualising different approaches to the provision of social protection. These include the Liberal welfare states of the United Kingdom and United States predominantly based on 'last resort', means-tested social protection; the Social Democratic (Nordic) countries offering universal protection, and Corporatist welfare states (Germany, France) based around social insurance accrued from employment participation. However, no categorisation is clear-cut. For example, the categorisation of Australia and Denmark has been contested and the post-war UK welfare state originally conceived around a social insurance model has been eroded over time, resulting in the current largely means-tested model. Additional typologies have been added over time to the original Global North-focused typology, including Southern European welfare states, South-East Asian and other Global South economies. For instance, China has faced challenges in moving from a communist to a hybrid market economy model alongside rapid industrialisation related to social protection coverage across the working age population and significantly different needs between urban and rural populations (Leung and Xu, 2015).

Attempts to reduce public expenditure on a specific domain of social protection – working age benefits – has been a preoccupation of a majority of government administrations. This is despite working age benefits usually comprising only a fraction of social protection expenditure – the majority being on pensions. This reflects perceptions of deservingness constructed by political and media discourses. For example, the othering of people outside the labour market as strivers (UK), or lifters (Australia) contrasts the lazy and feckless with strivers and leaners who work and earn (Hills, 2017). Drawing on Bacchi's (1999) policy problem representation argument, if the policy problem to be solved is viewed as being structural unemployment, the policy responses would not logically be constructed as supply-side focused and work first. Instead, they would involve economic stimuli and a focus on the demand-side (employers). However, if the policy problem is considered to be individuals' fecklessness that needs to be disciplined, supply-sided policies focused on coercion and sanctions would be rational.

Mechanisms to achieve reductions in spending on working age benefits have relied on two key policy instruments. Firstly, restricting eligibility to claim benefits to reduce in-flows. Secondly, ALMP in order to move away from 'passive' public spending on social protection benefits towards measures orientated around increasing the 'employability' of individuals by 'activating' them for work, thereby increasing outflows. Both instruments have pivoted on the modification of conditions ('conditionality') for receipt of benefits such as requiring claimants to participate in ALMP interventions, or face sanctions (reduction in their benefits) and enforcing more stringent requirements on individual, as well as temporal measures such as time limits on receipt of some benefits (for example, unemployment insurance in Denmark) or phased 'ramping up' of conditionality requirements according to duration of unemployment. Another feature has been the extension of ALMP beyond unemployed groups to other so-called 'economically inactive' cohorts (Gregg and Wadsworth, 2010), including individuals who may already be working in an unpaid capacity such as lone parents, disabled people and their carers. Such approaches are notably underpinned by ideological assumptions about participation in society being based on paid employment and not voluntary community activities or caring labour. Relatedly, a further feature of social protection systems is the extent to which they are structured along gendered or racialised lines, specifically whether systems are individualised (many countries) or household-based (a minority of countries, including the UK). At the more extreme ends of the spectrum, there has been implementation of more pure workfarist (work for your benefit) approaches (such as 'Work for the Dole' in Australia), significantly increased conditionality for benefits as well as financial sanctions. However, evidence suggests that such approaches are counterproductive with individuals being pushed further away from employment rather than closer to it (Department for Work and Pensions [DWP], 2023; Dwyer, 2019). Furthermore, conditionality drives inappropriate job applications which frustrate employers and result in them being less likely to use the public employment service (PES) for their workforce needs (Ingold, 2020). UK evidence suggests that sanctions cost more to the taxpayer than they save (NAO, 2016). Crucially, there are further under-examined economic and social costs to individuals and society, including those displaced to other domains of the public budget such as health and housing, as well as increases in child poverty.

Further recalibrations (Hemerijck, 2013) to social protections have been focused on improving incentives to employment by modifying benefit taper rates, earnings and tax thresholds that impact on benefit payments (see Table 27.1). Such modifications aim to offset the 'cliff edge' and poverty traps that often ensue when individuals move from benefits into employment, in order to maximise the number of individuals who exit (flow off) benefits. A further policy measure has been the use of in-work benefits to 'make work pay' through topping up of wages with partial benefit payments or tax credits, as well as allowing individuals to retain access to 'passported' benefits for a period of time when first entering employment (e.g. access to concessions), again to attempt to offset losses. In liberal market economies social protection benefits are not particularly generous in the first place but individuals are then pushed into often low-paid and poor-quality employment. Wage subsidies are also utilised however the international evidence base suggests that they lead to substitution effects (subsidised workers replace unsubsidised workers) and have limited effectiveness (Borland, 2016). Approaches to both social protection and ALMP are predicated on sticks or carrots (or a combination); the former is a punitive approach and the latter a coercive approach. Evidence suggests that it is counterproductive to force individuals to look for inappropriate survival jobs and employers become frustrated by poorly-targeted applications to meet conditionality requirements (Ingold, 2020). Research in the UK during 2020–2021 uncovered that, although conditionality was paused, claimants were still searching for employment (Geiger et al., 2020). Evidence internationally suggests that conditionality impacts the motivation of only a small minority of claimants, refuting the narrative of the feckless benefits scrounger. The majority of individuals prefer work over welfare.

The next section discusses the intensification of ALMP, beginning with the shift from 'passive' to 'active' welfare states in the context of rising unemployment in the 1990s. Within this narrative construct, passivity became associated with social protection and the more positive activity associated with activities to move individuals closer to employment. ALMP have been normalised and supra-national institutions have engaged in policy diffusion of ALMP across Global North and South. The section illustrates how paid employment is viewed as a universal good, a moral necessity, by government and citizens despite evidence of poor-quality conditions and low wages. Crucial to this analysis is the bringing back in of the demand-side dimension.

Active Labour Market Policies and Programmes

Although there is no accepted definition as such, ALMP aim

> to bring more people into the effective labour force, to counteract the potentially negative effects of unemployment and related benefits on work incentives by enforcing their conditionality on active job search and participation in measures to improve employability (Dwyer, 2019), and to manage employment services and other labour market measures so that they effectively promote and assist the return to work.
>
> (Martin, 2015: 3)

ALMP (policies being the broad framework and programmes being the specific defined plans) are designed by governments (national, regional, local). Policies and programmes tend to be referred to interchangeably as 'activation' (particularly in Northern Europe) and welfare to work (commonly used in the US, the UK and Australia). Some states prescribe the detail of programmes whereas others set out a broad framework for delivery. Most countries have some form of PES that delivers ALMP (or 'employment services') at the local level. A feature of ALMP cross-nationally is experimentation by governments to a greater or lesser degree with the commissioning of for-profit and non-profit organisations to deliver programmes, particularly for individuals furthest from the labour market with complex needs (Greer et al., 2017). Consequently, ALMP are delivered by the PES and by ALMP agencies, or providers who act as labour market intermediaries between employers and potential employees (Ingold and Valizade, 2017; Autor, 2009).

ALMP first emerged in the 1950s in Sweden as part of the 'Rehn-Meidner model' (Bonoli, 2010), their aims being equality of wage distribution, sustainable full employment, modernisation of Swedish industry and tackling labour shortage. ALMP as a policy instrument subsequently spread to France, Italy, Germany and elsewhere. Following stagflation in the 1970s, the aims of activation were modified to focusing on the provision of occupations and activities for the unemployed and to address mass unemployment, as well as on job creation through the provision of temporary jobs and training programmes in the public sector. In the 1990s a 'new wave' of 'active labour market policies and programmes' was diffused across EU and OECD countries (McBride et al., 2008) as critical policy solutions to rising unemployment. This led to some considerable 'contingent convergence' (Eichhorst and Konle-Seidl, 2008) of policy ideas translated (Ingold and Monaghan, 2016) across differing welfare state contexts. At the same time there was a 'reorientation' of ALMP away from job creation and towards the incentivisation of work over 'welfare' and the provision of employment assistance to address what was perceived as the key policy problem: the mismatch of workers with jobs.

In order to address this policy problem, ALMP typically involve a range of mechanisms, ranging from assistance with coaching and assistance with job search, employability skills training (CVs, interview skills), paid, subsidised or unpaid work placements/work trials, 'social activation' for non-employment-related obstacles to employments (e.g. housing, alcohol/drug use) through to pure workfare, or 'work for your benefit' schemes. Table 27.1 provides a summary of common active labour market programme interventions. ALMP approaches have been categorised as 'human capital' involving a focus on education, training or work experience, and 'work first' focused on moving individuals into any job in the most expedient way (Lindsay et al., 2007). In practice interventions are typically combined although liberal welfare states (the UK and Australia being key examples with similar commissioning models) have tended to adopt a 'work first' strategy. A feature of ALMP internationally is a form of 'sorting' of individuals into categories through some form of assessment process, often in addition to the process of being assessed for social protection. Ratings are focused on measuring readiness for employment or 'distance from the labour market' due to employment-related (gaps in work history, outdated skills or experience) or other 'barriers' or obstacles to employment including housing, health or caring responsibilities. Notably, this does not reflect demand-side barriers. This sorting is intended to direct appropriate support to individuals through tailored and personalised interventions, however in practice this is driven by the policy frameworks and expenditure limits. A critical point of difference between welfare states is with regard to the amount of public expenditure committed to ALMP, with the UK being a typically low spender on relatively cheap work first interventions, while Denmark has long invested more in human capital focused interventions.

Table 27.1 provides a summary of key public policy instruments in relation to social protection and ALMP. These are divided into 'hard' policy instruments based on a stick approach and 'soft' policy instruments based on carrots and sermons (Schneider and Ingram, 1990). It can be observed that these are largely targeted towards individuals rather than employers. The absence of inclusion of the demand-side is a key critique of ALMP. The next section considers this and other dimensions of critique in detail.

Critiques of Active Labour Market Policies and Programmes

ALMP have been viewed by governments across countries, as well as supra-national actors, as successful. However, international evidence suggests their efficacy has limitations.

Firstly, Peck and Theodore (2000) have argued that ALMP have merely led to a 'reshuffling' of the jobs queue at the lower end of the labour market. This is illustrated by evidence of a 'low-pay,

Table 27.1 Public policy instruments for individuals and employers

'Hard' policy instruments (sticks)	*'Soft' policy instruments (carrots and sermons)*
Means testing	Job counselling and job search assistance
Time limits on benefit receipt	Job preparation interventions
Reduction in benefit levels	Work experience, work trials
Stricter eligibility for benefits	Education, training, upskilling
Benefit conditionality and sanctions	Pre-employment schemes
Benefit taper rates	Wage subsidies to employers
Eligibility for work assessments	Post-placement support
Earnings thresholds required to exit benefit	Allied health and social activation (not directly related to employment)
Compulsory workfare schemes	In-work benefits to top up wages, e.g. tax credits and concessions
Anti-discrimination legislation	

Source: After Bonoli (2010: 441), Eichhorst and Konle-Seidl (2008), Etherington and Ingold (2012), Schneider and Ingram (1990) and Bredgaard, Ingold and van Berkel (2023).

no-pay cycle' in countries including the UK (Shildrick et al., 2012) where individuals cycle between ALMP and low-paid, insecure labour and unemployment. This is evident from 'churn' within ALMP whereby individuals return to programmes, arguably moving no closer to the labour market, or even further away (Scholz and Ingold, 2020). Secondly, coercing individuals into low-paid, short-term employment impacts not only individuals' behaviours but also employers' behaviours, as tax credits and other in-work benefits mean that employers assume that wages will be 'topped up' from public expenditure, thus impacting wage setting. Although evidence is still patchy, the Institute for Fiscal Studies (Hoynes et al, 2023) and others (Paul, 2016) have argued that in the UK it is likely that extension of more stringent conditionality requirements and modification of benefit levels to encourage people into work permits employers to pay lower wages than they otherwise would. This is exacerbated by lax labour regulation and a weak industrial relations system with collective bargaining restrictions that results in setting of minimum wage rates below the Living Wage. The cost of such top-up credits to the public purse is also significant, meaning that taxpayers are subsidising employers and employers are designing jobs to account for this subsidy (Jones and Carson, 2023). This further undermines the argument that a work first, conditionality-led approach saves public money.

Thirdly, Bonoli (2010: 448) has argued that unemployment is largely the result of the excess supply of low-skilled labour and a shortage of jobs (labour market slack). However, even during slack labour market conditions where there is an excess of job vacancies and a scarcity of workers there is, despite the preponderance of ALMP, a mismatch between labour market and supply. This is partly structural, illustrated by the link between ill health and long-term sickness and economic inactivity. High numbers of long-term sickness benefits claimants are concentrated in former industrial regions where manufacturing has been replaced by service sector employment, leading to a labour market mismatch (Beatty and Fothergill, 2020). The mismatch also relates to the adequate preparation of individuals for job vacancies through delivery of ALMP at the local level. This links to a fourth critique. This is the 'creaming' of the most job-ready on ALMP caseloads and the 'parking' of the hardest to help (Carter and Whitworth, 2015). This persistent issue is claimed to be a critical reason for the short-term achievements of ALMP in placing people into employment and related to contracted-out (quasi-marketised models). It also relates to a fifth criticism, namely the optimal design and monitoring of delivery of ALMP. Whether ALMP are delivered through the PES or through contracted providers, a performance framework is usually designed by the relevant government department. However, performance becomes a more complex issue to measure in outsourced contracts especially where there are multiple providers or complex supply chains. Whatever the context, measurement can drive behaviours at the level of delivery. As ALMP success is typically measured by job outcomes (often six months to one year), performance frameworks tend to be designed around such measures. Outcomes-based funding was introduced as a way of rewarding achievement of 'sustainable' (longer) job outcomes to overcome this limitation. There has been some interest in measuring 'softer' outcomes by measuring progression towards employment such as readiness for work (Dewson et al., 2000), particularly for groups who are considered 'harder to help, or 'furthest from the labour market' however this area is currently underexplored.

A final but significant limitation of ALMP to date has been the abject neglect of the demand-side. This is a serious omission given that ALMPs' success is measured on the number of individuals moved into employment and the cost of programmes versus their benefits to the public purse (seldom measured across policy domains). The absence of demand-side policies can be linked to the 'supply-side fundamentalism' (Peck and Theodore, 2000) that underpins ALMP. This speaks to the underpinnings of ALMP as being normatively predicated on the failings of individuals, whether that be outdated skills, gaps in employment history or more pejorative assumptions such as fecklessness or idleness (Jones and Kumar, 2022). However, the lens of scrutiny upon individuals ('jobseekers') has obscured the behaviours of employers including hiring behaviours and job design. It has also left largely obscured the impact of welfare policies on workplaces, such as the intensification of conditionality, leading to a supply of workers who are compelled to take any job, the associated driving down of wages and conditions and employers' shaping of job roles to account for benefit rules such as number of hours required to be employed to retain in-work benefits. The notion of 'skivers' and feckless individuals also reflects a deficit model that discourages employers from employing claimants and from using employment services (Ingold, 2013). A further recent development in the UK has been that of in-work progression (formerly 'in-work conditionality') in the context of Universal Credit, the single working age benefit. This requires individuals in employment to look for more employment either within their existing job or via another role (potentially requiring workers to take on more than one job), in order to increase pay and hours, with the aim of leaving benefit. This creates a new category of 'working claimants', further problematising those already in low-paid employment, which is a demand-side issue. Analyses (Jones and Carson, 2023; Griffiths, 2022) suggest that the policy has been developed absent of any recognition of the demand-side or the labour market context, meaning employers lack any knowledge or understanding of the policy. The instrument is also ignorant of contemporary developments around work including the common features of low-paid work such as precarity.

That is not to say that there are not examples of 'demand-side' interventions. For example, wage subsidies can be categorised as operating both on the demand- and supply-sides given that they reduce costs to employers (Robertshaw, 2024). However, in countries where employer 'engagement' in ALMP has been measured, it is clear that employers have little involvement in programmes, or use them for their hiring requirements (Ingold and Valizade, 2015; Bredgaard, 2018; Orton et al., 2019). Ingold and Valizade (2015) provide a useful review distinguishing between typologies that focus on categorising (1) the type of employer participation and (2) the motives for employer participation in activation policies. However, until attention is paid within policymaking to the demand-side dynamics of ALMP, important dimensions of the future of work will continue to be ignored, likely leading to exacerbation of inequalities for those already disadvantaged in the labour market. Swank and Martin (2001), Martin (2004), Martin and Swank (2004, 2012) were among the first to argue that a key determinant of employer involvement in social policies was the role of employers via employers' representative organisations (national and peak). However, not all countries have this mechanism, nor is it necessarily an effective way of involving employers (Valizade et al., 2022). However, the point stands that within welfare policymaking, employers have tended to be implicitly considered recipients of ALMP rather than key demand-side actors. This has led to a reinforcement of labour market inequalities (which may themselves have led to unemployment in the first place), poor workplace practices and low-paid, low-quality jobs (Fletcher, 2004).

Furthermore, despite the supply-side fundamentalism infusing them, ALMP themselves appear to have done little to improve labour market opportunities for the majority of under-served groups. Employers do not engage in ALMP for a variety of reasons including the plethora of programmes available. Employers also do not know how to engage, are not contacted by the PES or other providers, and are not aware of the potential benefits of engaging (Ingold et al, 2023). Additionally, while ALMP predominantly focus on job brokering (i.e. acquisition of vacancies) this does not provide a compelling value proposition for employers and means that ALMP are merely competing directly with other commercial job boards in the marketplace. The normative deficit model underpinning social protection and ALMP also fundamentally undermines demand-side strategies, presenting individuals as 'faulty' candidates for jobs whom employers are expected to employ. In this way, conditionality requirements for individuals to apply for jobs can lead to further employer frustration.

The next section proposes the factors that could feature in a demand-side activation strategy.

Critical Factors for a Demand-Side Activation Strategy

ALMP as currently conceived are focused on the supply-side and intensifying job search. Instead, they should be focused on (i) assisting people who struggle to get into paid employment; and (ii) assisting employers to access a more diverse talent pool. What follows is a roadmap to a demand-focused model for activation strategy that could underpin social protection and ALMP (and within this PES) and comprise a future of work welfare policy. The elements of this are summarised in Table 27.2.

At the macro level, the regulatory frameworks underpinning ALMP need to be as simple as possible, while ensuring value for public money. In designing ALMP, employers and industry bodies and trade unions need to be involved in the co-design of policies and engaged at this level on an ongoing basis. Joint commissioning of employment and skills would be optimal as these policy domains strongly intersect. Ingold and Valizade (2017) found that it was easier for Jobcentres in Denmark to engage employers in a sustained way because businesses are considered within the commissioning process (policy is steered by the Ministry but devolved to municipalities). By contrast, in the UK, with its weaker institutional framework, business engagement was much harder to achieve and needed more intensive outreach and relationship building by agencies. Not considering the demand-side of the labour market (employers) within the design or commissioning process at the institutional (macro) level means that providers have to retrofit their delivery to maximise the engagement of employers around their contractual and compliance requirements.

The optimal level of governance is at sub-national levels because labour markets are predominantly regional and local. Devolution means that ALMP are "designed in closer proximity to their sites of implementation, taking account of local labour market conditions and inherited institutional and governance structures and relations" (Etherington and Ingold, 2012: 33). A critical issue within

Table 27.2 A proposal for a demand-driven activation strategy

Governance level	*Actors*	*Activities*
Macro	Government at national level	Regulations relating to equality and labour laws Social protection legislation and the balancing of rights and duties Demand-informed ALMP based on accurate labour market intelligence Sets overarching framework for ALMP through design and/or commissioning of programmes focused on simplicity and incentivising of employer engagement Involvement of employers through employer associations, industry associations, trade unions Strategies for prevention of unemployment
Meso	Sectoral bodies Labour market intermediaries Regional and local government Local employer networks	Simplicity in programme operations Occupational progression maps Holistic human resource offer including recruitment, retention and progression strategies Co-production approach to employers
Micro	Individual organisations Hiring managers Diversity and inclusion managers	Inclusive human resource management Proactive recruitment strategies Innovative approaches to job design Partnerships with intermediaries Shared responsibility for local social outcomes

Source: After Bredgaard, Ingold and van Berkel (2023: 237).

outsourced services is that providers are already in competition with each other, which undermines effective employer engagement and creates a large number of less valuable, fragmented services to employers. Providing a bespoke and seamless service to businesses – collaboration amidst competition, or 'co-opetition' – requires collaboration between delivery partners. This requires the design and monitoring of contracts and performance frameworks that incentivise collaboration between the PES, ALMP agencies and providers to provide a better service to employers and individuals (Baker et al., 2023). Government should advertise the benefits of ALMP and clearly communicate to employers how they could engage with the PES or with delivery organisations in their relevant geographical area/s (Ingold and Knox, 2023).

There is a need for a rebalancing of rights and duties within social protection and ALMP. Over time, in neoliberal states the discourse and normative underpinnings have shifted away from rights and choice in equal measure (for example the relative balance in Denmark of the right and duty to be activated) towards the responsibilities of the individual over choice or rights. In particular, ALMP are relative outliers in terms of public policies that do not place personal choice at the centre. Personalised and tailored employment support involves ascertaining an individual's strengths, values and motivations and matching them to an occupation. However, despite espousal of personalisation and tailoring as a goal of ALMP, it this remains a challenge, particularly for the longer-term unemployed (Fuertes and Lindsay, 2016; O'Sullivan et al., 2021). Orton (2011) argues that drawing on the work of Sen and Nussbaum is instructive in relation to a reframing of ALMP and employability. This requires a normative shift towards a strengths-based model and away from a deficit model. Evidence is also clear that using a 'stick' approach of conditionality and financial sanctions is counterproductive for individuals and society (Dwyer, 2019) and should be used as a last resort.

Central to a new activation model is the interaction between the meso and micro levels. The former comprises labour market intermediaries, regional and local government and employer associations and sector bodies. The latter involves individual workplaces and hiring managers. This intersection centres around organisations and individuals delivering ALMP to build effective and sustainable relationships with employers, or what have been referred to as street-level bureaucrats and street-level organisations (SLOs) (Brodkin, 2013). They have a critical role to play in changing recruitment and talent acquisition practices so that hiring managers can gain access to the best talent and to access hidden talent pools that are usually overlooked (Ingold, 2018). Individuals and organisations delivering ALMP also need to be equipped with the skills to engage employers; such skills are qualitatively different to those required to engage with ALMP participants (Ingold and Stuart, 2014). This accords with what Bredgaard, Ingold and van Berkel (2023) have termed the 'negotiation' approach to employer engagement, one of three distinct 'varieties of employer engagement'. The others are regulation and facilitation. Regulation is the most basic level and involves sticks, i.e. legislation to outlaw discrimination, is focused on individuals further away from employment and conceptualisation of employers as passive recipients of ALMP and as utility maximisers. The second involves provision of adequate labour to serve the recruitment needs of employers with a focus on individuals close to employment ('job ready') and conceptualisation of employers as 'customers' of ALMP with a focus on 'carrots' such as subsidies. The negotiation approach involves collaboration with employers regarding job matching and recruitment approaches, job design and retention, primarily for individuals who face more significant barriers to employment and with a focus on information ('sermons'). This approach conceptualises employers as co-producers of ALMP and is based on fostering of relationships with employers and assisting them with education and information. Employers do not always know what their workforce needs are (or have the time to look at and interpret labour market data) so a diagnostic function is as important for employers as it is for participants of ALMP (job candidates). This is particularly critical as hiring managers often lack the necessary skills and information to adopt proactive rather than reactive approaches to recruitment including re-designing jobs to attract hidden talent in the labour supply pool, including parents and people with health conditions or disabilities. Organisations delivering ALMP need to have the confidence to challenge employers' conventional requirements for labour and traditional recruitment processes. Delivery organisations should refuse to partner with employers who exhibit poor workplace practices and not be penalised for this.

Bredgaard (2018) makes a critical distinction between employers' stated attitudes and their behaviours. This is critical in relation to what are referred to as 'disadvantaged groups'. Instead, a strengths-based approach would focus on the potential of 'priority groups' or 'under-served and overlooked' talent (Diversity Council Australia [DCA], 2022). For example, most employers state that they are willing to employ people with disabilities. However, the employment statistics demonstrate that most employers do not actually do this. A critical role for ALMP is therefore not only to assist employers to change their recruitment practices but to work with line managers who often lack expertise in inducting and supervising employees from priority groups. Employer education is critical and ALMP can provide this for the benefit of the wider organisation and its employees, not just individuals on ALMP caseloads. This can help to prepare organisations to receive under-served groups by creating appropriate processes and an organisational culture that is supportive and appropriate, reducing the likelihood of placements failing. Given that small- and medium-sized businesses comprise a majority of the business population yet often lack internal

HR expertise, there is a case for focusing more attention on these organisations, particularly for individuals furthest from employment. Another key dimension is the provision of post-placement/in-work support. Although in-work support offers clear benefits to newly recruited employees, it also has significant benefits for employers in relation to being able to support the individual.

With regard to measurement of the effectiveness of ALMP, job outcomes should not be the predominant focus, especially when predicated on a prescribed and relatively short length of time (e.g. six months) but needs to include a measure of job quality. This includes terms of employment; pay and other rewards; intrinsic characteristics of work; social support and cohesion; health and safety; work-life balance; representation and voice (Warhurst, Knox and Wright, 2024). Borghouts and Freese (2023) have argued for the expansion of strategic HRM to inclusive HRM focused on activities that facilitate labour market transitions across the life course and across organisations. They have also argued for the importance of prevention within social protection and ALMP strategies beyond rapid responses to redundancy often provided by the state and the PES.

Together, these elements constitute a new approach to demand-driven activation and an attempt to address at least some of the failings evidenced by critiques over the past few decades of intensification of this policy instrument across countries, not least the omission of the demand-side. The PES has a history going back over a century. Employment support is always going to be needed to assist individuals who struggle to enter paid employment or who experience interruptions to their employment trajectory due to caring, illness, or redundancy. Borghouts and Freese (2023) have put forward a model for a 'transitional-inclusive HRM-labour market model' that supports transitions between employment and unemployment and between jobs and careers. This intersects with the need to focus on careers rather than jobs including better joining up of skills and employment policies and funding within the broader employment ecosystem. A key part of this is the need for good quality information, advice and guidance to school leavers and those transitioning into different lifecourse phases related to work. Workfare instruments based on punishment are not a constructive dimension of such an approach. Eligibility rules for benefits, the conditionality associated with ongoing receipt and financial sanctions are 'sledgehammer to crack a nut' policy instruments that punish the majority in order to catch out a few transgressors. The social protection and ALMP systems that comprise welfare policy need to operate more effectively and efficiently for the majority and be recalibrated to meet the requirements of contemporary developments in the future of work.

Conclusion

This chapter has provided a critical account of welfare policy comprising social protection and ALMP and proposed a model that could comprise a future of work welfare policy involving demand-informed policy; an incentive model for ALMP based on job quality; a focus on rights and choice for individuals utilising ALMP; capacity-building of the sector to better engage employers in delivery; and engaged employers who embrace inclusive HRM in order to leverage overlooked talent.

Modified policy instruments are needed that better reflect the complexities and realities of working life in contemporary society. It is clear that an instrument such as in-work conditionality in the UK is ill-suited to these realities, as well as the reality of how organisations, HR and payroll operate. Alternative models for social protection have been put forward. These include Universal Basic Income (UBI) (Haagh, 2019), also referred to as 'Citizen's Income'. It is an idea that has been favoured by radically different ends of the political spectrum – from New Right thinker Charles Murray who considers UBI as a way of permanently replacing the welfare state (Murray, 2006) to political philosopher Phillippe van Parijs (2000), who favours a more utopian vision. Key features of UBI are that it is universal, unconditional and adequate to protect individuals from poverty. UBI would involve less bureaucracy than existing systems and would be flexible to allow individuals to participate in as much employment as they wish according to their preferences and changing circumstances. There have been experiments in countries including Finland and Kenya however they have been limited by size and lack of attention paid to scaling up. The second alternative model is the Four-Day Week (Barnes, 2020) which reduces the conventional five-day week to four, a future envisaged by both Marx and Keynes. There have been experiments in the UK, Ireland, US and New Zealand with benefits realised in terms of less stress, absenteeism and better retention of employees. Both models have merits but change needs to be at the larger scale which, depending on your perspective, could either emanate from macro levels of institutional policymaking or from a movement for change amongst organisations and individuals.

In closing, it is also worth noting the evolution of welfare policy, across both ALMP and social protection including the rise in digital service delivery (Considine et al., 2022). Digital tools can be used to automate routine tasks and free up time for coaches to develop relationships with candidates (and employers). However, widespread digital servicing poses challenges for both the most disadvantaged individuals and for employers, particularly smaller-sized employers (van Berkel et al., 2017). A further note of caution should be exercised in relation to the development of ALMP in jurisdictions in the Global South. Supra-national institutions have helped to diffuse the liberal model of ALMP (see Finn, 2020) however, in searching for good practice models the limitations of ALMP to date should be noted. Finally, in terms of a future research agenda, the majority of extant studies of ALMP have been within social and public policy and have tended to focus predominantly on either institutional or governance issues, or on individuals affected by policies or programmes, or on frontline actors involved in implementation. More recent attempts to illuminate the demand-side have fused HRM approaches with social and public policy literature (see Ingold and McGurk, 2023). Further inter-disciplinary approaches to scholarship are essential to the analysis of welfare policy if we are to better understand its role in the future of work.

References

Armingeon, K. and Bonoli, G. (2007) *The Politics of Post-Industrial Welfare States: Adapting Post-War Social Policies to New Social Risks*. London: Routledge.

Autor, D. (ed.) (2009) *Studies of Labor Market Intermediation*. Chicago, IL: University of Chicago Press.

Bacchi, C. L. (1999) *Women, Policy and Politics: The Construction of Policy Problems*. London: Sage.

Baker, O., Ingold, J., Crichton, E., and Carr, T. (2023) 'Practice case study: Programme commissioning and co-opetition in the UK and Australia,' in J. Ingold and P. McGurk (eds.) *Employer Engagement: Making Active Labour Market Policies Work*. Bristol: Bristol University Press, pp. 75–86.

Barnes, A. (with S. Jones) (2020) *The 4-Day Week: How the Flexible Work Revolution Can Increase Productivity, Profitability and Well-being, and Create a Sustainable Future*. Boston, MA: Little Brown.

Beatty, C. and Fothergill, S. (2020) 'The long shadow of job loss: Britain's older industrial towns in the 21st century,' *Frontiers in Sociology*. https://doi.org/10.3389/fsoc.2020.00054.

Bonoli, G. (2010) 'The political economy of active labour-market policy,' *Politics & Society* 38(4): 435–457.

Borghouts, I. and Freese, C. (2023) 'HRM and social security: It takes two to create a transitional labour market,' in J. Ingold and P. McGurk (eds.) *Employer Engagement: Making Active Labour Market Policies Work*. Bristol: Bristol University Press, pp. 182–200.

Borland, J. (2016) 'Wage subsidy programs: A primer,' *Australian Journal of Labour Economics* 19(3): 131–144.

Bredgaard, T. (2018) 'Employers and active labour market Policies: Typologies and evidence,' *Social Policy and Society* 17(3): 365–377.

Bredgaard, T., Ingold, J., and van Berkel, R. (2023) 'Varieties of policy approaches to employer engagement in activation policies,' in J. Ingold, P. McGurk P (eds.) *Employer Engagement: Making Active Labour Market Policies Work*. Bristol University Press, pp. 15–33.

Brodkin, E.Z. (2013) 'Street-level organizations and the welfare state,' in E. Brodkin and G. Marston (eds.) *Work and the Welfare State: Street-Level Organizations and Workfare Politics*. Washington, DC: Georgetown University Press, pp. 17–34.

Carter, E. and Whitworth, A. (2015) 'Creaming and parking in quasi-marketised welfare-to-work schemes: Designed out of or designed in to the UK work programme?' *Journal of Social Policy* 44(2): 277–296.

Considine, M., Mcgann, M., Ball, S. and Nguyen, P. (2022) 'Can robots understand welfare? Exploring machine bureaucracies in welfare-to-work,' *Journal of Social Policy* 51(3): 519–534.

Department for Work and Pensions (DWP) (2023) *The Impact of Benefit Sanctions on Employment Outcomes*. London: DWP. Available at: https://www.gov.uk/government/publications/the-impact-of-benefit-sanctions-on-employment-outcomes-draft-report/the-impact-of-benefit-sanctions-on-employment-outcomes

Dewson, S., Eccles, J., Tackey, N.D. and Jackson, A. (2000) *Guide to Measuring Soft Outcomes and Distance Travelled*. Brighton: Institute for Employment Studies.

Diversity Council Australia (DCA) (2022) Available at: https://www.dca.org.au/research/project/inclusive-recruitment-work [Accessed 24 March 2023].

Dwyer, P. (ed) (2019) *Dealing with Welfare Conditionality: Implementation and Effects*. Bristol: Policy Press.

Eichhorst, W. and Konle-Seidl, R. (2008) 'Contingent convergence: A comparative analysis of activation policies,' *IZA Discussion Paper No. 3905*. Available at SSRN. https://dx. doi.org/10.2139/ssrn.1318864

Esping-Andersen, G. (1990) *The Three Worlds of Welfare Capitalism*. Cambridge: Polity Press.

Etherington, D. and Ingold, J. (2012) 'Welfare to work and the inclusive labour market: A comparative study of activation policies for sickness benefit claimants in the UK and Denmark,' *Journal of European Social Policy* 22(1): 30–44.

Finn, D. (2020) *The Public Employment Service and Partnerships in China, Colombia, India and South Korea: Synthesis Report on Good Practices in using Partnerships for the delivery of Employment Services and Active Labour Market Programmes [preprint]*.

Fletcher, D. (2004) 'Demand-led programmes: Challenging labour market inequalities or reinforcing them?' *Environment and Planning C: Government and Policy* 22: 115–128.

Fuertes, V. and Lindsay, C. (2016) 'Personalization and street level-practice in activation: The case of the UK's Work Programme,' *Public Administration* 94: 526–541.

Geiger, B.B., Karagiannaki, E., Edmiston, D., Sullion, L. Summers, K., Ingold, J., Robertshaw, D. and Gibbons, A. (2020) *Claiming but Connected to Work*. Welfare at a (Social) Distance Rapid Report 1 (June 2020). Available at: https://eprints.whiterose.ac.uk/173176/ [Accessed: 27 March 2023].

Green, A, Sissons, P. (2023) The weakest link? Job quality and active labour market policy in the UK. in J. Ingold and P. McGurk, (eds.) *Employer Engagement: Making Active Labour Market Policies Work*. Bristol University Press. pp. 87–105.

Greer, I., Breidahl, K.N., Knuth, M. and Larsen, F. (2017) *The Marketisation of Employment Services: The Dilemmas of Europe's Work-First Welfare States*. Oxford: Oxford University Press.

Gregg, P. and Wadsworth, J. (2010) 'Unemployment and inactivity in the 2008–2009 recession,' *Economic Labour Market Review* 4: 44–450.

Griffiths, R. (2022) *Universal Credit, Working Claimants and the Government's Cost of Living Support, IPR Policy Brief*. Bath: Institute of Policy Research.

Grover, C. and Piggott, L. (2015) *Work, Welfare and Disabled People: Is Employment Really the Answer?* Bristol: Policy Press.

Guest, D., Knox, A. and Warhurst, C. (2021) 'Human relations virtual special issue: The quality of working life revisited,' *Human Relations*, 74(1): 153–156.

Haagh, L. (2019) *The Case for Universal Basic Income*. Hoboken, NJ: Wiley.

Hall, P.A. and Soskice, D. (2001) *Varieties of Capitalism: The Institutional Foundations of Comparative Advantage*. Oxford: Oxford University Press.

Hemerijck, A. (2013) *Changing Welfare States*. Oxford: Oxford University Press.

Hills, J. (2017) *Good Times, Bad Times: The Welfare Myth of Them and Us*. Bristol: Policy Press.

Hoynes H., Joyce, R., and Waters, T. (2023) *Benefits and Tax Credits*. London: Institute for Fiscal Studies. Available at: https://ifs.org.uk/publications/benefits-and-tax-credits

Ingold, J. (2013) *CERIC Blog: Government Rhetoric Is Likely to Turn Off Business and Undermine a Flagship Policy.* Available at: https://cericleeds.wordpress.com/page/2/ [Accessed 14 June 2013].

Ingold, J. (2018) 'Employer engagement in active labour market programmes: The role of boundary spanners,' *Public Administration* 96: 707–720.

Ingold, J. (2020) 'Employers' perspectives on benefit conditionality in the UK and Denmark,' *Social Policy & Administration* 54(2): 236–249.

Ingold, J. and McGurk, P. (eds.) (2023) *Employer Engagement: Making Active Labour Market Policies Work.* Bristol: Bristol University Press.

Ingold, J. and Monaghan, M. (2016) 'Evidence translation: An exploration of policymakers' use of evidence,' *Policy and Politics* 44(2): 171–190.

Ingold, J. and Stuart, M. (2014) *Employer engagement in the Work Programme. CERIC Policy Report No. 5.* Leeds: Centre for Employment Relations Innovation and Change.

Ingold, J. and Valizade, D. (2015) *Employer Angagement in Active Labour Market Policies in the UK and Denmark: A Survey of Employers, CERIC Policy Report No. 6.* Leeds: Centre for Employment Relations Innovation and Change.

Ingold, J. and Valizade, D. (2017) 'Employers' recruitment of disadvantaged groups: Exploring the effect of active labour market programme agencies as labour market intermediaries,' *Human Resource Management Journal* 27(4): 530–547.

Ingold, J., Knox, A., Macaulay, L., and Senewiratne, S. (2023) ''What about me?': An analysis of employers' engagement with employment service providers in Australia,' *Journal of Industrial Relations*, 65(3): 251–273. https://doi.org/10.1177/00221856231159512.

Jones, K. and Carson, C. (2023) *Universal Credit and Employers: Exploring the Demand-Side of UK Active Labour Market Policy: Final Report.* Manchester: Manchester Metropolitan University.

Jones, K. and Kumar, A. (2022) *Idleness.* Newcastle: Agenda Publishing.

Leung, J.C.B. and Xu, Y. (2015) *China's Social Welfare: The Third Turning Point.* Cambridge: Polity Press.

Lindsay, C., McQuaid, R.W. and Dutton, M. (2007) 'New approaches to employability in the UK: Combining 'human capital development' and 'work first' strategies?,' *Journal of Social Policy* 36(4): 539–560.

Martin, C.J. (2004) 'Reinventing welfare regimes employers and the implementation of active social policy,' *World Politics* 57(01): 39–69.

Martin, C.J. and Swank, D. (2004) 'Does the organization of capital matter? Employers and active labor market policy at the national and firm levels,' *The American Political Science Review* 98(4): 593–611.

Martin, C.J. and Swank, D. (2012) *The Political Construction of Business Interests: Coordination, Growth, and Equality.* Cambridge University Press.

Martin, J.P. (2015) 'Activation and active labour market policies in OECD countries: Stylised facts and evidence on their effectiveness,' *IZA Journal of Labor Policy* 4(4).

McBride, S., McNutt, K. and Williams, R.A. (2008) 'Policy learning? The OECD and its jobs strategy,' in R. Mahon and M. McBride (eds.) *The OECD and Transnational Governance.* Chicago, IL: University of Chicago Press, pp. 152–169.

Murray, C. (2006) *In Our Hands: A Plan to Replace the Welfare State.* Washington, DC: American Enterprise Institute.

NAO (2016) *Benefit Sanctions: HC 628 Session 1016–17 30 November 2016.* London: National Audit Office.

O'Sullivan, S., McGann, M. and Considine, M. (2021) *Buying and Selling the Poor: Inside Australia's Privatised Welfare-to-Work Market.* Sydney: Sydney University Press.

Orton, M. (2011) 'Flourishing lives: the capabilities approach as a framework for new thinking about employment, work and welfare in the 21st century,' *Work, Employment and Society* 25(2): 352–360. https://doi.org/10.1177/0950017011403848

Orton, M., Green, A., Atfield, G. and Barnes, S.A. (2019) 'Employer participation in active labour policy: From reactive gatekeepers to proactive strategic partners,' *Journal of Social Policy* 48(3): 511–528.

Paul, R. (2016) *Investigating the Relationship between Tax Credits and Wages Offered by Employers.* London: Civitas.

Peck, J. and Theodore, N. (2000) ''Work first': Workfare and the regulation of contingent labour markets,' *Cambridge Journal of Economics* 24: 119–138.

Robertshaw, DK. (2024) 'Lost in categorisation? Employment subsidies – bringing the beneficiaries back in,' *Journal of Social Policy* 53(1): 86–106. doi:10.1017/S0047279422000216

Schneider, A. and Ingram, H. (1990) 'Behavioural assumptions of policy tools,' *The Journal of Politics* 52(2): 510–529.

Scholz, F. and Ingold, J. (2020) 'Activating the 'ideal jobseeker': Experiences of individuals with mental health conditions on the UK Work Programme,' *Human Relations* 74(10): 1604–1627.

Shildrick, T., MacDonald, R., Webster, C. and Garthwaite, K. (2012) *Poverty and Insecurity: Life in Low-Pay, No-Pay Britain*. Bristol: Policy Press.

Swank, D. and Martin, C.J. (2001) 'Employers and the welfare state: The political economic organization of firms and social policy in contemporary capitalist democracies,' *Comparative Political Studies* 34(8): 889–923.

Taylor-Gooby, P. (ed.) (2004) *New Risks, New Welfare: The Transformation of the European Welfare State*. Oxford: Oxford University Press.

Titmuss, R.M. (1974) 'What is social policy?' in B. Abel-Smith and K. Titmuss (ed.) *Social Policy: An Introduction*. London: Allen & Unwin, pp. 33–38.

Valizade, D., Ingold, J. and Stuart, M. (2022) 'Employer participation in active labour market policies in the United Kingdom and Denmark: The effect of employer associations as social networks and the mediating role of collective voice,' *Work, Employment and Society*. https://doi.org/10.1177/09500170211063094

van Berkel, R., Ingold, J., McGurk, P., Bredgaard, T. and Boselie, P. (2017) 'An introduction to employer engagement in the field of HRM. Blending social policy and HRM research in promoting vulnerable groups' labour market participation,' *Human Resource Management* 27(4): 503–513.

van Parijs, P. (2000) 'A basic income for all,' *Boston Review*, 1 October 2000.

Warhurst, C., Knox, A. and Wright, S. (2024) Developing a standard measure of job quality. *Working Paper*. Coventry: University of Warwick.

Recommendations for Further Reading

Barnes, A. (with S. Jones) (2020) *The 4-Day Week: How the Flexible Work Revolution Can Increase Productivity, Profitability and Well-Being, and Create a Sustainable Future*. Boston, MA: Little Brown.

Cottam, H. (2019) *Radical Help: How We Can Remake the Relationships between Us & Revolutionise the Welfare State*. London: Little Brown.

Ingold, J. and McGurk, P. (eds.) (2023) *Employer Engagement: Making Active Labour Market Policies Work*. Bristol: Bristol University Press.

Torry, M. (2013) *Money for Everyone: Why We Need a Citizen's Income*. Bristol: Policy Press.

28

POLITICS AND THE FUTURE OF WORK

Routine Work, Automation Risk and Redistributive Preferences in the Age of Populism

Frederick Harry Pitts and M. Winter

Introduction: The Politics of Work between Economics and Culture

The volatile electoral and referendum outcomes of the past decade in the UK and the US have garnered considerable scholarly attention from political scientists and others interested in the future of work. Research has established a correlation between support for the populist political projects of Trumpism in the US and Brexit in the UK with a perceived risk of occupational automation, with those whose employment longevity or stability felt most threatened by automation more likely to vote in favour of these movements (Institute for the Future of Work 2019). Vital to this intersection of the future of work and political behaviour are methodological distinctions between job and task automation, between actual and perceived risk of automation, and between anticipated and experienced hardship. These, in turn, are found within the literature to shape preferences as regards redistributive policy solutions, and therefore the political strategies taken by actors in response to these preferences. Mapping this terrain, this chapter charts how these complex relationships between work, tasks, risk, perceptions of risk and political behaviour have been understood within political science over the period since a longstanding process of 'sociopolitical fracturing' (MacLeavy and Manley 2019) culminated in the populist upheavals of 2016.

In the context of recent populist upheavals, there has been an uptick of interest among comparative political economists and political sociologists in labour market dualisation and its consequences for political behaviour. The Institute for the Future of Work, for instance (2019), has used 'insider/outsider' theory to investigate the relationship between electoral outcomes and automation risk. Insider/outsider approaches understand inclusion to centre on the labour market, with those excluded subject to unemployment or precariousness. The Institute for the Future of Work's research suggested that automation generates a 'spectrum' of insiders and outsiders across this basic distinction. Similarly, Schwander differentiates between 'labour market status' approaches, which pit permanent fulltime employees against the unemployed and precarious but are seen as lacking complexity and explanatory power; and 'prospective risk exposure' approaches, which categorise collectives of workers along a spectrum of insider to outsider based on their exposure to the 'risk of vulnerable employment' (Schwander 2019, p. 17). Whichever frame is deployed, Schwander suggests that research tends to evidence the impact of employment stability and instability on voter preferences for, among insiders, job security, taxes, and higher wages and, among

 DOI: 10.4324/9781003327561-38

outsiders, benefits, job creation and income redistribution. However, this 'distributive conflict' has seldom been explored in the context of 'socio-cultural' dynamics, and it is less clear how these preferences, arising from objective risk, 'translate into political action' (Schwander 2019, pp. 15–18). It is this, as it relates to the future of work, that we explore in this chapter.

We show that the specific temporality of automation as an issue when compared to, say, the 'China shock' that resulted from globalisation in countries like the US, makes it difficult to estimate in the same way the immediate impacts on political sentiments of previous shifts; that is, 'if jobs are gradually eliminated over time and a significant proportion of affected workers manages to "survive" in an occupational environment of structural decline, the usual measures of economic hardship might not suffice to capture grievances among the disadvantaged' (Kurer and Palier 2019, p. 2). Existing studies show that routine workers do not experience the process of technological unemployment through direct, immediate exits and lay-offs, so much as a gradual decline in new entrants to replace natural attrition in the workforce (Im and Komp-Leukkunen 2021). Rather than a direct abolition or substitution of specific jobs, then 'technological change reshapes the employment structure and hence the relative importance and value attached to different kinds of work' (Kurer 2020, p. 1804).

Pivotal to the way the consequences of the threat of automation play out politically is not the experience of hardship but the fear of it. Those who remain in place in the slow and gradual process of turnover without replacement may experience stagnation in their living and working conditions but tend to maintain the status of labour market insiders, with higher-than-average pay packets and permanent contracts. It is this status that makes the 'political repercussions' of these shifts so dynamic, insofar as these workers represent a reasonably enfranchised group prepared to express their anxieties about losing their status at the ballot box (Kurer and Palier 2019, p. 3), rather than reacting to the experience of hardship itself. Thus, a sense of declining social status and societal recognition is a more profound trend than direct hardship through unemployment. This is because automation changes demand for nonroutine work relative to routine, and thus reorders the status, value and dignity accorded each, independent of any sharp material shifts.

Owing to these phenomena, the role of technology in occupational change and broader economic modernisation has been associated with the emergence of a generation of 'left behind' workers and voters that, Kurer (2020) observes, have been said to support greater social security (Thewissen and Rueda 2019), lash out at incumbent parties of all kinds (Frey et al 2018) or adopt a specifically right-wing anti-establishment populism (Im et al 2019). Other examples have disputed the salience of material interests and economic motives in driving political behaviour, stressing instead the cultural roots of contemporary populist upheavals (Inglehart and Norris 2016; Antonucci et al 2017; Gidron and Hall 2017). Along these lines, we chart how voter policy preferences in response to automation are not motivated by a narrowly economistic cost/benefit analysis, but also status concerns (Im and Komp-Leukunnen 2021). Populist right parties successfully win over voters exposed to automation risk by appealing to 'status anxiety'. In contrast, compensatory policies, such as benefits, have seemingly little effect on persuading voters (Gingrich 2019, p. 1).

The literature does evidence an interesting relationship between the threat of status decline and its realisation in direct economic hardship: while the former tends to drive the political dynamics discussed above, the latter potentially opens a narrow path to a politics more amenable to conventional centre-left positioning. Arguably, this has been witnessed in the political consequences of the cost-of-living crisis in some countries (Pakes and Pitts 2023). Ultimately compensatory policies alone will be insufficient, however, and policies to shore up status and dignity will also be required by any political strategy addressed to the consequences of the unfolding future of work (Im and Komp-Leukunnen 2021). This has specific import for forthcoming electoral events like the 2024 US presidential election, whereby, at the time of writing, there is no obvious and clear-cut Democrat advantage derived from the jobs and industries generated by investment in the rustbelt communities central to the Trump coalition. Indeed, it seems that some part of the voter constituency addressed by such policies still feel the siren call of a politics that has a more emotional character untouched by the material guarantees of so-called Bidenomics. This fundamental political question of the balance of cultural and material dynamics will continue as a feature of politics whichever path the future of work unfolds along.

Routine Workers and Automation Risk

Routine work cuts across conventionally blue- and white-collar occupations and represents some 25%–30% of employment in advanced capitalist democracies (Kurer 2020, p. 1799). It has generally been regarded as affording workers 'a decent standard of living and prospects of upward mobility' (Kurer 2020, p. 1799). However, automation is perceived as threatening the position of this work and those who do it, and there is evidence we are seeing increased routinisation synonymous with greater augmentation of work by technology without any improvements in control or discretion; indeed, it seems that it is granting greater control and discretion not to workers but to their bosses.

For the likes of Autor et al (2003) and Cortes (2016), routineness defines a job's susceptibility to automation. Rather than a synonym for simplicity, routineness describes compliance with a set of tasks that, whilst initially often the result of considerable skill and training, can thereafter be performed by following a series of 'rules and procedures'. This 'codifiability', suggest Acemoglu and Autor (2011), is the aspect that renders routine work susceptible to automation, whether it occurs in factories, in offices or elsewhere. The Routine Task Intensity Index has been used in various studies as a proxy for automation risk on the basis that the codified character of routine jobs renders them more susceptible to automation (Im and Komp-Leukkunen 2021). The trend, here, has been increasingly to decouple routine work from decent rates of pay.

However, whilst much of the popular discourse around automation has focused on the substitution of a worker with a robot and other autonomous technologies, the identification of routineness with the task composition of a job enables a more granular viewpoint that captures the complexity of worker journeys through a labour market characterised by declining job opportunities (Kurer 2020). Use of such approaches shows that, whilst nonroutine workers are set to be affected by the rollout of future technologies that threaten lower-skilled work, routine workers are presently the most susceptible to automation and mechanisation of production in recent decades has disproportionately impacted routine workers without higher education, owing to the advantage of robots, for instance, in performing well-defined tasks (Acemoglu and Restrepo 2020).

Recent technological change has had the greatest consequences for routine jobs in the middle of the income distribution (Gallego and Kurer 2022). In the US terminology, these are both 'blue-collar' industrial jobs and 'white-collar' desk-based jobs. However, we do not see the kind of 'end of work' scenario predicted in some of the hyperbolic discussion of automation in certain quarters of the academic and policy debate. One of the shortcomings of existing studies that Kurer and Gallego highlight is that technology is not an isolatable 'exogeneous' phenomenon that imposes itself upon national political and economic systems, but rather one that itself springs from and is shaped by 'economic considerations and political struggles' themselves (Gallego and Kurer 2022, p. 3).

This requires the more sophisticated theoretical models developed by the likes of Acemoglu and Restrepo (2018) and Caselli and Manning (2019), which, rather than treating new technology as exogenous to economy and society, refine the task-based approach that informs much of the best scholarship on automation to look at how the cost of labour and other factors condition the trajectory of automation in the workplace. These factors serve to place economics on a much more 'balanced growth trajectory' than that implied in some of the overblown prognostications about automation, because 'there are powerful self-correcting forces'. For instance, 'when automation increases too much, the cost of labour decreases, reducing incentives to continue automating whilst increasing incentives to create new tasks' that will be performed by humans. Hence predictions of technological unemployment have never come to pass in the past and are unlikely to do so today (Gallego and Kurer 2022, p. 4).

This kind of perspective enables us to see that, rather than laying waste to a great deal of human labour with the utopian or dystopian outcomes foreseen by some radical interpretations, automation has more likely caused a forced descent of workers from middle-income to low-income jobs, partly owing to a redesignation of formerly middle-income jobs to low-income jobs based on proximity to automation risk. Autor et al (2003), as well as Goos and Manning (2007), argue that the displacement of workers in routine and skilled occupations has polarised the labour market. As routine jobs have been impacted by automation, workers have also moved into lower-income service jobs less amenable to automation. The displacement of routine workers thus far has not generated any corresponding increase of employment opportunities among other groups or sectors, having the effect of hollowing out the middle of the income distribution, creating greater inequality in the process. But whenever new jobs are created by technology, those displaced are not usually in a position to take them up, instead dropping out of the labour market altogether or taking low-paid service sector employment shorn of collective bargaining and the other benefits and rights associated with secure manufacturing jobs (Wu 2022).

The specificity of this process relates to the way that susceptibility to automation does not play out in the short term, with the onset of technological change often very slow and gradual. Where automation is synonymous with a decline in job opportunities, it is because of those who exit lines of work not being replaced by new entrants. However, as Gallego and Kurer (2022) point out, the fact that many of the most extreme renditions of the future of work remain so far unfulfilled does not mean that technology wields no effect in the workplace and economy at large, materially underpinning wider political upheavals (see also Caprettini and Voth 2020). Independent of material impacts, the challenge posed to the apparent stability experienced by some voters manifests in a state of anxiety where the relative status of routine workers declines as 'other parts of society are catching up or pulling away' (Kurer 2020, p. 1800).

Due to the temporality of these dynamics, Im and Komp-Leukunnen (2021) find evidence that routine workers may not be fully aware of the actual extent to which their job is threatened by automation, not least because in the course of their individual careers they remain unlikely to face direct unemployment owing to it. Nevertheless, Gallego and Kurer (2022) summarise existing work suggesting that routine workers react to the negative impacts of technological change on their job prospects and social status by either rejecting the political status quo or supporting populist political parties. They also survey claims that those whose prospects and status benefit from digitalisation tend to support the political centre or status quo. This means that 'backlash' is not the only political consequence of technological change, but a much broader realignment.

A particular group pivotal to these realignments have been working-class men in traditional skilled occupations. As evidenced in a range of studies (Frey et al 2018; Acemoglu and Restrepo 2017; Kurer and Palier 2019; Gingrich 2019; Kurer 2020) the workers most affected by these shifts tend to be men without higher education who have nonetheless enjoyed a fair degree of security and stability in recent times. The male routine workers who have been found to be most impacted by the mechanisation of previous decades tend to play an active part in the political arena by means of regularly voting in elections. The evidence suggests that these workers are using this position to voice dissatisfaction about declining status and future prospects at the ballot box, with impacts that have cascaded through the political and economic sphere in recent years as these voters have been pivotal to electoral swings and parties have sought to tailor their rhetoric and policy offers in order to win them over.

Populist Upheavals and the Politics of Status

Azmanova (2011) suggests that the key political division in contemporary society is 'opportunity versus risk', specifically regarding globalisation and its impact on both economic and cultural perceptions. Where liberal and green parties have emphasised opportunity and possibility, populist and radical left parties have stressed risks and insecurities. This 'political mobilisation of the losers versus the winners restructures political competition' away from traditional left-right cleavages towards a 'risk-versus-opportunity axis' (Steenvoorden and Harteveld 2018, p. 32). Im et al (2019) find that the attraction of the radical right to routine workers rests in the promise to protect voters from risks – not only in terms of insulating working-class communities from globalisation, but also increasingly from technology too. Whilst very few respondents to large public surveys identify automation or technology as a key concern or issue and seem largely relaxed about the prospect of replacement by robots or machines, Wu (2022) uses survey data from the US to relate risk of automation to hostility to immigration and free trade, finding a strong correlation. This chimes with the findings of Frey et al (2018) and Im et al (2019), both affirming that voters at risk of automation were more likely to back the radical or populist right in recent elections.

Investigating whether the perception of having lost out to technology correlates with support for 'radical political change', Frey et al (2018, p. 418) discount offshoring and exposure to globalised free trade as explanations for Donald Trump's success among working-class voters, and find instead that his vote was higher in 'local labour markets more exposed to the adoption of robots', to the extent that, had exposure to robots not increased in a series of key electoral battlegrounds in the years preceding the 2016 election, Trump would not have won. They suggest that when polled voters display widespread fear of the computerisation and robotisation of work, and extensive support for restrictions upon the industrial application of machines (2018, p. 428). Acemoglu and Restrepo (2017) find that the introduction of robotics in the US has reduced wages and employment specifically among blue-collar workers without higher education – the group that decisively swung behind Trump in 2016. Trump stood to benefit from the anxieties of this group, Frey et al (2018) propose, because his promise to repatriate and restimulate manufacturing jobs in the US also implied resistance to automation.

The literature shows that these processes of realignment rest upon a politics of *status*. Drawing from social psychology, Kurer associates threat and anxiety about status with 'the development of socially conservative or even authoritarian character traits', and threats to the 'perceived value' of some forms of work and those that perform them with increased hostility to groups 'seen as competitors in the social hierarchy', as a means of achieving a relative stabilisation of their own status and value (Kurer 2020, p. 1805). Because social status is relative, these workers can shore up their status by 'maintaining their social distance' (Im and Komp-Leukkunen 2021, p. 458) from other groups and individuals perceived as occupying a lower status in the social order (see also Gidron and Hall 2019). Surviving in their existing jobs but nonetheless experiencing anxiety about the future risk of status decline owing to automation eroding the value of routine work in particular, routine workers are found to respond by drawing boundaries between them and groups like the unemployed, deemed less valuable and deserving. Rather than *objective* risk of automation, a far more profound driver here is the *subjective* risk of automation (Gallego et al 2021). In particular, the risk of status decline posed by automation leads routine workers to maintain a 'social distance' (Im and Komp-Leukkunen 2021, p. 458) between themselves and traditional outsider groups such as the unemployed or immigrants.

Whilst the evidence is clear that the 'losers' of technological change tend to vote for anti-establishment parties primarily of the right, then, the 'winners' – those who benefit from greater pay and opportunities in industries enjoying increased investment in new technology, for instance – show a propensity to support the political status quo (Gallego et al 2022). There is also evidence that in areas where technological change has meant the decline of industries like manufacturing and their replacement with more 'knowledge-intensive' professions and occupations, the tendency towards 'more progressive political values' (Gallego and Kurer 2022, p. 11) among such workers leads to greater voter support for the left (Schöll and Kurer 2021). As demonstrated among some centre-left parties in recent years, this creates obvious difficulties for parties seeking to articulate between the preferences of different groups of voters in order to compose successful electoral coalitions.

Anticipated Hardship and Absolute Hardship

Methodologically, using economic indicators of disadvantage like low income, unemployment or precariousness does not capture the specific position occupied by those who are reasonably well off yet threatened by the potential risk of automation. The literature on 'dualization' (Rueda 2005) cannot adequately capture the specificities of the situation because it is focused on existing labour market insiders and outsiders rather than the anxieties attached to movement between the two positions. Instead, we ought to consider how 'negative change in social identity or a sense of a loss of control', which is sometimes expressed in 'societal pessimism and nostalgia' or manifested in 'authoritarian and socially conservative preferences', drives demand for right-wing populism (Kurer and Palier 2019, p. 4). This literature (Ballard-Rosa et al 2018; Steenvoorden and Harteveld 2018) thus sheds light on how perceived or anticipated shifts in relative social position affect not only those already hard-up but those with the potential to lose what they have.

In contrast to prevailing attempts to extract the determinants of political behaviour from 'snapshot indicators of absolute economic hardship', Kurer (2020, p. 1086) thus centres on *trajectories* in the labour market and the *relative* adjustments in economic wellbeing that they imply. Kurer bases his study on the thesis that workers who 'move between occupational groups will differ in behaviour from their class of origin as well as from their class of destination and instead form preferences that lie somewhere in between'. For instance, 'upgraders' who find 'non-routine cognitive occupations' more immune to automation risk are considered as being more likely to back parties advocating free markets and a small state. Down-graders, meanwhile, respond to a declining state of economic and material survival in sometimes countervailing ways according to whether hardship is anticipated or experienced.

The results carve a middle path through the competing economic and non-economic emphases of the literature on populism by moving away from direct material hardship to a broader array of economic processes – associated with 'relative social decline' – that, in turn, manifest in non-economic political responses epitomised in 'socially conservative resentment' (Kurer 2020, pp. 1800–1801). This enables Kurer to differentiate between those who 'survive' in an 'increasingly vulnerable occupational environment' that 'activates concerns about status maintenance' and increases the appeal of nostalgic, socially conservative politics; and those who experience job loss and material hardship itself and thus reach for a politics geared towards economic compensation or security (Kurer 2020, p. 1800).

Along similar lines, Im et al (2019) find that increased perceived risk of automation is associated with greater propensity to vote for radical right parties, largely at the expense of mainstream right-wing parties. Whilst the decrease of support for the mainstream right is a trend across all groups perceiving such an increased risk of automation, this is specifically the case among those living comfortably or coping on present income. The central social group in the swing to the radical right, on this reading, are those who are coping on their current income but for whom the subjective risk of automation is increasing (2019, p. 4). In this way, right-wing populists have proved effective competitors for a 'contested stronghold' (Oesch and Rennwald 2018) previously the preserve of the left – routine workers currently 'surviving' (Kurer 2020, pp. 1818–1819). Kurer's evidence suggests that it is precisely the 'surviving' aspect that is here decisive, where hardship is something anticipated rather than experienced. The materialisation of anticipated hardship through impoverishment or unemployment, meanwhile, does not appear as a driver of support for socially conservative or right-wing populist parties, but rather 'pro-welfare' parties (Kurer 2020, pp. 1819–1820).

This account of how different trajectories of voters through the labour market play out in particular political responses resonates with a wider literature (Antonucci et al 2017; Gidron and Hall 2017) that pours cold water on claims that the populist upheavals of recent years bear a direct or inevitable relation to underpinning material and economic disadvantage or hardship. For instance, the average Leave voter was not the 'angry, unskilled and perhaps even unemployed outsider' some portrayed, but rather sourced from 'intermediate classes' concerned about declining economic position (Kurer and Palier 2019, p. 4). As Kurer argues (2020), it is often 'economic threat', rather than direct 'economic hardship', that influences the 'higher-than-average probability', according to Oesch and Rennwald (2018), that such workers back right-wing populists at the ballot box.

Compensatory Policies and the Politics of Distribution

The literature on the topics addressed in this chapter, Gingrich notes (2019), is currently divided between analyses (Thewissen and Rueda 2019) that demonstrate the insecurity and anxiety associated with automation risk encourages support for redistribution and thus the left, and analyses that stress the salience of 'non-material effects' in how automation risk translates into a political sentiment that favours the right. Thewissen and Rueda (2019) suggest that routine workers express more redistributive policy preferences when presented with the risk of automation, and redistributive policies like universal basic income or an 'automation tax' have been proposed as a means to 'decouple growth in automation from growth in inequality' (Jeffrey 2021, p. 417). However, it is fair to say that much of the available literature argues that government provision of compensatory redistribution measures does little to shift the dial leftwards (Gallego and Kurer 2022).

As we have seen, this latter literature (e.g. Gidron and Hall 2017; Kurer 2020) emphasises 'status anxiety', especially among male voters, as a 'strong predictor of populist voting'. Populist right parties have more effectively responded to these 'status concerns', whereas left parties have abandoned 'explicit class-based appeals' for an increasingly 'middle-class base' (Gingrich 2019, p. 3). As Wu (2022) argues, the fact that voters seem to behave in line with non-economic influences rather than economic shows the limits of compensatory approaches to redressing the harms of the material consequences of globalisation and industrial change.

However, as opposed to those who survive in routine work at the perceived threat of technological substitution, those who face a different trajectory – that of being expelled from employment or dropping out – face immediate material hardship and thus seek out compensatory policies not from the right but from the left – 'fear turns into experience' (Kurer 2020, p. 1806). Hence Gingrich hypothesises that parties of the left are best placed offering a compensatory approach that appeals to those voters whose material wellbeing is threatened by automation, in the process shoring up the left's position vis-à-vis the populist right (Gingrich 2019, p. 3).

While the psychological factors wrapped up in status anxiety do not necessarily cascade into 'economic or welfare demands' (Kurer 2020, p. 1805), then, other evidence does suggest that material disadvantage produces demand for redistributive remedies as a kind of compensation (Rehm 2009). In this sense, Gingrich (2019) considers whether each of the prevailing perspectives might simultaneously grasp something of the dynamics driving contemporary voter behaviour, insofar as automation impacts both 'the material wellbeing and social status of exposed workers', with each aspect driving voters in a different direction – material wellbeing to the left and social status to the populist right. Those responding to the experience of actual economic hardship with demands for redistributive measures are most likely to find this in the policy programmes offered by the left. Those seeking means to shore up their position in the social hierarchy, meanwhile, will be more likely to source this from the policy prospectus presently offered by the populist right (Kurer 2020).

However, contrary to the left's traditional assumption that material compensation poses a convincing response to the pressures driving populism, the evidence and analysis presented in most of these studies demonstrates that there is little sign more compensatory approaches reduce the populist temptation. In fact, in some cases, compensation may increase the propensity of exposed groups of workers to back populists at the ballot box. Whilst redistributive programmes of compensation may have proved effective in some limited circumstances in preventing radicalisation over the period where globalisation was reshaping working life in Western countries, and the populist 'backlash' may well be associated with the consequences of fiscal austerity in one fashion, they are likely to prove much less effective against the effects of automation on 'both income and status' (Gingrich 2019, p. 6).

Gingrich thus proposes that policy focuses not on after-the-fact solutions to 'experienced insecurity' and instead on the 'economic pressures' driving those insecurities, including 'how labour markets structure opportunities and choices for voters'. Thus, 'compensating the "losers" of change may not be enough to prevent the far-reaching political consequences of automation, instead we need to consider policies that makes more people "winners" in the new economic environment' (Gingrich 2019, p. 7).

The Role of Politics in Shaping Policy Preferences

Setting aside the specific policy offers that political parties use to respond to voter preferences in the context of the unfolding future of work, there is also the question of the strategies they deploy to shape these preferences. Jeffrey (2021) explores the role of political rhetoric in shaping voters' redistributive preferences against the backdrop of automation risk. As we have touched upon already, in recent years the direct material increase in inequality has not translated into growing support for redistributive policy offers. Even where voters stand to benefit from redistribution, beliefs, trust, and conceptions of fairness have all been identified as underpinning opposition to redistribution.

There is evidence that political rhetoric shapes these underpinning drivers of opposition to redistribution. When economic and labour market shocks occur explanations for hardship often involve misplaced anger directed towards immigrants or welfare claimants, for instance.

To investigate whether preferences for redistributive policies increase with perceived vulnerability to automation, Jeffrey (2021) conducted a survey experiment with a representative sample of 2,500 adults in the UK. Respondents were either asked to consider how vulnerable their jobs are to automation, or to conduct the same exercise along with exposure to political rhetoric that characterised automation in terms of the perceived fairness or unfairness of its outcomes and the individuals or groups who stand to benefit.

In line with the findings of many existing surveys, Jeffrey's participants tended to see automation as a societal threat, impacting others but not necessarily themselves or their families. However, the greater their perceived personal or familial vulnerability to automation, the greater the decline in their preference for redistributive cash transfers and minimum wage increases. Existing literature suggests that this may be because voters envisage themselves paying for rather than benefitting from such measures; or else a lack of trust in the state's capacity to govern. This relationship between vulnerability and aversion to compensatory and ameliorative cash transfers is suspended, Jeffrey finds, where the description of an automation shock is accompanied by political rhetoric identifying individuals or groups being to blame for, or benefitting from, technological unemployment. Moreover, whilst participants were found to respond to perceived vulnerability by turning against welfare programmes intended to protect the unemployed from direct economic hardship, they tended to be more favourably disposed towards policies that sought to protect workers from job losses in the first place, such as short-hours schemes that reduce working time for some workers to redistribute hours across the whole workforce in at-risk industries. Support for government protection for declining industries appeared to appeal to voters with both 'meritocratic' and 'egalitarian' perspectives, Jeffrey suggests, because it is generally seen to reward deserving groups and individuals.

This follows the insights of the literature on 'persuasive communication' in the spheres of politics and policy (Rodrik 2014). The implications are that the political consequences of automation are not confined to the terrain of employment, and that the kind of persuasive communication recently associated with populism may enable political actors to influence how these consequences play out. Jeffrey's (2021) study identifies 'more-educated' workers as a key battleground constituency in this respect, insofar as automation is forecast to impact on cognitive work much more comprehensively, they have a great propensity to express declining preference for redistributive measures in event of a potential automation shock, but also show a greater susceptibility to persuasive political rhetoric. This suggests, Jeffrey hypothesises, that rhetoric could strongly influence support for specific policy responses as these workers are influenced by future automation shocks.

Jeffrey thus adds to the growing literature on the relationship between automation, populism, and the radical right a better understanding of the relationship between automation and a broader array of redistributive political offers. As we have already seen, existing studies of the latter have found a correlation between automation risk and redistributive preferences (Thewissen and Rueda 2019), but others have found no substantial relationship (Dermont and Weisstanner 2020; Gallego et al 2021). The specific way in which Jeffrey adds to this literature is showing that automation shocks impact preferences not solely because of material labour market outcomes but rather through a combination of vulnerability and 'exposure to political rhetoric' (Jeffrey 2021, p. 419). This shows the capacity of politics to shape, as well as react to, the preferences of voters whether economic or cultural, material, or emotional.

Conclusion: Political Consequences of the Future of Work

The penultimate section has demonstrated that automation risk does not have an economically determined effect on voters, but rather its consequences are mediated by political rhetoric and policy offers. Political rhetoric can increase support for redistributive responses to automation shocks because it plays to a sense of fairness rather than material self-interest alone – something Jeffrey (2021) sees as potentially growing in significance as automation impacts upon more formally educated professional strata in the future, who are particularly susceptible to such rhetorical appeals.

This requires different approaches from politicians in addressing these issues. As Gallego and Kurer (2022) argue, the fact that subjective or objective automation risk shows no direct correlation with demand for specific policy responses could be because election campaigns seldom if ever address automation and digitisation directly. If they do, they do so positively, and thus voters are provided with few narratives through which to grasp the causes or consequences of technological change, seeking more tangible or concrete explanations for insecurity and loss of status for which there are clear policy responses – immigrants and border controls, for instance, or free trade and tariffs. Populist parties have prospered by offering explanations that connect economic, cultural, and political phenomena in this way, posing apparent solutions.

There are undoubtedly lessons to learn from this experience, and to apply in pursuit of other political values and objectives. However, there are difficulties in adapting responses to very different material and economic issues for the issue of automation. The real difference between automation and these other phenomena is the slow, gradual, and almost imperceptible way in which its effects are felt in everyday working life, which render it difficult to directly politicise when compared to phenomena whose effects may be more rapid and visible.

Rhetoric aside, concrete policy offers will nonetheless be important in creating the basis for these appeals. This will not be straightforward. If the analyses surveyed above are to be believed, the continued development of new technologies and their increased application in the workplace will reinforce the structural dynamics they describe above and thus render right-wing populism a constant part of the electoral landscape in post-industrial democracies. This will be exacerbated by the fact that it is difficult to imagine an 'adequate policy response' to voter concerns driven not by direct economic hardship but the expectation of it. In this way, '"more welfare" in the traditional sense might not help alleviate grievances' (Kurer 2020, p. 1826).

As Gingrich (2019) suggests, policy should focus on making more people 'winners' in the changed economic landscape, not merely offering after-the-fact compensatory solutions. Rather than financial support, the voters most impacted by automation risk desire safeguards on their social status – something the 'responsible centre-right and centre-left' face a 'strategic disadvantage' in addressing. Their 'mundane, precise and politically feasible policy reactions' struggle to offer a convincing alternative to the 'less tangible identity politics' offered by the populist right (Kurer 2020, p. 1826).

All in all, as Gallego and Kurer (2022, p. 15) warn, this terrain presents a uniquely difficult proposition for political organisation and policymaking, with a gap between everyday experience and large-scale structural change, as well as a lack of clarity as to the precise role of technology within this next to other factors. For political parties, trade unions and other relevant actors there are challenges in finding the right form of words through which to convince and campaign around the complex interrelationships that drive workplace change in an age of automation, and the policies required to regulate and direct them. Politicians may thus be left with little more than the identification of proxy groups and processes through which to target discontent with the fallout from the unfolding future of work. The danger, of course, is that 'wrong diagnoses…lead to misguided policy responses' (Kurer 2022, p. 15), with all of the political consequences that this implies.

Finally, there is evidence that the routinisation of work is increasing apace (see Gilbert's chapter in this volume), and this is likely to mean that the mediation of this dynamic in the swings of political sentiment outlined above will in some sense continue to shape electoral patterns of the foreseeable future. This should focus the minds of policymakers and parties seeking political power not only on vying for electoral advantage in the cultural and emotional landscape associated with displacement and status decline, but also how to reconfigure that landscape through policy interventions in job design and job quality. Politics is not simply downstream from technological shifts, but has the capacity to shape the latter. Through an active politics of work, the political can condition the unfolding future of work, rather than be conditioned by it.

Acknowledgements

This work was made possible by Knowledge Exchange Funding from Research England and the Office for Students, in partnership with the Institute for the Future of Work.

References

Acemoglu, D., & Autor, D. (2011). Skills, tasks and technologies: Implications for employment and earnings. In D. Card, & O. Ashenfelter (eds.). *Handbook of Labor Economics* (Vol. 4, pp. 1043–1171). Amsterdam: Elsevier.

Acemoglu, D., & Restrepo, P. (2017). *Robots, and Jobs: Evidence from US Labor Markets*, National Bureau of Economic Research, Working Paper 23285. https://www.nber.org/papers/w23285

Acemoglu, D., & Restrepo, P. (2018). The race between man and machine: Implications of technology for growth, factor shares, and employment. *American Economic Review*, 108(6), 1488–1542.

Acemoglu, D., & Restrepo, P. (2020). Robots and jobs: Evidence from US labor markets. *Journal of Political Economy*, 128, 2188–2244.

Antonucci, L., Horvath, L., Kutiyski, Y., et al. (2017). The malaise of the squeezed middle: Challenging the narrative of the 'left behind' Brexiter. *Competition & Change*, 21(3), 211–229.

Autor, D. H., Levy, F., & Murnane, R. J. (2003). The skill content of recent technological change: An empirical exploration. *The Quarterly Journal of Economics*, 118(4), 1279–1333.

Azmanova, A. (2011). After the left–right (dis)continuum: Globalization and the remaking of Europe's ideological geography. *International Political Sociology*, 5(4), 384–407.

Ballard-Rosa, C., Jensen, A., & Scheve, K. (2018). Economic decline, social identity, and authoritarian values in the United States. *International Studies Quarterly*. DOI: 10.1093/isq/sqab027.

Caprettini, B., & Voth, H.-J. (2020). Rage against the Machines: Labor-saving technology and unrest in industrializing England. *American Economic Review: Insights*, 2(3), 305–320.

Caselli, F., & Manning, A. (2019). Robot arithmetic: New technology and wages. *American Economic Review: Insights*, 1(1), 1–12.

Cortes, G. M. (2016). Where have the middle-wage workers gone? A study of polarization using panel data. *Journal of Labor Economics*, 34(1), 63–105.

Dermont, C., & Weisstanner, D. (2020). Automation and the future of the welfare state: Basic income as a response to technological change? *Political Research Exchange*, 2(1), 1757387.

Di Tella, R., & Rodrik, D. (2020). Labour market shocks and the demand for trade protection: Evidence from online surveys. *Economic Journal*, 130, 1008–1030.

Frey, C. B., & Osborne, M. A. (2017). The future of employment: How susceptible are jobs to computerisation? *Technological forecasting and social change*, 114, 254–280.

Frey, C.B., Berger, T, & Chen, C. (2018). Political machinery: did robots swing the 2016 US presidential election? *Oxford Review of Economic Policy*, 34(3), 418–442. https://doi.org/10.1093/oxrep/gry007

Gallego, A., & Kurer, T. (2022). Automation, digitalization, and artificial intelligence in the workplace: Implications for political behavior, *Annual Review of Political Science*, 25, 463–484.

Gallego, A., Kuo, A., Manzano, D., & Fernández-Albertos, J. (2022). Technological risk and policy preferences. *Comparative Political Studies*, 55(1), 60–92.

Gallego, A., Kurer, T., & Schöll, N. (2021). Neither left behind nor superstar: Ordinary winners of digitalization at the ballot box. *The Journal of Politics*, 84(1), 418–436.

Gidron, N., & Hall, P. A. (2017). The politics of social status: Economic and cultural roots of the populist right. *The British Journal of Sociology*, 68(S1), 57–84.

Gidron, N., & Hall, P. A. (2019). Populism as a problem of social integration. *Comparative Political Studies*, 53(7), 1027–1059.

Gingrich, J. (2019). Did state responses to automation matter for voters? *Research & Politics*, 6(1), 2053168019832745.

Goos, M., & Manning, A. (2007). Lousy and lovely jobs: The rising polarization of work in Britain. *Review of Economics and Statistics*, 89(1), 118–133.

Im, Z. J., & Komp-Leukkunen, K. (2021). Automation and public support for workfare. *Journal of European Social Policy*, 31(4), 457–472.

Im, Z. J., Mayer, N., Palier, B., & Rovny, J. (2019). The "losers of automation": A reservoir of votes for the radical right? *Research & Politics*, 6(1), 2053168018822395.

Inglehart, R. F., & Norris, P. (2016). Trump, Brexit, and the rise of populism: Economic have-nots and cultural backlash (HKS Working Paper No. RWP16-026).

Institute for the Future of Work (2019). Automation, Politics and the Future of Work: A Discussion Paper. https://www.ifow.org/publications/automation-politics-and-the-future-of-work

Jeffrey, K. (2021). Automation and the future of work: How rhetoric shapes the response in policy preferences. *Journal of Economic Behavior & Organization*, 192, 417–433.

Kaihovaara, A., & Im, Z. J. (2020). Jobs at risk? Task routineness, offshorability, and attitudes toward immigration. *European Political Science Review*, 12(3), 327–345.

Kurer, T. (2020). The declining middle: Occupational change, social status, and the populist right. *Comparative Political Studies*, 53(10–11), 1798–1835.

Kurer, T., & Palier, B. (2019). Shrinking and shouting: The political revolt of the declining middle in times of employment polarization. *Research & Politics*, 6(1), 2053168019831164.

MacLeavy, J., & Manley, D. (2019). Socio-political fracturing: Inequality, stalled social mobility and electoral outcomes. *Area*, 51(4), 681–688.

Oesch, D., & Rennwald, L. (2018). Electoral competition in Europe's new tripolar political space: Class voting for the left, centre-right and radical right. *European Journal of Political Research*, 57(4), 783–807.

Pakes, A., & Pitts, F. H. (2023). *A Progressive Politics of Work for the Age of Unpeace: What Labour Can Learn from the European Centre-Left*. Brussels: Foundation for European Progressive Studies.

Rehm, P. (2009). Risks and redistribution: An individual-level analysis. *Comparative Political Studies*, 42, 855–881.

Rodrik, D. (2014). When ideas trump interests: Preferences, worldviews, and policy innovations. *Journal of Economic Perspectives*, 28(1), 189–208.

Rueda, D. (2005). Insider–outsider politics in industrialized democracies: The challenge to social democratic parties. *American Political Science Review*, 99(1), 61–74.

Schöll, N., & Kurer, T. (2021). How technological change affects regional electorates. *Working Paper*, Barcelona: Barcelona School of Economics.

Schwander, H. (2019). Labor market dualization and insider–outsider divides: Why this new conflict matters. *Political Studies Review*, 17(1), 14–29.

Steenvoorden, E., & Harteveld, E. (2018). The appeal of nostalgia: The influence of societal pessimism on support for populist radical right parties. *West European Politics*, 41(1), 28–52.

Thewissen, S., & Rueda, D. (2019). Automation and the welfare state: Technological change as a determinant of redistribution preferences. *Comparative Political Studies*, 52(2), 171–208.

Wu, N. (2022). Misattributed blame? Attitudes toward globalization in the age of automation. *Political Science Research and Methods*, 10(3), 470–487.

Recommendations for Further Reading

Frey, C. B., Berger, T., & Chen, C. (2018). Political machinery: Did robots swing the 2016 US presidential election? *Oxford Review of Economic Policy*, 34(3), 418–442.

Gallego, A., & Kurer, T. (2022). Automation, digitalization and artificial intelligence in the workplace: Implications for political behaviour. *Annual Review of Political Science*, 25, 463–484.

Gingrich, J. (2019). Did state responses to automation matter for voters? *Research & Politics*, 6(1), 2053168019832745.

Jeffrey, K. (2021). Automation and the future of work: How rhetoric shapes the response in policy preferences. *Journal of Economic Behavior & Organization*, 192, 417–433.

Kurer, T. (2020). The declining middle: Occupational change, social status, and the populist right. *Comparative Political Studies*, 53(10–11), 1798–1835.

PART 11

Environment and the Future of Work

29

GREEN JOBS, JUST TRANSITION, AND THE FUTURE OF WORK

Ed Atkins

Introduction

> Today is "Climate Day" at the White House and — which means that today is "Jobs Day" at the White House.
>
> (President Joe Biden, 27 January 2021)

The above comment by US President Joe Biden before signing executive orders for climate action highlights an increasingly significant narrative of mitigating climate breakdown: namely the overlap between these policies and aspirations for job creation. Biden would say in the same remarks that "When I think of climate change, I think of — and the answers to it — I think of jobs" (White House, 2021). Biden's government's Inflation Reduction Act of 2022 provides further evidence of this overlap: pledging US$370 billion in tax credits to the renewable energy industry to stimulate the move away from fossil fuels and create new, 'secure', green jobs.

The promise of green jobs has become a key narrative of renewable energy transitions, with politicians and activists across the globe arguing that decarbonisation should yield the emergence of new, better jobs. Globally, it has been estimated that a shift to a low-carbon 'green' economy can create up to 24 million jobs (United Nations [UN], 2019). Decarbonisation is going to have important impacts on local, national and global labour markets. If climate targets to reduce global temperature change by 2°C by 2050 are to be met, the number of direct energy jobs globally could increase to 26 million – with renewable energy jobs replacing declining fossil fuel employment numbers and expanding further (Pai et al., 2021). According to some estimates, there could be as many as 42 million renewable energy jobs by 2050 – clustered in solar (18.7 million), bioenergy (14.1 million), and wind power (6.2 million) (Ferroukhi et al., 2020).

This potential for job creation holds immense significance as a crucial way to support diverse groups and communities experiencing change. However, despite this promise, its realisation remains incomplete. In many cases, 'green' jobs suffer from precariousness and inadequate compensation, and there are limited avenues for individuals to transition from carbon-heavy work to these positions, perpetuating the exclusion of many. In this chapter, I explore how solutions to these issues can be found in approaches to job creation and protections that place the future of green work within the wider importance of worker-environmentalist coalitions.

DOI: 10.4324/9781003327561-40

What's a 'Green' Job?

The concept of 'green jobs' in the context of a decarbonised economy encompasses various occupations and skills. Bowen et al. (2018) have proposed a classification of three types of green work that may emerge in the future:

- 'green increased demand' – or where existing jobs will change and become greener with limited changes to the skills required;
- 'green enhanced skills – or where existing jobs change but require new skills or knowledge for such a transition to take place; and
- 'green new and emerging' – or new, unique jobs that emerge in new green sectors.

Contemporary policy pledges focus on the latter category, particularly jobs related to renewable energy projects and electric vehicle manufacturing. The jobs promised vary in terms of required skills, educational levels, and employment conditions. While some roles may prioritise manual trades and require a lower level of formal education, others, such as those in planning, regulation, and management, may demand higher technical skills and scientific knowledge.

The International Trade Union Confederation offers a definition of green jobs that emphasises environmental sustainability, decent work, and workers' rights:

> A green job reduces the environmental impacts of enterprises and economic sectors to sustainable levels, whilst providing decent work and living conditions to all those involved in production, and ensures workers' rights are respected. Green jobs are not only those traditional jobs people think of as green – like making solar panels, manufacturing wind turbines, water conservation and sustainable forestry. They also include retrofitting related jobs in the construction and public transport sectors, and making energy efficiency improvements in manufacturing plants, along with services supporting all industries.
>
> (ITUC, 2012: 3)

This broad definition is essential for understanding the future of work in a decarbonised economy, particularly beyond the sectors of construction, manufacturing, and energy production. It highlights the need to understand the broader sectoral shifts that will accompany successful decarbonisation efforts. The wider structural and behavioural shifts required by climate reaction will change patterns and practices of work for many: from hospital cleaners to office workers. In the UK, the Labour for a Green New Deal movement has argued that any net-zero transition requires greater investment in social care and the creation of a National Care Service. This fuses the urgency for climate action to the need to support those vulnerable to climate shocks, such as heat stress. It also places workers who may at first be seen as distant from climate agendas – in this case, care workers – at the centre of a green future of work.

Any approach to future 'green' jobs should encompass a wide range of occupations and prioritise the principles of decent work, ensuring adequate incomes, social protection, safe working conditions, employment rights, and effective social dialogue (United Nations Framework Convention on Climate Change [UNFCCC], 2016; International Labour Organization [ILO], 2021). A notion of 'skilled and satisfying' work, as advocated by Stroud et al. (2014), emphasises the importance of high-quality, highly skilled jobs that maintain or improve working conditions. By embracing the concept of decent work, the goal is to avoid the creation of poorly paid, precarious, and low-skilled jobs that deviate from previous employment patterns in the transition to a green economy (see Chapter 8 which identifies an overarching trend towards precarious work).

Yet, for all the promises made about 'good, green jobs', renewable jobs aren't fulfilling their promise of a 'new industrial revolution' that enhances livelihoods and prosperity. Instead, they frequently end up facing similar challenges, such as precarious employment and the lack of protections commonly associated with the platform economy (Scheiber, 2021) (see Chapter 8). Existing jobs in renewable energies may offer wages and conditions far below those associated with fossil fuel work – for example, in New Jersey, the median wage paid to a solar installer is $43,620 compared to the $80,530 median annual salary of those working within power plants (Vachon, 2019).

The Global Energy Talent Index (2023) has shown that many jobs in the renewables sector can provide well-paid employment for many – for example, a permanently employed Maintenance Engineer working in the European renewables sector could earn an average of £67,524 a year. However, there is a great variety of pay within these sectors that should be taken into account. There are many cases of the renewables industry being implicated in instances of low wages, highlighting concerns about fair compensation. Several cases exemplify this issue. In the UK, for instance, reports reveal that ships involved in offshore wind installations off the coast have been paying poverty-level wages. The *Glomar Wave*, operating from Great Yarmouth in 2021, was found to pay a meagre daily rate of £47.35, equivalent to £3.94 per hour based on the 12-hour work shifts performed by the crew. This falls well below the state-mandated National Minimum Wage of £8.91 per hour (Rail, Maritime and Transport Workers [RMT], 2021). Similarly, catering staff aboard the Edda Passat, servicing the Race Bank wind farm in Grimsby, were compensated at a rate of £6.75 per hour (Daly, 2019). Crews of such vessels are often paid a set day rate, which depreciated on longer working days to complete set tasks, with limited protections in place to secure set working hours or potential overtime pay. Many of these workers, often international migrants employed within the industry, are bound by fixed-term contracts that do not adequately account for overtime resulting in depressed hourly rates. International workers in this sector are not necessarily covered by the collective bargaining secured by UK-based unions, leading to limited opportunities of challenging such poor practices and conditions.

While carbon-heavy industries are commonly associated with precarious employment as fluctuating demand and market prices lead to unpredictable employment patterns and economic precarity, which makes it harder for workers to campaign for improvements in their social and economic well-being, it is important to recognise that green jobs can also fall into the same pattern. In the recycling industry in parts of the United States, contracts are often temporary and subject to regular renewal (see Econie and Doughtery, 2019). Similarly, offshore wind jobs may be limited to the short-term future only, making it challenging for workers to maintain job security and stable income (Scottish Trade Unions Congress [STUC] and Transition Economics, 2021). This observation not only reflects the broader trend of increased casualisation and job precarity but also underscores the short-term nature of some green work. With the primary focus on reducing emissions, the construction of a wind farm, for instance, requires a surge of labour to manufacture, transport, and assemble the turbine components. The solar industry operates similarly, with workers assigned specific tasks for installing each respective panel across the site. Once these tasks are completed, labour demands decrease and become limited to maintenance roles only. Jobs are not necessarily lost; rather, contracts expire and opportunities diminish.

Who holds these jobs is also important. The dominance of white men in green jobs is evident from a study conducted in 2017, which revealed a higher likelihood of white men aged 35–64 with a high school education occupying these roles (McClure et al., 2017). In the United States, Black workers hold less than 10% of jobs in the sector (Muro et al., 2019), while Latinx workers represent approximately 17%, but both are often relegated to entry-level, low-income installation work (Jones, 2021). In the US solar industry, installation workers tend to receive lower wages compared to their counterparts in other areas of the industry (Interstate Renewable Energy Council [IREC], 2021). This disparity has been more pronounced in states in the Deep South characterised by racial inequities and tensions (Mock, 2013). Such underemployment compounds broader injustices, as Black and Latinx workers find themselves trapped in lower-paid and less secure employment (Reid and Rubin, 2003; Penner, 2008), and face a greater risk of redundancy during economic downturns (Weller, 2019). The lack of employment opportunities for racialised communities is yet another facet of environmental and energy injustices, already formed from the construction of fossil fuel energy projects in their communities and limited access to new renewable energy technologies.

In 2019, women accounted for 32% of the renewable energy workforce, in contrast to the oil and gas industry's 22% representation (International Renewable Energy Agency [IRENA], 2019). In the wind sector, women comprised 21% of the workforce, while in the US solar industry in 2017, women held 27% of the 250,000 roles across the sector (IRENA, 2019, 2020). Yet, of those women within the industry, many often occupy administrative positions rather than engineering or technical roles (Clancy and Feenstra, 2019). Administrative roles accounted for 45% of positions held by women in the sector in 2019, compared to 28% in STEM jobs (IRENA, 2019). Gender representation in management and leadership positions within the renewables sector is lacking (Allison et al., 2019). C3E International's research in 2019, based on data from 68 companies, revealed that women held only 18% of management positions.

The transition to renewable energy creates new employment opportunities but risks reinforcing traditional forms of labour market exclusion and division. IRENA has argued that the underrepresentation of women in the sector is rooted in structural factors, highlighting the influence of gender roles shaped by social and cultural norms as significant and ongoing barriers to increasing women's labour market participation (IRENA, 2020, 2021). Working conditions in the sector can also contribute to an unwelcoming environment for women, including issues such as appearance-based comments, sexualised remarks, complaints about their presence on-site, and a lack of role models in the industry (Allison et al., 2019; GWNET, 2019) (see Chapter 8). The lack of representation has substantial implications, as the absence of women often restricts the development of inclusive energy policies. Energy policies frequently adopt a gender-neutral approach, assuming that men and women experience and are impacted by energy transitions in identical ways – the persistence of this approach perpetuates inequities and inequalities in energy relations by overlooking crucial complexities (Mang-Benza, 2021) (see Chapter 14).

Just Transition Approaches

Part of the asserted potential of green jobs is rooted in their role as mitigating impacts of other processes of economic restructuring and the job losses that may come with them. For example, in Germany, the Green Party has argued that energy and digital transitions will replace many of the jobs lost to automation beyond the energy sector – including both administrative and manual roles (Martin, 2021). While the job losses driven by automation and artificial intelligence technologies are emergent, there is a greater clarity on how green job agendas can address the redundancy and precarity in carbon-heavy sectors caused by decarbonisation.

The adverse consequences of decarbonisation are not limited to fossil fuel companies and their executives, but also extend to communities that have built their lives, livelihoods, and local economies around carbon-intensive industries (see Chapter 30). The closure of the Hazelwood mine in the Latrobe Valley, Australia had a two-fold impact on employment. First, it led to the loss of 1,400 direct jobs. Second, the subsequent decline in spending had a ripple effect, leading to an additional 1,771 job losses (Sheldon et al., 2018). Such transitions will shape new energy relationships between individuals, communities, employment, livelihoods, and industry. Communities living near carbon-intensive and extractive activities often develop close ties due to shared employment and geographical proximity: yet, as the number of extractive jobs diminishes, the supporting roles and opportunities that have been created to sustain these industries also vanish.

Communities that heavily depend on carbon-intensive industries become ‘locked in’ to such sectors and at risk of being stranded within a low-carbon economy (Freudenberg, 1992). In the United States, Snyder (2018) identifies 30 counties at a higher risk due to their dependence on fossil fuel employment. One such example is Norton County, Virginia, where an estimated 53% of jobs rely on the fossil fuel industry. Similarly, cities and towns in the UK, such as Aberdeen and Grangemouth, face the challenge of potential stranding as their economies heavily rely on oil and gas (Diski, 2021). The risks of job losses due to decarbonisation are not limited to fossil fuel extraction industries but extend to sectors like steel, glass, and transport, with the Yorkshire and Humber region in the UK estimated to have around 360,000 jobs at risk (Diski et al., 2021).

In the United States, national energy policies have targeted support for communities left ‘stranded’ by a transition away from coal economies. This includes US$14 billion of investment in the economic renewal of ‘coal communities’, such as those in Appalachia (The White House, 2023). Communities in Appalachia have been heavily reliant on the coal industry, which has left them stranded as it declines. The coal mines in Appalachia played a vital role in fuelling the economic growth of the nation and were accompanied by entire settlements built by coal companies to house the workers. The communities developed around these mining operations, with the companies sponsoring local institutions such as schools. The industry’s decline not only resulted in job losses but also led to a decline in municipal income and significant changes in the local social fabric. Between 2000 and 2015, 23 out of the 25 counties in the region experienced rising rates of childhood poverty (Snyder, 2018). In Knott County, Kentucky, the loss of 90% of coal jobs over a 15-year period coincided with a nearly 15% increase in the child poverty rate, rising from 31.6% in 2000 to 46.4% in 2015 (Snyder, 2018). Concurrently, the region faced a devastating opioid epidemic, with some counties having an average of three opioid prescriptions per person in 2012 (Snyder, 2018). While job losses are not directly causes of the opioid epidemic, they can contribute to the underlying factors that increase the risk of substance abuse and addiction, by generating financial insecurity and economic distress, removing the social network and sense of purpose that work provides, and removing health insurance coverage. Mining is an industry with higher rates of workplace injury and physical pain, which workers may be prescribed opioids to manage. Job loss when it occurs can disrupt access to healthcare, including pain management, leading some individuals to seek alternative sources of opioids (itself driven by the broader fentanyl crisis in the United States) while also removing the possibility of alternative treatments, including for substance abuse issues and mental health concerns.

Climate activists now engage with these communities to advocate for decarbonisation and additional economic transformation. The histories and memories of deindustrialisation and job losses in these areas are crucial in shaping the localised values that impact the perceptions of these sustainability transitions. Due to past experiences where changes and restructuring were implemented without considering dissent or the adverse effects on affected places and communities, many workers are sceptical of a terminology and framework of ‘transition’ (Powell et al., 2019; Diski et al., 2021). As Carl Wood of the Utility Workers Union told the 2009 Good Jobs, Green Jobs national conference in Washington D.C. (2012) (Brecher, 2009), “Workers are used to be[ing] ground up and spat out by any change in society”. The word ‘transition’ remains a dirty word for many communities.

One way of addressing this in future green jobs policies is through a framework of 'just transition', which is rooted in the efforts of trade unions to balance workers' rights and protections with environmental and climate concerns. Initially articulated by Canadian uranium miners in the 1960s, it gained prominence when Tony Mazzocchi, the leader of the Oil, Chemical and Atomic Workers International Union in the United States, popularised the term through his advocacy for a 'Superfund for Workers' (see Galgósczi, 2020). Under Mazzocchi, a vocabulary of just transition emerged as a demand from workers who faced hazardous working conditions, environmental pollution, and plant closures, while also serving as a platform to foster alliances between environmental and labour groups (Just Transition Research Collaborative, 2018; Atkins, 2023a).

The call for a just transition represents an important effort to overcome the binary that pits climate action against job creation that was articulated by employers (Goddard and Farrelly, 2018). Demands for ecological health and protection emerged as part of a working-class environmentalism that challenged the notion of a trade-off between environmental protection and decent employment by linking working conditions to a healthy environment (Atkins, 2023a). Brian Kohler, a Canadian trade union leader from the Communications, Energy and Paper Workers Union (Just Transition Research Collaborative, 2018) later emphasised this view: "The real choice is not jobs or the environment. It is both or neither" (Kohler, 1996).

The concept and language of just transition have gained recognition and inclusion in international climate policy. It is referred to in key international documents, such as those of the International Labour Organization (ILO), the United Nations Environment Programme (UNEP), and the United Nations Framework Convention on Climate Change (UNFCCC). The 2015 Paris Agreement emphasised the importance of a just transition for the workforce and the creation of decent work and quality jobs aligned with national development priorities (UNFCCC, 2016: 2).

The Silesia Declaration at COP24 in Katowice, Poland, in 2018 highlighted the need for signatories to recognise and address the connections between climate change, climate policies, and the rights and futures of workers. This declaration marked a significant moment for the concept of just transition, as countries demonstrated their commitment to involving workers and communities in climate policy and action (Jenkins, 2019; Stevis et al., 2020). The inclusion of just transition language in these international climate documents represents a notable achievement for proponents of the framework, particularly trade unions, and underscores the increasing influence of these organisations in international climate policy. This represents an important act of codification of just transition – with the concept asserted as more than an 'add-on' and a means to appease worker groups (Abram et al., 2022). Instead, it becomes a broader policy priority – in which governments intervene to lessen the impacts of climate action on workers and the communities from which they are drawn.

The ILO (2015) has provided a set of guidelines for what a just transition would look like:

- National economic policies that prioritise employment generation.
- Targeted environmental regulations in specific sectors and industries.
- Fostering supportive business environments to enable the growth of 'green' enterprises.
- Social protection policies to safeguard workers against the adverse impacts of climate change and climate policies.
- Policies that promote job creation, minimise job losses, and facilitate a smooth transition to greener practices.
- Implementation of occupational health and safety policies to protect workers' well-being.
- Emphasis on skills development initiatives to equip workers with the necessary competencies for green jobs.

- Social dialogue to ensure the inclusion of all stakeholders affected by change and policies.
- Policy coherence by integrating sustainable development principles across various policy domains, fostering social dialogue, and coordinating efforts among different policy areas.

Lessons can be taken from previous policies that have responded to the consequences of economic transformations resulting from the gradual elimination of coal. A regularly cited example is that of policies introduced in Germany's Ruhr region to both protect employment and support workers leaving the coal industry. Coal production was the primary industry of the region, with the Ruhr at risk in the 1970s of becoming a stranded community and the closure of operations leading to mass unemployment. However, the regional government of North-Rhine Westphalia implemented several plans to mitigate the impacts of the end of the coal industry – including bridging payments for those close to retirement (providing wages for up to five years to support workers waiting to be able to claim their pensions) and the provision of new training and personal development programmes to support younger works find new work (Galgósczi, 2014) (see Chapter 25). Subsequent schemes in the following decades diversified the regional economy through high-tech businesses. One initiative between 1989 and 1999 involved 120 projects, the expenditure of the equivalent of €2.5 billion, and the creation of 5,000 jobs (Galgósczi, 2014). The concept of 'just transition' can become a mobilising force to promote future green jobs to ensure both employment for workers and environmental protection (Abraham, 2017; Just Transition Research Collaborative, 2018). This involves proactive green job creation policies, rather than merely reacting to change. A sustained focus on managing transition through job protections if applied in isolation neglects the broader consequences of decarbonisation. At the core of future green jobs policies should be the aspiration to create *better* jobs.

Better Jobs and Skills

In the UK, around 6.3 million jobs, equivalent to one in five jobs, are expected to undergo skill changes in the coming decades (UK Green Jobs Taskforce, 2021). The UNFCCC (2020) highlights that skills' shortages are already presenting significant barriers to transitioning to a low-carbon economy. Various factors are contributing to this situation, including an underestimation of the rate at which labour demands are increasing, shortages of skilled workers in high-demand sectors, negative perceptions of certain sectors despite their growth potential, and a lack of teachers and trainers needed to deliver skills-based training (Strietska-Ilina et al., 2011).

The UNFCCC (2020) has emphasised the importance of continuous education and training as well as lifelong learning, enabling individuals of all ages to reskill and transition across sectors. Given that highly skilled jobs tend to offer better pay, it is crucial to establish pathways or secure access to training for individuals lacking the necessary skills. Apprenticeships serve as a valuable means to achieve this objective. Apprenticeship schemes can simultaneously address the labour requirements for decarbonisation and provide excluded individuals with new employment opportunities. In the UK, Friends of the Earth (2021) has called for the expansion of existing apprenticeship programmes, aiming to create 250,000 'green' apprenticeships. This would have offered young people a generation disproportionately impacted by the COVID-19 pandemic, new avenues for employment and also provide a direct pathway to secure employment opportunities. Additional reforms in further education curricula can introduce bridge programmes that enhance skills and knowledge while guiding those entering the labour market towards future green employment. These programmes can also be modularised, allowing individuals with limited income or time constraints to participate intermittently or combine education with work commitments (Martinson et al., 2010).

Targeted skills training initiatives can be implemented to address specific forms of exclusion. The MillionTreesNYC programme in New York focused on providing skills training to individuals aged 18–24 from low-income communities who were unemployed or underemployed. Participants received a salary while engaging in a seven-month training programme that taught the necessary professional skills for environmental conservation and restoration. Upon completion, graduates were offered full-time jobs in local government and non-governmental organisations (Falxa-Raymond et al., 2013). Other projects like GRID Alternatives, funded by Sun Edison and located in Oakland, California, focus on targeted training programmes to improve diversity and inclusion in the solar energy sector. They specifically target women, Indigenous American groups, and people who have recently been released from prison (Stephens, 2021). These training programmes not only provide skills but also increase employment opportunities for participants by connecting them with the industry and fostering supportive work environments to ensure employee retention (Stephens, 2021).

In the United States, worker-led organisations are increasingly instrumental in advocating for green jobs that prioritise worker well-being and decent work. In New York, Climate Jobs in New York, a union-led organisation representing over 2.5 million workers, emerged as a prominent force in advancing a pro-worker and pro-climate agenda. A key aspect of their efforts is to secure project labour agreements for new wind projects in the state. These agreements involve wind farm developers partnering with local unions to employ union workers and ensure union wages throughout the project's construction phase. They may also include provisions for apprenticeship training programs, benefiting both the company by maintaining a steady labour supply and providing new opportunities for younger or underemployed workers. Crucially, these agreements foster dialogue between the company and the union, outlining the project timeline and discussing the number of workers required at each stage and each year. The widespread adoption of project labour agreements represents a significant triumph for the trade union movement, with states like Maine and Connecticut enacting legislation mandating labour standards for renewable energy projects above a certain megawatt capacity.

Climate Jobs Illinois, a branch of the Climate Jobs National Resource Center, and the Illinois Clean Jobs Coalition successfully advocated for the passage of the Climate and Equitable Jobs Act by the Illinois General Assembly in 2021. This legislation was driven by the realisation that trade unions had been excluded from previous energy policies in the state, leading to renewable energy projects relying on cheap, out-of-state labour (Roberts, 2021). The resulting bill, developed through close collaboration between lawmakers, community groups, trade unions, and other stakeholders, mandates project labour agreements, fair wages, and actions to enhance diversity and inclusion in the workforce for all utility-scale projects seeking qualification under the state's Renewable Portfolio Standard. Additionally, the Clean Jobs Workforce Network Hubs programme was established, allocating \$80 million per year to support training programs for low-income communities. In California, similar project labour agreements have facilitated the implementation of a state-wide apprenticeship system, leading to increased diversity in applications, particularly in terms of ethnicity (Luke et al., 2017). In Kern County, when solar projects are under construction, 43% of entry-level workers come from economically disadvantaged communities or communities with higher-than-average unemployment rates (Luke et al., 2017). Such initiatives demonstrate the potential for creating a more inclusive and diverse workforce within the green sector through dialogue between workers, government, and renewable energy companies.

These efforts by trade unions in the United States have prioritised safeguarding existing working conditions and preventing the bypassing of unionised labour. As a result, project labour agreements have been established, wherein renewable energy companies commit to collaborating with unions to create good, stable, well-compensated, and highly skilled green jobs. Furthermore, the focus extends beyond job creation within the renewable energy sector itself. The development of supply chains and manufacturing capacities for renewable energy components stimulates employment opportunities in other areas. The overall success of any transition and the provision of new job security hinges on the sustained vitality of local and regional economies. While energy transitions can take place in a top-down, government-led manner, doing so risks not only injustice but also a widespread suspicion of and opposition to such change. This broader perspective ensures the long-term benefits of green job initiatives by allowing for bottom-up approaches that centre transitions on inclusive, decent and secure work and collective bargaining.

Conclusion: What Future of Green Work?

The labour movement has a long-standing history of supporting environmental causes. Collaborations between labour and environmental groups have been instrumental in highlighting the shared interests of ecological conservation and worker health and safety. The United Automobile Workers (UAW) provided financial and logistical support for the inaugural Earth Day in 1970. More recently, trade union members, on average, demonstrate greater pro-environmental attitudes compared to the general population (Vachon and Brecher, 2016), and labour unions are increasingly active participants in global climate summits (Allan, 2020). Green jobs agendas represent the next stage in which demands for decent work and environmental and climate protections can be fused. Decarbonisation policies are an opportunity for society to become socially inclusive as well as emit less (Healy and Barry, 2017; Atkins, 2023b). Green jobs agendas have a significant role in this – guiding not only the futures of work but of communities and the climate itself.

Despite some progress in including workers in an energy transition, there is still work to be done. A survey conducted in the UK revealed that 81% of oil and gas workers would be open to transitioning out of the sector but that the primary concern stopping them was future job security. This is understandable: it is possible to decarbonise without generating a substantial number of jobs. A study commissioned by the Scottish Trade Union Congress has highlighted the significance of comprehensive policy measures in the energy sector. By implementing an active industrial strategy, embracing public ownership, and making substantial investments, Scotland has the potential to create as many as 367,000 jobs in the energy industry alone. However, if they approach prioritises business-as-usual without considering job security and the development of green skills, climate action may only result in the creation of 9,000 jobs (STUC and Transition Economics, 2021).

The transition towards the future of green work will not be smooth. Although the overall impact on the planet is expected to yield positive outcomes in terms of emissions, the consequences of decarbonisation will be varied and encompass both positive and negative aspects. Green jobs and their potential for shaping the future of work offer a crucial avenue for addressing these impacts. However, it is important to note that these *green* jobs aren't necessarily *good* jobs, as they can still be characterised by episodes of low pay, precarity and exclusion that are commonly associated with work in other sectors.

For a truly inclusive transition towards a green future of work, it is essential for governments to enact proactive frameworks that establish strong linkages between renewable energy jobs, skills development agendas, and trade unions. This approach empowers trade unions to contribute to the definition of future employment prospects. Neglecting these measures may result in renewable energy jobs becoming part of the group adversely affected by the process of decarbonisation. If we view climate action as synonymous with job creation, as President Joe Biden has expressed ('the climate equals jobs'), a green future of work must strive to minimise disparities between those who benefit and those who lose out. This can be achieved by mitigating past job losses, fostering new employment opportunities, and charting a clear and inclusive path for all individuals through the transition.

References

Abraham, J. (2017). Just transitions for the miners: Labor environmentalism in the Ruhr and Appalachian coalfields. *New Political Science*, 39(2): 218–240.

Abram, S., Atkins, E., Dietzel, A., Jenkins, K., Kiamba, L., Kirshner, J. et al. (2022). Just transition: Pathways to socially inclusive decarbonisation. *Climate Policy*, 22(8): 1033–1049.

Allan, J.I. (2020). *The New Climate Activism: NGO Authority and Participation in Climate Change Governances*. Toronto: University of Toronto Press.

Allison, J.E., McCrory, K. and Oxnevad, I. (2019). Closing the renewable energy gender gap in the United States and Canada: The role of women's professional networking. *Energy Research & Social Science*, 55: 35–34.

Atkins, E. (2023a). The structural power of workers in influencing energy transitions: Examples of the Green Bans (Australia) and the Lucas Plan (United Kingdom). *Energy Research and Social Science*, 96: 102944.

Atkins E. (2023b). *A Just Energy Transition: Getting Decarbonisation Right in a Time of Crisis*. Bristol: Bristol University Press.

Bowen, A., Kuralbaayeva, K. and Tipoe, E.L. (2018). Characterising green employment: The impacts of 'greening' on workforce composition. *Energy Economics*, 72: 263–275.

Brecher, J. (2009). *Will workers be left behind in a green transition?* Blog Entry 5 May. Available at: https://www.jeremybrecher.org/will-workers-be-left-behind-in-a-green-transition/

Clancy, J. and Feenstra, M. (2019). Women, gender equality and the energy transition in the EU. *European Union Policy Department for Citizens' Rights and Constitutional Affairs*, May 2019. Available at: https://www.europarl.europa.eu/RegData/etudes/STUD/2019/608867/IPOL_STU(2019)608867_EN.pdf

Daly, P. (2019). The reason why Grimsby offshore wind sector is allowed to pay staff less than the minimum wage. *Grimsby Live*, 2 May. Available at: https://www.grimsbytelegraph.co.uk/news/grimsby-news/offshore-wind-minimum-wage-grimsby-2819861 (Accessed 14/06/2023).

Diski, R. (2021). Preparing for a just transition in Yorkshire and the Humber. *New Economics Foundation*, 10 June. Available at: https://newec onomics.org/2021/06/preparing-for-a-just-transition-in-yorkshire-andthe-humber (Accessed 14/06/2023).

Diski, R., Chapman, A. and Kumar, C. (2021). Powering the just transition: Putting workers and unions at the centre of industrial change in Yorkshire and the Humber. London: New Economics Foundation, 9 June. Available at: https://neweconomics.org/2021/06/powering-the-just-transition (Accessed 14/06/2023).

Econie, A. and Doughtery, M.L. (2019). Contingent work in the US recycling industry: Permatemps and precarious green jobs. *Geoforum*, 99: 132–141.

Falxa-Raymond, N., Svendsen, E. and Campbell, L.K. (2013). From job training to green jobs: A case study for a young adult employment program centered on environmental restoration in New York City, US. *Urban Forestry & Urban Greening*, 12: 287–295.

Ferroukhi, R., Garcia Casals, X. and Parajuli, B. (2020). *Measuring the Socio-economics of Transition: Focus on Jobs*. Abu Dhabi: IRENA.

Freudenberg, W.R. (1992). Addictive economies: Extractive industries and vulnerable localities in a changing world economy. *Rural Sociology*, 57(3): 305–332.

Friends of the Earth (2021). *An Emergency Plan on Green Jobs for Young People*. London: Friends of the Earth.

Galgóczi, B. (2014). The long and winding road from black to green: Decades of structural change in the Ruhr region. *International Journal of Labour Research*, 6: 217.

Galgósczi, B. (2020). Just transition on the ground: Challenges and opportunities for social dialogue. *European Journal of Industrial Relations*, 26(4): 367–382.

Global Energy Talent Index (2023). *The Global Energy Talent Index Report 2023*. Available at: https://www.getireport.com/ (Accessed 14/06/2023).

Goddard, G. and Farrelly, M.A. (2018). Just transition management: Balancing just outcomes with just processes in Australian renewable energy transitions. *Applied Energy*, 225: 110–123.

GWNET [Global Women's Network for the Energy Transition] (2019). *Women for Sustainable Energy: Strategies to Foster Women's Talent for Transformational Change*. Vienna: GWNET.

Healy, N. and Barry, J. (2017). Politicizing energy justice and energy system transitions: Fossil fuel divestment and a "just transition". *Energy Policy*, 108: 451–459.

ILO [International Labor Organization] (2015). ILO adopts guidelines on sustainable development, decent work and green jobs. *International Labor Organization*, 5 November. Available at: https://www.ilo.org/global/topics/green-jobs/news/WCMS_422575/lang--en/index.htm (Accessed 14/06/2023).

ILO [International Labor Organization] (2021). Decent work. *International Labor Organization*, no date. Available at: https://www.ilo.org/global/topics/decent-work/lang--en/index.htm (Accessed 14/06/2023).

IREC [Interstate Renewable Energy Council] (2021). *National Solar Jobs Census 2020*. Albany, NY: Interstate Renewable Energy Council.

IRENA [International Renewable Energy Agency] (2019). *Renewable Energy: A Gender Perspective*. Abu Dhabi: International Renewable Energy Agency.

IRENA [International Renewable Energy Agency] (2020) *Renewable Energy and Jobs: Annual Review 2019*. Abu Dhabi: International Renewable Energy Agency.

IRENA [International Renewable Energy Agency] (2021). *Renewable energy and Jobs: Annual Review 2020*. Abu Dhabi: International Renewable Energy Agency.

ITUC [International Trade Unions Congress] (2012). *Growing Green and Decent Jobs*. Brussels: ITUC.

Jenkins, K. (2019). Implementing just transition after COP24. *Climate Strategies Policy Brief*, January 2019. Available at: https://climatestrategies. org/wp-content/uploads/2019/01/Implementing-Just-Transition-afterCOP24_FINAL.pdf (Accessed 14/06/2023).

Jones, C. (2021). As clean energy jobs grow, women and Black workers are at risk of being left behind. *USA Today*, 9 September. Available at: https://eu.usatoday.com/story/money/2021/09/09/clean-energy-jobs-womenblack-hispanic-workers-report/5776787001/ (Accessed 14/06/2023).

Just Transition Research Collaborative (2018). *Mapping Just Transition(s) to a Low-Carbon World*. UNRISD. Available at: https://www.uncclearn.org/wp-content/uploads/library/report-jtrc-2018.pdf (Accessed 14/06/2023).

Kohler, B. (1996). Sustainable development: A labor view. Presentation at 1996 *Persistent Organic Pollutants Conference*, 5 December 1996, University of Chicago. Available at: https://www.sdearthtimes.com/et0597/et0597s4.html (Accessed 14/06/2023).

Luke, N., Zabin, C., Velasco, D. and Collier, R. (2017). *Diversity in California's Clean Energy Workforce: Access to Jobs for Disadvantaged Workers in Renewable Energy Construction*. Berkeley: Center for Labor Research and Education, University of California.

Mang-Benza, C. (2021). Many shades of pink in the energy transition: Seeing women in energy extraction, production, distribution and consumption. *Energy Research & Social Science*, 73: 101901.

Martin, N. (2021). The Green Party's economic plans. *DW*, 21 April. Available at: https://www.dw.com/en/germany-the-green-partys-economic-plans/a-57275813 (Accessed 14/06/2023).

Martinson, K., Stanczyk, A. and Eyster, L. (2010). *Low-Skill Workers' Access to Quality Green Jobs. The Urban Institute, Brief 13*. Washington, DC: Urban Institute.

McClure, L.A., LeBlanc, W.G., Fernandez, C.A., Fleming, L.E., Lee, D.J., Moore, K.J. and Caban-Martinez, A.J. (2017). Green collar workers: An emerging workforce in the environmental sector. *Journal of Occupational and Environmental Medicine*, 59(5): 440–445.

Mock, B. (2013). *Civil Rights Through Green Jobs, In These Times*, 30 December. Available at: https://inthesetimes.com/article/civil-rights-through-green-jobs

Morena, E., Krause, D. and Stevis, D. (eds.) (2020). *Just Transitions: Social Justice in the Shift Towards a Low-Carbon World*. London: Pluto Press.

Muro, M., Tomer, A., Shivaram, R. and Kane, J. (2019). *Advancing Inclusion Through Clean Energy Jobs*, Washington D.C.: Brookings Institute.

Pai, S., Emmerling, J., Drouet, L., Zerriffi, H. and Jewell, J. (2021). Meeting well-below 2C target would increase energy sector jobs globally. *One Earth*, 4: 1026–1036.

Penner, A.M. (2008). Race and gender differences in wages: The role of occupational sorting at the point of hire. *The Sociological Quarterly*, 49(3): 597–614.

Powell, D., Balata, F., van Lerven, F. and Welsh, M. (2019). Trust in transition: Climate breakdown and high carbon workers. *New Economics Foundation*, 28 November. Available at: https://neweconomics.org/2019/11/trust-in-transition (Accessed 14/06/2023).

Reid, L.W. and Rubin, B.A. (2003). Integrating economic dualism and labor market segmentation: The effects of race, gender, and structural location on earnings, 1974–2000. *The Sociological Quarterly*, 44(3): 405–432.

RMT [Rail, Maritime and Transport Workers, National Union of] (2021). RMT uncovers illegal employment practices in the offshore supply chain. *RMT*, 13 May. Available at: https://www.rmt.org.uk/news/rmt-uncovers-illegal-employment-practices-in-the-offshore/ (Accessed 14/06/2023).

Roberts, D. (2021). Volts – Illinois' brilliant new climate, jobs, and justice bill. 22 September [Podcast]. Available at: https://www.volts.wtf/p/illinois-brilliant-new-climate-jobs#details (Accessed 14/06/2023).

Scheiber, N. (2021). Building solar farms may not build the middle class. *The New York Times*, 16 July. Available at: https://www.nytimes.com/2021/07/16/business/economy/green-energy-jobs-economy.html (Accessed 14/06/2023).

Sheldon, P., Junankar, R. and De Rosa Pontello, A. (2018). The Ruhr or Appalachia? Deciding the future of Australia's coal power workers and communities. *IRRC Report for CFMMEU Mining and Energy*. Available at: https://www.ituc-csi.org/IMG/pdf/ruhrorappalachia_report_final.pdf (Accessed 14/06/2023).

Snyder, B.F. (2018). Vulnerability to decarbonization in hydrocarbon intensive counties in the United States: A just transition to avoid postindustrial decay. *Energy Research & Social Science*, 42: 34–43.

Stephens, J.C. (2021). *Diversifying Power: Why We Need Antiracist, Feminist Leadership on Climate and Energy*. Washington, DC: Island Press.

Stevis, D., Morena, E., and Krause, D. (2020). Introduction: The genealogy and contemporary politics of just transitions. In Morena, E., Krause, D. and Stevis, D. (eds.) *Just Transitions: Social Justice in the Shift Towards a Low-Carbon World*. London: Pluto Press, pp. 1–31.

Strietska-Ilina, O., Hoffman, C., Durán Haro, M. and Jeon, S. (2011). *Skills for Green Jobs: A Global View*. Geneva: International Labour Organization.

Stroud, D., Fairbrother, P., Evans, C., and Blake, J. (2014). Skill development in the transition to a 'green economy': A 'varieties of capitalism' analysis. *The Economic and Labour Relations Review*, 25(1): 10–27.

STUC [Scottish Trade Unions Congress] and Transition Economics (2021). *Green Jobs in Scotland*. Glasgow: Scottish Trade Unions Congress.

UK Green Jobs Taskforce (2021). *Green Jobs Taskforce: Report to Government, Industry and the Skills Sector*. London: UK Government.

UN [United Nations] (2019). Green economy could create 24 million new jobs. United Nations, 3 April. Available at: https://www.un.org/sustainabledevelopment/blog/2019/04/green-economy-could-create-24-million-new-jobs/ (Accessed 14/06/2023).

UNFCCC [United Nations Framework Convention on Climate Change] (2016). Paris agreement. In UNFCCC COP Report Number 21, Addendum, at 21, U.N. Do. FCCC/CP/2015/10/Add.1.

UNFCCC [United Nations Framework Convention on Climate Change] (2020). *Just Transition of the Workforce, and the Creation of Decent Work and Quality Jobs*. UNFCCC Technical Paper, Bonn, Germany.

Vachon, T. (2019). The green transition: Renewable energy technology, climate change mitigation and the future of work in New Jersey. *Prepared for the New Jersey Governor's Task Force on the Future of Work*. Available at: https://fowtf.innovation.nj.gov/downloads/resources/Vachon_Climate_Jobs_Rep ort_RCS.pdf (Accessed 14/06/2023).

Vachon, T.E. and Brecher, J. (2016). Are union members more or less likely to be environmentalist? Some evidence from two national surveys. *Labor Studies Journal*, 41(2): 185–203.

Weller, C. (2019). Black workers at greater risk amid growing recession worries. *Forbes*, 9 March. Available at: https://www.forbes.com/sites/christianweller/2020/03/09/black-workers-at-greater-risk-amid-growing-recession-worries/?sh=36fe1a3825cc (Accessed 14/06/2023).

The White House (2021). Remarks by President Biden before signing executive actions on tackling climate change, creating jobs, and restoring scientific integrity. *The White House*, 27 January. Available at: https://www.whitehouse.gov/briefing-room/speeches-remarks/2021/01/27/remarks-by-president-biden-before-signing-executive-actions-on-tackling-climate-change-creating-jobs-and-restoring-scientific-integrity/ (Accessed 14/06/2023).

The White House (2023). Fact sheet: Biden-Harris Administration announces new clean energy projects to revitalize energy communities, support coal workers, and reduce reliance on competitors like China. *The White House*, 4 April. Available at: https://www.whitehouse.gov/briefing-room/statements-releases/2023/04/04/fact-sheet-biden-harris-administration-announces-new-clean-energy-projects-to-revitalize-energy-communities-support-coal-workers-and-reduce-reliance-on-competitors-like-china/ (Accessed 14/06/2023).

Recommendations for Further Reading

Abram, S., Atkins, E., Dietzel, A., Jenkins, K., Kiamba, L., Kirshner, J. et al. (2022). Just transition: Pathways to socially inclusive decarbonisation. *Climate Policy*, 22(8): 1033–1049. *(A review of recent literature on energy transitions and just transition processes).*

Galgóczi, B. (2020). Just transition on the ground: Challenges and opportunities for social dialogue. *European Journal of Industrial Relations*, 26(4): 367–382. *(An examination of regional just transition policies).*

Mang-Benza, C. (2021). Many shades of pink in the energy transition: Seeing women in energy extraction, production, distribution and consumption. *Energy Research & Social Science*, 73: 101901. *(An exploration of how 'gender-blindness' in the energy sector leads to certain types of policy – and how the sector can be more diverse).*

Morena, E., Krause, D. and Stevis, D. (eds.) (2020). *Just Transitions: Social Justice in the Shift towards a Low-Carbon World.* London: Pluto Press. *(A comprehensive account of just transition work and its history).*

Pai, S., Emmerling, J., Drouet, L., Zerriffi, H. and Jewell, J. (2021). Meeting well-below 2C target would increase energy sector jobs globally. *One Earth*, 4: 1026–1036. *(A short analysis of how many 'green' energy jobs may emergent in certain climate policy scenarios)*.

Stephens, J.C. (2021). *Diversifying Power: Why we Need Antiracist, Feminist Leadership on Climate and Energy.* Washington, DC: Island Press. *(An important call for a different type of climate policy)*.

30

ENERGY TRANSITIONS AND THE FUTURE OF DECENT WORK IN ASIAN GARMENT FACTORIES

Evie Gilbert

Introduction

The global garment industry has been subject to significant transformation, particularly around the rise of fast fashion in the 1990s and early 2000s (López et al., 2022), as has the labour force within it. The globalisation of garment manufacturing and the fragmentation into global value chains has restructured the garment sector and transformed production, purchasing and consumption. Defined as 'the race to the bottom', the transition of garment production to Global South facilities drove competition in the form of cheap labour and fast lead times for production. Asia in particular has become a key export market and an essential employer in the Global South. The sector employs over 60 million workers, of which the majority are women (Sharpe et al., 2022). However, existing structures are being threatened by factors such as automation, sustainability pressures and 'reshoring' (Ibid.). While these factors threaten the competitiveness of garment-producing countries in the Global South as a whole, these downward pressures are most harshly felt by garment workers on the factory floor (Hildingsson et al., 2019; Hafner et al., 2022; Ahmad et al., 2020; Dedeoğlu, 2010).

This chapter focuses on the garment sector in Asia, reviewing the future of work for garment workers in the face of energy transition pressures. In doing so, the chapter aims to address tensions between decarbonisation and decent work in Asian garment factories, focusing on the factory floor as a space where these phenomena meet and whereby tensions are felt by those with limited power. As exporters in Asia typically occupy the lower end of the value chain such as Cut-Make-Trim factories, workers usually are employed for low-skill repetitive tasks and are subject to pressures to reduce costs, which subsequently impacts worker wages and their working conditions (ILO, 2022). The upfront costs associated with decarbonisation, sustainable garment production and renewable energy transformations add to the financial pressures felt by exporters, who remain in competition with one another to keep the costs of production low for buyers (Jamali et al., 2017). This chapter, therefore, asks the following questions: as policies and practices transform the garment sector around energy transitions and decarbonisation in manufacturing processes, what is the consideration for the experience of decent work and the future of work of low-skilled garment workers?

The focus of this chapter on decent work and decarbonisation aims not to attribute barriers to decent work with energy transitions but to highlight how such pressures influence, exacerbate and

DOI: 10.4324/9781003327561-41

create new forms of challenges in achieving decent work. In the context of decarbonisation and garment manufacturing, there are a plethora of issues to address. However, this chapter homes in on tensions between decarbonisation efforts and decent work. The International Labour Organization (ILO) outlines multiple pillars of decent work, including rights at work, employment, social dialogue and social protection (ILO, 2017). Within these pillars, opportunities for work and wages are significant elements of decent work. This chapter argues that decarbonisation practices require significant investments from factories in Asia and therefore influence employment in decent work through increased downward pressures on wages for garment workers, but also encourage practices of subcontracting. Informal subcontracting factories already exhibit high barriers to decent work due to their hidden nature which permits poor working conditions, lower wages and limited access to worker rights and benefits (Goto, 2011). The complexity of garment value chains allows for the subcontracting of labour to informal factories, hiding both environmental and social abuses from the end consumer (Sweet, 2022).

Labour in the garment industry has been structured around buyer-driven global value chains and these structures have encouraged increasing fragmentation and networks of contracted factories and subcontracted factories across the manufacturing levels. Literature on the future of work centres on impending trends such as digitalisation, technological innovation, structural transformation and climate change (ILO, 2019; Schlogl et al., 2021). More specifically, discussions on the future of work in garment manufacturing pay close attention to the influence of pressures such as technology uptake for increased productivity but also sustainability (Licata and Kemp, 2020). The future of work and its uncertainties are widely recognised due to these pressures. This chapter will apply trends in future of work literature to the garment sector, highlighting female labourers as indirect victims of transformations of work.

Garment production is often located in emerging economies whereby demand for energy and electricity is not only felt at the industry level but at the level of the country as a whole. As a result, increasing local energy consumption driven by demand from export markets influences the decisions made on energy sources and therefore impacts the projected emissions. In a study on Bangladesh, Debnath and Mourshed (2022) find that electricity consumption increased by 526% between 2000 and 2021 and that projected demand in the country's transition towards an upper-middle-income country requires the government to consider the use of coal in the electricity mix. Bangladesh's garment industry has driven economic growth but also the demand for an energy-intensive economy. Garment factories are an energy-intensive step in the value chain due to the need for steam. Energy sources in these production centres are often derived from coal, natural gases or the burning of natural wood. To fuel boilers in garment factories in Cambodia, 70% of the wood burned comes from illegal harvesting contributing both to deforestation and to excessive CO_2 release as a result of burning 'non-sustainably managed forests' (Geres, 2019, p. 3).

In addition to the damaging environmental impacts of large production centres, the demanding nature of fast fashion and the global garment industry has facilitated processes of subcontracting to smaller factories. Factories subcontract to smaller informal production centres as a means of offsetting high upfront costs and managing changing seasonal demands for labour. However, adding links to the value chain inevitably reduces profitability and therefore increases pressure to reduce costs further, these pressures are almost always felt by the garment worker and transparency is obscured further (Alamgir and Banerjee, 2019). Measuring emissions and the climate impact of these smaller facilities is incredibly complex. As these firms exist on the periphery of the supply chain they fall beyond the gaze of sustainability efforts, have significantly fewer resources to be able to adapt to climate-conscious processes and therefore impact the industry's ability to reduce its overall environmental impact (Berry et al., 2022; Sweet, 2022). Sweet (2022), in particular questions whether existing informal labour structures which support the garment export industry in many Global South countries are a means of avoiding investing in clean energy whereby the environmental impact of small local production facilities is complicated to trace. Labourers engaged in this complex network are rarely at the forefront of strategies moving forward. Therefore, tensions between reducing environmental impact and ensuring decent labour practices persist.

In exploring these issues, the remainder of this chapter is structured as follows. Firstly, literature on the future of work in the garment sector is reviewed, outlining the emphasis on digitalisation, automation and new structures of labour. Literature on decent work in the future of garment manufacturing is also reviewed to outline imagined labour structures as the sector transforms. The chapter focuses on garment manufacturing in Asia due to the region's structures of low-cost labour-intensive production and significant energy demands required for garment exports to Western markets. Second, the chapter addresses key trends in energy transitions, focusing on decarbonisation and the circular economy in the global garment industry. Finally, the chapter addresses tensions between industrial decarbonisation efforts and decent work for factory workers, arguing that while environmental and social sustainability cannot be considered separately, the complexity of the global garment value chain encourages competitive behaviours which are inevitably felt by the labour force in the form of insecurity. This suggests that the future of work, and decent work in particular, in Asia's garment sector is uncertain and that the process of decarbonising the garment sector may perpetuate the experience of invisibility and insecurity for the garment worker in the Global South.

The Future of Garment Work

Asia has played a significant role in the global garment industry and continues to produce 55% of global garment exports (ILO, 2022). However, as the garment industry is restructured around new technologies central to the Industry 4.0 narrative, the role of Asia and the prominence of 'race to the bottom' labour-intensive manufacturing in the future is called into question. The future of garment work in Asia is uncertain, and the speculative nature of the future encourages dystopian thinking in academic and policy spheres, which often glorifies the role of digitalisation, robotics and AI in industry practice (Schlogl et al., 2021). However, for the garment sector, which has successfully created a labour force designed to fuel fast fashion, the future of work is ever more precarious. As climate and energy demands encourage new manufacturing processes, it is essential to highlight existing narratives on the future of work in Asia and the potential for existing labour forces to be included in wide-scale structural transformation.

The threat of mass displacement is a recurring theme in the discourse on the future of work in Asia's garment manufacturing sector. Chang et al. (2016) argue that labour in the TGF sector is most susceptible to technological displacement, including displacement by technologies designed to make the industry more sustainable. The transformation of garment manufacturing has been promoted as a means of improving productivity however, such processes increase the cost of production and it is widely recognised that manufacturers will continue to chase cheap labour despite sustainability pressures (Chang et al., 2016). Vashisht and Rani (2020) agree that whilst many jobs in garment manufacturing are displaceable, the feasibility of upgrading manufacturing in garment-producing countries is not as predicted. Due to the downward pressures faced by factories in the Global South and the complexity of the global value chain, the reality of upgrading to a fully automated production process is highly unlikely (Vashisht and Rani, 2020). This is particularly significant when looking at 'footloose factories' in Asia, whereby the ease of moving production across facilities and more significantly across borders is widely practised and incredibly beneficial for manufacturers seeking out low-cost labour. The Ministry of Economy and Finance in Cambodia is well aware of this tension between industry practices and the movement towards automation stating, "With the increasing pressure to adopt modern technology and increased use of machineries foreign investors might question where they should invest because one of the perks of the garment factories is they can move really quickly. They can move from one country to the next within aamybe a month or even less because all they do is shut down the factory and move all their equipment" (Ministry of Economy and Finance, Cambodia, 18/01/2023). This increases precarity for the garment worker on the factory floor. In looking at the future of work in garment manufacturing, characterised by investments in new technologies, the footloose approach disadvantages Asian factories as the high level of foreign investment does not look to sustain upgrading in-country but looks to relocate to more favourable environments (Calabrese and Balchin, 2022). Chang et al. (2016) highlight the future of fashion will require the ability to customise garments. Therefore, while garment manufacturing may remain labour-intensive in Asia, new technologies are being implemented in producing countries closer to the western consumer to deal with the pressure for customisation over mass manufacturing (Licata and Kemp, 2020). Montt et al. (2018) also argue that the transformation required to enforce environmental sustainability in manufacturing will inevitably shape the future of work.

The garment sector thus far has thrived on low-cost labour. However, this is becoming less important in guaranteeing competitiveness in the future (Huynh, 2015). The future of garment work in Asia is unlikely to completely transform around competitive technologies and is therefore subject to precarity and insecurity. The garment sector in Asia is a female-dominated labour force and future of work narratives tend to omit gender from such thinking (Howcroft and Rubery, 2019) (see Chapter 14 for more on gender). As a consequence, the impacts of future of work transformations are limited in their gendered analysis. For the female labour force in Asia's garment industry, this also limits the ability to assess the impact of energy transformations on the future of work through a gendered lens. Montt et al. (2018) argue that labour and the natural environment cannot be considered separately as industrial activity influences the natural environment, but also a push for decarbonisation in industrial sectors inevitably impacts the labour existing within it.

Decarbonising the Global Factory

Asia is still considered the 'garments and textiles factory of the world' (ILO, 2022, p. 1), contributing substantially to global exports but also to global emissions. Sustainability and decarbonisation are significant factors influencing the transformation of the garment sector and therefore, garment work in Asia. The global garment industry contributes between 6% and 8% of global carbon emissions (Sharpe et al., 2022), therefore the pressure put on the sector to decarbonise is unsurprising. The impact of the garment industry on the global climate through the release of Greenhouse Gas (GHG) emissions exists across the entire supply chain and the United Nations Framework Convention on Climate Change brought together stakeholders across the global garment sector to commit to the Fashion Industry Charter for Climate Action which aims to reduce carbon emissions by 30% by 2030 and net-zero by 2050 (Sharpe et al., 2022). It is not only GHG emissions released by the garment industry, but high water usage, chemical pollutants and textile waste, which are key factors in the sector's environmentally damaging portfolio (Deben et al., 2020). Deben et al. (2020) predict that if production and consumption of garments continue as is, by 2030 emissions from the garment sector alone will increase by 50%. Dyke et al. (2021) draw attention to the complications of 'net zero', stating that seeking out net zero can lead to an assumption that future technologies will solve carbon removal, thereby impeding decarbonisation strategies in the present.

Decarbonisation requires a transformation of the economic system to one which runs on an energy mix continuously reducing and offsetting carbon release (Bernstein and Hoffmann, 2018). Decarbonisation efforts have seen garment stakeholders commit to 30% emission reductions by 2030 through the Fashion Industry Charter for Climate Action. Dyeing, finishing and textile waste are energy-intensive activities carried out in garment manufacturing facilities across Asia and the electricity supply to these producing markets is carbon-intensive (Sharpe et al., 2022). The demand for energy in the ASEAN region has steadily been rising, and such needs have been met with the increasing use of fossil fuels, only 20% of which comes from renewable sources (EU-ASEAN Business Council, 2023). Therefore, global brands are increasingly pressuring producing countries to transition towards renewable energy sources. Current efforts to decarbonise the industry are insufficient to meet sustainability goals. With 70% of the garment industry's emissions coming from upstream activities, there needs to be a transformation of the manufacturing and production processes (Berg et al., 2020). The potential of decarbonising manufacturing in Asia is restricted by the high investment costs associated with reducing emissions during the manufacturing stages (Berg et al., 2020). The Ministry of Economy and Finance Cambodia, when asked about transitions to clean energy use in the garment sector raised financial concerns, "We have to take a cautious approach [to electricity] because if we force investment in clean energy too soon, which takes up a huge chunk of investment, I'm not sure if the factories can afford it in the short term" (Ministry of Economy and Finance, Phnom Penh, 18/01/2023). The EU-ASEAN Business Council (2023) highlights the challenges to decarbonisation in ASEAN specifically, these include: a shortage of financing for the transition to renewables, poor policy environments for fostering the growth of renewable energy use, the subsidisation of fossil fuels across the region, lack of infrastructure for increased demand for renewables and finally limited capacity to support communities impacted by energy transformations.

At the consumer level, and throughout downstream processes, there is a growing awareness of the environmental impacts of buying habits and therefore, the 'circular economy' (CE) has become an essential phenomenon for global fashion (Gazzola et al., 2020). The CE has gained traction among governments and policymakers, particularly in the EU for its solution to global linear economic flows (Korhonen et al., 2018b). The CE aims to transform production and consumption and promote sustainable development through a regenerative system whereby the closed loop reduces resource wastage and provides environmental and economic benefits (Koszewska, 2018). Moran et al. (2021) argue that the entire CE framework must be implemented to contribute to the reduction of carbon emissions and that currently limited transparency encourages greenwashing for many of the processes within the framework. The CE aims to promote higher quality products designed to last longer and be repaired and reused, which Sharpe (2017) argues can encourage near-shoring garment production closer to the consumer. The circular economy in garments aims to contribute to carbon reduction and the reuse of garments can reduce their footprint by 73% (Material Economics, 2018). This model passes on environmental mitigation strategies to the consumer as well as industry stakeholders. However, such processes can be Global North-centric and therefore it is essential to evaluate how such strategies may impact the work of those existing within linear, fast-fashion production structures. The following section addresses this issue, bringing forward the tension between decarbonisation policy and practices and the ability to secure decent work in Asia's garment sector.

Tensions for the Future of Work

The ability to act on international pressures for decarbonisation is limited by complicated power dynamics within garment value chains. Furthermore, the global garment industry has transformed around lead firms' ability to gain from limited labour and environmental regulation (Parsons et al., 2022), permitting the fast fashion industry to create a zero-sum game for both labour and the environment. This section aims to highlight the tensions between decarbonisation demands and a decent future of work for garment workers in Asia. The Western consumer's concern for the environmental impact of fashion encourages a focus on reducing the carbon footprint of garments in marketing and consequently can distort consumer perceptions around sustainability (Niinimäki, 2015). There exists a tension between consumer demands, consumer ethics and industrial reality. Furthermore, terms such as 'sustainability' in the fashion industry have become commonplace in marketing and encouraged the rise of greenwashing. The vague definition of sustainability, allows for the hiding of labour practices under the assumption that these terms reflect improvements both environmentally and socially. Such heavy focus on decarbonisation shifts the focus of sustainability to environmental impact, however, it is essential to include the garment worker in this narrative who often feel the pressure of tensions in the garment industry. Solidarity Centre Cambodia identified the need to look at the impact of climate change and environmental action in garment manufacturing on workers in the present but also in the future. This position encourages thinking about the social impact of decarbonisation efforts through the lens of the worker's experience on the factory floor,

> On the one hand our you know union members are being very negatively affected by the climate crisis in the present, so we want to ameliorate that. But we also need to think about, in the future how does this get better and if a demand comes saying 'shut down all your polluting factories', what's our position and how do we make sure that that doesn't negatively impact workers and cause mass and employment and lower wages.
>
> (Solidarity Centre, Phnom Penh, 17/01/23)

The factory floor is an ideal space to analyse tensions between future decent work and decarbonisation as it is the site in which vulnerable labourers, particularly women, experience the impacts of wider industry trends. Access to decent work is essential for the sustainability of women's participation in formal employment in the future however, in the context of the factory, there exists an imbalance between climate mitigation and the mitigation of pressures felt by labourers (Parsons et al., 2022). Barriers to decent work in existing experiences of garment labour are a product of the nature of the global garment value chain. Decisions by brands to locate production in the Global South whereby precarious working conditions, low-cost labour and constrained labour regulations have been normalised, exacerbate the obstacles to securing decent work for labourers in GVCs. There is an awareness within the literature on GVCs of the existing obstacles to decent work in the Global South and the complacency in remedying this experience for workers in the present (Hasle and Vang, 2021). Looking to the future of work we risk assuming that the development of new technologies designed with 'sustainability' in mind will also secure decent work across the supply chain. ILO. (2019) argue that emerging technologies designed to reduce environmental impact and improve efficiency and quality in manufacturing will create new forms of decent work deficits without resolving existing challenges.

Chasing low-cost labour in the garment sector has been key to ensuring high-profit margins; however, this has allowed for the most energy-intensive activities to take place in countries with weaker social and environmental industry standards, complicating the current push for decarbonisation. While Cantore et al. (2016) argue that there is no need for a trade-off between economic growth and decarbonisation, the investment in energy-efficient technologies can be a concern for garment-producing countries experiencing energy insecurity. Without increasing the price of exported garments, manufacturers in the Global South are not incentivised to invest in renewable alternatives, particularly in countries still concerned with energy security. Decarbonisation cannot be a priority for markets such as Bangladesh without first assuring rapid industrial growth, however, this growth continues to be stunted by the garment value chain's ability always to seek out cheaper alternatives (Debnath and Mourshed, 2022). Cantore et al. (2016) state that investing in energy-efficient technologies can promote productivity however, it is important to assess what this means for the experience of the labour force and how the benefits of these investments are felt globally.

Benefits associated with strategies designed to reduce environmental impact and improve social sustainability are often unequally distributed (Repp et al., 2021). For example, Geissdoerfer et al. (2017) argue that CE is often used interchangeably with 'sustainability' and that in research, authors tend to emphasise environmental elements over the economic and social dimensions of CE thinking. The circular economy has been promoted as a means of reducing the carbon footprint of garments, however, in a 2017 study, only 20% of publications on the CE promoted social sustainability as one of the core targets of the framework (Kirchherr et al., 2017). Muchangos (2022) argues that there is limited data on the impact of CE in the Global South, particularly due to key elements of the CE concept being more in line with production and consumption experiences in the Global North. Furthermore, the success of a true CE requires access to each step of the CE process. H&M, when asked about their approach to circularity in their production locations recognised that while some exporting countries in the Global South have potential for circularity, others lack key infrastructure,

> A purely circular garment space would be the growing or the creating of the raw material processing into yarn, processing the fabric, cutting trim, then either waste products from cut and trim and post-consumer waste going back into that process. In the Vietnamese context that is already achievable… every step of that process can be done domestically. Whereas the challenge in Cambodia is that, none of that happens… There's no tier 3 yarn production and there's no recycling facilities, either to turn pre and post-consumer waste back into yarn so it's impossible today to be circular in Cambodia.
>
> (H&M, 03/02/2023)

Repp et al. (2021) suggest that the CE framework needs to consider the impact on employment that a transition towards circular fashion may have particularly in the Global South. The success of a CE depends upon the resources The CE ideal is the creation of new jobs in addition to reducing emissions, however, hesitation to react to CE will limit the benefits for the labour force (The Ellen MacArthur Foundation, 2013; Larsson and Teigland, 2019). While a transition to the CE may create jobs in a Global North context, in the form of garment recycling and re-use due to the proximity to the consumer (Repp et al., 2021), Ahmed et al. (2022) speculate that in countries such as Bangladesh, CE implementation could reduce the workforce. As a consequence, the emphasis on the re-use of garment products suggests a decrease in employment, therefore an increase in job insecurity, in garment manufacturing countries in the Global South (Ahmed et al., 2022).

The rise of 'fast fashion' has contributed to the restructuring of garment manufacturing in which supply chains are increasingly obscured and therefore mitigating environmental impact becomes ever more challenging. The informal sector makes up a significant proportion of garment production in Asia and has consequences for both climate strategies and efforts to improve working conditions. The emphasis on automation and digitalisation in the future of garment work threatens to reshape the global garment industry. As transitions towards automated production decrease in cost, labour-intensive garment producers in Asia are at risk of losing out on their existing competitive advantage. ILO (2019) suggest that such competition is likely to increase the use of subcontracting factories as a means of facing pressures on wages and efficiency. The availability of work in subcontracting factories however makes it an attractive choice for garment workers despite the lack of monitoring and compliance. One worker commented on her experience working in a subcontracting factory,

> For non-standard factories, the working process is terrible. The workers are forced to work to reach the target however, bonus is rarely provided. I can earn more money in non-standard factory than that of big factories but it is hard to work in small factory.
>
> (Garment worker, Kandal, 02/11/22)

The complexity of garment value chains is already a barrier to accurate sustainability monitoring. Due to the prevalence of subcontracting factories across the Asian garment industry, formal factories are competing not only regionally but also internally against informal factories. In these cases, precarious forms of work are integrated into the value chain (Salmivaara, 2021). Parsons (2023) states that despite decarbonisation efforts and higher environmental and labour standard requirements, there exists a high risk that garments are subcontracted to another factory which may not follow the same level of compliance. Sweet (2022) argues that the use of informal factories harms environmental mitigation efforts due to the lack of transparency and therefore inability to trace critical environmental and social issues within the supply chain. A representative for a trade union in Cambodia commented on the role of subcontracting factories in the future, acknowledging the risks of non-compliance,

> I think the labour force will move towards subcontracting factories and I think the governemnt should look into regulating that as well, because the unregistered subcontractors don't have a legal contractual link to the buyers and it is one way to avoid responsibility.
>
> (Union representative, Phnom Penh, 14/12/22)

Sweet implies that ignoring the prominence of the informal sector in garment-producing countries could help firms avoid high upfront costs for more energy-efficient technologies (2022). This suggests that in markets where labour rights and working conditions are already called into question, a future of decent work falls in second place to price competitiveness (see Chapters 3 and 18), a trend visible across global value chains beyond just garments.

Conclusion

'Sustainability' encompasses a wide range of both environmental and social elements of industrial production. In order to effectively assess tensions between energy transitions and the future of work, this chapter has narrowed in on decarbonisation and its conflicts and interruptions with the experience of decent work for garment workers. This chapter has argued that pressures to decarbonise the garment industry are being felt in the employment experience of garment workers in the Global South, with investment requirements for a 'green' transition being felt on the factory floor by the industry's most vulnerable workers. Parsons et al. (2022) state that workers' voices have been silenced at the intersection of climate change and working conditions, and this has been exacerbated by efforts to decarbonise the industry.

ILO (2019, p. 18) argue that a decent future of work for garment workers is a 'distant aspiration' despite the growing concern for labour rights in garments, due to the competitive nature of GVCs and the continuation of manufacturing in the Global South. Furthermore, while there has been growing concern for sustainability, the demand for decarbonisation has shifted the global garment industry's attention towards environmental strategies. This is not to say that the social impacts of garment manufacturing have been neglected, but the consequences for the future of work as a result of decarbonisation efforts remain under-explored. Garment workers in Asia sit within complex, hidden value chains and often feel the pressures on the sector at an individual level. Tensions between producers and consumers are shaping this insecure future of work for garment workers in Asia. Pressure for a cleaner garment industry, whilst maintaining price competitiveness, is felt at the factory level and is made ever more challenging by the complex nature of the global garment value chain.

There is a lack of integration in research and policy on energy transitions and labour. Within the factory space decarbonisation and decent work are presented as oppositional phenomena but thinking forward they must be considered together. This chapter has narrowed in on the factory floor as a space whereby tensions between energy transition efforts and decent work are felt by those with limited power over the future of their work. For the labour force directly impacted by energy transition policies and strategies they remain invisible and therefore are often subject to indecent work. Chateau et al. (2018) find that low-skill workers are more likely to feel the effects of decarbonisation policies, including through changes in wages. In the context of Asian garment manufacturing, this chapter has argued that pressures for decarbonisation combined with high costs of implementing green technologies negatively impact employment and decent work for garment workers by encouraging precarious employment. If the drive for decarbonisation and decent work in the global garment industry continues to be approached as separate goals, garment workers in Asia will continue to feel the most damaging effects of this zero-sum game. The future of work in garment manufacturing remains uncertain for factory workers in Asia. However, as the future of work is continuously shaped around emerging technologies designed to reduce environmental impact, the social consequences of such efforts must be brought up to equal importance. Without considering the new pressures that will be felt by an already invisible workforce across precarious employment structures in Asia, the future of work for such garment labourers in 'green' garment manufacturing remains insecure and indecent.

References

Ahmed, Z., Mahmud, S. and Acet, H. (2022) 'Circular economy model for developing countries: Evidence from Bangladesh', *Heliyon*, 8(9), p. e09530.

Ahmad, S., Miskon, S., Alabdan, R. and Tlili, I. (2020) 'Towards sustainable textile and apparel industry: Exploring the role of business intelligence systems in the era of industry 4.0', *Sustainability*, 12(7), p. 2632.

Alamgir, F. and Banerjee, S.B. (2019) 'Contested compliance regimes in global production networks: Insights from the Bangladesh garment industry', *Human Relations*, 72(2), pp. 272–297.

Berg, A. Granskog, A., Lee, L. and Magnus, K.-H. (2020) *Fashion on climate—How the fashion industry can urgently act to reduce its greenhouse gas emissions*. New York: McKinsey & Company. Available at: https://www.mckinsey.com/industries/retail/our-insights/fashion-on-climate

Bernstein, S. and Hoffman, M. (2018) Decarbonisation: The Politics of Transformation, in: Jordan, A., Huitema, D., van Asselt, H. and Forster, J. (eds.) *Governing Climate Change: Polycentricity in Action?* Cambridge: Cambridge University Press, pp. 248–265.

Berry, F., Sharpe, S. and Martinez Fernandez, M.C. (2022) *Greening the sector: Environmental initiatives and tools in the garment sector in Asia.* Geneva: ILO. Available at: https://doi.org/10.54394/JRAN5992.

Calabrese, L. and Balchin, N. (2022) 'Foreign investment and upgrading in the garment sector in Africa and Asia', *Global Policy*, 13, pp. 34–44.

Cantore, N., Calì, M. and Velde, D.W. te (2016) 'Does energy efficiency improve technological change and economic growth in developing countries?', *Energy Policy*, 92, pp. 279–285. Available at: https://doi.org/10.1016/j.enpol.2016.01.040.

Chang, J.-H., Rynhart, G. and Huynh, P. (2016) *ASEAN in transformation: Textiles, clothing and footwear: Refashioning the future.* ILO: Geneva.

Chateau, J., Bibas, R. and Lanzi, E. (2018) 'Impacts of green growth policies on labour markets and wage income distribution: A general equilibrium application to climate and energy policies'. OECD Environment Working Paper 137, 21 November 2018. https://doi.org/10.1787/ea3696f4-en

Deben, L., McLachlan, C., Perry, P., Larkin, A., Broderick, J., Blakey, J., Paterson, M., Taylor, R., Barnes, M., Gough, C., Welfle, A., Bridle, S., Hoolohan, C., Browne, A. L., Bouzarovski, S. and Pincetl, S. (2020) 'On Net Zero: Analysis and ideas on Net Zero, curated by Policy@ Manchester'. Manchester: policy@manchester. Available at: https://pure.manchester.ac.uk/ws/portalfiles/portal/176491999/uom_on_net_zero.pdf

Debnath, K.B. and Mourshed, M. (2022) 'Why is Bangladesh's electricity generation heading towards a GHG emissions-intensive future?', *Carbon Management*, 13(1), pp. 216–237. Available at: https://doi.org/10.1080/17583004.2022.2068454.

Dedeoğlu, S. (2010) 'Visible hands–invisible women: Garment production in Turkey', *Feminist Economics*, 16(4), pp. 1–32.

Dyke, J., Watson, R. and Knorr, W. (2021) 'Climate scientists: Concept of net zero is a dangerous trap', *The Conversation*, 22 April 2021. Available at: https://theconversation.com/climate-scientists-concept-of-net-zero-is-a-dangerous-trap-157368 (Accessed: 21 September 2023).

ILO. (2019) *The future of work in textiles, clothing, leather and footwear.* ILO Working Paper 326, Geneva: ILO.

ILO (2022) 'Employment, wages and productivity trends in the Asian garment sector: data and policy insights for the future of work'.Available at: https://www.ilo.org/publications/employment-wages-and-productivity-asian-garment-sector-taking-stock-recent

EU-ASEAN Business Council (2023) Energy Transition in ASEAN, April 2023. Available at: https://www.eu-asean.eu/wp-content/uploads/2023/04/Energy-Transition-in-ASEAN-2023_5-April-2023.pdf

Gazzola, P. et al. (2020) 'Trends in the fashion industry. The perception of sustainability and circular economy: A gender/generation quantitative approach', *Sustainability*, 12(7), p. 2809.

Geissdoerfer, M., Savaget, P., Bocken, N.M.P. and Hultink, E.J. (2017) 'The circular economy–A new sustainability paradigm?', *Journal of Cleaner Production*, 143, pp. 757–768.

Goto, K. (2011) 'Competitiveness and decent work in Global Value Chains: Substitutionary or complementary?', *Development in Practice*, 21(7), pp. 943–958.

Group for the Environment, Renewable Energy and Solidarity (Geres) (2019) Sustainable Steam for Cambodian Garment Factories, Cambodia: Geres. Available at: https://www.geres.eu/wp-content/uploads/2019/10/Brochure_Garment_EN-1.pdf

Hafner, S., Speich, M., Bischofberger, P. and Ulli-Beer, S. (2022) 'Governing industry decarbonisation: Policy implications from a firm perspective', *Journal of Cleaner Production*, 375, p. 133884.

Hasle, P. and Vang, J. (2021) 'Designing better interventions: Insights from research on decent work', *Journal of Supply Chain Management*, 57(2), pp. 58–70.

Hildingsson, R., Kronsell, A. and Khan, J. (2019) 'The green state and industrial decarbonisation', *Environmental Politics*, 28(5), pp. 909–928. Available at: https://doi.org/10.1080/09644016.2018.1488484.

Howcroft, D. and Rubery, J. (2019) '"Bias in, Bias out": Gender equality and the future of work debate', *Labour & Industry: A Journal of the Social and Economic Relations of Work*, 29(2), pp. 213–227. Available at: https://doi.org/10.1080/10301763.2019.1619986.

Huynh, P. (2015) *Employment, wages and working conditions in Asia's garment sector: Finding new drivers of competitiveness.* ILO.

ILO (2017) *Decent work and the 2030 agenda for sustainable development.* Geneva: ILO.

Jamali, D., Lund-Thomsen, P. and Khara, N. (2017) 'CSR institutionalized myths in developing countries: An imminent threat of selective decoupling', *Business & Society*, 56(3), pp. 454–486.

Kirchherr, J., Reike, D. and Hekkert, M. (2017) 'Conceptualizing the circular economy: An analysis of 114 definitions', *Resources, Conservation and Recycling*, 127, pp. 221–232.

Korhonen, J., Honkasalo, A. and Seppälä, J. (2018a) 'Circular economy: The concept and its limitations', *Ecological Economics*, 143, pp. 37–46.

Korhonen, J., Nuur, C., Feldmann, A. and Birkie, SE. (2018b) 'Circular economy as an essentially contested concept,' *Journal of Cleaner Production*, 175, pp. 544–552. https://doi.org/10.1016/j.jclepro.2017.12.111

Koszewska, M. (2018) 'Circular economy—Challenges for the textile and clothing industry', *Autex Research Journal*, 18(4), pp. 337–347.

Material Economics (2018) The Circular Economy: A Powerful Force for Climate Mitigation, Stockholm: Sverige AB.Available at: https://www.sitra.fi/app/uploads/2018/05/material-economics-circular-economy.pdf

Larsson, A., and Teigland, R. (eds.) *The Digital Transformation of Labor: Automation, the Gig Economy and Welfare*, Routledge: Abingdon.

Licata, M. and Kemp, W. (2020). *The Future of Work in Fashion*, UN Today, 5 July 2020. Available at: https://untoday.org/the-future-of-work-in-fashion/

López, T. Riedler T, Köhnen, H. and Fütterer, M. (2022) 'Digital value chain restructuring and labour process transformations in the fast-fashion sector: Evidence from the value chains of Zara & H&M', *Global Networks*, 22(4), pp. 684–700. Available at: https://doi.org/10.1111/glob.12353.

MacArthur, E. (2013) 'Towards the circular economy', *Journal of Industrial Ecology*, 2(1), pp. 23–44.

Montt, G., Fraga, F. and Harsdorff, M. (2018) 'The future of work in a changing natural environment: Climate change, degradation and sustainability', Research Paper 4, 30 August 2018, *ILO Future of Work Research Paper Series,* Geneva: International Labour Organization

Moran, C.A., Eichelmann, E. and Buggy, C.J. (2021) 'The challenge of "Depeche Mode" in the fashion industry–Does the industry have the capacity to become sustainable through circular economic principles, a scoping review', *Sustainable Environment*, 7(1), p. 1975916.

Muchangos, L.S. dos (2022) 'Mapping the circular economy concept and the Global South', *Circular Economy and Sustainability*, 2(1), pp. 71–90.

Niinimäki, K. (2015) 'Ethical foundations in sustainable fashion', *Textiles and Clothing Sustainability*, 1(1), pp. 1–11.

Parsons, L., Lawreniuk, S., Sok, S. and Buckley, J. (2022) 'Hot trends: How the global garment industry shapes climate change vulnerability in Cambodia', *Royal Holloway, University of London and University of Nottingham.* Available at: https://www.solidaritycenter.org/wp-content/uploads/2022/07/Hot-Trends-Report.pdf

Repp, L., Hekkert, M. and Kirchherr, J. (2021) 'Circular economy-induced global employment shifts in apparel value chains: Job reduction in apparel production activities, job growth in reuse and recycling activities', *Resources, Conservation and Recycling*, 171, p. 105621.

Salmivaara, A. (2021) 'Precarious work and insecure lives. De facto informalization in Cambodia's garment factories', *Journal of Labor and Society*, 24(1), pp. 44–75.

Schlogl, L., Weiss, E. and Prainsack, B. (2021) 'Constructing the "Future of Work": An analysis of the policy discourse', *New Technology, Work and Employment*, 36(3), pp. 307–326. Available at: https://doi.org/10.1111/ntwe.12202.

Sharpe, S. (2017) 'Environmental scoping study decent work in the garment sector supply chains in Asia', Geneva: ILO

Sharpe, S., Dominish, E. and Fernandez, M.C.M. (2022) 'Taking climate action: Measuring carbon emissions in the garment sector in Asia', *ILO Working Paper-53*, Geneva: ILO, p. 32.

Sweet, S. (2022) 'Exploring the environmental and social impact of informal market practices in the apparel industry', in Bali Swain, R. and Kambhampati, U. (eds.), *The informal sector and the environment* London: Routledge, pp. 64–80. Available at: https://doi.org/10.4324/9781003223856-4.

Vashisht, P. and Rani, N. (2020) 'Automation and the future of garment sector jobs in India', *The Indian Journal of Labour Economics*, 63(2), pp. 225–246.

Recommendations for Further Reading

Howson, P., Astuti, R., Hensengerth, O. and Kindon, S. (2022, June). *Asia-Pacific ClimateScapes: Exploring opportunities, challenges and trade-offs toward just transitions for decarbonisation.* British Academy

Policy Report, June 2022. Available at: https://www.thebritishacademy.ac.uk/documents/4133/BA1098_JT_AP_Pete_Howson_-_Proof_FINAL_-_June_2022.pdf

Kreinin, H. and Aigner, E. (2022). 'From "Decent work and economic growth" to "Sustainable work and economic degrowth": A new framework for SDG 8', *Empirica*, 49(2), pp. 281–311.

Montt, G., Fraga, F. and Harsdorff, M. (2018) *The future of work in a changing natural environment: Climate change, degradation and sustainability*. ILO Future of Work Research Paper Series, Geneva: ILO

Parsons, L. (2023) *Carbon Colonialism. How rich countries export climate breakdown.* Manchester: Manchester University Press

Parsons, L., Lawreniuk, S., Sok, S. and Buckley, J. (2022) Hot trends: *How the global garment industry shapes climate change vulnerability in Cambodia. Royal Holloway*, University of London and University of Nottingham.

31

THERMAL FUTURES OF WORK

Intertwined Economic and Environmental Trajectories under Climate Change

Laurie Parsons

Thermal Futures of Work

In the summer of 2022, Europe was in the grip of a record-breaking heatwave. Everybody who could did what they were able to avoid it, seeking cool breezes, remaining at home, or watching the sweltering streets from the comfort of an air-conditioned office. But some, like José Antonio González, didn't have those options. As others were seeking shade in the glowering heat of the afternoon, he was starting his shift as a street-sweeper in Madrid. The temperature was a dangerous 104°F, but after a long time without a job, González couldn't afford to pass up a one-month summer contract to sweep the city, where he lived in a working-class neighbourhood. It was a decision that would prove fatal. Three hours after beginning his shift, the 60-year-old collapsed with heat stroke and was found lying in the street he was cleaning and died soon after arriving in hospital (Associated Press News, July 22nd, 2022).

Gonzalez's is a story that brings home a tragic reality of the climate crisis: heat kills. And under climate change it is doing so with ever greater frequency and intensity. Heat-related deaths worldwide increased by 74% between 1990 and 2016 (Hill and Babin, 2021), with the most extreme single heatwaves claiming tens of thousands of lives and orders of magnitude more requiring medical treatment or hospitalisation (Mitchell, 2021). Major heatwaves, especially in urban centres, have been described as 'the greatest threat climate change poses to human health' (Hutyra, 2022: 1). Yet exceptional events like this belie a more mundane, but deadlier, future. Without a major shift in course, more than three quarters of humanity will face the threat of dying from extreme heat by 2100 (Leahy, 2022). Moreover, 'a hotter planet will expose divides in the world of work' (O'Connor, 2022).

This is a vital, but counterintuitive point, because it doesn't always tally with the way that we think about heat. The temperature is in general a number attributed to an area: a figure we may see in a weather forecast for an entire city, or even a country. At its most local we may get a sense of temperature from a street thermometer. Yet despite these shifts in scale, heat tends to be viewed fundamentally as a quality of the atmosphere, of the very air around us and its energy. This perspective is valid, but inadequate. Just imagine the difference in how that same thermometer reading *feels*, when you are undertaking heavy, physical work, versus observing it from a café table. Imagine, similarly, how it *feels* when peering at the same thermometer through the window of an

DOI: 10.4324/9781003327561-42

unventilated room. In the latter case, it might well seem unbearable. Indeed, if you were unable to get up and open the window or the door, then it might well *be* unbearable. A lack of ventilation can result in serious health problems in high temperatures, especially when combined with heavy work, making the capacity to exercise agency over how your body interacts with its environment a crucial dimension of heat stress. If you were compelled, perhaps as a result of the work you were undertaking, to remain in context that accentuated, rather than relieved, the external temperature, then your personal health risk is many times higher. And yet outside, the 'headline' figure of the temperature remains the same.

All of which alludes to a vital insight around the human embodiment of heat: the external temperature is only one component of its impact on human bodies. Indeed, people rarely experience their environment in a direct sense at all. If they did, then the majority of the world would be uninhabitable because our bodies are able to function only in such a narrow thermal band. To avoid serious illness, our body temperature needs in a general sense to remain between 36.5°C and 37.1°C when we are not in motion, which – depending on humidity – means an air temperature of 27°C or a water temperature of 33°C (Science Norway, 2016). Our ability to survive in any latitude more than 30° North or South – an area with billions of human inhabitants – is thus inherently artificial. We can survive it only because of the ways in which we re-craft the environment around us to make it liveable. This can mean measures as simple as clothing or a roof, but it also means heating, cooling and insulation, all of which help to keep the skin beneath our jumpers, or underneath our parasols, as close as possible to the narrow tropical band in which we can survive.

Working practices are similarly adapted to our environment. An office meeting held outside in a Northern European January would, after all, be unlikely to be productive. Yet the provisions and protections which shape the world of work are not evenly distributed. Manual workers, generally those lower in the socioeconomic strata of a given context, tend to face a greater degree of exposure to the elements – whether in the form of hot or cold – than their better off counterparts. The best off in society face very little thermal discomfort, even when they reside in environments that are geographically inhospitable to humans without external intervention. Those who face the greatest degree of exposure to excess heat or cold, by contrast, are invariably the worst off: those with the least capacity to manage their working conditions and often the greatest propensity to longer-term health problems which make them more vulnerable to its effects.

The story of José Antonio González, with which this chapter opens, encapsulates this relationship. A vulnerable older worker, taking on low paid and unhealthy work due to long-term poverty: his is a story characteristic of the dangers of heat stress the world over. Those who have economic power have agency over their environment, whereas those who do not are at its mercy. As this tragic case and a great many more like it exemplify, the climate is not the great leveller. On the contrary, each person's experience of their environment has a great deal to do with their position in society and – on a basic level – the amount of money they possess.

This is not altogether unfamiliar. On the contrary, it is a point that the field of climate justice has engaged with extensively in recent years, both in a general sense and in the specific field of thermal inequity (Dialesandro et al., 2021; Mitchell and Chakraborty, 2015). Yet it is a point whose implications have yet to be fully fleshed out. Recognising that the human dangers of the climate are at least as much about social inequities as environmental ones means recognising that the human impacts of climate change will be underpinned as much by economic trajectories as climatic ones. We are facing, in other words, a world defined not only by rising temperatures, but by thermal futures of work.

Bridging the Environment-Economic Nexus

The human experience of the climate is shaped both by the environment we face and our capacity to alleviate it. This seems, in principle, like an intuitive statement, at least to anybody who has ever held an umbrella or put on a coat. Yet interpreting it along future trajectories is far more challenging. Addressing the intertwined dynamism of economic and environmental futures presents a number of obstacles, in both policy and scientific terms. It is easy enough to point to the outlier cases, such as Mr González, who appear to exemplify the nexus so clearly, yet attempting to scale this up to an entire population is fraught with difficulty. Even measuring the problem is hard, tackling it harder still.

The health threat of a hotter world necessitates policy action 'at every level of political and social life' (Hill and Babin, 2021: 1). Yet effective governance remains stymied by scientific limitations. Even as climate change has risen to the top of the global policy agenda, scholarship on the human impacts of heat remains an emerging field. To date, there has been no large-scale, systematic effort by climatologists to quantify the heat-related human health impacts of climate change (Vicedo-Cabrera et al., 2021), with only a handful of studies having considered the problem in depth (Mitchell, 2021). Most studies on the human impact of climate change have instead concentrated on the effects of extreme weather events like floods and typhoons, especially on rural communities, rather than increases in heat (Zander et al., 2018) in large part due to the complexity of measuring it (Kunz-Plapp et al., 2016). Thus, despite being one of the world's major global challenges it is a topic impeded by 'known barriers' centred on 'limitations in the availability of the relevant data and in their spatial and temporal resolution' (Gasparrini et al., 2022: 557).

In facing this challenge, bridges are urgently needed to connect thermal vulnerability science and people's experiences 'in a way that integrates multiple dimensions of vulnerability' (Hamstead et al., 2020: 219). This shift in thinking is 'essential' (Levi et al., 2018: 467), but requires a new approach to the study of heat, away from a geographically bounded, large-scale approach, towards an appreciation that 'it is not extreme heat that kills, but weak social safety systems and inequality' (Wang, 2021: 1).

Generating data on the embodied experience of heat is, however, rather easier said than done. For a start, the very complexity of the topic means that there are a great many ways to approach it. Even within a given house – or room – the temperature may vary widely, making the selection of an appropriate scale both challenging and somewhat subjective. Is the temperature of a workplace dangerous if one part of it is too hot, or the workplace as a whole? How about exposure to that heat? Does it matter how much time people spend there, at what time of day, or year? In reality the nature of exposure to excess heat depends on a great many things, from working conditions to built infrastructure to clothing to local environmental conditions, but only a few of these are linked to the climate and fewer still are shared by everybody in any given place.

Heat exposure – a person's physical risk from excess heat – is not just a question of temperature. Like cold exposure, it is socially produced: the result of economic, not behavioural inequalities. Indeed, to fully understand the landscape of risk from heat exposure, we have to look at its opposite. Risk to health from cold temperatures is, for now, far more obviously correlated to wealth in global Northern contexts. And this is a relationship we are familiar with. For those without the luxury of central heating, the experience of winter is visceral. People living in cold houses explain that 'when it's cold, it feels like the whole house has turned into a big block of ice. It feels like someone is rubbing ice on my nose' (BBC, 2016). This is a world away from the temperate world that most people in the UK inhabit; even on the coldest days, transitioning from warm house to warm car, to warm office and back means that the better off only experience cold, as it were, at a distance. It is a moment of frost on the skin, numb fingers on a walk back from the shops. The true, numbing, clawing, penetrating face of cold remains unknown. The increased risk of heart attacks and strokes, the respiratory illnesses, the poor diet due to 'heat or eat' choices, the impact on mental health issues, and the worsening of existing conditions are all absent. And yet outside the temperature is the same.

In other parts of the world, these same relationships are apparent with heat: an increasingly deadly force around the world. The health impacts of prolonged heat exposure range from acute impacts such as heatstroke, to less visible, chronic disease vulnerability, especially when high temperatures meet high humidity and even more so when combined with heavy work (Levi et al., 2018). However, as research is crucially beginning to emphasise, this risk is unevenly spread. Those who are relatively socially disadvantaged are likely to find themselves 'disproportionately affected by temperature extremes' (Hansen et al., 2013: 2), with ethnic and political disadvantages key focal points of negative heat impacts.

How, then, to make sense of this scientifically? On a basic level, measuring body temperature itself, rather than ambient temperature is an effective solution. A person's core temperature is, in effect, an aggregate of all the factors that shape exposure to heat stress; the end result of society, environment and climate all working in combination. Yet even measuring this is fraught with difficulty. The most accurate forms of measurement, swallowed temperature capsules, produce high quality data, but last only 24 hours. The next best thing, in-ear thermometer readings administered by medical professionals give an accurate reading, but require a persistent observational presence in the workplace, as well as periodic halting to the very workplace activities which contribute to elevated core temperatures in the first place. Newly developed body-worn core temperature measurement devices are an important addition to this methodological stable, but lack some of the accuracy of their alternatives.

And this is before we even begin to consider the far greater methodological conundrum facing researchers of human heat stress: acclimation, or getting used to, heat stress. The human body is adaptive and resilient. Workers in hazardous conditions are in many cases able to become used to conditions that would be dangerous to others (Malgoyre et al., 2020). Take brick workers in the global South, for example, who spend much of their working days in dangerously hot conditions, due to the combination of heavy work, high ambient temperatures and brick kilns that can reach up to 1,500° centigrade during firing. If brick workers' bodies responded to their working conditions in the same way as yours or mine, then very few bricks would end up being made (Hajizadeh et al., 2016).

Recent data from Cambodia shows that in some kilns brick workers spend over, 15% of their working day with a core body temperature elevated above 38°C, the generally agreed safe threshold (Parsons and Ly, 2020). In another brick kiln, workers spent on average 2% of their working hours with a core temperature over 39°C: clinically defined as a high fever. In one case, a worker spent 7% of their working hours – almost an hour and a half per day for a week – with core temperature over 40°C: clinical heat stroke, usually requiring immediate hospitalisation. Yet he did not go to hospital, immediately or otherwise. He continued to work and got up the next day to it all again (Parsons and Ly, 2023).

Extraordinary as this might sound it is in fact typical of the industry, where workers with hugely elevated core temperatures have been shown to exhibit far fewer of the immediate symptoms of heat stress than would be expected amongst the general population (Hajizadeh et al., 2016). And it isn't just the brick industry. Workers in agriculture (El Khayet et al., 2022) and construction (Acharya et al., 2018), many of whom work outdoors in high temperatures for long periods, by necessity become used to extremely high levels of heat stress on a daily basis. Even indoor work, such as the garment industry, which employs over 70 million people – mostly young women – worldwide, is beginning to be recognised as a major source of heat stress (see Chapter 30).

Workers interviewed as part of a recent study of Cambodia reported that 'before, the temperature was only 36 degrees Celsius. Nowadays, the weather is hotter than before. So, it affects our health. We catch a cold and feel sick most of the time' (Peakhadey, union representative in a Phnom Penh factory, cited in Parsons et al., 2022). Moreover, the impact of this extreme heat has a tangible and sometimes dramatic impact on worker health. Workers complain that 'the weather has been irregular recently. It has changed from hot to cold. I always catch a cold and have a cough nowadays. Most of the factory workers have the same issues' (Bora, union representative in a Kandal factory, cited in Parsons et al., 2022). As another worker expanded:

> [The temperature] has changed so much. It seems like we cannot accept this change…Sometimes, [workers] pass out. A garment worker passed out since it was sizzling, and then they had a convulsion.
>
> (Dara, union representative at a Kandal factory, cited in Parsons et al., 2022)

Though hugely important from the perspective of supply chain ethics, however, acute incidents of heat stress such as fainting and convulsions are not the norm. Despite the searing temperatures, most garment workers are nonetheless able to endure the heat stress they face and to persist with their work, at least in the short term. Faced with what initially seems unbearable, workers can become used to conditions to the extent that they continue to work relatively effectively.

This does not however mean that acclimated workers are unaffected by the conditions in which they work. On the contrary, it means instead that the effects of heat stress become more difficult to observe. Long-term exposure to high temperatures is linked to a variety of chronic conditions, from increased risk of heart attacks to strokes, to breathing problems and even sudden death. Indeed, in the working population the increased mortality risk is only 'a small part of the health impact' (Levi et al., 2018: 174). Much of the impact of workplace heat stress is long term, leaving 'little overtly observable physical damage' (Hamstead, 2020: 219). Exhaustion, reduced productivity, increased rates of disease, and chronic kidney disease are postulated in small-scale studies (Levi et al., 2018), but the implications of climate change for these prevalences are unclear (Vicedo-Cabrera et al., 2018).

Climate Change and Work: Uncertain Futures, Uncertain Tools

As temperatures both rise and become less predictable under climate change, the likelihood of health impacts from extreme temperatures is growing in every country worldwide. However, this is not an even trajectory. Exposure to both heat and cold is socioeconomically determined, the result of meteorological and socioeconomic factors interplaying in complex ways at human scales (Mitchell, 2021). From fans to rest breaks to air conditioning, the ability to evade heat is a key indicator of privilege and deprivation in the workplace. This means that that the most thermally vulnerable tend to also be the most socially marginalised (Mitchell and Chakraborty, 2014). Yet social vulnerability does not happen by accident. It is the product of long economic and political histories, through which processes it is continually maintained. Racial, gendered, social and economic inequities create and sustain the landscape of thermal precarity.

Whilst this is broadly agreed, however, interpreting this landscape under climate change is challenging. Even defining an extreme heat event is 'highly context dependent and can be a technical and contested exercise' (Turek-Hankins et al., 2021: 2), meaning that those studies that have emerged so far have tended to be limited to specific case studies (Dialesandro et al., 2021). Consequently, key questions around the small-scale, 'granular' (Hamstead et al., 2020) geography of heat vulnerability remain largely unanswered. How do workplace inequalities structure heat exposure on a human level, for example? How do these thermal dynamics shift throughout the day, or through the year? How is the landscape of thermal vulnerability reflected in exploitative, or precarious labour? Rather than relying on existing datasets, questions of this order require a set of approaches tailored to the challenges that answering them poses.

And in taking a human's eye view, these new perspectives raise questions at a scale hitherto unexplored in the analysis of thermal inequity. In order to understand the multi-scalar, global, and historical structures that give rise to these vulnerabilities, it is increasingly recognised, for example, that 'the relationship between industrialisation, colonialism, slavery and global capital accumulation are not neatly linear but...deeply entwined' (Klinsky and Mavrogianni, 2020: 414). Yet only recently has this recognition been extended to the impacts of climate change. The half of the world that is 'highly vulnerable to climate change' (IPCC, 2022) – and thus 15 times more likely to die from a flood, drought or storm than those who are not – do not find themselves in danger by accident. Nor, moreover, is their vulnerability merely a function of geography, but of an unfavourable position in a global economy dominated by the world's major carbon emitters. Although 1.1°C of warming since 1960 has undoubtedly increased the likelihood of temperature extremes, both hot and cold, each year, the climate is far from the only variable in environmental exposure. Recognising the global construction of local climatic vulnerability means recognising the historical and political origins of the economic inequalities that underpin them.

This recognition is about far more than mere speculation. When the UN Secretary General Antonio Guterres warned that planet was 'on a highway to climate hell' at COP 27 (Wingate, 2022), he invoked a powerful image of rapidly rising temperatures. Yet it is also a misleading one. The human impacts of climate change are not progressing along a linear trajectory, but in complex and unpredictable ways, articulated by social inequalities at multiple scales. Nevertheless, Guterres's metaphor reveals a wider characteristic of planning for rising temperatures: that 'the thermal discourse tends to focus on physical rather than social elements of vulnerability', limiting the effectiveness of interventions to assuage it (Hamstead et al., 2020: 229). Rather than viewing thermal vulnerability as an atmospheric problem, there is an urgent need to address the social inequities that underpin its worst effects.

There is ample momentum on which to build in this regard. The UN's July 2022 resolution establishing the human right to a clean, healthy and sustainable environment has drawn global attention to the environmental challenges faced by vulnerable populations. Coming in the wake of the COVID-19 pandemic, this builds on a widespread momentum to 'build back greener', as expressed both in the UK's Climate Change Strategy 2021–2024 (HM Government, 2021), and the UN Environment Programme's new 2022 strategy report.

However, how climate policy might better address the inequalities that structure thermal vulnerability is an open and largely untested question. There exists an urgent and pressing need for 'a better comparative understanding of the drivers of thermal inequity at the local scale, the efficacy of potential policy remedies in different places, and whether there are common barriers' (Byrne et al., 2016: 14–15). However, key uncertainties remain. How might climate policy intervene in social and economic inequalities? How might it reimagine the workplace as more equal and environmentally secure? It is these, as much as questions of carbon mitigation, that will shape the human experience of climate breakdown in the coming decades.

Answering these questions requires extending our understanding of climate vulnerability beyond the physical geography of landscape, to include the social geography of work: a lens through which scholars have only recently begun to peer. This is challenging not only because it is new, but because the conceptual and practical tools we possess are poorly suited to the granularity of the questions we need now to ask. We know, for example, that the geography of wealth underpins the geography of climate impacts. Yet this remains a partial picture. A growing body of scientific evidence demonstrates that excessively high heat levels are resulting in excess morbidity and mortality in the general population' (Levi et al., 2018). Yet 'in the working population the increased mortality risk is only a small part of the health impact' (Levi et al., 2018: 174). Much of the impact of workplace heat stress is long term, leaving 'little overtly observable physical damage' (Hamstead, 2020: 219). Exhaustion, reduced productivity, increased rates of disease, and chronic kidney disease are postulated in small-scale studies (Levi et al., 2018), but the implications of climate change for these prevalences are unclear (Vicedo-Cabrera et al., 2018).

Compounding this challenge is the need to account for how 'social factors contribute to a landscape which defines the level of heat exposure for individuals' (Mitchell and Chakraborty, 2018: 808). Even within a given workplace, heat stress is variegated by social and demographic factors, meaning that 'while climate heat increases the risk for all labour exposed to heat stress, this risk is differentiated among workers' (Newman and Humphrys, 2019: 565). An employee's working arrangements, in particular their relative security or precarity, shape both a worker's direct experience of heat stress and their ability to manage or mitigate it. Those in more formal employment are far more likely to work in an environment designed to mitigate the impacts of heat and more likely to be able to take personal measures to achieve the same effect (Newman and Humphrys, 2019; ILO, 2019a). With the world currently on divergent trajectories of workplace formalisation (ILO, 2019b), this unequal manifestation of heat stress is a growing reality of future work and presents a major obstacle to decent work in the global workplace.

Reconciling these trends with climatic analysis presents a major challenge and opportunity to climate scholarship, offering not only a new lens through which to understand the climate crisis, but also a fresh policy platform from which to effect adaptation to its impacts. And finally, it is something else too. In elucidating the workplace as the centre of climate breakdown and its impacts, this novel perspective offers the opportunity of a new site of resistance; a sense of shared risk, shared power and shared opportunity. After several decades of being disaggregated, disintegrated and disengaged by the baroque expansions of the global economy, thermal futures of work may provide a catalyst a renewed sense of cohesion amongst the workers of our global factory. In seeking granularity of perspective, this is a field that seeks not to individualise the problem of climate impacts, but to socialise them. Climate change is a force transforming the global workplace. A renewed focus on the worker will give labour a voice through which to participate in these transformations: adaptation, not as response, but as resistance.

References

Acharya, P., Boggess, B., & Zhang, K. (2018). Assessing heat stress and health among construction workers in a changing climate: A review. *International Journal of Environmental Research and Public Health*, 15(2), 247. https://doi.org/10.3390/ijerph15020247

Associated Press News (22/07/2022) *Spanish Worker's Death Shows Need to Adapt to Climate Change*. By Raquel Redondo and Barry Hatton. Available at: https://apnews.com/article/health-spain-madrid-b1e25a296c3c486ee15a9f0f2c4e8e37

BBC (20 March 2016). *Fuel poverty: An Anatomy of a Cold Home*. By Datshiane Navanayagam.

Byrne, J., Ambrey, C., Portanger, C., Lo, A., Matthews, T., Baker, D., & Davison, A. (2016). Could urban greening mitigate suburban thermal inequity?: the role of residents' dispositions and household practices. *Environmental Research Letters*, 11(9), 095014, 1–16.

Dialesandro, J., Brazil, N., Wheeler, S., & Abunnasr, Y. (2021). Dimensions of thermal inequity: neighborhood social demographics and urban heat in the Southwestern US. *International Journal of Environmental Research and Public Health*, 18(3), 941.

El Khayat, M., Halwani, D.A., Alameddine, I., Haidar, M. A., & Habib, R. R. (2022). Impacts of climate change and heat stress on farmworkers' health: A scoping review, *Frontiers in Public Health*, 10, 782811. https://doi.org/10.3389/fpubh.2022.782811

Gasparrini, A., Masselot, P., Scortichini, M., Schneider, R., Mistry, M. N., Sera, F., …, & Vicedo-Cabrera, A. M. (2022). Small-area assessment of temperature-related mortality risks in England and Wales: a case time series analysis. *The Lancet Planetary Health*, 6(7), e557–e564.

Hajizadeh, R., Golbabaei, F., Dehghan, S. F., Beheshti, M. H., Jafari, S. M., & Taheri, F. (2016). Validating the heat stress indices for using in heavy work activities in hot and dry climates. *Journal of Research in Health Sciences*, 16(2), 90–95.

Hamstead, Z., Coseo, P., AlKhaled, S., Boamah, E. F., Hondula, D. M., Middel, A., & Rajkovich, N. (2020). Thermally resilient communities: creating a socio-technical collaborative response to extreme temperatures. *Buildings and Cities*, 1(1), 218–232.

Hansen, A., Bi, L., Saniotis, A., & Nitschke, M. (2013). Vulnerability to extreme heat and climate change: is ethnicity a factor? *Global Health Action*, 6(1), 21364.

Hill, A. C., & Babin, M. (2021). *The Policy Challenge of Extreme Heat and Climate Change*. Think Global Health, 12 October 2021. Accessed on 14/11/2022 at [https://thinkglobalhealth.org].

HM Government (2021). *Net Zero Strategy: Build Back Greener.* United Kingdom: Crown Copyright. Accessed on 23/06/2023 at [https://www.gov.uk/government/publications].

Hutyra, L. cited in Holt, S. (23/09/2022). *What Is the Greatest Threat to Human Health from Climate Change? Boston University Arts and Sciences Newsletter.* The Big Question. Accessed on 29/11/2022 at [https://www.bu.edu.].

International Labour Organization (ILO) (2019a). *Working on a Warmer Planet: The Effect of Heat Stress on Productivity and Decent Work*. Geneva: ILO. Available at: https://www.ilo.org/global/publications/books/WCMS_711919/lang–en/index.htm

International Labour Organization (ILO) (2019b) *World Employment Social Outlook: Trends 2019*. Geneva: ILO. Available at: https://www.ilo.org/sites/default/files/wcmsp5/groups/public/@dgreports/@dcomm/@publ/documents/publication/wcms_670542.pdf

IPCC (2022). *Climate Change 2022: Impacts, Adaptation and Vulnerability*. IPCC Sixth Assessment Report. IPCC: Geneva.

Klinsky, S., & Mavrogianni, A. (2020). Climate justice and the built environment. *Buildings and Cities*, 1(1), 412–428.

Kunz-Plapp, T., Hackenbruch, J., & Schipper, J. W. (2016). Factors of subjective heat stress of urban citizens in contexts of everyday life. *Natural Hazards and Earth System Sciences*, 16(4), 977–994.

O'Connor, S. (2022). *A Hotter Planet Will Expose Divides in the World of Work, Financial Times*, 2 August 2022. Available at: https://www.ft.com/content/c51a38cd-2941-4eef-97af-8cc61849c04c

Leahy, S. (2022). By 2100, deadly heat may threaten majority of humankind. *National Geographic*. Accessed on 10/11/2022 at [https://nationalgeographic.org].

Levi, M., Kjellstrom, T., & Baldasseroni, A. (2018). Impact of climate change on occupational health and productivity: a systematic literature review focusing on workplace heat. *La Medicina del lavoro*, 109(3), 163.

Malgoyre, A., Siracusa, J., Tardo-Dino, P.E., Garcia-Vicencio, S., Koulmann, N., Epstein, Y., & Charlot, K. (2020). Four-month operational heat acclimatization positively affects the level of heat tolerance 6 months later. *Scientific Reports*, 10, 20260. https://doi.org/10.1038/ s41598-020-77358-7

Mathison, G (2014) *Humans are tropical animals, Science Norway*, 26 February 2014. Available at: https://www.sciencenorway.no/adaptation-body-temperature-forskningno/humans-are-tropical-animals/1397429

Mitchell, B. C., & Chakraborty, J. (2014). Urban heat and climate justice: A landscape of thermal inequity in pinellas county, Florida. *Geographical Review*, 104(4), 459–480. https://doi.org/10.1111/j.1931-0846.2014.12039.x

Mitchell, B. C., & Chakraborty, J. (2015). Landscapes of thermal inequity: disproportionate exposure to urban heat in the three largest US cities. *Environmental Research Letters*, 10(11), 115005.

Mitchell, B. C., & Chakraborty, J. (2018). Exploring the relationship between residential segregation and thermal inequity in 20 U.S. cities. *Local Environment*, 23(8), 796–813. https://doi.org/10.1080/13549839.2018.1474861

Newman, F., & Humphrys, E. (2020). Construction workers in a climate precarious world. *Critical Sociology*, 46(4), 557–572. https://doi.org/10.1177/0896920519880951

Parsons, L., & Ly, V. L. (2020). Thermal Working Paper 1: Heat Stress in the Cambodian Brick Sector, London: Royal Holloway. Available at: https://pure.royalholloway.ac.uk/ws/portalfiles/portal/58985512/Brick_Kiln_Thermal_Working_Paper_V2.pdf

Parsons, L., Lawreniuk, S., Sok, S., & Buckley, J. (2022). *Hot Trends: How the Global Garment Industry Shapes Climate Change Vulnerability in Cambodia.* Egham: Royal Holloway, University of London and University of Nottingham.

Turek-Hankins, L. L., de Perez, E. C., Scarpa, G., Ruiz-Diaz, R., Shwerdtle, P. N., Joe, E. T., … & Mach, K. J. (2021). Climate change adaptation to extreme heat: a global systematic review of implemented action. *Oxford Open Climate Change*, 1(1), kgab005. https://doi.org/10.1093/oxfclm/kgab005

United Nations Environment Programme [UNEP] (2022). *For People and Planet: The United Nations Environment Programme Strategy for Tackling Climate Change, Biodiversity and Nature Loss, and Pollution and Waste from 2022–2025.* Geneva: UNEP.

Vicedo-Cabrera, A.M., Guo, Y., Sera, F., et al. (2018). Temperature-related mortality impacts under and beyond Paris Agreement climate change scenarios. *Nature Climatic Change*, 150, 391–402. https://doi.org/10.1007/s10584-018-2274-3

Vicedo-Cabrera, A. M., Scovronick, N., Sera, F., Royé, D., Schneider, R., Tobias, A., …, & Gasparrini, A. (2021). The burden of heat-related mortality attributable to recent human-induced climate change. *Nature Climate Change*, 11(6), 492–500.

Wang, C. (2021). Extreme heat is deadly, but inequality is deadlier, Climate and Environment at Imperial Blog, 20 July 2021. Available at: https://granthaminstitute.com/2021/07/20/extreme-heat-is-deadly-but-inequality-is-deadlier/

Wingate, S. (2022). World on 'highway to climate hell with foot on the accelerator', UN head warns, The Independent, 7 November 2022. Available at: https://www.independent.co.uk/climate-change/news/antonio-guterres-prime-minister-world-boris-johnson-ukraine-b2219428.html

Zander, K. K., Cadag, J. R., Escarcha, J., & Garnett, S. T. (2018). Perceived heat stress increases with population density in urban Philippines. *Environmental Research Letters*, 13(8), 084009.

Recommendations for Further Reading

Hill, A. C., & Babin, M. (2021). The policy challenge of extreme heat and climate change. *Think Global Health*, 12 October 2021. Accessed on 14/11/2022 at [https://thinkglobalhealth.org].

Levi, M., Kjellstrom, T., & Baldasseroni, A. (2018). Impact of climate change on occupational health and productivity: a systematic literature review focusing on workplace heat. *La Medicina del lavoro*, 109(3), 163.

Mitchell, D. (2021). Climate attribution of heat mortality. *Nature Climate Change*, 11(6), 467–468

Parsons, L. (2021). Thermal inequality in a changing climate: heat, mobility, and precarity in the Cambodian brick sector. In Natarajan, N. and Parsons, L. (eds.). *Climate Change in the Global Workplace*. London: Routledge, 15–31.

Parsons, L. (2023). *Carbon Colonialism: How Rich Countries Export Climate Breakdown.* Manchester: Manchester University Press.

Parsons, L. (2023). *How Inequality Shapes Your Experience of a Heatwave*. The Conversation, 19 June 2023. https://theconversation.com/how-inequality-shapes-your-experience-of-a-heatwave-207774

Parsons, L., Lawreniuk, S., Sok, S., & Buckley, J. (2022). *Hot Trends: How the Global Garment Industry Shapes Climate Change Vulnerability in Cambodia.* Egham: Royal Holloway, University of London and University of Nottingham.

PART 12

Conclusion

32

CONCLUSIONS AND FUTURE CHALLENGES

The End of Work and the End of History

Frederick Harry Pitts and Julie MacLeavy

Introduction

We opened the book by considering how important it is to refocus the future of work debate not on far-flung abstractions, whether utopian or dystopian, but on the concrete futures that are being lived and experienced already in the here and now. We also contested the idea that the future of work is locked in and automatically determined by dint of the technological potentials at humanity's fingertips at any one point. There is the possibility of agency, control and change to emerge from outside sheer material and technological calculation and propel social and political transformation in ways suggestive of different futures, both good and bad. In our contemporary period of multiple intersecting crises – economic, geopolitical, not to mention ecological – the contingency that complicates a linear, sequential view of historical progress becomes plain to see (Gills 2020). However, the practical implications of this lack of predetermined destination for workers, social movements, political organisations and other emancipatory actors are much less clear.

In this conclusion, we wish to cap off the collection by considering some of the larger-scale shifts afoot in the world today, their relationship with both past and present futures of work (Kinsley 2019), and the potential shape of strategies to build different futures in the context of the changing political economies within which state, capital and labour relate in the contemporary time. This refocusing upon the changing role of the state, in particular, returns us to core concerns of labour geography and other disciplinary frames that have consistently noted the continuing relevance of the spatiality and specificity of the state in determining the world of work (Herod et al 2007) – even as globalisation apparently, and fleetingly, called it into question (Mann 1997).

Much of the debate around work futures in recent years, whether emanating from left, right or centre, is coloured by a belief that the unfolding technological forces command inevitable shifts in social, political and organisational relations. This deterministic and rationalistic understanding of history unites differing bodies of thought and practice, from traditional Marxism to mainstream liberalism. Every step is seen as part and parcel of the forward march of progress in a manner uncomplicated by agency and antagonism, and free of the complexities of real, concrete historical development. Contrary to both perspectives, progress is not guaranteed and political realism demands an acknowledgement of contingency and the potential for setbacks, in light of which the role of actual struggle and politics poses a response. Rather than a linear evolution, the material

DOI: 10.4324/9781003327561-44

world is shaped by the messy, troubling stuff of identity, ideology and irrationality. As actual history passes, concretely rather than abstractly, it becomes clearer that the real story within which the future of work will be forged is less a technological or material one as it is a geopolitical one, where shifts in global order based on competing powers and value systems are intertwined with other transformations – namely the competition to lead the world in the green transition necessitated by climate catastrophe.

The so-called 'end of the end of history' that has steadily dawned upon the world in recent years problematises the comfortable temporality within which much of the future of work debate has proceeded (Pitts 2022). With trade and military tensions between the US and China having gradually ratcheted up, the Russian invasion of Ukraine exposed the deep geopolitical fault lines that have ruptured the post-1989 world. At the tail end of a populist period where politics have often overdetermined economics, the Russian war against Ukraine and the Western response to it inaugurate a period where war and the threat of it are bringing about a new capitalism driven as much by the forces of destruction (Kurz 2011) as those of production. As Russia's belligerence in Eastern Europe lays bare, war and great-power conflicts place us very far from the predictable determinations of economic rationality. In Ukraine or Taiwan, for instance, this apparent 'new' or 'second' cold war (Achcar 2023; Schindler et al 2023) could easily end up running hotter and wider. Just as war and capitalist development have intertwined in the past, they give us tools to understand how they will, potentially, once again do so today, enabling us to understand the true conditions of the apparent 'post-neoliberal' turn in capitalism (Davies and Gane 2021) towards a 'neo-Keynesianism' of an ultimately military character reminiscent of the mid-twentieth century (Merchant 2023; see also Szalavetz 2015). Whether the confrontation between a US-led Western bloc with either party of the looser axis of Russia and China remains indirect or escalates further into a direct conflagration, the prospect of something resembling a 'second cold war' – or, better still, a 'world civil war' within the fraying global order (Pitts 2024; Kurz 2014) – is already leading to demands for sharp increases in spending on strategic industries and capacities that imply the necessity of certain jobs and skills in the economy. The tendencies defining contemporary capitalism and its work futures – and thus our own theorisations of it – cannot be cleanly separated from this military and geopolitical context.

Public and political conversation about the future of work tends towards economic rationalism and technological determinism, ignoring the uncomfortable reality of an increasingly fractious world riven by populism and great-power competition, and thus eliding the impact of geopolitical factors upon the changing workplace – what one of us has elsewhere termed 'workplace geopolitics' (Pitts and Thomas 2024). Today, hot and cold wars shape not only the creation and application of new technologies and the reconfiguration of industry for specific purposes, but also the relationship between the state, business and labour in regulating and coordinating the practice and management of production. On the surface, the transition to green jobs and industries has become a central focus of this policy imaginary, implying improvements in skills and wages and an industrial shift from services to sectors where productivity gains are more achievable (Rodrik 2023). But the superficially positive tale of the green transition is not the only story of industrial change in contemporary capitalism. For starters, the green transition itself is often justified by a requirement to become more self-sufficient in products and technologies (e.g. production of e-vehicles and batteries and mining of minerals) in order to avoid net zero representing nothing more than a handout to rival export-led economies.

This context of competition will likely also drive other shifts in the industrial character of contemporary capitalism. The greater role the state assumed in COVID-19 (Gerbaudo 2021; Nölke 2022) and the technocratic politics of green transition will be lent greater definition and purpose by the state-coordinated war economies arising around sanctions regimes, a reinvigorated military-industrial complex and great-power competition over technology and global markets. Rather than through the rational allocation of resources by capital operating in open markets, in our increasingly post-neoliberal age it is at the level of the state that the futures of work are being determined. The contemporary shifts in the balance of state, capital and labour, nationally and globally, will compel changes, both quick and slow, in the structure and character of the labour process, organisational life and everyday political economy. In this context we see the role of the state in shaping the future of work through national industrial policies compelled by geopolitical considerations (Schindler et al 2022). The new terrain on which the future of work will be fought over is a protectionist national economy driven by state intervention in strategic industries compelled by competition with systemic rivals. In this way, the geopolitical picture has become one of the key motivating principles of capitalist development and thus the unfolding future of work.

There is a transatlantic political consensus forming that jobs, skills and industry will be central to a new round of geopolitical competition between two military-economic blocs vying for markets and power – one arranged around the US and Europe, the other around China and Russia. The domestic expression of this in the West will likely be a stronger commitment to reshored manufacturing in critical industries associated with defence, security and dual-use civilian-military technologies. In this way, the looming presence of conflict continues to shape capitalist development, and work, in turn. Levitating on the leeway provided by the need to rally the national effort in a so-called 'second cold war' fought on economic and technological fronts, and concealing within a future-facing narrative a new spin on the same nostalgic politics that has lately characterised left and right, this promises voters a reconstruction of the conditions for the twentieth-century 'golden age' of capitalism: great-power rivalry between productive national economies based on stable, skilled, well-paid industrial labour.

Technological Entanglements

A particular area in which the context of a new cold war will shape capitalism will be on the technological frontier, which has dominated contemporary visions of changing capitalism and the prospect of a 'postcapitalist' alternative springing from it. These hopeful projections of impending booms in productive investment and splurges on labour-substituting and labour-augmenting technologies have tended to be based on an understanding of economic rationality that conceptually seals off the world of work from a wider array of factors which are now becoming clear. Where these visions have typically been undermined by the somewhat underwhelming track record of investment and innovation in capitalist economies, the context of a 'world civil war' promises to accomplish what peacetime could not. The power play of geopolitics may well shape how otherwise unresolved technological tendencies play out, with unfolding tendencies in the digital and technological transformation of work in countries like the UK and the US shaped by a policy and business context characterised by intensifying military and economic competition with rival countries like China and Russia.

In the Cold War period there was little economic entanglement between the West and the Soviet Union, maintaining a separation between trade policy, security concerns and military posture. Unlike the Soviet Union, however, China presents the West with the prospect of a serious commercial rival and economic challenger. At the same time as drawing up military plans to counterbalance China's rising power, US governments simultaneously facilitated the offshoring of a sizeable chunk of the country's industrial base to Chinese manufacturers. However, things changed with controversies around Huawei and other Chinese firms involved in the provision of technological infrastructure in the West – accusations of espionage and unfair competition casting a long shadow over what was once a hopeful vision of increased cooperation. Western governments, having imagined that greater and closer connections with the likes of China and Russia would reduce the potential for conflict, found that the rise of connectivity in the economy, technology and society had now become the means of the intensifying contest between world powers (Leonard 2021). Connectivity forces countries to converge, in part as a means to compete; but the closer everyone has drawn, the more they appear to want to be apart. This means that any 'new' or 'second' cold war combines geopolitical and geoeconomic dimensions to a much more substantial degree than the first.

Confronted with a new age of so-called 'systemic competition', Western governments today are once again playing catch up with the likes of China by investing in research and development (R&D), strategic industries, dual-use military-civilian technologies and driving productive investment in skills and productivity, mimicking the strategic support granted to sectors like electronics, nuclear, aerospace and computers in the second part of the twentieth century. As states face more insecurity, they invest ever greater resources into building up their capacity relative to the perceived existing strengths of other states, encouraging their counterparts to do likewise in a spiral of suspicion and securitisation (Peoples 2010). While in the postwar period of geopolitical competition, this manifested in expenditure on heavy weaponry (MacLeavy and Peoples 2009), today this also plays out in investment in digital and technological means to achieve what some call 'cyberpower' relative to a nation's rivals. A national security justification thus underpins new industrial strategies projecting a high-tech 'high road' to productivity and productive investment in skills and technology as a salvo in the emergent systemic competition with China. As the US has sought to contain China's global technological ambitions through tariffs and restrictions, China has responded by building up greater national self-sufficiency through subsidies and state intervention in the digital and tech sectors. In return, the US and other Western states have increasingly sought to themselves imitate China through a more interventionist industrial policy in key strategic sectors, including those that touch upon cyberpower.

More self-sufficient, coordinated and export-led national economies, trading in blocs of trusted allies, will increasingly prioritise 'on-shored' strategic industries like defence and high-tech manufacturing supported by vast sums of R&D spending. Alongside new national interests, this global combination of connectivity and conflict has given rise to new super-technology companies – Google, Amazon, Tencent and Meta (formerly Facebook), amongst others – embedding themselves further into our private lives, as well as the public sphere. The technological arms race between states is thus poised to have a profound impact upon citizens and societies, with innovations in artificial intelligence (AI) and algorithms being a key domain where many sense an absence of control over their lives and work. AI-powered social media algorithms, for instance, are suspected of prioritising content that fuels outrage and societal polarisation; their 'black box' quality rendering them impervious to human understanding or mastery for most. This gives rise to a feeling of powerlessness that follows through into politics at a national and global level by way of the ballot box and other means, sometimes acting to fuel the fire of division, discord and danger in the geopolitical arena. Hence, in a world defined by connectivity, convergence and conflict are mutually reinforcing, the one being produced by means of the other (Leonard 2021).

Undoubtedly, the Cold War, with its intense military-industrial-academic collaboration fuelled by large-scale state investment in higher education, gave rise to the information technology infrastructure that underpins this new socio-digital reality. But while contemporary technocratic visions of 'mission' and 'moonshot' economies (Mazzucato 2013, 2021), or postcapitalist red plenty (Mason 2015; Bastani 2019), paint a rosy picture of technological progress, they often fail to critically engage with the historical context that shapes their own ideas. These visions, forged from the ruptures of the present, demonstrably draw inspiration from the Cold War's rhetorical legacy, implicitly endorsing a similar model of innovation driven by national security concerns. The utopian futures these visions project can be interpreted as a yearning for the perceived stability of the Cold War's bipolar world order, which now seems strangely remote. However, this nostalgia conveniently erases the underlying reality of war and conflict as the very foundation upon which those futures were built. This truth is conveniently wished away in favour of framing these advancements as simply inevitable or morally justifiable.

Crucially, these contemporary visions both reveal and conceal a critical truth: the geopolitical fault lines that gave rise to the Cold War's technological advancements (and hence these futures past) are reemerging. This renewed competition begs the following questions: what new visions of the future will this generate, and who will hold sway over shaping them? And, at what human and societal cost will these futures be pursued by state and capital actors?

Crisis Corporatism?

Given that the future of work is more likely going to be conditioned by social and political factors than current technology-centric discussion suggests, what does this imply about the capacity of different actors, especially workers, to actively participate in shaping this unfolding future? The most positive, if imperfect, version of the answer may lie in a form of corporatism. Driven by external circumstances, this approach would integrate a discernible labour interest into the strategy of a changing state. At the national political-economic level, it would see a similar level of trust and confidence that a changing state grants industry in reckoning with rapid industrial and geopolitical change extended to workers as well. After all, they too weather the anxiety and uncertainty that attends these shifts in everyday life. And, the tumultuous post-2008 period, riven with crises – populism, Brexit, the pandemic, the Russian war on Ukraine and the wider West, and now dire stagflation – offers a compelling case for such collaboration: these events have arguably necessitated a form of 'crisis corporatism' from governments in order to render liberal democracies secure against the threats arranged against them (Coulter 2020; Meardi and Tassinari 2022).

However, the power of employers and governments to dictate the course of industrial relations is still overwhelming. There will be significant struggle needed to prevail upon the state to devolve countervailing power to workers and their unions in order to counterbalance the power of capital. Moreover, there must be a concerted effort to avoid the outcome sometimes associated with similar institution-building initiatives in the post-war period, whereby labour was effectively disciplined and constrained by an alienating bureaucracy (Panitch 1986). Where unions rejected similar proposals in the Seventies owing to the perception that they represented an accommodation to capital, today they start in a much weaker position and may be more willing to recognise the possible gains such a path provides. Countervailing power in the hands of workers and unions is required to make the rule of law in the workplace effective; especially where formal enforcement mechanisms on the side of labour are weak (Pakes and Pitts 2023).

Unfortunately, this cannot be as straightforward as a simple return to labour movement militancy driving modernisation, with trade union density and power having declined. A restoration of collective bargaining and worker voice at the level of the firm is neither a one-size-fits-all response to the specificities of a highly fissured economy nor a short-term overnight solution. Indeed, recent events bear out the irreconcilability of union demands and government willingness to construct compromises and bargains between labour and capital: entrenched positions on the part of firms, coupled with governments prioritising their interests, makes genuine bargaining between labour and capital exceedingly difficult. The Eurozone austerity measures enacted after the 2008 financial crisis vividly illustrate this dynamic. Implemented despite union opposition, these measures prioritised fiscal stability over worker protection, leading to job losses and stagnant wages (Baines and Cunningham 2021; MacLeavy 2025). And, in the post-pandemic period, long-term declines in real wages finally reached a point where they were intolerable for workers at precisely the time that employers were seeking to modernise in pursuit of their own profit margins, resulting in a wave of strike action in response to which many states sought strategies of repression rather than resolution in the name of any perceived 'national interest' (Edwards et al 2023; Greenhouse 2023; Laikola 2023; Oltermann 2023).

Despite these challenges, there are glimmers of hope for a more equitable future of work. Firstly, the recent wave of worker activism has demonstrated a renewed sense of worker solidarity and a willingness to fight for better conditions, even in adversarial circumstances. This renewed energy, coupled with the growing public concern about income inequality and worker precarity, could create a groundswell of public support for policies that strengthen worker rights and bargaining power. Secondly, technological advancements, often seen as a threat to workers, also have the potential to empower them. For instance, social media groups and messaging apps are being used by workers in diverse industries to share information, coordinate actions and build solidarity. Finally, there is a growing recognition amongst some policymakers and business leaders that, in this new geopolitical landscape, a more collaborative approach to labour relations is not just ethically sound but also potentially economically beneficial. A workforce with a voice and a stake in the economy's overall success may be more likely to be productive and engaged. Building trust and fostering cooperation between employers, workers, and governments is thus being seen as crucial to shaping a future of work that is both prosperous and just.

Final Reflections

The Handbook for the Future of Work has presented a multifaceted landscape, moulded by the complex interplay of technological advancements, geopolitical realignments and evolving worker demands: technological innovation is transforming labour markets through automation, fostering job creation in nascent sectors while displacing workers in established ones; geopolitical shifts, exemplified by the current 'world civil war', further complicate this equation, influencing national industrial policies and the relationship between governments, businesses and workers. One potential response, as we have sought to outline within this chapter, is 'crisis corporatism', a model that posits collaboration between stakeholders – governments, businesses and workers – as a means to navigate the challenges posed by this complex and shifting landscape. While concerns regarding power imbalances and undue corporate influence are valid, crisis corporatism also offers the possibility of a more unified approach to navigating the uncertainties of the future.

In closing we provide some further, final reflections on the book's cover art, which deliberately departs from the usual robot-dominated imagery associated with the 'future of work'. Featuring a sunlit industrial scene rendered in the socialist realist style, this artwork is intended to serve as a counterpoint to dominant narratives about technology, narratives which we have explained are too often fixated on anxieties about automation and worker displacement. Frequently, books and articles about work futures will use the sterile, robotic visions of a future where humans are replaced in part or whole by machines. We acknowledge that our choice might evoke historical tensions related to state control of the economy and potential limitations on worker freedoms. However, the optimistic and sunlit nature of the scene reminds us that, as Adorno put it, 'At every moment the ever-new is also the old lying close at hand. The new does not add itself to the old but remains the old in distress' (Adorno 2003, pp. 94–95). In this respect, present futures (Kinsley 2019) also contain within them glimpses of the past, both good and bad. With the ideological alternatives of the period implied in the image having long been foreclosed, and the industrial model of modernity it presents having been problematised by social and ecological contradictions, it reminds us of the continuing need for a contest over the values and visions that will shape the unfolding futures of work.

By choosing this cover art, we want to invite readers to consider these historical tensions alongside our written exploration of the future(s) of work and think further about the potential benefits and drawbacks of different approaches to work and the role of technology in shaping a more equitable future. Despite the inherent uncertainties, the rising sun on the cover we would like to suggest symbolises the potential for a brighter future. It is a future where collaboration, adaptability and a commitment to worker rights can pave the way for a more prosperous and just world of work. While the specific path remains unclear, the potential for a hopeful narrative exists for all participants in this ever-evolving story of work. Indeed, rather than any 'end' of work, the 'end of the end of history' may well give new importance to work and workers in the context of a changing capitalism.

References

Achcar, G. (2023). *The New Cold War: The United States, Russia, and China from Kosovo to Ukraine*. Chicago: Haymarket Books.

Adorno, T. W. (2003). Reflections on class theory, pp. 93–110, in: Tiedemann, R. (ed.) *Can One Live after Auschwitz? A Philosophical Reader*, trans. R. Livingstone, Redwood City: Stanford University Press.

Baines, D., and Cunningham, I. (2021). *Working in the Context of Austerity: Challenges and Struggles*. Bristol: University of Bristol Press.

Bastani, A. (2019). *Fully Automated Luxury Communism*. London: Verso.

Coulter, S. (2020). All in it together? The unlikely rebirth of Covid corporatism, *The Political Quarterly*, 91(3): 534–541.

Davies, W., and Gane, N. (2021). Post-neoliberalism? An introduction, *Theory, Culture & Society*, 38(6): 3–28.

Edwards, P., Baden-Fuller, C., Pissarides, C., Rubery, J., Crouch, C., and Taylor-Gooby, P. (2023). Inflation, wages and equality: Cross-disciplinary conversations, *Journal of the British Academy*, 11: 25–41.

Gerbaudo, P. (2021). *The Great Recoil: Politics after Populism and Pandemic*. London: Verso.

Gills, B. (2020). Deep restoration: From the Great Implosion to the Great Awakening, *Globalizations*, 17(4): 577–579.

Greenhouse, S. (2023). "It feels like it's strike summer": US unions flex muscles across industries, *The Guardian*. Available from: https://www.theguardian.com/us-news/2023/jul/26/strike-summer-us-unions-flex-muscles

Herod, A., Rainnie, A., and McGrath-Champ, S. (2007). Working space: Why incorporating the geographical is central to theorizing work and employment practices, *Work, Employment and Society*, 21(2): 247–264.

Kinsley, S. (2019). Present futures: Automation and the politics of anticipation, *Futures of Work*, 8. Available from: https://futuresofwork.co.uk/2019/07/31/imagining-automation-present-futures-and-the-politics-of-anticipation/

Kurz, R. (2011). The destructive origins of capitalism, *Libcom*, 14th June 2011. Available from: https://libcom.org/article/destructive-origins-capitalism-robert-kurz

Kurz, R. (2014). World power and world money: The economic function of the U.S. military machine within global capitalism and the background of the new financial crisis, pp. 187–200, in: Larsen, N., Nilges, M., Robinson, J., and Brown, N. (eds.) *Marxism and the Critique of Value*. Chicago, IL/Alberta: MCM.

Laikola, L. (2023). Finland set for weeks of strikes as unions rise up against cuts, *Bloomberg*. Available from: https://www.bloomberg.com/news/articles/2023-09-21/finland-set-for-weeks-of-strikes-as-unions-rise-up-against-cuts

Leonard, M. (2021). *The Age of Unpeace*. London: Bantam.

MacLeavy, J (2025). *Enduring Austerity: The Uneven Geographies of the Post-Welfare State*. Bristol: University of Bristol Press.
MacLeavy, J., and Peoples, C. (2009). Workfare–warfare: Neoliberalism, "active" welfare and the New American way of war, *Antipode*, 41(5): 890–915.
Mann, M. (1997). Has globalization ended the rise and rise of the nation-state? *Review of International Political Economy*, 4(3): 472–496.
Mason, P. (2015). *Postcapitalism*. London: Allen Lane.
Mazzucato, M. (2013). *The Entrepreneurial State*. London: Allen Lane.
Mazzucato, M. (2021). *Mission Economy*. London: Allen Lane.
Meardi, G., and Tassinari, A. (2022). Crisis corporatism 2.0? The role of social dialogue in the pandemic crisis in Europe, *Transfer: European Review of Labour and Research*, 28 (1): 83–100.
Merchant, J. (2023). The economic consequences of neo-Keynesianism, *Brooklyn Rail*. July/August. Available from: https://brooklynrail.org/2023/07/field-notes/The-Economic-Consequences-of-Neo-Keynesianism
Nölke, A. (2022). *Post-Corona Capitalism: The Alternatives Ahead*. Bristol: Bristol University Press
Oltermann, P. (2023). Millions of Germans face transport disruption in cost of living 'mega-strike', *The Guardian*. Available from: https://www.theguardian.com/world/2023/mar/27/millions-of-germans-face-transport-disruption-in-cost-of-living-mega-strike
Pakes, A., and Pitts, F. H. (2023). *A Progressive Politics of Work for the Age of Unpeace*. Brussels: Foundation for European Progressive Studies.
Panitch, L. (1986). *Working Class Politics in Crisis*. London: Verso.
Peoples, C. L. (2010). *Justifying Ballistic Missile Defence: Technology, Security and Culture*. Cambridge: Cambridge University Press.
Pitts, F. H. (2022). *The End of History and the Last Man,* 30 Years On. Bristol Ideas, 11th March. Available from: https://www.bristolideas.co.uk/read/end-of-history/
Pitts F. H. (2024). New cold war or 'world civil war'? Wertkritik and the critical theory of capitalism in an age of conflict, *European Journal of Social Theory*. DOI: 10.1177/13684310241247548
Pitts, F. H., and Thomas, H. (2024). Future of work and global trends: Reframing the debate in an age of state capitalism and systemic competition, in Moore, M., van der Linden, M., and Scherrer, C. (eds.) *The Elgar Companion to Decent Work and the Sustainable Development Goals*. Cheltenham: Edward Elgar. In Press.
Rodrik, D. (2023). On productivism, *HKS Faculty Research Working Paper Series.*
Schindler, S., Alami, I., and Jepson, N. (2022). Goodbye Washington Confusion, hello Wall Street Consensus: Contemporary state capitalism and the spatialisation of industrial strategy, *New Political Economy.* DOI: 10.1080/13563467.2022.2091534
Schindler, S., Alami, I., DiCarlo, J., Jepson, N., Rolfe, S., Bayırbağ, M. K., Cyuzuzo, L., DeBoom, M., Farahani, A. F., Liu, I. T., McNicol, H., Miao, J. T., Nock, P., Teri, G., Seoane, M. F. V., Ward, K., Zajontz, T., and Zhao, Y. (2023). The Second Cold War: US-China competition for centrality in infrastructure, digital, production, and finance networks, *Geopolitics*. DOI: 10.1080/14650045.2023.2253432
Szalavetz, A. (2015). Post-crisis approaches to state intervention: New developmentalism or industrial policy as usual? *Competition & Change*, 19(1): 70–83.

INDEX

Note: Page numbers followed by "n" denote endnotes.

accelerationism 60
Acemoglu, Daron 57, 218, 361, 363
active labour market policies and programmes (ALMP) 344–351; *see also* workfare
activism 123–129, 296, 416
Adkins, Lisa 162, 166–167, 169
affective economy 175–181
age 8–9, 181, 199, 201, 253, 315, 324, 346, 350
agile economy 175–181
agile management 37, 179
agrifood 237–248
AIDS 187, 191
Airbnb 108, 112
algo-activism 10, 124–129
algorithms 98–101, 123–129
Amazon 48, 114, 118, 318, 323, 333, 334, 414; Amazon Mechanical Turk 99, 108; Amazon Prime Video 117
Android 108
Apple 48, 118, 226; Apple TV+ 117
Application Programming Interface (API) 110
artificial intelligence (AI) 25, 57–59, 69, 82–83, 138, 200, 212, 219, 294–295, 414
assets 112, 163–167
augmentation 58; high-discretion 82–83; low-discretion 83–84
austerity 316–317
Australia 225–234, 382
automation 3, 69–86, 130–138, 213, 218, 359–369
autonomy 83, 85, 109, 116, 127, 135, 164, 178, 197, 248, 278–280
Autor, David H. 361–362

Beck, Ulrich 24–25
Benanav, Aaron 6, 64, 70, 213, 214, 217
Biden, Joe 375, 384
big data 217, 219
Big Tech 48
Bitcoin 137
Bolt 138
Bosworth, Barry 215, 217
Braverman, Harry 36, 81
Brenner, Robert 213–214
burnout 150, 199, 258

Canada 302–307
capitalist society 8, 31, 70, 175
care 129, 177–179, 195–203, 277
casino capitalism 64
Chang, Jae-Hee 390–391
ChatGPT 70, 178
Child Poverty Action Group (CPAG) 324
circular economy (CE) 390, 392, 394
Citizens' Advice Bureau 315, 317
city-regions 314–325
class 10, 116, 161–170
Clean Jobs Workforce Network Hubs programme 382
Climate and Equitable Jobs Act [Illinois] 382
climate change 400–407
Climate Jobs National Resource Center 382
cloud computing 29, 217
cloud work 112
coal production 381
cognitive technology 79–86

Cold War 226, 230, 413–415
Cole, Matthew 59, 65
Community 200, 244, 321–323
Conservative Party [UK] 21
corporatism 415–416
COVID-19 pandemic 7, 9, 46, 84–85, 94, 103, 147, 149, 197, 203, 218, 225–228, 232, 234, 244, 256, 258, 267, 299–301, 306, 307, 332, 335, 381, 405, 412
crowdsourcing 93–94, 112, 295
crowdwork 94, 96–103, 112, 278–280
cultural and creative industries (CCIs) 116–118
culture 18, 33, 244, 359–361
cyber-physical systems (CPS) 29, 217
cyberviolence 98–101

Davenport, Thomas 75–76
decent work 388–396
#DeclineNow movement 124, 126, 128
Deliveroo 103, 108, 112, 269
demographic changes 155–157
Department of Work and Pensions (DWP) [UK] 316
deprofessionalisation 257–258
digital divide 302, 308
digital labour 135–142
digital literacy 308
digitalisation 93, 155–157, 197–200, 300
disability 145–157; Disability Confident scheme 152, 157n1; Disability Employment Charter 156, 157, 157n1 Disability Living Allowance (DLA) 318; Disability Sheffield 316–317; Disabled People Against the Cuts (DPAC) 322
disconnected capitalism thesis (DCT) 44
discrimination 99–101, 149, 164, 189, 255, 280
diversity and inclusion 257, 382; Diversity Council Australia (DCA) 353
Documentary Film Movement (DFM) 20–21
DoorDash 124–126, 280
Dor, Lynford 137, 140
Dowling, Emma 196, 201
Dyer-Witheford, Nick 57, 62

eBay 110
economic geography 300–304
economics 11, 58, 149–151, 161, 203, 211, 227–228, 231, 259–260, 276, 299, 301, 359–361, 365, 400–407
The Economist 226–229
education and training 22, 36, 168, 190, 381
efficiency in industrial relations 331–339
Electronic Data Interchange (EDI) 289
end of work 24–25, 411–417
Energy & Climate Summit 232
energy transitions: in Asian garment factories 388–396; and future of decent work 388–396
Engels, Friedrich 19, 26
entrepreneurship 280
environment 202, 400–407
equality 155, 157, 167–168, 175, 331–339
Equality Act [UK] 145, 146, 255, 316
Equality and Human Rights Commission (EHRC) 156
Equal Pay Act [UK] 255
Esping-Andersen, Gøsta 345
European Commission 226
European Labour Force Survey 275
EU-SEAN Business Council 392
extractive capitalism 227

Facebook 49, 108, 111, 124, 198, 414
Fair Pay Agreements Bill [UK] 338
Fashion Industry Charter for Climate Action 391, 392
feminisation of labour 289
financialisation 42–50
First Nations People 227
flexibility 151, 199, 277–278
Food Regime Theory 237–238
Fordism 17, 34, 36, 163
FOREX 137
Fourth Industrial Revolution (4IR) 25, 29–38, 58, 60, 65–67, 135, 217, 226
freelancing 93, 269–270
Frey, Carl Benedikt 62, 64, 70, 73, 80, 186, 363
full-employment 254
fully automated luxury communism 60

Gallego, Aina 362, 368
garment industry 388–392, 395–396; garment factories 388–396
gender 85, 98–101, 116, 175–181, 189–190; gendered divisions of labour 176
General Purpose Transformers (GPTs) 80, 82
geography of work 299–308
gig economy 93–104, 113, 138, 155–157
global economy 161, 169, 215, 217, 335, 405
Global Energy Talent Index 377
Global Financial Crisis 256
globalisation 4, 8–9, 24, 36, 179, 219, 225, 255, 360, 363, 366
Global North 35, 38, 135, 169, 177, 179, 185, 274, 279
global production 289–296
Global South 36–37, 82, 85, 94–95, 135, 279, 294, 390
Global Value Chains (GVC) 228
Global Women's Network for the Energy Transition (GWNET) 378
Goldthorpe, John H. 21–22
González, José Antonio 400–402
Google 48, 111, 333, 414
Gorz, Andre 24–25

GPS tracking system 199
Graeber, David 6, 25
Great Financial Crisis/Great Recession 95, 149–150, 255, 257
green economy 375
Greenhouse Gas (GHG) emissions 391
green jobs 375–384; green work 383–384
Green New Deal movement 376
GrubHub 124

harassment: sexual 100, 333; workplace 255
Hennessy, Rosemary 188, 191
heteronormativity 191
Hlatshwayo, Mondli 136–137
Hochschild, Arlie Russell 115, 268
home officing 197–198
homo oeconomicus 202
Hospitality 114–116
Howcroft, Debra 112, 135, 187
human resources (HR) 239, 345
Huws, Ursula 141, 200, 201
Huxley, Aldous 19–20

IBM 110
Im, Zhen Jie 362–363, 365
immaterial labour 60–61
Independent Professionals (I-PROs) 274, 276, 283
Individual Placement and Support in Primary Care Initiative 151
industrial development 30, 33, 226
industrial policy 227–228, 231
industrial relations 331–339
Industry 4.0 217, 226–227
Industry 5.0 (i5.0) 225–234
Inequality 6, 116, 123–129, 259
Inflation Reduction Act [US] 232, 375
informal work 118, 186, 264–265
information and computer technologies (ICTs) 35–36, 217
infrastructure 33, 46–47, 69, 103, 110, 141, 156, 212, 217, 233
Ingold, Jo 350, 351, 353
Innovations 29, 33–35, 58, 80, 214–215, 226, 239, 300
insecurity 316–317
Instagram 198
Institute for Fiscal Studies 349
Institute of Future of Work (IFOW) 337
International Conference of Labour Statisticians 265
International Labour Organization (ILO) 93, 162, 265, 295, 335, 380, 389, 395
International Renewable Energy Agency (IRENA) 378
International Standard Industrial Classification (ISIC) divisions 212
International Trade Union Confederation (ITUC) 331, 376
Internet of Things (IoT) 58; Internet of Things and Services (IoTS) 217
Interstate Renewable Energy Council (IREC) 378

Jeffrey, Karen. 366–368
Jennings, Humphrey 18–19
Jobcentre 321
job displacement 60, 80–82, 302
job quality 253–260
job satisfaction 145, 149, 152, 166, 303
job security 8, 44, 162, 167, 256, 269, 339, 377, 383
Jonas, Hans 239, 245–246
Jones, Melanie 148, 150
just-in-time 289–296
just transition 375–384

kafala system [UAE] 266
kanban system 291
Keynesianism 162
Kickstarter 108
Kirby, Julia 75–76
Kurer, Thomas 360, 362, 364–365, 368

Labour Force Survey (LFS) 146
labour market 253–260, 344–354, 359
Labour Process Theory 62
Labour Theory of Value 65
Latimer, Heather 167–168
learning 50, 110, 138, 212, 218, 265–268
LGBTQ movements 186–190
LinkedIn 117
lithium and battery production 229–230
Logistics 140–141
low-carbon economy 379

machine learning 10, 29, 36, 57, 69, 73–76, 82, 290, 294
Maffie, Michael David 113, 119
Manning, Alan 361, 362
Manufacturing 225–234
Marx, Karl 19, 26, 60, 62, 69, 71, 81
Marxist political economy 212
Mazzucato, Mariana 57, 226
McKinsey & Co. 59, 227
meaningful work 25, 238
mental health 103, 244, 379, 403
Meta 48–49, 414
Microsoft 48, 82
migration 300–301; migrant workers 11, 139, 178, 239, 292, 294
Modern Manufacturing Initiative (MMI) 228, 230
Modern Times 20
Morozov, Evgeny 62, 63
Morris, William 18–19

"Mums 4 Housing" movement 191
Munck, Ronaldo 163–164

National Care Service [UK] 376
National Manufacturing Priorities [Australia] 228–229
National Minimum Wage [UK] 377
neoliberalism 164, 180, 214, 226, 237, 314, 324
Neo-Luddism 62
Neo-Schumpeterian economists 59
Netflix 108, 117
new economy 232, 234
non-labour platforms 108–120

Office for Budget Responsibility (OBR) [UK] 156
Office for National Statistics [UK] 147
Office of Federal Contract Compliance Programs [US] 153
on-demand economy/labour 93, 123, 292–294
OpenAI 70
oppression 30, 142
Osborne, Michael A. 62, 64, 80, 186
Oswin, Natalie 186–187
outsourcing 95, 138, 140–141, 201, 290, 292, 295, 333–345

Pahl, Ray 22–23
Paris Agreement 380
PayPal 108
Peoples Assembly [UK] 325
performance management 115
Personal Independence Payment (PIP) [UK] 318
personal protective equipment (PPE) 228
platform capitalism 64, 119, 217, 278
platform economy 93–101, 108, 110, 114–119
platformisation 57, 65, 109, 110, 114, 119–120, 218, 283
platform labour 93–104, 112, 138–140
platforms 95–98, 108–119, 123–129, 278–280
PlayStation 108
politics 359–369
populism 359–369
post-capitalism 38
post-growth 244–248
post-scarcity society 38
post-war period 254, 415
power resources approach 137
precariat 162–163
precariousness 8, 23, 25, 98–101, 139, 161–164, 268, 277–278, 314, 317–321
'Preston Model' 258
privacy 103, 111, 178, 180–181, 198–199
private equity (PE) 46–48
privilege 35, 48, 164, 168, 178, 201, 216, 264, 302
Productivity Commission [Australia] 228–229
productivity-tracking software 245
Public Services (Social Value) Act [UK] 154

quantified self 179–181
queer: approaches 186–192

race 116, 135–142
racial capitalism 135–142
racial inequality 116
Ramtin, Ramin 60, 71, 76
Reddit 124
redundancy 12, 96, 354, 378
regional development 301–303
Rehabilitation Act (1973) [US] 153
Rehn-Meidner model 348
remote work 299–308
renewable energy 232–233
reproductive labour 175–176
research and development (R&D) 215, 414
resistance 9, 12, 32, 94, 102, 109, 123, 142, 186, 302, 314–325, 334
Resolution Foundation 315
Restrepo, Pascual 218, 363
Retail 114–116
Rifkin, Jeremy 24, 195
robotics 25, 29, 32, 58, 137, 195, 226, 234, 267
'Routine-Biased Technological Change' (RBTC) 81
routine work 359–369
Rubery, Jill 135, 187, 314, 337
rural development 299, 301

Schor, Juliet B. 113, 200
Schumpeter, Joseph A. 60
Schwab, Klaus 29, 58
Scottish Trade Unions Congress (STUC) 377, 383
Second Industrial Revolution 34–35
second machine age 217
self-employment 268–269
Services 211–219
sexual harassment 100, 333
Shaikh, Anwar 59, 62
sharing economy 113, 119
Sheffield: City Council 316; Sheffield Equality Hubs 315; Sheffield Needs A Pay Rise (SNAP) campaign 315; Sheffield Occupational Health Advisory Service (SOHA) 316–317; Sheffield Trades Union Council (STUC) 315, 322
Silesia Declaration 380
skills 381–383
Skype 198

Smith, Adam 18
Smith, Jason E. 64, 217
Snapchat 198
social capital 274, 280–281
social class *see* class
social media 338
social mobility 161–170
social protection 344–354
social reproduction 185–192
social value 154–155
Sohn-Rethel, Alfred 69, 72
Solow Paradox 216
Soroui, Sarah T. 303
South Africa 136–142
South Yorkshire economy 315–316: austerity and 316–317; insecurity and 316–317
Spotify 108, 118
Srnicek, Nick 5, 111
Standing, Guy 5, 25
Steinhoff, James 61, 62
Strauss, Kendra 162, 266
street-level organisations (SLOs) 353
surveillance 10, 37, 47, 74–75, 85, 109, 110, 119, 139, 141, 177–179, 198
sustainability 46, 227, 232, 238, 282, 376, 389, 390, 392–395
Sweet, Susanne 389, 395
systemic competition 414

TaskRabbit 112
Taylor, Phil 112, 315
taylorism 73–74, 83, 141
techno-feudalism 63
technology 5, 30–35, 48–50, 57–66, 80, 175–177, 195, 214–215, 237–248, 300, 308, 413–415
temporary work agencies (TWAs) 292
Tencent 414
thermal future of work 400–407
Third Industrial Revolution 33–35, 65
Thompson, Edward Palmer 18–19
TikTok 198
Toyota Production System (TPS) 290–292
Trades Council Conference 324
Trade Union Congress (TUC) 314, 325
trade unions 140, 155, 157, 321–323, 377; Bakers Food and Allied Workers Union (BFAWU) 322; Canadian Freelance Union 269; Energy and Paper Workers Union 380; European Transport Workers' Federation (ETF) 336; Independent Workers Union of Great Britain (IWGB) 123, 338; National Union of Metal and Allied Workers of South Africa (NUMSA) 136; Public and Commercial Services union 321; United Automobile Workers (UAW) 383; Unite Community 321–322, 324–325; Utility Workers Union 379
TripAdvisor 108, 114, 119
Triplett, Jack E. 215, 217
Twitter 108, 111

Uber 100, 108, 112, 138; Uber Eats 124
underemployment 82, 214, 378
unemployment 3, 5, 7, 17, 21–22, 359–360, 362, 364, 382
unfreedom 266–267, 270
unions *see* trade unions
United Nations Convention on the Rights of Persons with Disabilities (UNCRPD) 146
United Nations Environment Programme (UNEP) 380, 405
United Nations Framework Convention on Climate Change (UNFCCC) 376, 380, 381, 391
United Nations Conference on Trade and Development (UNCTAD) 214, 335
Universal Basic Income (UBI) 5–7, 38, 344, 354
universal caregiver model 201
Universal Credit (UC) [UK] 314–315
Universal Labour Guarantee 338
unpaid work 264–270
Upwork 100
urbanisation 33, 301, 304–305
UTS Institute for Sustainable Futures for the Clean Energy Council 233

Valizade, Danat. 350, 351
Value Theory of Labour 65
van Dijck, José 109–111
Varoufakis, Yanis 63–64
Vidal, Matt 63, 82
volunteering 267–268

wage-effort bargain 333
wages 3, 8, 22, 29, 33–36, 58–59, 102–103, 135, 138–141, 161–167, 214–219
Warwick, Dennis 23–24
Webster, Edward 136–137, 139
WeClock 102
Weibo 108
welfare policy 317–321, 344–354
welfare state 17, 95, 162–163, 166–167, 345, 348
wellbeing 366
WhatsApp groups 129, 138–139
Williams, Alex 5, 60
Williams, Raymond 18–19
Wood, Alex. J. 112, 279
Work and Health Programme [UK] 151
Work Capability Assessment (WCA) [UK] 318
worker rights 95, 389, 416–417

workfare 266, 319, 348, 354
Workforce Disability Equality Standard (WDES) [UK] 153
work-life balance 98, 336, 354
Workplace Employment Relations Study (WERS) 149–151
work-related stress 140, 164, 198, 303
World Bank 339
World Economic Forum (WEF) 29, 58
World War I 21
World War II 21–22
Wu, Nicole 363, 365

Yelp 114, 119
young workers 253–260
youth 168, 253–258, 260
YouTube 117, 118

Zoom 198
Zuboff, Shoshana 74, 111

For Product Safety Concerns and Information please contact our EU representative GPSR@taylorandfrancis.com Taylor & Francis Verlag GmbH, Kaufingerstraße 24, 80331 München, Germany